Official American Bar Association Guide to Approved Law Schools

1999 Edition

Prepared by the Section of Legal Education and Admissions to the Bar in cooperation with the Office of the Consultant on Legal Education to the American Bar Association

Editors:

Rick L. Morgan

Kurt Snyder, Esq.

MACMILLAN • USA

Opinions expressed in this publication are not to be deemed to represent the views of the ABA or the Section unless and until adopted pursuant to their Bylaws.

1999 Edition

Macmillan General Reference
A Simon & Schuster Macmillan Company
1633 Broadway
New York, NY 10019-6785

Macmillan Publishing books may be purchased for business or sales promotional use. For information please write: Special Markets Department, Macmillan Publishing USA, 1633 Broadway, New York, NY 10019.

Library of Congress Number: 97-80998

ISBN: 0-02-862192-1

Manufactured in the United States of America

10 9 8 7 6 5 4 3 2 1

Table of Contents

Please Read!!!

The information made available through this publication was collected from questionnaires completed during the Fall 1997 academic semester and submitted by American Bar Association ("ABA") approved law schools to the ABA's Consultant on Legal Education as part of the accreditation process. The completed questionnaires provided to the Consultant's Office are certified by the Dean of each law school. Each certification is submitted to the Consultant's Office as an assurance that the information provided accurately reflects prevailing conditions at the law school for which the certification is given. However, the Consultant's Office conducts no audit to verify the accuracy of the information submitted by the respective institutions.

This book contains information concerning law schools that were operating as of October 1, 1997 and were approved by the ABA to confer the first degree in law. The approval status of an individual law school can change. Therefore, if you would like to confirm whether an individual law school is approved by the ABA at a specific time after October 1, you should contact the ABA directly. You can also access this information on the Section of Legal Education and Admissions to the Bar's website: http://www.abanet.org/legaled. For example, on February 3, 1998, just prior to the publication of this book, the ABA House of Delegates granted provisional approval to Chapman University School of Law and the University of the District of Columbia School of Law. Moreover, the Council of the Section acquiesced in advance degree programs from the following schools after October 1, 1997: American University School of Law, California Western School of Law, Golden Gate University School of Law, John Marshall Law School, University of Missouri-Columbia School of Law, University of Chicago School of Law, and Yeshiva University School of Law. For updates or corrections to this book, please visit the Section's website: http://www.abanet.org/legaled.

In addition to the information submitted by the respective law schools, this publication also includes material provided by various organizations with an interest in legal education. The views expressed in this book are not necessarily those of the ABA, the Section of Legal Education and Admissions to the Bar, or the Consultant's Office. Opinions expressed in this publication are not to be deemed to represent the views of the ABA or the Section unless and until adopted pursuant to their Bylaws.

Thank You!!!

James P. White, Consultant on Legal Education to the American Bar Association, and the Consultant's Staff would like to thank the various organizations, law schools, authors, bar examiners, and volunteers without whose assistance this book would not have become a reality. In particular, we owe much gratitude to the following individuals for volunteering their many hours of work: Associate Dean Paul Ciraulo, St. John's University School of Law; Dean Rudolph C. Hasl, St. John's University School of Law; Dean Steven R. Smith, California Western School of Law; and Associate Dean Peter A. Winograd, University of New Mexico School of Law. Furthermore, we would like to thank the following people and organizations: Linda Bernbach, Editorial Director and Charles A. Wall, Vice President, Editor-in-Chief, Macmillan General Reference; Jeffrey E. Hanson, Director, Debt Management Services at the Access Group[SM]; Bill Kennish, Micron Systems; Erica Moeser, Esq., President of the National Conference of Bar Examiners; Paula A. Patton, Esq., Executive Director of the National Association for Law Placement; Natalie Auberry and Kenneth A. Harshey, students at the Indiana University School of Law - Indianapolis; Philip D. Shelton, Esq., Executive Director and President of the Law School Admission Council; and David R. Stewart, Esq. of Sidley & Austin. And finally, the editors of the book, Rick L. Morgan and Kurt Snyder, Esq., would like to thank their spouses, Terrie Morgan and Debbie Snyder, for supporting them in this endeavor.

To order additional copies of this book,
please call the ABA Service Center, at (800) 285-2221.

Office of the Consultant on Legal Education
550 West North Street, Suite 349
Indianapolis, Indiana 46202
http://www.abanet.org/legaled

James P. White, Consultant
Arthur R. Gaudio, Deputy Consultant
Kurt Snyder, Assistant Consultant
Marilyn S. Shannon, Executive Administrator
Cathy A. Schrage, Executive Assistant
Rick L. Morgan, Data Specialist
Mary D. Barron, Senior Administrative Secretary
Claudia S. Fisher, Administrative Secretary
Kimberly S. Massie, Administrative Secretary
Mary L. Kronoshek, Administrative Secretary
Kirsten Iverson, Administrative Secretary

Section of Legal Education and
Admissions to the Bar
750 North Lake Shore Drive
Chicago, Illinois 60611
http://www.abanet.org/legaled

Michelle Deanne Ekanemesang, Administrative Assistant

COUNCIL OF THE SECTION OF LEGAL EDUCATION AND ADMISSIONS TO THE BAR, 1997-98

Officers

BEVERLY TARPLEY
Chairperson
Scarborough, Tarpley & Fouts
Abilene, Texas

RANDALL T. SHEPARD
Chairperson-Elect
Chief Justice, Indiana Supreme Court
Indianapolis, Indiana

ROBERT K. WALSH
Vice-Chairperson
Dean, Wake Forest University School of Law
Winston-Salem, North Carolina

DIANE C. YU
Secretary
Managing Counsel, Monsanto Company
St. Louis, Missoui

RUDOLPH C. HASL
Past Chairperson
Dean, St. John's University School of Law
Jamaica, New York

JOSE GARCIA-PEDROSA
Section Delegate to the House of Delegates
City Manager, City of Miami
Miami, Florida

NORMAN REDLICH
Section Delegate to the House of Delegates
Wachtell, Lipton, Rosen & Katz
New York, New York

GORDON D. SCHABER (deceased)
Secretary Emeritus
University Counsel and Former Dean, McGeorge School of Law
Sacramento, California

Members of the Council

MARTHA W. BARNETT
Holland & Knight
Tallahassee, Florida

LAURA N. GASAWAY
Professor, University of North Carolina School of Law
Chapel Hill, North Carolina

HERMA HILL KAY
Dean, U. of California School of Law - Berkeley
Berkeley, California

JOHN R. KRAMER
Professor and Former Dean, Tulane University School of Law
New Orleans, Louisiana

ELIZABETH B. LACY
Justice, Virginia Supreme Court
Richmond, Virginia

NANCY NEUMAN (Public Member)
Lewisburg, Pennsylvania

SOLOMON OLIVER, JR.
Judge, United States District Court, Northern District of Ohio
Cleveland, Ohio

GARY H. PALM
Professor, University of Chicago School of Law
Chicago, Illinois

WILLIAM R. RAKES
Gentry, Locke, Rakes & Moore
Roanoke, Virginia

MARÍA RAMÍREZ (Public Member)
Executive Director, International P.A.C.E.
Clifton Park, New York

DOROTHY S. RIDINGS (Public Member)
President, Council on Foundations
Washington, D.C.

STEVEN R. SMITH
Dean and President, California Western School of Law
San Diego, California

E. THOMAS SULLIVAN
Dean, University of Minnesota School of Law
Minneapolis, Minnesota

GERALD W. VANDEWALLE
Chief Justice, North Dakota Supreme Court
Bismarck, North Dakota

Liaisons:

SARA AUSTIN
Young Lawyers Division Liaison
York, Pennsylvania

MARK E. MORICE
Law Student Division Liaison
Student, Loyola -- New Orleans
New Orleans, Louisiana

ROY A. HAMMER
Board of Governors Liaison
Hemenway & Barnes
Boston, Massachusetts

ACCREDITATION COMMITTEE OF THE SECTION OF LEGAL EDUCATION AND ADMISSIONS TO THE BAR, 1997-98

Officers

JEFFREY E. LEWIS
Chairperson
Professor and Dean *Emeritus*, University of Florida College of Law
Gainesville, Florida

LIZABETH A. MOODY
Vice-Chairperson
Dean, Stetson University College of Law
St. Petersburg, Florida

Members of the Accreditation Committee

BERNARD F. ASHE
Private Practice, retired
Delmar, New York

HULETT H. ASKEW
Director, Office of Bar Admissions
Atlanta, Georgia

JOSEPH F. BACA
Justice, Supreme Court of New Mexico
Santa Fe, New Mexico

J. MARTIN BURKE
Professor, University of Montana
Missoula, Montana

MICHAEL J. DAVIS
Professor, University of Kansas School of Law
Lawrence, Kansas
Stinson, Mag, & Fizzell
Kansas City, Missouri

STEVEN P. FRANKINO
Professor, Villanova University School of Law
Villanova, Pennsylvania

DAN J. FREEHLING
Professor, Director of Law Library
Boston University School of Law
Boston, Massachusetts

HARRY E. GROVES
Professor *Emeritus*, University of North Carolina School of Law
Chapel Hill, North Carolina

JAMES J. HANKS, JR.
Ballard, Spahr, Andrews, & Ingersoll
Baltimore, Maryland

JAMES M. KLEIN
Professor, University of Toledo College of Law
Toledo, Ohio

JOHN L. LAHEY (Public Member)
President, Quinnipiac College
Hamden, Connecticut

SOLOMON OLIVER, JR.
Judge, United States District Court, Northern District of Ohio
Cleveland, Ohio

MARÍA RAMÍREZ (Public Member)
Executive Director, International P.A.C.E.
Clifton Park, New York

SHARREN B. ROSE
Nelson & Schmeling
Green Bay, Wisconsin

LEONARD P. STRICKMAN
Dean, University of Arkansas School of Law
Fayetteville, Arkansas

DAVID G. TRAGER
Judge, United States District Court, Eastern District of New York
Brooklyn, New York

TO: **Law School Applicants**

FROM: **164 American Law School Deans**

DATE: **January 7, 1998**

RE: **"Law School Rankings May Be Hazardous To Your Health!"**

Dear Law School Applicant:

It is easy to feel overwhelmed about the mass of material available to help you decide which law schools would best suit your needs, interests, and aspirations. You may be tempted to trim your research by resorting to some commercial ranking that purports to reduce to one easily digestible number — from #1 to #180 — how each ABA-accredited law school stacks up against the others. As deans of schools that range across the full spectrum of several such rating systems, we strongly urge you to minimize the influence of rankings on your own judgment. These rankings leave many important variables out of account, arbitrarily weight others, and are generally unreliable as a guide to those qualities of different schools that a candidate should consider when applying to law school. In the recent words of Newsweek *editor Kenneth Auchincloss, "Rankings generate huge hype, which is far more likely to serve the publisher's purpose than the readers'. . . .Applicants need help in widening their knowledge of schools that may be right for them, not narrowing their choices according to a ranking system."*

Appended to this letter is a more detailed analysis of why you should be wary of ranking systems. The key problem with all law school rating systems is that the final rankings are not based primarily on any hard underlying data. The range of performance among law schools based on most hard variables is actually fairly narrow. Rankings result chiefly from the value judgments that transform a limited range of data into an evaluative scheme. After the ranking "authority" decides which variables are relevant to the ranking, each variable must be given a weight. But the choices of variables and, even more dramatically, the choice of weights to be given those variables can be conspicuously arbitrary.

It would be better to proceed as follows: First, you should make a personal list of the things you care about in a potential law school. As you do further research, this list may grow or shrink, but you should start your search by asking yourself the fundamental questions, "Why do I want to go to law school? Which law schools will equip me to achieve my objectives?" That analysis may lead you to select as many as several dozen law schools in which you might be interested. Your second step, therefore, should be to gather detailed information about those schools.[1] *Third, after you have narrowed your list, you should take the time to visit the schools in which you are most interested or, at least, to talk to some faculty, staff, students, alumni, and legal employers who can give you current information about the school and what you can expect. This process is time-consuming and can be costly, but it will not be as costly as deciding to invest several years of your life and thousands of dollars of tuition in a school that is not well suited to you.*

You are about to make a substantial investment of time, money, energy — and soul — in pursuit of a legal education that meets your needs and will help you to fulfill your dreams. In the face of so important a decision, you owe it to yourself to avoid the temptation of relying on rankings and to undertake the kind of search we have outlined. We hope you make the right choice for you.

---

[1] Helpful publications include the *LSAC Official Guide to Law Schools,* and the *Official American Bar Association Guide to Approved Law Schools*, published by the American Bar Association Section of Legal Education and Admissions to the Bar. They can show you, through readily comparable data tables, much of the basic information for each law school in which you may be interested. You can get much additional information through the Internet — most law schools have web sites (accessible through **http://www.abanet.org/legaled/approved.html**), or you can write to the schools for their latest recruitment publications.

Signatories of Deans' Letter: "Law School Rankings May Be Hazardous To Your Health!"

Richard L. Aynes
University of Akron

Thomas H. Sponsler
Albany Law School

Claudio Grossman
American University
Washington College of Law

Joel Seligman
University of Arizona

Alan Matheson
Arizona State University

Leonard Strickman
University of Arkansas at Fayetteville

Rodney K. Smith
University of Arkansas at Little Rock

John A. Sebert
University of Baltimore

Bradley J. B. Toben
Baylor University

Aviam Soifer
Boston College

Ronald A. Cass
Boston University

H. Reese Hansen
Brigham Young University

Joan G. Wexler
Brooklyn Law School

Herma Hill Kay
University of California at Berkeley
Boalt Hall

Bruce A. Wolk
University of California at Davis

Mary Kay Kane
University of California
Hastings College of the Law

Susan Westerberg Prager
Univ. of California at Los Angeles

Steven R. Smith
California Western

Stephen C. Bahls
Capital University

Gerald Korngold
Case Western Reserve University

Bernard Dobranski
Catholic University of America
Columbus School of Law

Joseph P. Tomain
University of Cincinnati

Steven H. Steinglass
Cleveland State University
Cleveland-Marshall College of Law

David W. Leebron
Columbia University

Harold H. Bruff
University of Colorado

Hugh C. Macgill
University of Connecticut

Russell K. Osgood
Cornell Law School

Lawrence Raful
Creighton University

Francis J. Conte
University of Dayton

Robert Yegge
University of Denver

Teree E. Foster
DePaul University

Stephen A. Mazurak
University of Detroit Mercy

William L. Robinson
District of Columbia

C. Peter Goplerud, III
Drake University

Pamela B. Gann
Duke University

Nicholas P. Cafardi
Duquesne University

Howard O. Hunter
Emory University

Richard Matasar
University of Florida

Paul A. LeBel
Florida State University

James E. Duggan
Franklin Pierce Law Center

Jack H. Friedenthal
George Washington University

Judith C. Areen
Georgetown University

Edward D. Spurgeon
University of Georgia

Janice C. Griffith
Georgia State University

Anthony J. Pagano
Golden Gate University

John E. Clute
Gonzaga University

Raymond R. Krause
Hamline University

Lawrence C. Foster
University of Hawaii

Stuart Rabinowitz
Hofstra University

Stephen Zamora
University of Houston

Alice Gresham Bullock
Howard University

John A. Miller
University of Idaho

Thomas M. Mengler
University of Illinois

Alfred C. Aman, Jr.
Indiana University - Bloomington

Norman Lefstein
Indiana University - Indianapolis

Henry H. Perritt, Jr.
Illinois Institute of Technology
Chicago-Kent Law School

Carlos E. Ramos-González
Interamerican University
of Puerto Rico

N. William Hines
University of Iowa

Robert Gilbert Johnston
The John Marshall Law School

Michael H. Hoeflich
University of Kansas

David E. Shipley
University of Kentucky

James L. Huffman
Lewis and Clark Northwestern

Donald L. Burnett, Jr.
University of Louisville
Louis D. Brandeis School of Law

Gerald T. McLaughlin
Loyola Law School — Los Angeles

John Makdisi
Loyola University -- New Orleans

Donald L. Zillman
University of Maine

Howard B. Eisenberg
Marquette University

Donald G. Gifford
University of Maryland

Donald J. Polden
University of Memphis
Cecil C. Humphreys School of Law

R. Lawrence Dessem
Mercer University

Samuel C. Thompson
University of Miami

Jeffrey S. Lehman
University of Michigan

Jeremy T. Harrison
Michigan State University-Detroit

E. Thomas Sullivan
University of Minnesota

J. Richard Hurt
Mississippi College

Samuel M. Davis
University of Mississippi

Timothy J. Heinsz
University of Missouri-Columbia

Burnele V. Powell
University of Missouri-Kansas City

E. Edwin Eck
University of Montana

Harvey Perlman
University of Nebraska

John F. O'Brien
New England School of Law

Robert J. Desiderio
University of New Mexico

Kristin Booth Glen
City University of New York

Barry B. Boyer
State University of New York
at Buffalo

Harry Wellington
New York Law School

Signatories of Deans' Letter: "Law School Rankings May Be Hazardous To Your Health!"

John E. Sexton
New York University

Judith W. Wegner
University of North Carolina

Percy R. Luney, Jr.
North Carolina Central University

W. Jeremy Davis
University of North Dakota

David Hall
Northeastern University

LeRoy Pernell
Northern Illinois University

David C. Short
Northern Kentucky University
Salmon P. Chase College of Law

David T. Link
University of Notre Dame

Joseph D. Harbaugh
Nova Southeastern University

Victor L. Streib
Ohio Northern University

Gregory H. Williams
Ohio State University

Andrew M. Coats
University of Oklahoma

Jay Conison
Oklahoma City University

Rennard Strickland
University of Oregon

Richard L. Ottinger
Pace University

Gerald Caplan
University of the Pacific
McGeorge School of Law

Colin S. Diver
University of Pennsylvania

Peter G. Glenn
Pennsylvania State University
Dickinson School of Law

Richardson R. Lynn
Pepperdine University

Peter M. Shane
University of Pittsburgh

Antonio Garcia-Padilla
University of Puerto Rico

Neil Cogan
Quinnipiac College

J. Nelson Happy
Regent University

John E. Ryan
Roger Williams University

Jay M. Feinman
Rutgers University - Camden

Roger I. Abrams
Rutgers University - Newark

Rudolph C. Hasl
St. John's University

John B. Attanasio
St. Louis University

Barbara Bader Aldave
St. Mary's University

Daniel J. Morrissey
St. Thomas University

Barry A. Currier
Samford University
Cumberland School of Law

Grant H. Morris
University of San Diego

H. Jay Folberg
University of San Francisco

Mack A. Player
Santa Clara University

James Bond
Seattle University

John E. Montgomery
University of South Carolina

Barry R. Vickrey
University of South Dakota

Frank T. Read
South Texas College of Law

Scott H. Bice
University of Southern California

Thomas F. Guernsey
Southern Illinois University

Harvey Wingo
Southern Methodist University

Leigh H. Taylor
Southwestern University

Paul A. Brest
Stanford University

Lizabeth A. Moody
Stetson University

John E. Fenton, Jr.
Suffolk University

Daan Braveman
Syracuse University

Robert J. Reinstein
Temple University

Richard T. Wirtz
University of Tennessee

M. Michael Sharlot
University of Texas

McKen V. Carrington
Texas Southern University

W. Frank Newton
Texas Tech University

Frank K. Walwer
Texas Wesleyan University

Don LeDuc
Thomas M. Cooley Law School

Kenneth J. Vandevelde
Thomas Jefferson School of Law

Albert T. Quick
University of Toledo

Howard A. Glickstein
Touro University

Edward F. Sherman
Tulane University

Martin H. Belsky
University of Tulsa

Lee E. Teitelbaum
University of Utah

Ivan E. Bodensteiner
Valparaiso University

Kent Syverud
Vanderbilt University

L. Kinvin Wroth
Vermont Law School

Mark Sargent
Villanova University

Robert E. Scott
University of Virginia

Dorsey D. Ellis, Jr.
Washington University of St. Louis

James K. Robinson
Wayne State University

John W. Fisher, II
West Virginia University

Donald J. Dunn
Western New England College of Law

John A. FitzRandolph
Whittier Law School

Arthur N. Frakt
Widener University — Delaware and at Harrisburg

Robert K. Walsh
Wake Forest University

James M. Concannon
Washburn University

Roland L. Hjorth
University of Washington

Barry Sullivan
Washington & Lee University

Robert M. Ackerman
Willamette University

Paul Marcus
College of William and Mary
Marshall-Wythe School of Law

Harry J. Haynsworth, IV
William Mitchell College of Law

John M. Burman
University of Wyoming

Anthony T. Kronman
Yale University

(Deans' Letter Continued)

APPENDIX: WHAT'S WRONG WITH LAW SCHOOL RANKING SYSTEMS — A BRIEF ANALYSIS

There exists within legal education a consensus about the foundational requirements for a sound program. This consensus is embodied in the accreditation standards of the American Bar Association. But among the law schools that meet these standards, the variety is enormous. The aspects of that variety that a student will actually care about depend deeply on the circumstances of the individual student. Consider the following illustrative sampling (lower left) of some of the variables that applicants find important in choosing a law school:

Breadth and support of alumni network

Loan Repayment Assistance for low-income lawyers

Breadth of curriculum

Location

Clinical programs

Part-time enrollment option

Collaborative research opportunities with faculty

Public interest programs

Commitment to innovative technology

Quality of teaching

Cost

Racial and gender diversity within the faculty and student body

Externship options

Faculty accessibility

Religious orientation or commitment in curricular design

Intensity of writing instruction

Size of first-year classes

Interdisciplinary programs

Skills instruction

International programming

Specialized areas of faculty expertise

Chances are that some, but not all of these, matter to you. And it is probable that, of the variables that matter, some matter more to you than others. But none of them — ***not a single one*** *— is a separate factor in the most highly publicized of the current ranking systems, the list published by* U.S. News & World Report*. If the list above includes variables that you consider important, it does not make sense to defer to a system of ranking that ignores them.*

One of these systems — the ranking published by U.S. News & World Report *— well illustrates the weaknesses of all ratings schemes, including the* Gourman Report *rankings associated with* Princeton Review*. Like all such systems,* U.S. News *focuses predominantly on those aspects of law schools that can easily be counted, despite the far greater importance of those aspects that cannot easily be counted. Moreover, like all such systems,* U.S. News *attaches arbitrary weights to those few factors that it does include.*

For example, according to U.S. News*, the median undergraduate GPA of a law school's most recent entering class is five times more important in assessing a school's quality than a school's bar exam success. But why five times, instead of six times, or four times more important, or more important at all?* U.S. News *similarly assumes, by implication, that the quality of your experience as a law student depends four times more on the LSAT scores of your classmates than on a school's student-teacher ratio. Does that reflect your concerns?* U.S. News *weighs a school's overhead budget twice as heavily as its library size. What do you think? In fact, the weights attached to all the variables are just* U.S. News & World Report *inventions. Even minor adjustments in this weighting would change some rankings significantly, and the assigned weights are dubious.*

There is also no guarantee that any particular ranking source is accurate, logical, consistent, and honest in the way it gathers and reports data. For example, in 1997, U.S. News *rated each school in part according to its comparative bar passage rate in the state in which most of its recent graduates took the bar exam. But* U.S. News *did not require each school to report its performance on the same exam. Hence, one school might be treated as more successful than another in the same state simply because it reported its results on a different bar exam on which its graduates were more successful. It is logically indefensible to rate two law schools' bar exam performance rates based on different exams given at different times.*

There are more reasons to be cautious. U.S. News *says it bases 12 per cent of each school's overall score on the percentage of its second-most-recent class employed by February 15 of the year following its graduation. (In other words, the placement rate relevant to the 1997 rankings was the percentage of each school's 1995 graduates who were placed by February 15, 1996.) If you read the fine print, however, the actual placement rate is not the basis for many schools' scores. That's because the number of employed graduates attributed to each school is the total number of graduates actually reporting employment plus 25 per cent of the number of graduates who failed to report their employment status at all. This calculation is just a* U.S. News *invention. Moreover, for schools that failed entirely to report their placement data, U.S. News estimated a figure.*

There is much else wrong with the details of the U.S. News *and other rankings, but the major point is this: In deciding on your own education, you should not substitute someone else's ranking system for your own best judgment. You are simply being misled if you treat some rankings, of which* U.S. News *is a prominent example, as even a competent and conscientious presentation of the limited information they purport to convey.*

Chapter One

Introduction

The American Bar Association's Section of Legal Education and Admissions to the Bar, as part of the information process relating to the accreditation of American law schools, proudly presents the 1999 edition of the *Official American Bar Association Guide to Approved Law Schools*. In 1893 the ABA created its first section, the Section of Legal Education and Admissions to the Bar. The mission of the Section is "to be a creative national force in providing leadership and services to those responsible for, and those who benefit from, a sound program of legal education and bar admissions; to provide a fair, effective, and efficient accrediting system for American law schools that promotes quality legal education; and to continue to serve, through its Council, as the nationally recognized accrediting body for American law schools."

Since the adoption of the first law school accreditation Standards by the ABA in 1921, state supreme courts and other bar admitting authorities have encouraged the ABA's accreditation efforts, and the vast majority of states rely upon ABA accreditation to determine whether the law school that an applicant attended meets the educational requirements for the applicant's admission to the bar. Graduation from a law school that is not ABA approved may qualify a person to take the bar examination in the state in which the school is located, but may not qualify the person for the examination in other states.

The purpose of accreditation is not only to review a law school's compliance with the Standards, but also to provide a vehicle for sharing information relating to ongoing developments in legal education. One facet of the accreditation process is a detailed Annual Questionnaire completed by each approved school. The information from the questionnaire is utilized to prepare comparative statistics on all phases of law school operations and is used by the Accreditation Committee and Council in their accreditation review process. Careful analysis of these data serves to identify problems a school may be experiencing that call for a special visit or some other form of assistance. It also identifies trends in legal education. Moreover, Standard 509 of the Standards for Approval of Law Schools, as adopted by the ABA House of Delegates in August, 1996, states: "A law school shall publish basic consumer information. The information shall be published in a fair and accurate manner reflective of actual practice." This book satisfies a law school's obligation to provide basic consumer information under Standard 509.

This book is designed to provide consumers with basic information in a simple format that will facilitate comparisons between schools. Please note that applicants should not use this book as the sole source of information regarding application and admission. Rather, this book should supplement other avenues of evaluating respective schools, including making direct contact with admissions officers, professors, students, alumni or prelaw advisors. In addition to statistics on all ABA approved law schools, this book contains information intended to help individuals prepare for the rigors and costs associated with attending law school.

The ABA does not condone, approve, or sanction the use of the data contained herein to rank law schools. In fact, the ABA disapproves of any and all rankings. In the front of this book is a statement signed by 164 deans giving their view on rankings. The official ABA view on rankings is as follows, *"No rating of law schools beyond the simple statement of their accreditation status is attempted or advocated by the American Bar Association. Qualities that make one kind of school good for one student may not be as important to another. The American Bar Association and its Section of Legal Education and Admissions to the Bar have issued disclaimers of any law school rating system. Prospective law students should consider a variety of factors in making their choice among approved schools."*

As of October 1, 1997, a total of 180 institutions were approved by the American Bar Association: 179 confer the first degree in law (the J.D. degree); the other ABA approved school is the U.S. Army Judge Advocate General's School, which offers an officer's resident graduate course, a specialized program beyond the first degree in law. One of the 179 ABA approved law schools (Widener) also has a branch campus. As of October 1, 1997, three of the 179 law schools were provisionally approved: Texas Wesleyan University School of Law, Thomas Jefferson School of Law, and the District of Columbia School of Law. It is the position of the ABA that students at provisionally approved law schools and persons who graduate while a school is provisionally approved should be entitled to the same recognition accorded under the ABA Standards to students and graduates of fully approved law schools.

This book contains information concerning law schools that were operating as of October 1, 1997 and were approved by the ABA to confer the first degree in law. The approval status of an individual law school can change. Therefore, if you would like to confirm whether an individual law school is approved by the ABA at a specific time after October 1, you should contact the ABA directly. You can also access this information on the Section of Legal Education and Admissions to the Bar's website: http://www.abanet.org/legaled. For example, on February 3, 1998, just prior to the publication of this book, the ABA House of Delegates granted provisional approval to Chapman University School of Law and the University of the District of Columbia School of Law. In addition the Council of the Section acquiesced in advance degree programs from the following schools after October 1, 1997: American University School of Law, California Western School of Law, Golden Gate University School of Law, John Marshall Law School, University of Missouri-Columbia School of Law, University of Chicago School of Law, and Yeshiva University School of Law. For updates or corrections to this book, please visit the Section's website: http://www.abanet.org/legaled.

Other Organizations

Association of American Law Schools (AALS)

Founded in 1900, the nonprofit AALS has grown to 160 member law schools. The purpose of the Association is "the improvement of the legal profession through legal education." To carry out this mission, the AALS serves as the learned society for law teachers. It facilitates excellence in legal education through workshops, conferences, a quarterly newsletter and other publications, including the *AALS Directory of Law Teachers*, provided to law teachers and law schools. In addition, the AALS is legal education's principal representative to the federal government and to other national higher education organizations and learned societies.

Association of American Law Schools
1201 Connecticut Avenue, NW
Suite 800
Washington, DC 20036-2605
(202) 296-8851
http://www.aals.org

National Conference of Bar Examiners (NCBE)

The nonprofit NCBE was formed in 1931. Its mission is to "work with other institutions to develop, maintain, and apply reasonable and uniform standards of education and character for eligibility for admission to the practice of law." The NCBE assists bar authorities in the various jurisdictions by providing uniform, high quality standardized examinations for testing applicants for admission to the practice of law, disseminating information concerning admission standards and practices and conducting educational programs for members and staffs of bar authorities. The NCBE also provides character and fitness services to the various bar authorities. NCBE tests include the Multistate Bar Exam and the Multistate Professional Responsibility Examination. In conjunction with the ABA, the NCBE publishes the *Comprehensive Guide to Bar Admission Requirements* containing bar admission requirements in all U.S. jurisdictions.

National Conference of Bar Examiners
333 North Michigan Avenue
Suite 1025
Chicago, Illinois 60601
(312) 641-0963
http://www.ncbex.org

Law School Admission Council (LSAC)

LSAC is a nonprofit corporation whose members are 194 U.S. and Canadian law schools. It is best known as the sponsor of the Law School Admission Test (LSAT). Its other services include the Law School Data Assembly Service, which summarizes applicants' prior academic work and distributes that information to the law schools to which each candidate applies; Law School Forums--recruitment fairs, free-of-charge to applicants, held in seven American cities each year; and a host of outreach programs targeted to minorities underrepresented in the legal profession. For additional information about LSAC, please see chapter four or visit their website.

Law School Admission Council
Box 2000
Newtown, PA 18940-0998
(215) 968-1001
http://www.lsac.org

National Association for Law Placement (NALP)

Since its founding in 1971, the National Association for Law Placement (NALP) has served the legal community as a nonprofit organization dedicated to meeting the needs of the participants in the legal employment process. NALP provides information, coordination and standards that pertain to the hiring of law students and attorneys, and fosters fair and informed decision-making in legal career planning, recruiting and employment.

Virtually all of the ABA accredited law schools and approximately 850 legal employers, including most of the largest law firms, corporations, public interest and government agencies are NALP members.

NALP is widely respected for its ability to provide essential research data on legal recruiting and employment. NALP's research spans more than two decades and is extensively referenced throughout the legal community. Additionally, NALP publishes definitive print and electronic resources designed to support clear and accurate communication between and education of all participants in the legal hiring process.

National Association for Law Placement
1666 Connecticut Avenue, Suite 325
Washington, DC 20009-1039
(202) 667-1666
http://www.nalp.org

Chapter Two

ABA's Role in the Accreditation Process

Law schools approved by the American Bar Association (ABA) provide a legal education which meets a minimum set of standards as promulgated by the ABA. The ABA Standards for Approval of Law Schools (Standards) are designed, developed, and implemented by the judiciary, practicing bar, and the professorate for the purpose of advancing the basic goal of providing a sound program of legal education. As a result, every jurisdiction in the United States has determined that graduates of ABA approved law schools are able to sit for the bar in their respective jurisdictions. Responsibility for administering the ABA's accreditation process has been placed with the Council of the Section of Legal Education and Admissions to the Bar, which is recognized by the U.S. Department of Education as the "nationally recognized accrediting agency for schools of law." The Consultant on Legal Education to the American Bar Association and his staff assist the Council in administering the accreditation process. The role that the ABA plays as the national accrediting body has enabled accreditation to become unified and national in scope rather than fragmented, with the potential for inconsistency, among the fifty states, the District of Columbia, the Commonwealth of Puerto Rico, and other territories.

Since its inception in 1878, the American Bar Association has been concerned with improving the quality of legal education throughout the country. Following numerous studies of the educational programs available in the late 1880s and early 1900s, it was determined that a national process must be developed for ensuring the quality of the education of the prospective lawyer. Consequently, in 1921, the ABA adopted a statement for minimum standards of legal education and instituted a policy of publishing a list of law schools that complied with those standards. As of October 1, 1997 there were 180 law schools on the list of ABA approved law schools.

Since the early 1920s, the Standards, which govern the accreditation process, have evolved into a fairly comprehensive set of criteria to ensure that graduates of ABA approved law schools receive a sound education. The Section conducts an ongoing validation process to review the Standards, Interpretations, and Rules of Procedure. As part of this review process, the Standards were revised in August of 1996 and the Rules of Procedure in August of 1997.

Today, the Standards provide that the purpose of the accreditation process is not only to review a law school's compliance with the Standards, but also to provide a vehicle for sharing information relating to ongoing developments in legal education. Moreover, the process requires schools to evaluate themselves, their goals, and to determine if they are fulfilling their mission. Furthermore, the Standards require schools to seek to exceed the minimum requirements of the Standards. Ultimately, it is the hope of the ABA that the Standards will facilitate the ability of American law schools to provide a sound education that enables graduates to practice both competently and effectively.

The Need For a Centralized Accrediting Agency

In order to obtain a license to practice law, almost all law school graduates must apply for bar admission through a state board of bar examiners. Usually this board is an agency of the highest state court in the jurisdiction, but occasionally the board is connected more closely to the state's bar association. The criteria for eligibility to take the bar examination or to otherwise qualify for bar admission are set by each state, not by the Council or ABA. In order to sit for the bar examination, most states require an applicant to hold a degree from a law school that meets acceptable established educational standards. Most states, however, are not willing to commit the resources to handle the daunting task of accrediting law schools throughout the United States to determine if individuals have satisfied the requisite educational qualifications. Maintaining an accreditation process is both fiscally and administratively demanding. As a result, the vast majority of bar admission authorities in the United States rely upon ABA approval to determine whether their legal education requirement for admission to the bar is satisfied. Education at an ABA approved law school meets the requirements in every jurisdiction in the United States.

The ABA accreditation process obviates any need for an individual state court to evaluate law schools throughout the United States. The Standards, with which all ABA approved schools must comply, are the minimum requirements designed, developed, and implemented for the purpose of advancing the basic goal of providing a sound program of legal education. States can rely on the ABA to administer the accreditation process because they know that the ABA requires schools to be in full compliance with the Standards to remain on the list of approved schools. As a result, the ABA, as the national accrediting body, has enabled accreditation to become unified and national in scope rather than fragmented, with the potential for inconsistency, among the fifty states, the District of Columbia, the Commonwealth of Puerto Rico, and other territories.

Thus, the benefits of a nationally recognized accrediting agency for law schools are many. States are not burdened with maintaining an accreditation process, schools are not burdened with over 50 accrediting agencies, and students can be confident that their particular school satisfies the educational requirements of every state. Above all, the profession and the public are given assurances that lawyers have completed a course of study designed to provide them with a sound education that enables them to practice competently and effectively.

The Accreditation Process

The approval process is initiated when a school files an application, and approval will be granted only after a finding that the school offers a sound program of legal education which complies

with the Standards. The accreditation process involves a regularly scheduled on-site evaluation, careful analysis of self-study data, and emphasis on the steady improvement of the quality of the law school's educational program. Provisionally approved law schools are evaluated every year and fully approved schools every seven years, unless a situation arises requiring a more frequent review at an earlier time. Approval is granted or continued based upon the school's compliance with the ABA Standards. Responsibility for administering the ABA's program of accreditation has been placed with the Council of the Section of Legal Education and Admissions to the Bar, which is assisted by the Consultant on Legal Education to the American Bar Association and his staff.

A law school that has completed at least one full year of successful operation may apply for provisional approval. A law school is granted provisional approval when it establishes that it substantially complies with each of the Standards and gives assurances that it will be in full compliance with all of the Standards within three years after receiving provisional approval. A law school that has been provisionally approved for two years may be considered for full approval by the House of Delegates of the ABA upon a finding by the Council that the school fully meets each of the Standards, as interpreted by the Council. The school must insure continued compliance with the letter and the spirit of the Standards, with particular emphasis on a steady improvement in the quality of its educational program.

The ABA Standards provide that students at provisionally approved law schools and those who graduate while a school is provisionally approved are entitled to the same recognition accorded under the Standards to students and graduates of fully approved law schools.

Since 1971, the number of approved law schools offering the first degree in law has grown from 147 to 180. Total J.D. enrollment in approved schools has gone from approximately 91,225 students to 128,623 students within that period. In that same period female enrollment has increased from 8,567 to 57,123 and minority enrollment has increased from 5,568 to 25,279.

As part of the accreditation process, each school completes a detailed Questionnaire that serves several important functions. The data from the submitted questionnaires from all the ABA approved law schools are utilized to prepare comparative statistics on all phases of law school operation. The information is also used by the Accreditation Committee and the Council in their accreditation review process. The comparative data are also distributed to approved law schools that subscribe to the law school statistical service. Careful analysis of this information may identify problems a school is experiencing that calls for a special visit or some other form of assistance. They also identify trends in legal education.

Site evaluation teams are generally composed of legal educators (including law librarians, professional skills teachers, and other persons with specialized expertise), one or more practicing lawyers or members of the judiciary, and a university administrator. The site visit itself typically takes three to four days and includes fact finding about all aspects of the school's educational program, including the curriculum, academic program, resources, and physical plant. Conferences with faculty members, members of the bench and bar, law school administrators, and students are part of the process. Site evaluation teams visit classes, and review law school policies and procedures. Prior to the site visit, team members review a detailed site evaluation questionnaire, several annual questionnaires, and an institutional self-study — all prepared by representatives of the school.

Following the visit, a report of the facts ascertained in the visit is prepared and sent to the Consultant on Legal Education for transmittal to the law school and the Accreditation Committee of the Section. Upon receiving the initial report, a school is provided an opportunity to respond, correct and/or clarify any factual errors.

The Accreditation Committee is composed of members from the academic community, the judiciary, the profession, and the public. The initial decision to continue provisional or full approval of a school is made by the Accreditation Committee. However, when the granting or removal of provisional or full approval is involved, the Accreditation Committee makes a recommendation to the Council. The Council, in turn, makes its recommendation to the ABA's House of Delegates, which makes the final determination.

The Standards

The Standards are founded primarily on the fact that law schools are the gateway to the legal profession. They are minimum requirements designed, developed, and implemented for the purpose of advancing the basic goal of providing a sound program of legal education. Graduates of approved law schools can become members of the bar in all United States jurisdictions, representing all members of the public in important interests. Therefore, an approved law school must provide an opportunity for its students to study in a diverse educational environment and, in order to protect the interests of the public, law students, and the profession, it must provide an educational program that ensures that its graduates:

(1) understand their ethical responsibilities as representatives of clients, officers of the courts, and public citizens responsible for the quality and availability of justice;

(2) receive basic education through a curriculum that develops:

(i) understanding of the theory, philosophy, role, and ramifications of the law and its institutions;

(ii) skills of legal analysis, reasoning, and problem solving; oral and written communication; legal research; and other fundamental skills necessary to participate effectively in the legal profession;

(iii) understanding of the basic principles of public and private law; and

(3) understand the law as a public profession calling for performance of pro bono legal services.

The Standards have evolved since their inception into a comprehensive statement by which legal education programs may be evaluated. The Standards define the minimum criteria for acceptable legal education and training needed to qualify students to enter the practice of law. The Standards, as developed by the Council and adopted by the House of Delegates, are published and available through the ABA Service Center, which can be reached at (800) 285-2221. They are also available *via* the Section's website at http://www.abanet.org/legaled.

The Standards have been developed and revised through an ongoing evaluation process conducted through the participation of legal educators, practitioners, and judges. The Standards Review Committee of the Section continually reviews the Standards and makes suggestions for changes to the Council. Amendments are adopted after a process that involves advice from a variety of constituencies, with public hearings and other opportunities for interested parties to comment. In 1994, the Section, through its Standards Review Committee, undertook a total revision of the Standards and Interpretations. The Committee conducted public hearings and sought the views of members of various constituencies interested in legal education. This process culminated in a comprehensive set of revised Standards and Interpretations that was unanimously approved by the House of Delegates in August 1996. In the following year, the Council, through its Standards Review Committee, undertook a revision of the Rules of Procedure that was adopted by the House of Delegates in August 1997.

Foreign Study

The ABA approves foreign study programs of ABA approved law schools and individual foreign study programs for students who are currently enrolled in ABA approved law schools. The Council has adopted Criteria for Approval of Foreign Summer Programs, Criteria for Approval of Semester Abroad Programs, Criteria for Approval of Cooperative Programs for Foreign Study, and Criteria for Approval of Individual Student Study Abroad for Academic Credit.

Students currently enrolled at an ABA approved law school who desire to receive credit toward their J.D. degree for studies in a foreign program should read carefully the applicable criteria for their course of study. Typically, these programs are only open to students who have successfully completed their first year of study in law school. Students have four options to earn credit for foreign study in an ABA approved foreign program. They may (1) enroll in an approved summer program through an ABA approved law school; (2) enroll in an approved semester abroad program through an ABA approved law school; (3) earn credit from the ABA approved law school they are attending by participating in its ABA approved cooperative program with a foreign institution; and (4) establish their own semester course of study with the approval of the ABA *and* the ABA approved law school they are attending. Additional information on this subject may be obtained on the Section's website at http://www.abanet.org/legaled.

Post J.D. Programs and Other Programs in Addition to the J.D.

The Standards require all ABA approved law schools to obtain acquiescence from the Council prior to establishing a degree in addition to its J.D. degree program. A law school may not establish a degree program in addition to its J.D. degree program unless the school is fully approved and the quality of its J.D. degree program exceeds the requirements of the Standards. The additional degree program may not detract from a law school's ability to maintain a sound J.D. degree program.

About the ABA

The American Bar Association is the national organization of the legal profession. While encouraging professional development among its members and providing leadership in the improvement of the law, the ABA focuses a significant portion of its efforts and resources on a wide range of activities to improve the administration of justice and the delivery of legal services to the public.

Public service activities take place in such varied areas as environmental and energy law; election reform; housing and urban growth; juvenile justice; judicial reform; protection of legal rights of prisoners, the mentally disabled, and the elderly; and delivery of legal services to the poor.

Founded on August 21, 1878, the American Bar Association is the largest voluntary professional organization in the world, with a current membership of more than 350,000 -- representing about half the lawyers in the United States. In addition, the Law Student Division has more than 35,000 members.

ABA membership is open to lawyers admitted to practice and in good standing before the bar of any state or territory of the United States. Members include judges, professors, government officials, court administrators, business executives, and lawyers working in other fields. Eligible to affiliate with the ABA as associates are nonlawyer judges, administrators, federal court and bar association executives, criminal justice professionals, and others in law related areas. Members of the legal profession in other nations can become international associates.

The ABA is committed to keeping its members and the general public informed of the latest developments in the law and law-related fields. To accomplish this goal, it publishes numerous books and pamphlets and, on a regular basis, a variety of magazines, journals, and newsletters. To order an ABA publication call the ABA Service Center at (800) 285-2221.

American Bar Association Headquarters
750 North Lake Shore Drive
Chicago, Illinois 60611
(312) 988-5000
http://www.abanet.org

Chapter Three

Prelaw Preparation

Written by The Prelaw Committee of the ABA Section of Legal Education and Admissions to the Bar

(What follows is a statement on preparation for legal education drafted by the Prelaw Committee of the ABA Section of Legal Education and Admissions to the Bar. It addresses the course of study and skills necessary to obtain admission into law school and to be a successful lawyer.)

Students who are successful in law school, and who become accomplished attorneys or use their legal education successfully in other areas of professional life, come to their legal education from widely differing educational and experiential backgrounds. As undergraduate students, some have majored in subjects that are traditionally considered paths to law school, such as history, English, philosophy, political science, economics or business. Other successful law students, however, have focused their undergraduate studies in areas as diverse as art, music theory, computer science, engineering, nursing or education. Many law students enter law school directly from their undergraduate studies and without having had any substantial work experience. Others begin their legal education significantly later in life, and they bring to their law school education the insights and perspectives gained from those life experiences.

Thus the ABA does **not** recommend any particular group of undergraduate majors, or courses that should be taken by those wishing to prepare for legal education; developing such a list is neither possible nor desirable. The law is too multifaceted, and the human mind too adaptable, to permit such a linear approach to preparing for law school or the practice of law. Nonetheless, there are important skills and values, and significant bodies of knowledge, that can be acquired prior to law school and that will provide a sound foundation for a sophisticated legal education. This statement presents the recommendations of the American Bar Association Section of Legal Education and Admissions to the Bar concerning preparation for a good law school experience.

Prospective law students should also consult closely with the prelaw advisor at their undergraduate institution. That individual may be able to assist current students in selecting courses or professors that will particularly assist in developing the skills and knowledge foundation that is emphasized in this statement. Taking difficult courses from demanding instructors is the best generic preparation for legal education. The prelaw advisor can also assist current and former students in choosing law schools to which to apply that are appropriate in light of a prospective student's interests and credentials. Finally, prospective law students should also consult the publications and admissions personnel of the schools to which they are considering applying for any specific recommendations that individual schools may have concerning preparation for law school.

There are numerous skills and values that are essential to success in law school and to competent lawyering. There also is a large body of information that law students, and attorneys, should possess. The three or four years that a student spends in obtaining a quality legal education can and do provide much of the information that a lawyer needs. Good legal education also aids in developing the many skills and values essential to competent lawyering. Sound legal education, however, must build upon and further refine skills, values and knowledge that the student already possesses. Even though a student may well be able to acquire in law school some specific fundamental skills and knowledge that the student's pre-law school experience has not provided, the student who comes to law school lacking a broad range of basic skills and knowledge will face an extremely difficult task.

Skills and Values

The core skills and values that are essential for competent lawyering include analytic and problem solving skills, critical reading abilities, writing skills, oral communication and listening abilities, general research skills, task organization and management skills, and the values of serving faithfully the interests of others while also promoting justice.[1] Thus, individuals who wish to prepare adequately for legal education, and for a career in law or for other professional service that involves the use of lawyering skills, should seek educational, extracurricular and life experiences that will assist them in developing those attributes.[2] Some brief comments about each of the listed skills and values follow.

Analytic and Problem Solving Skills

Students should seek courses and other experiences that will engage them in critical thinking about important issues, that will engender in them tolerance for uncertainty, and that will give them experience in structuring and evaluating arguments for and against propositions that are susceptible to reasoned debate. Students also should seek courses and other experiences that require them to apply previously developed principles or theories to new situations, and that demand that they develop solutions to new problems. Good legal education teaches students to "think like a lawyer," but the analytic and problem-solving skills required of attorneys are not fundamentally different from those employed by other professionals. The law school experience will develop and refine those crucial skills, but one must enter law school with a reasonably well developed set of analytic and problem solving abilities.

Critical Reading Abilities

Preparation for legal education should include substantial experience at close reading and critical analysis of complex textual material, for much of what law students and attorneys do involves careful reading and sophisticated comprehension of judicial opinions,

statutes, documents, and other written materials. As with the other skills discussed in this statement, the requisite critical reading abilities may be acquired in a wide range of experiences, including the close reading of complex material in literature, political or economic theory, philosophy, or history. The particular nature of the materials examined is not crucial; what is important is that law school not be the first time that a student has been rigorously engaged in the enterprise of carefully reading and understanding, and critically analyzing, complex written material of substantial length. Potential law students should also be aware that the study and practice of law require the ability to read and assimilate large amounts of material, often in a short period of time.

Writing Skills

Those seeking to prepare for legal education should develop a high degree of skill at written communication. Language is the most important tool of a lawyer, and lawyers must learn to express themselves clearly and concisely. Legal education provides good training in writing, and particularly in the specific techniques and forms of written expression that are common in the law. Fundamental writing skills, however, should be acquired and refined before one enters law school. Those preparing for legal education should seek as many experiences as possible that will require rigorous and analytical writing, including preparing original pieces of substantial length and revising written work in response to constructive criticism.

Oral Communication and Listening Abilities

The ability to speak clearly and persuasively is another skill that is essential to success in law school and the practice of law. Lawyers also must have excellent listening skills if they are to understand their clients and others with whom they must interact daily. As with writing skills, legal education provides excellent opportunities for refining oral communication skills, and particularly for practicing the forms and techniques of oral expression that are most common in the practice of law. Before coming to law school, however, individuals should seek to develop their basic speaking and listening skills, such as by engaging in debate, making formal presentations in class, or speaking before groups in school, the community, or the workplace.

General Research Skills

Although there are many research sources and techniques that are specific to the law, an individual need not have developed any familiarity with these specific skills or materials before entering law school. However, the individual who comes to law school without ever having undertaken a project that requires significant library research and the analysis of large amounts of information obtained from that research will be at a severe disadvantage. Those wishing to prepare for legal education should select courses and seek experiences that will require them to plan a research strategy, to undertake substantial library research, and to analyze, organize and present a reasonably large amount of material. A basic ability to use a personal computer is also increasingly important for law students, both for word processing and for computerized legal research.

Task Organization and Management Skills

The study and practice of law require the ability to organize large amounts of information, to identify objectives, and to create a structure for applying that information in an efficient way in order to achieve desired results. Many law school courses, for example, are graded primarily on the basis of one examination at the end of the course, and many projects in the practice of law require the compilation of large amounts of information from a wide variety of sources, frequently over relatively brief periods of time. Thus those entering law school must be prepared to organize and assimilate large amounts of information in a manner that facilitates the recall and application of that information in an effective and efficient manner. Some of the requisite experience can be obtained through undertaking school projects that require substantial research and writing, or through the preparation of major reports for an employer, a school, or a civic organization.

Serving Others and Promoting Justice

Each member of the legal profession should be dedicated both to the objectives of serving others honestly, competently, and responsibly, and to the goals of improving fairness and the quality of justice in the legal system. Those thinking of entering this profession would be well served by having some significant experience, before coming to law school, in which they devoted substantial effort toward assisting others. Participation in public service projects or similar efforts at achieving objectives established for common purposes can be particularly helpful.

Knowledge

In addition to these fundamental skills and values, there are some basic areas of knowledge that are important to a sophisticated legal education and to the development of a competent attorney. As law becomes more pervasive in our society, an increasingly broad range of knowledge and information from other disciplines become relevant to lawyering and to any full understanding of the legal system. Some of that knowledge, particularly that most directly relevant to particular areas of the law, can be acquired in law school or when necessary for a particular project.

There are, however, generic types of knowledge that one should possess in order to have a full appreciation of the legal system in general, to understand how disputes might be resolved, to understand and apply various legal principles and standards, and to appreciate the context in which a legal problem or dispute arises. Some of the types of knowledge that are most useful, and that would most pervasively affect one's ability to derive the maximum benefit from legal education, include the following:

> A broad understanding of history, particularly American history, and the various factors (social, political,

economic, and cultural) that have influenced the development of the pluralistic society that presently exists in the United States;

A fundamental understanding of political thought and theory, and of the contemporary American political system;

A basic understanding of ethical theory and theories of justice;

A grounding in economics, particularly elementary micro-economic theory, and an understanding of the interaction between economic theory and public policy;

Some basic mathematical and financial skills, such as an understanding of basic precalculus mathematics and an ability to analyze financial data;

A basic understanding of human behavior and social interaction; and

An understanding of diverse cultures within and beyond the United States, of international institutions and issues, and of the increasing interdependence of the nations and communities within our world.

As law has become more woven into the fabric of our society, and as that society is increasingly influenced by disparate national and global forces, a broad knowledge base is essential for success in law school and for competence in the legal profession. Knowledge of specific areas of law can and will be acquired during a good legal education, but students must come to law school with much fundamental knowledge upon which legal education can build. Thus, those considering law school should focus their substantive preparation on acquiring the broad knowledge and perspectives outlined above.

Conclusion

The skills, values and knowledge discussed in this statement may be acquired in a wide variety of ways. One may take undergraduate, graduate, or even high school courses that can assist an individual in acquiring much of the requisite information, skills and perspectives. One may also gain much of this essential background through self-learning (another essential lawyering skill), by reading, in the workplace, or through various other life experiences. Moreover, it is not essential that everyone come to law school having fully developed all of the skills, values and knowledge suggested in this statement. Some of that foundation can be acquired during the initial years of law school. However, one who begins law school having already acquired most of the skills, values and knowledge listed in this statement will have a significant advantage and will be well prepared to benefit fully from a sophisticated and challenging legal education.

---

[1] These core skill and value areas are drawn, in substantial part, from the Statement of Skills and Values contained in the 1992 Report of the American Bar Association Task Force on Law Schools and the Profession, *Legal Education and Professional Development — An Educational Continuum.*

[2] People with various disabilities, such as visual or hearing limitations, have been successful in law school and in the practice of law. Persons with such disabilities, however, should be cognizant of the particular challenges that they may face in law school and in the profession.

Rating of Law Schools

No rating of law schools beyond the simple statement of their accreditation status is attempted or advocated by the American Bar Association. Qualities that make one kind of school good for one student may not be as important to another. The American Bar Association and its Section of Legal Education and Admissions to the Bar have issued disclaimers of any law school rating system. Prospective law students should consider a variety of factors in making their choice among approved schools.

Chapter Four

Admissions Process

Written by Philip D. Shelton, Executive Director and President of the Law School Admission Council (LSAC)

Law school applicants can expect the admissions process to be quite competitive. Most law schools receive more than enough applications from highly qualified candidates, many of whom would be perfectly capable of completing a law school education. The dilemma for admission committees is that limited space and resources mandate the denial of admission to many of these candidates.

Your Credentials

No concrete principles exist for predicting who will perform well in school. In order to be fair, schools rely heavily upon selection criteria that bear on expected performance in law school and can be applied objectively to all candidates. Law schools consider a variety of factors in admitting their students, and no single qualification will independently guarantee acceptance or rejection. However, the two factors that usually outweigh the rest are prior academic performance and the Law School Admission Test score.

Undergraduate performance is generally an important indicator of how someone is likely to perform in law school. Hence, many law schools look closely at college grades when considering individual applications. Course selection also can make a difference in admission evaluations. Applicants who have taken difficult or advanced courses in their undergraduate study often are evaluated in a more favorable light than students who have concentrated on easier or less advanced subjects.

Many law schools consider undergraduate-performance trends along with a student's numerical average. Thus, they may discount a slow start in a student's undergraduate career if he or she performs exceptionally well in the later school years. Similarly, admission committees may see an undergraduate's strong start followed by a mediocre finish as an indication of lesser potential to do well in law school. Candidates are advised to comment on irregular grade trends in the personal statement section of the application.

Choosing Schools

When selecting law schools to which you will apply, the general philosophy is that you should have a threefold plan: dream a little, be realistic, and be safe. Most applicants have no trouble selecting dream schools--those that are almost, but not quite, beyond their grasp--or safe schools--those for which admission is virtually certain. Applicants often have difficulty being realistic about their qualifications and their chances of being accepted at particular law schools.

Unquestionably, the number one strategic error in law school admission is a candidate's failure to evaluate realistically his or her own credentials.

Check your qualifications against the admission profile of the law schools to which you aspire with the information contained in this publication. Most schools publish statistics in this book on the GPA and LSAT 75th percentile and 25th percentile of the most recent entering class. You may use these data to help you determine where you should apply. Apply to those law schools whose student body profiles most closely match your personal profile. Those schools will be as eager to accept you as you are to be admitted.

Other Sources of Information

The school's admission office. This is a good source for general information about your chances for admission. Do not hesitate to request admission counseling. Be sure to obtain current catalogs from each law school you are considering.

Your college or university prelaw advisor. Your prelaw advisor can often provide you with reliable information about which law schools fit your personal profile. He or she may also be able to tell you which law schools have accepted students from your school in the past and provide you with an overview of the admitted students' credentials. However, you should not necessarily narrow your focus to only those law schools where others from your undergraduate school have been admitted.

School representatives and alumni. Take advantage of opportunities to talk with law school representatives and alumni. When you talk with alumni, remember that law schools sometimes change fairly quickly. Try to talk to a recent graduate or to one who is active in alumni affairs and therefore knowledgeable about the school as it is today.

School visits. You can learn a surprising amount about a school from talks with students and faculty members. Many law schools have formal programs in which a currently enrolled student will take you on a tour of the campus and answer your questions. Such a first-hand experience can be quite valuable in assessing how you would fit into the school.

Internet. The internet is a great source of information for learning more about law schools. You can visit the LSAC homepage at http://www.lsac.org or you can visit the homepage for the Section of Legal Education and Admissions to the Bar at http://www.abanet.org/legaled.

Admission Mechanics

Many law schools operate what is known as a rolling admission process: the school evaluates applications and informs candidates of admission decisions on a continuous basis over several months, usually beginning in late fall and extending to midsummer for waiting-list admissions.

At such schools, it is especially important for you to apply at the earliest possible date. The earlier you apply, the more places the school will have available. Most schools try to make comparable decisions throughout the admission season, even those that practice rolling admission. Still, it is disadvantageous to be one of the last applicants to complete a file. Furthermore, the more decisions you receive from law schools early in the process, the better able you will be to make your own decisions, such as whether to apply to more law schools or whether to accept a particular school's offer.

The average applicant applies to four or five law schools. You should be sure to place your applications at schools representing a range of admission standards. Even if you have top qualifications, you should apply to at least one safety school where you are almost certain of being admitted. This is your insurance policy. If you apply to a safety school in November, and are accepted in January or February, you may be disappointed but not panicked if you are later rejected by your top choices.

If you have strong qualifications, but you do not quite meet the competition of those currently being admitted at a particular law school, you may be placed on a waiting list for possible admission at a later date. The law school will send you a letter notifying you of its decision as early as April or as late as July.

It is up to you whether you wish to wait for a decision from a school that has put you on a waiting list or accept an offer from a school that has already accepted you.

Many law schools use seat deposits to help keep track of their new classes. For example, a school may require an initial acceptance fee of $200, which is credited to your first-term tuition if you actually register at the school; if you do not register, the deposit may be forfeited or partially refunded. A school may require a larger deposit around July 1, which is also credited to tuition. If you decline the offer of admission after you have paid your deposit, a portion of the money may be refunded, depending on the date you actually decline the offer. At some schools none of the deposit may be refunded.

Where to Attend

For some people, the choice of which law school to attend is an easy one. The most outstanding students will probably be able to go anywhere, and they will select the schools they perceive to be the most prestigious or which offer a program of particular interest. Others who need to stay in a particular area, perhaps because they have a family or a job they do not want to leave, will choose nearby schools or schools with part-time programs.

However, the majority of applicants will have to weigh a variety of personal and academic factors to come up with a list of potential schools. Then, once they have a list and more than one acceptance letter, they will have to choose a school. Applicants should consider carefully the offerings of each law school before making a decision. The quality of a law school is certainly a major consideration; however, estimations of quality are very subjective. Factors such as the campus atmosphere, the school's devotion to teaching and learning, and the applicant's enthusiasm for the school are very important. Remember that the law school is going to be your home for three or four years. Adjusting to law school and the general attitudes of a professional school is difficult enough without the additional distraction of culture shock.

All ABA approved law schools and many non ABA approved law schools require that you take the LSAT. The test consists of five 35-minute sections of multiple-choice questions, in three different areas. A 30-minute unscored writing sample is administered at the end of the test. The LSAT is designed to measure skills considered essential for success in law school: the reading and comprehension of complex texts with accuracy and insight; the organization and management of information and the ability to draw reasonable inferences from it; the ability to think critically; and, the analysis and evaluation of the reasoning and argument of others.

Most law school applicants familiarize themselves with test mechanics and question types, practice on sample tests, and study the information available on test-taking techniques and strategies. Though it is difficult to say when examinees are sufficiently prepared, very few people achieve their full potential without some preparation.

The most difficult admission decisions are those regarding candidates who are neither so well qualified nor so deficient as to present a clear-cut case for acceptance or rejection. These applicants constitute the majority of the applicant pool at many law schools and are the candidates that most law schools spend the bulk of their time reviewing.

Law school admission committees also consider other criteria: undergraduate course of study; graduate work, if any; college attended; improvement in grades and grade distribution; college curricular and extracurricular activities; ethnic/racial background; individual character and personality; letters of recommendation; personal statement or essay; work experience or other post undergraduate experiences; community activities; motivation to study and reasons for deciding to study law; state of residency; difficulties overcome; pre-college preparation; past accomplishments and leadership; and anything else that would distinguish you as a candidate.

(Excerpted, with permission, from The Official Guide to U.S. Law Schools, Law School Admission Council, Inc. (1999).)

See the next page for more information about the LSAT, LSAC, Law Services, or LSDAS -- or contact LSAC directly.

Law School Admission Council
Box 2000
Newtown, PA 18940-0998
(215) 968-1001
http://www.lsac.org

Law School Admission Council (LSAC)

Excerpted, with permission, from* The Official Guide to U.S. Law Schools, *Law School Admission Council, Inc. (1999)

Working with LSAC

LSAC administers the LSAT and serves as a liaison for much of the communication between you and the law schools. You are expected to send your individual law school application **directly to each law school** to which you apply; however, your test scores, transcripts, and other academic information and biographical data are sent to the law schools through the Law School Data Assembly Services (LSDAS).

Comprehensive information about LSAT registration and LSDAS subscription is set forth in complete detail in the *LSAT/LSDAS Registration and Information Book*, published annually. This publication is available at no charge through LSAC or any of 3,500 national distribution sites located on undergraduate campuses (principally prelaw advising offices and career centers) and at law schools. (LSAC operators will provide a list of distribution locations nearest your zip code; call 215-968-1001.)

You need not subscribe to the LSDAS at the same time you register for the LSAT, but doing so will simplify the process. Application deadlines for the law schools to which you apply dictate when you should subscribe to the LSDAS.

Planning Ahead for Law School Deadlines

Most law schools have a variety of application requirements and deadlines that you must meet to be considered for admission. Many of the deadlines are listed in this book. If you are applying to a number of schools, the various deadlines and requirements can be confusing. It probably will be helpful if you set up a detailed calendar that will remind you of when and what you must do to complete an application.

You will also want to be sure you can make an LSAT score available to a law school before its application deadline. In registering for the LSAT, be sure to give yourself enough time to select a convenient testing location and prepare for the actual test.

Below is a chart listing all the scheduled test administrations, including alternate dates for Saturday Sabbath observers, along with corresponding deadlines.

Basic LSAT Date and Deadline Information (1998-1999)

All scheduled administrations of the LSAT, both for regular test takers and test takers who are Saturday Sabbath observers, are listed below along with corresponding regular registration deadlines. Dates shown represent postmark deadlines for mail registrations and receipt deadlines for telephone and online registration. The basic fee for the LSAT is $86 (published test centers only).

For information on deadlines and fees for late registrations and nonpublished test centers (domestic and foreign), partial refunds, and early score reporting by telephone (TelScore), please refer to the current *LSAT/LSDAS Registration and Information Book*, or call LSAC directly at 215-968-1001. You can also find complete registration information on their World Wide Web site at *http://www.lsac.org*.

LSAT Test Dates

Regular	Monday June 15, 1998	Saturday September 26, 1998	Saturday December 5, 1998	Saturday February 6, 1999
Saturday Sabbath Observers		Monday September 28, 1998	Monday December 7, 1998	Monday February 8, 1999
Score Report Mailed (Approx.)	July 14, 1998	October 26, 1998	January 7, 1999	March 4, 1999
Regular Registration Deadlines (Mail, telephone, and online)				
Domestic	May 15, 1998	August 28, 1998	November 6, 1998	January 8, 1999
Foreign	May 8, 1998	August 21, 1998	October 30, 1998	January 2, 1999

Law School Forums Sponsored by LSAC

If you are considering law school -- attend a Law School Forum. Free admission. No preregistration. In one place, you can talk with representatives of LSAC-member law schools from across the United States; obtain admission materials, catalogs, and financial aid information; view video programs about the law school admission process, legal education and careers, and minority perspectives on legal education; attend informational sessions on the law school admission process, financing a legal education, and issues of importance to minority applicants, and purchase LSAC publications and LSAT® preparation materials. Forum hours are generally from 2 P.M. to 8 P.M. on Fridays and from 10 A.M. to either 4 P.M. or 5 P.M. on Saturdays, **depending on the city**. To confirm times and learn further details, call (215) 968-1001. Check the LSAC Web site at http://www.lsac.org, or watch for ads in your local media preceding the event. For further information contact: Law School Forums, LSAC, Box 40, Newtown, PA 18940-0040. The locations of the Law School Forums for 1998 are listed below.

Law School Forum Locations & Dates

Atlanta, Georgia
Friday, October 2-Saturday, October 3
Omni Hotel at CNN Center
100 CNN Center
Atlanta, GA

Boston, Massachusetts
Friday, October 30-Saturday, October 31
Marriott Copley Place
110 Huntington Avenue
Boston, MA

Chicago, Illinois
Friday, November 13 -Saturday, November 14
Chicago Hilton and Towers
720 South Michigan Avenue
Chicago, IL

Dallas, Texas
Saturday, October 10
Hotel Inter-Continental Dallas
15201 Dallas Parkway
Dallas, TX

Los Angeles, California
Friday, November 6-Saturday, November 7
Los Angeles Airport Marriot
5855 West Century Blvd.
Los Angeles, CA

New York, New York
Friday, September 18-Saturday, September 19
New York Marriott World Trade Center
Three World Trade Center
New York, NY

Washington, DC
Saturday, July 18
Omni Shoreham Hotel
2500 Calvert Street, N.W.
Washington, DC

Chapter Five

Finance & Debt Management*

Written by Jeffrey E. Hanson, Director, Debt Management Services, The Access Group, Box 7430, Wilmington, Delaware 19803-0430, (800) 282-1550 http://www.accessgrp.org

Introduction: Your Educational Investment

Your education is a major investment in yourself. Getting an education requires an investment of both time and money. *It is the expenditure of your scarce (limited) resources now, in the hope that you will realize a positive return on your investment in the future.* You must consider the time and money you'll invest in your education, along with the personal and professional goals you've set for yourself. Then, make the best investment you can. Your goal should be to borrow the minimum amount necessary to achieve your degree at the school you attend. This should both maximize the net return on your investment, and help you realize your financial and career goals.

How you pay for your education is an important decision that will impact your financial future and the lifestyle you can afford once you graduate. It also will influence how quickly you achieve your financial goals. Unless you currently have enough money in the bank to pay for school, you will need to **finance** your educational investment. In other words, you will be dependent on others to help you pay for your education. Just as you investigate which schools have the best programs for you, so too, you must gather information about how best to finance your degree. Deciding how you finance your degree should involve you, your family, and, unless your family can finance the full cost of your education, the school you want to attend. Note that you should be able to obtain financial assistance up to the estimated cost of attendance if you need it so long as:

- you do not have credit problems, and
- you are a U.S. citizen or permanent resident.

Conversely, sufficient financing may be difficult to obtain if you have credit problems and/or are an international student. Therefore, it is important to become well-informed about your financing options as soon as possible, and to act responsibly in the financing of your education.

Financing Your Education in a Responsible Manner

You will have financed your education in a responsible manner if you borrow the minimum amount necessary to achieve your educational goal, repay your student loans according to the repayment schedule, learn how to manage your financial affairs in a timely and efficient manner, have no regrets once you graduate about spending the resources that are required to obtain your degree, maximize the net return on your educational investment, succeed in getting the career opportunity you want once you graduate, and are able to afford the lifestyle you want once you graduate. In order to finance your education responsibly, and to maximize your educational investment, you need to get into some good financial habits.

Good Habits to a Sound Financial Future: *"The Borrower's Dozen"*

For most people, bad habits are hard to break and it is difficult to get into good habits, particularly when it comes to money. The following ***"Borrower's Dozen"*** is a listing of 13 good financial habits that should help you achieve your goals and guide you in financing your education responsibly. It's not too early to get into these habits if you haven't already done so. The longer you wait, the more difficult it will be to get into these habits.

1. Identify your goals.
2. Make well-informed choices about how you use your scarce resources.
3. Don't live a lifestyle you can't afford. Live *below* your means while in school so that you can afford to live like a professional once you graduate.
4. Budget your money just as carefully as your time; get on a monthly budget and stick to it.
5. Save a little each month (even if only $5), and plan for your financial future.
6. Keep accurate, well-organized records of your financial activities.
7. Establish and maintain a strong credit history; review your credit report annually.
8. Borrow the minimum amount you need.
9. Pay the interest on unsubsidized loans when it accrues, if possible.
10. Be a well-informed borrower. Not all loans are alike; know the differences and borrow wisely.
11. Pay your credit card balance in full each month. Charge only what you know you can repay when the bill arrives.
12. Limit the number of credit cards you have and your available credit.
13. Be realistic about how much money you'll earn once you graduate — don't count on any immediate financial windfalls.

It may not be easy for you to get into these habits, but if you can, you should have greater success achieving your financial goals. Some suggestions follow about how you can get into each of these habits.

Habit #1. *Identify your goals.*

You need to identify your long-term personal, professional, and financial goals. You should attempt to answer the following questions as you go about setting your goals.

- How do I want to use what I have learned?
- What do I want to accomplish in my career?
- Where do I want to work?
- How much do I hope to earn each year?
- Where do I want to live?
- What kind of lifestyle do I want?
- What are my hopes for a family?
- When do I want to retire?
- What kind of lifestyle do I want once I retire?

The worksheet in Figure 1 is an example of one way you can decide upon your goals. There also are books and software products available on the subject of personal finance that include sections on goal setting. Whatever approach works best for you, setting goals is an important step in financing your education responsibly.

Habit #2. *Make well-informed choices about how you use your scarce resources.*

The cost of your education really is up to you. How much you "spend" getting your degree is a function of the choices or decisions you make. In other words, the cost of your degree is a matter of ***CHOICE***. For example:

- cost of tuition depends on the school you **CHOOSE**;
- cost of housing depends on where you **CHOOSE** to live;
- cost of food depends on how/where/what you **CHOOSE** to eat;
- cost of entertainment depends on what you **CHOOSE** to do for fun;
- cost of transportation depends on what mode of transportation you **CHOOSE** to use.

Once you make a choice, you must pay the required "cost." **As such, YOU are responsible for the choices you make.** No one else can claim that responsibility — not your parents, not your friends, not your siblings, not your financial aid officer, etc. You need to make the most well-informed choices you can through sound financial planning and careful budgeting of your scarce resources. Careful budget planning is required in order to make choices that will maximize the long-term net return on your educational investment.

Habit #3. *Don't live a lifestyle you can't afford. Live below your means while in school so that you can live like a professional once you graduate.*

If you live like someone with an advanced degree while you're in school, you may have to live like a student once you graduate! Live *below* your means as a student; be thrifty! For example, go to half-priced movies, buy your clothes at outlet or second-hand stores, use public transportation, live with a roommate (you should be able to reduce your housing expenses by at least $200 per month if you live with a roommate), rent videos rather than going out, use your school's recreational facilities rather than joining a health club. Remember, you must repay every dollar you borrow (*plus interest*) and this will reduce your disposable income (*the money you use to pay for food, rent, transportation, fun, etc.*) once you graduate.

Habit #4. *Budget your money just as carefully as your time; get on a monthly budget and stick to it.*

Your personal budget is like a road map. It is a worksheet describing your lifestyle. It tells you who you are financially, where you are currently, and where it is you want to be. In other words, it can be used to show you where you're going financially and how to get there. Your budget can guide you in knowing how much debt or credit you can safely afford. It can help motivate you to reduce your discretionary consumer borrowing (i.e., use of credit cards).

Your personal budget is an important component of any financial planning you do. In fact, the first step any financial planner will take in advising you about your investments and finances will be to develop a comprehensive personal budget. It also is an important element in applying for personal and business loans.

The best way to develop your personal budget is to use worksheets. There are a number of self-help books on the market that have alternative versions of a budget worksheet. You also can use one of the available software products like *Access Advisor*, *Quicken*, or *Microsoft Money*. *Access Advisor* is an integrated debt management software package that is available on the Access Group® Web site at **http://www.accessgrp.org**.

The important thing to remember in developing your budget is that your goal is to determine how much you spend each **MONTH** on the various items you purchase. It should be detailed and as accurate as possible. You can use receipts or monthly billing statements to help quantify your expenses on discretionary items such as food, entertainment and clothing. You also can keep a daily journal of how you spent your money that day on these items. If you choose to use a daily journal, set up a worksheet with columns corresponding to the items in your budget (for example, food, clothing, transportation, entertainment). Then, each day, write down how much you spend in each category. You don't need to describe the purchase or indicate how you paid for it, just write in the amount (and perhaps, the date). KEEP IT SIMPLE — otherwise you may not stay with it! Tally each column on your worksheet at the end of the month and add it to your fixed (non-discretionary) payments such as rent, loan payments, etc. Repeat the process for several months to get an average, or do it every month.

You also need to follow a few "budgeting don'ts" in order to be successful in creating and living within your budget. The follow-

ing suggested things to avoid are taken from *Your Personal Financial Fitness Program, 1991-92* Edition by E.S. Lewin (1991, Facts on File, New York): (1) don't be dictatorial, work out the budget with yourself and other family members; (2) don't be in a hurry, you can't do it in an hour or a single sitting, it takes time; (3) don't go by what others spend (that is, don't keep up with the Joneses); (4) don't expect miracles, a budget is a tool to help manage more effectively; by itself, it will not give you more money or cut your spending; (5) don't nickel and dime it, round figures up or down to the nearest dollar or $10; (6) don't overdo the paperwork, report the essentials, that's all; and (7) don't be inflexible.

Habit #5. *Save a little each month (even if only $5), and plan for your financial future.*

Financial planners advise that it is essential to have savings. You need to have readily available funds for emergencies and other financial goals you want to achieve. Savings can provide the financial means to meet these needs. There are four steps you can take that should help you establish a successful savings program.

First, determine your savings and investment goal(s). Identify why you're saving money by establishing your savings goal(s). Determine what you are saving for (e.g., Bar exam expenses), how much you need or want to save (e.g., $1,000), and by when you need to have the money saved (e.g., graduation). This should make it much easier to discipline yourself in saving funds and in establishing the savings habit.

Second, "Pay yourself first!" Put money into your savings and/or investment account(s) at the beginning of the month or on payday. Don't wait until the end of the month thinking that you'll save whatever is leftover. If you plan to save only what is left, you'll find that there's nothing left! Another trick is to have the amount you want to save/invest taken directly from your checking account by your bank and transferred electronically to your savings or investment account(s). This way you don't have to remember to "Pay yourself first," and you'll not be tempted to put it off.

Third, make it inconvenient to withdraw funds. Establish your savings/investment account at a different bank or credit union from where you have your checking account. This will help reduce the temptation to withdraw funds for purposes other than the goal(s) you've set for yourself. Furthermore, don't get an ATM card or checks that you can use to withdraw funds from your savings/investment account. Make sure the only way you can withdraw funds is to go where you have your account(s) and withdraw the funds personally with a cashier's check or money order. This, too, will help minimize the chance you'll spend your savings on something other than your goal(s).

Fourth, earn as much as you can with your savings and investments without being uncomfortable with the level of financial risk. Make certain you're earning interest and/or dividends on the money you're saving/investing. You need to assess how much risk you're willing to take in deciding how to save/invest your funds. The greater the return, the higher the risk, and vice versa. In essence, you need to set up a savings or investment plan that will earn the maximum amount possible subject to the level of risk with which you are comfortable.

Habit #6. *Keep accurate, well organized records of your financial activities.*

You should keep copies of all documents relating to your financial activities. For example, you should retain copies of loan documents (e.g., applications, promissory notes, lender correspondence), receipts for major purchases (e.g., appliances, furniture, cars, any items with warranties), income tax returns and all the documentation used to prepare those returns (both federal and state), and your will. Remember, it is important to retain any documents related to the preparation of your tax returns until you're certain they will not be required for an audit of your return. Many tax experts suggest you should hold onto these documents for at least five (5) years.

You also should keep a log or journal of all conversations with the lender(s) and servicer(s) of any loans you borrow. This log should include: (1) the date and time you called, (2) the reason for the call, (3) any expected follow-up, and (4) the full name of the person with whom you spoke. You can maintain a notebook-style log or maintain the log on your personal computer. Whatever form you use, it may come in handy if there ever is a dispute about the conversation.

You need to develop a record-keeping system that will work for you. There are many books and software products available in bookstores on personal finance that you can use. These items contain information about how to set up your system. For example, you can use individual file folders, portfolios, three-ring binders, manila envelopes, or a filing cabinet approach. You also may want to consider developing a spreadsheet program on your personal computer (if you have one) to maintain your phone log, track expenses, etc. One such program is the "Access Advisor." "Access Advisor" is an integrated debt management software package that is available on the Access Group® Web site at **http://www.accessgrp.org**.

Whatever record-keeping system you choose, make certain that your approach is something you will maintain on a regular basis. You need to be well-organized and efficient in this process. Maintaining your record-keeping system may not be fun, but doing so can be a lifesaver if you ever get audited by the Internal Revenue Service or have other problems associated with the management of your financial affairs by a bank or other institution. In maintaining your record-keeping system, remember the **3-S's**: **S**imple — make it simple to use; **S**ustainable — make it sustainable, i.e., something you'll maintain over the long-term; **S**ecure — make it secure, your records need to be safe from fire or theft.

Habit #7. *Establish and maintain a strong credit history; review your credit report annually.*

Your credit report is your "**financial transcript**." It's comparable to your academic transcript and much more important when it comes to achieving your financial goals. Just as you are concerned about the quality and accuracy of your academic transcript, you should be concerned about the quality and accuracy of your financial transcript — i.e., your credit report. You can request a copy of your credit report by sending a written request (*typed or printed*) to one of the three national credit reporting agencies at the addresses listed below. You also may be able to order a copy of your credit report by phone or via the Internet. Thus, you may want to call the company before making your request so that you can select the procedure that is best suited to your needs.

If you submit a written request to obtain a copy of your credit report, it should include the following information: (1) your full name, including generation (e.g., Jr., Sr., I., II., III.); (2) your spouse's first name, if married; (3) your current address, including zip code; (4) any previous address(es) you have had in the past five years, including zip code(s); (5) your social security number; (6) your date of birth; (7) your current employer (if unemployed, say so); and (8) your daytime telephone number. Your request must be signed and should include a photocopy of documentation showing proof of your current address, for example, a recent billing statement from a major credit card company, a recent utility bill, or your valid driver's license.

Most credit reporting agencies charge a fee to obtain a credit report except in states where it is not permitted. Fees can vary by state based on state regulations. The maximum fee currently is $8.00 per report unless you have been denied credit within the last 60 days. It that case, you're entitled to a free copy of your report from the credit reporting agency that provided the report to the creditor who denied your request for credit. It's a good idea to call the company from which you are requesting a credit report in order to verify what fee you need to pay (as well as the correct procedure to follow). You also can ask what form(s) of payment they accept at the time you call. The addresses and toll-free telephone numbers of the three national credit reporting agencies are given below.

Equifax
P.O. Box 105873
Atlanta, GA 30348
(800) 685-1111

Experian *(formerly TRW)*
P.O. Box 8030
Layton, UT 84041-8030
(800) 682-7654

Trans Union
P.O. Box 390
Springfield, PA 19064-0390
(800) 888-4213

Be advised that credit criteria used to review/approve student loans can include the following: (1) absence of negative credit; (2) no bankruptcies, foreclosures, repossessions, charge-offs, or open judgments; (3) no prior education loan defaults unless paid in full or making satisfactory progress in repayment; and (4) absence of numerous past due accounts, i.e., no 30-, 60-, or 90-day delinquencies on consumer loans or revolving charge accounts within the past two years. You can call the Federal Trade Commission at (202) 326-2222 if you need help resolving credit problems.

Habit #8. *Borrow the minimum amount you need to achieve your goals.*

Although often it is necessary to borrow money to invest in your education or to buy a home, you should always borrow the minimum amount you need, and the loan(s) should have the lowest possible cost in terms of the interest rate and fees that you may be charged. **Every time you borrow money, whether an educational loan or from your credit card(s), you are influencing your financial future.** Remember, when you're financing your education with loans, you're essentially taking out an *"educational mortgage"* that you will need to repay with your future income. In repaying the money you have borrowed, you will reduce your future discretionary income. Therefore, you should ask yourself, "Do I really need this now?" every time you make a discretionary purchase with your borrowed funds or with a credit card. Think about the tradeoffs and make certain that the decision to borrow now will be a decision you won't regret when the bill to repay the debt arrives. Borrowing money to finance an investment is not a bad thing; it can be a very good financial decision. But remember, you should always maximize the net return on your investment, and this requires that you minimize what you pay for it, particularly with regard to the cost(s) associated with borrowing funds.

Habit #9. *Pay the interest on unsubsidized loans when it accrues, if possible.*

You can greatly reduce the amount of your educational debt when you enter repayment if you pay the interest that accrues on unsubsidized loans while you're in school, and during periods of eligible deferment and forbearance. Interest that accrues on unsubsidized federal and private loans during these periods will be capitalized (that is, added to the principal balance) at some point before they enter repayment. Once that interest is added to the principal, it also begins accruing interest. This can significantly increase the total principal and amount of total finance charges you will pay. As such, not paying the interest as it accrues will further reduce the amount of discretionary income you will have available to pay your living expenses once you graduate. Even paying just a portion of the interest as it accrues can help you achieve your financial goals more quickly, and reduce the financial burden of your educational loans.

Habit #10. *Be a well-informed borrower. Not all loans are alike; know the differences and borrow wisely.*

Educate yourself about the loans you borrow. The promissory note for your loan is the "contract" between you and the lender. It stipulates all the terms and conditions of a loan as well as your rights and responsibilities as a borrower. As such, the promissory note is the best source of information about each loan you borrow. You should read any promissory note you are required to sign before you sign it. **Remember, it is very important that you keep copies of all promissory notes you sign.**

Habit #11. *Pay your credit card balance in full each month. Charge only what you know you can repay when the bill arrives.*

"Use credit cards only for convenience, never for credit." This quote is taken from H. Jackson Brown, Jr., *Life's Little Instruction Book*, Rutledge Hill Press, 1991. You're using a credit card for convenience only when you pay the bill **IN FULL** each and every month. If you don't pay the bill in full each month, you're using your credit card for credit and that means you're living beyond your means. In other words, you're living a lifestyle you can't afford at that point in time. Doing so is not responsible behavior and in the long run, likely will prevent you from achieving your financial goals. If you can't pay the balance in full on an account, at least stop making further charges on the credit card.

Also remember to pay your credit card and all other bills by the stated due date. This is essential if you want to avoid getting into credit problems.

Habit #12. *Limit the number of credit cards you have and your available credit.*

Your credit rating can be affected by the number of credit cards you have. You don't need numerous credit cards while in school. You can reduce your overall credit rating if you have more than a few credit cards, even if you owe nothing on the surplus cards. Creditors like to see that you have been offered credit, have it available, but do not use it.

Which card(s) should you keep? The choice is up to you. You can keep the card with the lowest limit, the card with NO annual fee, the card that provides frequent flyer miles based on usage, etc. The best choice, however, probably is the card that has the lowest limit. You only need cards with limits of $1,000 to $2,000 to have sufficient credit for those emergencies that may occur. By keeping several cards with lower limits, you are less likely to build up a balance beyond what you can afford to repay in full each month.

Habit #13. *Be realistic about how much money you will earn once you graduate; don't count on any immediate financial windfalls.*

You may not be offered as much money as you expect when you graduate. Educate yourself about the job market in the field you plan to pursue. Plan for the future by estimating realistically now what your discretionary (after-tax) income will be after you complete your training. It may not be as much, or go as far, as you expect. The worksheet provided in Figure 1 can be used to help you estimate how far your paycheck will go once you graduate.

It also is important not to view your future income as a "financial windfall." The money you will be earning simply will be replacing the borrowed funds you have been living on while you are a student. Although you may be earning more than what you borrowed, your expenses also will be higher. Your budget once you start working will be larger, in part, because you'll have new expenses as a professional, and because you'll need to be repaying the educational loans you borrowed while in school. Thus, be very careful in your use of credit now. Using the expectation of a financial windfall when you graduate as justification for using your credit cards to enjoy a better lifestyle while in school, probably will be a decision you'll regret once you graduate and realize how much consumer debt you have accumulated. It also will make it more difficult to achieve your financial goals.

Financing Your Education: Questions To Ask Before Borrowing

You should get answers to the following 13 questions as you plan the financing of your education. Some of these questions are general and apply to any school you might attend; others are more specific to the programs, policies, and procedures of each school you're considering. You should evaluate these issues as you explore your financial options, regardless of where you plan to attend school. Remember, financing your education involves a collaboration of yourself, your family, the school you attend, and your lender(s). Answering these questions should give you the information you'll need to make well-informed choices about how to finance your education, and to make the most of your educational investment. The 13 questions are as follows.

1. What should I be doing now to prepare for meeting the cost of my education?
2. What eligibility requirements must I meet in order to obtain financing for my degree?
3. What financing options/programs are available to me at the school(s) I am considering attending?
4. What is the purpose of financial aid, and what do I need to know about the process?
5. How do I apply for financial assistance, and what application(s) is(are) needed?
6. When should I apply for financial assistance, and what are the application deadlines?
7. Will my parents be expected to provide any of their financial information and/or contribute to the cost of my education?
8. What is done with the information I (and my parents) provide?
9. What should I know about the assistance I am offered, such as grants, loans, work study?
10. What can I do to reduce the amount I have to borrow, yet still attend the school of my choice?
11. What can I do, once I arrive on campus, to minimize how much I borrow?

12. What options will I have to work while obtaining my degree?
13. What impact will the loan(s) I borrow have on me after I complete my education?

Where can you find the answers to these questions?

Each of these questions is discussed below in more detail. Additional information and answers should be available from a number of sources. The financial aid staff at the schools you're considering probably are your most important resource to use in answering these questions. You also can utilize publications from funding groups, such as federal and state governments, lenders, scholarship-granting organizations, and financial aid guidebooks that are available from your local bookstore. Another useful and timely source of answers to these questions is the Internet. Many schools have their own Web sites that often include information about financial aid. Contact any school you're considering, to see if it has a Web site. Many lenders and other funding organizations also have Web sites. For example, the Web site for the Access Group is **www.accessgrp.org**. Finally, there are several Web sites that have been established by government agencies and other organizations to assist students with the financing of their education. The following two sites may be a good place to start your search: **www.finaid.org** and **www.ed.gov**.

Question #1. What should I be doing now to prepare for meeting the cost of my education?

There are five steps you can take now to prepare for the cost of law school. These are steps that should be taken even before you have applied to and/or been admitted by a law school. They involve conversations with your family and with the financial aid staff at the schools you're considering attending, as well as specific actions you should take.

First, you should determine what resources you will be able to contribute toward your educational expenses. Your resources include contributions from your family (and spouse, if married), the funds you will have saved by the time you enroll, and any scholarship funds you're awarded by private foundations, associations, or other organizations. This will require that you discuss the cost of law school with your family (and spouse), and determine the extent to which they plan to assist you financially. You also will need to save as much money as you can before entering law school, and explore opportunities for scholarships/fellowships from private foundations, organizations, and associations, as well as federal, state, and local government agencies.

The second step is to contact the law schools you are interested in attending to find out the expected cost of attendance so that you can determine if you will have sufficient funds to pay for your education or if you will need to seek additional assistance through the financial aid program offered by the school(s). If you think you will need additional financial assistance from the school, you'll need to determine what assistance is offered, the required application procedures, and any applicable deadlines. You should find out how to obtain the necessary application forms and take the necessary steps to get them once they are available.

The third step is to make certain you don't have credit problems. You should contact one of the three national credit reporting agencies—Equifax, Experian (formerly TRW), or Trans Union Corporation—to obtain a copy of your credit report. If you think you may have credit problems, you should review your credit history with the financial aid staff at the law school you want to attend before you apply for loans. You can obtain a copy of your credit report by following the procedure described above in **Habit #7**.

The fourth step is to be careful how you use your credit cards. Consumer credit is not an investment; it's simply a means of improving your standard of living on a temporary basis. Credit card debt is bad debt. Get your credit card and other consumer debts paid off as quickly as possible. You will not be able to borrow additional student loan funds to pay your credit card bills.

Finally, plan now and prepare yourself for the financial future you want when you complete law school by getting into the good financial habits described above.

Question #2. What are the eligibility requirements in order to get financing for my degree?

There are several criteria that you must satisfy in order to participate in the federal financial aid programs. You must be enrolled at least half-time at an eligible institution pursuing a degree or certificate. You must be a U.S. citizen or eligible noncitizen (e.g., permanent resident). You cannot currently be in default on any prior federal student loans you may have borrowed nor owe a refund on a federal grant program. You also cannot have been charged with a drug offense. Failure to meet any of these criteria will make you ineligible to receive funding from any of the federal assistance programs. It is very important that you contact the financial aid office at the school(s) you're considering if you think you do not meet all the criteria listed above. There may be steps that can be taken to correct the problem. If you are an international student, please note that there currently are no federal financial aid programs available to you.

Privately guaranteed educational loan programs require all of the above criteria in addition to the requirement that you do not have credit problems. Lenders offering privately guaranteed student loans will check your credit history before approving a loan for you. The credit criteria that are used vary from one lender to the next. Most look primarily at your prior pattern of payment on your credit obligations. Consequently, it is a very good idea that you obtain current copies of your credit report from each of the three national credit reporting agencies if you think you'll need to apply for a privately

guaranteed student loan to help finance your educational expenses. Refer to **Habit #7** above for instructions on how to obtain a copy of your credit report.

Contact the financial aid office at the schools you're considering, once you have copies of your credit reports, if you think you have problems that might prevent you from being able to borrow a privately guaranteed loan. The financial aid staff may be able to offer assistance, or guide you to an agency like the Consumer Credit Counseling Service (CCCS) to help you repair your credit.

Question #3. What financing options/programs are available to me at the school(s) I am considering attending?

Important Disclosure: *As of the printing of this material, information regarding all aid programs is correct. Please note, however, that the specific details of these programs may change at any time due to changes in government legislation/regulation.*

There are three general financing options available if you cannot pay the full cost of law school from your own resources and those of your family: (1) grants/scholarships, (2) loans, and (3) work study. The sources of these funding options include federal and state governments; the school you attend; banks and other lending organizations; and private foundations, civic organizations, and other associations. Note that education loans are the most common and abundant source of funding available to law students.

Grants/Scholarships

Grants and scholarships are funds you do not have to repay. Availability of these funds is limited. In some instances, a service commitment is required in order to receive funding. There are three principal sources for grant and scholarship funding: (1) government, (2) institutional, and (3) private/civic sources.

Grant and scholarship assistance from government sources (federal/state) is dependent on the availability of funding and, in the case of state programs, the state in which you reside/attend law school. Not all states offer grant/scholarship assistance to law students. You should contact the financial aid office at the school you plan to attend to inquire about the availability of federal and state grant assistance. Be advised that some of these programs require a service commitment in order to receive the funding. Service typically requires that you practice law (oftentimes in the public interest) in a particular location for a specific period of time (usually one year of service for each year of funding support) immediately following graduation and passage of the Bar.

The institution you attend may award scholarship and/or grant assistance to students who meet their eligibility requirements. These scholarships/grants typically are funded from endowments and gifts given to the school as well as from general institutional revenues. Recipients usually have to meet specific requirements such as a strong undergraduate academic record (referred to as merit-based aid), demonstrated financial need (referred to as need-based aid), special career objectives, or a combination of these and/or other factors. In some cases, all students are considered for funding. In other cases, you may need to submit a specific application by a particular date. You should contact the school(s) you are considering, to find out if they have any special application procedures and/or deadlines you need to follow in order to be considered for an institutional grant/scholarship.

There are a number of civic organizations and other groups that provide scholarship funding to qualified law students. Many law schools have compiled a listing of such programs that have funded students attending their institutions. You should contact the financial aid office at the school(s) you're considering, to obtain information about these private sources of grant/scholarship funding. You also can check the Internet and local bookstore for other sources of information on scholarships and grants.

Loan Programs

There are four general types of education loan programs: (1) federally guaranteed loans, (2) state-sponsored loans, (3) institutionally funded loans, and (4) privately guaranteed supplemental loans offered by private lenders. Federally guaranteed loans include the Federal Stafford Loan and the Federal Perkins Loan.

All law schools participate in the federal student loan programs sponsored by the U.S. Department of Education. U.S. citizens and eligible noncitizens pursuing a degree or certificate at least half-time can participate in these programs, provided they are not currently in default nor owe a refund to any federal student aid program from which they previously received assistance. These federally guaranteed programs are summarized below.

Federal Loan Programs

Federal Stafford Loan (Subsidized/Unsubsidized)

Federal Stafford Loans are low-cost education loans that are guaranteed by the federal government. They are available through the William D. Ford Federal Direct Loan (FDL) Program and the Federal Family Education Loan (FFEL) Program. The terms and conditions for the FDL and FFEL programs are similar. The source of loan funds, portions of the application process, and the repayment plans available to borrowers are the major differences between the two programs. The FDL Program is funded directly by the U.S. Government whereas the FFEL Program is funded by, and the loans borrowed from, commercial lenders such as banks, credit unions, and organizations such as the Access Group. The school you attend determines whether you borrow from the FDL or FFEL programs. If your school does not participate in the FDL Program, you will borrow your Federal Stafford Loans through the FFEL Program. The financial aid staff at the school you attend will explain the application process and differences in repayment options.

The Federal Stafford Loan is available in two forms: *subsidized* and *unsubsidized*. Both forms are low-cost loans that are guaranteed by the federal government. In other words, the federal government agrees to repay your lender if you fail to do so. It is because of this federal guaranty that lenders are willing and able to offer these loans to you at such affordable rates. The *subsidized* Federal Stafford Loan is a need-based loan in which interest is paid by the federal government (i.e., subsidized) until you begin repayment and during approved deferment periods. The *unsubsidized* Federal Stafford Loan is not based on financial need. Interest on the *unsubsidized* Federal Stafford Loan is **NOT** paid by the federal government, and thus, must be paid by you — the borrower. You can pay the interest when billed or allow it to accrue and capitalize (i.e., be added to the principal) while in school. You can use the *unsubsidized* Federal Stafford Loan to meet financial need not covered by other sources and/or to replace an expected family contribution.

The maximum *subsidized* Federal Stafford Loan per year currently is $8,500 or the amount of your unmet financial need, whichever is less. The current combined annual maximum for *subsidized* and *unsubsidized* Federal Stafford Loans is $18,500, or your cost of attendance minus any other financial aid, whichever is less. Therefore, the maximum *unsubsidized* Federal Stafford Loan you can borrow in a given year is the difference between the combined annual maximum (typically, $18,500) and your *subsidized* Federal Stafford Loan eligibility. The cumulative maximum is $138,500, of which no more than $65,500 can be *subsidized* funds..

The interest rate for all Federal Stafford Loans (both *subsidized* and *unsubsidized*) disbursed on or after July 1, 1994, is variable, with a cap of 8.25%. This variable rate applies both to new borrowers (i.e., those with no outstanding Federal Stafford Loans) and to those who have outstanding loans with a fixed interest rate. In other words, **all** Federal Stafford Loans made after June 30, 1994 have a variable interest rate. The rate is adjusted annually on July 1. The Federal Stafford Loan in-school interest rate for the period July 1, 1997 to June 30, 1998 is **7.66%**. The rate in repayment is **8.25%**.

You are charged two fees when borrowing a Federal Stafford Loan: (1) an origination fee, and (2) a guarantee fee. The origination fee is paid to the federal government and currently is three percent (3%) of the total amount borrowed. The guarantee fee is paid to the guarantee agency if borrowing from the FFEL Program and to the federal government if borrowing from the FDL Program. The amount of this fee varies depending upon the guarantor/lender, but cannot exceed one percent (1%) of the total amount borrowed. Both fees are deducted from each disbursement of your loan.

Repayment of principal is deferred on both the *subsidized* and *unsubsidized* Federal Stafford Loans so long as you are enrolled at least half-time as a student pursuing a degree or certificate. Repayment of principal (and interest on the *subsidized* loan) begins six months after you cease to be enrolled at least half-time (remember that interest on *unsubsidized* loans begins accruing as soon as funds are disbursed by your lender). This six-month period is called the "grace period." You should receive repayment information from your lender prior to or during the grace period. The repayment period extends from 5 to 10 years. There is no penalty for prepayment.

A deferment or forbearance may be available under certain conditions once repayment begins if you need to postpone repayment of your loan(s). A deferment is a temporary suspension of payment on your loan. Interest is subsidized during a deferment on *subsidized* Federal Stafford Loans. It is not subsidized on *unsubsidized* loans during a deferment, and thus, continues to accrue. A forbearance is a temporary suspension or reduction of payment of your loan that is granted by your lender due to economic hardship. Interest continues to accrue during a forbearance regardless of loan type. You must negotiate with your lender on the type and amount of forbearance that will be granted to you. See the Federal Stafford Loan promissory note for more information.

Alternative repayment options (including graduated repayment, income contingent repayment and income sensitive repayment), and refinancing of your loans through the federal loan consolidation program, also are available. These programs reduce the amount that must be paid each month, at least temporarily, and typically are used when the borrower anticipates that he or she will be unable to pay the minimum loan amount required under the fixed monthly payment plan. Using one of these options, however, will increase the total cost of the loan because of increased finance charges accruing on the loan principal. Thus, you should analyze your situation carefully before selecting an alternative repayment plan or consolidating your loans. More information on each of these programs is available from your financial aid office and/or your lender/servicer.

Federal Perkins Loan

The Federal Perkins Loan is both a federally guaranteed and federally subsidized loan program administered by the school you are attending. Funds for this program are provided by the federal government, with your school acting as the lender. The Federal Perkins Loan Program is designed to provide need-based, low interest financial assistance to students demonstrating high financial need. The exact loan amount offered to a student depends upon the availability of funds and the amount of his or her financial need, but cannot exceed $5,000 per year. The cumulative maximum for this program is $30,000 and includes both undergraduate and graduate borrowing. Principal and interest are deferred during the in-school years. Repayment begins following a grace period of either six or nine months depending on when you received your first Federal Perkins Loan (for most students it will be nine months). The Federal Perkins Loan interest rate currently is fixed at **5.0%**.

The repayment period can last up to 10 years. Deferments and forbearances are available under certain situations once you enter repayment (refer to the Federal Perkins Loan promissory note for details) if you need to postpone repayment of your loan(s). Federal Perkins Loans also can be refinanced in the Federal Loan Consolidation Program with Federal Stafford Loans you may have borrowed. It is best not to consolidate Federal Perkins Loans if you can avoid it, however, because the interest rate will increase significantly when they are refinanced.

State-Funded Loan Programs

Some states offer education loan programs. Eligibility for these loans may or may not be based on financial need. Information about the availability, terms, and application procedures for these loans can be obtained from the financial aid office at the school(s) you're considering attending.

Institutional Loans

Many law schools have limited institutional loan funds available for qualified students. These loans may be used in limited amounts to cover financial need not met by federal loans. In other cases, they may be used as "loans of last resort" to assist those students who have difficulty obtaining assistance from other sources. Whatever the case, it usually is up to the financial aid staff to determine who is eligible to apply for these loans. Contact the financial aid staff at the school(s) you're considering, if you are interested in obtaining information about the availability and likelihood of being awarded an institutional loan.

Privately Guaranteed Supplemental Loans

There are a number of privately guaranteed student loan programs (e.g., Law Access® Loan Program, LawLoans, GradExcel, Professional Education Plan (PEP), GradAssist Loan). These loan programs are not based on financial need and tend to have higher fees/ interest rates. They are intended to supplement the other financial assistance you are receiving. The financial aid staff at the school(s) you're considering attending can provide more detailed information about the various privately guaranteed supplemental loan programs available to law students. It is important to remember that you should borrow the minimum amount necessary, and that you cannot receive financial assistance in excess of the cost of attendance determined by the financial aid office.

Federal Work-Study

The Federal Work-Study (FWS) Program provides employment for law students who have demonstrated financial need. It allows you to earn money to help pay for your educational expenses. Community service work and work related to your course of study are encouraged. Eligibility for FWS funding depends on the availability of work-study funds at the school you are attending, the policies of the school, when you apply for financial assistance, and your level of financial need. These funds may be paid on an hourly basis or you may receive a salary from the institution you are attending. You can earn only up to the amount of your total FWS award. Be advised that not all law schools have work-study funding. To inquire about the availability of this program, contact the financial aid office at the school(s) you're considering.

Question #4. What is the purpose of financial aid, and what do I need to know about the process?

Financial aid programs are designed to assist you and your family in financing your educational investment. You are permitted by current federal regulations to receive assistance up to the estimated cost of attendance for your degree program, as established by the financial aid office at the school you attend. It is necessarily a very bureaucratic process. You should get answers to the following questions about the financial aid program at each school you are interested in attending before you make any final decisions about how you finance your education. The financial aid staff at each school you are considering should be able to provide the answers you need.

1. What is the philosophy of financial aid at the institution?
2. What grant and loan resources are available to meet my financial need?
3. Can I meet my full financial need using those resources?
4. Will my parents be expected to provide financial information and/or contribute to my educational expenses? (In other words, will I be considered financially dependent or independent in terms of receiving institutional funding?) What options will I have if my parents refuse?
5. What is the financial aid process?
6. How do I apply for assistance?
7. What are the application deadlines?
8. What is done with all the information I provide?
9. Will my credit history affect my ability to get financial assistance?
10. What should I know about the loans I am offered?

Question #5. How do I apply for financial assistance, and what application(s) is(are) needed?

Applying for financial assistance is a cooperative effort including you, your family, the financial aid staff at the school you are attending, and the lender(s) from which you borrow education loan funds. Financing your education with financial aid involves multiple steps and requires that you submit various application documents. As stated previously, these steps are bureaucratic and can be very frustrating (particularly if you do not complete all required application materials correctly and/or do not adhere to established application deadlines).

The specific application procedures and deadlines can vary from one school to another based on the availability of institutional resources and the financial aid operation at the school you attend. The basic procedure, however, typically includes the following initial six steps.

1. Contact the school(s) you are considering attending to obtain information about their application procedures, deadlines, and any application materials they supply directly to

you. *This should be done around the time you are applying for admission.*

2. Obtain and complete the financial aid applications that are required by the school(s) you're considering.

• You will need to complete the *Free Application for Federal Student Aid* (*FAFSA*) if you are applying for federal student aid, regardless of which school you attend.

You can apply either by completing and mailing the paper version of the *FAFSA*, by applying electronically (through your school), or by using the U.S. Department of Education's new *FAFSA Express* software. You can obtain a *FAFSA* from any financial aid office or from the Federal Student Aid Information Center at P.O. Box 84, Washington, D.C. 20044. You also can call the Federal Student Aid Information Center at 1-800-4-FED-AID (1-800-433-3243). Note that if you applied for federal student aid in the current academic year, you probably will receive a *Renewal Free Application for Federal Student Aid (Renewal FAFSA)* for the next academic year. That form can be used in place of the options described above.

• Complete any supplemental application materials that are required by the school(s) you're considering (note that not all schools require supplemental application materials).

The supplemental application typically requests information not contained on the *FAFSA/Renewal FAFSA* and is used for the purpose of awarding institutional funds. Some schools use fee-based supplemental applications such the Need Access Application Diskette or the College Scholarship Service (CSS) Profile . Others use an institutional application and/or a combination of both a fee-based application and an institutional form. Whatever procedure is used, it is important to contact the financial aid office at the schools you're considering, to obtain the necessary application material(s)/instructions.

• Submit a copy of your most recent federal income tax return, if instructed to do so on your SAR and/or if required by the school(s) you're considering attending.

It is very important to complete your federal income tax return as soon as possible for the calendar year preceding the academic year for which you are applying for financial aid so that you will have the necessary information to complete the *FAFSA/Renewal FAFSA* and other application materials.

Complete all application materials and submit them as directed by the deadline date. **Remember to keep a copy of all application materials for future reference and in case they get lost or mishandled.** Make certain to obtain information about any application deadline dates from the financial aid staff at the school(s) you considering attending. You should apply as soon as possible even if there are no application deadlines, however, to avoid delays in receiving your financial aid award packet.

3. Review the *Student Aid Report (SAR)* that you receive from the federal processor once your *FAFSA/Renewal FAFSA* has been processed to make certain the data you provided on your application has been entered correctly.

• Follow any instructions contained on the SAR. The financial aid office at the school(s) you listed on your *FAFSA/Renewal FAFSA* also should receive the information electronically. They will use it to determine your eligibility for federal student aid funding.

Your eligibility for assistance will be determined by the financial aid staff once all the application information has been received and reviewed. Then you will be sent a financial aid award notice/packet informing you of the assistance you are eligible to receive. It may take a number of weeks from the time you submit your application documents until you receive a financial aid award announcement/packet. Processing of your application materials (and those of all other students) can be a very time-consuming process.

4. Respond to your financial aid award announcement and return it to the financial aid office, as instructed, once you receive it.

• Typically you must indicate which portions of the award you accept and which portions you reject. Then you must return a copy of your award announcement to the financial aid office. Be certain to follow any deadline dates.

Be aware that the financial aid staff has offered the most affordable financial aid package they can, based upon your financial situation, available resources, federal/state regulations, and institutional policies. If you feel you need additional assistance, contact the financial aid office.

5. Apply for any loans you need to borrow that you have been offered by the financial aid office.

• You will need to complete and submit the appropriate application(s), as instructed, for any funds you wish to borrow.

In some cases, you may be able to apply for your loan(s) electronically. You should be provided with specific instructions by the financial aid office on how to complete the loan application process. Adhere to any deadline dates and borrow the minimum amount you need. Remember, every dollar you borrow must be repaid with interest. This will have an impact on your financial future.

6. Sign the promissory note(s) for your loan(s) if not part of the original loan application, and submit them to your lender(s).

- The promissory note(s) for your loan(s) may not be part of the loan application. If so, you will need to sign the promissory note(s) once the loan(s) has(have) been processed and approved. Loan funds cannot be disbursed to you until you have signed the promissory note for the loan. The promissory note is the legally binding contract between you and your lender.

Important reminders in applying for assistance:

- Complete all required forms—neatly!
- Be consistent when completing all forms.
- Answer all questions completely.
- Apply as early as possible.
- Adhere to all published deadlines.
- Keep copies of all forms.

Question #6. When should I apply for financial assistance, and what are the application deadlines?

Follow all deadlines established by the school(s) you're considering. Each school can provide specific deadline information. You should apply as early as possible once application materials are available. **Be advised, however, that you cannot submit the federal application, i.e., *FAFSA/Renewal FAFSA*, before January 1st of the year in which the academic year of your enrollment will begin.**

Question #7. Will my parents be expected to provide any of their financial information and/or contribute to the cost of my education?

The basic philosophy of the system is to provide you with an opportunity to attend the school of your choice without regard to your financial circumstances. Some schools, however, may not have the means to meet your full financial need. Many schools also have criteria that require your parents to contribute to the extent possible before institutional resources will be offered to meet a portion of your financial need. You will want to ask the financial aid staff at each school you are considering attending about the school's policy on financial independence.

Although you will be considered by the federal government to be financially independent for the purposes of receiving federal funds, you may be considered financially *dependent* on your parents by the law school you are attending for the purposes of receiving institutional funds such as grants and scholarships. The institutional policy regarding financial independence typically is more stringent than the corresponding federal regulations. It may be based on one or more factors, including your age, your prior work experience, and your status on your parents' tax returns. The institutional policy is needed because there generally are insufficient school resources to fund all students adequately with grant and/or scholarship assistance. Thus, institutional dependency policies are designed to guarantee that the distribution of these scarce institutional dollars is fair and equitable.

Question #8. What is done with the information I (and my parents) provide?

Your "family contribution" is determined by the financial aid staff based on the financial information provided by you and your family using guidelines established by Congress and the law school. Your "financial need" is calculated as the difference between the estimated "cost of attendance" for your degree program and the "family contribution" determined by the financial aid staff, as illustrated below. It is this "financial need" figure that will be used by the financial aid staff to determine what assistance you are eligible to receive.

Cost of Attendance

minus

Family Contribution

equals

Financial Need

Your financial aid information is considered confidential and will be treated as such by the financial aid staff and your lender(s). Only those individuals responsible for processing your application materials will have access to the documents you and your family submit.

Question #9. What should I know about the assistance (e.g., grants, loans, work-study) I am offered?

Grants/Scholarships

You should know the answers to the following questions about any grant or scholarship award you receive.

- Will it be automatically renewed in subsequent years? If so, will it be renewed for the same amount or will the amount be adjusted?
- If it will not be automatically renewed, can you reapply for another grant or scholarship?
- Will your academic performance in law school affect the amount of your grant or scholarship award in subsequent years?
- Will you be required to provide any service in order to receive the grant or scholarship? If so, what type of service will be required and when will you need to provide it?

Loans

You should know the following information about each of the loans you are offered before you actually apply for the funds.

Loan amount offered and maximum loan eligibility

You should get answers to the following questions about the loan amount you've been offered and your maximum annual and cumulative loan eligibility in the program: Have you been offered the maximum amount from the loan program or can you apply for more funds from the program if you need additional assistance later in the academic year? In borrowing the offered amount, how close will you be to your cumulative maximum in this loan program if such a maximum exists? Will you exhaust your loan eligibility in this program before you complete your degree?

Co-signer requirements, if any

Although no federal loan programs currently require you to have a co-signer or co-borrower, some state, institutional, and privately guaranteed loan programs do require that you obtain a creditworthy co-signer in order to apply for the loan. In other cases, applying with a co-signer can reduce the cost of the loan. Whatever the situation, you should determine what co-signer requirements exist, if any, and the credit approval criteria for the loan. If you do not have someone who is willing or able to serve as your co-signer, you will need to find an alternative to the loan that is offered.

Interest rate

The interest rate is the percentage rate you are charged to borrow the loan. You should know when interest starts accruing and at what rate. You also should know whether the loan has a fixed or variable rate. If the rate is variable, you should know how it is calculated, how frequently it is adjusted, if it has a cap (in other words, an upper limit) and when the rate changes. Remember, the lower the rate, the less your loan will cost.

Impact of your credit history on loan approval

Federal regulations currently do not require a review of your credit history in order for you to borrow federally guaranteed loans. Institutional and privately guaranteed supplemental loans, however, typically do require that your credit record be analyzed before your loan application can be approved. You should obtain a copy of your credit report using the steps given above in **Habit #7** so that you can check on the current status of your credit. If you have credit problems, you may have trouble obtaining the loan financing you need to attend school. The financial aid staff at the school(s) you're considering may be able to counsel you about alternative financing options if you have credit problems and/or on methods to repair your credit. Having a copy of your credit report will help them advise you.

Availability of alternatives

Are there alternative loan options if you cannot meet the application and/or approval requirements of the loans you've been offered? It is important to answer this question early in the application process so that you can plan carefully for the financing of your education costs. The financial aid staff at the school(s) you're considering should be able to advise you about any financing alternatives.

Repayment terms/grace period

It is very important that you understand the terms and conditions of each loan you borrow. This will allow you to make well-informed borrowing decisions. You should borrow the minimum amount you need at the lowest possible cost with the best possible repayment terms in order to maximize the investment in your education. The loan application and promissory note should provide the information you need. Remember to keep copies of these materials for future reference.

Deferment and forbearance options

You may need to temporarily postpone repayment of your loans once you graduate. Therefore, it is important to know the deferment and forbearance options for each loan you borrow. This information should be contained in the application materials and the promissory note.

Reputation of lender

An important aspect of borrowing an education loan is the relationship you hope to have with your lender. As such, there are a number of questions you should answer regarding the reputation of your lender before you make a final decision on which lender you will use. What is the reputation of the lender offering the loan you need to borrow? How easy is it to solve problems with the lender? How accessible is customer assistance? Does the lender provide a toll-free number you can call to get help? Does the lender specialize in making loans to law students? Does the lender offer any repayment incentives that can reduce the cost of your loan(s) once you begin repaying the borrowed funds? The financial aid staff at the school(s) you're considering may be able to help you answer these questions. You should also contact each potential lender for answers to these questions. Another source of information may be currently enrolled students who are borrowing from the lender in question.

Question #10. What can I do to reduce the amount I have to borrow, yet still attend the school of my choice?

You should consider applying for scholarships and grant offered by private organizations, foundations, and associations. You also should discuss the financing of your education with your family

to determine the extent to which they can and will help you finance your education. It also is important to evaluate the tradeoffs associated with attending school at night so that you can work during the day versus attending school full-time during the day. Attending school part-time at night will allow you to borrow less money, but it will take longer to complete your training. Finally, you should adopt the financial habits described above so that you can manage your personal finances responsibly and minimize your need to borrow funds.

Question #11. What can I do once I arrive on campus to minimize what I borrow?

Be thrifty. Live as cheaply as you can. Remember, you are a student. You'll enjoy a more comfortable lifestyle once you've graduated if you minimize your borrowing while in school. Getting into the good habits listed above is one way to minimize your borrowing. Some additional suggestions include the following.

- Consider living with a roommate. Doing so can probably reduce what you have to borrow by at least $200 per month. Over three years that's a savings of nearly $7,500 in total borrowing and a savings of at least $100 in monthly payments once you start repaying your loans.

- Pay the **FULL** amount due for any credit card bill(s) you receive and don't charge more on your card(s) than you know you will repay when the bill arrives.

- Pay any interest that accrues on loans you are offered while in school if you can afford to do so, rather than let the interest accrue and capitalize. This will reduce the total cost of the loans you are borrowing and save you money once you enter repayment.

- Follow the budget you establish for yourself.

Question #12. What options will I have to work while obtaining my degree?

Current ABA guidelines strongly discourage first-year law students from working during the academic year. Working in the second and third year of law school, however, is not discouraged and, in fact, is an important strategy for gaining a job once you graduate. Working five to twenty hours a week during the school year can reduce the amount you need to borrow. Five hours per week should net you at least $1,000 for the year, which means you can reduce your borrowing by $1,000. Many schools offer part-time employment that also may provide an opportunity for you to study or get valuable professional experience.

Question #13. What impact will the loan(s) I borrow have on me after I complete my education?

Your education loans must be repaid. This will reduce your disposable income during repayment. Remember, you are borrowing funds now that you will repay with your future income once you graduate.

What happens if I don't repay my loan(s)?

Failure to repay your loans will prevent you from achieving your financial goals, at least in the near term. When you fail to repay your loan(s) according to the repayment schedule, your lender will follow the collection procedures required by the government. If your account is not brought current, your delinquency will be reported to all national credit bureaus. Defaulted loans will affect your credit rating and jeopardize your future ability to borrow funds for any purpose. You also will be liable for any collection expenses that are incurred.

How can I effectively manage my loan portfolio?

1. Make a file folder for all your financial records. You should keep all documents in one place for easy reference. Some students keep a separate file folder for each loan type, and in some cases, a separate file for each lender if more than one lender is used for a particular loan. The types of materials to keep are: your copies of the loan applications, promissory notes, disclosure statements, and copies of all correspondence with the lender.

2. Keep a cumulative record of your education loans. This type of record keeping also enables you to estimate your projected debt level and monthly payments. It is important to keep this record up to date.

3. Keep lenders informed of any changes in your name, address and/or registration status. This must be done in writing.

4. Confirm all of your telephone conversations with your lenders with a follow-up letter. This is a sound practice in any business transaction.

What should I do if I experience difficulty repaying my loan(s)?

The most important action to take is to contact your lender quickly before you go into default. Your lender may be willing to offer you a forbearance period under certain conditions. To qualify, you must demonstrate that you are willing to make the loan payments, but you are unable to do so because of extraordinary circumstances.

What if my monthly loan payments are not manageable? Is there a way to reduce the burden?

Yes, you should contact your lender about refinancing your federal loan portfolio. You can refinance your federal loans by paying them off with a consolidation loan. There are two consolidation programs, the Federal Consolidation Loan offered by FFEL program lenders and the Federal Direct Consolidation Loan offered by the FDL program. In both cases, a consolidation loan will stretch your payments over a longer period of time and reduce your monthly installments into one manageable monthly repayment. You gain more disposable income by refinancing your federal loans into a new single loan. Doing so will reduce your monthly loan payments, thereby making the repayment of your education loan debt less difficult. The total amount you will repay increases, however, because of the extended repayment period and the potentially higher interest rate. To consolidate your loans, you must be in repayment or the grace period, and you cannot be more than 90 days delinquent on the loans you are consolidating. You can consolidate any portion of your Federal Stafford, Federal SLS, Federal Perkins and other federal student loan portfolio. It is best, however, not to consolidate your Federal Perkins loans, if possible, as the increase in interest rate greatly adds to the overall cost of these loans.

Refinancing of supplemental loans borrowed from private lenders also may be available. Information on consolidating these loans should be available from the lenders and usually is described in the application materials for the loan. It is important to note, however, that these privately guaranteed loans cannot be consolidated with your federally guaranteed loans.

Where can I get more information?

The best place to start when looking for more information is the financial aid office at the school(s) you're considering attending. The financial aid staff are professionals who are trained to serve your educational financing needs. Several additional sources of useful information are listed below.

For general information about the federal student aid process/ programs, refer to the following free U.S. Department of Education publication.:

The Student Guide: Financial Aid from the U.S. Dept. of Education.

This publication and other general information is available on the U.S. Department of Education Web site: **www.ed.gov**, or can be obtained by contacting:

Federal Student Aid Information Center
P.O. Box 84
Washington, D.C. 20044
1-800-4-FED-AID
(1-800-433-3243)

The toll-free TDD number is: **1-800-730-8913**

To inquire about the processing status of your *Free Application for Federal Student Aid (FAFSA)/Renewal FAFSA*, contact:

Federal Student Aid Information Center
1-319-337-5665

This is a toll call. Collect calls will not be accepted and you cannot inquire about the status of your *FAFSA/Renewal FAFSA* using the toll-free number. Also be aware that the financial aid staff will not be able to determine the status of your *FAFSA/Renewal FAFSA* before your application has been processed and the results have been forwarded to the school by the federal processing center.

There is a Web site on the Internet that provides useful, up-to-date information about the financial aid process. It includes additional references and resources. The name of the Web site is "FINAID: The Financial Aid Information Page." You can access it at: **http://www.finaid.org.** There are several Web sites that offer information about individual spending and consumption behavior that may help you learn more about how to develop good financial habits. They all can be found at **http://www.abanet.org/legaled**.

Spending Personality Assessment
http://www.ns.net/cash/selftest/selftest.html

The Seven Spending Personalities
http://www.ns.net/cash/selftest/7sp_info.html#fanatical

What is Your Financial Personality
http://www.minnesotamutual.com/personal/perstest.html

Consumer World Links to Over 1,200 Sites
http://www.consumerworld.org

Summary

Remember, your legal education is an INVESTMENT in your future, and something in which you can take pride. It can be a professionally rewarding and financially enriching experience if you:

- devise your long-term financial plan and manage your resources in a responsible manner while in school;
- make good, cost-effective, and well-informed CHOICES;
- develop a budget and live within that budget while in school;
- borrow the minimum amount needed to achieve your educational goal(s);
- avoid using credit cards except in emergencies or in situations where you'll pay the full balance when the bill arrives;
- work with the advisors in your financial aid office to obtain the financial assistance you need and follow the directions they provide to you regarding your education loans.

Your education is an important key to your financial future and to your success. The questions answered here provide a guide on how to make the financing of your legal education more manageable. Knowing these answers should allow you to make responsible, well-informed financial decisions.

FIGURE 1: PLANNING FOR YOUR FUTURE

Step 1:
What are my short-term needs and long-term goals?

(These are the things I WANT to pay for.)

Short-Term Needs *(e.g., housing, food, transportation, clothing, entertainment)*	Estimated Monthly Cost
1.	$
2.	$
3.	$
4.	$
5.	$
6.	$
Total Cost of Short-Term Needs	$ (1)

Long-Term Goals *(e.g.,housing, investments, retirement planning)*	Estimated Monthly Cost
1.	$
2.	$
3.	$
4.	$
5.	$
6.	$
Total Cost of Long-Term Goals	$ (2)

TOTAL cost of all the things I want to pay for: *[(1) + (2)]* $______________ (3)

Step 2:

How far will my paycheck go?

INCOME

My annual salary/wages: $____________

My spouse's salary/wages: $____________

Other income: ____________________________ $____________

Total annual income: *(sum of above)* $____________

Monthly Income: *(Total annual income ÷ 12)* **$____________ (4)**

WHAT I HAVE TO PAY FOR

Taxes: *(assume 1/3 of Total monthly income)* $____________

Malpractice insurance and/or other professional expense(s): $____________

My monthly student loan payment: $____________ ☞
(assume a monthly payment of $125 for every $10,000 you owe)

My spouse's monthly student loan payment: $____________

My total monthly credit card payment: $____________ ☞
(assume monthly payment is 2% of total credit card balance and include all other personal debt payments)

My spouse's total monthly credit card payment: $____________

Total of What I Have to Pay Each Month: *(sum of above)* **$____________ (5)**

DISCRETIONARY MONTHLY INCOME

Total monthly income: $____________ (4)

Total monthly required payments: $____________ (5)

Total Discretionary Income Available to Satisfy My Needs & Goals: *[(4) - (5)]* **$____________ (6)**

Step 3:

My financial balance sheet

Item	Amount	
Total Discretionary Income Available to Satisfy Needs & Goals:	$	**(6)**
Total Cost of All Things I Want to Pay for:	$	**(3)**
Total Amount of Money Left Over Each Month: *[(6) - (3)]*	$	**(7)**

- What happens if the amount of money left over each month [i.e., amount (7)] is NEGATIVE? What should you do?

- What happens if the amount of money left over each month [i.e., amount (7)] is POSITIVE? What should you do?

Chapter Six

Bar Admissions

Written by Erica Moeser, President of the National Conference of Bar Examiners

General Information

In order to obtain a license to practice law, almost all law school graduates must apply for bar admission through a state board of bar examiners. Most often this board is an agency of the highest state court in the jurisdiction, but occasionally the board is connected more closely to the state's bar association. The criteria for eligibility to take the bar examination or to otherwise qualify for bar admission are set by each state.

Licensing involves a demonstration of worthiness in two distinct areas. The first is competence. For initial licensure, competence is ordinarily established by a showing that the applicant holds an acceptable educational credential (with rare exception, a J.D. degree) from a law school that meets acceptable or established educational standards, and by achieving a passing score on the bar examination.

The most common testing configuration consists of a two-day bar examination, one day of which is devoted to the Multistate Bar Examination, a standardized 200-item test covering six areas (Constitutional Law, Contracts, Criminal Law, Evidence, Real Property, and Torts). The second day of testing is typically comprised of locally-crafted essays and multiple choice questions from a broader range of subject matters, although in some states, nationally developed tests such as the Multistate Essay Examination and the Multistate Performance Test are used to round out the test.

In addition, almost all jurisdictions require that the applicant present an acceptable score on the Multistate Professional Responsibility Examination, which is separately administered three times each year.

The second area of inquiry by bar examiners involves the character and fitness of applicants for a law license. In this regard, bar examiners seek background information concerning each applicant that is relevant to the appropriateness of granting a professional credential. Because law is a public profession, and because the degree of harm a lawyer, once licensed, can inflict is substantial, decisions about who should be admitted to practice law are made carefully by bar examining boards.

Boards of bar examiners in most jurisdictions expect to hear from prospective candidates during the final year of law school. Bar examinations are ordinarily offered at the end of February and July, with considerably more applicants taking the summer test because it falls after graduation from law school.

Some boards offer or require law student registration at an earlier point in law school. This preliminary processing, where available, permits the board to review character and fitness issues in advance.

As state-specific information is so important (and so variable) in the lawyer licensing process, law students are well-advised to contact the board in the jurisdiction(s) in which they are most likely to practice law.

Using the Charts in this Book

The charts provided in this book permit prospective law school applicants to learn something about the basic requirements for bar admission in each jurisdiction and to compare the performance of recent graduates from each school on the bar examination in those jurisdictions in which the law schools' graduates took the test. Note that the information provided relates to persons who took the bar examination in the state for the first time.

This information allows the reader to consider the following questions:

— Did graduates of one law school perform as well as the graduates of other law schools? For example, if 90% of one law school's graduates who took the test as first-time-takers passed the test compared to 60% from another law school, the prospective applicant may be validly concerned about whether the admissions policies of the second school are sufficiently selective, or whether the second school offers an education that will reasonably assure success on a licensing examination after three years of study.

— How does the passing percentage for first-time-takers at a law school compare with the overall pass rate for first-time-takers in the state? For example, while a law school with a passing percentage of 75% may be doing relatively well in a jurisdiction with an overall pass rate of 60%, a 75% pass rate may be of some concern in a jurisdiction in which the overall pass rate is 93%.

Of course, there are many reasons why one law school may outperform another in the long- or the short-run, and bar performance alone should not be used as the sole measure of assessing law school quality. Because each state's bar examining board sets its own passing score on the bar examination, comparisons of the passing percentages for law schools across state lines may not be as useful to prospective applicants.

In any event, the material appearing with regard to bar admissions offers needed insight into the performance of each law school's graduates. As it is necessary to obtain a license in order to practice law, applicants are better equipped to make application and attendance decisions when armed with bar passage information.

BAR ADMISSIONS

	Generally, is graduation from an ABA approved law school required?*	Registration of law students required?	May students take the bar exam prior to graduation?	Certain law school courses required for admission?	Require Multistate Bar Exam?	Require Multistate Professional Responsibility Exam?	Bar Passage Rates		
							% of First Time Takers Passing - Summer 1996	% of First Time Takers Passing - Winter 1997	% of First Time Takers Passing - Combined Summer 1996 Winter 1997
Alabama	NO	YES	NO	NO	YES	YES	78%	66%	74%
Alaska	YES	NO	NO	NO	YES	YES	83%	67%	77%
Arizona	YES	NO	NO	NO	YES	YES	83%	81%	82%
Arkansas	YES	NO	NO	NO	YES	YES	84%	77%	82%
California	NO	YES	NO	NO	YES	YES	69%	62%	67%
Colorado	YES	NO	NO	NO	YES	YES	89%	82%	87%
Connecticut	NO	NO	NO	NO	YES	YES	84%	84%	84%
Delaware	YES	YES	NO	NO	YES	YES	NA	No Test	NA
Florida	YES	NO	NO	NO	YES	YES	84%	85%	84%
Georgia	NO	NO	NO	NO	YES	YES	88%	76%	83%
Hawaii	YES	NO	NO	NO	YES	YES	76%	57%	70%
Idaho	YES	NO	NO	NO	YES	YES	81%	68%	76%
Illinois	YES	YES	NO	NO	YES	YES	86%	84%	86%
Indiana	YES	NO	YES	YES	NO	YES	78%	88%	80%
Iowa	YES	YES	YES	NO	YES	YES	78%	80%	78%
Kansas	YES	NO	YES	NO	YES	YES	87%	93%	90%
Kentucky	YES	NO	NO	YES	YES	YES	84%	82%	83%
Louisiana	YES	NO	NO	NO	NO	YES	69%	54%	66%
Maine	NO	NO	NO	NO	YES	YES	81%	84%	82%
Maryland	YES	YES	NO	NO	YES	NO	76%	79%	76%
Massachusetts	YES	NO	NO	NO	YES	YES	83%	76%	81%
Michigan	YES	NO	NO	NO	YES	YES	84%	86%	85%
Minnesota	YES	NO	NO	NO	YES	YES	92%	84%	91%
Mississippi	YES	YES	YES	NO	YES	YES	94%	84%	91%
Missouri	YES	YES	NO	NO	YES	YES	83%	81%	82%
Montana	YES	NO	NO	NO	YES	YES	94%	No Test	94%
Nebraska	YES	NO	YES	NO	YES	YES	97%	87%	95%

* Graduation from a state-approved law school which is not ABA approved may qualify a person to take the bar examination in the state in which the school is located, but may not qualify the person for the examination in other states. You may wish to contact the bar admission authorities in the state(s) in which you intend to practice for more information on whether graduation from a law school that is not approved will qualify you to take the bar examination in that state. Please note that many jurisdictions have exceptions to the general rule. For example, many jurisdictions will allow individuals who did not graduate from an ABA approved law school to sit for the bar exam if they have been admitted to practice law in another state for a set amount of years. The state of Alabama allows graduates of non-ABA approved schools to sit for the bar exam if the schools are located in the state of Alabama. Connecticut will allow graduates of law schools approved by the Connecticut Bar Examiner Committee to sit for the bar exam.

BAR ADMISSIONS

	Generally, is graduation from an ABA approved law school required?*	Registration of law students required?	May students take the bar exam prior to graduation?	Certain law school courses required for admission?	Require Multistate Bar Exam?	Require Multistate Professional Responsibility Exam?	Bar Passage Rates		
							% of First Time Takers Passing - Summer 1996	% of First Time Takers Passing - Winter 1997	% of First Time Takers Passing - Combined Summer 1996 Winter 1997
Nevada	YES	NO	YES	NO	YES	YES	69%	No Test	69%
New Hampshire	YES	NO	NO	NO	YES	YES	77%	77%	77%
New Jersey	YES	NO	NO	YES	YES	YES	78%	68%	77%
New Mexico	YES	NO	NO	NO	YES	YES	89%	94%	91%
New York	YES	NO	NO	NO	YES	YES	78%	67%	77%
North Carolina	YES	NO	YES	NO	YES	YES	81%	76%	80%
North Dakota	YES	YES	NO	NO	YES	YES	85%	No Test	85%
Ohio	YES	YES	NO	YES	YES	YES	90%	89% [1]	90%
Oklahoma	YES	YES	NO	NO	YES	YES	84%	88%	85%
Oregon	YES	NO	NO	NO	YES	YES	77%	74%	77%
Pennsylvania	YES	NO	NO	NO	YES	YES	75%	76%	75%
Rhode Island	YES	NO	NO	NO	YES	YES	67%	88%	72%
South Carolina	YES	NO	NO	NO	YES	YES	90%	82%	88%
South Dakota	YES	NO	NO	NO	YES	YES	86%	88%	86%
Tennessee	YES	NO	NO	NO	YES	YES	81%	72%	79%
Texas	YES	YES	YES	NO	YES	YES	84%	81%	84%
Utah	YES	NO	NO	NO	YES	YES	92%	95%	93%
Vermont	YES	NO	YES	NO	YES	YES	88%	67%	79%
Virginia	YES	NO	YES	NO	YES	YES	80%	66%	77%
Washington	YES	NO	NO	NO	NO	NO	73%	82%	76%
West Virginia	YES	NO	NO	NO	YES	YES	80%	64%	79%
Wisconsin	YES	NO	YES	NO	YES	NO	93%	90%	92%
Wyoming	YES	YES	NO	NO	YES	YES	76%	75%	76%
Guam	YES	NO	NO	NO	YES	YES	NA	NA	NA
N. Mariana Isl.	YES	NO	NO	NO	YES	YES	23%	67%	41%
Puerto Rico	YES	NO	NO	NO	NO	NO	71%	53%	68%
Virgin Islands	YES	NO	NO	NO	YES	YES	NA	NA	NA

* Graduation from a state-approved law school which is not ABA approved may qualify a person to take the bar examination in the state in which the school is located, but may not qualify the person for the examination in other states. You may wish to contact the bar admission authorities in the state(s) in which you intend to practice for more information on whether graduation from a law school that is not approved will qualify you to take the bar examination in that state. Please note that many jurisdictions have exceptions to the general rule. For example, many jurisdictions will allow individuals who did not graduate from an ABA approved law school to sit for the bar exam if they have been admitted to practice law in another state for a set amount of years. The state of Alabama allows graduates of non-ABA approved schools to sit for the bar exam if the schools are located in the state of Alabama. Connecticut will allow graduates of law schools approved by the Connecticut Bar Examiner Committee to sit for the bar exam.

1 The Winter bar passage rate for Ohio is slightly lower on this chart when compared to the two page spread for the Ohio schools. This is a result of a last minute correction -- the 89% figure is correct.

STATE BAR EXAMINERS

ALABAMA
Board of Bar Examiners
Alabama State Bar
P.O. Box 671
Montgomery, AL 36101
TEL: 205/269-1515
admit@alabar/prg

ALASKA
Committee of Law Examiners
Alaska Bar Association
P.O. Box 100279
Anchorage, AK 99510-0279
TEL: 907/272-7469
www.alaskabar.org

ARIZONA
Committee on Examinations
and Character and Fitness
111 W. Monroe
Phoenix, AZ 85003-1742
TEL: 602/340-7295

ARKANSAS
State Board of Law Examiners
2400 Justice Building
625 Marshall
Little Rock, AR 72201
TEL: 501/374-1855
www.state.ar.us/supremecourt/

CALIFORNIA
The State Bar of California
Office of Admissions
555 Franklin Street
San Francisco, CA 94102
TEL: 415/561-8303
www.calbar.org

COLORADO
Supreme Court
Board of Law Examiners
600 17th St., Ste. 520-S
Denver, CO 80202
TEL: 303/893-8096

CONNECTICUT
Connecticut Bar Examining
Committee
287 Main Street
East Hartford, CT 06118-1885
TEL: 860/568-3450

DELAWARE
Board of Bar Examiners for
the State of Delaware
200 W. Ninth St., Ste. 300-B
Wilmington, DE 19801
TEL: 302/577-7038

DIST. OF COLUMBIA
Director of Admissions
D.C. Court of Appeals
Room 4200
500 Indiana Avenue, N.W.
Washington, DC 20001
TEL: 202/879-2710

FLORIDA
Florida Board of Bar Examiners
1891 Eider Court
Tallahassee, FL 32399-1750
TEL: 904/487-1292

GEORGIA
Supreme Court of Georgia
Office of Bar Admissions
P.O. Box 38466
Atlanta, GA 30334-0466
TEL: 404/656-3490
www.state.ga.us/courts/
supreme

GUAM
Superior Court of Guam
Guam Judicial Center
120 West O'Brien Drive
Agana, GU 96910
TEL: 671/475-3510

HAWAII
Bar Admission Attorney
Supreme Court of Hawai'i
Ali'i lani Hale
417 South King Street
Honolulu, HI 96813-2912
TEL: 808/539-4919, 4977

IDAHO
Admissions Administrator
Idaho State Bar
PO Box 895
525 West Jefferson
Boise, ID 83701
TEL: 208/334-4500
cmcdonal@isb.id.us

ILLINOIS
Illinois Board of Admissions
to the Bar
430 First of America Center
Springfield, IL 62701
TEL: 217/522-5917

INDIANA
Indiana State Board of
Law Examiners
National City Center
Suite 1070, South. Tower
115 W. Washington St., #1070
Indianapolis, IN 46204-3417
TEL: 317/232-2552

IOWA
Clerk
Supreme Court of Iowa
State Capitol Building
Des Moines, IA 50319
TEL: 515/281-5911

KANSAS
Kansas Board of Law
Examiners
Kansas Judicial Center
301 S. West 10th Ave., Rm.374
Topeka, KS 66612-1507
TEL: 785/296-8410

KENTUCKY
Kentucky Board of Bar
Examiners
1510 Newtown Pike, Suite X
Lexington, KY 40511
TEL: 606/246-2381

LOUISIANA
Louisiana Committee on
Bar Admissions
601 St. Charles Avenue
New Orleans, LA 70130
TEL: 504/566-1600

MAINE
Maine Board of Bar Examiners
P.O. Box 30
Augusta, ME 04332-0030
TEL: 207/623-2464

MARYLAND
State Board of Law Examiners
People's Resource Center
100 Community Pl., Rm. 1.210
Crownsville, MD 21032-2026
TEL: 410/514-7044

MASSACHUSETTS
Massachusetts Board of Bar
Examiners
77 Franklin Street
Boston, MA 02110
TEL: 617/482-4466, 4467

MICHIGAN
Michigan Board of Law
Examiners
200 Washington Square North
P.O. Box 30104
Lansing, MI 48909
TEL: 517/334-6992

MINNESOTA
Minnesota State Board of
Law Examiners
Minnesota Judicial Center
25 Constitution Avenue
Suite 110
St. Paul, MN 55155
TEL: 612/297-1800

MISSISSIPPI
Mississippi Board of
Bar Admissions
P.O. Box 1449
Jackson, MS 39215-1449
TEL: 601/354-6055

MISSOURI
Missouri State Board of
Law Examiners
P.O. Box 150
Jefferson City, MO 65102
TEL: 573/751-4144

MONTANA
Board of Bar Examiners
Room 315, Justice Building
215 North Sanders
Helena, MT 59620
TEL: 406/444-2621

NEBRASKA
Nebraska State Bar Commission
635 South 14th Street
P.O. Box 81809
Lincoln, NE 68501
TEL: 402/475-7091

NEVADA
State Bar of Nevada
201 Las Vegas Blvd. South
Suite 200
Las Vegas, NV 89101
TEL: 702/382-2200

NEW HAMPSHIRE
Clerk of the Supreme Court
Supreme Court Building
Concord, NH 03301
TEL: 603/271-2646

NEW JERSEY
New Jersey Board of Bar Examiners
P.O. Box 973
Trenton, NJ 08625-0973
TEL: 609/984-7785

NEW MEXICO
New Mexico State Board of Bar Examiners
9420 Indian School Rd. NE
Albuquerque, NM 87112
TEL: 505/271-9706
www.nmexam.org
cskiba@nmexam.org

NEW YORK
New York State Board of Law Examiners
7 Executive Centre Drive
Albany, NY 12203
TEL: 518/452-8700
www.nybarexam.org

NORTH CAROLINA
Board of Bar Examiners
P.O. Box 2946
208 Fayetteville Street
Raleigh, NC 27602
TEL: 919/828-4886

NORTH DAKOTA
State Bar Board
1st Floor, Judicial Wing
600 East Boulevard Avenue
Bismarck, ND 58505-0530
TEL: 701/328-4201
PennyM@sc3.court.state.nd.us

NORTHERN MARIANA ISLANDS
Supreme Court of the Commonwealth of the Northern Mariana Islands
P.O. Box 2165
Saipan, MP 96950
TEL: 670/234-5175, 5176, 5177

OHIO
Ohio Board of Bar Examiners
State Office Tower
30 East Broad Street, 2nd Floor
Columbus, OH 43215-3414
TEL: 614/466-1541
www.sconet.ohio.gov

OKLAHOMA
Oklahoma Board of Bar Examiners
P.O. Box 53036
Oklahoma City, OK 73152
TEL: 405/524-2365

OREGON
Admissions Director
5200 SW Meadows Road
P.O. Box 1689
Lake Oswego, OR 97035-0889
TEL: 503/620-0222 ext. 410

PENNSYLVANIA
Pennsylvania Board of Law Examiners
5035 Ritter Road, Suite 1100
Mechanicsburg, PA 17055
TEL: 717/795-7270

PUERTO RICO
Commonwealth of Puerto Rico Supreme Court
P.O. Box 2392
San Juan, PR 00902-2392
TEL: 787/725-5030

RHODE ISLAND
Rhode Island Board of Bar Examiners
Supreme Court
250 Benefit Street
Providence, RI 02903
TEL: 401/222-3272
brburns@ids.net

SOUTH CAROLINA
South Carolina State Board of Law Examiners
P.O. Box 11330
Columbia, SC 29211
TEL: 803/734-1080

SOUTH DAKOTA
South Dakota Board of Bar Examiners
500 East Capitol
Pierre, SD 57501
TEL: 605/773-4898

TENNESSEE
Tennessee Board of Law Examiners
706 Church Street, Suite 100
Nashville, TN 37243-0740
TEL: 615/741-3234

TEXAS
Texas Board of Law Examiners
P.O. Box 13486
Austin, TX 78711-3486
TEL: 512/463-1621

UTAH
Utah State Bar
645 South 200 East
Salt Lake City, UT 84111-3834
TEL: 801/531-9077

VERMONT
Board of Bar Examiners
109 State Street
Montpelier, VT 05609-0702
TEL: 802/828-3281
www.state.ut.us/courts
joann@supreme.crt.state.vt.us

VIRGIN ISLANDS
Committee of Bar Examiners
Territorial Court of the Virgin Islands
P.O. Box 70
Charlotte Amalie,
St. Thomas, VI 00804
TEL: 809/774-5480

VIRGINIA
Virginia Board of Bar Examiners
Shockoe Center, Suite 225
11 South 12th Street
Richmond, VA 23219
TEL: 804/786-7490

WASHINGTON
Washington State Bar Association
2101 Fourth Avenue, 4th Fl.
Seattle, WA 98121-2330
TEL: 206/727-8210
www.wsba/prg
license@wsbar.org

WEST VIRGINIA
West Virginia Board of Law Examiners
Building 1, E-400
1900 Kanawha Blvd., E.
Charleston, WV 25305-0837
TEL: 304/558-7815
www.state.wv.us/wvsca

WISCONSIN
Board of Bar Examiners
119 Martin Luther King, Jr. Boulevard, Room 405
Madison, WI 53703-3355
TEL: 608/266-9760

WYOMING
State Board of Law Examiners of Wyoming
P.O. Box 109
Cheyenne, WY 82003-0109
TEL: 307/632-9061

Chapter Seven

Career Outlook

Written by the National Association for Law Placement (NALP)*

Just as every law school is unique in its curricular offerings and campus culture, each differs in the range of services provided for career planning and employment. However, all career services offices and the professionals who administer them have at least one thing in common — law students and graduates are their most important concern.

Career services administrators and staff know the search for employment in today's competitive legal marketplace requires a great deal of forethought, a significant investment of time, use of a variety of communication and technological tools, and development of critical job-search related skills. It is through the law school career services program that students and new professionals can acquire the tools they need to prepare for and obtain satisfying, rewarding careers as lawyers.

Programs and Activities of Career Services Offices

Law school career services offices are very important resource partners for students who take responsibility for their own careers and take the lead in their career planning and job search effort. Career services offices cannot and do not "broker" students into jobs, nor can they offer a guarantee of a job upon graduation. Instead, they provide specialized career counseling, collect and distribute vital information and resources, and offer critical skills training, while leading the efforts of the law school to establish relationships with employers. In performing these tasks, the career services office becomes a major marketing and outreach program for its law school, as well as an invaluable resource for both law students and graduates as they chart their career paths.

Career Planning, Advising and Counseling Services

Career planning and counseling services are valuable resources law students can use to enhance their job search activities. Career planning and counseling can be of great assistance if tailored to the needs of groups of students (first years, third years, part-time, etc.), as well as individual students. These services typically include an exploration of the many career options available to lawyers and a self-inventory experience to gain insight about career aspirations. Career counseling may also provide assistance in managing educational or consumer debt.

Job Search Assistance

The development of a successful job search and career plan requires law students and graduates to assume personal responsibility for charting their search and implementing a plan to undertake it. However, the law school career services office significantly aids students in that effort: it can offer training in job prospecting, networking, resume writing, and interviewing; use of informational and technological resources to learn about employers and job opportunities; job postings and resume forwarding to assist students in connecting with employers who may not recruit locally; administration of on-campus interview programs; and management of mentoring programs between law students and alumni.

Alumni Career Resources

Some law schools have the resources to offer continuing support to law school graduates — most of whom, if true to statistical data, will change jobs at least seven times during their professional careers. Law school alumni turn to their career planning offices for advice on resumes, referrals and resources, information on the hiring needs of specific employers, and access to career-related publications. Some career services programs publish newsletters especially for alumni, offer counseling services, and organize special networking or other activities.

Past Employment Experiences, Law Student and Lawyer Employment

Prior work experience may help define interest in a future career as a lawyer. Successful work experiences demonstrating capacity for learning, business acumen and ability to interact with clients are especially relevant to that future. However, no matter what the law students or graduates did prior to law school, they are still "new lawyers" and thus, their compensation as lawyers will generally be similar to that of others who accept jobs of the same type. A student's background can be advantageous, however, by attracting the interest of employers looking for a particular type of student or a special skill.

Summer Jobs During Law School

Summer offers an opportunity for many law students to gain real world experience as a paid or unpaid clerk in a law firm, government agency, public interest organization or law related business. Internships, externships, and clerkships with law firms are ways to acquire work experience as is serving as a research assistant for a member of the law faculty. Law students who hope to work for a large law firm after graduation should be aware those firms hire entry-level lawyers primarily from their summer clerk programs. Moreover, summer jobs are important opportunities for law students to establish contacts and to receive evaluation of their work product.

School Term Employment

Students may choose to work during the school term — perhaps to gain experience or financial support. In accordance with ABA standards, full-time law students may not be employed for more than 20 hours per week by a legal employer; however, evening division students often continue the employment they had before they entered law school. These students will need to consider the relationship of their current career with law and may need to acquire legal work experience prior to graduation. This is particularly true if evening division students anticipate making a transition into law practice.

Graduates Acquire Jobs at Various Times

The search for a full-time job is a process that is dictated not only by the effort and commitment of the candidate but also by the unique recruiting practices of various types of employers. Large firms tend to be more structured and predictable than smaller firms.

Summer Clerkship May Lead to First-Year Associate Offer

Some law firms (typically the large firms which can predict their needs well in advance) interview on campus in the fall to hire students for the following summer. If a student's performance is acceptable and the hiring needs of the firm have remained consistent with the size of the summer class, the student may receive an offer for a full-time job following graduation. Students receiving such offers make a decision on whether to accept such an offer during the fall of their third year of law school. Some government agencies (typically Department of Justice and other large agencies) have Honors programs which work in a similar manner, although few of those agencies actually conduct on-campus interviews.

Employers Hire in Spring From Third Year Class

Smaller private practice employers and a significant number of public interest and government agencies interview and hire third-year law students during the spring of the students third year. This timetable enables them to predict more accurately their hiring needs and offers both employers and students an additional semester of law school for hiring/career decisions.

Judicial Clerkships are a Source of Post-Graduation Employment

Jobs as clerks for judges at the local, state or federal level provide postgraduate employment for about 12 percent of law graduates. These job offers typically encompass one or two years and provide invaluable experience in the court system. Judicial clerks balance the advantages of the clerkship experience with the delay of entering full-time practice.

Offers of Employment Occur After Graduation or Bar Passage

Many private practice employers, public interest agencies, and most government employers extend offers of employment after graduation from law school and bar passage. Thus, graduates may not acquire their first job until six to nine months after graduation. Understanding hiring practices of the broad range of legal employers enables job seekers to interpret a law school's data on employment more accurately. Law schools whose graduates are employed by a significant number of government or small firm employers will naturally have statistical data showing fewer graduates employed at graduation while schools whose graduates are employed primarily in large law firms will have statistical data that shows more graduates employed at graduation.

Principles and Standards Guide Job Offers and Responses

Both employers and students are guided in the employment process by NALP's *Principles and Standards for Law Placement and Recruitment Activities.* These guidelines are promulgated to ensure that students have an adequate opportunity to make decisions about offers of employment without undue pressure and that employers will receive responses from students in a timely manner. Copies of the *Principles and Standards* are available through each law school or by contacting NALP.

Graduates Choose Jobs According to Interests

Members of each graduating class acquire full and part-time jobs with an array of public and private, legal and nonlegal organizations. By definition, a "legal" job is a position requiring a *juris doctor* and requiring substantial use of legal skills and training. In contrast, "nonlegal" jobs are positions that do not require a *juris doctor* and may or may not make specific use of legal skills and background. Law graduates have in the past obtained legal, nonlegal, full and part-time jobs from these five general types of employers:

Private Practice — includes all positions within a law firm, including solo practitioner, associate, law clerk, paralegal and administrative or support staff.

Public Interest — includes positions funded by the Legal Services Corporation and others providing civil legal and indigent services as well as positions with nonprofit advocacy or cause-related organizations.

Government — includes all levels and branches of government, including public defender and prosecutor positions, positions with the military, and all other agencies such as the Small Business Administration, state or local transit authorities, congressional committees, law enforcement, and social services.

Judicial Clerkship — a one- or two-year appointment clerking for a judge on the federal, state, or local level.

Business and Industry — includes positions in accounting firms, insurance companies, banking and financial institutions, corporations, companies and organizations of all sizes such as private hospitals, retail establishments, consulting and public relations firms, political campaigns, trade associations and labor unions.

Academic — includes work as a law professor, law librarian, administrator or faculty member in higher education or other academic settings, including elementary and secondary schools.

Employment Outlook for New Lawyers

Making an informed choice to pursue a career in the law must include an examination of law school curricula, student services and admission requirements. Of equal importance is undertaking a comprehensive self-inventory on career aspirations and realistically and

candidly assessing the options and prospects for employment after graduation.

The latter assessment requires a basic understanding of how the legal profession has evolved during recent years, including the changes in the ways in which law is practiced, and how the growth of the profession will affect the employment prospects and experiences of future lawyers.

The legal profession has experienced significant changes in its demographic composition, during the past two decades.

Since the early 1970s the composition of what was once known as "the gentlemanly profession" has been transformed by the entry of a substantial number of women and, to a lesser degree, minorities into the nation's law schools and ultimately into the practicing bar. In 1996, 43 percent of law graduates were women, a substantial increase over the 15 percent who graduated in 1975. Minorities comprised 17.9 percent of the 1996 graduating class as compared to 5.4 percent of the 1975 class.

Since 1991, the percentage of graduates accepting legal positions as their first jobs has diminished from more than 84% to 76.1% for the Class of 1996. Private practice employment decreased from 62% in 1990 to the current rate of 55.7%.

The increased frequency with which graduates initially acquire nonlegal jobs after law school has been documented by NALP data — and anecdotal information also suggests that attorneys leaving the practice of law to pursue nonlegal entrepreneurial or business careers has increased dramatically in recent years.

Law firm structure and strategies for hiring and growth have changed in response to the market economy.

In 1996 approximately 350 law firms employed more than 100 lawyers, a sharp contrast to the "less than a dozen firms in 1960" or the 47 firms doing so in 1978. Some analysts project that the number of large firms will continue to increase as a result of mergers and the competitive advantage offered by a national or international presence.

Today, legal employers carefully plan for growth and hire entry level, lateral and summer clerks accordingly. Some law firms only grow "internally" — meaning they hire only entry-level attorneys, monitoring and grooming them for partnership in their seventh or eighth year. This strategy precipitates the outplacement of a predict-

Initial Employment by Type of Employer

Class of 1996 - As of February 15, 1997

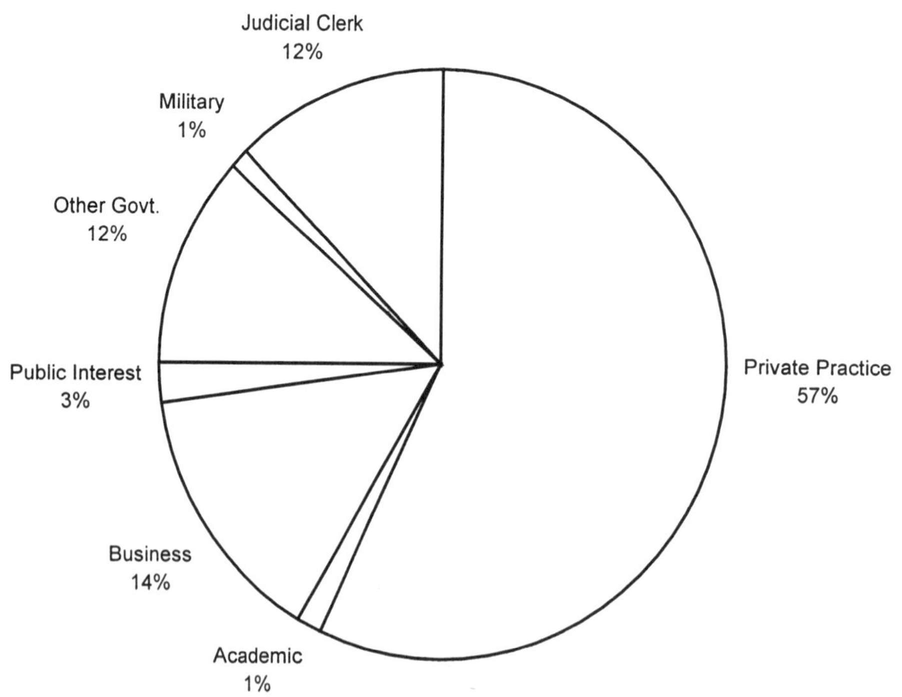

able percentage of associates each year — those who are judged not to be of partnership caliber.

Some firms grow through the expansion or creation of practice groups — a strategy that may predicate aggressive recruitment or "cherry picking" of lateral associates and experienced partners. Associates in today's legal market frequently make several lateral moves before settling into a partnership track at a firm and partners with a substantial book of business now move from firm to firm, an occurrence rare before the 1980s.

The business operations of law firms have changed in response to client demand and the need to be profitable.

In many respects, the law profession has been forced to conduct itself as a business. Managing partners must sustain "profitability" in order to retain partners who could, ostensibly, take their talent and clientele to other firms. Recruitment and accounting practices, like attorney overhead and billables, are carefully scrutinized for cost effectiveness. Thus an attorney's success is tied to a certain extent, to his profitability and his ability to cultivate clients.

Government and public interest hiring has declined during recent years due to budget restraints and calls for smaller and more efficient governments at the federal, state and local levels.

Law graduates who are dedicated to public service employment have generally been successful in obtaining jobs — but sometimes only because they acted in an entrepreneurial manner and utilized special grant programs to fund their jobs. Graduates of the future are likely to find that the opportunities in public service will remain somewhat limited and that median compensation is less likely to equal or exceed that for other employment.

Employment Experiences of Distinctive Graduates

Women and Minorities

Data on the Class of 1996 shows that fewer women entered private practice than in the past whereas more obtained government, clerkship and public interest positions. The same was true for minorities compared to non-minorities, although the percentage of minorities obtaining clerkship positions was somewhat lower. About

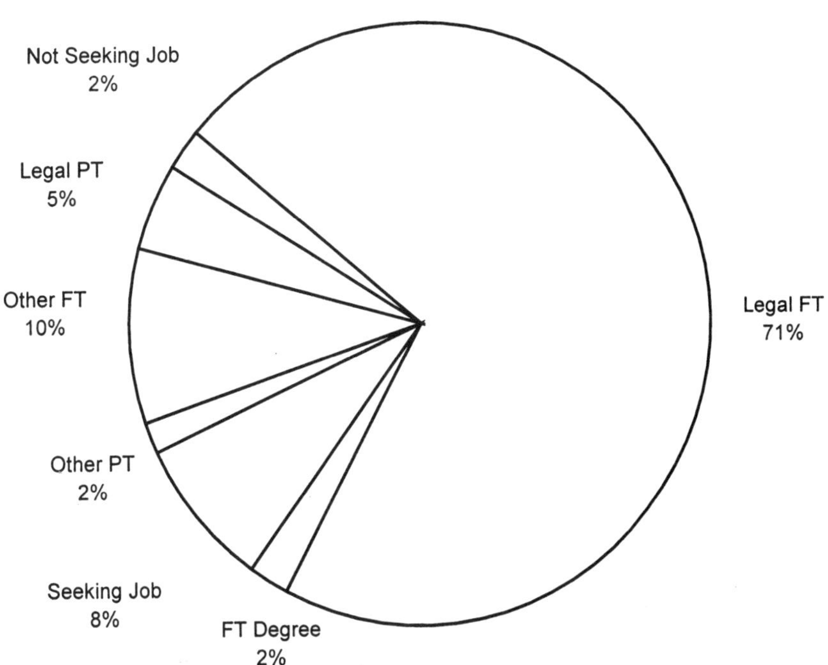

47% of employed minority women obtained jobs in private practice compared with 54.2% of non-minority women. Among minority men, 52.8% obtained private practice jobs compared with 59.5% of non-minority men. Viewed from another perspective, minorities — who as a group constituted about 18% of the Class of 1996 — obtained 14.4% of all law firm jobs obtained by the Class of 1996.

Graduates with Disabilities

NALP data on the Class of 1996 included a total of 264 graduates with disabilities. Compared to non-disabled graduates, disabled graduates were more likely to be unemployed six months after graduation and those who were employed were less likely to be employed in full-time legal positions. Less than half of the employed disabled graduates obtained jobs in private practice, while 17.2% obtained government jobs and 4.7% obtained public interest positions. Business and clerkships accounted for 17.2% and 13.0% of jobs, respectively. The median salary for disabled graduates was $35,180 compared to the national median for all graduates of $40,000.

Older Graduates

The median age of the Class of 1996 was 26. Compared to their counterparts age 30 or younger, those 31 or older were far less likely to be employed in a full-time legal job and far more likely to be employed in a nonlegal position. Unemployment rates were somewhat higher among graduates age 41 or older, but a larger portion of those who were unemployed reported that they were not seeking employment.

Jobs in business and academic settings were considerably more common among older employed graduates. While only 9.6% of employed graduates in the 20-25 age bracket acquired jobs in business and industry, over one-fifth of those age 36 or older did so.

Women age 31-35 reported median salaries of $41,000 and men age 31-35 reported median salaries of $48,000. Similarly, women age 41-45 reported median salaries of $40,000 while men in that same age bracket reported salaries of $45,000.

Geography Impacts Employment and Compensation of New Graduates

Two regions, the Mid-Atlantic and South Atlantic (US Census Bureau Regions) dominated the job market for new graduates, accounting for a plurality (40%) of the jobs of the Class of 1996 for which a location was reported. The East North Central and Pacific states each accounted for an additional 14-15% of jobs. The East South Central and Mountain states provided the fewest jobs.

Median starting salaries were generally higher and more dispersed in regions supporting more jobs. Among these large regions, the median starting salary was the highest in the Pacific states and at $48,000 it was considerably above the $43,000 average starting salary in the Mid-Atlantic region, the one that had the most jobs.

Five Year Overview

During the past few years, the legal profession has weathered an economic recession which affected the employment of recent law school graduates. Since 1990, the number of law school graduates has increased while the percentage of graduates acquiring jobs in private practice has declined. Compensation levels have plateaued, with the 1992 figure of $40,000 compared to $36,000 for 1991 accounted for by the increased percentage of jobs acquired in smaller and medium-sized firms — firms which typically compensate at somewhat lower levels than larger private practice organizations. The chart to the lower right on page 51 illustrates the nature of the recent job market.

---

*The National Association for Law Placement is a nonprofit educational organization dedicated to meeting the needs of all participants in the legal employment process — law schools, legal employers, and law students and graduates. Contributors to the preceding information include: Susan Benson, Director of Career Services, University of San Diego School of Law; Kathleen Brady, Assistant Dean of Career Planning and Placement, Fordham University School of Law; Deborah Hirsch, Assistant Dean for Career Services, University of Houston Law Center; Beth Kirch, Director of Career Services, University of Georgia School of Law; Nancy Krieger, formerly Director of Career Services, now Director of Alumni Services, University of Michigan Law School; Pam Malone, Assistant Dean for Career Services, Vanderbilt University School of Law; Cynthia L. Rold, Assistant Dean for Admissions and Financial Aid, Duke University School of Law; and Ellen Wayne, Assistant Dean and Director of Career Services, Columbia University Law School.

National Association for Law Placement (NALP) Charts

1996 Employment by Type

	Number of Jobs Acquired	Salary Median
Academic	390	$35,000
Business / Industry	4,149	$45,000
Judicial Clerkships	3,350	$35,000
Government	3,687	$34,500
Public Interest	725	$30,000
Private Practice All Sizes	16,312	$50,000
Private Practice 2 - 10 Attorneys	5,592	$34,000
Private Practice 11 - 25 Attorneys	1,683	$40,000
Private Practice 26 - 50 Attorneys	1,054	$49,000
Private Practice 51 - 100 Attorneys	1,059	$55,000
Private Practice 101 - 250 Attorneys	1,700	$62,000
Private Practice 250 + Attorneys	2,260	$74,000

1996 Employment by Region

	Number of Jobs Reported in Region	Median Salary for All Jobs
New England	1,767	$37,668
Mid Atlantic	5,557	$45,000
East North Central	4,284	$40,000
West North Central	1,817	$42,000
South Atlantic	5,476	$38,000
East South Central	1,107	$36,000
West South Central	2,311	$42,000
Mountain	1,295	$36,000
Pacific	3,901	$48,000

Six Year Overview

	Class of 1991	Class of 1992	Class of 1993	Class of 1994	Class of 1995	Class of 1996
Number of Graduates	38,800	39,405	39,914	39,305	39,199	39,920
Percent employed six months post-graduation	85.9%	83.5%	83.4%	84.7%	86.7%	87.4%
Percent employed in Private Practice jobs	60.8%	59%	57.1%	55%	56.1%	55.7%
Compensation Medians (All jobs)	$40,000	$36,000	$36,000	$37,000	$40,000	$40,000
Most frequently reported salaries	NA	NA	NA	$30,000 (6.6%) $35,000 (5.4%)	$30,000 (7.4%) $35,000 (5.1%)	$30,000 (7.3%) $30,000 (5.1%)

Chapter Eight

Values of the Profession

(What follows is Part II, without comments, of the Statement of Fundamental Lawyering Skills and Professional Values, written by the ABA's Section of Legal Education and Admissions to the Bar's Task Force on Law Schools and the Profession: Narrowing the Gap, chaired by Robert MacCrate. The purpose of the group was to study and improve the process by which new members of the profession are prepared for the practice of law. The Task Force was a diverse group, reflecting the various segments of the profession. It included members of the federal and state judiciary, deans and faculty members of law schools, and members of the practicing bar.)

1. Provision of Competent Representation

As a member of a profession dedicated to the service of clients, a lawyer should be committed to the values of:

1.1 *Attaining a Level of Competence in One's Own Field of Practice, including:*

(a) With regard to lawyering skills, developing a degree of proficiency that is sufficient to enable the lawyer to represent the client competently or to acquire whatever additional degree of proficiency is needed within the time available for doing so and without inappropriately burdening the client's resources;

(b) With regard to substantive knowledge (including both knowledge of the law and familiarity with the fields and disciplines other than law), acquiring sufficient knowledge to enable the lawyer to represent clients competently or to acquire whatever additional knowledge is needed within the time available for doing so and without inappropriately burdening the client's resources;

(c) Developing a realistic sense of the limits of the lawyer's own skills and knowledge;

(d) Developing practices that will enable the lawyer to represent clients consistently with the ethical rules of the profession, including the rules that require a lawyer:

(i) Work diligently and zealously on a client's behalf;

(ii) Avoid conflicts of interest that undermine or appear to undermine the lawyer's loyalty to a client;

(iii) Preserve a client's confidences and secrets;

(iv) Refrain from handling matters that are beyond the lawyer's range of competence (*see* Value §§ 1.3(a)(ii), 1.3(b)(ii) *infra*);

1.2 *Maintaining a Level of Competence in One's Own Field of Practice, including:*

(a) With regard to lawyering skills, engaging in whatever forms of study and learning are necessary to attain the degree of expertise that may be expected of any competent practitioner at the lawyer's level of experience;

(b) With regard to substantive knowledge, attending to new developments in the law or other relevant fields or disciplines, and engaging in whatever forms of study and learning are necessary to attain the degree of expertise that may be expected of any competent practitioner at the lawyer's level of experience;

(c) As the lawyer improves his or her skills and expands his or her knowledge of the field, maintaining a realistic sense of the new limits of his or her skills and knowledge;

(d) Maintaining the conditions of physical and mental alertness necessary for competence, including:

(i) Remaining constantly alert to the existence of problems that may impede or impair the lawyer's ability to provide competent representation (such as alcohol abuse, drug abuse, psychological or emotional problems, senility, or other types of health problems);

(ii) To the extent that the lawyer's ability to provide competent representation is impeded or impaired, taking whatever steps are necessary to ensure competent representation of his or her clients, including, when appropriate:

(A) Seeking treatment to remedy the problems that have resulted in the impairment of the lawyer's abilities;

(B) Until the lawyer has regained competence, enlisting whatever aid is necessary (including aid from other lawyers) to allow the lawyer to competently represent his or her clients;

(C) If the lawyer is unable to competently represent a client even with assistance, withdrawing from the representation and referring the client to another lawyer;

1.3 *Representing Clients in a Competent Manner, including,*

(a) With regard to lawyering skills:

(i) Applying his or her skills in a competent manner;

(ii) If the representation of a particular client requires types of skills or a degree of proficiency that the lawyer does not presently possess:

(A) Assessing whether the client would be best served by the lawyer's acquisition of the requisite skills (assuming it is possible to do so within the time available and without inappropriately burdening the client's resources), or by the lawyer's enlisting the aid of other lawyers or other individuals, or by referring the client to another lawyer;

(B) Advising the client of the limits of the lawyer's skills and the steps the lawyer intends to take to overcome or compensate for his or her limitations;

(b) With regard to substantive knowledge of the law or of other fields or disciplines:

(i) Applying his or her knowledge in a competent manner;

(ii) If the representation of a particular client requires knowledge that the lawyer does not presently possess:

(A) Assessing whether the client would best be served by the lawyer's acquisition of the requisite knowledge (assuming it is possible to do so with the time available and without inappropriately burdening the client's resources), or by the lawyer's enlisting the aid of other lawyers or experts from other fields, or by referring the client to another lawyer;

(B) Advising the client of the limits of the lawyer's knowledge and the steps the lawyer intends to take to overcome or compensate for his or her limitations;

(c) Devoting the time, effort, and resources necessary to competently represent the client;

(d) Representing the client in a manner that is consistent with the ethical rules of the profession.

2. Striving to Promote Justice, Fairness, and Morality

2.1 *Promoting Justice, Fairness, and Morality in One's Own Daily Practice, including:*

(a) To the extent required or permitted by the ethical rules of the profession, acting in conformance with considerations of justice, fairness, or morality when making decisions or acting on behalf of a client;

(b) To the extent required or permitted by the ethical rules of the profession, counseling clients to take considerations of justice, fairness, and morality in account when the client makes decisions or engages in conduct that may have an adverse effect on other individuals or on society;

(c) Treating other people (including clients, other attorneys, and support personnel) with dignity and respect;

2.2 *Contributing to the Profession's Fulfillment of its Responsibility to Ensure that Adequate Legal Services Are Provided to Those Who Cannot Afford to Pay for Them*;

2.3 *Contributing to the Profession's Fulfillment of its Responsibility to Enhance the Capacity of Law and Legal Institutions to Do Justice.*

3. Striving to Improve the Profession

As a member of a "self-governing" profession (AMERICAN BAR ASSOCIATION, MODEL RULES OF PROFESSIONAL CONDUCT, Preamble (1983)), a lawyer should be committed to the values of:

3.1 *Participating in Activities Designed to Improve the Profession*;

3.2 *Assist in the Training and Preparation of New Lawyers and the Continuing Education of the Bar*;

3.3 *Striving to Rid the Profession of Bias Based on Race, Religion, Ethnic Origin, Gender, Sexual Orientation, Age, or Disability, and to Rectify the Effects of These Biases.*

4. Professional Self-Development

As a member of a "learned profession" (AMERICAN BAR ASSOCIATION, MODEL RULES OF PROFESSIONAL CONDUCT, Preamble (1983)), a lawyer should be committed to the values of:

4.1 *Seeking Out and Taking Advantage of Opportunities to Increase One's Own Knowledge and Improve One's Own Skills, including:*

(a) Making use of the process of reflecting upon and learning from experience, which entails:

(i) Critically assessing one's performance so as to evaluate:

(A) The quality of the preparation for the performance, including:

(I) An assessment of the appropriateness of the goals set for the performance and an analysis of whether it would have been possible and desirable to define the goals differently;

(II) An assessment of the appropriateness of the means chosen to pursue the goals and an analysis of whether it would have been possible and desirable to employ different means;

(III) The extent to which the planning process correctly anticipated the contingencies that arose and effectively prepared for these contingencies;

(IV) The accuracy of one's assessments of the likely perspectives, concerns, and reactions of any individuals with whom one interacted (such as, for example, clients, other lawyers, judges, mediators, legislators, and government officials);

(B) The quality of the performance itself, including:

(I) The effectiveness of any applications of the lawyering skills;

(II) The quality of the execution of the plans for the performance;

(III) The appropriateness and effectiveness of one's reactions to any unexpected events;

(C) The extent to which ethical issues were properly identified and resolved;

(ii) Identifying practices that will make it possible to replicate effective aspects of the performance in the future and/or guard against repetition of ineffective ones, including:

(A) Methods of thinking or analysis that will make it possible to plan more effectively for performances;

(B) Methods of improving future performances, including one's applications of lawyering skills;

(C) Methods of improving one's own abilities to perceive or resolve ethical issues;

(b) Taking advantage of courses of study for increasing one's knowledge of one's own field of practice, other fields of legal practice, and other relevant disciplines;

(c) Employing a consistent practice of reading about new developments in the law or other relevant fields or disciplines;

(d) Periodically meeting with other lawyers in one's own field of practice or other fields for the purpose of discussing substantive law, techniques, or topical issues;

4.2 *Selecting and Maintaining Employment That Will Allow the Lawyer to Develop As A Professional and To Pursue His or Her Professional and Personal Goals.*

Chapter Nine

Geographic Location

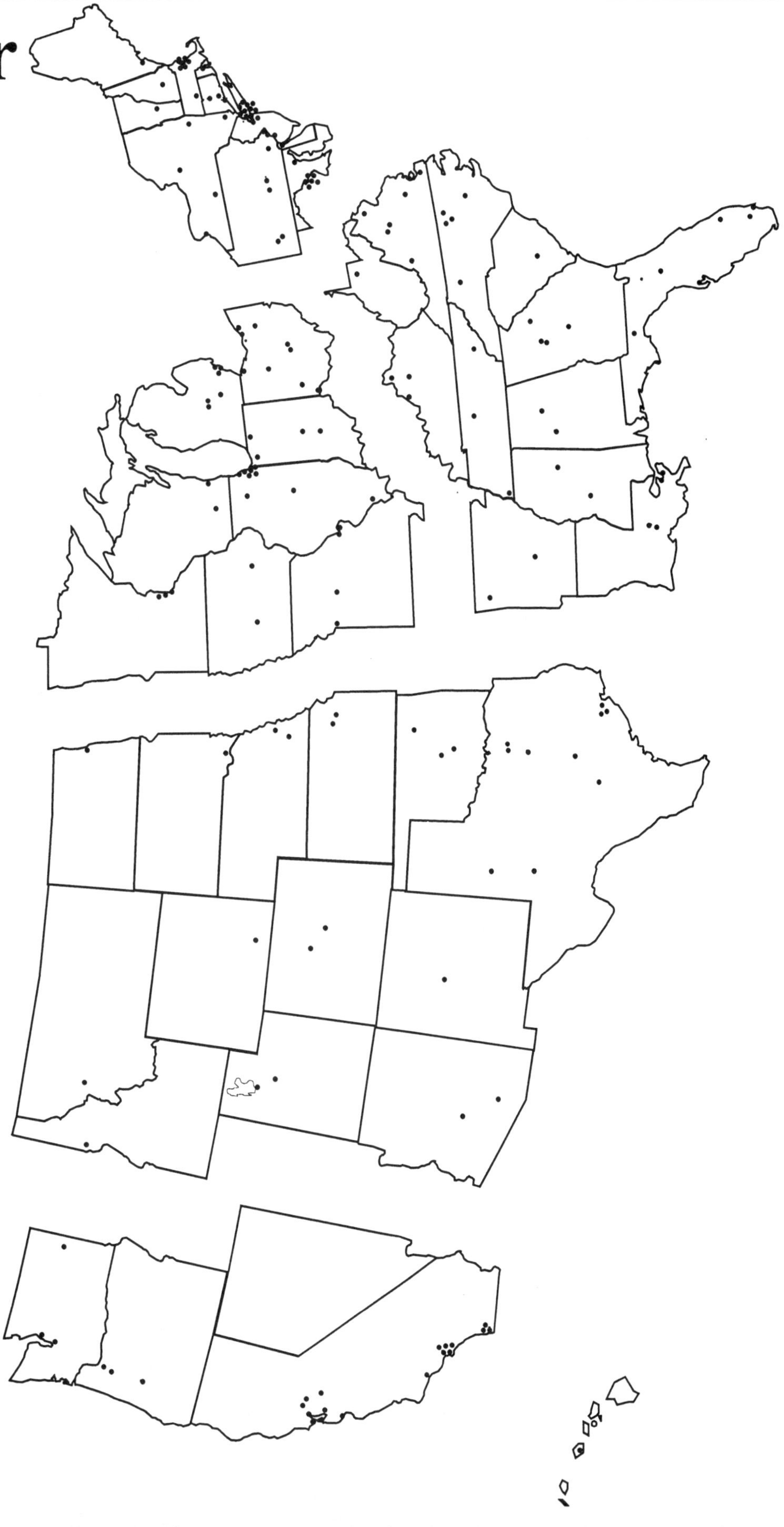

Northeast

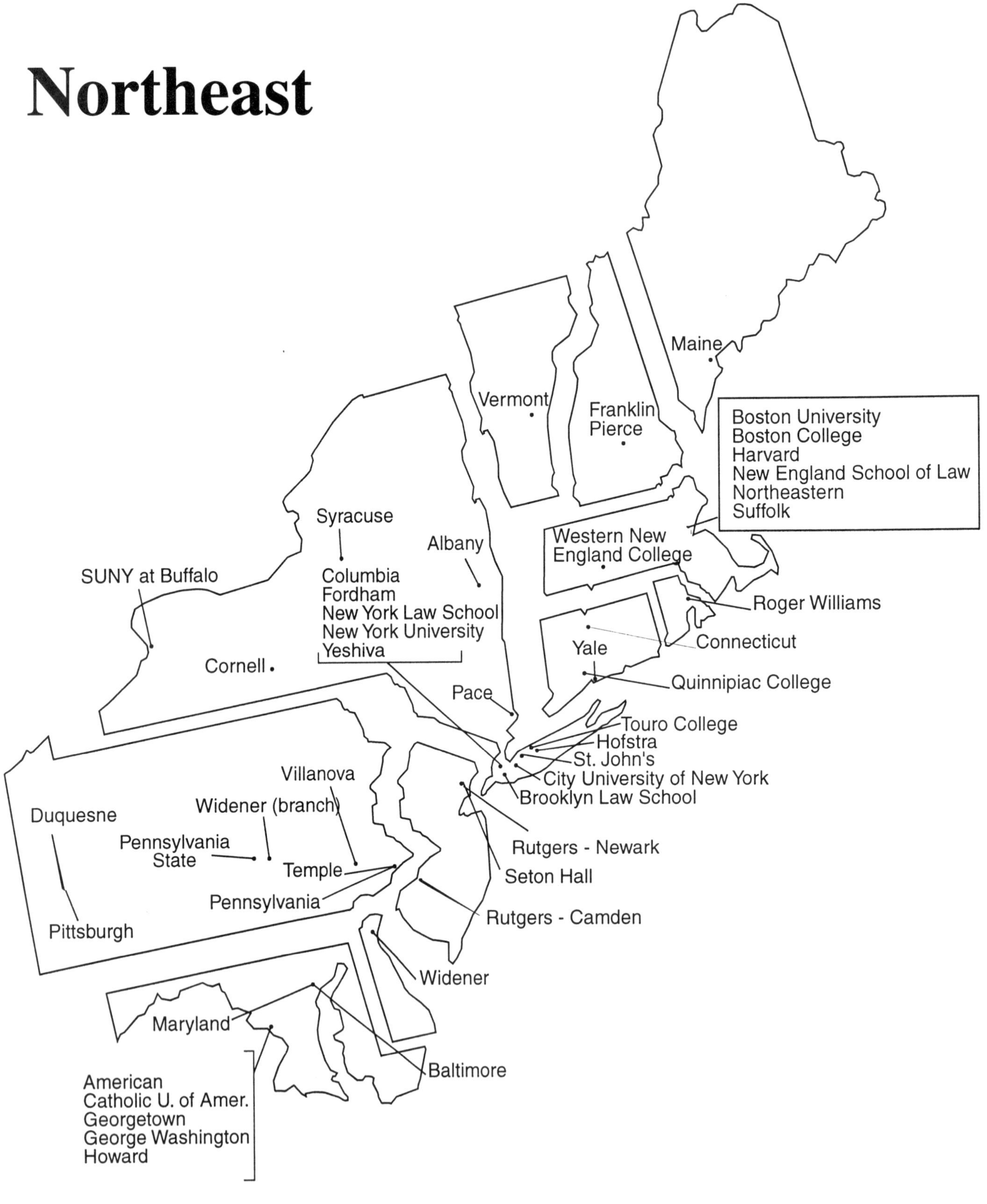

Maine

Vermont

Franklin Pierce

Boston University
Boston College
Harvard
New England School of Law
Northeastern
Suffolk

Western New England College

Roger Williams

Connecticut

Yale

Quinnipiac College

Syracuse

Albany

SUNY at Buffalo

Columbia
Fordham
New York Law School
New York University
Yeshiva

Cornell

Pace

Touro College

Hofstra

St. John's

City University of New York

Brooklyn Law School

Rutgers - Newark

Seton Hall

Rutgers - Camden

Villanova

Widener (branch)

Duquesne

Pennsylvania State

Temple

Pennsylvania

Pittsburgh

Widener

Maryland

Baltimore

American
Catholic U. of Amer.
Georgetown
George Washington
Howard

Midwest

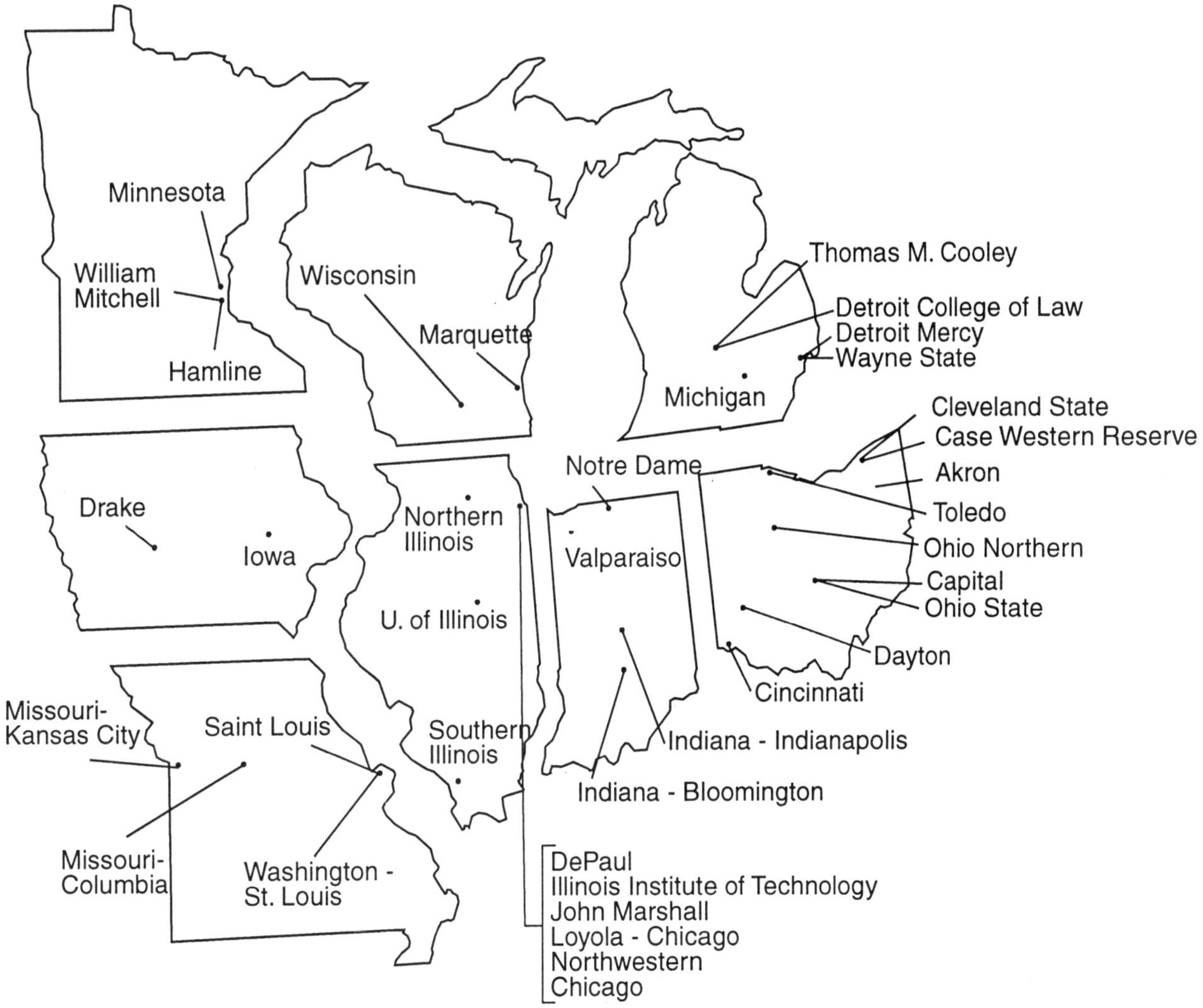

Minnesota
William Mitchell
Hamline
Wisconsin
Marquette
Michigan
Thomas M. Cooley
Detroit College of Law
Detroit Mercy
Wayne State
Drake
Iowa
Northern Illinois
U. of Illinois
Southern Illinois
Notre Dame
Valparaiso
Indiana - Indianapolis
Indiana - Bloomington
Cleveland State
Case Western Reserve
Akron
Toledo
Ohio Northern
Capital
Ohio State
Dayton
Cincinnati
Missouri-Kansas City
Saint Louis
Missouri-Columbia
Washington - St. Louis
DePaul
Illinois Institute of Technology
John Marshall
Loyola - Chicago
Northwestern
Chicago

Southeast

West Virginia
George Mason
Virginia
Judge Advocate General's School
Washington and Lee
William & Mary
Regent
Richmond
Northern Kentucky
Kentucky
Louisville
Vanderbilt
Duke
North Carolina Central
North Carolina
Campbell
Wake Forest
Tennessee
Arkansas-Fayetteville
Memphis
Arkansas-Little Rock
South Carolina
Emory
Samford
U. of Mississippi
Alabama
Mercer
Georgia
Georgia State
Mississippi College
Southern
Louisiana State
Loyola-New Orleans
Tulane
Florida
Florida State
Stetson
Nova Southeastern
St. Thomas
Miami
U. of Puerto Rico
Inter-American U. of Puerto Rico
Catholic U. of Puerto Rico

Montana
North Dakota
Idaho
South Dakota
Wyoming
Creighton
Utah
Brigham Young
Nebraska
Colorado
U. of Denver
Washburn
Kansas
Tulsa
New Mexico
Oklahoma City Univ.
Arizona State U.
Oklahoma
U. of Arizona
Texas Tech
Texas Wesleyan
Southern Methodist
Baylor
U. of Texas
Houston
St. Mary's
South Texas College
Texas Southern

Mid-Continent

West Coast

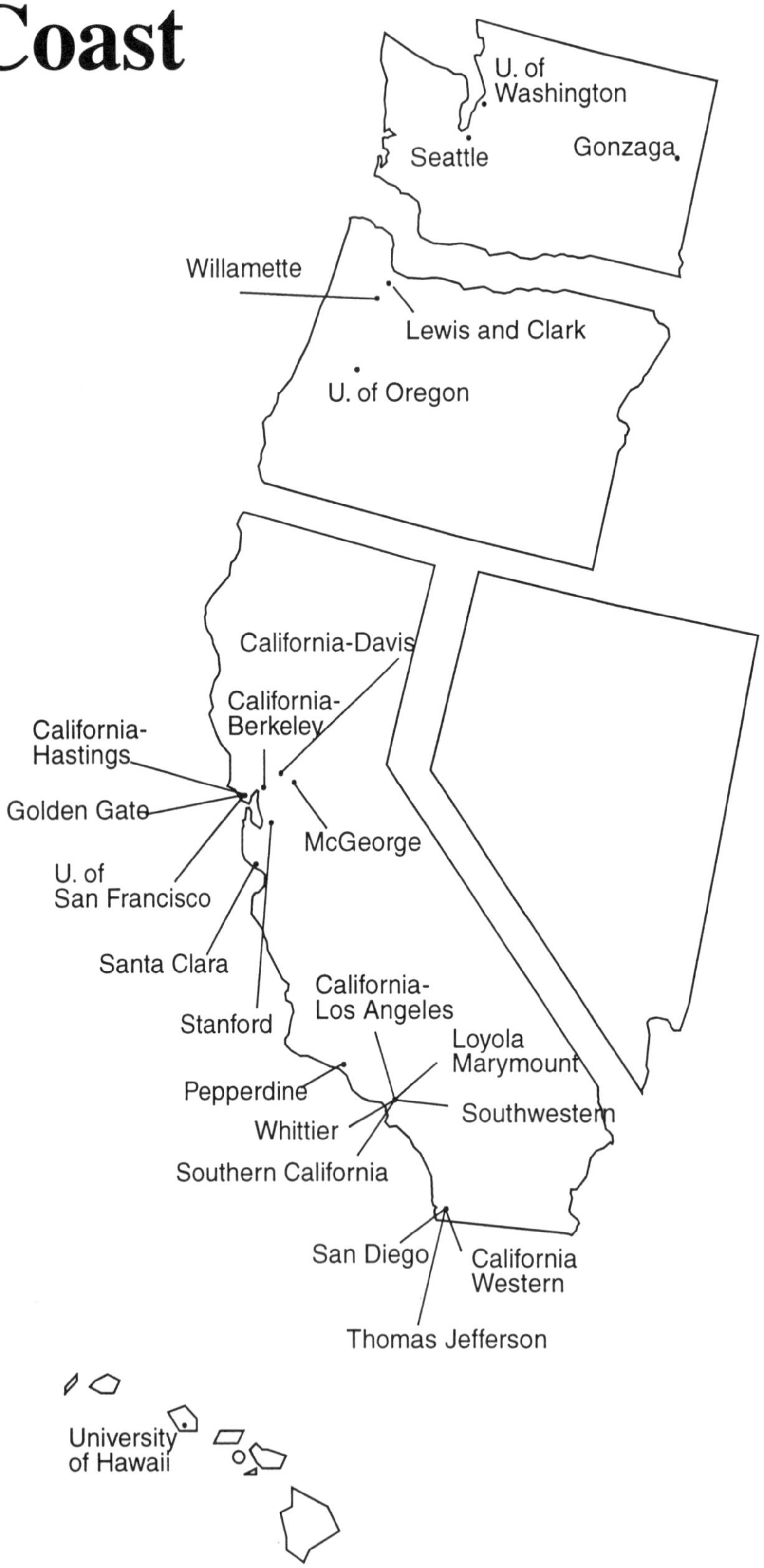

U. of Washington
Seattle
Gonzaga
Willamette
Lewis and Clark
U. of Oregon
California-Davis
California-Berkeley
California-Hastings
Golden Gate
McGeorge
U. of San Francisco
Santa Clara
Stanford
California-Los Angeles
Loyola Marymount
Pepperdine
Southwestern
Whittier
Southern California
San Diego
California Western
Thomas Jefferson
University of Hawaii

Chapter Ten

About the Data

This book is designed to provide consumers with basic information in a simple format that will facilitate comparisons between schools. Please note that applicants should not use this book as the sole source of information regarding application and admission. Rather, this book should supplement other avenues of evaluating respective schools, including making direct contact with admissions officers, professors, students, alumni or prelaw advisors.

The information made available through this publication was collected from questionnaires completed during the Fall 1997 academic semester and submitted by American Bar Association ("ABA") approved law schools to the ABA's Consultant on Legal Education as part of the accreditation process. The completed questionnaires provided to the Consultant's Office are certified by the Dean of each law school. Each certification is submitted to the Consultant's Office as an assurance that the information provided accurately reflects prevailing conditions at the law school for which the certification is given. However, the Consultant's Office conducts no audit to verify the accuracy of the information submitted by the respective institutions.

The information contained in this book is only a small portion of what is collected in the questionnaire for accreditation purposes. Standard 509 for approved law schools, which was developed from Department of Education requirements, requires that basic information should be available to consumers. As a result of these requirements, this book contains a two-page spread on each law school approved by the ABA. Each page is divided into different segments as discussed below. In addition, much of the same data are displayed on three other charts (apart from the two-page spreads) to facilitate side by side comparisons.

SCHOOL NAME (Provisional Approval)

The law schools are arranged in alphabetical order by each institution's primary name. (Please note that some schools are known by more than one name.) A law school that has completed at least one full year of successful operation may apply for provisional approval. A law school is granted provisional approval when it establishes that it substantially complies with each of the Standards and gives assurances that it will be in full compliance with all of the Standards within three years after receiving provisional approval. The students at provisionally approved law schools and persons who graduate while a school is provisionally approved are entitled to the same recognition as students and graduates of fully approved law schools. Schools listed in this publication with "Provisional" next to their name were provisionally approved as of October 1, 1997.

THE BASICS

The "Basics" section contains a variety of general information, sorted into the categories listed below.

Type of School: All ABA approved law schools are either public or private. "Public" means that the school receives money from the state in which the school is located. "Private" indicates the school is not operated by the state.

Application Deadline: Not all schools have specific deadlines for admission applications. If the item was left blank in the questionnaire completed by the school, the term "Rolling" appears.

Financial Aid Deadline: Indicates the deadline for the school's financial aid form. (The school deadline may not be the same as Federal and State deadlines.) If the item was left blank in the questionnaire completed by the school, the term "Rolling" appears.

Student/Faculty Ratio: Indicates the number of students relative to the number of instructors. The ratio is calculated by comparing faculty full-time equivalency (FTE) to FTE of JD enrollment. A general definition of Faculty FTE is as follows: Total "Full-time" faculty, plus "Additional Instructional Resources." Additional instructional resources include administrators who teach, as well as part-time faculty. Teaching administrators and part-time faculty are included in the faculty FTE at differing weighted factors ranging from .2 to .7. FTE of JD enrollment is calculated as follows: Full-time JD enrollment plus two-thirds of part-time JD enrollment less enrollment in semester-abroad programs.

First Year Can Start Other Than Fall: Indicates whether the school has an entering class other than in the fall term.

Student Housing: Indicates whether there is housing restricted to law students and whether there is graduate housing for which law students are eligible.

Term: Indicates whether the school operates on a semester, quarter or trimester system.

FACULTY & ADMINISTRATORS

This section of the two-page spread contains detailed information on the number, gender, and race of the teachers at the school for both semesters. For fall, the information is reported as of October 1, 1997; for spring, the information is an estimate. The five categories of faculty are mutually exclusive. Teachers on "leave" or sabbatical during the Fall 1997 term are not included in the full-time faculty count. The "Full-time" row indicates tenured or tenure-track faculty. "Other full-time" indicates nontenured Professional Skills Instructors and nontenured Legal Writing Instructors. "Deans, librarians,

& others who teach" are law school administrators who teach at least halftime. Administrators who neither teach nor hold faculty rank are not included in these numbers. Administrators who teach are typically at the school and available to students during the entire year. For this reason they are counted in fall and spring regardless of their teaching load. "Part-time during the fall semester" includes: Adjuncts, Permanent Part-time, Faculty from Another Unit, Part-time Professional Skills, and Emeritus Part-time. It should be noted that some schools may have low part-time numbers in the fall semester because at their school most of the part-time instruction occurs in the spring semester. The "Total" row combines figures from the "Full-time" row through the "Part-time" row. "Deans, librarians, & others who teach < half" are law school administrators who teach less than halftime in the fall or spring.

J.D. ENROLLMENT & ETHNICITY

This section represents the JD enrollment by ethnic category, gender, year in school, and full-time/part-time status. Students are classified for purposes of enrollment statistics on the basis of whether they are carrying a full load in the division in which they are enrolled. Minority group enrollment is the total enrollment of students who classify themselves as African American, American Indian or Alaskan Native; Asian or Pacific Islander; Mexican American; Puerto Rican; and other Hispanic-American. Although Puerto Rican law students enrolled in the three approved law schools in Puerto Rico are not classified as minority students in the "Survey of Minority Group Students Enrolled in J.D. Programs in Approved Law Schools," they are counted as minorities in all other areas. Nonresident alien students ("Foreign Nationals") are not included as minority students.

JD Degrees Awarded: This indicates the total number of JD degrees awarded during the 1996-97 academic year.

CURRICULUM

All information in this category is based on the 12-month period beginning at the close of the prior academic year (e.g. June 1996 through May 1997). In courses where there was enrollment by both full-time and part-time students, schools were asked to classify each of those courses as "full-time" or "part-time" based on time of day and relative enrollment of full-time and part-time students. Some schools which have a part-time program experienced difficulty providing curriculum information which distinguished between full-time and part-time. In those cases, the part-time column contains zeros. A "small section" means a section of a substantive law course, which may include a legal writing component; "small section" does not mean a legal writing section standing alone. A simulation course is one in which a substantial portion of the instruction is accomplished through the use of role playing or drafting exercises, e.g., trial advocacy, corporate planning and drafting, negotiations, and estate planning and drafting. The "number of course titles beyond the first year curriculum," refers only to classroom courses offered the previous year not to clinical or field placement possibilities. If a title is offered in both the full-time program and part-time program, the school could count it once in each column. Seminars are defined as courses requiring a written work product and having an enrollment limited to no more than 25. "Faculty-supervised clinics" are those courses or placements with other agencies in which full-time faculty have primary professional responsibility for all cases on which students are working. "Field placements" is a term in which someone other than full-time faculty has primary responsibility to the client; they are frequently called "externships" or "internships." Schools were also asked not to double count a single course by classifying it both as full-time and part-time. "Number involved in law journals/in moot court or trial competitions" reflected those students beyond the first year who participated in those activities during the previous year regardless of whether the student received credit.

GPA & LSAT SCORES

This section of the two-page spread contains statistics on the 1997 entering class. All persons in the particular category, regardless of whether they were admitted through any special admissions program rather than through the normal admissions process, were included. The admissions year was calculated from October 1, 1996 through September 30, 1997. Schools which admit in the spring and/or summer were to include those students in the totals. Figures on matriculants include all students who attended at least one class during the first week of the term in which they were admitted. For George Washington, applications and admitted applicants are not identified by the school as full-time or part-time. Therefore, "N/A" appears under the full-time and part-time columns, and the total application and admission offers were entered under the total column.

Percentiles of GPA and LSAT: The GPA and LSAT scores represent the 75th and 25th percentile of the entering class. For example, if the entering class has 100 students, the 75th and 25th percentile could be determined by ranking the students with the best scores first and the worst scores last. The 25th highest score would indicate the 75th percentile, whereas the 25th lowest score would indicate the 25th percentile. This computation is done separately for both the LSAT and the GPA. The 75th and 25th percentiles are a better indication of the quality of a class as compared to a median.

FINANCIAL AID

This indicates the number and percentage of students receiving internal grants or scholarships from law school or university sources. External grants such as state grants are not included. The percentage for full-time and part-time are based on the total number of full-time and part-time students, respectively. The total column percentage is based on total J.D. enrollment. All ABA approved law schools give grants of some kind. However, a few schools did not submit any data for financial aid. Thus, if a school has reported $0 for the median grant amount, the school should be contacted directly to ascertain the correct figure.

INFORMATIONAL & LIBRARY RESOURCES

This section of the two-page spread contains basic information about the law library. In addition, it contains brief information about the physical size of the school and the number of computers available.

Number of volume & volume equivalents: "Volumes" refers to the total number of law and law-related books held by the law school at the end of the 1996-97 fiscal year. "Volume equivalents" is also the number held at the end of the 1996-97 fiscal year. Volume equivalents are computed as follows: Microfiche, Six fiche = 1 volume. Microfilm, 1 roll = 5 volumes.

Title: Each item for which a separate shelf bibliographic unit record has been made.

Active serial subscription: Subscriptions where pieces/parts/updates have been received on a regular or irregular basis during the last two years.

Study seating capacity inside the library: This indicates the number of study seats available for library users.

Square feet of law library: This is the total sq. footage of the library.

Square feet of law school (Excluding Library): This is the result of subtracting the square footage of the library from the total square footage of the law school, including the library.

Number of professional staff: This is the number of professional librarians, including librarians who teach or hold faculty rank.

Hours per week with professional staff: This indicates the number of hours per week that professional staff are on duty in the library.

Hours per week without professional staff: This indicates the number of hours per week the library is open (regular schedule) minus the number of hours per week professional staff are on duty. Please note that many schools also allow students to have access to the library twenty-four hours a day.

Number of student computer workstations: This indicates the number of workstations (networked or stand alone) inside the library and elsewhere in the law school that are available to students. Some ABA approved law schools require their students to possess their own personal computers -- which would not be counted for these purposes.

Number of additional networked connections: This number indicates the number of additional network ports (excluding those listed above) available to students inside the library and elsewhere in the law school. These are not computer workstations; this number represents the number of network ports.

Require Laptop Computer: This section simply indicates whether the school requires students entering the law school in the fall 1997 to have a laptop computer.

J.D. ATTRITION (Prior Year)

Attrition percentages were based on Fall 1996 enrollment. "Other attrition" includes: Transfers, Health, Financial, and other.

TUITION & FEES

Full-time tuition: This represents the full-time tuition (plus annual fees) for the academic year for a typical first year student.

Part-time tuition: This represents the part-time tuition (plus annual fees) for the academic year for a typical first year student. Please note that some schools elected to report part-time tuition on a "per credit hour" basis.

LIVING EXPENSES

This represents the 1997-98 academic year total living expenses (room, board, etc.) and book expenses for full-time, single, resident students for "Living on campus," "Living off campus," and "Living at home." Tuition and fee charges are not included. The figures are used in analyzing law student budgets for loan purposes. Many schools use the same budget amount for all three categories.

PLACEMENT

This section represents statistics on the employment status of the 1996 graduating class six months after gradation. The employment percentages are based on the graduates whose employment status was "known." Hence, for the schools reporting a large percentage of graduates in which the employment status is unknown, the actual percentage employed may be significantly different -- higher or lower. "Type of Employment" and "Geographic Location" percentages are based on the number of students "Employed."

BAR PASSAGE RATES

This section refers to numbers and percentages of 1996 graduates who took the Summer 1996 and the February 1997 examinations. The states' overall pass rates for first time takers were obtained by an independent survey of each state bar authority with the assistance of the National Conference of Bar Examiners. Please note that bar exam rates often vary slightly because of the varying methodology utilized. For this book, schools reported data for the jurisdiction(s) in which they had the largest number of first-time takers. Reporting the second highest jurisdiction was optional. Wisconsin allows graduates of the University of Wisconsin Law School and Marquette University Law School to exercise the "diploma privilege" and be admitted to the bar without taking the examination.

Chapter Eleven

Comparison Charts

This book contains information concerning law schools that were operating as of October 1, 1997 and were approved by the ABA to confer the first degree in law. The approval status of an individual law school can change. Therefore, if you would like to confirm whether an individual law school is approved by the ABA at a specific time after October 1, you should contact the ABA directly. You can also access this information on the Section of Legal Education and Admissions to the Bar's website: http://www.abanet.org/legaled. For example, on February 3, 1998, just prior to the publication of this book, the ABA House of Delegates granted provisional approval to Chapman University School of Law and the University of the District of Columbia School of Law. In addition the Council of the Section acquiesced in advance degree programs from the following schools after October 1, 1997: American University School of Law, California Western School of Law, Golden Gate University School of Law, John Marshall Law School, University of Missouri-Columbia School of Law, University of Chicago School of Law, and Yeshiva University School of Law. For updates or corrections to this book, please visit the Section's website: http://www.abanet.org/legaled.

SECTION OF LEGAL EDUCATION AND ADMISSIONS TO THE BAR • ESTABLISHED 1893 • ABA

	CAREER PLACEMENT														BAR PASSAGE *		
	Employment Status					Type of Employment						Location					
School	% Employment Status Known	% Employed	% Pursuing Graduate Degree	% Unemployed - Seeking	% Unemployed - Not Seeking	% in Law Firms	% in Business & Industry	% in Government	% in Public Interest	% in Judicial Clerkships	% in Academia	% Employed in State	# of States where Employed	% Employed in Foreign Nations	State where most take exam	Pass Rate for first-time test takers	State's Overall Pass Rate for first-time test takers
*** Alabama ***																	
Alabama	100.0	90.9	5.4	2.2	1.6	68.0	5.9	8.3	1.8	14.2	1.8	79.9	11	0.0	AL	90.6	74
Samford	97.2	90.3	2.4	3.9	3.4	67.2	8.6	9.7	1.1	11.8	0.5	53.2	15	0.0	AL	89.1	74
*** Arizona ***																	
Arizona	98.1	89.0	2.6	5.2	3.2	49.6	13.9	11.7	5.1	18.2	1.5	70.1	20	0.7	AZ	87.2	82
Arizona State	88.5	88.6	1.6	6.5	3.3	37.6	14.7	27.5	1.8	15.6	1.8	90.8	9	0.0	AZ	85.8	82
*** Arkansas ***																	
Arkansas-Fayettville	97.4	84.2	4.4	7.0	4.4	52.1	20.8	13.5	2.1	9.4	2.1	72.9	14	4.2	AR	83.2	82
Arkansas-Little Rock	98.4	91.3	4.7	2.4	1.6	52.6	11.2	20.7	2.6	8.6	3.4	86.2	10	0.9	AR	87.2	82
*** California ***																	
California - Hastings	90.0	92.1	2.9	4.1	0.9	55.7	12.0	10.1	7.6	11.7	2.8	68.4	22	1.9	CA	80.1	67
California Western School of Law	88.5	80.9	1.5	12.2	5.3	59.4	14.2	18.4	1.4	2.8	0.9	74.5	20	0.9	CA	75.7	67
California-Berkeley	96.7	94.7	1.1	2.3	1.9	62.7	4.0	6.7	5.6	15.1	0.8	75.0	18	0.4	CA	90.9	67
California-Davis	98.0	93.1	0.7	4.2	2.1	53.7	15.7	16.4	4.5	6.7	3.0	93.3	6	0.7	CA	87.1	67
California-Los Angeles	99.7	89.2	1.9	5.1	3.8	67.4	12.1	8.9	3.9	6.0	1.8	86.9	14	1.1	CA	88.6	67
Golden Gate	86.8	76.2	4.6	15.9	3.3	56.5	21.7	8.7	6.1	4.3	0.9	93.9	4	0.0	CA	68.9	67
Loyola-Los Angeles	97.8	88.5	0.8	9.9	0.8	64.8	20.2	7.8	3.2	3.5	0.6	68.3	8	0.0	CA	75.7	67
McGeorge	79.1	78.7	3.4	17.9	0.0	59.7	12.9	23.6	0.4	2.6	0.9	84.1	14	1.7	CA	74.6	67
Pepperdine	67.6	73.2	4.2	22.5	0.0	58.7	23.1	13.5	0.0	4.8	0.0	67.3	17	0.0	CA	71.8	67
San Diego	88.2	86.3	3.6	6.9	3.2	64.9	15.1	14.6	0.8	4.6	0.0	77.8	16	0.0	CA	78.7	67
San Francisco	87.1	81.1	2.3	9.7	6.9	57.7	18.3	12.7	2.1	5.6	1.4	90.8	10	0.0	CA	82.0	67
Santa Clara	79.8	85.1	2.1	9.3	3.6	64.8	23.6	8.5	1.2	1.8	0.0	84.8	7	1.2	CA	71.1	67
Southern California	95.8	94.2	1.5	1.9	2.4	69.6	9.8	5.2	5.7	9.8	0.0	79.9	12	2.1	CA	82.2	67
Southwestern	94.7	79.6	0.6	7.2	12.5	55.9	28.7	10.6	2.4	1.2	1.2	92.5	13	0.8	CA	62.9	67

* Bar Passage Data is for the Summer 96 and Winter 97 Exams.

	CAREER PLACEMENT														BAR PASSAGE *		
	Employment Status					Type of Employment						Location					
	% Employment Status Known	% Employed	% Pursuing Graduate Degree	% Unemployed - Seeking	% Unemployed - Not Seeking	% in Law Firms	% in Business & Industry	% in Government	% in Public Interest	% in Judicial Clerkships	% in Academia	% Employed in State	# of States where Employed	% Employed in Foreign Nations	State where most take exam	Pass Rate for first-time test takers	State's Overall Pass Rate for first-time test takers
*** California ***																	
Stanford	98.0	96.4	3.1	0.5	0.0	54.3	11.8	5.4	2.2	25.8	0.5	57.0	23	2.7	CA	87.7	67
Thomas Jefferson School of Law	67.5	86.4	1.2	8.6	3.7	58.6	2.9	22.9	0.0	0.0	0.0	91.4	2	0.0	CA	55.1	67
Whittier College	89.8	76.7	2.0	10.0	11.3	58.3	26.1	7.0	1.7	2.6	3.5	79.1	13	0.9	CA	62.5	67
*** Colorado ***																	
Colorado	96.0	89.0	0.0	9.0	2.1	54.3	10.9	15.5	4.7	14.7	0.0	72.9	17	0.8	CO	91.3	87
Denver	50.7	84.7	2.0	11.3	2.0	48.8	20.5	13.4	1.6	12.6	0.8	82.7	5	0.0	CO	83.5	87
*** Connecticut ***																	
Connecticut	96.9	91.6	0.5	6.3	1.6	46.6	24.7	17.8	2.3	6.3	2.3	72.4	16	0.0	CT	87.8	84
Quinnipiac College	84.5	88.2	2.2	9.1	0.5	51.2	18.3	16.5	0.6	9.1	1.8	50.0	16	0.6	CT	82.1	84
Yale	99.5	98.4	0.5	1.1	0.0	36.9	5.6	3.4	5.6	47.5	0.6	11.2	31	0.0	NY	95.1	77
*** Delaware ***																	
Widener	92.1	79.7	1.4	17.7	1.1	39.4	22.9	12.9	0.4	17.9	1.1	18.3	16	0.0	PA	67.5	75
*** District of Columbia ***																	
American	78.1	85.2	4.4	8.5	1.8	42.0	15.6	20.8	6.1	13.4	0.4	45.0	31	0.9	MD	75.5	76
Catholic University of America	100.0	89.4	2.3	4.2	4.2	39.6	22.6	19.1	3.0	13.2	1.7	43.4	30	0.9	MD	73.4	76
George Washington	85.8	96.2	1.0	2.5	0.3	54.8	9.7	15.7	2.3	12.3	0.5	39.7	31	0.5	MD	94.3	76
Georgetown	97.3	96.4	1.2	1.9	0.5	63.1	8.6	8.6	5.0	11.5	1.8	44.7	41	1.3	NY	86.9	77
Howard	78.3	88.0	1.9	10.2	0.0	28.4	20.0	29.5	5.3	14.7	1.1	33.7	21	2.1	MD	41.2	76
*** Florida ***																	
Florida	95.6	86.6	1.7	8.1	3.5	63.1	6.0	17.1	1.0	3.4	0.0	80.5	13	1.0	FL	88.3	84
Florida State	92.4	88.3	4.7	5.8	1.2	54.3	7.9	23.2	8.6	4.6	1.3	76.2	7	0.0	FL	87.3	84
Miami	94.1	69.1	3.3	26.5	1.1	58.1	8.3	13.4	0.8	5.1	2.0	77.1	27	0.0	FL	84.5	84
Nova Southeastern	74.8	82.7	2.4	13.5	1.4	57.0	9.9	20.9	1.7	0.6	2.3	85.5	10	0.6	FL	80.4	84
St. Thomas	84.5	87.0	5.3	3.8	3.8	57.0	11.4	27.2	1.8	0.0	2.6	93.9	15	0.0	FL	79.3	84

* Bar Passage Data is for the Summer 96 and Winter 97 Exams.

SECTION OF LEGAL EDUCATION AND ADMISSIONS TO THE BAR · ESTABLISHED 1893 · ABA	CAREER PLACEMENT														BAR PASSAGE *		
	Employment Status					Type of Employment						Location					
	% Employment Status Known	% Employed	% Pursuing Graduate Degree	% Unemployed - Seeking	% Unemployed - Not Seeking	% in Law Firms	% in Business & Industry	% in Government	% in Public Interest	% in Judicial Clerkships	% in Academia	% Employed in State	# of States where Employed	% Employed in Foreign Nations	State where most take exam	Pass Rate for first-time test takers	State's Overall Pass Rate for first-time test takers
*** Florida ***																	
Stetson	87.5	91.2	2.7	6.0	0.0	57.2	7.2	19.3	1.8	11.4	3.0	84.3	13	0.0	FL	91.2	84
*** Georgia ***																	
Emory	95.6	90.7	2.3	6.9	0.0	62.8	19.4	7.7	0.5	8.7	1.0	67.9	25	1.5	GA	91.0	83
Georgia	96.0	93.9	1.9	3.3	0.9	68.2	7.5	9.0	1.5	12.9	0.0	80.1	19	1.0	GA	97.0	83
Georgia State	95.2	92.8	0.0	5.0	2.2	60.5	17.1	12.4	4.7	3.9	1.6	95.3	5	0.8	GA	88.0	83
Mercer	97.9	89.1	2.9	8.0	0.0	65.9	6.5	16.3	0.0	9.8	1.6	70.7	13	0.0		0.0	0
*** Hawaii ***																	
Hawaii	100.0	89.0	1.4	5.5	4.1	36.9	10.8	12.3	3.1	36.9	0.0	86.2	3	9.2	HI	90.3	70
*** Idaho ***																	
Idaho	94.5	91.3	4.3	1.4	2.9	36.5	12.7	20.6	1.6	25.4	0.0	76.2	9	1.6	ID	89.3	76
*** Illinois ***																	
Chicago	100.0	96.2	2.2	1.6	0.0	68.5	2.2	2.2	2.2	24.7	0.0	30.3	30	0.0	IL	100.0	86
Depaul	90.7	86.3	1.9	9.9	1.9	52.2	23.3	14.8	0.7	2.6	1.9	84.4	16	1.1	IL	87.6	86
Illinois	99.5	91.4	3.2	4.9	0.5	68.0	13.0	5.3	1.2	8.3	4.1	65.1	23	0.6	IL	95.6	86
Illinois Institute of Technology	97.4	82.6	1.3	7.1	9.0	52.1	30.0	9.9	2.6	4.5	1.0	82.7	28	0.3	IL	86.4	86
John Marshall Law School	95.4	84.4	3.3	11.7	0.6	54.4	17.8	19.6	1.1	4.6	1.1	81.9	12	0.0	IL	78.0	86
Loyola-Chicago	100.0	96.9	0.9	0.9	1.3	56.4	18.2	18.6	1.8	2.7	2.3	84.5	16	0.9	IL	83.6	86
Northern Illinois	96.5	88.0	2.4	8.4	1.2	57.5	12.3	26.0	1.4	2.7	0.0	79.5	11	0.0	IL	75.3	86
Northwestern	97.0	96.9	0.0	0.5	2.6	72.9	8.0	5.9	1.1	11.7	0.5	56.4	23	1.1	IL	92.9	86
Southern Illinois	92.7	88.1	0.0	11.9	0.0	61.8	7.9	13.5	4.5	4.5	1.1	61.8	13	0.0	IL	83.1	86
*** Indiana ***																	
Indiana-Bloomington	97.8	89.9	4.5	4.5	1.1	50.0	17.5	13.1	3.1	13.1	3.1	49.4	27	3.7	IN	86.9	80
Indiana-Indianapolis	95.2	91.2	0.8	4.6	3.4	61.8	16.1	13.4	2.8	4.1	1.8	88.5	13	0.5	IN	83.8	80
Notre Dame	96.0	91.1	3.0	3.6	2.4	61.0	9.7	9.7	1.9	15.6	1.9	11.7	30	1.9	IL	95.2	86

* Bar Passage Data is for the Summer 96 and Winter 97 Exams.

	CAREER PLACEMENT														BAR PASSAGE *		
	Employment Status					Type of Employment						Location					
	% Employment Status Known	% Employed	% Pursuing Graduate Degree	% Unemployed - Seeking	% Unemployed - Not Seeking	% in Law Firms	% in Business & Industry	% in Government	% in Public Interest	% in Judicial Clerkships	% in Academia	% Employed in State	# of States where Employed	% Employed in Foreign Nations	State where most take exam	Pass Rate for first-time test takers	State's Overall Pass Rate for first-time test takers
*** Indiana ***																	
Valparaiso	91.0	96.0	2.0	1.3	0.7	51.0	15.9	13.8	0.0	6.2	2.8	46.2	19	0.0	IN	73.9	80
*** Iowa ***																	
Drake	100.0	92.0	1.0	6.5	0.5	54.1	18.0	15.3	3.3	6.6	1.6	43.2	27	0.0	IA	81.2	78
Iowa	98.1	90.5	1.4	5.2	2.8	59.2	12.0	10.5	4.2	12.6	1.6	36.6	30	0.5	IA	78.2	78
*** Kansas ***																	
Kansas	91.4	89.2	4.1	4.1	2.7	48.5	27.3	12.9	2.3	6.8	1.5	49.2	17	0.8	KS	89.7	90
Washburn	96.6	85.9	3.5	6.3	4.2	43.4	18.9	26.2	5.7	4.9	0.8	66.4	21	1.6	KS	80.2	90
*** Kentucky ***																	
Kentucky	100.0	97.1	2.2	0.0	0.7	57.8	11.9	11.9	1.5	16.3	0.7	78.5	13	1.5	KY	86.2	83
Louisville	98.0	91.8	0.0	5.2	3.1	59.6	18.0	11.2	3.4	5.6	2.2	79.8	8	0.0	KY	87.8	83
Northern Kentucky	87.4	94.6	1.8	1.8	1.8	61.9	19.0	8.6	1.0	2.9	1.0	47.6	7	0.0	KY	69.9	83
*** Louisiana ***																	
Louisiana State	94.8	96.7	1.6	1.6	0.0	61.9	10.2	8.0	0.0	19.9	0.0	85.8	7	0.0	LA	79.5	66
Loyola-New Orleans	81.8	84.2	2.2	9.8	3.8	36.1	9.7	3.9	0.0	5.2	0.6	43.2	12	0.0	LA	65.7	66
Southern	88.5	80.5	11.7	7.8	0.0	43.5	11.3	27.4	0.0	14.5	3.2	90.3	5	0.0	LA	35.7	66
Tulane	96.0	78.6	3.9	11.3	6.2	55.7	9.8	14.0	3.4	15.9	0.8	36.4	34	2.7	LA	68.1	66
*** Maine ***																	
Maine	97.7	76.7	1.2	16.3	5.8	66.7	16.7	9.1	6.1	27.3	4.5	74.2	14	0.0	ME	84.7	82
*** Maryland ***																	
Baltimore	82.4	87.9	1.2	9.3	1.6	39.9	18.8	17.4	2.8	21.1	0.0	83.5	12	0.0	MD	75.8	76
Maryland	92.6	87.4	2.1	8.4	2.1	42.3	18.3	11.5	5.8	20.7	1.4	78.8	17	0.0	MD	82.9	76
*** Massachusetts ***																	
Boston	98.0	85.0	4.6	10.1	0.3	61.2	15.3	9.9	1.7	7.8	1.4	34.7	21	0.7	MA	80.8	81
Boston College	94.8	92.2	0.0	6.6	1.2	66.1	8.1	9.7	2.1	13.1	0.8	55.9	26	0.4	MA	92.3	81
Harvard	99.6	96.3	1.3	2.2	0.2	63.4	3.6	0.8	3.4	28.4	0.4	8.6	43	1.3	NY	92.5	77

* Bar Passage Data is for the Summer 96 and Winter 97 Exams.

	CAREER PLACEMENT														BAR PASSAGE *		
	Employment Status					Type of Employment						Location					
	% Employment Status Known	% Employed	% Pursuing Graduate Degree	% Unemployed - Seeking	% Unemployed - Not Seeking	% in Law Firms	% in Business & Industry	% in Government	% in Public Interest	% in Judicial Clerkships	% in Academia	% Employed in State	# of States where Employed	% Employed in Foreign Nations	State where most take exam	Pass Rate for first-time test takers	State's Overall Pass Rate for first-time test takers
***** Massachusetts *****																	
New England School of Law	80.3	87.2	1.9	9.7	1.2	48.7	23.2	16.1	0.4	8.9	2.7	61.2	20	0.0	MA	81.2	81
Northeastern	86.7	87.6	1.8	8.9	1.8	45.9	8.1	6.8	17.6	21.6	0.0	58.8	23	2.0	MA	88.1	81
Suffolk	75.9	87.4	0.8	9.2	2.6	43.8	27.0	17.1	2.1	6.9	2.1	85.9	19	0.0	MA	80.3	81
Western New England	92.6	87.5	0.0	9.5	3.0	38.9	30.9	21.1	2.9	5.1	1.1	34.9	18	0.0	MA	75.9	81
***** Michigan *****																	
Detroit College of Law at Michigan State	85.5	88.3	1.2	9.4	1.2	53.6	21.2	9.9	1.3	6.0	1.3	92.1	6	3.3	MI	83.6	85
Detroit Mercy	31.3	97.3	1.4	1.4	0.0	49.3	19.7	19.7	0.0	11.3	0.0	94.4	4	1.4	MI	78.5	85
Michigan	96.6	93.0	0.5	5.9	0.5	65.8	6.4	4.1	2.3	20.6	0.6	21.7	32	1.2	MI	85.4	85
Thomas M. Cooley Law School	59.5	82.6	4.8	9.3	3.3	62.8	13.5	15.7	0.9	4.9	1.8	37.7	31	0.0	MI	85.0	85
Wayne State	66.3	91.4	1.6	6.2	0.8	58.1	17.1	12.8	4.3	7.7	0.0	94.9	5	0.9	MI	95.6	85
***** Minnesota *****																	
Hamline	95.0	86.5	2.3	8.2	2.9	34.5	29.1	9.5	7.4	17.6	2.0	74.3	15	0.7	MN	86.2	91
Minnesota	99.6	91.1	1.5	2.6	4.8	39.4	15.4	12.2	4.1	26.0	1.2	63.4	30	0.4	MN	97.8	91
William Mitchell College of Law	89.5	93.0	1.2	5.8	0.0	46.9	27.2	13.8	0.4	10.0	0.0	86.6	14	1.3	MN	84.6	91
***** Mississippi *****																	
Mississippi	99.3	90.6	4.3	2.2	2.9	63.5	9.5	9.5	0.8	15.9	0.0	71.4	18	0.0	MS	95.4	91
Mississippi College	92.0	86.5	4.8	2.9	5.8	70.0	0.0	8.9	2.2	17.8	1.1	58.9	14	0.0	MS	84.8	91
***** Missouri *****																	
Missouri-Columbia	67.5	90.4	1.0	8.7	0.0	52.1	5.3	20.2	1.1	21.3	0.0	87.2	9	0.0	MO	87.6	82
Missouri-Kansas City	97.8	92.6	0.0	5.1	2.2	55.6	15.9	16.7	0.8	8.7	2.4	77.8	11	0.0	MO	68.6	82
St. Louis	91.7	92.3	1.4	4.5	1.8	51.2	19.7	14.3	1.0	9.4	1.0	72.4	18	0.0	MO	80.1	82
Washington University	96.8	89.6	2.7	6.0	1.6	63.2	13.5	11.7	3.7	8.0	0.0	47.9	19	0.6	MO	87.8	82

* Bar Passage Data is for the Summer 96 and Winter 97 Exams.

	CAREER PLACEMENT														BAR PASSAGE *		
	Employment Status					Type of Employment						Location					
	% Employment Status Known	% Employed	% Pursuing Graduate Degree	% Unemployed - Seeking	% Unemployed - Not Seeking	% in Law Firms	% in Business & Industry	% in Government	% in Public Interest	% in Judicial Clerkships	% in Academia	% Employed in State	# of States where Employed	% Employed in Foreign Nations	State where most take exam	Pass Rate for first-time test takers	State's Overall Pass Rate for first-time test takers
*** Montana ***																	
Montana	95.9	93.0	2.8	2.8	1.4	59.1	3.0	15.2	0.0	19.7	3.0	87.9	8	1.5	MT	95.6	94
*** Nebraska ***																	
Creighton	96.5	85.5	1.8	10.9	1.8	52.5	22.0	13.5	4.3	7.1	0.7	39.7	32	0.0	NE	94.4	95
Nebraska	98.6	92.5	2.7	3.4	1.4	53.3	18.5	20.7	3.0	6.7	0.7	64.4	23	1.5	NE	98.0	95
*** New Hampshire ***																	
Franklin Pierce Law Center	89.7	86.7	0.0	12.4	0.9	63.3	19.4	9.2	3.1	2.0	3.1	40.8	20	2.0	NH	81.1	77
*** New Jersey ***																	
Rutgers-Camden	93.9	92.5	0.0	4.0	3.5	39.8	12.9	10.8	3.2	30.6	2.7	61.8	15	1.6	NJ	78.0	77
Rutgers-Newark	91.0	91.6	1.0	5.9	1.5	38.2	19.9	8.6	5.9	24.2	1.6	73.7	10	0.5	NJ	74.0	77
Seton Hall	95.0	91.2	0.5	7.0	1.3	40.7	14.3	7.7	0.8	34.6	0.0	69.8	25	0.0	NJ	76.0	77
*** New Mexico ***																	
New Mexico	82.1	86.5	3.1	9.4	1.0	47.0	4.8	31.3	4.8	10.8	1.2	83.1	9	0.0	NM	86.6	91
*** New York ***																	
Albany Law School	99.6	83.1	3.4	7.3	6.1	52.1	21.2	19.8	1.8	3.7	0.9	84.3	18	0.5	NY	84.8	77
Brooklyn Law School	85.5	86.3	1.6	12.1	0.0	52.8	17.8	20.9	2.2	6.2	0.0	92.2	11	0.0	NY	84.2	77
City U. of New York	70.1	82.2	0.0	16.8	1.0	31.3	21.7	14.5	27.7	3.6	1.2	78.3	13	0.0	NY	55.7	77
Columbia	99.2	98.3	0.6	0.9	0.3	68.5	4.3	1.7	3.5	21.1	0.9	63.9	28	1.4	NY	91.8	77
Cornell Law School	92.2	94.6	3.6	1.8	0.0	67.5	1.9	5.7	2.5	17.2	5.1	24.8	27	0.6	NY	91.9	77
Fordham	90.2	92.8	1.3	4.9	1.1	56.3	17.0	13.1	0.7	5.7	0.7	83.0	17	0.5	NY	85.9	77
Hofstra	89.8	90.7	2.8	4.0	2.4	65.2	14.7	10.7	3.1	6.2	0.0	75.0	15	0.9	NY	76.7	77
New York Law School	85.3	91.5	0.3	5.3	2.8	47.9	24.0	15.1	1.4	4.1	0.7	63.0	15	0.7	NY	67.1	77
New York University	99.3	99.5	0.5	0.0	0.0	70.8	4.6	3.0	4.6	16.1	0.2	67.6	28	0.0	NY	93.6	77
Pace	83.3	89.1	0.5	7.6	2.7	56.1	22.6	12.2	0.6	4.3	0.6	59.1	14	0.6	NY	70.0	77
St. John's	83.1	92.9	1.4	3.4	2.4	52.7	16.1	23.4	0.4	6.2	0.0	85.0	11	0.0	NY	86.8	77

* Bar Passage Data is for the Summer 96 and Winter 97 Exams.

Section of Legal Education and Admissions to the Bar • Established 1893 • ABA	CAREER PLACEMENT														BAR PASSAGE *		
	Employment Status					Type of Employment						Location					
	% Employment Status Known	% Employed	% Pursuing Graduate Degree	% Unemployed - Seeking	% Unemployed - Not Seeking	% in Law Firms	% in Business & Industry	% in Government	% in Public Interest	% in Judicial Clerkships	% in Academia	% Employed in State	# of States where Employed	% Employed in Foreign Nations	State where most take exam	Pass Rate for first-time test takers	State's Overall Pass Rate for first-time test takers
*** New York ***																	
State U. of New York at Buffalo	98.9	84.7	5.7	4.2	5.4	57.0	11.8	13.6	7.7	4.5	5.0	80.5	18	1.8	NY	73.2	77
Syracuse	98.2	90.3	3.0	5.6	1.1	54.1	22.7	11.6	1.7	7.4	2.5	42.6	27	2.9	NY	68.6	77
Touro College	88.9	87.5	0.0	10.9	1.6	55.4	23.8	13.1	3.0	1.8	3.0	91.1	10	0.0	NY	68.9	77
Yeshiva	80.7	91.1	1.6	4.9	2.4	58.5	19.2	10.7	4.5	6.2	0.9	90.2	8	0.9	NY	76.7	77
*** North Carolina ***																	
Campbell	91.0	100.0	0.0	0.0	0.0	79.1	3.3	11.0	1.1	5.5	0.0	85.7	0	0.0	NC	93.3	80
Duke	100.0	98.4	1.1	0.5	0.0	81.3	2.2	2.7	1.1	12.6	0.0	7.7	31	0.0	NC	95.1	80
North Carolina	97.5	94.4	2.1	3.0	0.4	56.8	12.7	13.2	3.2	12.3	1.8	63.6	24	1.8	NC	89.4	80
North Carolina Central	80.0	79.4	4.4	16.2	0.0	37.0	29.6	18.5	13.0	0.0	1.9	74.1	10	0.0	NC	64.5	80
Wake Forest	96.2	96.1	0.0	3.3	0.7	59.9	12.9	17.0	0.7	13.6	0.0	65.3	21	0.0	NC	90.0	80
*** North Dakota ***																	
North Dakota	92.8	84.4	6.2	4.7	4.7	51.9	11.1	3.7	5.6	27.8	0.0	68.5	11	1.9	ND	89.1	85
*** Ohio ***																	
Akron	99.4	87.1	2.9	2.3	7.6	44.3	23.5	17.4	2.7	9.4	2.7	72.5	15	0.7	OH	83.0	90
Capital	97.0	90.3	1.8	4.9	3.1	49.0	24.0	20.1	3.9	4.4	0.0	85.3	20	0.0	OH	91.3	90
Case Western Reserve	98.6	79.0	2.4	13.3	5.2	57.8	20.5	13.3	1.8	6.0	0.6	63.9	21	1.8	OH	89.4	90
Cincinnati	100.0	89.0	3.1	5.5	2.4	50.4	20.4	8.0	1.8	11.5	0.0	75.2	15	0.0	OH	93.2	90
Cleveland State	96.4	88.9	3.7	4.5	2.9	49.1	28.7	12.5	1.9	2.8	4.2	89.4	13	0.0	OH	89.4	90
Dayton	96.2	87.6	0.0	9.8	2.6	50.0	21.6	14.2	6.0	7.5	0.7	60.4	21	0.0	OH	91.2	90
Ohio Northern	81.2	75.8	6.6	15.4	2.2	56.5	8.7	17.4	4.3	7.2	1.4	36.2	24	0.0	OH	74.5	90
Ohio State	97.3	89.7	1.4	8.0	0.9	53.4	10.5	17.3	3.1	11.0	2.1	72.8	23	0.5	OH	92.9	90
Toledo	89.6	88.4	1.1	9.4	1.1	54.4	18.1	15.6	3.1	5.6	3.1	57.5	19	0.6	OH	89.8	90

* Bar Passage Data is for the Summer 96 and Winter 97 Exams.

	CAREER PLACEMENT														BAR PASSAGE *		
	Employment Status					Type of Employment						Location					
	% Employment Status Known	% Employed	% Pursuing Graduate Degree	% Unemployed - Seeking	% Unemployed - Not Seeking	% in Law Firms	% in Business & Industry	% in Government	% in Public Interest	% in Judicial Clerkships	% in Academia	% Employed in State	# of States where Employed	% Employed in Foreign Nations	State where most take exam	Pass Rate for first-time test takers	State's Overall Pass Rate for first-time test takers
*** Oklahoma ***																	
Oklahoma	98.7	84.1	0.0	15.9	0.0	82.2	4.9	9.2	0.5	2.2	0.0	71.4	9	0.5	OK	89.7	85
Oklahoma City	83.6	77.7	2.7	19.6	0.0	77.4	20.0	14.8	0.0	0.9	1.7	58.3	21	0.0	OK	84.4	85
Tulsa	96.6	80.2	5.6	13.2	1.0	55.1	24.7	13.3	3.8	3.2	0.0	62.0	26	0.0	OK	79.8	85
*** Oregon ***																	
Lewis & Clark College	97.3	84.2	0.5	12.6	2.8	51.4	12.7	18.8	6.6	9.4	1.1	61.3	21	5.0	OR	82.1	77
Oregon	94.8	85.8	4.7	5.5	3.9	49.5	7.3	11.9	5.5	22.0	3.7	67.0	14	1.8	OR	73.3	77
Willamette	95.0	85.7	3.0	10.5	0.8	62.3	17.5	7.9	3.5	7.0	1.8	56.1	18	0.9	OR	73.7	77
*** Pennsylvania ***																	
Duquesne	98.8	87.4	0.0	11.4	1.2	47.9	26.0	10.3	4.1	10.3	1.4	89.0	9	0.0	PA	74.7	75
Pennsylvania	98.2	96.3	0.9	1.4	1.4	72.3	5.8	1.5	2.4	16.5	0.0	25.2	20	1.0	NY	92.8	77
Pennsylvania State Dickinson	94.4	91.5	2.0	5.2	1.3	48.6	2.1	16.4	1.4	20.0	0.0	66.4	13	0.0	PA	87.9	75
Pittsburgh	90.4	81.5	3.7	12.7	2.1	51.3	13.0	8.4	3.9	14.9	0.6	61.0	17	0.0	PA	86.2	75
Temple	97.2	93.5	1.2	3.5	1.8	53.0	17.6	11.6	4.4	12.9	0.6	61.1	23	0.0	PA	71.6	75
Villanova	87.2	88.4	2.6	8.9	0.0	58.9	13.7	4.2	0.0	23.2	0.0	71.4	13	0.6	PA	79.5	75
Widener-Harrisburg	96.1	75.5	2.0	20.5	2.0	38.3	17.6	17.6	1.6	18.1	2.1	58.5	12	0.0	PA	64.6	75
*** Puerto Rico ***																	
Inter American U. of Puerto Rico	97.2	87.1	2.9	8.2	1.8	57.7	18.1	15.4	8.7	13.4	1.3	98.7	2	0.7	PR	58.5	68
Pontifical Catholic U. of Puerto Rico	33.0	50.0	11.8	38.2	0.0	41.2	0.0	17.6	0.0	35.3	5.9	100.0	0	0.0	PR	56.8	68
Puerto Rico	61.4	91.4	5.7	2.9	0.0	48.4	28.1	6.2	4.7	9.4	3.1	100.0	1	0.0	PR	74.1	68
*** Rhode Island ***																	
Roger Williams	72.9	96.8	0.0	3.2	0.0	56.7	26.7	8.3	0.0	8.3	0.0	56.7	8	0.0	RI	54.2	72

* Bar Passage Data is for the Summer 96 and Winter 97 Exams.

	CAREER PLACEMENT														BAR PASSAGE *		
	Employment Status					Type of Employment						Location					
	% Employment Status Known	% Employed	% Pursuing Graduate Degree	% Unemployed - Seeking	% Unemployed - Not Seeking	% in Law Firms	% in Business & Industry	% in Government	% in Public Interest	% in Judicial Clerkships	% in Academia	% Employed in State	# of States where Employed	% Employed in Foreign Nations	State where most take exam	Pass Rate for first-time test takers	State's Overall Pass Rate for first-time test takers
*** South Carolina ***																	
South Carolina	96.9	88.8	4.0	5.2	2.0	51.1	9.0	15.8	1.4	21.7	0.9	86.4	12	0.9	SC	91.4	88
*** South Dakota ***																	
South Dakota	100.0	94.4	2.8	2.8	0.0	36.8	14.7	20.6	0.0	26.5	1.5	60.3	17	0.0	SD	80.9	86
*** Tennessee ***																	
Memphis	74.4	95.7	1.1	1.1	2.2	59.6	20.2	9.0	0.0	4.5	2.2	74.2	10	2.2	TN	90.6	79
Tennessee	98.1	87.9	2.5	5.1	4.5	63.0	14.5	7.2	1.4	12.3	1.4	84.8	11	0.0	TN	84.8	79
Vanderbilt	98.9	94.9	2.2	1.1	1.7	68.6	8.3	9.5	2.4	10.7	0.6	29.6	28	0.6	TN	93.0	79
*** Texas ***																	
Baylor	97.2	95.7	0.0	2.9	1.4	65.4	6.8	11.3	0.0	15.0	0.8	85.0	12	0.0	TX	92.6	84
Houston	88.0	88.7	2.0	5.1	4.3	65.2	18.5	8.4	0.9	5.7	1.3	93.0	11	0.0	TX	91.1	84
South Texas College of Law	52.9	77.3	1.8	20.5	0.5	57.1	12.9	5.9	0.0	7.6	1.8	71.8	5	0.0	TX	83.2	84
Southern Methodist	93.4	85.1	5.3	7.0	2.6	74.2	13.9	7.2	0.5	3.6	0.5	68.0	26	0.0	TX	86.0	84
St. Mary's	82.3	87.3	0.5	11.8	0.5	60.1	12.4	14.0	1.7	9.6	2.2	93.3	0	0.0	TX	73.8	84
Texas	87.4	90.3	0.9	7.1	1.7	64.3	6.8	9.4	0.3	10.5	1.0	61.2	31	1.3	TX	95.8	84
Texas Southern	78.4	93.1	4.6	0.0	2.3	43.2	8.6	1.2	0.0	2.5	0.0	48.1	6	0.0	TX	75.0	84
Texas Tech	90.5	84.9	0.0	15.1	0.0	86.3	0.7	4.8	0.7	7.5	0.0	96.6	3	0.0	TX	86.7	84
Texas Wesleyan	70.9	76.0	3.0	10.0	11.0	52.6	30.3	9.2	0.0	2.6	5.3	98.7	2	0.0	TX	57.3	84
*** Utah ***																	
Brigham Young	100.0	93.6	3.8	1.3	1.3	50.7	18.5	9.6	0.0	15.1	3.4	45.2	25	1.4	UT	92.1	93
Utah	99.1	94.8	0.9	0.9	3.5	56.9	15.6	12.8	0.9	13.8	0.0	72.5	14	1.8	UT	93.1	93
*** Vermont ***																	
Vermont Law School	98.7	79.6	2.0	16.3	2.0	49.6	15.4	12.8	5.1	12.8	0.9	20.5	32	0.9	VT	82.8	79

* Bar Passage Data is for the Summer 96 and Winter 97 Exams.

SECTION OF LEGAL EDUCATION AND ADMISSIONS TO THE BAR · ESTABLISHED 1893 · ABA

	CAREER PLACEMENT														BAR PASSAGE *		
	Employment Status					Type of Employment						Location					
	% Employment Status Known	% Employed	% Pursuing Graduate Degree	% Unemployed - Seeking	% Unemployed - Not Seeking	% in Law Firms	% in Business & Industry	% in Government	% in Public Interest	% in Judicial Clerkships	% in Academia	% Employed in State	# of States where Employed	% Employed in Foreign Nations	State where most take exam	Pass Rate for first-time test takers	State's Overall Pass Rate for first-time test takers
***** Virginia *****																	
George Mason	89.4	91.0	0.0	3.4	5.6	37.9	17.4	26.7	3.7	14.3	0.0	42.9	14	0.0	VA	83.5	77
Regent	79.0	91.6	1.2	4.8	2.4	51.3	14.5	21.1	6.6	5.3	1.3	32.9	26	0.0	VA	69.2	77
Richmond	96.1	85.8	1.4	6.8	6.1	55.9	13.4	11.0	3.1	15.7	0.8	72.4	16	0.8	VA	77.8	77
Virginia	98.9	97.6	1.1	0.8	0.5	59.3	8.5	5.8	3.8	21.4	0.3	19.5	33	1.1	VA	90.7	77
Washington & Lee	99.2	93.4	1.6	4.9	0.0	56.1	6.1	8.8	0.9	27.2	0.9	32.5	26	0.9	VA	78.2	77
William & Mary	98.8	92.9	2.9	1.8	2.4	60.8	8.2	8.2	3.2	18.4	1.3	39.2	27	0.0	VA	92.5	77
***** Washington *****																	
Gonzaga	97.0	79.6	11.7	6.2	2.5	55.8	10.9	14.7	1.6	10.1	3.1	46.5	22	0.0	WA	85.4	76
Seattle	93.0	81.7	0.8	14.7	2.8	54.9	16.0	19.4	0.5	4.9	1.0	85.4	20	0.0	WA	80.6	76
Washington, U. of	98.6	85.8	5.0	9.2	0.0	55.4	12.4	13.2	6.6	9.1	3.3	80.2	11	1.7	WA	86.8	76
***** West Virginia *****																	
West Virginia	93.5	90.8	3.8	4.6	0.8	66.1	9.3	15.3	3.4	4.2	1.7	89.0	8	0.0	WV	78.2	79
***** Wisconsin *****																	
Marquette	98.7	89.2	1.3	7.6	1.9	58.9	15.6	16.3	1.4	5.0	0.0	72.3	17	0.7	WI	100.0	92
Wisconsin	91.5	91.9	2.0	5.3	0.8	57.7	11.5	15.4	4.4	8.8	1.3	65.2	21	0.9	WI	100.0	92
***** Wyoming *****																	
Wyoming	89.2	81.8	1.5	16.7	0.0	44.4	11.1	20.4	5.6	18.5	0.0	64.8	0	0.0	WY	81.0	76

* Bar Passage Data is for the Summer 96 and Winter 97 Exams.

SECTION OF LEGAL EDUCATION AND ADMISSIONS TO THE BAR • ESTABLISHED 1893 • ABA	EXPENSES				FACULTY						STUDENT BODY					
	Res Non-Res Full-Time Tuition	Res Non-Res Part-Time Tuition	Expenses: on-campus	Expenses: off-campus	Student-Faculty Ratio	# Full-Time Faculty	# Part-Time Faculty	% Men	% Women	% Minorities	# of Full-Time Students	# of Part-Time Students	% Men	% Women	% Minorities	First Year Attrition Rate
***** Alabama *****																
Alabama	$3,758 $8,382	$0 $0	$7,574	$8,230	19.7/1	24	30	71	29	8	568	0	59.3	40.7	8.3	4.1%
Samford	$17,700 $17,700	$0 $0	N/A	$11,089	20.3/1	26	14	81	19	12	616	0	65.9	34.1	7.8	5.7%
***** Arizona *****																
Arizona	$4,060 $10,712	$0 $0	$8,030	$11,740	16.6/1	23	32	65	35	13	458	0	51.7	48.3	23.6	0.0%
Arizona State	$4,059 $10,711	$0 $0	$10,765	$10,765	16.6/1	23	12	74	26	13	458	0	50.7	49.3	24.9	9.0%
***** Arkansas *****																
Arkansas-Fayettville	$3,613 $8,101	$0 $0	$10,464	$10,464	14.3/1	22	8	68	32	18	377	0	59.9	40.1	9.5	19%
Arkansas-Little Rock	$4,206 $9,274	$3,040 $6,660	N/A	$9,517	14.7/1	20	11	70	30	10	253	151	51.5	48.5	11.6	11%
***** California *****																
California - Hastings	$11,167 $19,559	$0 $0	$15,704	$15,704	20.9/1	46	73	72	28	22	1,156	0	51.9	48.1	28.2	5.2%
California Western School of Law	$19,820 $19,820	$0 $0	N/A	$13,120	21.5/1	27	32	63	37	11	692	8	47.7	52.3	26.0	30%
California-Berkeley	$10,800 $19,784	$0 $0	$12,344	$12,344	16.7/1	41	43	78	22	10	820	0	48.8	51.2	29.9	3.4%
California-Davis	$10,843 $19,827	$0 $0	$10,530	$10,263	17.4/1	23	17	65	35	17	481	0	48.6	51.4	28.7	2.6%
California-Los Angeles	$10,917 $19,901	$0 $0	$11,524	$13,838	15.9/1	56	8	75	25	13	1,004	0	52.8	47.2	36.9	5.2%
Golden Gate	$19,074 $19,074	$13,224 $13,224	N/A	$11,030	16.7/1	30	49	63	37	17	502	152	43.7	56.3	25.1	12%
Loyola-Los Angeles	$20,734 $0	$13,922 $0	N/A	$13,445	22.0/1	45	32	64	36	24	927	393	53.8	46.2	40.1	6.9%
McGeorge	$18,378 $18,378	$11,326 $11,326	$13,910	$13,910	23.4/1	36	34	81	19	8	817	322	52.9	47.1	23.1	12%
Pepperdine	$21,900 $21,900	$0 $0	$15,234	$15,234	18.8/1	28	22	82	18	14	657	0	55.3	44.7	16.6	4.9%
San Diego	$19,980 $19,980	$14,180 $14,180	$12,538	$12,538	15.9/1	46	33	76	24	15	695	279	58.9	41.1	21.8	14%
San Francisco	$20,000 $20,000	$14,275 $14,275	$10,910	$12,850	20.2/1	25	31	72	28	20	525	125	47.5	52.5	26.3	12%
Santa Clara	$19,810 $19,810	$13,800 $13,800	N/A	$15,164	25.3/1	28	23	64	36	21	697	231	52.4	47.6	34.5	13%
Southern California	$23,862 $23,862	$0 $0	$11,098	$12,024	15.5/1	34	15	71	29	15	619	0	56.1	43.9	40.1	2.4%
Southwestern	$20,050 $20,050	$12,735 $12,735	N/A	$11,430	19.2/1	40	23	70	30	15	703	326	49.8	50.2	35.5	19%
Stanford	$24,276 $24,276	$0 $0	$11,136	$15,369	18.3/1	25	32	76	24	8	550	0	58.0	42.0	28.2	0.6%
Thomas Jefferson School of Law	$16,256 $16,256	$11,640 $11,640	N/A	$13,973	19.1/1	21	28	52	48	5	297	281	62.6	37.4	21.8	33%

SECTION OF LEGAL EDUCATION • AND ADMISSIONS TO THE BAR • ESTABLISHED 1893 ABA

	EXPENSES				FACULTY						STUDENT BODY					
	Res Non-Res Full-Time Tuition	Res Non-Res Part-Time Tuition	Expenses: on-campus	Expenses: off-campus	Student-Faculty Ratio	# Full-Time Faculty	# Part-Time Faculty	% Men	% Women	% Minorities	# of Full-Time Students	# of Part-Time Students	% Men	% Women	% Minorities	First Year Attrition Rate
***** California *****																
Whittier College	$20,014 $20,014	$12,022 $12,022	N/A	$14,958	21.6/1	21	23	62	38	14	369	266	50.4	49.6	37.3	24%
***** Colorado *****																
Colorado	$4,953 $16,171	$0 $0	$8,730	$10,633	14.7/1	29	9	83	17	14	510	2	51.0	49.0	17.6	6.1%
Denver	$17,970 $17,970	$13,478 $13,478	$11,663	$11,663	23.6/1	34	75	74	26	9	787	269	50.9	49.1	11.4	9.7%
***** Connecticut *****																
Connecticut	$10,928 $22,718	$7,658 $15,878	N/A	$12,248	14.1/1	32	27	78	22	9	439	165	51.8	48.2	15.2	11%
Quinnipiac College	$19,323 $19,323	$16,175 $16,175	N/A	$13,075	18.7/1	31	23	68	32	13	540	238	61.6	38.4	10.8	8.8%
Yale	$23,940 $23,940	$0 $0	$11,090	$11,090	11.1/1	43	28	79	21	12	573	0	57.4	42.6	29.5	0.0%
***** Delaware *****																
Widener	$17,820 $17,820	$13,380 $13,380	$11,620	$11,620	24.8/1	35	36	66	34	0	749	445	54.3	45.7	6.7	16%
***** District of Columbia *****																
American	$21,894 $21,894	$15,405 $15,405	$12,734	$12,734	20.6/1	44	96	61	39	11	882	313	41.0	59.0	24.0	0.3%
Catholic University of America	$22,412 $22,412	$17,065 $17,065	$12,790	$12,790	19.0/1	37	48	70	30	14	659	282	52.5	47.5	19.2	7.7%
George Washington	$22,959 $22,959	$16,200 $16,200	$13,587	$13,587	17.7/1	64	111	69	31	13	1,215	217	56.8	43.2	27.8	2.4%
Georgetown	$23,375 $23,375	$0 $16,200	$14,575	$14,575	19.3/1	83	110	63	37	10	1,605	485	53.4	46.6	25.0	1.7%
Howard	$12,425 $12,425	$0 $0	$10,957	$13,198	16.6/1	21	19	71	29	81	419	0	45.3	54.7	92.6	13%
***** Florida *****																
Florida	$4,036 $12,942	$0 $0	$7,840	$9,110	20.5/1	45	10	73	27	16	1,107	0	58.2	41.8	24.2	2.4%
Florida State	$4,386 $13,930	$0 $0	$14,034	$14,034	20.5/1	26	11	73	27	15	638	2	56.9	43.1	25.3	2.5%
Miami	$21,458 $21,458	$15,450 $15,450	$14,665	$14,665	24.4/1	45	113	76	24	16	1,133	277	56.7	43.3	28.8	1.6%
Nova Southeastern	$19,400 $19,400	$14,550 $14,550	$11,659	$12,664	18.2/1	40	27	63	38	18	780	140	58.8	41.2	24.6	13%
St. Thomas	$18,985 $18,985	$0 $0	$12,015	$14,120	25.9/1	17	16	76	24	29	528	0	60.6	39.4	32.6	22%
Stetson	$19,110 $19,110	$0 $0	$10,690	$12,470	17.7/1	30	24	70	30	10	634	5	48.0	52.0	17.2	8.1%

	EXPENSES				FACULTY						STUDENT BODY					
	Res Non-Res Full-Time Tuition	Res Non-Res Part-Time Tuition	Expenses: on-campus	Expenses: off-campus	Student-Faculty Ratio	# Full-Time Faculty	# Part-Time Faculty	% Men	% Women	% Minorities	# of Full-Time Students	# of Part-Time Students	% Men	% Women	% Minorities	First Year Attrition Rate
***** Georgia *****																
Emory	$22,700 $22,700	$0 $0	$9,946	$9,946	19.1/1	28	43	89	11	7	638	5	53.7	46.3	22.9	0.5%
Georgia	$3,757 $12,357	$0 $0	$7,054	$9,328	18.7/1	29	8	79	21	7	652	0	54.1	45.9	11.3	6.2%
Georgia State	$3,345 $10,429	$2,537 $7,597	$11,552	$12,705	16.6/1	28	8	68	32	11	392	249	50.7	49.3	25.4	13%
Mercer	$17,990 $17,990	$8,995 $8,995	N/A	$11,000	16.9/1	20	5	80	20	10	405	0	59.8	40.2	11.9	12%
***** Hawaii *****																
Hawaii	$7,115 $13,547	$0 $0	$7,200	$9,700	11.8/1	16	12	63	38	19	226	0	49.6	50.4	66.4	8.8%
***** Idaho *****																
Idaho	$3,882 $9,682	$0 $0	$10,106	$10,106	14.5/1	17	7	65	35	0	296	0	65.9	34.1	8.1	2.4%
***** Illinois *****																
Chicago	$24,138 $24,138	$0 $0	$14,342	$14,342	19.1/1	24	6	79	21	4	550	0	57.8	42.2	22.9	3.9%
Depaul	$18,810 $18,810	$12,710 $12,710	$12,558	$12,558	20.7/1	39	58	69	31	13	765	309	51.7	48.3	13.5	5.4%
Illinois	$7,646 $17,718	$0 $0	$9,632	$9,632	15.8/1	32	19	69	31	16	605	0	59.5	40.5	28.8	7.1%
Illinois Institute of Technology	$19,930 $19,930	$14,400 $14,400	N/A	$15,670	21.4/1	42	77	67	33	12	862	325	51.7	48.3	17.7	5.2%
John Marshall Law School	$16,600 $16,600	$11,880 $11,880	N/A	$12,924	14.7/1	54	96	74	26	7	700	385	57.3	42.7	17.3	14%
Loyola-Chicago	$20,856 $20,856	$15,668 $15,668	N/A	$13,250	20.9/1	26	64	69	31	15	516	207	43.6	56.4	18.1	12%
Northern Illinois	$5,938 $10,976	$0 $0	$7,662	$8,462	14.4/1	16	8	81	19	13	260	24	63.4	36.6	20.1	9.6%
Northwestern	$22,638 $0	$0 $0	$14,178	$14,808	14.6/1	36	111	81	19	6	629	0	57.6	42.4	21.9	5.0%
Southern Illinois	$5,300 $13,924	$0 $0	$8,060	$8,060	13.3/1	23	5	70	30	13	353	0	62.0	38.0	16.4	9.9%
***** Indiana *****																
Indiana-Bloomington	$6,162 $15,268	$0 $0	$6,298	$6,562	16.8/1	32	13	81	19	6	640	9	57.3	42.7	17.9	3.1%
Indiana-Indianapolis	$5,612 $13,380	$4,059 $9,608	$8,106	$11,576	18.5/1	34	16	71	29	6	563	292	53.8	46.2	11.0	5.4%
Notre Dame	$20,427 $20,427	$0 $0	$5,150	$5,150	17.3/1	24	21	88	13	13	522	0	63.0	37.0	18.8	2.9%
Valparaiso	$16,920 $16,920	$12,940 $12,940	$10,390	$10,390	18.2/1	18	15	67	33	11	367	39	53.4	46.6	17.7	1.8%

SECTION OF LEGAL EDUCATION AND ADMISSIONS TO THE BAR • ESTABLISHED 1893 • ABA	EXPENSES				FACULTY						STUDENT BODY					
	Res Non-Res Full-Time Tuition	Res Non-Res Part-Time Tuition	Expenses: on-campus	Expenses: off-campus	Student-Faculty Ratio	# Full-Time Faculty	# Part-Time Faculty	% Men	% Women	% Minorities	# of Full-Time Students	# of Part-Time Students	% Men	% Women	% Minorities	First Year Attrition Rate
*** Iowa ***																
Drake	$16,330 $16,330	$550 $550	N/A	$10,679	16.8/1	20	16	70	30	5	395	11	57.4	42.6	10.3	2.5%
Iowa	$5,974 $15,324	$0 $0	$7,998	$9,320	13.3/1	44	16	70	30	9	657	0	57.8	42.2	20.5	7.0%
*** Kansas ***																
Kansas	$4,553 $11,260	$0 $0	$10,391	$10,391	17.5/1	26	13	77	23	12	533	0	61.4	38.6	10.7	1.1%
Washburn	$6,396 $9,476	$0 $0	$11,316	$11,316	16.0/1	23	16	65	35	26	441	0	56.5	43.5	11.1	8.3%
*** Kentucky ***																
Kentucky	$4,956 $12,796	$0 $0	$9,898	$9,898	16.8/1	21	17	81	19	5	423	0	58.6	41.4	5.7	6.1%
Louisville	$4,850 $12,690	$4,060 $10,590	$7,646	$9,090	14.4/1	25	12	72	28	12	365	90	55.8	44.2	8.1	7.3%
Northern Kentucky	$5,200 $13,040	$4,340 $10,880	$6,304	$10,500	13.2/1	21	33	81	19	5	199	204	64.3	35.7	6.7	9.4%
*** Louisiana ***																
Louisiana State	$3,936 $8,923	$2,643 $6,011	$10,550	$18,950	19.6/1	26	14	88	12	8	610	0	54.4	45.6	10.2	33%
Loyola-New Orleans	$16,870 $16,870	$12,166 $12,166	$11,200	$11,200	17.7/1	30	18	67	33	27	516	157	52.7	47.3	22.7	12%
Southern	$3,128 $7,728	$0 $0	$8,314	$9,504	12.3/1	24	7	58	42	58	326	0	55.2	44.8	64.4	18%
Tulane	$22,940 $0	$0 $0	$11,200	$11,200	21.7/1	37	53	73	27	14	959	5	52.1	47.9	19.0	8.9%
*** Maine ***																
Maine	$8,378 $15,994	$6,010 $11,450	$7,900	$7,900	20.4/1	12	9	67	33	0	294	0	57.8	42.2	5.4	7.7%
*** Maryland ***																
Baltimore	$8,352 $14,480	$6,878 $11,318	N/A	$10,480	18.9/1	39	60	62	38	10	659	344	50.5	49.5	19.3	2.3%
Maryland	$9,219 $16,603	$6,919 $12,455	$9,741	$12,630	14.2/1	47	36	64	36	13	614	262	47.5	52.5	26.8	4.5%
*** Massachusetts ***																
Boston	$22,268 $22,268	$0 $0	$12,532	$12,532	18.4/1	45	54	64	36	11	996	0	54.6	45.4	17.6	7.1%
Boston College	$22,360 $22,360	$0 $0	N/A	$12,225	16.1/1	43	33	63	37	19	829	0	48.7	51.3	19.3	0.0%
Harvard	$23,466 $23,466	$0 $0	$12,695	$12,695	21.6/1	64	19	88	13	13	1,658	0	58.1	41.9	25.5	0.0%
New England School of Law	$14,450 $14,450	$10,880 $10,880	N/A	$13,450	19.8/1	34	44	74	26	9	549	392	51.5	48.5	16.2	7.3%
Northeastern	$21,300 $21,300	$0 $0	$12,700	$12,700	21.2/1	23	17	57	43	22	585	0	32.3	67.7	26.3	3.2%
Suffolk	$19,036 $19,036	$14,278 $14,278	N/A	$14,581	23.8/1	52	54	83	17	8	1,000	739	50.4	49.6	9.9	5.1%

SECTION OF LEGAL EDUCATION AND ADMISSIONS TO THE BAR • ESTABLISHED 1893 • ABA	EXPENSES				FACULTY						STUDENT BODY					
	Res Non-Res Full-Time Tuition	Res Non-Res Part-Time Tuition	Expenses: on-campus	Expenses: off-campus	Student-Faculty Ratio	# Full-Time Faculty	# Part-Time Faculty	% Men	% Women	% Minorities	# of Full-Time Students	# of Part-Time Students	% Men	% Women	% Minorities	First Year Attrition Rate
***** Massachusetts *****																
Western New England	$17,366 $17,366	$0 $12,820	N/A	$8,750	18.1/1	26	16	81	19	8	381	251	51.6	48.4	8.5	17%
***** Michigan *****																
Detroit College of Law at Michigan State	$14,732 $14,732	$11,050 $11,050	$9,910	$13,655	26.6/1	21	30	57	43	10	517	231	60.4	39.6	12.2	2.8%
Detroit Mercy	$15,450 $15,450	$11,046 $11,046	N/A	$11,853	18.5/1	18	26	83	17	6	269	237	52.4	47.6	13.2	31%
Michigan	$17,332 $23,332	$0 $0	$12,900	$12,250	15.9/1	54	15	81	19	9	1,035	0	58.6	41.4	20.8	0.6%
Thomas M. Cooley Law School	$14,110 $14,110	$10,090 $10,090	N/A	$15,571	18.6/1	50	83	70	30	10	228	1,345	60.9	39.1	16.0	27%
Wayne State	$6,578 $13,802	$4,738 $9,898	$9,404	$9,404	26.4/1	21	23	71	29	19	518	226	52.7	47.3	16.8	12%
***** Minnesota *****																
Hamline	$15,545 $15,545	$11,197 $11,197	$7,573	$10,120	17.6/1	24	38	67	33	8	494	20	51.2	48.8	9.9	4.8%
Minnesota	$9,230 $15,274	$0 $0	$8,849	$8,849	16.3/1	39	54	74	26	8	762	0	57.9	42.1	17.2	4.0%
William Mitchell College of Law	$16,280 $16,280	$11,830 $11,830	N/A	$10,508	23.1/1	31	76	74	26	10	508	531	53.2	46.8	11.3	6.6%
***** Mississippi *****																
Mississippi	$3,181 $7,103	$118 $314	$9,600	$9,600	21.8/1	19	5	84	16	21	496	3	59.5	40.5	12.4	18%
Mississippi College	$12,610 $0	$0 $0	$10,186	$13,816	21.8/1	16	8	63	38	13	418	0	62.4	37.6	11.2	0.6%
***** Missouri *****																
Missouri-Columbia	$8,555 $16,588	$0 $0	$9,072	$11,675	17.9/1	25	8	76	24	4	538	0	61.7	38.3	8.9	5.2%
Missouri-Kansas City	$8,548 $16,581	$6,154 $11,892	$10,130	$12,460	17.1/1	24	11	67	33	4	463	32	54.3	45.7	10.7	3.4%
St. Louis	$18,205 $18,205	$13,580 $13,580	$8,900	$9,700	17.6/1	34	16	76	24	9	545	262	56.4	43.6	16.9	0.0%
Washington University	$21,715 $21,715	$0 $0	N/A	$10,490	15.3/1	34	44	59	41	12	622	4	56.7	43.3	22.4	7.1%
***** Montana *****																
Montana	$6,046 $11,048	$0 $0	$7,540	$7,540	15.1/1	13	10	62	38	8	235	0	57.4	42.6	7.7	1.2%
***** Nebraska *****																
Creighton	$15,446 $15,446	$10,052 $10,052	$11,120	$11,120	16.8/1	22	26	68	32	5	432	17	59.5	40.5	10.9	13%
Nebraska	$3,920 $8,386	$0 $0	$6,885	$9,005	14.1/1	22	14	86	14	9	372	1	57.1	42.9	7.5	13%

Section of Legal Education and Admissions to the Bar • Established 1893 • ABA	EXPENSES				FACULTY						STUDENT BODY					
	Res Non-Res Full-Time Tuition	Res Non-Res Part-Time Tuition	Expenses: on-campus	Expenses: off-campus	Student-Faculty Ratio	# Full-Time Faculty	# Part-Time Faculty	% Men	% Women	% Minorities	# of Full-Time Students	# of Part-Time Students	% Men	% Women	% Minorities	First Year Attrition Rate
*** New Hampshire ***																
Franklin Pierce Law Center	$15,857 $0	$0 $0	N/A	$11,800	22.5/1	15	24	80	20	0	403	0	62.8	37.2	14.6	12%
*** New Jersey ***																
Rutgers-Camden	$10,062 $14,288	$7,940 $11,500	$8,995	$11,295	21.8/1	25	27	76	24	12	548	159	53.9	46.1	18.7	10%
Rutgers-Newark	$10,037 $14,263	$6,436 $9,284	$9,375	$11,675	15.9/1	34	30	62	38	21	502	221	54.4	45.6	31.5	13%
Seton Hall	$18,631 $18,631	$0 $13,285	N/A	$16,565	26.0/1	36	74	69	31	19	914	320	56.6	43.4	16.1	6.3%
*** New Mexico ***																
New Mexico	$3,612 $12,116	$0 $0	$7,895	$10,304	11.3/1	25	12	52	48	24	341	0	49.3	50.7	39.6	7.3%
*** New York ***																
Albany Law School	$18,905 $18,905	$14,206 $14,206	$8,800	$10,070	22.2/1	27	17	70	30	15	690	42	47.4	52.6	15.6	7.6%
Brooklyn Law School	$20,740 $20,740	$15,580 $15,580	$16,506	$16,506	20.6/1	52	61	52	48	8	936	534	53.9	46.1	17.8	2.8%
City U. of New York	$6,452 $9,682	$0 $0	N/A	$10,351	13.1/1	29	23	41	59	41	456	0	40.1	59.9	39.5	20%
Columbia	$25,666 $25,666	$0 $0	$13,800	$13,800	15.8/1	58	38	76	24	9	1,105	0	55.2	44.8	33.9	0.0%
Cornell Law School	$23,100 $23,100	$0 $0	$11,850	$11,850	11.1/1	43	10	67	33	5	536	0	58.2	41.8	27.8	1.1%
Fordham	$22,699 $22,699	$17,029 $17,029	$16,995	$16,995	21.5/1	50	95	78	22	12	1,055	355	55.7	44.3	24.1	1.7%
Hofstra	$21,182 $21,182	$0 $0	$13,280	$16,788	23.4/1	29	15	86	14	14	814	2	54.4	45.6	18.3	0.8%
New York Law School	$21,060 $21,060	$15,793 $15,793	$13,945	$13,945	23.3/1	43	66	70	30	12	880	488	53.7	46.3	20.9	5.5%
New York University	$25,685 $25,685	$0 $0	$16,225	$16,225	14.8/1	74	68	73	27	12	1,317	0	53.5	46.5	19.4	1.4%
Pace	$20,640 $20,640	$15,490 $15,490	$9,760	$13,210	16.2/1	36	36	64	36	8	494	310	48.8	51.2	16.8	8.5%
St. John's	$21,000 $21,000	$15,750 $15,750	N/A	$12,740	17.3/1	48	26	69	31	10	770	289	61.3	38.7	24.2	1.9%
State U. of New York at Buffalo	$8,075 $12,725	$0 $0	$9,855	$9,855	18.4/1	32	31	69	31	13	708	0	51.7	48.3	17.5	6.7%
Syracuse	$21,136 $21,136	$18,249 $0	$12,094	$12,094	16.9/1	36	26	58	42	11	716	24	55.4	44.6	20.3	1.2%
Touro College	$19,600 $19,600	$15,300 $15,300	$15,545	$15,545	17.7/1	29	20	62	38	7	399	331	56.4	43.6	22.6	16%
Yeshiva	$20,000 $20,000	$0 $0	N/A	$18,038	17.7/1	43	48	70	30	7	914	0	53.1	46.9	19.7	5.9%

SECTION OF LEGAL EDUCATION • AND ADMISSIONS TO THE BAR • ESTABLISHED 1893 ABA	EXPENSES				FACULTY						STUDENT BODY					
	Res Non-Res Full-Time Tuition	Res Non-Res Part-Time Tuition	Expenses: on-campus	Expenses: off-campus	Student-Faculty Ratio	# Full-Time Faculty	# Part-Time Faculty	% Men	% Women	% Minorities	# of Full-Time Students	# of Part-Time Students	% Men	% Women	% Minorities	First Year Attrition Rate
***** North Carolina *****																
Campbell	$15,733 $15,733	$0 $0	$26,285	$29,305	19.8/1	14	11	93	7	0	332	0	54.2	45.8	6.0	6.7%
Duke	$24,537 $24,537	$0 $0	$11,610	$11,610	15.4/1	33	24	70	30	12	611	0	59.2	40.8	15.9	4.5%
North Carolina	$2,881 $14,743	$0 $0	$8,950	$8,950	19.5/1	30	11	70	30	7	687	0	51.4	48.6	20.7	2.1%
North Carolina Central	$2,072 $11,034	$2,072 $11,034	$7,783	$10,650	25.1/1	11	6	36	64	64	253	118	44.2	55.8	49.9	11%
Wake Forest	$19,500 $19,500	$0 $0	N/A	$11,700	13.8/1	28	20	71	29	4	456	14	61.7	38.3	9.6	7.5%
***** North Dakota *****																
North Dakota	$4,097 $8,533	$0 $0	$7,300	$7,300	14.5/1	11	5	55	45	0	192	0	60.9	39.1	5.2	4.5%
***** Ohio *****																
Akron	$6,249 $10,746	$4,509 $7,721	$10,537	$10,537	25.0/1	18	28	61	39	17	402	209	55.8	44.2	8.0	20%
Capital	$14,993 $14,993	$9,823 $9,823	$10,585	$10,585	22.5/1	26	32	69	31	15	458	369	54.9	45.1	10.8	14%
Case Western Reserve	$19,540 $0	$813 $0	$10,430	$10,430	19.2/1	28	42	82	18	0	634	15	55.9	44.1	15.3	0.0%
Cincinnati	$7,245 $14,076	$0 $0	$10,256	$10,256	14.9/1	20	18	70	30	10	354	4	45.5	54.5	10.3	5.7%
Cleveland State	$7,145 $14,250	$5,495 $10,960	$7,934	$9,760	20.1/1	32	30	69	31	9	579	292	54.5	45.5	12.3	10%
Dayton	$18,280 $18,280	$0 $0	$8,800	$8,800	21.5/1	19	21	74	26	5	490	0	60.2	39.8	15.7	14%
Ohio Northern	$18,980 $18,980	$0 $0	$7,450	$8,700	16.8/1	17	6	76	24	6	329	0	66.0	34.0	14.3	20%
Ohio State	$7,022 $15,968	$0 $0	$9,569	$9,569	16.9/1	33	30	79	21	9	668	4	55.8	44.2	16.4	3.7%
Toledo	$6,970 $13,406	$5,808 $11,172	N/A	$9,639	17.5/1	25	13	72	28	8	417	164	54.2	45.8	9.5	11%
***** Oklahoma *****																
Oklahoma	$4,492 $13,260	$0 $0	$9,294	$10,932	18.8/1	24	14	75	25	8	542	0	52.2	47.8	14.9	3.6%
Oklahoma City	$13,488 $13,488	$9,680 $9,680	$6,741	$9,094	18.2/1	23	12	78	22	9	389	171	61.4	38.6	14.6	21%
Tulsa	$15,314 $15,314	$10,264 $10,264	$5,610	$7,050	15.0/1	30	51	57	43	17	453	132	56.4	43.6	17.8	11%
***** Oregon *****																
Lewis & Clark College	$17,395 $17,395	$13,045 $13,045	N/A	$11,200	13.5/1	36	31	69	31	3	464	163	54.5	45.5	14.5	7.2%
Oregon	$10,004 $13,642	$0 $0	$7,032	$7,515	16.8/1	26	7	62	38	15	524	0	51.7	48.3	14.1	1.2%
Willamette	$17,100 $17,100	$0 $0	$10,820	$10,820	18.6/1	18	5	78	22	0	398	5	52.4	47.6	10.2	13%

SECTION OF LEGAL EDUCATION AND ADMISSIONS TO THE BAR · ESTABLISHED 1893 · ABA	EXPENSES				FACULTY						STUDENT BODY					
	Res Non-Res Full-Time Tuition	Res Non-Res Part-Time Tuition	Expenses: on-campus	Expenses: off-campus	Student-Faculty Ratio	# Full-Time Faculty	# Part-Time Faculty	% Men	% Women	% Minorities	# of Full-Time Students	# of Part-Time Students	% Men	% Women	% Minorities	First Year Attrition Rate
							*** Pennsylvania ***									
Duquesne	$14,414 $14,414	$11,020 $11,020	$8,332	$8,332	24.3/1	19	19	74	26	11	337	330	56.7	43.3	5.5	21%
Pennsylvania	$24,530 $24,530	$0 $0	$12,000	$12,000	17.7/1	34	32	82	18	9	721	0	58.3	41.7	25.2	0.0%
Pennsylvania State Dickinson	$14,600 $14,600	$0 $0	$9,955	$12,155	26.3/1	16	43	75	25	6	503	4	58.8	41.2	8.5	5.7%
Pittsburgh	$11,898 $18,346	$0 $0	N/A	$10,180	22.2/1	26	21	62	38	15	693	0	58.3	41.7	9.5	0.4%
Temple	$8,900 $15,414	$7,182 $12,392	$12,984	$12,984	18.4/1	44	74	73	27	23	770	339	51.3	48.7	27.6	3.8%
Villanova	$18,780 $18,780	$0 $0	$11,000	$13,440	21.0/1	27	27	85	15	11	680	0	54.7	45.3	15.9	3.0%
Widener-Harrisburg	$17,820 $17,820	$13,380 $13,380	N/A	$11,620	22.3/1	15	11	47	53	13	305	147	61.1	38.9	4.2	15%
							*** Puerto Rico ***									
Inter American U. of Puerto Rico	$10,495 $10,495	$7,895 $0	N/A	$8,900	23.9/1	20	24	60	40	100	375	300	44.9	55.1	100.0	13%
Pontifical Catholic U. of Puerto Rico	$8,768 $8,768	$6,256 $0	$6,811	$8,927	21.4/1	17	13	59	41	100	319	174	48.7	51.3	100.0	19%
Puerto Rico	$2,320 $3,570	$1,570 $3,500	$7,544	$6,044	24.5/1	16	33	81	19	100	332	210	43.7	56.3	100.0	7.5%
							*** Rhode Island ***									
Roger Williams	$18,080 $18,080	$13,873 $13,873	$12,704	$13,610	14.4/1	22	20	59	41	14	246	202	58.0	42.0	7.1	29%
							*** South Carolina ***									
South Carolina	$6,964 $13,706	$0 $0	$11,009	$11,009	20.9/1	35	0	89	11	29	764	0	58.5	41.5	9.0	4.0%
							*** South Dakota ***									
South Dakota	$4,715 $9,979	$0 $0	$6,233	$8,429	15.2/1	12	1	83	17	8	219	0	61.2	38.8	5.5	5.5%
							*** Tennessee ***									
Memphis	$4,182 $10,360	$3,320 $8,144	$11,090	$11,090	20.8/1	20	25	70	30	5	479	31	56.7	43.3	10.6	18%
Tennessee	$4,204 $10,496	$0 $0	$10,816	$10,816	16.5/1	25	24	68	32	8	494	0	54.7	45.3	10.5	6.7%
Vanderbilt	$21,971 $21,971	$0 $0	$11,800	$11,800	18.1/1	25	20	84	16	0	542	0	60.1	39.9	16.8	0.5%
							*** Texas ***									
Baylor	$11,839 $11,839	$0 $0	$7,995	$12,330	21.1/1	16	8	75	25	6	400	0	65.8	34.3	10.0	9.0%
Houston	$5,505 $9,705	$4,049 $7,049	$7,680	$9,670	21.0/1	35	38	86	14	3	741	213	57.7	42.3	21.4	3.1%
South Texas College of Law	$14,700 $14,700	$10,000 $10,000	N/A	$12,024	20.3/1	45	23	73	27	13	790	423	57.5	42.5	20.9	15%
Southern Methodist	$19,534 $19,534	$14,200 $14,200	$6,573	$4,965	26.7/1	24	59	83	17	29	755	22	54.3	45.7	19.0	4.7%

SECTION OF LEGAL EDUCATION AND ADMISSIONS TO THE BAR · ESTABLISHED 1893 · ABA	EXPENSES				FACULTY						STUDENT BODY					
	Res Non-Res Full-Time Tuition	Res Non-Res Part-Time Tuition	Expenses: on-campus	Expenses: off-campus	Student-Faculty Ratio	# Full-Time Faculty	# Part-Time Faculty	% Men	% Women	% Minorities	# of Full-Time Students	# of Part-Time Students	% Men	% Women	% Minorities	First Year Attrition Rate
***** Texas *****																
St. Mary's	**$14,916 $14,916**	**$0 $0**	**$9,492**	**$12,296**	**22.1/1**	**29**	**34**	**72**	**28**	**17**	**768**	**0**	**52.7**	**47.3**	**39.1**	**3.4%**
Texas	**$6,300 $13,300**	**$0 $0**	**$8,734**	**$10,306**	**20.6/1**	**57**	**39**	**81**	**19**	**7**	**1,465**	**0**	**55.6**	**44.4**	**22.6**	**3.4%**
Texas Southern	**$4,367 $8,007**	**$0 $0**	**$2,734**	**$9,872**	**19.1/1**	**26**	**7**	**81**	**19**	**81**	**596**	**0**	**53.5**	**46.5**	**84.1**	**40%**
Texas Tech	**$6,195 $10,335**	**$0 $0**	**$9,190**	**$9,190**	**24.9/1**	**22**	**6**	**77**	**23**	**14**	**637**	**0**	**58.2**	**41.8**	**13.0**	**8.8%**
Texas Wesleyan	**$12,074 $12,074**	**$8,674 $8,674**	**$6,541**	**$8,506**	**22.4/1**	**21**	**18**	**81**	**19**	**19**	**381**	**277**	**59.4**	**40.6**	**19.3**	**20%**
***** Utah *****																
Brigham Young	**$4,970 $7,450**	**$275 $412**	**$11,000**	**$10,940**	**15.2/1**	**24**	**20**	**83**	**17**	**13**	**439**	**0**	**67.2**	**32.8**	**12.3**	**0.0%**
Utah	**$4,445 $9,946**	**$0 $0**	**$8,149**	**$8,149**	**14.3/1**	**21**	**6**	**86**	**14**	**19**	**358**	**0**	**64.8**	**35.2**	**13.4**	**3.1%**
***** Vermont *****																
Vermont Law School	**$18,565 $18,565**	**$0 $0**	**N/A**	**$13,375**	**17.4/1**	**22**	**14**	**50**	**50**	**5**	**459**	**0**	**51.9**	**48.1**	**6.3**	**8.0%**
***** Virginia *****																
George Mason	**$7,448 $17,990**	**$5,320 $12,850**	**N/A**	**$14,953**	**21.7/1**	**23**	**34**	**83**	**17**	**9**	**378**	**337**	**62.0**	**38.0**	**10.1**	**4.1%**
Regent	**$13,872 $13,872**	**$0 $0**	**$10,793**	**$10,793**	**19.5/1**	**17**	**23**	**82**	**18**	**18**	**398**	**0**	**64.1**	**35.9**	**8.5**	**11%**
Richmond	**$18,170 $18,170**	**$0 $0**	**$7,920**	**$10,170**	**16.4/1**	**24**	**40**	**71**	**29**	**8**	**471**	**1**	**54.2**	**45.8**	**16.1**	**13%**
Virginia	**$13,954 $19,870**	**$0 $0**	**$10,760**	**$10,760**	**16.0/1**	**62**	**38**	**77**	**23**	**8**	**1,127**	**0**	**63.4**	**36.6**	**12.6**	**0.6%**
Washington & Lee	**$17,211 $17,211**	**$0 $0**	**$10,085**	**$10,085**	**11.4/1**	**29**	**7**	**79**	**21**	**7**	**367**	**0**	**59.4**	**40.6**	**9.3**	**2.5%**
William & Mary	**$7,758 $17,574**	**$0 $0**	**$12,830**	**$12,830**	**21.7/1**	**20**	**21**	**60**	**40**	**15**	**520**	**0**	**54.0**	**46.0**	**19.8**	**4.0%**
***** Washington *****																
Gonzaga	**$17,030 $17,030**	**$10,250 $10,250**	**$12,050**	**$12,050**	**20.7/1**	**20**	**17**	**75**	**25**	**5**	**484**	**19**	**60.6**	**39.4**	**15.1**	**14%**
Seattle	**$17,086 $17,086**	**$14,232 $14,232**	**N/A**	**$11,008**	**22.8/1**	**28**	**21**	**64**	**36**	**11**	**641**	**189**	**50.1**	**49.9**	**19.0**	**11%**
Washington, U. of	**$5,388 $13,293**	**$0 $0**	**$11,271**	**$11,271**	**12.8/1**	**36**	**14**	**56**	**44**	**11**	**509**	**1**	**47.6**	**52.4**	**29.2**	**0.0%**
***** West Virginia *****																
West Virginia	**$5,062 $12,104**	**$0 $0**	**$8,302**	**$10,212**	**15.2/1**	**24**	**15**	**63**	**38**	**13**	**425**	**13**	**54.3**	**45.7**	**4.3**	**4.7%**

Section of Legal Education and Admissions to the Bar • Established 1893 • ABA	EXPENSES				FACULTY						STUDENT BODY					
	Res Non-Res Full-Time Tuition	Res Non-Res Part-Time Tuition	Expenses: on-campus	Expenses: off-campus	Student-Faculty Ratio	# Full-Time Faculty	# Part-Time Faculty	% Men	% Women	% Minorities	# of Full-Time Students	# of Part-Time Students	% Men	% Women	% Minorities	First Year Attrition Rate
***** Wisconsin *****																
Marquette	**$17,830** **$17,830**	**$14,800** **$14,800**	**$11,990**	**$11,990**	**14.5/1**	**26**	**22**	**65**	**35**	**12**	**415**	**59**	**57.6**	**42.4**	**10.8**	**0.0%**
Wisconsin	**$5,910** **$15,442**	**$4,924** **$12,869**	**$9,725**	**$9,725**	**16.3/1**	**40**	**42**	**65**	**35**	**10**	**748**	**64**	**53.2**	**46.8**	**23.2**	**1.0%**
***** Wyoming *****																
Wyoming	**$4,234** **$9,322**	**$0** **$0**	**$7,076**	**$7,076**	**15.3/1**	**12**	**5**	**67**	**33**	**0**	**213**	**0**	**55.9**	**44.1**	**2.8**	**13%**

ADMISSIONS

			FULL-TIME						PART-TIME						TOTAL	
	Application Deadline	Application Fee	75% GPA	25% GPA	75% LSAT	25% LSAT	% Accepted	# of Matriculants	75% GPA	25% GPA	75% LSAT	25% LSAT	% Accepted	# of Matriculants	Total % Admitted	Total Matriculants
***** Alabama *****																
Alabama	03/01	$25	3.65	3.08	160	154	44	209	0.00	0.00	0	0	N/A	0	44	209
Samford	05/01	$40	3.28	2.75	154	148	58	212	0.00	0.00	0	0	N/A	0	58	212
***** Arizona *****																
Arizona	03/01	$45	3.66	3.11	164	155	30	151	0.00	0.00	0	0	N/A	0	30	151
Arizona State	03/01	$35	3.61	3.00	163	153	22	158	0.00	0.00	0	0	N/A	0	22	158
***** Arkansas *****																
Arkansas-Fayettville	04/01	$0	3.53	2.97	157	149	49	131	0.00	0.00	0	0	N/A	0	49	131
Arkansas-Little Rock	04/01	$40	3.62	3.02	156	148	57	81	3.40	2.65	155	148	41	50	51	131
***** California *****																
California - Hastings	02/16	$40	3.56	3.08	165	158	35	311	0.00	0.00	0	0	N/A	0	35	311
California Western School of Law	04/01	$45	3.34	2.65	152	145	71	347	0.00	0.00	0	0	N/A	0	71	347
California-Berkeley	02/01	$40	3.86	3.66	171	163	21	268	0.00	0.00	0	0	N/A	0	21	268
California-Davis	02/01	$40	3.64	3.25	162	156	38	172	0.00	0.00	0	0	N/A	0	38	172
California-Los Angeles	01/15	$40	3.73	3.42	165	159	25	381	0.00	0.00	0	0	N/A	0	25	381
Golden Gate	04/15	$40	3.27	2.75	156	148	59	178	3.21	2.64	154	148	50	52	58	230
Loyola-Los Angeles	02/01	$50	3.47	3.01	160	153	40	365	3.44	2.99	158	152	42	119	40	484
McGeorge	05/15	$40	3.31	2.82	155	149	69	291	3.18	2.71	157	149	64	96	68	387
Pepperdine	03/01	$50	3.51	3.02	159	153	46	243	0.00	0.00	0	0	N/A	0	46	243
San Diego	02/01	$40	3.36	2.79	161	157	43	243	3.24	2.73	157	154	87	91	47	334
San Francisco	04/01	$40	3.32	2.79	159	152	43	172	3.24	2.67	156	150	47	46	43	218
Santa Clara	03/01	$40	3.42	2.96	160	153	50	242	3.35	2.82	161	153	49	56	50	298
Southern California	02/01	$60	3.60	3.20	166	159	27	200	0.00	0.00	0	0	N/A	0	27	200
Southwestern	06/30	$50	3.24	2.67	154	150	55	256	3.31	2.57	153	149	44	78	53	334
Stanford	02/01	$65	3.87	3.60	171	165	12	177	0.00	0.00	0	0	N/A	0	12	177
Thomas Jefferson School of Law	Rolling	$35	3.07	2.37	150	143	82	151	3.17	2.41	152	144	77	39	81	190

Section of Legal Education and Admissions to the Bar • ABA • Established 1893	ADMISSIONS																
			FULL-TIME						PART-TIME						TOTAL	
	Application Deadline	Application Fee	75% GPA	25% GPA	75% LSAT	25% LSAT	% Accepted	# of Matriculants	75% GPA	25% GPA	75% LSAT	25% LSAT	% Accepted	# of Matriculants	Total % Admitted	Total Matriculants
*** California ***																
Whittier College	03/15	$50	3.19	2.55	154	148	59	158	3.21	2.59	153	145	59	117	59	275
*** Colorado ***																
Colorado	02/15	$45	3.72	3.33	164	158	35	186	0.00	0.00	0	0	N/A	0	35	186
Denver	05/01	$45	3.38	2.85	157	151	63	254	3.45	2.87	158	151	62	77	63	331
*** Connecticut ***																
Connecticut	03/15	$30	3.48	3.08	160	154	48	140	3.33	2.83	158	152	42	55	46	195
Quinnipiac College	Rolling	$40	3.15	2.47	152	145	58	197	3.18	2.55	151	145	40	101	55	298
Yale	02/15	$65	3.96	3.78	175	168	7	188	0.00	0.00	0	0	N/A	0	7	188
*** Delaware ***																
Widener	05/15	$60	3.22	2.72	151	145	75	259	3.25	2.66	152	145	68	127	73	386
*** District of Columbia ***																
American	03/01	$55	3.46	3.04	159	153	41	286	3.40	2.79	154	148	57	95	43	381
Catholic University of America	03/01	$55	3.30	3.10	157	151	50	219	3.30	2.60	155	149	50	83	50	302
George Washington	03/01	$55	3.57	3.23	163	159	N/A	377	3.42	3.09	161	154	N/A	59	N/A	436
Georgetown	03/01	$60	3.75	3.26	168	163	29	510	3.62	3.14	167	159	34	125	30	635
Howard	04/30	$60	3.30	2.71	154	148	36	127	0.00	0.00	0	0	N/A	0	36	127
*** Florida ***																
Florida	02/01	$20	3.78	3.38	162	154	28	202	0.00	0.00	0	0	N/A	0	28	202
Florida State	02/15	$20	3.56	3.05	159	152	34	221	0.00	0.00	0	0	N/A	0	34	221
Miami	07/31	$45	3.45	2.91	157	151	64	354	3.29	2.67	152	146	72	128	65	482
Nova Southeastern	03/01	$50	3.15	2.57	151	143	55	248	3.20	2.45	151	145	55	67	55	315
St. Thomas	04/30	$40	3.04	2.46	152	147	56	205	0.00	0.00	0	0	N/A	0	56	205
Stetson	03/01	$45	3.40	2.90	155	148	47	237	0.00	0.00	0	0	N/A	0	47	237

Section of Legal Education and Admissions to the Bar · Established 1893 · ABA	ADMISSIONS															
			FULL-TIME						PART-TIME						TOTAL	
	Application Deadline	Application Fee	75% GPA	25% GPA	75% LSAT	25% LSAT	% Accepted	# of Matriculants	75% GPA	25% GPA	75% LSAT	25% LSAT	% Accepted	# of Matriculants	Total % Admitted	Total Matriculants
*** Georgia ***																
Emory	03/01	$50	3.60	3.23	163	158	38	207	0.00	0.00	0	0	N/A	0	38	207
Georgia	03/01	$30	3.73	3.33	164	158	26	233	0.00	0.00	0	0	N/A	0	26	233
Georgia State	03/15	$30	3.40	2.87	160	154	23	121	3.59	2.91	161	154	31	79	25	200
Mercer	03/15	$45	3.51	2.82	157	151	45	151	0.00	0.00	0	0	N/A	0	45	151
*** Hawaii ***																
Hawaii	03/01	$30	3.53	3.07	160	154	37	77	0.00	0.00	0	0	N/A	0	37	77
*** Idaho ***																
Idaho	02/01	$30	3.42	2.90	155	152	69	128	0.00	0.00	0	0	N/A	0	69	128
*** Illinois ***																
Chicago	Rolling	$60	3.80	3.50	172	165	25	175	0.00	0.00	0	0	N/A	0	25	175
Depaul	04/01	$40	3.37	2.91	156	151	70	259	3.20	2.58	154	149	58	79	68	338
Illinois	03/15	$40	3.75	3.20	164	157	34	200	0.00	0.00	0	0	N/A	0	34	200
Illinois Institute of Technology	04/01	$40	3.43	2.92	156	150	66	282	3.38	2.76	157	148	55	102	64	384
John Marshall Law School	03/01	$50	3.23	2.67	152	145	63	232	3.08	2.42	154	146	51	135	60	367
Loyola-Chicago	04/01	$45	3.56	2.97	161	155	36	169	3.39	2.75	157	150	54	72	39	241
Northern Illinois	05/15	$35	3.27	2.71	157	152	42	82	2.90	2.65	156	151	48	5	42	87
Northwestern	02/16	$80	3.68	3.33	166	161	21	206	0.00	0.00	0	0	N/A	0	21	206
Southern Illinois	03/01	$25	3.53	2.77	157	150	57	120	0.00	0.00	0	0	N/A	0	57	120
*** Indiana ***																
Indiana-Bloomington	03/01	$35	3.68	3.03	162	155	41	203	0.00	0.00	0	0	100	2	41	205
Indiana-Indianapolis	03/01	$35	3.49	2.96	157	151	59	186	3.55	2.94	158	151	40	82	54	268
Notre Dame	03/01	$65	3.66	3.15	165	160	28	180	0.00	0.00	0	0	N/A	0	28	180
Valparaiso	04/15	$30	3.40	2.69	154	147	64	119	3.14	2.47	155	147	45	7	63	126

SECTION OF LEGAL EDUCATION AND ADMISSIONS TO THE BAR • ABA • ESTABLISHED 1893

	ADMISSIONS																
			FULL-TIME						PART-TIME						TOTAL	
	Application Deadline	Application Fee	75% GPA	25% GPA	75% LSAT	25% LSAT	% Accepted	# of Matriculants	75% GPA	25% GPA	75% LSAT	25% LSAT	% Accepted	# of Matriculants	Total % Admitted	Total Matriculants
*** Iowa ***																
Drake	03/01	$35	3.51	2.89	156	151	45	120	0.00	0.00	0	0	14	3	44	123
Iowa	03/01	$20	3.73	3.09	163	154	47	231	0.00	0.00	0	0	N/A	0	47	231
*** Kansas ***																
Kansas	03/15	$40	3.63	3.12	158	152	50	180	0.00	0.00	0	0	N/A	0	50	180
Washburn	03/15	$30	3.45	2.88	154	147	60	148	0.00	0.00	0	0	N/A	0	60	148
*** Kentucky ***																
Kentucky	03/01	$25	3.70	3.14	160	154	44	142	0.00	0.00	0	0	N/A	0	44	142
Louisville	02/15	$30	3.46	2.82	160	152	34	91	3.66	3.07	159	152	39	33	35	124
Northern Kentucky	05/15	$35	3.26	2.76	155	151	37	68	3.65	2.99	159	151	47	56	39	124
*** Louisiana ***																
Louisiana State	02/01	$25	3.53	3.06	157	148	54	244	0.00	0.00	0	0	N/A	0	54	244
Loyola-New Orleans	08/20	$20	3.25	2.70	154	149	54	172	3.33	2.64	157	150	53	44	54	216
Southern	03/31	$0	3.00	2.42	147	141	27	119	0.00	0.00	0	0	N/A	0	27	119
Tulane	Rolling	$45	3.50	3.00	162	155	54	304	0.00	0.00	0	0	N/A	0	54	304
*** Maine ***																
Maine	02/15	$25	3.49	3.03	159	150	51	97	0.00	0.00	0	0	N/A	0	51	97
*** Maryland ***																
Baltimore	04/01	$35	3.25	2.69	153	147	55	217	3.26	2.71	155	149	49	82	54	299
Maryland	03/01	$42	3.60	3.06	159	151	39	212	3.53	2.96	161	152	33	62	39	274
*** Massachusetts ***																
Boston	03/01	$50	3.56	3.03	163	158	40	322	0.00	0.00	0	0	N/A	0	40	322
Boston College	03/01	$65	3.68	3.25	163	157	30	289	0.00	0.00	0	0	N/A	0	30	289
Harvard	02/02	$65	3.93	3.73	173	166	14	556	0.00	0.00	0	0	N/A	0	14	556
New England School of Law	06/01	$50	3.29	2.59	153	145	67	187	3.32	2.52	154	145	74	99	68	286
Northeastern	03/01	$55	3.50	3.04	158	151	36	176	0.00	0.00	0	0	N/A	0	36	176
Suffolk	03/03	$50	3.42	2.90	154	147	74	348	3.41	2.86	156	147	71	190	73	538

	ADMISSIONS															
			FULL-TIME						PART-TIME						TOTAL	
SECTION OF LEGAL EDUCATION AND ADMISSIONS TO THE BAR · ESTABLISHED 1893 · ABA	Application Deadline	Application Fee	75% GPA	25% GPA	75% LSAT	25% LSAT	% Accepted	# of Matriculants	75% GPA	25% GPA	75% LSAT	25% LSAT	% Accepted	# of Matriculants	Total % Admitted	Total Matriculants
*** Massachusetts ***																
Western New England	Rolling	$35	3.27	2.79	151	144	71	131	3.29	2.63	151	144	70	74	71	205
*** Michigan ***																
Detroit College of Law at Michigan State	04/15	$50	3.39	2.80	155	147	62	139	3.46	2.74	155	146	57	39	61	178
Detroit Mercy	04/15	$50	3.30	2.72	151	144	59	92	3.32	2.59	150	145	68	55	61	147
Michigan	02/15	$70	3.69	3.33	169	163	34	339	0.00	0.00	0	0	N/A	0	34	339
Thomas M. Cooley Law School	Rolling	$50	3.15	2.63	147	140	75	209	3.12	2.55	147	140	76	550	76	759
Wayne State	03/15	$20	3.46	3.00	158	151	60	163	3.45	3.04	160	151	46	64	57	227
*** Minnesota ***																
Hamline	05/15	$30	3.45	2.89	152	150	54	138	0.00	0.00	0	0	N/A	4	54	142
Minnesota	03/01	$40	3.77	3.28	164	158	43	245	0.00	0.00	0	0	N/A	0	43	245
William Mitchell College of Law	07/01	$45	3.49	2.90	156	147	74	200	3.31	2.74	157	148	N/A	135	74	335
*** Mississippi ***																
Mississippi	03/01	$20	3.63	3.02	157	150	35	170	0.00	0.00	0	0	N/A	0	35	170
Mississippi College	05/01	$25	3.27	2.67	152	145	69	142	0.00	0.00	0	0	N/A	0	69	142
*** Missouri ***																
Missouri-Columbia	03/01	$40	3.58	3.04	158	152	57	192	0.00	0.00	0	0	N/A	0	57	192
Missouri-Kansas City	Rolling	$25	3.40	2.81	156	150	61	156	3.61	3.22	156	151	46	15	60	171
St. Louis	03/01	$40	3.51	3.01	157	148	63	182	3.26	2.66	156	147	63	72	63	254
Washington University	03/01	$50	3.57	3.07	163	155	56	197	0.00	0.00	0	0	N/A	0	56	197
*** Montana ***																
Montana	03/01	$60	3.63	3.01	160	153	54	82	0.00	0.00	0	0	N/A	0	54	82
*** Nebraska ***																
Creighton	05/01	$40	3.31	2.83	152	146	74	150	3.18	2.40	160	148	38	6	73	156
Nebraska	03/01	$25	3.67	3.13	158	150	52	142	0.00	0.00	0	0	N/A	0	52	142

SECTION OF LEGAL EDUCATION AND ADMISSIONS TO THE BAR • ESTABLISHED 1893 • ABA

	ADMISSIONS															
			FULL-TIME						PART-TIME						TOTAL	
	Application Deadline	Application Fee	75% GPA	25% GPA	75% LSAT	25% LSAT	% Accepted	# of Matriculants	75% GPA	25% GPA	75% LSAT	25% LSAT	% Accepted	# of Matriculants	Total % Admitted	Total Matriculants
***** New Hampshire *****																
Franklin Pierce Law Center	05/01	$45	3.20	2.66	156	145	68	133	0.00	0.00	0	0	N/A	4	68	137
***** New Jersey *****																
Rutgers-Camden	03/01	$40	3.49	3.04	155	150	50	191	3.35	2.64	158	149	N/A	45	50	236
Rutgers-Newark	03/15	$40	3.50	3.06	159	153	34	152	3.55	2.66	159	150	25	59	33	211
Seton Hall	04/15	$50	3.36	2.81	157	151	50	321	3.41	2.67	157	150	32	64	47	385
***** New Mexico *****																
New Mexico	02/16	$40	3.52	2.80	160	151	34	118	0.00	0.00	0	0	N/A	0	34	118
***** New York *****																
Albany Law School	03/15	$50	3.32	2.86	153	145	74	250	0.00	0.00	0	0	N/A	0	74	250
Brooklyn Law School	Rolling	$60	3.50	3.00	159	153	49	275	3.35	2.86	154	149	51	210	49	485
City U. of New York	03/15	$40	3.35	2.70	152	142	38	167	0.00	0.00	0	0	N/A	0	38	167
Columbia	02/15	$65	3.71	3.39	171	165	21	358	0.00	0.00	0	0	N/A	0	21	358
Cornell Law School	02/01	$65	3.78	3.39	166	163	29	182	0.00	0.00	0	0	N/A	0	29	182
Fordham	03/01	$60	3.62	3.09	164	159	31	321	3.55	2.93	161	155	32	121	31	442
Hofstra	04/15	$60	3.50	2.95	157	149	49	291	0.00	0.00	0	0	N/A	0	49	291
New York Law School	04/01	$50	3.33	2.85	154	148	52	332	3.43	2.72	154	146	35	127	48	459
New York University	02/01	$65	3.81	3.55	170	166	24	393	0.00	0.00	0	0	N/A	0	24	393
Pace	02/15	$55	3.36	2.83	155	147	50	181	3.15	2.65	154	147	49	103	50	284
St. John's	03/01	$50	3.29	2.68	160	151	47	235	3.41	2.58	158	151	36	67	45	302
State U. of New York at Buffalo	02/01	$50	3.55	2.99	158	152	52	214	0.00	0.00	0	0	N/A	0	52	214
Syracuse	04/01	$50	3.43	2.94	154	148	66	247	3.02	2.87	153	147	44	6	66	253
Touro College	05/01	$50	3.19	2.49	151	145	52	131	3.28	2.57	151	145	50	103	52	234
Yeshiva	04/01	$60	3.55	2.99	159	151	46	329	0.00	0.00	0	0	N/A	0	46	329

SECTION OF LEGAL EDUCATION AND ADMISSIONS TO THE BAR · ESTABLISHED 1893 · ABA	ADMISSIONS															
			FULL-TIME						PART-TIME						TOTAL	
	Application Deadline	Application Fee	75% GPA	25% GPA	75% LSAT	25% LSAT	% Accepted	# of Matriculants	75% GPA	25% GPA	75% LSAT	25% LSAT	% Accepted	# of Matriculants	Total % Admitted	Total Matriculants
*** North Carolina ***																
Campbell	Rolling	$40	3.42	2.83	157	152	32	112	0.00	0.00	0	0	N/A	0	32	112
Duke	02/01	$65	3.78	3.29	169	161	29	205	0.00	0.00	0	0	N/A	0	29	205
North Carolina	02/01	$60	3.73	3.23	164	156	34	230	0.00	0.00	0	0	N/A	0	34	230
North Carolina Central	04/15	$30	3.30	2.60	152	146	20	99	3.30	2.80	160	152	22	34	21	133
Wake Forest	03/15	$60	3.53	2.96	162	157	43	163	0.00	0.00	0	0	N/A	0	43	163
*** North Dakota ***																
North Dakota	04/01	$35	3.52	2.97	154	147	67	65	0.00	0.00	0	0	N/A	0	67	65
*** Ohio ***																
Akron	04/01	$35	3.48	2.78	155	148	52	130	3.41	2.76	156	150	52	71	52	201
Capital	05/01	$35	3.29	2.66	151	144	75	166	3.35	2.74	157	147	65	116	72	282
Case Western Reserve	04/01	$40	3.53	3.02	159	152	70	234	3.66	3.02	161	151	22	8	66	242
Cincinnati	04/01	$35	3.66	3.04	163	155	40	123	0.00	0.00	0	0	N/A	0	40	123
Cleveland State	04/01	$35	3.41	2.88	153	145	59	186	3.33	2.63	155	147	51	102	58	288
Dayton	05/01	$40	3.41	2.79	154	146	61	178	0.00	0.00	0	0	N/A	0	61	178
Ohio Northern	Rolling	$40	3.19	2.47	152	143	77	131	0.00	0.00	0	0	N/A	0	77	131
Ohio State	03/15	$30	3.69	3.23	161	153	43	213	0.00	0.00	0	0	N/A	0	43	213
Toledo	03/15	$30	3.44	2.86	155	148	66	152	3.23	2.59	152	147	55	40	65	192
*** Oklahoma ***																
Oklahoma	04/15	$50	3.51	3.01	156	149	59	210	0.00	0.00	0	0	N/A	0	59	210
Oklahoma City	07/15	$35	3.23	2.53	150	143	68	149	3.28	2.49	150	143	75	41	69	190
Tulsa	Rolling	$30	3.33	2.75	154	146	69	151	3.43	2.61	154	145	80	39	70	190
*** Oregon ***																
Lewis & Clark College	03/15	$50	3.47	2.99	163	157	55	179	3.46	2.95	160	154	52	41	55	220
Oregon	04/01	$50	3.58	3.16	159	152	58	194	0.00	0.00	0	0	N/A	0	58	194
Willamette	03/15	$50	3.50	3.00	158	150	74	158	0.00	0.00	0	0	100	2	74	160

SECTION OF LEGAL EDUCATION AND ADMISSIONS TO THE BAR · ESTABLISHED 1893 · ABA	ADMISSIONS															
			FULL-TIME						PART-TIME						TOTAL	
	Application Deadline	Application Fee	75% GPA	25% GPA	75% LSAT	25% LSAT	% Accepted	# of Matriculants	75% GPA	25% GPA	75% LSAT	25% LSAT	% Accepted	# of Matriculants	Total % Admitted	Total Matriculants
*** Pennsylvania ***																
Duquesne	04/01	$50	3.41	2.78	154	149	79	152	3.33	2.58	156	147	64	87	75	239
Pennsylvania	03/01	$65	3.73	3.39	167	163	30	230	0.00	0.00	0	0	N/A	0	30	230
Pennsylvania State Dickinson	03/01	$50	3.45	2.86	157	152	53	176	0.00	0.00	0	0	N/A	0	53	176
Pittsburgh	03/01	$40	3.50	2.90	158	152	68	222	0.00	0.00	0	0	N/A	0	68	222
Temple	03/01	$50	3.49	3.00	159	151	40	287	3.37	2.75	159	151	38	83	40	370
Villanova	01/31	$75	3.79	3.14	162	154	56	242	0.00	0.00	0	0	N/A	0	56	242
Widener-Harrisburg	05/15	$60	3.31	2.57	151	144	79	88	3.45	2.65	156	147	76	40	78	128
*** Puerto Rico ***																
Inter American U. of Puerto Rico	03/31	$63	3.26	2.82	144	137	38	122	3.31	2.70	142	136	33	104	36	226
Pontifical Catholic U. of Puerto Rico	04/15	$25	3.33	2.87	141	134	45	110	3.20	2.72	142	133	40	58	43	168
Puerto Rico	02/16	$15	3.84	3.30	151	143	27	100	3.51	3.10	150	142	14	50	21	150
*** Rhode Island ***																
Roger Williams	05/15	$60	3.33	2.79	151	144	62	91	3.29	2.61	151	142	69	48	63	139
*** South Carolina ***																
South Carolina	02/15	$35	3.49	2.93	159	152	40	242	0.00	0.00	0	0	N/A	0	40	242
*** South Dakota ***																
South Dakota	03/01	$15	3.54	2.78	154	149	62	90	0.00	0.00	0	0	N/A	0	62	90
*** Tennessee ***																
Memphis	02/15	$15	3.38	2.66	160	147	56	188	3.10	2.86	157	143	69	17	57	205
Tennessee	02/01	$15	3.74	3.27	159	152	34	182	0.00	0.00	0	0	N/A	0	34	182
Vanderbilt	02/01	$50	3.81	3.43	165	158	33	186	0.00	0.00	0	0	N/A	0	33	186
*** Texas ***																
Baylor	03/01	$40	3.75	3.12	162	157	38	75	0.00	0.00	0	0	N/A	0	38	75
Houston	02/01	$50	3.57	3.05	161	154	43	254	3.58	2.98	161	155	34	70	42	324
South Texas College of Law	03/01	$40	3.21	2.66	155	151	60	292	3.26	2.74	157	152	66	146	62	438
Southern Methodist	02/01	$50	3.48	2.94	160	155	39	235	2.95	2.90	164	156	17	2	39	237

	ADMISSIONS															
			FULL-TIME						PART-TIME						TOTAL	
	Application Deadline	Application Fee	75% GPA	25% GPA	75% LSAT	25% LSAT	% Accepted	# of Matriculants	75% GPA	25% GPA	75% LSAT	25% LSAT	% Accepted	# of Matriculants	Total % Admitted	Total Matriculants
*** Texas ***																
St. Mary's	03/01	$45	3.11	2.58	153	147	58	276	0.00	0.00	0	0	N/A	0	58	276
Texas	02/01	$65	3.73	3.40	165	159	31	460	0.00	0.00	0	0	N/A	0	31	460
Texas Southern	04/01	$40	2.89	2.38	145	140	47	260	0.00	0.00	0	0	N/A	0	47	260
Texas Tech	02/01	$50	3.62	3.18	158	152	48	205	0.00	0.00	0	0	N/A	0	48	205
Texas Wesleyan	03/15	$50	3.14	2.56	152	147	56	136	3.09	2.75	152	146	54	75	55	211
*** Utah ***																
Brigham Young	02/01	$30	3.70	3.20	163	157	33	139	0.00	0.00	0	0	N/A	0	33	139
Utah	02/01	$40	3.74	3.27	163	153	42	128	0.00	0.00	0	0	N/A	0	42	128
*** Vermont ***																
Vermont Law School	02/01	$50	3.30	2.80	158	150	64	146	0.00	0.00	0	0	N/A	0	64	146
*** Virginia ***																
George Mason	03/01	$35	3.31	2.84	159	155	43	135	3.19	2.57	161	155	33	78	40	213
Regent	04/01	$40	3.41	2.70	155	147	57	143	0.00	0.00	0	0	N/A	0	57	143
Richmond	02/01	$35	3.31	2.77	159	154	42	167	0.00	0.00	0	0	N/A	0	42	167
Virginia	01/15	$40	3.78	3.50	168	163	30	362	0.00	0.00	0	0	N/A	0	30	362
Washington & Lee	02/01	$40	3.64	3.04	167	161	36	128	0.00	0.00	0	0	N/A	0	36	128
William & Mary	03/01	$40	3.53	3.00	165	159	30	171	0.00	0.00	0	0	N/A	0	30	171
*** Washington ***																
Gonzaga	03/15	$40	3.38	2.72	154	148	75	168	0.00	0.00	0	0	N/A	2	75	170
Seattle	04/01	$50	3.61	3.06	159	151	67	173	3.40	2.64	152	145	73	89	68	262
Washington, U. of	01/15	$50	3.78	3.36	165	158	27	166	0.00	0.00	0	0	N/A	0	27	166
*** West Virginia ***																
West Virginia	03/01	$45	3.61	3.06	156	150	49	146	3.50	2.71	154	152	100	5	50	151

	ADMISSIONS															
SECTION OF LEGAL EDUCATION AND ADMISSIONS TO THE BAR • ESTABLISHED 1893 • ABA			FULL-TIME						PART-TIME						TOTAL	
	Application Deadline	Application Fee	75% GPA	25% GPA	75% LSAT	25% LSAT	% Accepted	# of Matriculants	75% GPA	25% GPA	75% LSAT	25% LSAT	% Accepted	# of Matriculants	Total % Admitted	Total Matriculants
*** Wisconsin ***																
Marquette	04/01	$35	3.33	2.80	157	151	54	141	3.33	2.70	157	152	43	46	53	187
Wisconsin	02/01	$38	3.68	3.27	163	154	38	216	3.76	2.89	161	154	N/A	9	38	225
*** Wyoming ***																
Wyoming	04/01	$35	3.41	2.75	158	149	61	82	0.00	0.00	0	0	N/A	0	61	82

Chapter Twelve

School Profiles

All ABA Approved Law Schools

pages 96-453

This book contains information concerning law schools that were operating as of October 1, 1997 and were approved by the ABA to confer the first degree in law. The approval status of an individual law school can change. Therefore, if you would like to confirm whether an individual law school is approved by the ABA at a specific time after October 1, you should contact the ABA directly. You can also access this information on the Section of Legal Education and Admissions to the Bar's website: http://www.abanet.org/legaled. For example, on February 3, 1998, just prior to the publication of this book, the ABA House of Delegates granted provisional approval to Chapman University School of Law and the University of the District of Columbia School of Law. In addition the Council of the Section acquiesced in advance degree programs from the following schools after October 1, 1997: American University School of Law, California Western School of Law, Golden Gate University School of Law, John Marshall Law School, University of Missouri-Columbia School of Law, University of Chicago School of Law, and Yeshiva University School of Law. For updates or corrections to this book, please visit the Section's website: http://www.abanet.org/legaled.

AKRON, UNIVERSITY OF

C. Blake McDowell Law Center
Akron, OH 44325-2901
800-4akron-u
http://www.uakron.edu/law/index.html

ABA Approved Since 1961

The Basics

Type of School: Public   Term: Semester
Application deadline: 04/01 (Preferred)
Application fee: $35
Financial Aid deadline: 05/01 (Preferred)
Can first year start other than Fall? No
Student faculty ratio: 25.0 to 1
Does the University offer:
- housing restricted to law students? No
- graduate student housing for which law students are eligible? Yes

Faculty & Administrators

	Total		Men		Women		Minorities	
	Fall	Spr	Fall	Spr	Fall	Spr	Fall	Spr
Full-time	18	18	11	11	7	7	3	3
Other Full-Time	0	0	0	0	0	0	0	0
Deans, librarians, & others who teach > 1/2	4	4	2	2	2	2	1	1
Part-time	28	27	12	15	16	12	0	2
Total	50	49	25	28	25	21	4	6
Deans, librarians, & others who teach < 1/2	4	4	3	3	1	1	0	0

Curriculum

	Full time	Part time
Typical first-year section size	51	62
Is there typically a "small section" of the first year class, other than Legal Writing, taught by full-time faculty?	No	No
If yes, typical size offered last year	N/A	N/A
# of classroom course titles beyond 1st year curriculum	36	48
# of upper division courses, excluding seminars, with an enrollment:		
Under 25	25	28
25 - 49	6	16
50 - 74	11	10
75 - 99	6	1
100 +	0	0
# of seminars	10	4
# of seminar positions available	306	
# of seminar positions filled	172	55
# of positions available in simulation courses	246	
# of simulation positions filled	113	96
# of positions available in faculty supervised clinical courses	150	
# of fac. sup. clin. positions filled	63	18
# involved in field placements	63	18
# involved in law journals	38	4
# in moot court or trial competitions	27	6
# of credit hrs required to graduate	88	

J.D. Enrollment & Ethnicity

	Men		Women		Fl-Time		Pt-Time		1st Yr		2nd Yr		3rd Yr		4th Yr		Total		JD Degrees Awarded
	#	%	#	%	#	%	#	%	#	%	#	%	#	%	#	%	#	%	
African-American	12	3.5	11	4.1	17	4.2	6	2.9	13	6.6	6	3.4	4	2.0	0	0.0	23	3.8	6
American Indian	1	0.3	1	0.4	2	0.5	0	0.0	0	0.0	0	0.0	2	1.0	0	0.0	2	0.3	1
Asian American	2	0.6	12	4.4	12	3.0	2	1.0	5	2.6	4	2.3	5	2.5	0	0.0	14	2.3	4
Mexican American	0	0.0	1	0.4	1	0.2	0	0.0	1	0.5	0	0.0	0	0.0	0	0.0	1	0.2	0
Puerto Rican	0	0.0	0	0.0	0	0.0	0	0.0	0	0.0	0	0.0	0	0.0	0	0.0	0	0.0	0
Hispanic American	6	1.8	3	1.1	5	1.2	4	1.9	4	2.0	0	0.0	4	2.0	1	2.7	9	1.5	2
Total Minorities	21	6.2	28	10.4	37	9.2	12	5.7	23	11.7	10	5.6	15	7.5	1	2.7	49	8.0	13
Foreign Nationals	2	0.6	3	1.1	5	1.2	0	0.0	1	0.5	3	1.7	1	0.5	0	0.0	5	0.8	2
Caucasian	318	93.3	239	88.5	360	89.6	197	94.3	172	87.8	164	92.7	185	92.0	36	97.3	557	91.2	151
Total	341	55.8	270	44.2	402	65.8	209	34.2	196	32.1	177	29.0	201	32.9	37	6.1	611		166

GPA & LSAT Scores

	Full Time	Part Time	Total
# of apps	939	197	1,136
# admits	484	103	587
# of matrics	130	71	201
75% GPA	3.48	3.41	
25% GPA	2.78	2.76	
75% LSAT	155	156	
25% LSAT	148	150	

Tuition & Fees

	Resident	Non-resident
Full-Time	$6,249	$10,746
Part-Time	$4,509	$7,721

Living Expenses

Estimated living expenses for Singles		
Living on campus	Living off campus	Living at home
$10,537	$10,537	$10,537

Employment

	Total	%
Employment status known	171	99.4
Employment status unknown	1	0.6
Employed	149	87.1
Pursuing graduate degrees	5	2.9
Unemployed seeking employment	4	2.3
Unemployed not seeking employment	13	7.6
Type of Employment		
# employed in law firms	66	44.3
# employed in business & industry	35	23.5
# employed in government	26	17.4
# employed in public interest	4	2.7
# employed as judicial clerks	14	9.4
# employed in academia	4	2.7
Geographic Location		
# employed in state	108	72.5
# employed in foreign countries	1	0.7
# of states where employed	15	

Financial Aid

	Full-time		Part-time		Total	
	#	%	#	%	#	%
Total # of Students	402		209		611	
Total # receiving grants	108	26.9	46	22.0	154	25.2
Less than 1/2 tuition	58	14.4	36	17.2	94	15.4
Half to full tuition	20	5.0	8	3.8	28	4.6
Full tuition	30	7.5	2	1.0	32	5.2
More than full tuition	0	0.0	0	0.0	0	0.0
Median Grant Amount	$2,500		$1,000			

Informational & Library Resources

# of volumes & volume equivalents	250,968	# of professional staff	5
# of titles	52,403	Hours per week with professional staff	79
# of active serial subscriptions	3,364	Hours per week without professional staff	19
Study seating capacity inside the library	295	# of student computer work stations for entire law school	47
Square feet of law library	34,634	# of additional networked connections	0
Square feet of law school (excl. Library)	54,709	Require Laptop Computer?	N

J.D. Attrition (Prior Year)

	Academic	Other	TOTALS	
	#	#	#	%
1st Year	13	31	44	20%
2nd Year	1	12	13	6.1%
3rd Year	0	0	0	0.0%
4th Year	0	1	1	2.9%
TOTALS	14	44	58	9.1%

Bar Passage Rates

Jurisdiction	Ohio		
Exam	Sum 96	Win 97	Total
# from school taking bar for the first time	107	28	135
School's pass rate for all first-time takers	80%	93%	83%
State's pass rate for all first-time takers	90%	90%	90%

ALABAMA, UNIVERSITY OF

P.O. Box 870382
Tuscaloosa, AL 35487
(205)348-5117
http://www.law.ua.edu

ABA Approved Since 1926

The Basics

Type of School: Public   Term: Semester
Application deadline: 03/01
Application fee: $25
Financial Aid deadline: Rolling
Can first year start other than Fall? No
Student faculty ratio: 19.7 to 1
Does the University offer:
- housing restricted to law students? No
- graduate student housing for which law students are eligible? Yes

Faculty & Administrators

	Total		Men		Women		Minorities	
	Fall	Spr	Fall	Spr	Fall	Spr	Fall	Spr
Full-time	24	22	17	16	7	6	2	2
Other Full-Time	4	4	2	2	2	2	1	1
Deans, librarians, & others who teach > 1/2	1	1	1	1	0	0	0	0
Part-time	30	28	22	23	7	5	2	2
Total	59	55	42	42	16	13	5	5
Deans, librarians, & others who teach < 1/2	4	4	4	4	0	0	0	0

Curriculum

	Full time	Part time
Typical first-year section size	98	0
Is there typically a "small section" of the first year class, other than Legal Writing, taught by full-time faculty?	No	No
If yes, typical size offered last year	N/A	N/A
# of classroom course titles beyond 1st year curriculum	87	0
# of upper division courses, excluding seminars, with an enrollment:		
Under 25	50	0
25 - 49	16	0
50 - 74	17	0
75 - 99	9	0
100 +	1	0
# of seminars	18	0
# of seminar positions available	216	
# of seminar positions filled	183	0
# of positions available in simulation courses	288	
# of simulation positions filled	264	0
# of positions available in faculty supervised clinical courses	61	
# of fac. sup. clin. positions filled	52	0
# involved in field placements	29	0
# involved in law journals	96	0
# in moot court or trial competitions	113	0
# of credit hrs required to graduate	90	

J.D. Enrollment & Ethnicity

	Men		Women		Fl-Time		Pt-Time		1st Yr		2nd Yr		3rd Yr		4th Yr		Total		JD Degrees Awarded
	#	%	#	%	#	%	#	%	#	%	#	%	#	%	#	%	#	%	
African-American	14	4.2	22	9.5	36	6.3	0	0.0	13	6.3	7	3.7	16	9.1	0	0.0	36	6.3	19
American Indian	3	0.9	2	0.9	5	0.9	0	0.0	4	1.9	0	0.0	1	0.6	0	0.0	5	0.9	0
Asian American	2	0.6	2	0.9	4	0.7	0	0.0	1	0.5	2	1.1	1	0.6	0	0.0	4	0.7	2
Mexican American	0	0.0	0	0.0	0	0.0	0	0.0	0	0.0	0	0.0	0	0.0	0	0.0	0	0.0	0
Puerto Rican	0	0.0	0	0.0	0	0.0	0	0.0	0	0.0	0	0.0	0	0.0	0	0.0	0	0.0	0
Hispanic American	1	0.3	1	0.4	2	0.4	0	0.0	1	0.5	1	0.5	0	0.0	0	0.0	2	0.4	1
Total Minorities	20	5.9	27	11.7	47	8.3	0	0.0	19	9.2	10	5.3	18	10.3	0	0.0	47	8.3	22
Foreign Nationals	0	0.0	0	0.0	0	0.0	0	0.0	0	0.0	0	0.0	0	0.0	0	0.0	0	0.0	0
Caucasian	317	94.1	204	88.3	521	91.7	0	0.0	187	90.8	177	94.7	157	89.7	0	0.0	521	91.7	158
Total	337	59.3	231	40.7	568	100.0	0	0.0	206	36.3	187	32.9	175	30.8	0	0.0	568		180

GPA & LSAT Scores

	Full Time	Part Time	Total
# of apps	744	0	744
# admits	326	0	326
# of matrics	209	0	209
75% GPA	3.65	0.00	
25% GPA	3.08	0.00	
75% LSAT	160	0	
25% LSAT	154	0	

Tuition & Fees

	Resident	Non-resident
Full-Time	$3,758	$8,382
Part-Time	$0	$0

Living Expenses

Estimated living expenses for Singles

Living on campus	Living off campus	Living at home
$7,574	$8,230	$6,484

Financial Aid

	Full-time		Part-time		Total	
	#	%	#	%	#	%
Total # of Students	568		0		568	
Total # receiving grants	123	21.7	0	0.0	123	21.7
Less than 1/2 tuition	28	4.9	0	0.0	28	4.9
Half to full tuition	53	9.3	0	0.0	53	9.3
Full tuition	27	4.8	0	0.0	27	4.8
More than full tuition	15	2.6	0	0.0	15	2.6
Median Grant Amount	$2,000		$0			

Informational & Library Resources

# of volumes & volume equivalents	356,552	# of professional staff	7
# of titles	78,038	Hours per week with professional staff	57
# of active serial subscriptions	3,148	Hours per week without professional staff	45
Study seating capacity inside the library	562	# of student computer work stations for entire law school	61
Square feet of law library	65,950	# of additional networked connections	0
Square feet of law school (excl. Library)	75,892	Require Laptop Computer?	N

Employment

	Total	%
Employment status known	186	100.0
Employment status unknown	0	0.0
Employed	169	90.9
Pursuing graduate degrees	10	5.4
Unemployed seeking employment	4	2.2
Unemployed not seeking employment	3	1.6
Type of Employment		
# employed in law firms	115	68.0
# employed in business & industry	10	5.9
# employed in government	14	8.3
# employed in public interest	3	1.8
# employed as judicial clerks	24	14.2
# employed in academia	3	1.8
Geographic Location		
# employed in state	135	79.9
# employed in foreign countries	0	0.0
# of states where employed	11	

J.D. Attrition (Prior Year)

	Academic	Other	TOTALS	
	#	#	#	%
1st Year	1	7	8	4.1%
2nd Year	1	4	5	2.8%
3rd Year	0	0	0	0.0%
4th Year	0	0	0	0.0%
TOTALS	2	11	13	2.4%

Bar Passage Rates

Jurisdiction	Alabama		
Exam	Sum 96	Win 97	Total
# from school taking bar for the first time	144	15	159
School's pass rate for all first-time takers	92%	73%	91%
State's pass rate for all first-time takers	78%	66%	74%

ALBANY LAW SCHOOL

80 New Scotland Avenue
Albany, NY 12208
(518)445-2311
http://www.als.edu

ABA Approved Since 1930

The Basics

Type of School: Private — Term: Semester
Application deadline: 03/15
Application fee: $50
Financial Aid deadline: Rolling
Can first year start other than Fall? No
Student faculty ratio: 22.2 to 1
Does the University offer:
- housing restricted to law students? Yes
- graduate student housing for which law students are eligible? No

Faculty & Administrators

	Total		Men		Women		Minorities	
	Fall	Spr	Fall	Spr	Fall	Spr	Fall	Spr
Full-time	27	29	19	21	8	8	4	5
Other Full-Time	5	5	1	1	4	4	0	0
Deans, librarians, & others who teach > 1/2	5	5	1	1	4	4	0	0
Part-time	17	20	13	17	3	3	2	2
Total	54	59	34	40	19	19	6	7
Deans, librarians, & others who teach < 1/2	4	4	4	4	0	0	0	0

Curriculum

	Full time	Part time
Typical first-year section size	82	0
Is there typically a "small section" of the first year class, other than Legal Writing, taught by full-time faculty?	Yes	No
If yes, typical size offered last year	49	N/A
# of classroom course titles beyond 1st year curriculum	99	0
# of upper division courses, excluding seminars, with an enrollment:		
Under 25	36	0
25 - 49	23	0
50 - 74	10	0
75 - 99	8	0
100 +	10	0
# of seminars	31	0
# of seminar positions available	757	
# of seminar positions filled	438	0
# of positions available in simulation courses	383	
# of simulation positions filled	256	0
# of positions available in faculty supervised clinical courses	118	
# of fac. sup. clin. positions filled	68	0
# involved in field placements	289	0
# involved in law journals	123	0
# in moot court or trial competitions	306	0
# of credit hrs required to graduate	87	

J.D. Enrollment & Ethnicity

	Men		Women		Fl-Time		Pt-Time		1st Yr		2nd Yr		3rd Yr		4th Yr		Total		JD Degrees Awarded
	#	%	#	%	#	%	#	%	#	%	#	%	#	%	#	%	#	%	
African-American	16	4.6	31	8.1	45	6.5	2	4.8	15	6.0	16	6.7	15	6.4	1	11.1	47	6.4	18
American Indian	4	1.2	0	0.0	3	0.4	1	2.4	2	0.8	1	0.4	0	0.0	1	11.1	4	0.5	1
Asian American	11	3.2	24	6.2	35	5.1	0	0.0	14	5.6	5	2.1	16	6.8	0	0.0	35	4.8	18
Mexican American	0	0.0	1	0.3	1	0.1	0	0.0	0	0.0	1	0.4	0	0.0	0	0.0	1	0.1	0
Puerto Rican	6	1.7	8	2.1	13	1.9	1	2.4	6	2.4	8	3.4	0	0.0	0	0.0	14	1.9	2
Hispanic American	4	1.2	9	2.3	12	1.7	1	2.4	3	1.2	5	2.1	5	2.1	0	0.0	13	1.8	6
Total Minorities	41	11.8	73	19.0	109	15.8	5	11.9	40	15.9	36	15.1	36	15.4	2	22.2	114	15.6	45
Foreign Nationals	5	1.4	5	1.3	10	1.4	0	0.0	3	1.2	4	1.7	3	1.3	0	0.0	10	1.4	2
Caucasian	301	86.7	307	79.7	571	82.8	37	88.1	208	82.9	198	83.2	195	83.3	7	77.8	608	83.1	203
Total	347	47.4	385	52.6	690	94.3	42	5.7	251	34.3	238	32.5	234	32.0	9	1.2	732		250

GPA & LSAT Scores

	Full Time	Part Time	Total
# of apps	1,155	0	1,155
# admits	849	0	849
# of matrics	250	0	250
75% GPA	3.32	0.00	
25% GPA	2.86	0.00	
75% LSAT	153	0	
25% LSAT	145	0	

Tuition & Fees

	Resident	Non-resident
Full-Time	$18,905	$18,905
Part-Time	$14,206	$14,206

Living Expenses

Estimated living expenses for Singles		
Living on campus	Living off campus	Living at home
$8,800	$10,070	$6,250

Employment

	Total	%
Employment status known	261	99.6
Employment status unknown	1	0.4
Employed	217	83.1
Pursuing graduate degrees	9	3.4
Unemployed seeking employment	19	7.3
Unemployed not seeking employment	16	6.1
Type of Employment		
# employed in law firms	113	52.1
# employed in business & industry	46	21.2
# employed in government	43	19.8
# employed in public interest	4	1.8
# employed as judicial clerks	8	3.7
# employed in academia	2	0.9
Geographic Location		
# employed in state	183	84.3
# employed in foreign countries	1	0.5
# of states where employed	18	

Financial Aid

	Full-time		Part-time		Total	
	#	%	#	%	#	%
Total # of Students	690		42		732	
Total # receiving grants	325	47.1	5	11.9	330	45.1
Less than 1/2 tuition	264	38.3	5	11.9	269	36.7
Half to full tuition	54	7.8	0	0.0	54	7.4
Full tuition	7	1.0	0	0.0	7	1.0
More than full tuition	0	0.0	0	0.0	0	0.0
Median Grant Amount	$4,000		$2,300			

Informational & Library Resources

# of volumes & volume equivalents	512,768	# of professional staff	7
# of titles	75,637	Hours per week with professional staff	71
# of active serial subscriptions	3,697	Hours per week without professional staff	33
Study seating capacity inside the library	482	# of student computer work stations for entire law school	121
Square feet of law library	53,056	# of additional networked connections	0
Square feet of law school (excl. Library)	46,288	Require Laptop Computer?	N

J.D. Attrition (Prior Year)

	Academic	Other	TOTALS	
	#	#	#	%
1st Year	3	16	19	7.6%
2nd Year	0	16	16	6.5%
3rd Year	1	0	1	0.4%
4th Year	0	0	0	0.0%
TOTALS	4	32	36	4.8%

Bar Passage Rates

Jurisdiction	New York		
Exam	Sum 96	Win 97	Total
# from school taking bar for the first time	239	17	256
School's pass rate for all first-time takers	85%	76%	85%
State's pass rate for all first-time takers	78%	67%	77%

AMERICAN UNIVERSITY

4801 Massachusetts Ave, NW
Washington, DC 20016
(202)274-4004
http://www.wcl.american.edu

ABA Approved Since 1940

The Basics

Type of School: Private Term: Semester
Application deadline: 03/01
Application fee: $55
Financial Aid deadline: 03/01
Can first year start other than Fall? No
Student faculty ratio: 20.6 to 1
Does the University offer:
- housing restricted to law students? No
- graduate student housing for which law students are eligible? Yes

Faculty & Administrators

	Total		Men		Women		Minorities	
	Fall	Spr	Fall	Spr	Fall	Spr	Fall	Spr
Full-time	44	47	27	29	17	18	5	5
Other Full-Time	5	4	1	1	4	3	0	0
Deans, librarians, & others who teach > 1/2	4	4	3	3	1	1	0	0
Part-time	96	108	68	77	28	31	6	8
Total	149	163	99	110	50	53	11	13
Deans, librarians, & others who teach < 1/2	1	1	1	1	0	0	1	1

Curriculum

	Full time	Part time
Typical first-year section size	95	95
Is there typically a "small section" of the first year class, other than Legal Writing, taught by full-time faculty?	No	No
If yes, typical size offered last year	N/A	N/A
# of classroom course titles beyond 1st year curriculum	160	67
# of upper division courses, excluding seminars, with an enrollment:		
Under 25	83	40
25 - 49	15	13
50 - 74	8	9
75 - 99	9	3
100 +	0	2
# of seminars	67	21
# of seminar positions available	1,732	
# of seminar positions filled	663	154
# of positions available in simulation courses	520	
# of simulation positions filled	251	163
# of positions available in faculty supervised clinical courses	201	
# of fac. sup. clin. positions filled	187	14
# involved in field placements	228	13
# involved in law journals	303	24
# in moot court or trial competitions	150	0
# of credit hrs required to graduate	86	

J.D. Enrollment & Ethnicity

	Men		Women		Fl-Time		Pt-Time		1st Yr		2nd Yr		3rd Yr		4th Yr		Total		JD Degrees Awarded
	#	%	#	%	#	%	#	%	#	%	#	%	#	%	#	%	#	%	
African-American	34	6.9	63	8.9	61	6.9	36	11.5	44	11.4	26	7.2	21	5.7	6	7.7	97	8.1	29
American Indian	3	0.6	8	1.1	7	0.8	4	1.3	3	0.8	5	1.4	3	0.8	0	0.0	11	0.9	5
Asian American	46	9.4	71	10.1	96	10.9	21	6.7	35	9.0	37	10.2	43	11.7	2	2.6	117	9.8	26
Mexican American	10	2.0	9	1.3	12	1.4	7	2.2	10	2.6	3	0.8	2	0.5	4	5.1	19	1.6	4
Puerto Rican	3	0.6	3	0.4	2	0.2	4	1.3	3	0.8	1	0.3	2	0.5	0	0.0	6	0.5	1
Hispanic American	12	2.4	25	3.5	29	3.3	8	2.6	15	3.9	10	2.8	11	3.0	1	1.3	37	3.1	13
Total Minorities	108	22.0	179	25.4	207	23.5	80	25.6	110	28.4	82	22.7	82	22.2	13	16.7	287	24.0	78
Foreign Nationals	6	1.2	5	0.7	8	0.9	3	1.0	0	0.0	5	1.4	5	1.4	1	1.3	11	0.9	4
Caucasian	376	76.7	521	73.9	667	75.6	230	73.5	277	71.6	274	75.9	282	76.4	64	82.1	897	75.1	248
Total	490	41.0	705	59.0	882	73.8	313	26.2	387	32.4	361	30.2	369	30.9	78	6.5	1195		330

GPA & LSAT Scores

	Full Time	Part Time	Total
# of apps	3,792	617	4,409
# admits	1,562	350	1,912
# of matrics	286	95	381
75% GPA	3.46	3.40	
25% GPA	3.04	2.79	
75% LSAT	159	154	
25% LSAT	153	148	

Tuition & Fees

	Resident	Non-resident
Full-Time	$21,894	$21,894
Part-Time	$15,405	$15,405

Living Expenses

Estimated living expenses for Singles		
Living on campus	Living off campus	Living at home
$12,734	$12,734	$12,734

Employment

	Total	%
Employment status known	271	78.1
Employment status unknown	76	21.9
Employed	231	85.2
Pursuing graduate degrees	12	4.4
Unemployed seeking employment	23	8.5
Unemployed not seeking employment	5	1.8
Type of Employment		
# employed in law firms	97	42.0
# employed in business & industry	36	15.6
# employed in government	48	20.8
# employed in public interest	14	6.1
# employed as judicial clerks	31	13.4
# employed in academia	1	0.4
Geographic Location		
# employed in state	104	45.0
# employed in foreign countries	2	0.9
# of states where employed	31	

Financial Aid

	Full-time		Part-time		Total	
	#	%	#	%	#	%
Total # of Students	882		313		1195	
Total # receiving grants	246	27.9	0	0.0	246	20.6
Less than 1/2 tuition	212	24.0	0	0.0	212	17.7
Half to full tuition	34	3.9	0	0.0	34	2.8
Full tuition	0	0.0	0	0.0	0	0.0
More than full tuition	0	0.0	0	0.0	0	0.0
Median Grant Amount	$7,506		$0			

Informational & Library Resources

# of volumes & volume equivalents	412,309	# of professional staff	9
# of titles	160,057	Hours per week with professional staff	82
# of active serial subscriptions	5,773	Hours per week without professional staff	37
Study seating capacity inside the library	623	# of student computer work stations for entire law school	48
Square feet of law library	55,000	# of additional networked connections	600
Square feet of law school (excl. Library)	84,420	Require Laptop Computer?	N

J.D. Attrition (Prior Year)

	Academic	Other	TOTALS	
	#	#	#	%
1st Year	1	0	1	0.3%
2nd Year	1	21	22	5.7%
3rd Year	0	2	2	0.6%
4th Year	0	0	0	0.0%
TOTALS	2	23	25	2.1%

Bar Passage Rates

Jurisdiction	Maryland		
Exam	Sum 96	Win 97	Total
# from school taking bar for the first time	138	25	163
School's pass rate for all first-time takers	72%	92%	75%
State's pass rate for all first-time takers	76%	79%	76%

ARIZONA STATE UNIVERSITY

P.O. Box 877906
Tempe, AZ 85287-7906
(602)965-6181
http://www.asu.edu/law

ABA Approved Since 1969

The Basics

Type of School: Public
Term: Semester
Application deadline: 03/01
Application fee: $35
Financial Aid deadline: 03/01
Can first year start other than Fall? No
Student faculty ratio: 16.6 to 1
Does the University offer:
- housing restricted to law students? No
- graduate student housing for which law students are eligible? Yes

Faculty & Administrators

	Total		Men		Women		Minorities	
	Fall	Spr	Fall	Spr	Fall	Spr	Fall	Spr
Full-time	23	26	17	20	6	6	3	2
Other Full-Time	2	2	0	0	2	2	0	0
Deans, librarians, & others who teach > 1/2	6	5	4	3	2	2	1	1
Part-time	12	15	12	13	0	2	1	2
Total	43	48	33	36	10	12	5	5
Deans, librarians, & others who teach < 1/2	0	0	0	0	0	0	0	0

Curriculum

	Full time	Part time
Typical first-year section size	135	0
Is there typically a "small section" of the first year class, other than Legal Writing, taught by full-time faculty?	Yes	No
If yes, typical size offered last year	31	N/A
# of classroom course titles beyond 1st year curriculum	92	0
# of upper division courses, excluding seminars, with an enrollment:		
Under 25	28	0
25 - 49	26	0
50 - 74	8	0
75 - 99	2	0
100 +	0	0
# of seminars	37	0
# of seminar positions available	551	
# of seminar positions filled	395	0
# of positions available in simulation courses	104	
# of simulation positions filled	101	0
# of positions available in faculty supervised clinical courses	111	
# of fac. sup. clin. positions filled	108	0
# involved in field placements	87	0
# involved in law journals	132	0
# in moot court or trial competitions	55	0
# of credit hrs required to graduate	87	

J.D. Enrollment & Ethnicity

	Men		Women		Fl-Time		Pt-Time		1st Yr		2nd Yr		3rd Yr		4th Yr		Total		JD Degrees Awarded
	#	%	#	%	#	%	#	%	#	%	#	%	#	%	#	%	#	%	
African-American	8	3.4	12	5.3	20	4.4	0	0.0	8	5.0	6	4.1	6	3.9	0	0.0	20	4.4	9
American Indian	14	6.0	15	6.6	29	6.3	0	0.0	16	10.1	2	1.4	11	7.1	0	0.0	29	6.3	8
Asian American	8	3.4	8	3.5	16	3.5	0	0.0	4	2.5	5	3.4	7	4.5	0	0.0	16	3.5	12
Mexican American	19	8.2	23	10.2	42	9.2	0	0.0	14	8.8	11	7.6	17	11.0	0	0.0	42	9.2	10
Puerto Rican	0	0.0	0	0.0	0	0.0	0	0.0	0	0.0	0	0.0	0	0.0	0	0.0	0	0.0	2
Hispanic American	3	1.3	4	1.8	7	1.5	0	0.0	1	0.6	2	1.4	4	2.6	0	0.0	7	1.5	3
Total Minorities	52	22.4	62	27.4	114	24.9	0	0.0	43	27.0	26	17.9	45	29.2	0	0.0	114	24.9	44
Foreign Nationals	4	1.7	6	2.7	10	2.2	0	0.0	6	3.8	3	2.1	1	0.6	0	0.0	10	2.2	1
Caucasian	176	75.9	158	69.9	334	72.9	0	0.0	110	69.2	116	80.0	108	70.1	0	0.0	334	72.9	108
Total	232	50.7	226	49.3	458	100.0	0	0.0	159	34.7	145	31.7	154	33.6	0	0.0	458		153

GPA & LSAT Scores

	Full Time	Part Time	Total
# of apps	1,754	0	1,754
# admits	391	0	391
# of matrics	158	0	158
75% GPA	3.61	0.00	
25% GPA	3.00	0.00	
75% LSAT	163	0	
25% LSAT	153	0	

Tuition & Fees

	Resident	Non-resident
Full-Time	$4,059	$10,711
Part-Time	$0	$0

Living Expenses

Estimated living expenses for Singles

Living on campus	Living off campus	Living at home
$10,765	$10,765	$10,765

Employment

	Total	%
Employment status known	123	88.5
Employment status unknown	16	11.5
Employed	109	88.6
Pursuing graduate degrees	2	1.6
Unemployed seeking employment	8	6.5
Unemployed not seeking employment	4	3.3
Type of Employment		
# employed in law firms	41	37.6
# employed in business & industry	16	14.7
# employed in government	30	27.5
# employed in public interest	2	1.8
# employed as judicial clerks	17	15.6
# employed in academia	2	1.8
Geographic Location		
# employed in state	99	90.8
# employed in foreign countries	0	0.0
# of states where employed	9	

Financial Aid

	Full-time		Part-time		Total	
	#	%	#	%	#	%
Total # of Students	458		0		458	
Total # receiving grants	211	46.1	0	0.0	211	46.1
Less than 1/2 tuition	97	21.2	0	0.0	97	21.2
Half to full tuition	14	3.1	0	0.0	14	3.1
Full tuition	59	12.9	0	0.0	59	12.9
More than full tuition	41	9.0	0	0.0	41	9.0
Median Grant Amount	$3,541		$0			

Informational & Library Resources

# of volumes & volume equivalents	359,471	# of professional staff	9
# of titles	109,897	Hours per week with professional staff	70
# of active serial subscriptions	6,423	Hours per week without professional staff	40
Study seating capacity inside the library	558	# of student computer work stations for entire law school	54
Square feet of law library	60,000	# of additional networked connections	17
Square feet of law school (excl. Library)	59,645	Require Laptop Computer?	N

J.D. Attrition (Prior Year)

	Academic	Other	TOTALS	
	#	#	#	%
1st Year	3	11	14	9.0%
2nd Year	0	2	2	1.4%
3rd Year	0	0	0	0.0%
4th Year	0	0	0	0.0%
TOTALS	3	13	16	3.5%

Bar Passage Rates

Jurisdiction	Arizona		
Exam	Sum 96	Win 97	Total
# from school taking bar for the first time	110	24	134
School's pass rate for all first-time takers	89%	71%	86%
State's pass rate for all first-time takers	83%	81%	82%

ARIZONA, UNIVERSITY OF

James E. Rogers Law Center
P.O. Box 210176
Tucson, AZ 85721-0176
(520)621-1373
http://www.law.arizona.edu

ABA Approved Since 1930

The Basics

Type of School: Public — Term: Semester

Application deadline: 03/01

Application fee: $45

Financial Aid deadline: 03/01

Can first year start other than Fall? No

Student faculty ratio: 16.6 to 1

Does the University offer:
- housing restricted to law students? No
- graduate student housing for which law students are eligible? No

Faculty & Administrators

	Total		Men		Women		Minorities	
	Fall	Spr	Fall	Spr	Fall	Spr	Fall	Spr
Full-time	23	28	15	20	8	8	3	3
Other Full-Time	2	2	2	2	0	0	0	0
Deans, librarians, & others who teach > 1/2	3	2	2	2	1	0	0	0
Part-time	32	27	21	17	11	10	2	1
Total	60	59	40	41	20	18	5	4
Deans, librarians, & others who teach < 1/2	0	0	0	0	0	0	0	0

Curriculum

	Full time	Part time
Typical first-year section size	75	0
Is there typically a "small section" of the first year class, other than Legal Writing, taught by full-time faculty?	Yes	No
If yes, typical size offered last year	25	N/A
# of classroom course titles beyond 1st year curriculum	97	0
# of upper division courses, excluding seminars, with an enrollment:		
Under 25	63	0
25 - 49	22	0
50 - 74	5	0
75 - 99	4	0
100 +	2	0
# of seminars	25	0
# of seminar positions available	415	
# of seminar positions filled	274	0
# of positions available in simulation courses	315	
# of simulation positions filled	259	0
# of positions available in faculty supervised clinical courses	27	
# of fac. sup. clin. positions filled	19	0
# involved in field placements	106	0
# involved in law journals	79	0
# in moot court or trial competitions	61	0
# of credit hrs required to graduate	85	

J.D. Enrollment & Ethnicity

	Men		Women		Fl-Time		Pt-Time		1st Yr		2nd Yr		3rd Yr		4th Yr		Total		JD Degrees Awarded
	#	%	#	%	#	%	#	%	#	%	#	%	#	%	#	%	#	%	
African-American	8	3.4	6	2.7	14	3.1	0	0.0	5	3.3	5	3.4	4	2.5	0	0.0	14	3.1	9
American Indian	6	2.5	6	2.7	12	2.6	0	0.0	7	4.7	2	1.4	3	1.9	0	0.0	12	2.6	4
Asian American	13	5.5	15	6.8	28	6.1	0	0.0	10	6.7	7	4.7	11	6.9	0	0.0	28	6.1	10
Mexican American	13	5.5	12	5.4	25	5.5	0	0.0	10	6.7	9	6.1	6	3.8	0	0.0	25	5.5	8
Puerto Rican	3	1.3	0	0.0	3	0.7	0	0.0	2	1.3	1	0.7	0	0.0	0	0.0	3	0.7	0
Hispanic American	18	7.6	8	3.6	26	5.7	0	0.0	7	4.7	10	6.8	9	5.6	0	0.0	26	5.7	19
Total Minorities	61	25.7	47	21.3	108	23.6	0	0.0	41	27.3	34	23.0	33	20.6	0	0.0	108	23.6	50
Foreign Nationals	0	0.0	3	1.4	3	0.7	0	0.0	1	0.7	2	1.4	0	0.0	0	0.0	3	0.7	1
Caucasian	176	74.3	171	77.4	347	75.8	0	0.0	108	72.0	112	75.7	127	79.4	0	0.0	347	75.8	107
Total	237	51.7	221	48.3	458	100.0	0	0.0	150	32.8	148	32.3	160	34.9	0	0.0	458		158

GPA & LSAT Scores

	Full Time	Part Time	Total
# of apps	1,459	0	1,459
# admits	442	0	442
# of matrics	151	0	151
75% GPA	3.66	0.00	
25% GPA	3.11	0.00	
75% LSAT	164	0	
25% LSAT	155	0	

Tuition & Fees

	Resident	Non-resident
Full-Time	$4,060	$10,712
Part-Time	$0	$0

Living Expenses

Estimated living expenses for Singles

Living on campus	Living off campus	Living at home
$8,030	$11,740	$5,960

Financial Aid

	Full-time		Part-time		Total	
	#	%	#	%	#	%
Total # of Students	458		0		458	
Total # receiving grants	248	54.1	0	0.0	248	54.1
Less than 1/2 tuition	51	11.1	0	0.0	51	11.1
Half to full tuition	152	33.2	0	0.0	152	33.2
Full tuition	33	7.2	0	0.0	33	7.2
More than full tuition	12	2.6	0	0.0	12	2.6
Median Grant Amount	$2,175		$0			

Informational & Library Resources

# of volumes & volume equivalents	369,567	# of professional staff	8
# of titles	62,989	Hours per week with professional staff	71
# of active serial subscriptions	4,158	Hours per week without professional staff	34
Study seating capacity inside the library	368	# of student computer work stations for entire law school	45
Square feet of law library	39,604	# of additional networked connections	84
Square feet of law school (excl. Library)	43,221	Require Laptop Computer?	N

Employment

	Total	%
Employment status known	154	98.1
Employment status unknown	3	1.9
Employed	137	89.0
Pursuing graduate degrees	4	2.6
Unemployed seeking employment	8	5.2
Unemployed not seeking employment	5	3.2
Type of Employment		
# employed in law firms	68	49.6
# employed in business & industry	19	13.9
# employed in government	16	11.7
# employed in public interest	7	5.1
# employed as judicial clerks	25	18.2
# employed in academia	2	1.5
Geographic Location		
# employed in state	96	70.1
# employed in foreign countries	1	0.7
# of states where employed	20	

J.D. Attrition (Prior Year)

	Academic	Other	TOTALS	
	#	#	#	%
1st Year	0	0	0	0.0%
2nd Year	0	7	7	4.6%
3rd Year	0	3	3	1.8%
4th Year	0	0	0	0.0%
TOTALS	0	10	10	2.1%

Bar Passage Rates

Jurisdiction	Arizona		
Exam	Sum 96	Win 97	Total
# from school taking bar for the first time	99	18	117
School's pass rate for all first-time takers	89%	78%	87%
State's pass rate for all first-time takers	83%	81%	82%

ARKANSAS, FAYETTEVILLE, UNIVERSITY OF

Waterman Hall
Leflar Law Center
Fayetteville, AR 72701-1201
(501)575-5601
http://law-gopher.uark.edu/arklaw

ABA Approved Since 1926

The Basics

Type of School: Public   Term: Semester
Application deadline: 04/01
Application fee: $0
Financial Aid deadline: 04/01
Can first year start other than Fall? No
Student faculty ratio: 14.3 to 1
Does the University offer:
- housing restricted to law students? No
- graduate student housing for which law students are eligible? No

Faculty & Administrators

	Total		Men		Women		Minorities	
	Fall	Spr	Fall	Spr	Fall	Spr	Fall	Spr
Full-time	22	22	15	15	7	7	4	3
Other Full-Time	6	6	2	2	4	4	0	0
Deans, librarians, & others who teach > 1/2	2	2	2	2	0	0	0	0
Part-time	8	12	7	10	1	2	1	1
Total	38	42	26	29	12	13	5	4
Deans, librarians, & others who teach < 1/2	2	2	2	2	0	0	0	0

Curriculum

	Full time	Part time
Typical first-year section size	70	0
Is there typically a "small section" of the first year class, other than Legal Writing, taught by full-time faculty?	Yes	No
If yes, typical size offered last year	25	N/A
# of classroom course titles beyond 1st year curriculum	101	0
# of upper division courses, excluding seminars, with an enrollment:		
Under 25	59	0
25 - 49	19	0
50 - 74	3	0
75 - 99	5	0
100 +	0	0
# of seminars	7	0
# of seminar positions available	105	
# of seminar positions filled	92	0
# of positions available in simulation courses	128	
# of simulation positions filled	116	0
# of positions available in faculty supervised clinical courses	108	
# of fac. sup. clin. positions filled	87	0
# involved in field placements	9	0
# involved in law journals	40	0
# in moot court or trial competitions	140	0
# of credit hrs required to graduate	90	

J.D. Enrollment & Ethnicity

	Men		Women		Fl-Time		Pt-Time		1st Yr		2nd Yr		3rd Yr		4th Yr		Total		JD Degrees Awarded
	#	%	#	%	#	%	#	%	#	%	#	%	#	%	#	%	#	%	
African-American	7	3.1	14	9.3	21	5.6	0	0.0	6	4.6	10	7.6	5	4.4	0	0.0	21	5.6	3
American Indian	3	1.3	3	2.0	6	1.6	0	0.0	0	0.0	3	2.3	3	2.6	0	0.0	6	1.6	2
Asian American	4	1.8	3	2.0	7	1.9	0	0.0	4	3.1	1	0.8	2	1.8	0	0.0	7	1.9	1
Mexican American	0	0.0	0	0.0	0	0.0	0	0.0	0	0.0	0	0.0	0	0.0	0	0.0	0	0.0	0
Puerto Rican	0	0.0	0	0.0	0	0.0	0	0.0	0	0.0	0	0.0	0	0.0	0	0.0	0	0.0	0
Hispanic American	2	0.9	0	0.0	2	0.5	0	0.0	1	0.8	0	0.0	1	0.9	0	0.0	2	0.5	0
Total Minorities	16	7.1	20	13.2	36	9.5	0	0.0	11	8.4	14	10.6	11	9.6	0	0.0	36	9.5	6
Foreign Nationals	4	1.8	0	0.0	4	1.1	0	0.0	2	1.5	2	1.5	0	0.0	0	0.0	4	1.1	1
Caucasian	206	91.2	131	86.8	337	89.4	0	0.0	118	90.1	116	87.9	103	90.4	0	0.0	337	89.4	129
Total	226	59.9	151	40.1	377	100.0	0	0.0	131	34.7	132	35.0	114	30.2	0	0.0	377		136

ARKANSAS, FAYETTEVILLE, UNIVERSITY OF

GPA & LSAT Scores

	Full Time	Part Time	Total
# of apps	647	0	647
# admits	317	0	317
# of matrics	131	0	131
75% GPA	3.53	0.00	
25% GPA	2.97	0.00	
75% LSAT	157	0	
25% LSAT	149	0	

Tuition & Fees

	Resident	Non-resident
Full-Time	$3,613	$8,101
Part-Time	$0	$0

Living Expenses

Estimated living expenses for Singles		
Living on campus	Living off campus	Living at home
$10,464	$10,464	$10,464

Financial Aid

	Full-time		Part-time		Total	
	#	%	#	%	#	%
Total # of Students	377		0		377	
Total # receiving grants	98	26.0	0	0.0	98	26.0
Less than 1/2 tuition	36	9.5	0	0.0	36	9.5
Half to full tuition	27	7.2	0	0.0	27	7.2
Full tuition	1	0.3	0	0.0	1	0.3
More than full tuition	34	9.0	0	0.0	34	9.0
Median Grant Amount	$2,817		$0			

Informational & Library Resources

# of volumes & volume equivalents	243,962	# of professional staff	6
# of titles	87,595	Hours per week with professional staff	60
# of active serial subscriptions	2,240	Hours per week without professional staff	47
Study seating capacity inside the library	355	# of student computer work stations for entire law school	40
Square feet of law library	25,500	# of additional networked connections	0
Square feet of law school (excl. Library)	54,500	Require Laptop Computer?	N

Employment

	Total	%
Employment status known	114	97.4
Employment status unknown	3	2.6
Employed	96	84.2
Pursuing graduate degrees	5	4.4
Unemployed seeking employment	8	7.0
Unemployed not seeking employment	5	4.4
Type of Employment		
# employed in law firms	50	52.1
# employed in business & industry	20	20.8
# employed in government	13	13.5
# employed in public interest	2	2.1
# employed as judicial clerks	9	9.4
# employed in academia	2	2.1
Geographic Location		
# employed in state	70	72.9
# employed in foreign countries	4	4.2
# of states where employed	14	

J.D. Attrition (Prior Year)

	Academic	Other	TOTALS	
	#	#	#	%
1st Year	8	22	30	19%
2nd Year	0	0	0	0.0%
3rd Year	0	0	0	0.0%
4th Year	0	0	0	0.0%
TOTALS	8	22	30	7.6%

Bar Passage Rates

Jurisdiction	Arkansas		
Exam	Sum 96	Win 97	Total
# from school taking bar for the first time	84	17	101
School's pass rate for all first-time takers	82%	88%	83%
State's pass rate for all first-time takers	84%	77%	82%

ARKANSAS, LITTLE ROCK, UNIVERSITY OF

1201 McAlmont Street
Little Rock, AR 72202-5142
(501)324-9434
http://www.ualr.edu/~lawsch/index.htm

ABA Approved Since 1969

The Basics

Type of School: Public   Term: Semester

Application deadline: 04/01

Application fee: $40

Financial Aid deadline: 03/01

Can first year start other than Fall? No

Student faculty ratio: 14.7 to 1

Does the University offer:
- housing restricted to law students? No
- graduate student housing for which law students are eligible? No

Faculty & Administrators

	Total		Men		Women		Minorities	
	Fall	Spr	Fall	Spr	Fall	Spr	Fall	Spr
Full-time	20	20	14	14	6	6	2	2
Other Full-Time	3	3	0	0	3	3	1	1
Deans, librarians, & others who teach > 1/2	2	2	1	1	1	1	0	0
Part-time	11	9	9	9	2	0	1	1
Total	36	34	24	24	12	10	4	4
Deans, librarians, & others who teach < 1/2	0	0	0	0	0	0	0	0

Curriculum

	Full time	Part time
Typical first-year section size	82	45
Is there typically a "small section" of the first year class, other than Legal Writing, taught by full-time faculty?	No	No
If yes, typical size offered last year	N/A	N/A
# of classroom course titles beyond 1st year curriculum	47	35
# of upper division courses, excluding seminars, with an enrollment:		
Under 25	19	21
25 - 49	8	21
50 - 74	7	0
75 - 99	2	0
100 +	0	0
# of seminars	4	3
# of seminar positions available	86	
# of seminar positions filled	42	24
# of positions available in simulation courses	208	
# of simulation positions filled	123	42
# of positions available in faculty supervised clinical courses	42	
# of fac. sup. clin. positions filled	22	0
# involved in field placements	0	0
# involved in law journals	62	21
# in moot court or trial competitions	33	7
# of credit hrs required to graduate	87	

J.D. Enrollment & Ethnicity

	Men		Women		Fl-Time		Pt-Time		1st Yr		2nd Yr		3rd Yr		4th Yr		Total		JD Degrees Awarded
	#	%	#	%	#	%	#	%	#	%	#	%	#	%	#	%	#	%	
African-American	15	7.2	19	9.7	19	7.5	15	9.9	15	10.9	11	8.3	5	4.6	3	11.5	34	8.4	6
American Indian	2	1.0	1	0.5	2	0.8	1	0.7	0	0.0	0	0.0	3	2.8	0	0.0	3	0.7	1
Asian American	1	0.5	0	0.0	1	0.4	0	0.0	0	0.0	1	0.8	0	0.0	0	0.0	1	0.2	2
Mexican American	0	0.0	0	0.0	0	0.0	0	0.0	0	0.0	0	0.0	0	0.0	0	0.0	0	0.0	0
Puerto Rican	0	0.0	0	0.0	0	0.0	0	0.0	0	0.0	0	0.0	0	0.0	0	0.0	0	0.0	0
Hispanic American	5	2.4	4	2.0	8	3.2	1	0.7	3	2.2	4	3.0	2	1.8	0	0.0	9	2.2	3
Total Minorities	23	11.1	24	12.2	30	11.9	17	11.3	18	13.1	16	12.1	10	9.2	3	11.5	47	11.6	12
Foreign Nationals	0	0.0	1	0.5	1	0.4	0	0.0	1	0.7	0	0.0	0	0.0	0	0.0	1	0.2	0
Caucasian	185	88.9	171	87.2	222	87.7	134	88.7	118	86.1	116	87.9	99	90.8	23	88.5	356	88.1	105
Total	208	51.5	196	48.5	253	62.6	151	37.4	137	33.9	132	32.7	109	27.0	26	6.4	404		117

GPA & LSAT Scores

	Full Time	Part Time	Total
# of apps	290	170	460
# admits	164	70	234
# of matrics	81	50	131
75% GPA	3.62	3.40	
25% GPA	3.02	2.65	
75% LSAT	156	155	
25% LSAT	148	148	

Tuition & Fees

	Resident	Non-resident
Full-Time	$4,206	$9,274
Part-Time	$3,040	$6,660

Living Expenses

Estimated living expenses for Singles		
Living on campus	Living off campus	Living at home
N/A	$9,517	$7,193

Financial Aid

	Full-time		Part-time		Total	
	#	%	#	%	#	%
Total # of Students	253		151		404	
Total # receiving grants	61	24.1	8	5.3	69	17.1
Less than 1/2 tuition	37	14.6	5	3.3	42	10.4
Half to full tuition	6	2.4	0	0.0	6	1.5
Full tuition	2	0.8	0	0.0	2	0.5
More than full tuition	16	6.3	3	2.0	19	4.7
Median Grant Amount	$1,250		$858			

Informational & Library Resources

# of volumes & volume equivalents	257,002	# of professional staff	5
# of titles	28,018	Hours per week with professional staff	78
# of active serial subscriptions	2,795	Hours per week without professional staff	21
Study seating capacity inside the library	385	# of student computer work stations for entire law school	52
Square feet of law library	52,973	# of additional networked connections	32
Square feet of law school (excl. Library)	50,166	Require Laptop Computer?	N

Employment

	Total	%
Employment status known	127	98.4
Employment status unknown	2	1.6
Employed	116	91.3
Pursuing graduate degrees	6	4.7
Unemployed seeking employment	3	2.4
Unemployed not seeking employment	2	1.6
Type of Employment		
# employed in law firms	61	52.6
# employed in business & industry	13	11.2
# employed in government	24	20.7
# employed in public interest	3	2.6
# employed as judicial clerks	10	8.6
# employed in academia	4	3.4
Geographic Location		
# employed in state	100	86.2
# employed in foreign countries	1	0.9
# of states where employed	10	

J.D. Attrition (Prior Year)

	Academic	Other	TOTALS	
	#	#	#	%
1st Year	3	15	18	11%
2nd Year	6	12	18	15%
3rd Year	0	0	0	0.0%
4th Year	0	0	0	0.0%
TOTALS	9	27	36	8.6%

Bar Passage Rates

Jurisdiction	Arkansas		
Exam	Sum 96	Win 97	Total
# from school taking bar for the first time	82	27	109
School's pass rate for all first-time takers	89%	81%	87%
State's pass rate for all first-time takers	84%	77%	82%

BALTIMORE, UNIVERSITY OF

1420 North Charles Street
Baltimore, MD 21201
(410)837-4459
http://www.ubalt.edu/www/law

ABA Approved Since 1972

The Basics

Type of School: Public Term: Semester
Application deadline: 04/01
Application fee: $35
Financial Aid deadline: 04/01
Can first year start other than Fall? No
Student faculty ratio: 18.9 to 1
Does the University offer:
- housing restricted to law students? No
- graduate student housing for which law students are eligible? No

Faculty & Administrators

	Total		Men		Women		Minorities	
	Fall	Spr	Fall	Spr	Fall	Spr	Fall	Spr
Full-time	39	37	24	23	15	14	4	4
Other Full-Time	2	2	1	1	1	1	1	1
Deans, librarians, & others who teach > 1/2	3	4	3	4	0	0	0	0
Part-time	60	74	43	55	17	19	6	5
Total	104	117	71	83	33	34	11	10
Deans, librarians, & others who teach < 1/2	1	1	1	1	0	0	0	0

Curriculum

	Full time	Part time
Typical first-year section size	75	75
Is there typically a "small section" of the first year class, other than Legal Writing, taught by full-time faculty?	No	No
If yes, typical size offered last year	N/A	N/A
# of classroom course titles beyond 1st year curriculum	69	82
# of upper division courses, excluding seminars, with an enrollment:		
Under 25	35	53
25 - 49	23	15
50 - 74	17	16
75 - 99	5	12
100 +	0	0
# of seminars	14	10
# of seminar positions available	380	
# of seminar positions filled	232	79
# of positions available in simulation courses	760	
# of simulation positions filled	405	291
# of positions available in faculty supervised clinical courses	108	
# of fac. sup. clin. positions filled	87	17
# involved in field placements	73	23
# involved in law journals	164	56
# in moot court or trial competitions	28	12
# of credit hrs required to graduate	90	

J.D. Enrollment & Ethnicity

	Men		Women		Fl-Time		Pt-Time		1st Yr		2nd Yr		3rd Yr		4th Yr		Total		JD Degrees Awarded
	#	%	#	%	#	%	#	%	#	%	#	%	#	%	#	%	#	%	
African-American	46	9.1	84	16.9	71	10.8	59	17.2	31	10.4	42	13.3	33	11.5	24	23.5	130	13.0	32
American Indian	4	0.8	3	0.6	6	0.9	1	0.3	1	0.3	5	1.6	0	0.0	1	1.0	7	0.7	0
Asian American	15	3.0	21	4.2	28	4.2	8	2.3	8	2.7	14	4.4	12	4.2	2	2.0	36	3.6	1
Mexican American	0	0.0	0	0.0	0	0.0	0	0.0	0	0.0	0	0.0	0	0.0	0	0.0	0	0.0	0
Puerto Rican	0	0.0	0	0.0	0	0.0	0	0.0	0	0.0	0	0.0	0	0.0	0	0.0	0	0.0	0
Hispanic American	9	1.8	12	2.4	19	2.9	2	0.6	6	2.0	12	3.8	3	1.0	0	0.0	21	2.1	3
Total Minorities	74	14.6	120	24.2	124	18.8	70	20.3	46	15.4	73	23.2	48	16.7	27	26.5	194	19.3	36
Foreign Nationals	6	1.2	7	1.4	12	1.8	1	0.3	4	1.3	5	1.6	4	1.4	0	0.0	13	1.3	2
Caucasian	427	84.2	369	74.4	523	79.4	273	79.4	249	83.3	237	75.2	235	81.9	75	73.5	796	79.4	273
Total	507	50.5	496	49.5	659	65.7	344	34.3	299	29.8	315	31.4	287	28.6	102	10.2	1003		311

GPA & LSAT Scores

	Full Time	Part Time	Total
# of apps	1,331	353	1,684
# admits	728	174	902
# of matrics	217	82	299
75% GPA	3.25	3.26	
25% GPA	2.69	2.71	
75% LSAT	153	155	
25% LSAT	147	149	

Tuition & Fees

	Resident	Non-resident
Full-Time	$8,352	$14,480
Part-Time	$6,878	$11,318

Living Expenses

Estimated living expenses for Singles		
Living on campus	Living off campus	Living at home
N/A	$10,480	$7,242

Employment

	Total	%
Employment status known	248	82.4
Employment status unknown	53	17.6
Employed	218	87.9
Pursuing graduate degrees	3	1.2
Unemployed seeking employment	23	9.3
Unemployed not seeking employment	4	1.6
Type of Employment		
# employed in law firms	87	39.9
# employed in business & industry	41	18.8
# employed in government	38	17.4
# employed in public interest	6	2.8
# employed as judicial clerks	46	21.1
# employed in academia	0	0.0
Geographic Location		
# employed in state	182	83.5
# employed in foreign countries	0	0.0
# of states where employed	12	

Financial Aid

	Full-time		Part-time		Total	
	#	%	#	%	#	%
Total # of Students	659		344		1003	
Total # receiving grants	57	8.6	32	9.3	89	8.9
Less than 1/2 tuition	50	7.6	29	8.4	79	7.9
Half to full tuition	7	1.1	3	0.9	10	1.0
Full tuition	0	0.0	0	0.0	0	0.0
More than full tuition	0	0.0	0	0.0	0	0.0
Median Grant Amount	$1,500		$1,200			

Informational & Library Resources

# of volumes & volume equivalents	287,125	# of professional staff	7
# of titles	27,056	Hours per week with professional staff	86
# of active serial subscriptions	3,306	Hours per week without professional staff	24
Study seating capacity inside the library	314	# of student computer work stations for entire law school	75
Square feet of law library	30,000	# of additional networked connections	0
Square feet of law school (excl. Library)	88,095	Require Laptop Computer?	N

J.D. Attrition (Prior Year)

	Academic	Other	TOTALS	
	#	#	#	%
1st Year	2	5	7	2.3%
2nd Year	2	14	16	5.3%
3rd Year	0	0	0	0.0%
4th Year	0	0	0	0.0%
TOTALS	4	19	23	2.2%

Bar Passage Rates

Jurisdiction	Maryland		
Exam	Sum 96	Win 97	Total
# from school taking bar for the first time	221	56	277
School's pass rate for all first-time takers	74%	84%	76%
State's pass rate for all first-time takers	76%	79%	76%

BAYLOR UNIVERSITY

P.O. Box 97288
1400 S. 5th Street
Waco, TX 76798-7288
(254)710-1911
http://www.baylor.edu/~Law

ABA Approved Since 1931

The Basics

Type of School: Private Term: Quarter

Application deadline: 03/01

Application fee: $40

Financial Aid deadline: 03/01

Can first year start other than Fall? Yes

Student faculty ratio: 21.1 to 1

Does the University offer:
- housing restricted to law students? No
- graduate student housing for which law students are eligible? No

Faculty & Administrators

	Total		Men		Women		Minorities	
	Fall	Spr	Fall	Spr	Fall	Spr	Fall	Spr
Full-time	16	16	12	12	4	4	1	1
Other Full-Time	0	0	0	0	0	0	0	0
Deans, librarians, & others who teach > 1/2	2	2	1	1	1	1	0	0
Part-time	8	17	7	15	1	2	0	1
Total	26	35	20	28	6	7	1	2
Deans, librarians, & others who teach < 1/2	2	2	1	1	1	1	0	0

Curriculum

	Full time	Part time
Typical first-year section size	73	0
Is there typically a "small section" of the first year class, other than Legal Writing, taught by full-time faculty?	Yes	No
If yes, typical size offered last year	45	N/A
# of classroom course titles beyond 1st year curriculum	67	0
# of upper division courses, excluding seminars, with an enrollment:		
Under 25	63	0
25 - 49	28	0
50 - 74	10	0
75 - 99	9	0
100 +	0	0
# of seminars	3	0
# of seminar positions available	65	
# of seminar positions filled	65	0
# of positions available in simulation courses	1,271	
# of simulation positions filled	1,271	0
# of positions available in faculty supervised clinical courses	6	
# of fac. sup. clin. positions filled	6	0
# involved in field placements	79	0
# involved in law journals	79	0
# in moot court or trial competitions	28	0
# of credit hrs required to graduate	120	

J.D. Enrollment & Ethnicity

	Men		Women		Fl-Time		Pt-Time		1st Yr		2nd Yr		3rd Yr		4th Yr		Total		JD Degrees Awarded
	#	%	#	%	#	%	#	%	#	%	#	%	#	%	#	%	#	%	
African-American	1	0.4	3	2.2	4	1.0	0	0.0	2	1.0	2	1.8	0	0.0	0	0.0	4	1.0	3
American Indian	1	0.4	2	1.5	3	0.8	0	0.0	2	1.0	1	0.9	0	0.0	0	0.0	3	0.8	2
Asian American	4	1.5	1	0.7	5	1.3	0	0.0	3	1.4	2	1.8	0	0.0	0	0.0	5	1.3	2
Mexican American	19	7.2	5	3.6	24	6.0	0	0.0	10	4.8	9	8.3	5	6.1	0	0.0	24	6.0	11
Puerto Rican	0	0.0	0	0.0	0	0.0	0	0.0	0	0.0	0	0.0	0	0.0	0	0.0	0	0.0	0
Hispanic American	3	1.1	1	0.7	4	1.0	0	0.0	3	1.4	1	0.9	0	0.0	0	0.0	4	1.0	1
Total Minorities	28	10.6	12	8.8	40	10.0	0	0.0	20	9.6	15	13.8	5	6.1	0	0.0	40	10.0	19
Foreign Nationals	0	0.0	0	0.0	0	0.0	0	0.0	0	0.0	0	0.0	0	0.0	0	0.0	0	0.0	0
Caucasian	235	89.4	125	91.2	360	90.0	0	0.0	189	90.4	94	86.2	77	93.9	0	0.0	360	90.0	149
Total	263	65.8	137	34.3	400	100.0	0	0.0	209	52.3	109	27.3	82	20.5	0	0.0	400		168

GPA & LSAT Scores

	Full Time	Part Time	Total
# of apps	797	0	797
# admits	302	0	302
# of matrics	75	0	75
75% GPA	3.75	0.00	
25% GPA	3.12	0.00	
75% LSAT	162	0	
25% LSAT	157	0	

Tuition & Fees

	Resident	Non-resident
Full-Time	$11,839	$11,839
Part-Time	$0	$0

Living Expenses

Estimated living expenses for Singles		
Living on campus	Living off campus	Living at home
$7,995	$12,330	$7,941

Financial Aid

	Full-time		Part-time		Total	
	#	%	#	%	#	%
Total # of Students	400		0		400	
Total # receiving grants	319	79.8	0	0.0	319	79.8
Less than 1/2 tuition	257	64.3	0	0.0	257	64.3
Half to full tuition	47	11.8	0	0.0	47	11.8
Full tuition	0	0.0	0	0.0	0	0.0
More than full tuition	15	3.8	0	0.0	15	3.8
Median Grant Amount	$3,134		$0			

Informational & Library Resources

# of volumes & volume equivalents	178,096	# of professional staff	6
# of titles	20,142	Hours per week with professional staff	55
# of active serial subscriptions	2,120	Hours per week without professional staff	55
Study seating capacity inside the library	303	# of student computer work stations for entire law school	32
Square feet of law library	17,861	# of additional networked connections	8
Square feet of law school (excl. Library)	37,413	Require Laptop Computer?	N

Employment

	Total	%
Employment status known	139	97.2
Employment status unknown	4	2.8
Employed	133	95.7
Pursuing graduate degrees	0	0.0
Unemployed seeking employment	4	2.9
Unemployed not seeking employment	2	1.4
Type of Employment		
# employed in law firms	87	65.4
# employed in business & industry	9	6.8
# employed in government	15	11.3
# employed in public interest	0	0.0
# employed as judicial clerks	20	15.0
# employed in academia	1	0.8
Geographic Location		
# employed in state	113	85.0
# employed in foreign countries	0	0.0
# of states where employed	12	

J.D. Attrition (Prior Year)

	Academic	Other	TOTALS	
	#	#	#	%
1st Year	0	18	18	9.0%
2nd Year	0	1	1	1.0%
3rd Year	0	1	1	0.9%
4th Year	0	0	0	0.0%
TOTALS	0	20	20	4.9%

Bar Passage Rates

Jurisdiction	Texas		
Exam	Sum 96	Win 97	Total
# from school taking bar for the first time	98	51	149
School's pass rate for all first-time takers	93%	92%	93%
State's pass rate for all first-time takers	84%	81%	84%

BOSTON COLLEGE

885 Centre Street
Newton Centre, MA 02159
(617)552-8550
http://www.bc.edu/lawschool

ABA Approved Since 1932

The Basics

Type of School: Private — Term: Semester
Application deadline: 03/01
Application fee: $65
Financial Aid deadline: 03/15
Can first year start other than Fall? No
Student faculty ratio: 16.1 to 1
Does the University offer:
- housing restricted to law students? No
- graduate student housing for which law students are eligible? No

Faculty & Administrators

	Total		Men		Women		Minorities	
	Fall	Spr	Fall	Spr	Fall	Spr	Fall	Spr
Full-time	43	41	27	26	16	15	8	8
Other Full-Time	3	3	0	0	3	3	0	0
Deans, librarians, & others who teach > 1/2	1	1	1	1	0	0	0	0
Part-time	33	42	28	30	5	12	2	0
Total	80	87	56	57	24	30	10	8
Deans, librarians, & others who teach < 1/2	12	12	4	4	8	8	0	0

Curriculum

	Full time	Part time
Typical first-year section size	100	0
Is there typically a "small section" of the first year class, other than Legal Writing, taught by full-time faculty?	Yes	No
If yes, typical size offered last year	32	N/A
# of classroom course titles beyond 1st year curriculum	122	0
# of upper division courses, excluding seminars, with an enrollment:		
Under 25	90	0
25 - 49	38	0
50 - 74	10	0
75 - 99	3	0
100 +	5	0
# of seminars	45	0
# of seminar positions available	896	
# of seminar positions filled	540	0
# of positions available in simulation courses	452	
# of simulation positions filled	407	0
# of positions available in faculty supervised clinical courses	210	
# of fac. sup. clin. positions filled	168	0
# involved in field placements	6	0
# involved in law journals	93	0
# in moot court or trial competitions	134	0
# of credit hrs required to graduate	85	

J.D. Enrollment & Ethnicity

	Men		Women		Fl-Time		Pt-Time		1st Yr		2nd Yr		3rd Yr		4th Yr		Total		JD Degrees Awarded
	#	%	#	%	#	%	#	%	#	%	#	%	#	%	#	%	#	%	
African-American	26	6.4	38	8.9	64	7.7	0	0.0	20	6.9	26	9.5	18	6.7	0	0.0	64	7.7	11
American Indian	0	0.0	1	0.2	1	0.1	0	0.0	1	0.3	0	0.0	0	0.0	0	0.0	1	0.1	1
Asian American	17	4.2	37	8.7	54	6.5	0	0.0	22	7.6	16	5.9	16	6.0	0	0.0	54	6.5	13
Mexican American	7	1.7	9	2.1	16	1.9	0	0.0	6	2.1	2	0.7	8	3.0	0	0.0	16	1.9	1
Puerto Rican	1	0.2	5	1.2	6	0.7	0	0.0	2	0.7	4	1.5	0	0.0	0	0.0	6	0.7	4
Hispanic American	11	2.7	8	1.9	19	2.3	0	0.0	7	2.4	6	2.2	6	2.2	0	0.0	19	2.3	9
Total Minorities	62	15.3	98	23.1	160	19.3	0	0.0	58	20.1	54	19.8	48	17.9	0	0.0	160	19.3	39
Foreign Nationals	3	0.7	4	0.9	7	0.8	0	0.0	4	1.4	3	1.1	0	0.0	0	0.0	7	0.8	2
Caucasian	339	83.9	323	76.0	662	79.9	0	0.0	226	78.5	216	79.1	220	82.1	0	0.0	662	79.9	231
Total	404	48.7	425	51.3	829	100.0	0	0.0	288	34.7	273	32.9	268	32.3	0	0.0	829		272

GPA & LSAT Scores

	Full Time	Part Time	Total
# of apps	4,089	0	4,089
# admits	1,237	0	1,237
# of matrics	289	0	289
75% GPA	3.68	0.00	
25% GPA	3.25	0.00	
75% LSAT	163	0	
25% LSAT	157	0	

Tuition & Fees

	Resident	Non-resident
Full-Time	$22,360	$22,360
Part-Time	$0	$0

Living Expenses

Estimated living expenses for Singles		
Living on campus	Living off campus	Living at home
N/A	$12,225	$12,225

Financial Aid

	Full-time		Part-time		Total	
	#	%	#	%	#	%
Total # of Students	829		0		829	
Total # receiving grants	355	42.8	0	0.0	355	42.8
Less than 1/2 tuition	177	21.4	0	0.0	177	21.4
Half to full tuition	178	21.5	0	0.0	178	21.5
Full tuition	0	0.0	0	0.0	0	0.0
More than full tuition	0	0.0	0	0.0	0	0.0
Median Grant Amount	$8,541		$0			

Informational & Library Resources

# of volumes & volume equivalents	371,611	# of professional staff	10
# of titles	52,242	Hours per week with professional staff	76
# of active serial subscriptions	6,133	Hours per week without professional staff	30
Study seating capacity inside the library	617	# of student computer work stations for entire law school	97
Square feet of law library	49,488	# of additional networked connections	475
Square feet of law school (excl. Library)	72,464	Require Laptop Computer?	N

Employment

	Total	%
Employment status known	256	94.8
Employment status unknown	14	5.2
Employed	236	92.2
Pursuing graduate degrees	0	0.0
Unemployed seeking employment	17	6.6
Unemployed not seeking employment	3	1.2
Type of Employment		
# employed in law firms	156	66.1
# employed in business & industry	19	8.1
# employed in government	23	9.7
# employed in public interest	5	2.1
# employed as judicial clerks	31	13.1
# employed in academia	2	0.8
Geographic Location		
# employed in state	132	55.9
# employed in foreign countries	1	0.4
# of states where employed	26	

J.D. Attrition (Prior Year)

	Academic	Other	TOTALS	
	#	#	#	%
1st Year	0	0	0	0.0%
2nd Year	0	20	20	7.4%
3rd Year	0	19	19	6.9%
4th Year	0	0	0	0.0%
TOTALS	0	39	39	4.8%

Bar Passage Rates

Jurisdiction	Massachusetts		
Exam	Sum 96	Win 97	Total
# from school taking bar for the first time	182	14	196
School's pass rate for all first-time takers	93%	79%	92%
State's pass rate for all first-time takers	83%	76%	81%

BOSTON UNIVERSITY

765 Commonwealth Ave
Boston, MA 02215
(617)353-3112
http://www.bu.edu/LAW

ABA Approved Since 1925

The Basics

Type of School: Private Term: Semester
Application deadline: 03/01
Application fee: $50
Financial Aid deadline: 04/01
Can first year start other than Fall? No
Student faculty ratio: 18.4 to 1
Does the University offer:
- housing restricted to law students? No
- graduate student housing for which law students are eligible? No

Faculty & Administrators

	Total		Men		Women		Minorities	
	Fall	Spr	Fall	Spr	Fall	Spr	Fall	Spr
Full-time	45	45	29	29	16	16	5	5
Other Full-Time	0	0	0	0	0	0	0	0
Deans, librarians, & others who teach > 1/2	7	7	6	6	1	1	0	0
Part-time	54	46	34	30	20	16	5	3
Total	106	98	69	65	37	33	10	8
Deans, librarians, & others who teach < 1/2	2	2	2	2	0	0	0	0

Curriculum

	Full time	Part time
Typical first-year section size	80	0
Is there typically a "small section" of the first year class, other than Legal Writing, taught by full-time faculty?	No	No
If yes, typical size offered last year	N/A	N/A
# of classroom course titles beyond 1st year curriculum	112	0
# of upper division courses, excluding seminars, with an enrollment:		
Under 25	48	0
25 - 49	23	0
50 - 74	14	0
75 - 99	13	0
100 +	11	0
# of seminars	43	0
# of seminar positions available	770	
# of seminar positions filled	556	0
# of positions available in simulation courses	240	
# of simulation positions filled	222	0
# of positions available in faculty supervised clinical courses	172	
# of fac. sup. clin. positions filled	147	0
# involved in field placements	20	0
# involved in law journals	340	0
# in moot court or trial competitions	252	0
# of credit hrs required to graduate	84	

J.D. Enrollment & Ethnicity

	Men		Women		Fl-Time		Pt-Time		1st Yr		2nd Yr		3rd Yr		4th Yr		Total		JD Degrees Awarded
	#	%	#	%	#	%	#	%	#	%	#	%	#	%	#	%	#	%	
African-American	8	1.5	20	4.4	28	2.8	0	0.0	9	2.8	11	3.4	8	2.3	0	0.0	28	2.8	16
American Indian	3	0.6	5	1.1	8	0.8	0	0.0	1	0.3	2	0.6	5	1.4	0	0.0	8	0.8	2
Asian American	43	7.9	55	12.2	98	9.8	0	0.0	39	12.1	28	8.6	31	8.9	0	0.0	98	9.8	35
Mexican American	2	0.4	1	0.2	3	0.3	0	0.0	2	0.6	1	0.3	0	0.0	0	0.0	3	0.3	5
Puerto Rican	2	0.4	0	0.0	2	0.2	0	0.0	2	0.6	0	0.0	0	0.0	0	0.0	2	0.2	4
Hispanic American	19	3.5	17	3.8	36	3.6	0	0.0	13	4.0	7	2.2	16	4.6	0	0.0	36	3.6	17
Total Minorities	77	14.2	98	21.7	175	17.6	0	0.0	66	20.4	49	15.1	60	17.2	0	0.0	175	17.6	79
Foreign Nationals	6	1.1	3	0.7	9	0.9	0	0.0	3	0.9	2	0.6	4	1.1	0	0.0	9	0.9	4
Caucasian	461	84.7	351	77.7	812	81.5	0	0.0	254	78.6	274	84.3	284	81.6	0	0.0	812	81.5	279
Total	544	54.6	452	45.4	996	100.0	0	0.0	323	32.4	325	32.6	348	34.9	0	0.0	996		362

GPA & LSAT Scores

	Full Time	Part Time	Total
# of apps	4,103	0	4,103
# admits	1,651	0	1,651
# of matrics	322	0	322
75% GPA	3.56	0.00	
25% GPA	3.03	0.00	
75% LSAT	163	0	
25% LSAT	158	0	

Tuition & Fees

	Resident	Non-resident
Full-Time	$22,268	$22,268
Part-Time	$0	$0

Living Expenses

Estimated living expenses for Singles		
Living on campus	Living off campus	Living at home
$12,532	$12,532	$8,576

Financial Aid

	Full-time		Part-time		Total	
	#	%	#	%	#	%
Total # of Students	996		0		996	
Total # receiving grants	493	49.5	0	0.0	493	49.5
Less than 1/2 tuition	307	30.8	0	0.0	307	30.8
Half to full tuition	186	18.7	0	0.0	186	18.7
Full tuition	0	0.0	0	0.0	0	0.0
More than full tuition	0	0.0	0	0.0	0	0.0
Median Grant Amount	$9,393		$0			

Informational & Library Resources

# of volumes & volume equivalents	525,069	# of professional staff	9
# of titles	67,497	Hours per week with professional staff	77
# of active serial subscriptions	6,389	Hours per week without professional staff	25
Study seating capacity inside the library	797	# of student computer work stations for entire law school	6
Square feet of law library	37,000	# of additional networked connections	64
Square feet of law school (excl. Library)	64,452	Require Laptop Computer?	N

Employment

	Total	%
Employment status known	346	98.0
Employment status unknown	7	2.0
Employed	294	85.0
Pursuing graduate degrees	16	4.6
Unemployed seeking employment	35	10.1
Unemployed not seeking employment	1	0.3
Type of Employment		
# employed in law firms	180	61.2
# employed in business & industry	45	15.3
# employed in government	29	9.9
# employed in public interest	5	1.7
# employed as judicial clerks	23	7.8
# employed in academia	4	1.4
Geographic Location		
# employed in state	102	34.7
# employed in foreign countries	2	0.7
# of states where employed	21	

J.D. Attrition (Prior Year)

	Academic	Other	TOTALS	
	#	#	#	%
1st Year	0	24	24	7.1%
2nd Year	2	6	8	2.2%
3rd Year	2	1	3	0.8%
4th Year	0	0	0	0.0%
TOTALS	4	31	35	3.3%

Bar Passage Rates

Jurisdiction	Massachusetts			New York		
Exam	Sum 96	Win 97	Total	Sum 96	Win 97	Total
# from school taking bar for the first time	167	15	182	123	8	131
School's pass rate for all first-time takers	81%	73%	81%	83%	63%	82%
State's pass rate for all first-time takers	83%	76%	81%	78%	67%	77%

BRIGHAM YOUNG UNIVERSITY

Provo, UT 84602
(801)378-4274
http://www.law.byu.edu

ABA Approved Since 1974

The Basics

Type of School: Private Term: Semester
Application deadline: 02/01
Application fee: $30
Financial Aid deadline: 06/01
Can first year start other than Fall? No
Student faculty ratio: 15.2 to 1
Does the University offer:
- housing restricted to law students? No
- graduate student housing for which law students are eligible? No

Faculty & Administrators

	Total		Men		Women		Minorities	
	Fall	Spr	Fall	Spr	Fall	Spr	Fall	Spr
Full-time	24	24	20	20	4	4	3	3
Other Full-Time	0	0	0	0	0	0	0	0
Deans, librarians, & others who teach > 1/2	4	4	3	3	1	1	0	0
Part-time	20	19	16	12	4	7	0	0
Total	48	47	39	35	9	12	3	3
Deans, librarians, & others who teach < 1/2	0	0	0	0	0	0	0	0

Curriculum

	Full time	Part time
Typical first-year section size	110	0
Is there typically a "small section" of the first year class, other than Legal Writing, taught by full-time faculty?	Yes	No
If yes, typical size offered last year	25	N/A
# of classroom course titles beyond 1st year curriculum	47	0
# of upper division courses, excluding seminars, with an enrollment:		
Under 25	19	0
25 - 49	22	0
50 - 74	2	0
75 - 99	4	0
100 +	5	0
# of seminars	65	0
# of seminar positions available	1,777	
# of seminar positions filled	1,124	0
# of positions available in simulation courses	328	
# of simulation positions filled	206	0
# of positions available in faculty supervised clinical courses	125	
# of fac. sup. clin. positions filled	39	0
# involved in field placements	83	0
# involved in law journals	123	0
# in moot court or trial competitions	91	0
# of credit hrs required to graduate	90	

J.D. Enrollment & Ethnicity

	Men		Women		Fl-Time		Pt-Time		1st Yr		2nd Yr		3rd Yr		4th Yr		Total		JD Degrees Awarded
	#	%	#	%	#	%	#	%	#	%	#	%	#	%	#	%	#	%	
African-American	2	0.7	0	0.0	2	0.5	0	0.0	0	0.0	1	0.7	1	0.7	0	0.0	2	0.5	1
American Indian	6	2.0	3	2.1	9	2.1	0	0.0	2	1.4	4	2.6	3	2.1	0	0.0	9	2.1	1
Asian American	12	4.1	9	6.3	21	4.8	0	0.0	8	5.7	7	4.6	6	4.1	0	0.0	21	4.8	6
Mexican American	12	4.1	0	0.0	12	2.7	0	0.0	5	3.6	3	2.0	4	2.7	0	0.0	12	2.7	3
Puerto Rican	0	0.0	1	0.7	1	0.2	0	0.0	1	0.7	0	0.0	0	0.0	0	0.0	1	0.2	0
Hispanic American	4	1.4	5	3.5	9	2.1	0	0.0	3	2.1	4	2.6	2	1.4	0	0.0	9	2.1	5
Total Minorities	36	12.2	18	12.5	54	12.3	0	0.0	19	13.6	19	12.4	16	11.0	0	0.0	54	12.3	16
Foreign Nationals	4	1.4	0	0.0	4	0.9	0	0.0	0	0.0	3	2.0	1	0.7	0	0.0	4	0.9	1
Caucasian	255	86.4	126	87.5	381	86.8	0	0.0	121	86.4	131	85.6	129	88.4	0	0.0	381	86.8	137
Total	295	67.2	144	32.8	439	100.0	0	0.0	140	31.9	153	34.9	146	33.3	0	0.0	439		154

GPA & LSAT Scores

	Full Time	Part Time	Total
# of apps	685	0	685
# admits	226	0	226
# of matrics	139	0	139
75% GPA	3.70	0.00	
25% GPA	3.20	0.00	
75% LSAT	163	0	
25% LSAT	157	0	

Tuition & Fees

	LDS	Non-LDS
Full-Time	$4,970	$7,450
Part-Time	$275	$412

Living Expenses

Estimated living expenses for Singles		
Living on campus	Living off campus	Living at home
$11,000	$10,940	$7,750

Financial Aid

	Full-time		Part-time		Total	
	#	%	#	%	#	%
Total # of Students	439		0		439	
Total # receiving grants	242	55.1	0	0.0	242	55.1
Less than 1/2 tuition	185	42.1	0	0.0	185	42.1
Half to full tuition	51	11.6	0	0.0	51	11.6
Full tuition	4	0.9	0	0.0	4	0.9
More than full tuition	2	0.5	0	0.0	2	0.5
Median Grant Amount	$1,400		$0			

Informational & Library Resources

# of volumes & volume equivalents	408,785	# of professional staff	10
# of titles	145,686	Hours per week with professional staff	45
# of active serial subscriptions	5,843	Hours per week without professional staff	59
Study seating capacity inside the library	813	# of student computer work stations for entire law school	85
Square feet of law library	90,605	# of additional networked connections	431
Square feet of law school (excl. Library)	28,073	Require Laptop Computer?	N

Employment

	Total	%
Employment status known	156	100.0
Employment status unknown	0	0.0
Employed	146	93.6
Pursuing graduate degrees	6	3.8
Unemployed seeking employment	2	1.3
Unemployed not seeking employment	2	1.3
Type of Employment		
# employed in law firms	74	50.7
# employed in business & industry	27	18.5
# employed in government	14	9.6
# employed in public interest	0	0.0
# employed as judicial clerks	22	15.1
# employed in academia	5	3.4
Geographic Location		
# employed in state	66	45.2
# employed in foreign countries	2	1.4
# of states where employed	25	

J.D. Attrition (Prior Year)

	Academic	Other	TOTALS	
	#	#	#	%
1st Year	0	0	0	0.0%
2nd Year	0	0	0	0.0%
3rd Year	0	0	0	0.0%
4th Year	0	0	0	0.0%
TOTALS	0	0	0	0.0%

Bar Passage Rates

Jurisdiction	Utah			California		
Exam	Sum 96	Win 97	Total	Sum 96	Win 97	Total
# from school taking bar for the first time	82	7	89	18	6	24
School's pass rate for all first-time takers	91%	100%	92%	83%	50%	75%
State's pass rate for all first-time takers	92%	95%	93%	69%	62%	67%

BROOKLYN LAW SCHOOL

250 Joralemon Street
Brooklyn, NY 11201
(718)625-2200
http://www.brooklaw.edu

ABA Approved Since 1937

The Basics

Type of School: Private
Term: Semester
Application deadline: Rolling
Application fee: $60
Financial Aid deadline: 04/15
Can first year start other than Fall? No
Student faculty ratio: 20.6 to 1
Does the University offer:
- housing restricted to law students? Yes
- graduate student housing for which law students are eligible? No

Faculty & Administrators

	Total		Men		Women		Minorities	
	Fall	Spr	Fall	Spr	Fall	Spr	Fall	Spr
Full-time	52	48	27	26	25	22	4	4
Other Full-Time	1	1	0	0	1	1	0	0
Deans, librarians, & others who teach > 1/2	1	1	1	1	0	0	0	0
Part-time	61	66	35	44	26	22	4	3
Total	115	116	63	71	52	45	8	7
Deans, librarians, & others who teach < 1/2	7	7	2	2	5	5	0	0

Curriculum

	Full time	Part time
Typical first-year section size	96	109
Is there typically a "small section" of the first year class, other than Legal Writing, taught by full-time faculty?	Yes	No
If yes, typical size offered last year	37	N/A
# of classroom course titles beyond 1st year curriculum	68	61
# of upper division courses, excluding seminars, with an enrollment:		
Under 25	56	45
25 - 49	35	18
50 - 74	22	13
75 - 99	11	4
100 +	8	4
# of seminars	16	14
# of seminar positions available	559	
# of seminar positions filled	351	123
# of positions available in simulation courses	776	
# of simulation positions filled	549	181
# of positions available in faculty supervised clinical courses	269	
# of fac. sup. clin. positions filled	254	15
# involved in field placements	650	54
# involved in law journals	160	28
# in moot court or trial competitions	47	10
# of credit hrs required to graduate	86	

J.D. Enrollment & Ethnicity

	Men		Women		Fl-Time		Pt-Time		1st Yr		2nd Yr		3rd Yr		4th Yr		Total		JD Degrees Awarded
	#	%	#	%	#	%	#	%	#	%	#	%	#	%	#	%	#	%	
African-American	28	3.5	49	7.2	34	3.6	43	8.1	26	5.4	24	5.4	21	4.7	6	6.3	77	5.2	17
American Indian	2	0.3	1	0.1	2	0.2	1	0.2	1	0.2	2	0.4	0	0.0	0	0.0	3	0.2	2
Asian American	55	6.9	54	8.0	76	8.1	33	6.2	36	7.4	36	8.0	34	7.7	3	3.2	109	7.4	32
Mexican American	1	0.1	3	0.4	1	0.1	3	0.6	1	0.2	1	0.2	2	0.5	0	0.0	4	0.3	0
Puerto Rican	10	1.3	13	1.9	15	1.6	8	1.5	10	2.1	2	0.4	9	2.0	2	2.1	23	1.6	5
Hispanic American	19	2.4	27	4.0	27	2.9	19	3.6	15	3.1	18	4.0	10	2.3	3	3.2	46	3.1	7
Total Minorities	115	14.5	147	21.7	155	16.6	107	20.0	89	18.4	83	18.5	76	17.2	14	14.7	262	17.8	63
Foreign Nationals	6	0.8	1	0.1	6	0.6	1	0.2	3	0.6	3	0.7	1	0.2	0	0.0	7	0.5	1
Caucasian	671	84.7	530	78.2	775	82.8	426	79.8	392	81.0	362	80.8	366	82.6	81	85.3	1201	81.7	373
Total	792	53.9	678	46.1	936	63.7	534	36.3	484	32.9	448	30.5	443	30.1	95	6.5	1470		437

GPA & LSAT Scores

	Full Time	Part Time	Total
# of apps	2,071	755	2,826
# admits	1,008	388	1,396
# of matrics	275	210	485
75% GPA	3.50	3.35	
25% GPA	3.00	2.86	
75% LSAT	159	154	
25% LSAT	153	149	

Tuition & Fees

	Resident	Non-resident
Full-Time	$20,740	$20,740
Part-Time	$15,580	$15,580

Living Expenses

Estimated living expenses for Singles		
Living on campus	Living off campus	Living at home
$16,506	$16,506	$10,296

Employment

	Total	%
Employment status known	371	85.5
Employment status unknown	63	14.5
Employed	320	86.3
Pursuing graduate degrees	6	1.6
Unemployed seeking employment	45	12.1
Unemployed not seeking employment	0	0.0
Type of Employment		
# employed in law firms	169	52.8
# employed in business & industry	57	17.8
# employed in government	67	20.9
# employed in public interest	7	2.2
# employed as judicial clerks	20	6.2
# employed in academia	0	0.0
Geographic Location		
# employed in state	295	92.2
# employed in foreign countries	0	0.0
# of states where employed	11	

Financial Aid

	Full-time		Part-time		Total	
	#	%	#	%	#	%
Total # of Students	936		534		1470	
Total # receiving grants	433	46.3	119	22.3	552	37.6
Less than 1/2 tuition	405	43.3	105	19.7	510	34.7
Half to full tuition	25	2.7	12	2.2	37	2.5
Full tuition	3	0.3	2	0.4	5	0.3
More than full tuition	0	0.0	0	0.0	0	0.0
Median Grant Amount	$5,616		$3,924			

Informational & Library Resources

# of volumes & volume equivalents	465,022	# of professional staff	9
# of titles	57,416	Hours per week with professional staff	86
# of active serial subscriptions	3,416	Hours per week without professional staff	20
Study seating capacity inside the library	702	# of student computer work stations for entire law school	80
Square feet of law library	78,082	# of additional networked connections	313
Square feet of law school (excl. Library)	191,798	Require Laptop Computer?	N

J.D. Attrition (Prior Year)

	Academic	Other	TOTALS	
	#	#	#	%
1st Year	0	13	13	2.8%
2nd Year	2	16	18	4.0%
3rd Year	1	4	5	1.1%
4th Year	1	0	1	1.1%
TOTALS	4	33	37	2.5%

Bar Passage Rates

Jurisdiction	New York		
Exam	Sum 96	Win 97	Total
# from school taking bar for the first time	382	11	393
School's pass rate for all first-time takers	85%	64%	84%
State's pass rate for all first-time takers	78%	67%	77%

CALIFORNIA WESTERN SCHOOL OF LAW

225 Cedar Street
San Diego, CA 92101-3046
(619)239-0391
http://www.cwsl.edu

ABA Approved Since 1962

The Basics

Type of School: Private Term: Trimester
Application deadline: 04/01
Application fee: $45
Financial Aid deadline: 03/18
Can first year start other than Fall? Yes
Student faculty ratio: 21.5 to 1
Does the University offer:
- housing restricted to law students? No
- graduate student housing for which law students are eligible? No

Faculty & Administrators

	Total		Men		Women		Minorities	
	Fall	Spr	Fall	Spr	Fall	Spr	Fall	Spr
Full-time	27	31	17	19	10	12	3	6
Other Full-Time	3	3	1	1	2	2	0	0
Deans, librarians, & others who teach > 1/2	1	1	0	0	1	1	0	0
Part-time	32	21	21	14	11	7	4	2
Total	63	56	39	34	24	22	7	8
Deans, librarians, & others who teach < 1/2	5	5	2	2	3	3	0	0

Curriculum

	Full time	Part time
Typical first-year section size	70	0
Is there typically a "small section" of the first year class, other than Legal Writing, taught by full-time faculty?	No	No
If yes, typical size offered last year	N/A	N/A
# of classroom course titles beyond 1st year curriculum	122	0
# of upper division courses, excluding seminars, with an enrollment:		
Under 25	87	0
25 - 49	28	0
50 - 74	20	0
75 - 99	6	0
100 +	2	0
# of seminars	19	0
# of seminar positions available	497	
# of seminar positions filled	332	0
# of positions available in simulation courses	1,680	
# of simulation positions filled	1,274	0
# of positions available in faculty supervised clinical courses	0	
# of fac. sup. clin. positions filled	0	0
# involved in field placements	148	0
# involved in law journals	69	0
# in moot court or trial competitions	44	0
# of credit hrs required to graduate	89	

J.D. Enrollment & Ethnicity

	Men		Women		Fl-Time		Pt-Time		1st Yr		2nd Yr		3rd Yr		4th Yr		Total		JD Degrees Awarded
	#	%	#	%	#	%	#	%	#	%	#	%	#	%	#	%	#	%	
African-American	10	3.0	14	3.8	21	3.0	3	37.5	9	3.1	10	4.8	5	2.5	0	0.0	24	3.4	11
American Indian	2	0.6	8	2.2	10	1.4	0	0.0	5	1.7	4	1.9	1	0.5	0	0.0	10	1.4	2
Asian American	32	9.6	44	12.0	76	11.0	0	0.0	32	11.1	20	9.5	24	11.9	0	0.0	76	10.9	19
Mexican American	22	6.6	26	7.1	47	6.8	1	12.5	25	8.7	9	4.3	14	7.0	0	0.0	48	6.9	8
Puerto Rican	0	0.0	5	1.4	5	0.7	0	0.0	3	1.0	2	1.0	0	0.0	0	0.0	5	0.7	0
Hispanic American	10	3.0	9	2.5	19	2.7	0	0.0	8	2.8	7	3.3	4	2.0	0	0.0	19	2.7	6
Total Minorities	76	22.8	106	29.0	178	25.7	4	50.0	82	28.4	52	24.8	48	23.9	0	0.0	182	26.0	46
Foreign Nationals	5	1.5	3	0.8	8	1.2	0	0.0	4	1.4	3	1.4	1	0.5	0	0.0	8	1.1	3
Caucasian	253	75.7	257	70.2	506	73.1	4	50.0	203	70.2	155	73.8	152	75.6	0	0.0	510	72.9	189
Total	334	47.7	366	52.3	692	98.9	8	1.1	289	41.3	210	30.0	201	28.7	0	0.0	700		238

CALIFORNIA WESTERN SCHOOL OF LAW

GPA & LSAT Scores

	Full Time	Part Time	Total
# of apps	1,948	0	1,948
# admits	1,383	0	1,383
# of matrics	347	0	347
75% GPA	3.34	0.00	
25% GPA	2.65	0.00	
75% LSAT	152	0	
25% LSAT	145	0	

Tuition & Fees

	Resident	Non-resident
Full-Time	$19,820	$19,820
Part-Time	$0	$0

Living Expenses

Estimated living expenses for Singles		
Living on campus	Living off campus	Living at home
N/A	$13,120	$8,520

Financial Aid

	Full-time		Part-time		Total	
	#	%	#	%	#	%
Total # of Students	692		8		700	
Total # receiving grants	172	24.9	0	0.0	172	24.6
Less than 1/2 tuition	61	8.8	0	0.0	61	8.7
Half to full tuition	49	7.1	0	0.0	49	7.0
Full tuition	62	9.0	0	0.0	62	8.9
More than full tuition	0	0.0	0	0.0	0	0.0
Median Grant Amount	$9,875		$0			

Informational & Library Resources

# of volumes & volume equivalents	257,781	# of professional staff	8
# of titles	41,727	Hours per week with professional staff	90
# of active serial subscriptions	3,420	Hours per week without professional staff	29
Study seating capacity inside the library	487	# of student computer work stations for entire law school	55
Square feet of law library	27,370	# of additional networked connections	16
Square feet of law school (excl. Library)	109,344	Require Laptop Computer?	N

Employment

	Total	%
Employment status known	262	88.5
Employment status unknown	34	11.5
Employed	212	80.9
Pursuing graduate degrees	4	1.5
Unemployed seeking employment	32	12.2
Unemployed not seeking employment	14	5.3
Type of Employment		
# employed in law firms	126	59.4
# employed in business & industry	30	14.2
# employed in government	39	18.4
# employed in public interest	3	1.4
# employed as judicial clerks	6	2.8
# employed in academia	2	0.9
Geographic Location		
# employed in state	158	74.5
# employed in foreign countries	2	0.9
# of states where employed	20	

J.D. Attrition (Prior Year)

	Academic	Other	TOTALS	
	#	#	#	%
1st Year	47	27	74	30%
2nd Year	0	6	6	2.5%
3rd Year	0	0	0	0.0%
4th Year	0	0	0	0.0%
TOTALS	47	33	80	12%

Bar Passage Rates

Jurisdiction	California			Nevada		
Exam	Sum 96	Win 97	Total	Sum 96	Win 97	Total
# from school taking bar for the first time	126	109	235	25	0	25
School's pass rate for all first-time takers	75%	76%	76%	72%		72%
State's pass rate for all first-time takers	69%	62%	67%	69%	0%	69%

CALIFORNIA-BERKELEY, UNIVERSITY OF

221 Boalt Hall
Berkeley, CA 94720
(510)642-1741
http://www.law.berkeley.edu

ABA Approved Since 1923

The Basics

Type of School: Public   Term: Semester

Application deadline: 02/01

Application fee: $40

Financial Aid deadline: 03/01

Can first year start other than Fall? No

Student faculty ratio: 16.7 to 1

Does the University offer:
- housing restricted to law students? No
- graduate student housing for which law students are eligible? Yes

Faculty & Administrators

	Total		Men		Women		Minorities	
	Fall	Spr	Fall	Spr	Fall	Spr	Fall	Spr
Full-time	41	43	32	34	9	9	4	5
Other Full-Time	4	1	1	1	3	0	1	0
Deans, librarians, & others who teach > 1/2	7	7	5	5	2	2	0	0
Part-time	43	56	34	40	9	16	3	5
Total	95	107	72	80	23	27	8	10
Deans, librarians, & others who teach < 1/2	2	2	1	1	1	1	0	0

Curriculum

	Full time	Part time
Typical first-year section size	90	0
Is there typically a "small section" of the first year class, other than Legal Writing, taught by full-time faculty?	Yes	No
If yes, typical size offered last year	30	N/A
# of classroom course titles beyond 1st year curriculum	119	0
# of upper division courses, excluding seminars, with an enrollment:		
Under 25	43	0
25 - 49	25	0
50 - 74	12	0
75 - 99	10	0
100 +	10	0
# of seminars	40	0
# of seminar positions available	777	
# of seminar positions filled	551	0
# of positions available in simulation courses	258	
# of simulation positions filled	237	0
# of positions available in faculty supervised clinical courses	172	
# of fac. sup. clin. positions filled	98	0
# involved in field placements	89	0
# involved in law journals	279	0
# in moot court or trial competitions	143	0
# of credit hrs required to graduate	85	

J.D. Enrollment & Ethnicity

	Men		Women		Fl-Time		Pt-Time		1st Yr		2nd Yr		3rd Yr		4th Yr		Total		JD Degrees Awarded
	#	%	#	%	#	%	#	%	#	%	#	%	#	%	#	%	#	%	
African-American	17	4.3	26	6.2	43	5.2	0	0.0	1	0.4	21	7.9	21	7.3	0	0.0	43	5.2	27
American Indian	4	1.0	5	1.2	9	1.1	0	0.0	0	0.0	4	1.5	5	1.7	0	0.0	9	1.1	2
Asian American	43	10.8	70	16.7	113	13.8	0	0.0	38	14.2	39	14.7	36	12.6	0	0.0	113	13.8	45
Mexican American	30	7.5	26	6.2	56	6.8	0	0.0	6	2.2	21	7.9	29	10.1	0	0.0	56	6.8	25
Puerto Rican	0	0.0	0	0.0	0	0.0	0	0.0	0	0.0	0	0.0	0	0.0	0	0.0	0	0.0	0
Hispanic American	11	2.8	13	3.1	24	2.9	0	0.0	8	3.0	6	2.3	10	3.5	0	0.0	24	2.9	9
Total Minorities	105	26.3	140	33.3	245	29.9	0	0.0	53	19.8	91	34.2	101	35.3	0	0.0	245	29.9	108
Foreign Nationals	0	0.0	0	0.0	0	0.0	0	0.0	0	0.0	0	0.0	0	0.0	0	0.0	0	0.0	0
Caucasian	295	73.8	280	66.7	575	70.1	0	0.0	215	80.2	175	65.8	185	64.7	0	0.0	575	70.1	175
Total	400	48.8	420	51.2	820	100.0	0	0.0	268	32.7	266	32.4	286	34.9	0	0.0	820		283

CALIFORNIA-BERKELEY, UNIVERSITY OF

GPA & LSAT Scores

	Full Time	Part Time	Total
# of apps	4,171	0	4,171
# admits	860	0	860
# of matrics	268	0	268
75% GPA	3.86	0.00	
25% GPA	3.66	0.00	
75% LSAT	171	0	
25% LSAT	163	0	

Tuition & Fees

	Resident	Non-resident
Full-Time	$10,800	$19,784
Part-Time	$0	$0

Living Expenses

Estimated living expenses for Singles		
Living on campus	Living off campus	Living at home
$12,344	$12,344	$12,344

Financial Aid

	Full-time		Part-time		Total	
	#	%	#	%	#	%
Total # of Students	820		0		820	
Total # receiving grants	508	62.0	0	0.0	508	62.0
Less than 1/2 tuition	348	42.4	0	0.0	348	42.4
Half to full tuition	132	16.1	0	0.0	132	16.1
Full tuition	7	0.9	0	0.0	7	0.9
More than full tuition	21	2.6	0	0.0	21	2.6
Median Grant Amount	$6,000		$0			

Informational & Library Resources

# of volumes & volume equivalents	760,526	# of professional staff	17
# of titles	207,494	Hours per week with professional staff	65
# of active serial subscriptions	7,401	Hours per week without professional staff	29
Study seating capacity inside the library	401	# of student computer work stations for entire law school	140
Square feet of law library	88,902	# of additional networked connections	48
Square feet of law school (excl. Library)	85,833	Require Laptop Computer?	N

Employment

	Total	%
Employment status known	266	96.7
Employment status unknown	9	3.3
Employed	252	94.7
Pursuing graduate degrees	3	1.1
Unemployed seeking employment	6	2.3
Unemployed not seeking employment	5	1.9
Type of Employment		
# employed in law firms	158	62.7
# employed in business & industry	10	4.0
# employed in government	17	6.7
# employed in public interest	14	5.6
# employed as judicial clerks	38	15.1
# employed in academia	2	0.8
Geographic Location		
# employed in state	189	75.0
# employed in foreign countries	1	0.4
# of states where employed	18	

J.D. Attrition (Prior Year)

	Academic	Other	TOTALS	
	#	#	#	%
1st Year	1	8	9	3.4%
2nd Year	1	16	17	6.3%
3rd Year	1	5	6	2.0%
4th Year	0	0	0	0.0%
TOTALS	3	29	32	3.8%

Bar Passage Rates

Jurisdiction	California		
Exam	Sum 96	Win 97	Total
# from school taking bar for the first time	222	8	230
School's pass rate for all first-time takers	91%	88%	91%
State's pass rate for all first-time takers	69%	62%	67%

CALIFORNIA-DAVIS, UNIVERSITY OF

School of Law
400 Mrak Hall Drive
Davis, CA 95616-5201
(530)752-0243
http://www.kinghall.ucdavis.edu

ABA Approved Since 1968

The Basics

Type of School: Public Term: Semester
Application deadline: 02/01
Application fee: $40
Financial Aid deadline: 03/02
Can first year start other than Fall? No
Student faculty ratio: 17.4 to 1
Does the University offer:
- housing restricted to law students? No
- graduate student housing for which law students are eligible? Yes

Curriculum

	Full time	Part time
Typical first-year section size	80	0
Is there typically a "small section" of the first year class, other than Legal Writing, taught by full-time faculty?	Yes	No
If yes, typical size offered last year	25	N/A
# of classroom course titles beyond 1st year curriculum	79	0
# of upper division courses, excluding seminars, with an enrollment:		
Under 25	20	0
25 - 49	23	0
50 - 74	8	0
75 - 99	7	0
100 +	0	0
# of seminars	17	0
# of seminar positions available	266	
# of seminar positions filled	182	0
# of positions available in simulation courses	370	
# of simulation positions filled	279	0
# of positions available in faculty supervised clinical courses	160	
# of fac. sup. clin. positions filled	83	0
# involved in field placements	96	0
# involved in law journals	109	0
# in moot court or trial competitions	102	0
# of credit hrs required to graduate	88	

Faculty & Administrators

	Total		Men		Women		Minorities	
	Fall	Spr	Fall	Spr	Fall	Spr	Fall	Spr
Full-time	23	24	15	16	8	8	4	5
Other Full-Time	0	0	0	0	0	0	0	0
Deans, librarians, & others who teach > 1/2	1	1	1	1	0	0	0	0
Part-time	17	15	12	9	5	6	3	3
Total	41	40	28	26	13	14	7	8
Deans, librarians, & others who teach < 1/2	2	2	2	2	0	0	0	0

J.D. Enrollment & Ethnicity

	Men		Women		Fl-Time		Pt-Time		1st Yr		2nd Yr		3rd Yr		4th Yr		Total		JD Degrees Awarded
	#	%	#	%	#	%	#	%	#	%	#	%	#	%	#	%	#	%	
African-American	9	3.8	8	3.2	17	3.5	0	0.0	6	3.5	6	3.8	5	3.3	0	0.0	17	3.5	6
American Indian	1	0.4	7	2.8	8	1.7	0	0.0	3	1.7	1	0.6	4	2.6	0	0.0	8	1.7	2
Asian American	37	15.8	34	13.8	71	14.8	0	0.0	20	11.6	19	12.2	32	21.1	0	0.0	71	14.8	24
Mexican American	12	5.1	17	6.9	29	6.0	0	0.0	5	2.9	13	8.3	11	7.2	0	0.0	29	6.0	12
Puerto Rican	0	0.0	1	0.4	1	0.2	0	0.0	0	0.0	1	0.6	0	0.0	0	0.0	1	0.2	0
Hispanic American	5	2.1	7	2.8	12	2.5	0	0.0	2	1.2	3	1.9	7	4.6	0	0.0	12	2.5	5
Total Minorities	64	27.4	74	30.0	138	28.7	0	0.0	36	20.8	43	27.6	59	38.8	0	0.0	138	28.7	49
Foreign Nationals	4	1.7	4	1.6	8	1.7	0	0.0	4	2.3	3	1.9	1	0.7	0	0.0	8	1.7	0
Caucasian	166	70.9	169	68.4	335	69.6	0	0.0	133	76.9	110	70.5	92	60.5	0	0.0	335	69.6	115
Total	234	48.6	247	51.4	481	100.0	0	0.0	173	36.0	156	32.4	152	31.6	0	0.0	481		164

GPA & LSAT Scores

	Full Time	Part Time	Total
# of apps	2,095	0	2,095
# admits	805	0	805
# of matrics	172	0	172
75% GPA	3.64	0.00	
25% GPA	3.25	0.00	
75% LSAT	162	0	
25% LSAT	156	0	

Tuition & Fees

	Resident	Non-resident
Full-Time	$10,843	$19,827
Part-Time	$0	$0

Living Expenses

Estimated living expenses for Singles		
Living on campus	Living off campus	Living at home
$10,530	$10,263	N/A

Employment

	Total	%
Employment status known	144	98.0
Employment status unknown	3	2.0
Employed	134	93.1
Pursuing graduate degrees	1	0.7
Unemployed seeking employment	6	4.2
Unemployed not seeking employment	3	2.1
Type of Employment		
# employed in law firms	72	53.7
# employed in business & industry	21	15.7
# employed in government	22	16.4
# employed in public interest	6	4.5
# employed as judicial clerks	9	6.7
# employed in academia	4	3.0
Geographic Location		
# employed in state	125	93.3
# employed in foreign countries	1	0.7
# of states where employed	6	

Financial Aid

	Full-time		Part-time		Total	
	#	%	#	%	#	%
Total # of Students	481		0		481	
Total # receiving grants	371	77.1	0	0.0	371	77.1
Less than 1/2 tuition	47	9.8	0	0.0	47	9.8
Half to full tuition	307	63.8	0	0.0	307	63.8
Full tuition	2	0.4	0	0.0	2	0.4
More than full tuition	15	3.1	0	0.0	15	3.1
Median Grant Amount	$5,572		$0			

Informational & Library Resources

# of volumes & volume equivalents	398,113	# of professional staff	4
# of titles	82,722	Hours per week with professional staff	78
# of active serial subscriptions	5,208	Hours per week without professional staff	0
Study seating capacity inside the library	375	# of student computer work stations for entire law school	70
Square feet of law library	35,521	# of additional networked connections	0
Square feet of law school (excl. Library)	29,278	Require Laptop Computer?	N

J.D. Attrition (Prior Year)

	Academic	Other	TOTALS	
	#	#	#	%
1st Year	0	4	4	2.6%
2nd Year	1	7	8	5.3%
3rd Year	0	2	2	1.1%
4th Year	0	0	0	0.0%
TOTALS	1	13	14	2.9%

Bar Passage Rates

Jurisdiction	California		
Exam	Sum 96	Win 97	Total
# from school taking bar for the first time	135	5	140
School's pass rate for all first-time takers	88%	60%	87%
State's pass rate for all first-time takers	69%	62%	67%

CALIFORNIA-HASTINGS, UNIVERSITY OF

200 McAllister Street
San Francisco, CA 94102
(415)565-4600
http://www.uchastings.edu

ABA Approved Since 1939

The Basics

Type of School: Public
Term: Semester
Application deadline: 02/16
Application fee: $40
Financial Aid deadline: 02/16
Can first year start other than Fall? No
Student faculty ratio: 20.9 to 1
Does the University offer:
- housing restricted to law students? Yes
- graduate student housing for which law students are eligible? Yes

Faculty & Administrators

	Total		Men		Women		Minorities	
	Fall	Spr	Fall	Spr	Fall	Spr	Fall	Spr
Full-time	46	49	33	31	13	18	10	9
Other Full-Time	0	0	0	0	0	0	0	0
Deans, librarians, & others who teach > 1/2	4	4	3	3	1	1	1	1
Part-time	73	55	43	38	30	17	10	0
Total	123	108	79	72	44	36	21	10
Deans, librarians, & others who teach < 1/2	2	2	0	0	2	2	0	0

Curriculum

	Full time	Part time
Typical first-year section size	84	0
Is there typically a "small section" of the first year class, other than Legal Writing, taught by full-time faculty?	Yes	No
If yes, typical size offered last year	42	N/A
# of classroom course titles beyond 1st year curriculum	130	0
# of upper division courses, excluding seminars, with an enrollment:		
Under 25	14	0
25 - 49	18	0
50 - 74	9	0
75 - 99	25	0
100 +	8	0
# of seminars	48	0
# of seminar positions available	1,052	
# of seminar positions filled	698	0
# of positions available in simulation courses	851	
# of simulation positions filled	666	0
# of positions available in faculty supervised clinical courses	184	
# of fac. sup. clin. positions filled	172	0
# involved in field placements	108	0
# involved in law journals	410	0
# in moot court or trial competitions	42	0
# of credit hrs required to graduate	86	

J.D. Enrollment & Ethnicity

	Men		Women		Fl-Time		Pt-Time		1st Yr		2nd Yr		3rd Yr		4th Yr		Total		JD Degrees Awarded
	#	%	#	%	#	%	#	%	#	%	#	%	#	%	#	%	#	%	
African-American	19	3.2	25	4.5	44	3.8	0	0.0	9	2.9	27	5.6	8	2.2	0	0.0	44	3.8	20
American Indian	5	0.8	6	1.1	11	1.0	0	0.0	3	1.0	4	0.8	4	1.1	0	0.0	11	1.0	1
Asian American	96	16.0	98	17.6	194	16.8	0	0.0	45	14.7	97	20.1	52	14.2	0	0.0	194	16.8	61
Mexican American	19	3.2	21	3.8	40	3.5	0	0.0	11	3.6	23	4.8	6	1.6	0	0.0	40	3.5	20
Puerto Rican	1	0.2	3	0.5	4	0.3	0	0.0	1	0.3	2	0.4	1	0.3	0	0.0	4	0.3	3
Hispanic American	18	3.0	15	2.7	33	2.9	0	0.0	7	2.3	17	3.5	9	2.5	0	0.0	33	2.9	20
Total Minorities	158	26.3	168	30.2	326	28.2	0	0.0	76	24.8	170	35.2	80	21.8	0	0.0	326	28.2	125
Foreign Nationals	2	0.3	2	0.4	4	0.3	0	0.0	1	0.3	3	0.6	0	0.0	0	0.0	4	0.3	3
Caucasian	440	73.3	386	69.4	826	71.5	0	0.0	229	74.8	310	64.2	287	78.2	0	0.0	826	71.5	271
Total	600	51.9	556	48.1	1156	100.0	0	0.0	306	26.5	483	41.8	367	31.7	0	0.0	1156		399

CALIFORNIA-HASTINGS, UNIVERSITY OF

GPA & LSAT Scores

	Full Time	Part Time	Total
# of apps	3,605	0	3,605
# admits	1,278	0	1,278
# of matrics	311	0	311
75% GPA	3.56	0.00	
25% GPA	3.08	0.00	
75% LSAT	165	0	
25% LSAT	158	0	

Tuition & Fees

	Resident	Non-resident
Full-Time	$11,167	$19,559
Part-Time	$0	$0

Living Expenses

Estimated living expenses for Singles		
Living on campus	Living off campus	Living at home
$15,704	$15,704	$15,704

Employment

	Total	%
Employment status known	343	90.0
Employment status unknown	38	10.0
Employed	316	92.1
Pursuing graduate degrees	10	2.9
Unemployed seeking employment	14	4.1
Unemployed not seeking employment	3	0.9
Type of Employment		
# employed in law firms	176	55.7
# employed in business & industry	38	12.0
# employed in government	32	10.1
# employed in public interest	24	7.6
# employed as judicial clerks	37	11.7
# employed in academia	9	2.8
Geographic Location		
# employed in state	216	68.4
# employed in foreign countries	6	1.9
# of states where employed	22	

Financial Aid

	Full-time		Part-time		Total	
	#	%	#	%	#	%
Total # of Students	1156		0		1156	
Total # receiving grants	915	79.2	0	0.0	915	79.2
Less than 1/2 tuition	854	73.9	0	0.0	854	73.9
Half to full tuition	58	5.0	0	0.0	58	5.0
Full tuition	0	0.0	0	0.0	0	0.0
More than full tuition	3	0.3	0	0.0	3	0.3
Median Grant Amount	$3,991		$0			

Informational & Library Resources

# of volumes & volume equivalents	597,499	# of professional staff	9
# of titles	182,393	Hours per week with professional staff	64
# of active serial subscriptions	8,350	Hours per week without professional staff	38
Study seating capacity inside the library	1,295	# of student computer work stations for entire law school	174
Square feet of law library	82,750	# of additional networked connections	200
Square feet of law school (excl. Library)	120,070	Require Laptop Computer?	N

J.D. Attrition (Prior Year)

	Academic	Other	TOTALS	
	#	#	#	%
1st Year	2	24	26	5.2%
2nd Year	0	5	5	1.3%
3rd Year	0	1	1	0.3%
4th Year	0	0	0	0.0%
TOTALS	2	30	32	2.5%

Bar Passage Rates

Jurisdiction	California		
Exam	Sum 96	Win 97	Total
# from school taking bar for the first time	334	23	357
School's pass rate for all first-time takers	81%	65%	80%
State's pass rate for all first-time takers	69%	62%	67%

CALIFORNIA-LOS ANGELES, UNIVERSITY OF

405 Hilgard Avenue
Los Angeles, CA 90095
(310)825-4841
http://www.law.ucla.edu

ABA
Approved
Since
1950

The Basics

Type of School: Public   Term: Semester
Application deadline: 01/15
Application fee: $40
Financial Aid deadline: 03/01
Can first year start other than Fall? No
Student faculty ratio: 15.9 to 1
Does the University offer:
- housing restricted to law students? No
- graduate student housing for which law students are eligible? Yes

Faculty & Administrators

	Total		Men		Women		Minorities	
	Fall	Spr	Fall	Spr	Fall	Spr	Fall	Spr
Full-time	56	56	42	43	14	13	7	5
Other Full-Time	5	5	2	2	3	3	0	0
Deans, librarians, & others who teach > 1/2	2	2	0	0	2	2	0	0
Part-time	8	19	7	14	1	5	0	0
Total	71	82	51	59	20	23	7	5
Deans, librarians, & others who teach < 1/2	2	2	0	0	2	2	0	0

Curriculum

	Full time	Part time
Typical first-year section size	80	0
Is there typically a "small section" of the first year class, other than Legal Writing, taught by full-time faculty?	Yes	No
If yes, typical size offered last year	30	N/A
# of classroom course titles beyond 1st year curriculum	105	0
# of upper division courses, excluding seminars, with an enrollment:		
Under 25	43	0
25 - 49	26	0
50 - 74	16	0
75 - 99	6	0
100 +	12	0
# of seminars	27	0
# of seminar positions available	375	
# of seminar positions filled	309	0
# of positions available in simulation courses	71	
# of simulation positions filled	71	0
# of positions available in faculty supervised clinical courses	164	
# of fac. sup. clin. positions filled	151	0
# involved in field placements	62	0
# involved in law journals	546	0
# in moot court or trial competitions	190	0
# of credit hrs required to graduate	87	

J.D. Enrollment & Ethnicity

	Men		Women		Fl-Time		Pt-Time		1st Yr		2nd Yr		3rd Yr		4th Yr		Total		JD Degrees Awarded
	#	%	#	%	#	%	#	%	#	%	#	%	#	%	#	%	#	%	
African-American	24	4.5	27	5.7	51	5.1	0	0.0	10	2.6	20	6.2	21	6.9	0	0.0	51	5.1	39
American Indian	9	1.7	1	0.2	10	1.0	0	0.0	1	0.3	6	1.9	3	1.0	0	0.0	10	1.0	6
Asian American	81	15.3	118	24.9	199	19.8	0	0.0	81	21.4	52	16.1	66	21.8	0	0.0	199	19.8	67
Mexican American	52	9.8	52	11.0	104	10.4	0	0.0	39	10.3	45	13.9	20	6.6	0	0.0	104	10.4	41
Puerto Rican	0	0.0	0	0.0	0	0.0	0	0.0	0	0.0	0	0.0	0	0.0	0	0.0	0	0.0	3
Hispanic American	1	0.2	5	1.1	6	0.6	0	0.0	0	0.0	0	0.0	6	2.0	0	0.0	6	0.6	11
Total Minorities	167	31.5	203	42.8	370	36.9	0	0.0	131	34.7	123	38.1	116	38.3	0	0.0	370	36.9	167
Foreign Nationals	2	0.4	3	0.6	5	0.5	0	0.0	2	0.5	2	0.6	1	0.3	0	0.0	5	0.5	2
Caucasian	361	68.1	268	56.5	629	62.6	0	0.0	245	64.8	198	61.3	186	61.4	0	0.0	629	62.6	157
Total	530	52.8	474	47.2	1004	100.0	0	0.0	378	37.6	323	32.2	303	30.2	0	0.0	1004		326

CALIFORNIA-LOS ANGELES, UNIVERSITY OF

GPA & LSAT Scores

	Full Time	Part Time	Total
# of apps	3,957	0	3,957
# admits	1,007	0	1,007
# of matrics	381	0	381
75% GPA	3.73	0.00	
25% GPA	3.42	0.00	
75% LSAT	165	0	
25% LSAT	159	0	

Tuition & Fees

	Resident	Non-resident
Full-Time	$10,917	$19,901
Part-Time	$0	$0

Living Expenses

Estimated living expenses for Singles		
Living on campus	Living off campus	Living at home
$11,524	$13,838	$7,129

Financial Aid

	Full-time		Part-time		Total	
	#	%	#	%	#	%
Total # of Students	1004		0		1004	
Total # receiving grants	478	47.6	0	0.0	478	47.6
Less than 1/2 tuition	231	23.0	0	0.0	231	23.0
Half to full tuition	234	23.3	0	0.0	234	23.3
Full tuition	1	0.1	0	0.0	1	0.1
More than full tuition	12	1.2	0	0.0	12	1.2
Median Grant Amount	$5,478		$0			

Informational & Library Resources

# of volumes & volume equivalents	525,128	# of professional staff	10
# of titles	180,123	Hours per week with professional staff	61
# of active serial subscriptions	6,967	Hours per week without professional staff	37
Study seating capacity inside the library	271	# of student computer work stations for entire law school	100
Square feet of law library	42,346	# of additional networked connections	35
Square feet of law school (excl. Library)	64,750	Require Laptop Computer?	N

Employment

	Total	%
Employment status known	316	99.7
Employment status unknown	1	0.3
Employed	282	89.2
Pursuing graduate degrees	6	1.9
Unemployed seeking employment	16	5.1
Unemployed not seeking employment	12	3.8
Type of Employment		
# employed in law firms	190	67.4
# employed in business & industry	34	12.1
# employed in government	25	8.9
# employed in public interest	11	3.9
# employed as judicial clerks	17	6.0
# employed in academia	5	1.8
Geographic Location		
# employed in state	245	86.9
# employed in foreign countries	3	1.1
# of states where employed	14	

J.D. Attrition (Prior Year)

	Academic	Other	TOTALS	
	#	#	#	%
1st Year	1	15	16	5.2%
2nd Year	2	8	10	3.5%
3rd Year	2	1	3	0.9%
4th Year	0	0	0	0.0%
TOTALS	5	24	29	3.2%

Bar Passage Rates

Jurisdiction	California			New York		
Exam	Sum 96	Win 97	Total	Sum 96	Win 97	Total
# from school taking bar for the first time	277	20	297	10	8	18
School's pass rate for all first-time takers	89%	85%	89%	100%	88%	94%
State's pass rate for all first-time takers	69%	62%	67%	78%	67%	77%

CAMPBELL UNIVERSITY

P.O. Box 158
Buies Creek, NC 27506
(910)893-1750
http://webster.campbell.edu/culawsch

ABA Approved Since 1979

The Basics

Type of School: Private

Term: Semester

Application deadline: Rolling

Application fee: $40

Financial Aid deadline: Rolling

Can first year start other than Fall? No

Student faculty ratio: 19.8 to 1

Does the University offer:
- housing restricted to law students? No
- graduate student housing for which law students are eligible? Yes

Faculty & Administrators

	Total		Men		Women		Minorities	
	Fall	Spr	Fall	Spr	Fall	Spr	Fall	Spr
Full-time	14	13	13	12	1	1	0	0
Other Full-Time	1	1	1	1	0	0	0	0
Deans, librarians, & others who teach > 1/2	3	3	3	3	0	0	0	0
Part-time	11	14	8	9	3	5	0	0
Total	29	31	25	25	4	6	0	0
Deans, librarians, & others who teach < 1/2	0	0	0	0	0	0	0	0

Curriculum

	Full time	Part time
Typical first-year section size	50	0
Is there typically a "small section" of the first year class, other than Legal Writing, taught by full-time faculty?	Yes	No
If yes, typical size offered last year	37	N/A
# of classroom course titles beyond 1st year curriculum	61	0
# of upper division courses, excluding seminars, with an enrollment:		
Under 25	27	0
25 - 49	11	0
50 - 74	4	0
75 - 99	4	0
100 +	8	0
# of seminars	8	0
# of seminar positions available	336	
# of seminar positions filled	196	0
# of positions available in simulation courses	103	
# of simulation positions filled	103	0
# of positions available in faculty supervised clinical courses	0	
# of fac. sup. clin. positions filled	0	0
# involved in field placements	30	0
# involved in law journals	90	0
# in moot court or trial competitions	48	0
# of credit hrs required to graduate	90	

J.D. Enrollment & Ethnicity

	Men		Women		Fl-Time		Pt-Time		1st Yr		2nd Yr		3rd Yr		4th Yr		Total		JD Degrees Awarded
	#	%	#	%	#	%	#	%	#	%	#	%	#	%	#	%	#	%	
African-American	3	1.7	6	3.9	9	2.7	0	0.0	4	3.6	0	0.0	5	4.8	0	0.0	9	2.7	4
American Indian	2	1.1	2	1.3	4	1.2	0	0.0	3	2.7	1	0.9	0	0.0	0	0.0	4	1.2	0
Asian American	1	0.6	2	1.3	3	0.9	0	0.0	2	1.8	0	0.0	1	1.0	0	0.0	3	0.9	3
Mexican American	0	0.0	0	0.0	0	0.0	0	0.0	0	0.0	0	0.0	0	0.0	0	0.0	0	0.0	0
Puerto Rican	1	0.6	0	0.0	1	0.3	0	0.0	1	0.9	0	0.0	0	0.0	0	0.0	1	0.3	0
Hispanic American	2	1.1	1	0.7	3	0.9	0	0.0	1	0.9	2	1.7	0	0.0	0	0.0	3	0.9	0
Total Minorities	9	5.0	11	7.2	20	6.0	0	0.0	11	9.8	3	2.6	6	5.8	0	0.0	20	6.0	7
Foreign Nationals	0	0.0	2	1.3	2	0.6	0	0.0	0	0.0	1	0.9	1	1.0	0	0.0	2	0.6	1
Caucasian	171	95.0	139	91.4	310	93.4	0	0.0	101	90.2	112	96.6	97	93.3	0	0.0	310	93.4	92
Total	180	54.2	152	45.8	332	100.0	0	0.0	112	33.7	116	34.9	104	31.3	0	0.0	332		100

GPA & LSAT Scores

	Full Time	Part Time	Total
# of apps	620	0	620
# admits	201	0	201
# of matrics	112	0	112
75% GPA	3.42	0.00	
25% GPA	2.83	0.00	
75% LSAT	157	0	
25% LSAT	152	0	

Tuition & Fees

	Resident	Non-resident
Full-Time	$15,733	$15,733
Part-Time	$0	$0

Living Expenses

Estimated living expenses for Singles		
Living on campus	Living off campus	Living at home
$26,285	$29,305	N/A

Financial Aid

	Full-time		Part-time		Total	
	#	%	#	%	#	%
Total # of Students	332		0		332	
Total # receiving grants	105	31.6	0	0.0	105	31.6
Less than 1/2 tuition	90	27.1	0	0.0	90	27.1
Half to full tuition	9	2.7	0	0.0	9	2.7
Full tuition	6	1.8	0	0.0	6	1.8
More than full tuition	0	0.0	0	0.0	0	0.0
Median Grant Amount	$2,000		$0			

Informational & Library Resources

# of volumes & volume equivalents	162,450	# of professional staff	5
# of titles	18,858	Hours per week with professional staff	45
# of active serial subscriptions	2,336	Hours per week without professional staff	61
Study seating capacity inside the library	412	# of student computer work stations for entire law school	55
Square feet of law library	28,143	# of additional networked connections	0
Square feet of law school (excl. Library)	50,140	Require Laptop Computer?	N

Employment

	Total	%
Employment status known	91	91.0
Employment status unknown	9	9.0
Employed	91	100.0
Pursuing graduate degrees	0	0.0
Unemployed seeking employment	0	0.0
Unemployed not seeking employment	0	0.0
Type of Employment		
# employed in law firms	72	79.1
# employed in business & industry	3	3.3
# employed in government	10	11.0
# employed in public interest	1	1.1
# employed as judicial clerks	5	5.5
# employed in academia	0	0.0
Geographic Location		
# employed in state	78	85.7
# employed in foreign countries	0	0.0
# of states where employed	8	

J.D. Attrition (Prior Year)

	Academic	Other	TOTALS	
	#	#	#	%
1st Year	7	1	8	6.7%
2nd Year	0	0	0	0.0%
3rd Year	0	0	0	0.0%
4th Year	0	0	0	0.0%
TOTALS	7	1	8	2.4%

Bar Passage Rates

Jurisdiction	North Carolina		
Exam	Sum 96	Win 97	Total
# from school taking bar for the first time	87	3	90
School's pass rate for all first-time takers	93%	100%	93%
State's pass rate for all first-time takers	81%	76%	80%

CAPITAL UNIVERSITY

303 East Broad Street
Columbus, OH 43215
(614)236-6500
http://www.law.capital.edu

ABA Approved Since 1950

The Basics

Type of School: Private — Term: Semester
Application deadline: 05/01
Application fee: $35
Financial Aid deadline: 04/01
Can first year start other than Fall? No
Student faculty ratio: 22.5 to 1
Does the University offer:
- housing restricted to law students? No
- graduate student housing for which law students are eligible? No

Faculty & Administrators

	Total		Men		Women		Minorities	
	Fall	Spr	Fall	Spr	Fall	Spr	Fall	Spr
Full-time	26	26	18	18	8	8	4	4
Other Full-Time	1	1	1	1	0	0	0	0
Deans, librarians, & others who teach > 1/2	4	4	2	2	2	2	0	0
Part-time	32	21	28	18	4	3	3	2
Total	63	52	49	39	14	13	7	6
Deans, librarians, & others who teach < 1/2	1	1	1	1	0	0	0	0

Curriculum

	Full time	Part time
Typical first-year section size	87	98
Is there typically a "small section" of the first year class, other than Legal Writing, taught by full-time faculty?	No	No
If yes, typical size offered last year	N/A	N/A
# of classroom course titles beyond 1st year curriculum	36	73
# of upper division courses, excluding seminars, with an enrollment:		
Under 25	29	57
25 - 49	8	17
50 - 74	15	10
75 - 99	7	9
100 +	0	0
# of seminars	8	7
# of seminar positions available	225	
# of seminar positions filled	129	53
# of positions available in simulation courses	240	
# of simulation positions filled	144	38
# of positions available in faculty supervised clinical courses	60	
# of fac. sup. clin. positions filled	40	4
# involved in field placements	97	14
# involved in law journals	27	8
# in moot court or trial competitions	13	3
# of credit hrs required to graduate	86	

J.D. Enrollment & Ethnicity

	Men		Women		Fl-Time		Pt-Time		1st Yr		2nd Yr		3rd Yr		4th Yr		Total		JD Degrees Awarded
	#	%	#	%	#	%	#	%	#	%	#	%	#	%	#	%	#	%	
African-American	27	5.9	30	8.0	34	7.4	23	6.2	23	8.0	20	8.4	8	3.8	6	6.6	57	6.9	12
American Indian	2	0.4	0	0.0	2	0.4	0	0.0	2	0.7	0	0.0	0	0.0	0	0.0	2	0.2	0
Asian American	7	1.5	5	1.3	8	1.7	4	1.1	5	1.7	5	2.1	1	0.5	1	1.1	12	1.5	3
Mexican American	0	0.0	0	0.0	0	0.0	0	0.0	0	0.0	0	0.0	0	0.0	0	0.0	0	0.0	0
Puerto Rican	0	0.0	0	0.0	0	0.0	0	0.0	0	0.0	0	0.0	0	0.0	0	0.0	0	0.0	0
Hispanic American	7	1.5	11	2.9	13	2.8	5	1.4	2	0.7	6	2.5	10	4.8	0	0.0	18	2.2	2
Total Minorities	43	9.5	46	12.3	57	12.4	32	8.7	32	11.1	31	13.1	19	9.0	7	7.7	89	10.8	17
Foreign Nationals	4	0.9	3	0.8	4	0.9	3	0.8	5	1.7	1	0.4	0	0.0	1	1.1	7	0.8	1
Caucasian	407	89.6	324	86.9	397	86.7	334	90.5	252	87.2	205	86.5	191	91.0	83	91.2	731	88.4	199
Total	454	54.9	373	45.1	458	55.4	369	44.6	289	34.9	237	28.7	210	25.4	91	11.0	827		217

GPA & LSAT Scores

	Full Time	Part Time	Total
# of apps	598	232	830
# admits	449	151	600
# of matrics	166	116	282
75% GPA	3.29	3.35	
25% GPA	2.66	2.74	
75% LSAT	151	157	
25% LSAT	144	147	

Tuition & Fees

	Resident	Non-resident
Full-Time	$14,993	$14,993
Part-Time	$9,823	$9,823

Living Expenses

Estimated living expenses for Singles		
Living on campus	Living off campus	Living at home
$10,585	$10,585	$10,585

Financial Aid

	Full-time		Part-time		Total	
	#	%	#	%	#	%
Total # of Students	458		369		827	
Total # receiving grants	236	51.5	79	21.4	315	38.1
Less than 1/2 tuition	227	49.6	56	15.2	283	34.2
Half to full tuition	5	1.1	16	4.3	21	2.5
Full tuition	4	0.9	7	1.9	11	1.3
More than full tuition	0	0.0	0	0.0	0	0.0
Median Grant Amount	$3,000		$4,000			

Informational & Library Resources

# of volumes & volume equivalents	238,699	# of professional staff	6
# of titles	44,668	Hours per week with professional staff	50
# of active serial subscriptions	2,385	Hours per week without professional staff	47
Study seating capacity inside the library	484	# of student computer work stations for entire law school	67
Square feet of law library	40,500	# of additional networked connections	180
Square feet of law school (excl. Library)	61,400	Require Laptop Computer?	N

Employment

	Total	%
Employment status known	226	97.0
Employment status unknown	7	3.0
Employed	204	90.3
Pursuing graduate degrees	4	1.8
Unemployed seeking employment	11	4.9
Unemployed not seeking employment	7	3.1
Type of Employment		
# employed in law firms	100	49.0
# employed in business & industry	49	24.0
# employed in government	41	20.1
# employed in public interest	8	3.9
# employed as judicial clerks	9	4.4
# employed in academia	0	0.0
Geographic Location		
# employed in state	174	85.3
# employed in foreign countries	0	0.0
# of states where employed	20	

J.D. Attrition (Prior Year)

	Academic	Other	TOTALS	
	#	#	#	%
1st Year	9	28	37	14%
2nd Year	10	2	12	5.5%
3rd Year	0	0	0	0.0%
4th Year	0	0	0	0.0%
TOTALS	19	30	49	6.1%

Bar Passage Rates

Jurisdiction	Ohio			Pennsylvania		
Exam	Sum 96	Win 97	Total	Sum 96	Win 97	Total
# from school taking bar for the first time	156	27	183	9	1	10
School's pass rate for all first-time takers	93%	81%	91%	89%	100%	90%
State's pass rate for all first-time takers	90%	90%	90%	75%	76%	75%

CASE WESTERN RESERVE UNIVERSITY

Gund Hall
11075 East Blvd
Cleveland, OH 44106-7148
(216)368-6350
http://lawwww.cwru.edu

ABA Approved Since 1923

The Basics

Type of School: Private   Term: Semester
Application deadline: 04/01
Application fee: $40
Financial Aid deadline: 05/01
Can first year start other than Fall? No
Student faculty ratio: 19.2 to 1
Does the University offer:
- housing restricted to law students? No
- graduate student housing for which law students are eligible? Yes

Faculty & Administrators

	Total		Men		Women		Minorities	
	Fall	Spr	Fall	Spr	Fall	Spr	Fall	Spr
Full-time	28	32	23	25	5	7	0	1
Other Full-Time	4	4	3	3	1	1	0	0
Deans, librarians, & others who teach > 1/2	2	2	2	2	0	0	1	1
Part-time	42	44	31	32	10	12	2	3
Total	76	82	59	62	16	20	3	5
Deans, librarians, & others who teach < 1/2	2	2	1	1	1	1	0	0

Curriculum

	Full time	Part time
Typical first-year section size	72	0
Is there typically a "small section" of the first year class, other than Legal Writing, taught by full-time faculty?	No	No
If yes, typical size offered last year	N/A	N/A
# of classroom course titles beyond 1st year curriculum	97	0
# of upper division courses, excluding seminars, with an enrollment:		
Under 25	63	0
25 - 49	23	0
50 - 74	18	0
75 - 99	6	0
100 +	1	0
# of seminars	15	0
# of seminar positions available	180	
# of seminar positions filled	148	0
# of positions available in simulation courses	256	
# of simulation positions filled	242	0
# of positions available in faculty supervised clinical courses	62	
# of fac. sup. clin. positions filled	58	0
# involved in field placements	35	0
# involved in law journals	126	0
# in moot court or trial competitions	90	0
# of credit hrs required to graduate	88	

J.D. Enrollment & Ethnicity

	Men		Women		Fl-Time		Pt-Time		1st Yr		2nd Yr		3rd Yr		4th Yr		Total		JD Degrees Awarded
	#	%	#	%	#	%	#	%	#	%	#	%	#	%	#	%	#	%	
African-American	21	5.8	30	10.5	50	7.9	1	6.7	14	5.8	17	7.7	20	10.6	0	0.0	51	7.9	18
American Indian	1	0.3	1	0.3	2	0.3	0	0.0	0	0.0	2	0.9	0	0.0	0	0.0	2	0.3	0
Asian American	21	5.8	16	5.6	37	5.8	0	0.0	12	5.0	9	4.1	16	8.5	0	0.0	37	5.7	16
Mexican American	0	0.0	0	0.0	0	0.0	0	0.0	0	0.0	0	0.0	0	0.0	0	0.0	0	0.0	0
Puerto Rican	0	0.0	0	0.0	0	0.0	0	0.0	0	0.0	0	0.0	0	0.0	0	0.0	0	0.0	0
Hispanic American	8	2.2	1	0.3	9	1.4	0	0.0	5	2.1	2	0.9	2	1.1	0	0.0	9	1.4	1
Total Minorities	51	14.0	48	16.8	98	15.5	1	6.7	31	12.9	30	13.6	38	20.2	0	0.0	99	15.3	35
Foreign Nationals	1	0.3	3	1.0	4	0.6	0	0.0	3	1.3	0	0.0	1	0.5	0	0.0	4	0.6	0
Caucasian	311	85.7	235	82.2	532	83.9	14	93.3	206	85.8	191	86.4	149	79.3	0	0.0	546	84.1	175
Total	363	55.9	286	44.1	634	97.7	15	2.3	240	37.0	221	34.1	188	29.0	0	0.0	649		210

CASE WESTERN RESERVE UNIVERSITY

GPA & LSAT Scores

	Full Time	Part Time	Total
# of apps	1,148	94	1,242
# admits	804	21	825
# of matrics	234	8	242
75% GPA	3.53	3.66	
25% GPA	3.02	3.02	
75% LSAT	159	161	
25% LSAT	152	151	

Tuition & Fees

	Resident	Non-resident
Full-Time	$19,540	$0
Part-Time	$813	$0

Living Expenses

Estimated living expenses for Singles		
Living on campus	Living off campus	Living at home
$10,430	$10,430	$10,430

Employment

	Total	%
Employment status known	210	98.6
Employment status unknown	3	1.4
Employed	166	79.0
Pursuing graduate degrees	5	2.4
Unemployed seeking employment	28	13.3
Unemployed not seeking employment	11	5.2
Type of Employment		
# employed in law firms	96	57.8
# employed in business & industry	34	20.5
# employed in government	22	13.3
# employed in public interest	3	1.8
# employed as judicial clerks	10	6.0
# employed in academia	1	0.6
Geographic Location		
# employed in state	106	63.9
# employed in foreign countries	3	1.8
# of states where employed	21	

Financial Aid

	Full-time		Part-time		Total	
	#	%	#	%	#	%
Total # of Students	634		15		649	
Total # receiving grants	236	37.2	0	0.0	236	36.4
Less than 1/2 tuition	98	15.5	0	0.0	98	15.1
Half to full tuition	107	16.9	0	0.0	107	16.5
Full tuition	31	4.9	0	0.0	31	4.8
More than full tuition	0	0.0	0	0.0	0	0.0
Median Grant Amount	$9,900		$0			

Informational & Library Resources

# of volumes & volume equivalents	351,576	# of professional staff	9
# of titles	84,443	Hours per week with professional staff	63
# of active serial subscriptions	4,679	Hours per week without professional staff	45
Study seating capacity inside the library	446	# of student computer work stations for entire law school	73
Square feet of law library	31,495	# of additional networked connections	0
Square feet of law school (excl. Library)	64,909	Require Laptop Computer?	N

J.D. Attrition (Prior Year)

	Academic	Other	TOTALS	
	#	#	#	%
1st Year	0	0	0	0.0%
2nd Year	0	9	9	4.4%
3rd Year	1	0	1	0.5%
4th Year	0	0	0	0.0%
TOTALS	1	9	10	1.6%

Bar Passage Rates

Jurisdiction	Ohio		
Exam	Sum 96	Win 97	Total
# from school taking bar for the first time	125	7	132
School's pass rate for all first-time takers	89%	100%	89%
State's pass rate for all first-time takers	90%	90%	90%

CATHOLIC UNIVERSITY OF AMERICA

Washington, DC 20064
(319)319-5140
http://www.law.cua.edu

ABA Approved Since 1925

The Basics

Type of School: Private   Term: Semester
Application deadline: 03/01
Application fee: $55
Financial Aid deadline: 03/15
Can first year start other than Fall? No
Student faculty ratio: 19.0 to 1
Does the University offer:
- housing restricted to law students? No
- graduate student housing for which law students are eligible? Yes

Faculty & Administrators

	Total		Men		Women		Minorities	
	Fall	Spr	Fall	Spr	Fall	Spr	Fall	Spr
Full-time	37	38	26	27	11	11	5	5
Other Full-Time	6	6	3	3	3	3	0	0
Deans, librarians, & others who teach > 1/2	1	1	0	0	1	1	1	1
Part-time	48	63	35	44	13	19	4	4
Total	92	108	64	74	28	34	10	10
Deans, librarians, & others who teach < 1/2	2	2	2	2	0	0	0	0

Curriculum

	Full time	Part time
Typical first-year section size	70	70
Is there typically a "small section" of the first year class, other than Legal Writing, taught by full-time faculty?	Yes	Yes
If yes, typical size offered last year	35	35
# of classroom course titles beyond 1st year curriculum	83	73
# of upper division courses, excluding seminars, with an enrollment:		
Under 25	52	40
25 - 49	24	17
50 - 74	16	2
75 - 99	12	2
100 +	0	0
# of seminars	5	6
# of seminar positions available	224	
# of seminar positions filled	77	82
# of positions available in simulation courses	355	
# of simulation positions filled	158	141
# of positions available in faculty supervised clinical courses	140	
# of fac. sup. clin. positions filled	105	20
# involved in field placements	214	31
# involved in law journals	121	41
# in moot court or trial competitions	45	15
# of credit hrs required to graduate	84	

J.D. Enrollment & Ethnicity

	Men		Women		Fl-Time		Pt-Time		1st Yr		2nd Yr		3rd Yr		4th Yr		Total		JD Degrees Awarded
	#	%	#	%	#	%	#	%	#	%	#	%	#	%	#	%	#	%	
African-American	38	7.7	67	15.0	62	9.4	43	15.2	42	13.9	29	10.1	28	9.7	6	9.7	105	11.2	17
American Indian	0	0.0	0	0.0	0	0.0	0	0.0	0	0.0	0	0.0	0	0.0	0	0.0	0	0.0	0
Asian American	17	3.4	20	4.5	25	3.8	12	4.3	13	4.3	9	3.1	11	3.8	4	6.5	37	3.9	11
Mexican American	5	1.0	7	1.6	9	1.4	3	1.1	4	1.3	4	1.4	4	1.4	0	0.0	12	1.3	1
Puerto Rican	3	0.6	4	0.9	4	0.6	3	1.1	1	0.3	2	0.7	4	1.4	0	0.0	7	0.7	1
Hispanic American	12	2.4	8	1.8	18	2.7	2	0.7	8	2.6	7	2.4	5	1.7	0	0.0	20	2.1	2
Total Minorities	75	15.2	106	23.7	118	17.9	63	22.3	68	22.4	51	17.8	52	17.9	10	16.1	181	19.2	32
Foreign Nationals	4	0.8	7	1.6	6	0.9	5	1.8	5	1.7	3	1.0	3	1.0	0	0.0	11	1.2	1
Caucasian	415	84.0	334	74.7	535	81.2	214	75.9	230	75.9	232	81.1	235	81.0	52	83.9	749	79.6	278
Total	494	52.5	447	47.5	659	70.0	282	30.0	303	32.2	286	30.4	290	30.8	62	6.6	941		311

CATHOLIC UNIVERSITY OF AMERICA

GPA & LSAT Scores

	Full Time	Part Time	Total
# of apps	1,773	388	2,161
# admits	887	193	1,080
# of matrics	219	83	302
75% GPA	3.30	3.30	
25% GPA	3.10	2.60	
75% LSAT	157	155	
25% LSAT	151	149	

Tuition & Fees

	Resident	Non-resident
Full-Time	$22,412	$22,412
Part-Time	$17,065	$17,065

Living Expenses

Estimated living expenses for Singles		
Living on campus	Living off campus	Living at home
$12,790	$12,790	$12,790

Employment

	Total	%
Employment status known	263	100.0
Employment status unknown	0	0.0
Employed	235	89.4
Pursuing graduate degrees	6	2.3
Unemployed seeking employment	11	4.2
Unemployed not seeking employment	11	4.2
Type of Employment		
# employed in law firms	93	39.6
# employed in business & industry	53	22.6
# employed in government	45	19.1
# employed in public interest	7	3.0
# employed as judicial clerks	31	13.2
# employed in academia	4	1.7
Geographic Location		
# employed in state	102	43.4
# employed in foreign countries	2	0.9
# of states where employed	30	

Financial Aid

	Full-time		Part-time		Total	
	#	%	#	%	#	%
Total # of Students	659		282		941	
Total # receiving grants	238	36.1	24	8.5	262	27.8
Less than 1/2 tuition	233	35.4	24	8.5	257	27.3
Half to full tuition	3	0.5	0	0.0	3	0.3
Full tuition	2	0.3	0	0.0	2	0.2
More than full tuition	0	0.0	0	0.0	0	0.0
Median Grant Amount	$3,000		$2,500			

Informational & Library Resources

# of volumes & volume equivalents	277,899	# of professional staff	8
# of titles	79,705	Hours per week with professional staff	86
# of active serial subscriptions	5,378	Hours per week without professional staff	29
Study seating capacity inside the library	502	# of student computer work stations for entire law school	72
Square feet of law library	50,000	# of additional networked connections	405
Square feet of law school (excl. Library)	68,575	Require Laptop Computer?	N

J.D. Attrition (Prior Year)

	Academic	Other	TOTALS	
	#	#	#	%
1st Year	3	20	23	7.7%
2nd Year	1	1	2	0.7%
3rd Year	0	1	1	0.3%
4th Year	0	0	0	0.0%
TOTALS	4	22	26	2.7%

Bar Passage Rates

Jurisdiction	Maryland		
Exam	Sum 96	Win 97	Total
# from school taking bar for the first time	104	20	124
School's pass rate for all first-time takers	75%	65%	73%
State's pass rate for all first-time takers	76%	79%	76%

CHICAGO, UNIVERSITY OF

1111 East 60th Street
Chicago, IL 60637
(773)702-9494
http://www.law.uchicago.edu

ABA Approved Since 1923

The Basics

Type of School: Private
Term: Quarter
Application deadline: Rolling
Application fee: $60
Financial Aid deadline: 04/15
Can first year start other than Fall? No
Student faculty ratio: 19.1 to 1
Does the University offer:
- housing restricted to law students? No
- graduate student housing for which law students are eligible? Yes

Faculty & Administrators

	Total		Men		Women		Minorities	
	Fall	Spr	Fall	Spr	Fall	Spr	Fall	Spr
Full-time	24	23	19	19	5	4	1	0
Other Full-Time	6	6	4	4	2	2	0	0
Deans, librarians, & others who teach > 1/2	2	2	2	2	0	0	1	1
Part-time	6	17	4	11	2	6	2	1
Total	38	48	29	36	9	12	4	2
Deans, librarians, & others who teach < 1/2	0	0	0	0	0	0	0	0

Curriculum

	Full time	Part time
Typical first-year section size	88	0
Is there typically a "small section" of the first year class, other than Legal Writing, taught by full-time faculty?	No	No
If yes, typical size offered last year	N/A	N/A
# of classroom course titles beyond 1st year curriculum	69	0
# of upper division courses, excluding seminars, with an enrollment:		
Under 25	18	0
25 - 49	24	0
50 - 74	12	0
75 - 99	5	0
100 +	10	0
# of seminars	53	0
# of seminar positions available	910	
# of seminar positions filled	720	0
# of positions available in simulation courses	70	
# of simulation positions filled	53	0
# of positions available in faculty supervised clinical courses	85	
# of fac. sup. clin. positions filled	85	0
# involved in field placements	0	0
# involved in law journals	97	0
# in moot court or trial competitions	42	0
# of credit hrs required to graduate	105	

J.D. Enrollment & Ethnicity

	Men		Women		Fl-Time		Pt-Time		1st Yr		2nd Yr		3rd Yr		4th Yr		Total		JD Degrees Awarded
	#	%	#	%	#	%	#	%	#	%	#	%	#	%	#	%	#	%	
African-American	13	4.1	27	11.6	40	7.3	0	0.0	10	5.7	15	7.8	15	8.2	0	0.0	40	7.3	12
American Indian	1	0.3	0	0.0	1	0.2	0	0.0	0	0.0	0	0.0	1	0.5	0	0.0	1	0.2	0
Asian American	30	9.4	26	11.2	56	10.2	0	0.0	17	9.7	19	9.8	20	11.0	0	0.0	56	10.2	15
Mexican American	12	3.8	2	0.9	14	2.5	0	0.0	6	3.4	5	2.6	3	1.6	0	0.0	14	2.5	5
Puerto Rican	5	1.6	0	0.0	5	0.9	0	0.0	2	1.1	3	1.6	0	0.0	0	0.0	5	0.9	0
Hispanic American	4	1.3	6	2.6	10	1.8	0	0.0	3	1.7	3	1.6	4	2.2	0	0.0	10	1.8	1
Total Minorities	65	20.4	61	26.3	126	22.9	0	0.0	38	21.7	45	23.3	43	23.6	0	0.0	126	22.9	33
Foreign Nationals	0	0.0	2	0.9	2	0.4	0	0.0	1	0.6	0	0.0	1	0.5	0	0.0	2	0.4	1
Caucasian	253	79.6	169	72.8	422	76.7	0	0.0	136	77.7	148	76.7	138	75.8	0	0.0	422	76.7	152
Total	318	57.8	232	42.2	550	100.0	0	0.0	175	31.8	193	35.1	182	33.1	0	0.0	550		186

GPA & LSAT Scores

	Full Time	Part Time	Total
# of apps	2,520	0	2,520
# admits	631	0	631
# of matrics	175	0	175
75% GPA	3.80	0.00	
25% GPA	3.50	0.00	
75% LSAT	172	0	
25% LSAT	165	0	

Tuition & Fees

	Resident	Non-resident
Full-Time	$24,138	$24,138
Part-Time	$0	$0

Living Expenses

Estimated living expenses for Singles		
Living on campus	Living off campus	Living at home
$14,342	$14,342	$14,342

Financial Aid

	Full-time		Part-time		Total	
	#	%	#	%	#	%
Total # of Students	550		0		550	
Total # receiving grants	236	42.9	0	0.0	236	42.9
Less than 1/2 tuition	175	31.8	0	0.0	175	31.8
Half to full tuition	61	11.1	0	0.0	61	11.1
Full tuition	0	0.0	0	0.0	0	0.0
More than full tuition	0	0.0	0	0.0	0	0.0
Median Grant Amount	$9,000		$0			

Informational & Library Resources

# of volumes & volume equivalents	619,753	# of professional staff	8
# of titles	241,069	Hours per week with professional staff	57
# of active serial subscriptions	7,708	Hours per week without professional staff	33
Study seating capacity inside the library	445	# of student computer work stations for entire law school	50
Square feet of law library	75,002	# of additional networked connections	247
Square feet of law school (excl. Library)	65,111	Require Laptop Computer?	N

Employment

	Total	%
Employment status known	185	100.0
Employment status unknown	0	0.0
Employed	178	96.2
Pursuing graduate degrees	4	2.2
Unemployed seeking employment	3	1.6
Unemployed not seeking employment	0	0.0
Type of Employment		
# employed in law firms	122	68.5
# employed in business & industry	4	2.2
# employed in government	4	2.2
# employed in public interest	4	2.2
# employed as judicial clerks	44	24.7
# employed in academia	0	0.0
Geographic Location		
# employed in state	54	30.3
# employed in foreign countries	0	0.0
# of states where employed	30	

J.D. Attrition (Prior Year)

	Academic	Other	TOTALS	
	#	#	#	%
1st Year	0	7	7	3.9%
2nd Year	0	1	1	0.6%
3rd Year	0	0	0	0.0%
4th Year	0	0	0	0.0%
TOTALS	0	8	8	1.5%

Bar Passage Rates

Jurisdiction	Illinois			New York		
Exam	Sum 96	Win 97	Total	Sum 96	Win 97	Total
# from school taking bar for the first time	56	9	65	36	0	36
School's pass rate for all first-time takers	100%	100%	100%	97%		97%
State's pass rate for all first-time takers	86%	84%	86%	78%	67%	77%

CINCINNATI, UNIVERSITY OF

P.O. Box 210040
Cincinnati, OH 45221-0040
(513)556-6805
http://www.law.uc.edu

ABA Approved Since 1923

The Basics

Type of School: Public   Term: Semester
Application deadline: 04/01
Application fee: $35
Financial Aid deadline: 03/01
Can first year start other than Fall? No
Student faculty ratio: 14.9 to 1
Does the University offer:
- housing restricted to law students? No
- graduate student housing for which law students are eligible? Yes

Faculty & Administrators

	Total		Men		Women		Minorities	
	Fall	Spr	Fall	Spr	Fall	Spr	Fall	Spr
Full-time	20	20	14	13	6	7	2	2
Other Full-Time	3	3	1	1	2	2	1	1
Deans, librarians, & others who teach > 1/2	1	1	0	0	1	1	0	0
Part-time	18	27	16	20	2	7	0	2
Total	42	51	31	34	11	17	3	5
Deans, librarians, & others who teach < 1/2	2	2	1	1	1	1	0	0

Curriculum

	Full time	Part time
Typical first-year section size	23	0
Is there typically a "small section" of the first year class, other than Legal Writing, taught by full-time faculty?	Yes	No
If yes, typical size offered last year	23	N/A
# of classroom course titles beyond 1st year curriculum	107	0
# of upper division courses, excluding seminars, with an enrollment:		
Under 25	45	0
25 - 49	14	0
50 - 74	7	0
75 - 99	4	0
100 +	0	0
# of seminars	37	0
# of seminar positions available	503	
# of seminar positions filled	414	0
# of positions available in simulation courses	175	
# of simulation positions filled	175	0
# of positions available in faculty supervised clinical courses	175	
# of fac. sup. clin. positions filled	175	0
# involved in field placements	111	0
# involved in law journals	97	0
# in moot court or trial competitions	52	0
# of credit hrs required to graduate	88	

J.D. Enrollment & Ethnicity

	Men		Women		Fl-Time		Pt-Time		1st Yr		2nd Yr		3rd Yr		4th Yr		Total		JD Degrees Awarded
	#	%	#	%	#	%	#	%	#	%	#	%	#	%	#	%	#	%	
African-American	12	7.4	19	9.7	31	8.8	0	0.0	14	11.7	9	7.6	8	6.7	0	0.0	31	8.7	11
American Indian	0	0.0	0	0.0	0	0.0	0	0.0	0	0.0	0	0.0	0	0.0	0	0.0	0	0.0	0
Asian American	3	1.8	0	0.0	3	0.8	0	0.0	3	2.5	0	0.0	0	0.0	0	0.0	3	0.8	1
Mexican American	0	0.0	0	0.0	0	0.0	0	0.0	0	0.0	0	0.0	0	0.0	0	0.0	0	0.0	1
Puerto Rican	1	0.6	0	0.0	1	0.3	0	0.0	0	0.0	1	0.8	0	0.0	0	0.0	1	0.3	0
Hispanic American	2	1.2	0	0.0	2	0.6	0	0.0	1	0.8	0	0.0	1	0.8	0	0.0	2	0.6	3
Total Minorities	18	11.0	19	9.7	37	10.5	0	0.0	18	15.0	10	8.4	9	7.6	0	0.0	37	10.3	16
Foreign Nationals	1	0.6	1	0.5	2	0.6	0	0.0	0	0.0	0	0.0	2	1.7	0	0.0	2	0.6	0
Caucasian	144	88.3	175	89.7	315	89.0	4	100.0	102	85.0	109	91.6	108	90.8	0	0.0	319	89.1	114
Total	163	45.5	195	54.5	354	98.9	4	1.1	120	33.5	119	33.2	119	33.2	0	0.0	358		130

GPA & LSAT Scores

	Full Time	Part Time	Total
# of apps	1,008	0	1,008
# admits	406	0	406
# of matrics	123	0	123
75% GPA	3.66	0.00	
25% GPA	3.04	0.00	
75% LSAT	163	0	
25% LSAT	155	0	

Tuition & Fees

	Resident	Non-resident
Full-Time	$7,245	$14,076
Part-Time	$0	$0

Living Expenses

Estimated living expenses for Singles		
Living on campus	Living off campus	Living at home
$10,256	$10,256	$10,256

Employment

	Total	%
Employment status known	127	100.0
Employment status unknown	0	0.0
Employed	113	89.0
Pursuing graduate degrees	4	3.1
Unemployed seeking employment	7	5.5
Unemployed not seeking employment	3	2.4
Type of Employment		
# employed in law firms	57	50.4
# employed in business & industry	23	20.4
# employed in government	9	8.0
# employed in public interest	2	1.8
# employed as judicial clerks	13	11.5
# employed in academia	0	0.0
Geographic Location		
# employed in state	85	75.2
# employed in foreign countries	0	0.0
# of states where employed	15	

Financial Aid

	Full-time		Part-time		Total	
	#	%	#	%	#	%
Total # of Students	354		4		358	
Total # receiving grants	188	53.1	0	0.0	188	52.5
Less than 1/2 tuition	97	27.4	0	0.0	97	27.1
Half to full tuition	42	11.9	0	0.0	42	11.7
Full tuition	47	13.3	0	0.0	47	13.1
More than full tuition	2	0.6	0	0.0	2	0.6
Median Grant Amount	$4,000		$0			

Informational & Library Resources

# of volumes & volume equivalents	373,135	# of professional staff	11
# of titles	172,720	Hours per week with professional staff	61
# of active serial subscriptions	2,411	Hours per week without professional staff	46
Study seating capacity inside the library	401	# of student computer work stations for entire law school	45
Square feet of law library	49,227	# of additional networked connections	0
Square feet of law school (excl. Library)	48,836	Require Laptop Computer?	N

J.D. Attrition (Prior Year)

	Academic	Other	TOTALS	
	#	#	#	%
1st Year	3	4	7	5.7%
2nd Year	0	0	0	0.0%
3rd Year	0	0	0	0.0%
4th Year	0	0	0	0.0%
TOTALS	3	4	7	1.9%

Bar Passage Rates

Jurisdiction	Ohio		
Exam	Sum 96	Win 97	Total
# from school taking bar for the first time	97	6	103
School's pass rate for all first-time takers	93%	100%	93%
State's pass rate for all first-time takers	90%	90%	90%

CITY UNIVERSITY OF NEW YORK

65-21 Main Street
Flushing, NY 11367
(718)340-4200
http://web.law.cuny.edu

ABA Approved Since 1985

The Basics

Type of School: Public   Term: Semester

Application deadline: 03/15

Application fee: $40

Financial Aid deadline: 05/01

Can first year start other than Fall? No

Student faculty ratio: 13.1 to 1

Does the University offer:
- housing restricted to law students? No
- graduate student housing for which law students are eligible? No

Faculty & Administrators

	Total		Men		Women		Minorities	
	Fall	Spr	Fall	Spr	Fall	Spr	Fall	Spr
Full-time	29	30	12	13	17	17	12	12
Other Full-Time	2	3	1	2	1	1	1	1
Deans, librarians, & others who teach > 1/2	0	0	0	0	0	0	0	0
Part-time	23	17	8	5	15	12	4	5
Total	54	50	21	20	33	30	17	18
Deans, librarians, & others who teach < 1/2	2	2	1	1	1	1	0	0

Curriculum

	Full time	Part time
Typical first-year section size	80	0
Is there typically a "small section" of the first year class, other than Legal Writing, taught by full-time faculty?	Yes	No
If yes, typical size offered last year	20	N/A
# of classroom course titles beyond 1st year curriculum	67	0
# of upper division courses, excluding seminars, with an enrollment:		
Under 25	39	0
25 - 49	14	0
50 - 74	8	0
75 - 99	7	0
100 +	1	0
# of seminars	8	0
# of seminar positions available	160	
# of seminar positions filled	147	0
# of positions available in simulation courses	480	
# of simulation positions filled	467	0
# of positions available in faculty supervised clinical courses	89	
# of fac. sup. clin. positions filled	89	0
# involved in field placements	57	0
# involved in law journals	24	0
# in moot court or trial competitions	27	0
# of credit hrs required to graduate	91	

J.D. Enrollment & Ethnicity

	Men		Women		Fl-Time		Pt-Time		1st Yr		2nd Yr		3rd Yr		4th Yr		Total		JD Degrees Awarded
	#	%	#	%	#	%	#	%	#	%	#	%	#	%	#	%	#	%	
African-American	24	13.1	49	17.9	73	16.0	0	0.0	27	15.9	27	19.9	19	12.7	0	0.0	73	16.0	27
American Indian	3	1.6	0	0.0	3	0.7	0	0.0	2	1.2	0	0.0	1	0.7	0	0.0	3	0.7	0
Asian American	26	14.2	25	9.2	51	11.2	0	0.0	26	15.3	13	9.6	12	8.0	0	0.0	51	11.2	12
Mexican American	0	0.0	0	0.0	0	0.0	0	0.0	0	0.0	0	0.0	0	0.0	0	0.0	0	0.0	0
Puerto Rican	11	6.0	11	4.0	22	4.8	0	0.0	6	3.5	8	5.9	8	5.3	0	0.0	22	4.8	8
Hispanic American	16	8.7	15	5.5	31	6.8	0	0.0	14	8.2	10	7.4	7	4.7	0	0.0	31	6.8	2
Total Minorities	80	43.7	100	36.6	180	39.5	0	0.0	75	44.1	58	42.6	47	31.3	0	0.0	180	39.5	49
Foreign Nationals	3	1.6	3	1.1	6	1.3	0	0.0	3	1.8	3	2.2	0	0.0	0	0.0	6	1.3	2
Caucasian	100	54.6	170	62.3	270	59.2	0	0.0	92	54.1	75	55.1	103	68.7	0	0.0	270	59.2	96
Total	183	40.1	273	59.9	456	100.0	0	0.0	170	37.3	136	29.8	150	32.9	0	0.0	456		147

CITY UNIVERSITY OF NEW YORK

GPA & LSAT Scores

	Full Time	Part Time	Total
# of apps	1,441	0	1,441
# admits	543	0	543
# of matrics	167	0	167
75% GPA	3.35	0.00	
25% GPA	2.70	0.00	
75% LSAT	152	0	
25% LSAT	142	0	

Tuition & Fees

	Resident	Non-resident
Full-Time	$6,452	$9,682
Part-Time	$0	$0

Living Expenses

Estimated living expenses for Singles		
Living on campus	Living off campus	Living at home
N/A	$10,351	$5,451

Employment

	Total	%
Employment status known	101	70.1
Employment status unknown	43	29.9
Employed	83	82.2
Pursuing graduate degrees	0	0.0
Unemployed seeking employment	17	16.8
Unemployed not seeking employment	1	1.0
Type of Employment		
# employed in law firms	26	31.3
# employed in business & industry	18	21.7
# employed in government	12	14.5
# employed in public interest	23	27.7
# employed as judicial clerks	3	3.6
# employed in academia	1	1.2
Geographic Location		
# employed in state	65	78.3
# employed in foreign countries	0	0.0
# of states where employed	13	

Financial Aid

	Full-time		Part-time		Total	
	#	%	#	%	#	%
Total # of Students	456		0		456	
Total # receiving grants	280	61.4	0	0.0	280	61.4
Less than 1/2 tuition	272	59.6	0	0.0	272	59.6
Half to full tuition	2	0.4	0	0.0	2	0.4
Full tuition	6	1.3	0	0.0	6	1.3
More than full tuition	0	0.0	0	0.0	0	0.0
Median Grant Amount	$775		$0			

Informational & Library Resources

# of volumes & volume equivalents	242,632	# of professional staff	9
# of titles	25,329	Hours per week with professional staff	49
# of active serial subscriptions	2,619	Hours per week without professional staff	8
Study seating capacity inside the library	397	# of student computer work stations for entire law school	72
Square feet of law library	33,475	# of additional networked connections	0
Square feet of law school (excl. Library)	62,977	Require Laptop Computer?	N

J.D. Attrition (Prior Year)

	Academic	Other	TOTALS	
	#	#	#	%
1st Year	11	21	32	20%
2nd Year	5	2	7	4.6%
3rd Year	0	1	1	0.7%
4th Year	0	0	0	0.0%
TOTALS	16	24	40	8.6%

Bar Passage Rates

Jurisdiction	New York		
Exam	Sum 96	Win 97	Total
# from school taking bar for the first time	111	20	131
School's pass rate for all first-time takers	62%	20%	56%
State's pass rate for all first-time takers	78%	67%	77%

CLEVELAND STATE UNIVERSITY

Cleveland-Marshall College of Law
1801 Euclid Avenue
Cleveland, OH 44115-2223
(216)687-2344
http://www.law.csuohio.edu

ABA Approved Since 1957

The Basics

Type of School: Public   Term: Semester

Application deadline: 04/01

Application fee: $35

Financial Aid deadline: 04/01

Can first year start other than Fall? No

Student faculty ratio: 20.1 to 1

Does the University offer:
- housing restricted to law students? Yes
- graduate student housing for which law students are eligible? Yes

Faculty & Administrators

	Total		Men		Women		Minorities	
	Fall	Spr	Fall	Spr	Fall	Spr	Fall	Spr
Full-time	32	34	22	24	10	10	3	3
Other Full-Time	9	9	4	4	5	5	0	0
Deans, librarians, & others who teach > 1/2	5	3	2	1	3	2	0	0
Part-time	30	33	24	29	6	4	2	2
Total	76	79	52	58	24	21	5	5
Deans, librarians, & others who teach < 1/2	2	2	2	2	0	0	1	1

Curriculum

	Full time	Part time
Typical first-year section size	61	35
Is there typically a "small section" of the first year class, other than Legal Writing, taught by full-time faculty?	No	No
If yes, typical size offered last year	N/A	N/A
# of classroom course titles beyond 1st year curriculum	44	55
# of upper division courses, excluding seminars, with an enrollment:		
Under 25	31	36
25 - 49	30	37
50 - 74	8	7
75 - 99	4	2
100 +	0	0
# of seminars	6	9
# of seminar positions available	209	
# of seminar positions filled	40	124
# of positions available in simulation courses	279	
# of simulation positions filled	103	144
# of positions available in faculty supervised clinical courses	61	
# of fac. sup. clin. positions filled	42	5
# involved in field placements	50	4
# involved in law journals	36	17
# in moot court or trial competitions	16	8
# of credit hrs required to graduate	87	

J.D. Enrollment & Ethnicity

	Men		Women		Fl-Time		Pt-Time		1st Yr		2nd Yr		3rd Yr		4th Yr		Total		JD Degrees Awarded
	#	%	#	%	#	%	#	%	#	%	#	%	#	%	#	%	#	%	
African-American	29	6.1	45	11.4	42	7.3	32	11.0	24	8.8	22	8.9	21	7.5	7	10.0	74	8.5	16
American Indian	2	0.4	1	0.3	3	0.5	0	0.0	2	0.7	0	0.0	1	0.4	0	0.0	3	0.3	1
Asian American	11	2.3	10	2.5	13	2.2	8	2.7	10	3.6	5	2.0	3	1.1	3	4.3	21	2.4	6
Mexican American	0	0.0	0	0.0	0	0.0	0	0.0	0	0.0	0	0.0	0	0.0	0	0.0	0	0.0	0
Puerto Rican	0	0.0	0	0.0	0	0.0	0	0.0	0	0.0	0	0.0	0	0.0	0	0.0	0	0.0	0
Hispanic American	3	0.6	6	1.5	8	1.4	1	0.3	4	1.5	3	1.2	2	0.7	0	0.0	9	1.0	9
Total Minorities	45	9.5	62	15.7	66	11.4	41	14.0	40	14.6	30	12.1	27	9.6	10	14.3	107	12.3	32
Foreign Nationals	6	1.3	2	0.5	8	1.4	0	0.0	7	2.6	1	0.4	0	0.0	0	0.0	8	0.9	0
Caucasian	424	89.3	332	83.8	505	87.2	251	86.0	227	82.8	216	87.4	253	90.4	60	85.7	756	86.8	210
Total	475	54.5	396	45.5	579	66.5	292	33.5	274	31.5	247	28.4	280	32.1	70	8.0	871		242

CLEVELAND STATE UNIVERSITY

GPA & LSAT Scores

	Full Time	Part Time	Total
# of apps	1,052	278	1,330
# admits	623	142	765
# of matrics	186	102	288
75% GPA	3.41	3.33	
25% GPA	2.88	2.63	
75% LSAT	153	155	
25% LSAT	145	147	

Tuition & Fees

	Resident	Non-resident
Full-Time	$7,145	$14,250
Part-Time	$5,495	$10,960

Living Expenses

Estimated living expenses for Singles		
Living on campus	Living off campus	Living at home
$7,934	$9,760	$9,760

Employment

	Total	%
Employment status known	243	96.4
Employment status unknown	9	3.6
Employed	216	88.9
Pursuing graduate degrees	9	3.7
Unemployed seeking employment	11	4.5
Unemployed not seeking employment	7	2.9
Type of Employment		
# employed in law firms	106	49.1
# employed in business & industry	62	28.7
# employed in government	27	12.5
# employed in public interest	4	1.9
# employed as judicial clerks	6	2.8
# employed in academia	9	4.2
Geographic Location		
# employed in state	193	89.4
# employed in foreign countries	0	0.0
# of states where employed	13	

Financial Aid

	Full-time		Part-time		Total	
	#	%	#	%	#	%
Total # of Students	579		292		871	
Total # receiving grants	298	51.5	75	25.7	373	42.8
Less than 1/2 tuition	273	47.2	65	22.3	338	38.8
Half to full tuition	23	4.0	9	3.1	32	3.7
Full tuition	2	0.3	1	0.3	3	0.3
More than full tuition	0	0.0	0	0.0	0	0.0
Median Grant Amount	$1,000		$1,000			

Informational & Library Resources

# of volumes & volume equivalents	425,131	# of professional staff	14
# of titles	121,364	Hours per week with professional staff	88
# of active serial subscriptions	2,580	Hours per week without professional staff	7
Study seating capacity inside the library	483	# of student computer work stations for entire law school	65
Square feet of law library	84,670	# of additional networked connections	300
Square feet of law school (excl. Library)	52,487	Require Laptop Computer?	N

J.D. Attrition (Prior Year)

	Academic	Other	TOTALS	
	#	#	#	%
1st Year	4	22	26	10%
2nd Year	4	6	10	3.7%
3rd Year	2	4	6	2.3%
4th Year	0	0	0	0.0%
TOTALS	10	32	42	4.8%

Bar Passage Rates

Jurisdiction	Ohio		
Exam	Sum 96	Win 97	Total
# from school taking bar for the first time	172	55	227
School's pass rate for all first-time takers	92%	80%	89%
State's pass rate for all first-time takers	90%	90%	90%

COLORADO, UNIVERSITY OF

Campus Box 401
Boulder, CO 80309-0401
(303)492-7203
http://www.colorado.edu/law

ABA Approved Since 1923

The Basics

Type of School: Public　　Term: Semester
Application deadline: 02/15
Application fee: $45
Financial Aid deadline: 03/01
Can first year start other than Fall? No
Student faculty ratio: 14.7 to 1
Does the University offer:
- housing restricted to law students? No
- graduate student housing for which law students are eligible? No

Faculty & Administrators

	Total		Men		Women		Minorities	
	Fall	Spr	Fall	Spr	Fall	Spr	Fall	Spr
Full-time	29	29	24	24	5	5	4	5
Other Full-Time	3	3	1	1	2	2	0	0
Deans, librarians, & others who teach > 1/2	2	2	1	1	1	1	0	0
Part-time	9	13	8	9	1	4	0	2
Total	43	47	34	35	9	12	4	7
Deans, librarians, & others who teach < 1/2	3	3	2	2	1	1	1	1

Curriculum

	Full time	Part time
Typical first-year section size	70	0
Is there typically a "small section" of the first year class, other than Legal Writing, taught by full-time faculty?	Yes	No
If yes, typical size offered last year	28	N/A
# of classroom course titles beyond 1st year curriculum	89	0
# of upper division courses, excluding seminars, with an enrollment:		
Under 25	63	0
25 - 49	36	0
50 - 74	15	0
75 - 99	1	0
100 +	0	0
# of seminars	15	0
# of seminar positions available	188	
# of seminar positions filled	162	0
# of positions available in simulation courses	284	
# of simulation positions filled	282	0
# of positions available in faculty supervised clinical courses	116	
# of fac. sup. clin. positions filled	82	0
# involved in field placements	65	0
# involved in law journals	95	0
# in moot court or trial competitions	60	0
# of credit hrs required to graduate	89	

J.D. Enrollment & Ethnicity

	Men		Women		Fl-Time		Pt-Time		1st Yr		2nd Yr		3rd Yr		4th Yr		Total		JD Degrees Awarded
	#	%	#	%	#	%	#	%	#	%	#	%	#	%	#	%	#	%	
African-American	10	3.8	11	4.4	21	4.1	0	0.0	7	3.8	6	3.9	8	4.6	0	0.0	21	4.1	12
American Indian	4	1.5	10	4.0	14	2.7	0	0.0	4	2.2	3	1.9	7	4.0	0	0.0	14	2.7	3
Asian American	8	3.1	10	4.0	18	3.5	0	0.0	7	3.8	6	3.9	5	2.9	0	0.0	18	3.5	8
Mexican American	6	2.3	12	4.8	17	3.3	1	50.0	5	2.7	4	2.6	9	5.2	0	0.0	18	3.5	8
Puerto Rican	0	0.0	1	0.4	1	0.2	0	0.0	1	0.5	0	0.0	0	0.0	0	0.0	1	0.2	1
Hispanic American	10	3.8	8	3.2	18	3.5	0	0.0	6	3.3	5	3.2	7	4.0	0	0.0	18	3.5	0
Total Minorities	38	14.6	52	20.7	89	17.5	1	50.0	30	16.3	24	15.6	36	20.7	0	0.0	90	17.6	32
Foreign Nationals	0	0.0	0	0.0	0	0.0	0	0.0	0	0.0	0	0.0	0	0.0	0	0.0	0	0.0	0
Caucasian	223	85.4	199	79.3	421	82.5	1	50.0	154	83.7	130	84.4	138	79.3	0	0.0	422	82.4	124
Total	261	51.0	251	49.0	510	99.6	2	0.4	184	35.9	154	30.1	174	34.0	0	0.0	512		156

GPA & LSAT Scores

	Full Time	Part Time	Total
# of apps	1,846	0	1,846
# admits	650	0	650
# of matrics	186	0	186
75% GPA	3.72	0.00	
25% GPA	3.33	0.00	
75% LSAT	164	0	
25% LSAT	158	0	

Tuition & Fees

	Resident	Non-resident
Full-Time	$4,953	$16,171
Part-Time	$0	$0

Living Expenses

Estimated living expenses for Singles		
Living on campus	Living off campus	Living at home
$8,730	$10,633	$6,691

Employment

	Total	%
Employment status known	145	96.0
Employment status unknown	6	4.0
Employed	129	89.0
Pursuing graduate degrees	0	0.0
Unemployed seeking employment	13	9.0
Unemployed not seeking employment	3	2.1
Type of Employment		
# employed in law firms	70	54.3
# employed in business & industry	14	10.9
# employed in government	20	15.5
# employed in public interest	6	4.7
# employed as judicial clerks	19	14.7
# employed in academia	0	0.0
Geographic Location		
# employed in state	94	72.9
# employed in foreign countries	1	0.8
# of states where employed	17	

Financial Aid

	Full-time		Part-time		Total	
	#	%	#	%	#	%
Total # of Students	510		2		512	
Total # receiving grants	244	47.8	0	0.0	244	47.7
Less than 1/2 tuition	157	30.8	0	0.0	157	30.7
Half to full tuition	19	3.7	0	0.0	19	3.7
Full tuition	54	10.6	0	0.0	54	10.5
More than full tuition	14	2.7	0	0.0	14	2.7
Median Grant Amount	$1,500		$0			

Informational & Library Resources

# of volumes & volume equivalents	357,468	# of professional staff	6
# of titles	123,646	Hours per week with professional staff	64
# of active serial subscriptions	3,660	Hours per week without professional staff	45
Study seating capacity inside the library	333	# of student computer work stations for entire law school	49
Square feet of law library	36,000	# of additional networked connections	0
Square feet of law school (excl. Library)	68,185	Require Laptop Computer?	N

J.D. Attrition (Prior Year)

	Academic	Other	TOTALS	
	#	#	#	%
1st Year	0	10	10	6.1%
2nd Year	0	8	8	4.8%
3rd Year	0	0	0	0.0%
4th Year	0	0	0	0.0%
TOTALS	0	18	18	3.6%

Bar Passage Rates

Jurisdiction	Colorado		
Exam	Sum 96	Win 97	Total
# from school taking bar for the first time	107	8	115
School's pass rate for all first-time takers	92%	88%	91%
State's pass rate for all first-time takers	89%	82%	87%

COLUMBIA UNIVERSITY

435 West 116th Street
New York, NY 10027
(212)854-2640
http://www.columbia.edu/cu/law

ABA Approved Since 1923

The Basics

Type of School: Private Term: Semester

Application deadline: 02/15

Application fee: $65

Financial Aid deadline: 03/01

Can first year start other than Fall? No

Student faculty ratio: 15.8 to 1

Does the University offer:
- housing restricted to law students? Yes
- graduate student housing for which law students are eligible? Yes

Faculty & Administrators

	Total		Men		Women		Minorities	
	Fall	Spr	Fall	Spr	Fall	Spr	Fall	Spr
Full-time	58	57	44	45	14	12	5	6
Other Full-Time	10	11	5	6	5	5	0	0
Deans, librarians, & others who teach > 1/2	3	3	2	2	1	1	1	1
Part-time	38	52	35	44	3	8	1	5
Total	109	123	86	97	23	26	7	12
Deans, librarians, & others who teach < 1/2	4	4	2	2	2	2	0	0

Curriculum

	Full time	Part time
Typical first-year section size	118	0
Is there typically a "small section" of the first year class, other than Legal Writing, taught by full-time faculty?	Yes	No
If yes, typical size offered last year	30	N/A
# of classroom course titles beyond 1st year curriculum	76	0
# of upper division courses, excluding seminars, with an enrollment:		
Under 25	27	0
25 - 49	27	0
50 - 74	11	0
75 - 99	6	0
100 +	20	0
# of seminars	97	0
# of seminar positions available	18	
# of seminar positions filled	1,521	0
# of positions available in simulation courses	607	
# of simulation positions filled	601	0
# of positions available in faculty supervised clinical courses	141	
# of fac. sup. clin. positions filled	138	0
# involved in field placements	93	0
# involved in law journals	529	0
# in moot court or trial competitions	91	0
# of credit hrs required to graduate	83	

J.D. Enrollment & Ethnicity

	Men		Women		Fl-Time		Pt-Time		1st Yr		2nd Yr		3rd Yr		4th Yr		Total		JD Degrees Awarded
	#	%	#	%	#	%	#	%	#	%	#	%	#	%	#	%	#	%	
African-American	54	8.9	81	16.4	135	12.2	0	0.0	45	12.6	47	12.3	43	11.8	0	0.0	135	12.2	31
American Indian	3	0.5	4	0.8	7	0.6	0	0.0	3	0.8	2	0.5	2	0.5	0	0.0	7	0.6	1
Asian American	72	11.8	76	15.4	148	13.4	0	0.0	47	13.1	52	13.6	49	13.5	0	0.0	148	13.4	53
Mexican American	15	2.5	21	4.2	36	3.3	0	0.0	12	3.4	11	2.9	13	3.6	0	0.0	36	3.3	8
Puerto Rican	8	1.3	13	2.6	21	1.9	0	0.0	3	0.8	8	2.1	10	2.7	0	0.0	21	1.9	8
Hispanic American	17	2.8	11	2.2	28	2.5	0	0.0	12	3.4	8	2.1	8	2.2	0	0.0	28	2.5	11
Total Minorities	169	27.7	206	41.6	375	33.9	0	0.0	122	34.1	128	33.4	125	34.3	0	0.0	375	33.9	112
Foreign Nationals	22	3.6	18	3.6	40	3.6	0	0.0	15	4.2	16	4.2	9	2.5	0	0.0	40	3.6	10
Caucasian	419	68.7	271	54.7	690	62.4	0	0.0	221	61.7	239	62.4	230	63.2	0	0.0	690	62.4	231
Total	610	55.2	495	44.8	1105	100.0	0	0.0	358	32.4	383	34.7	364	32.9	0	0.0	1105		353

GPA & LSAT Scores

	Full Time	Part Time	Total
# of apps	5,080	0	5,080
# admits	1,086	0	1,086
# of matrics	358	0	358
75% GPA	3.71	0.00	
25% GPA	3.39	0.00	
75% LSAT	171	0	
25% LSAT	165	0	

Tuition & Fees

	Resident	Non-resident
Full-Time	$25,666	$25,666
Part-Time	$0	$0

Living Expenses

Estimated living expenses for Singles		
Living on campus	Living off campus	Living at home
$13,800	$13,800	$3,725

Financial Aid

	Full-time		Part-time		Total	
	#	%	#	%	#	%
Total # of Students	1105		0		1105	
Total # receiving grants	360	32.6	0	0.0	360	32.6
Less than 1/2 tuition	243	22.0	0	0.0	243	22.0
Half to full tuition	103	9.3	0	0.0	103	9.3
Full tuition	7	0.6	0	0.0	7	0.6
More than full tuition	7	0.6	0	0.0	7	0.6
Median Grant Amount	$8,755		$0			

Informational & Library Resources

# of volumes & volume equivalents	964,628	# of professional staff	19
# of titles	335,440	Hours per week with professional staff	74
# of active serial subscriptions	6,055	Hours per week without professional staff	28
Study seating capacity inside the library	417	# of student computer work stations for entire law school	120
Square feet of law library	71,225	# of additional networked connections	400
Square feet of law school (excl. Library)	109,971	Require Laptop Computer?	N

Employment

	Total	%
Employment status known	352	99.2
Employment status unknown	3	0.8
Employed	346	98.3
Pursuing graduate degrees	2	0.6
Unemployed seeking employment	3	0.9
Unemployed not seeking employment	1	0.3
Type of Employment		
# employed in law firms	237	68.5
# employed in business & industry	15	4.3
# employed in government	6	1.7
# employed in public interest	12	3.5
# employed as judicial clerks	73	21.1
# employed in academia	3	0.9
Geographic Location		
# employed in state	221	63.9
# employed in foreign countries	5	1.4
# of states where employed	28	

J.D. Attrition (Prior Year)

	Academic	Other	TOTALS	
	#	#	#	%
1st Year	0	0	0	0.0%
2nd Year	0	1	1	0.3%
3rd Year	0	0	0	0.0%
4th Year	0	0	0	0.0%
TOTALS	0	1	1	0.1%

Bar Passage Rates

Jurisdiction	New York		
Exam	Sum 96	Win 97	Total
# from school taking bar for the first time	272	19	291
School's pass rate for all first-time takers	92%	95%	92%
State's pass rate for all first-time takers	78%	67%	77%

CONNECTICUT, UNIVERSITY OF

55 Elizabeth Street
Hartford, CT 06105
(860)570-5127
http://www.law.uconn.edu

ABA Approved Since 1933

The Basics

Type of School: Public   Term: Semester
Application deadline: 03/15
Application fee: $30
Financial Aid deadline: 03/15
Can first year start other than Fall? No
Student faculty ratio: 14.1 to 1
Does the University offer:
- housing restricted to law students? No
- graduate student housing for which law students are eligible? No

Faculty & Administrators

	Total		Men		Women		Minorities	
	Fall	Spr	Fall	Spr	Fall	Spr	Fall	Spr
Full-time	32	29	25	25	7	4	3	2
Other Full-Time	3	3	1	1	2	2	0	0
Deans, librarians, & others who teach > 1/2	1	1	1	1	0	0	0	0
Part-time	27	25	23	20	4	5	1	0
Total	63	58	50	47	13	11	4	2
Deans, librarians, & others who teach < 1/2	2	2	1	1	1	1	0	0

Curriculum

	Full time	Part time
Typical first-year section size	63	64
Is there typically a "small section" of the first year class, other than Legal Writing, taught by full-time faculty?	Yes	Yes
If yes, typical size offered last year	25	21
# of classroom course titles beyond 1st year curriculum	70	38
# of upper division courses, excluding seminars, with an enrollment:		
Under 25	29	9
25 - 49	18	10
50 - 74	7	18
75 - 99	0	1
100 +	0	0
# of seminars	31	11
# of seminar positions available	705	
# of seminar positions filled	415	166
# of positions available in simulation courses	133	
# of simulation positions filled	83	34
# of positions available in faculty supervised clinical courses	86	
# of fac. sup. clin. positions filled	73	0
# involved in field placements	80	6
# involved in law journals	85	7
# in moot court or trial competitions	31	0
# of credit hrs required to graduate	86	

J.D. Enrollment & Ethnicity

	Men		Women		Fl-Time		Pt-Time		1st Yr		2nd Yr		3rd Yr		4th Yr		Total		JD Degrees Awarded
	#	%	#	%	#	%	#	%	#	%	#	%	#	%	#	%	#	%	
African-American	18	5.8	15	5.2	21	4.8	12	7.3	9	4.7	8	4.3	12	6.2	4	11.1	33	5.5	11
American Indian	0	0.0	3	1.0	3	0.7	0	0.0	1	0.5	1	0.5	1	0.5	0	0.0	3	0.5	1
Asian American	19	6.1	15	5.2	31	7.1	3	1.8	14	7.4	10	5.4	10	5.2	0	0.0	34	5.6	9
Mexican American	2	0.6	1	0.3	3	0.7	0	0.0	1	0.5	0	0.0	2	1.0	0	0.0	3	0.5	0
Puerto Rican	1	0.3	7	2.4	7	1.6	1	0.6	1	0.5	3	1.6	4	2.1	0	0.0	8	1.3	2
Hispanic American	7	2.2	4	1.4	6	1.4	5	3.0	8	4.2	2	1.1	1	0.5	0	0.0	11	1.8	4
Total Minorities	47	15.0	45	15.5	71	16.2	21	12.7	34	17.9	24	13.0	30	15.5	4	11.1	92	15.2	27
Foreign Nationals	0	0.0	1	0.3	1	0.2	0	0.0	1	0.5	0	0.0	0	0.0	0	0.0	1	0.2	1
Caucasian	266	85.0	245	84.2	367	83.6	144	87.3	155	81.6	161	87.0	163	84.5	32	88.9	511	84.6	168
Total	313	51.8	291	48.2	439	72.7	165	27.3	190	31.5	185	30.6	193	32.0	36	6.0	604		196

GPA & LSAT Scores

	Full Time	Part Time	Total
# of apps	836	312	1,148
# admits	401	130	531
# of matrics	140	55	195
75% GPA	3.48	3.33	
25% GPA	3.08	2.83	
75% LSAT	160	158	
25% LSAT	154	152	

Tuition & Fees

	Resident	Non-resident
Full-Time	$10,928	$22,718
Part-Time	$7,658	$15,878

Living Expenses

Estimated living expenses for Singles		
Living on campus	Living off campus	Living at home
N/A	$12,248	$6,112

Financial Aid

	Full-time		Part-time		Total	
	#	%	#	%	#	%
Total # of Students	439		165		604	
Total # receiving grants	223	50.8	0	0.0	223	36.9
Less than 1/2 tuition	154	35.1	0	0.0	154	25.5
Half to full tuition	40	9.1	0	0.0	40	6.6
Full tuition	2	0.5	0	0.0	2	0.3
More than full tuition	27	6.2	0	0.0	27	4.5
Median Grant Amount	$4,800		$0			

Informational & Library Resources

# of volumes & volume equivalents	458,434	# of professional staff	15
# of titles	146,928	Hours per week with professional staff	70
# of active serial subscriptions	5,716	Hours per week without professional staff	22
Study seating capacity inside the library	797	# of student computer work stations for entire law school	55
Square feet of law library	94,724	# of additional networked connections	396
Square feet of law school (excl. Library)	60,813	Require Laptop Computer?	N

Employment

	Total	%
Employment status known	190	96.9
Employment status unknown	6	3.1
Employed	174	91.6
Pursuing graduate degrees	1	0.5
Unemployed seeking employment	12	6.3
Unemployed not seeking employment	3	1.6
Type of Employment		
# employed in law firms	81	46.6
# employed in business & industry	43	24.7
# employed in government	31	17.8
# employed in public interest	4	2.3
# employed as judicial clerks	11	6.3
# employed in academia	4	2.3
Geographic Location		
# employed in state	126	72.4
# employed in foreign countries	0	0.0
# of states where employed	16	

J.D. Attrition (Prior Year)

	Academic	Other	TOTALS	
	#	#	#	%
1st Year	0	20	20	11%
2nd Year	0	2	2	1.0%
3rd Year	0	0	0	0.0%
4th Year	0	0	0	0.0%
TOTALS	0	22	22	3.5%

Bar Passage Rates

Jurisdiction	Connecticut		
Exam	Sum 96	Win 97	Total
# from school taking bar for the first time	135	29	164
School's pass rate for all first-time takers	87%	93%	88%
State's pass rate for all first-time takers	84%	84%	84%

CORNELL LAW SCHOOL

Myron Taylor Hall
Ithaca, NY 14853-4901
(607)255-5141
www.law.cornell.edu/admit/admit.htm

ABA Approved Since 1923

The Basics

Type of School: Private   Term: Semester

Application deadline: 02/01

Application fee: $65

Financial Aid deadline: 03/16

Can first year start other than Fall? No

Student faculty ratio: 11.1 to 1

Does the University offer:

- housing restricted to law students? Yes
- graduate student housing for which law students are eligible? Yes

Curriculum

	Full time	Part time
Typical first-year section size	75	0
Is there typically a "small section" of the first year class, other than Legal Writing, taught by full-time faculty?	Yes	No
If yes, typical size offered last year	27	N/A
# of classroom course titles beyond 1st year curriculum	123	0
# of upper division courses, excluding seminars, with an enrollment:		
Under 25	28	0
25 - 49	16	0
50 - 74	10	0
75 - 99	5	0
100 +	6	0
# of seminars	35	0
# of seminar positions available	576	
# of seminar positions filled	529	0
# of positions available in simulation courses	185	
# of simulation positions filled	139	0
# of positions available in faculty supervised clinical courses	75	
# of fac. sup. clin. positions filled	71	0
# involved in field placements	46	0
# involved in law journals	239	0
# in moot court or trial competitions	76	0
# of credit hrs required to graduate	84	

Faculty & Administrators

	Total		Men		Women		Minorities	
	Fall	Spr	Fall	Spr	Fall	Spr	Fall	Spr
Full-time	43	34	29	25	14	9	2	3
Other Full-Time	3	2	1	1	2	1	0	0
Deans, librarians, & others who teach > 1/2	3	3	2	2	1	1	0	0
Part-time	10	9	10	9	0	0	0	1
Total	59	48	42	37	17	11	2	4
Deans, librarians, & others who teach < 1/2	0	0	0	0	0	0	0	0

J.D. Enrollment & Ethnicity

	Men		Women		Fl-Time		Pt-Time		1st Yr		2nd Yr		3rd Yr		4th Yr		Total		JD Degrees Awarded
	#	%	#	%	#	%	#	%	#	%	#	%	#	%	#	%	#	%	
African-American	14	4.5	26	11.6	40	7.5	0	0.0	12	6.7	15	8.2	13	7.5	0	0.0	40	7.5	10
American Indian	9	2.9	6	2.7	15	2.8	0	0.0	5	2.8	5	2.7	5	2.9	0	0.0	15	2.8	1
Asian American	33	10.6	32	14.3	65	12.1	0	0.0	21	11.7	28	15.3	16	9.2	0	0.0	65	12.1	21
Mexican American	5	1.6	4	1.8	9	1.7	0	0.0	3	1.7	3	1.6	3	1.7	0	0.0	9	1.7	1
Puerto Rican	5	1.6	4	1.8	9	1.7	0	0.0	2	1.1	1	0.5	6	3.4	0	0.0	9	1.7	3
Hispanic American	7	2.2	4	1.8	11	2.1	0	0.0	5	2.8	3	1.6	3	1.7	0	0.0	11	2.1	5
Total Minorities	73	23.4	76	33.9	149	27.8	0	0.0	48	26.8	55	30.1	46	26.4	0	0.0	149	27.8	41
Foreign Nationals	10	3.2	12	5.4	22	4.1	0	0.0	10	5.6	4	2.2	8	4.6	0	0.0	22	4.1	8
Caucasian	229	73.4	136	60.7	365	68.1	0	0.0	121	67.6	124	67.8	120	69.0	0	0.0	365	68.1	144
Total	312	58.2	224	41.8	536	100.0	0	0.0	179	33.4	183	34.1	174	32.5	0	0.0	536		193

GPA & LSAT Scores

	Full Time	Part Time	Total
# of apps	2,980	0	2,980
# admits	864	0	864
# of matrics	182	0	182
75% GPA	3.78	0.00	
25% GPA	3.39	0.00	
75% LSAT	166	0	
25% LSAT	163	0	

Tuition & Fees

	Resident	Non-resident
Full-Time	$23,100	$23,100
Part-Time	$0	$0

Living Expenses

Estimated living expenses for Singles		
Living on campus	Living off campus	Living at home
$11,850	$11,850	N/A

Employment

	Total	%
Employment status known	166	92.2
Employment status unknown	14	7.8
Employed	157	94.6
Pursuing graduate degrees	6	3.6
Unemployed seeking employment	3	1.8
Unemployed not seeking employment	0	0.0
Type of Employment		
# employed in law firms	106	67.5
# employed in business & industry	3	1.9
# employed in government	9	5.7
# employed in public interest	4	2.5
# employed as judicial clerks	27	17.2
# employed in academia	8	5.1
Geographic Location		
# employed in state	39	24.8
# employed in foreign countries	1	0.6
# of states where employed	27	

Financial Aid

	Full-time		Part-time		Total	
	#	%	#	%	#	%
Total # of Students	536		0		536	
Total # receiving grants	258	48.1	0	0.0	258	48.1
Less than 1/2 tuition	213	39.7	0	0.0	213	39.7
Half to full tuition	45	8.4	0	0.0	45	8.4
Full tuition	0	0.0	0	0.0	0	0.0
More than full tuition	0	0.0	0	0.0	0	0.0
Median Grant Amount	$7,225		$0			

Informational & Library Resources

# of volumes & volume equivalents	585,501	# of professional staff	7
# of titles	173,628	Hours per week with professional staff	61
# of active serial subscriptions	6,159	Hours per week without professional staff	24
Study seating capacity inside the library	404	# of student computer work stations for entire law school	81
Square feet of law library	51,534	# of additional networked connections	8
Square feet of law school (excl. Library)	96,956	Require Laptop Computer?	

J.D. Attrition (Prior Year)

	Academic	Other	TOTALS	
	#	#	#	%
1st Year	0	2	2	1.1%
2nd Year	0	6	6	3.2%
3rd Year	0	2	2	1.1%
4th Year	0	0	0	0.0%
TOTALS	0	10	10	1.8%

Bar Passage Rates

Jurisdiction	New York			Massachusetts		
Exam	Sum 96	Win 97	Total	Sum 96	Win 97	Total
# from school taking bar for the first time	92	7	99	22	0	22
School's pass rate for all first-time takers	91%	100%	92%	100%		100%
State's pass rate for all first-time takers	78%	67%	77%	83%	76%	81%

CREIGHTON UNIVERSITY

2500 California Plaza
Omaha, NE 68178
(402)280-2872
http://www.creighton.edu/culaw

ABA
Approved
Since
1924

The Basics

Type of School: Private Term: Semester
Application deadline: 05/01
Application fee: $40
Financial Aid deadline: 07/20
Can first year start other than Fall? Yes
Student faculty ratio: 16.8 to 1
Does the University offer:
- housing restricted to law students? No
- graduate student housing for which law students are eligible? Yes

Curriculum

	Full time	Part time
Typical first-year section size	78	0
Is there typically a "small section" of the first year class, other than Legal Writing, taught by full-time faculty?	Yes	No
If yes, typical size offered last year	26	N/A
# of classroom course titles beyond 1st year curriculum	66	0
# of upper division courses, excluding seminars, with an enrollment:		
Under 25	34	0
25 - 49	31	0
50 - 74	14	0
75 - 99	4	0
100 +	0	0
# of seminars	10	0
# of seminar positions available	174	
# of seminar positions filled	156	0
# of positions available in simulation courses	288	
# of simulation positions filled	275	0
# of positions available in faculty supervised clinical courses	30	
# of fac. sup. clin. positions filled	22	0
# involved in field placements	65	0
# involved in law journals	39	0
# in moot court or trial competitions	48	0
# of credit hrs required to graduate	94	

Faculty & Administrators

	Total		Men		Women		Minorities	
	Fall	Spr	Fall	Spr	Fall	Spr	Fall	Spr
Full-time	22	22	15	15	7	7	1	1
Other Full-Time	0	0	0	0	0	0	0	0
Deans, librarians, & others who teach > 1/2	6	6	3	3	3	3	0	0
Part-time	26	28	15	18	11	10	1	1
Total	54	56	33	36	21	20	2	2
Deans, librarians, & others who teach < 1/2	0	0	0	0	0	0	0	0

J.D. Enrollment & Ethnicity

	Men		Women		Fl-Time		Pt-Time		1st Yr		2nd Yr		3rd Yr		4th Yr		Total		JD Degrees Awarded
	#	%	#	%	#	%	#	%	#	%	#	%	#	%	#	%	#	%	
African-American	6	2.2	7	3.8	13	3.0	0	0.0	6	3.8	3	2.0	4	2.8	0	0.0	13	2.9	2
American Indian	2	0.7	1	0.5	3	0.7	0	0.0	2	1.3	1	0.7	0	0.0	0	0.0	3	0.7	0
Asian American	6	2.2	6	3.3	12	2.8	0	0.0	3	1.9	6	3.9	3	2.1	0	0.0	12	2.7	2
Mexican American	4	1.5	2	1.1	6	1.4	0	0.0	4	2.6	2	1.3	0	0.0	0	0.0	6	1.3	1
Puerto Rican	1	0.4	0	0.0	1	0.2	0	0.0	1	0.6	0	0.0	0	0.0	0	0.0	1	0.2	0
Hispanic American	9	3.4	5	2.7	14	3.2	0	0.0	5	3.2	4	2.6	5	3.5	0	0.0	14	3.1	3
Total Minorities	28	10.5	21	11.5	49	11.3	0	0.0	21	13.5	16	10.5	12	8.5	0	0.0	49	10.9	8
Foreign Nationals	1	0.4	0	0.0	1	0.2	0	0.0	0	0.0	0	0.0	1	0.7	0	0.0	1	0.2	1
Caucasian	238	89.1	161	88.5	382	88.4	17	100.0	135	86.5	136	89.5	128	90.8	0	0.0	399	88.9	150
Total	267	59.5	182	40.5	432	96.2	17	3.8	156	34.7	152	33.9	141	31.4	0	0.0	449		159

GPA & LSAT Scores

	Full Time	Part Time	Total
# of apps	692	24	716
# admits	514	9	523
# of matrics	150	6	156
75% GPA	3.31	3.18	
25% GPA	2.83	2.40	
75% LSAT	152	160	
25% LSAT	146	148	

Tuition & Fees

	Resident	Non-resident
Full-Time	$15,446	$15,446
Part-Time	$10,052	$10,052

Living Expenses

Estimated living expenses for Singles		
Living on campus	Living off campus	Living at home
$11,120	$11,120	$11,120

Financial Aid

	Full-time		Part-time		Total	
	#	%	#	%	#	%
Total # of Students	432		17		449	
Total # receiving grants	141	32.6	0	0.0	141	31.4
Less than 1/2 tuition	80	18.5	0	0.0	80	17.8
Half to full tuition	40	9.3	0	0.0	40	8.9
Full tuition	20	4.6	0	0.0	20	4.5
More than full tuition	1	0.2	0	0.0	1	0.2
Median Grant Amount	$6,000		$0			

Informational & Library Resources

# of volumes & volume equivalents	238,467	# of professional staff	6
# of titles	35,904	Hours per week with professional staff	71
# of active serial subscriptions	3,966	Hours per week without professional staff	33
Study seating capacity inside the library	243	# of student computer work stations for entire law school	32
Square feet of law library	28,325	# of additional networked connections	0
Square feet of law school (excl. Library)	52,250	Require Laptop Computer?	N

Employment

	Total	%
Employment status known	165	96.5
Employment status unknown	6	3.5
Employed	141	85.5
Pursuing graduate degrees	3	1.8
Unemployed seeking employment	18	10.9
Unemployed not seeking employment	3	1.8
Type of Employment		
# employed in law firms	74	52.5
# employed in business & industry	31	22.0
# employed in government	19	13.5
# employed in public interest	6	4.3
# employed as judicial clerks	10	7.1
# employed in academia	1	0.7
Geographic Location		
# employed in state	56	39.7
# employed in foreign countries	0	0.0
# of states where employed	32	

J.D. Attrition (Prior Year)

	Academic	Other	TOTALS	
	#	#	#	%
1st Year	9	14	23	13%
2nd Year	0	1	1	0.7%
3rd Year	0	1	1	0.6%
4th Year	0	0	0	0.0%
TOTALS	9	16	25	5.2%

Bar Passage Rates

Jurisdiction	Nebraska		
Exam	Sum 96	Win 97	Total
# from school taking bar for the first time	63	8	71
School's pass rate for all first-time takers	97%	75%	94%
State's pass rate for all first-time takers	97%	87%	95%

DAYTON, UNIVERSITY OF

300 College Park Ave.
Dayton, OH 45469-2772
(937)229-3211
http://www.udayton.edu/~law

ABA Approved Since 1975

The Basics

Type of School: Private Term: Semester
Application deadline: 05/01
Application fee: $40
Financial Aid deadline: 03/01
Can first year start other than Fall? No
Student faculty ratio: 21.5 to 1
Does the University offer:
- housing restricted to law students? Yes
- graduate student housing for which law students are eligible? Yes

Faculty & Administrators

	Total		Men		Women		Minorities	
	Fall	Spr	Fall	Spr	Fall	Spr	Fall	Spr
Full-time	19	18	14	13	5	5	1	1
Other Full-Time	3	3	0	0	3	3	1	1
Deans, librarians, & others who teach > 1/2	2	2	2	2	0	0	0	0
Part-time	21	23	14	20	7	3	1	1
Total	45	46	30	35	15	11	3	3
Deans, librarians, & others who teach < 1/2	0	0	0	0	0	0	0	0

Curriculum

	Full time	Part time
Typical first-year section size	90	0
Is there typically a "small section" of the first year class, other than Legal Writing, taught by full-time faculty?	No	No
If yes, typical size offered last year	N/A	N/A
# of classroom course titles beyond 1st year curriculum	49	0
# of upper division courses, excluding seminars, with an enrollment:		
Under 25	27	0
25 - 49	15	0
50 - 74	8	0
75 - 99	9	0
100 +	3	0
# of seminars	13	0
# of seminar positions available	260	
# of seminar positions filled	147	0
# of positions available in simulation courses	244	
# of simulation positions filled	201	0
# of positions available in faculty supervised clinical courses	36	
# of fac. sup. clin. positions filled	36	0
# involved in field placements	60	0
# involved in law journals	36	0
# in moot court or trial competitions	25	0
# of credit hrs required to graduate	87	

J.D. Enrollment & Ethnicity

	Men		Women		Fl-Time		Pt-Time		1st Yr		2nd Yr		3rd Yr		4th Yr		Total		JD Degrees Awarded
	#	%	#	%	#	%	#	%	#	%	#	%	#	%	#	%	#	%	
African-American	20	6.8	21	10.8	41	8.4	0	0.0	16	9.0	16	9.3	9	6.4	0	0.0	41	8.4	8
American Indian	1	0.3	1	0.5	2	0.4	0	0.0	1	0.6	1	0.6	0	0.0	0	0.0	2	0.4	0
Asian American	11	3.7	5	2.6	16	3.3	0	0.0	9	5.1	5	2.9	2	1.4	0	0.0	16	3.3	2
Mexican American	0	0.0	0	0.0	0	0.0	0	0.0	0	0.0	0	0.0	0	0.0	0	0.0	0	0.0	0
Puerto Rican	1	0.3	1	0.5	2	0.4	0	0.0	0	0.0	0	0.0	2	1.4	0	0.0	2	0.4	1
Hispanic American	10	3.4	6	3.1	16	3.3	0	0.0	7	4.0	7	4.1	2	1.4	0	0.0	16	3.3	3
Total Minorities	43	14.6	34	17.4	77	15.7	0	0.0	33	18.6	29	16.9	15	10.6	0	0.0	77	15.7	14
Foreign Nationals	1	0.3	1	0.5	2	0.4	0	0.0	1	0.6	1	0.6	0	0.0	0	0.0	2	0.4	0
Caucasian	251	85.1	160	82.1	411	83.9	0	0.0	143	80.8	142	82.6	126	89.4	0	0.0	411	83.9	142
Total	295	60.2	195	39.8	490	100.0	0	0.0	177	36.1	172	35.1	141	28.8	0	0.0	490		156

GPA & LSAT Scores

	Full Time	Part Time	Total
# of apps	1,350	0	1,350
# admits	830	0	830
# of matrics	178	0	178
75% GPA	3.41	0.00	
25% GPA	2.79	0.00	
75% LSAT	154	0	
25% LSAT	146	0	

Tuition & Fees

	Resident	Non-resident
Full-Time	$18,280	$18,280
Part-Time	$0	$0

Living Expenses

Estimated living expenses for Singles		
Living on campus	Living off campus	Living at home
$8,800	$8,800	$8,800

Financial Aid

	Full-time		Part-time		Total	
	#	%	#	%	#	%
Total # of Students	490		0		490	
Total # receiving grants	185	37.8	0	0.0	185	37.8
Less than 1/2 tuition	86	17.6	0	0.0	86	17.6
Half to full tuition	90	18.4	0	0.0	90	18.4
Full tuition	8	1.6	0	0.0	8	1.6
More than full tuition	1	0.2	0	0.0	1	0.2
Median Grant Amount	$9,500		$0			

Informational & Library Resources

# of volumes & volume equivalents	258,941	# of professional staff	5
# of titles	35,628	Hours per week with professional staff	61
# of active serial subscriptions	4,214	Hours per week without professional staff	41
Study seating capacity inside the library	501	# of student computer work stations for entire law school	71
Square feet of law library	46,130	# of additional networked connections	1305
Square feet of law school (excl. Library)	78,401	Require Laptop Computer?	N

Employment

	Total	%
Employment status known	153	96.2
Employment status unknown	6	3.8
Employed	134	87.6
Pursuing graduate degrees	0	0.0
Unemployed seeking employment	15	9.8
Unemployed not seeking employment	4	2.6
Type of Employment		
# employed in law firms	67	50.0
# employed in business & industry	29	21.6
# employed in government	19	14.2
# employed in public interest	8	6.0
# employed as judicial clerks	10	7.5
# employed in academia	1	0.7
Geographic Location		
# employed in state	81	60.4
# employed in foreign countries	0	0.0
# of states where employed	21	

J.D. Attrition (Prior Year)

	Academic	Other	TOTALS	
	#	#	#	%
1st Year	9	17	26	14%
2nd Year	3	3	6	4.2%
3rd Year	0	0	0	0.0%
4th Year	0	0	0	0.0%
TOTALS	12	20	32	6.5%

Bar Passage Rates

Jurisdiction	Ohio		
Exam	Sum 96	Win 97	Total
# from school taking bar for the first time	81	10	91
School's pass rate for all first-time takers	91%	90%	91%
State's pass rate for all first-time takers	90%	90%	90%

DENVER, UNIVERSITY OF

7039 East 18th Street
Denver, CO 80220
(303)871-6000
gopher://gopher.cair.du.edu/1

ABA Approved Since 1928

The Basics

Type of School: Private Term: Semester
Application deadline: 05/01
Application fee: $45
Financial Aid deadline: 02/15
Can first year start other than Fall? No
Student faculty ratio: 23.6 to 1
Does the University offer:
- housing restricted to law students? Yes
- graduate student housing for which law students are eligible? Yes

Faculty & Administrators

	Total		Men		Women		Minorities	
	Fall	Spr	Fall	Spr	Fall	Spr	Fall	Spr
Full-time	34	36	25	27	9	9	3	4
Other Full-Time	4	4	0	0	4	4	0	0
Deans, librarians, & others who teach > 1/2	3	3	2	2	1	1	1	1
Part-time	75	65	54	43	21	22	10	13
Total	116	108	81	72	35	36	14	18
Deans, librarians, & others who teach < 1/2	0	0	0	0	0	0	0	0

Curriculum

	Full time	Part time
Typical first-year section size	87	68
Is there typically a "small section" of the first year class, other than Legal Writing, taught by full-time faculty?	No	No
If yes, typical size offered last year	N/A	N/A
# of classroom course titles beyond 1st year curriculum	75	59
# of upper division courses, excluding seminars, with an enrollment:		
Under 25	33	44
25 - 49	20	17
50 - 74	11	7
75 - 99	13	4
100 +	1	1
# of seminars	11	5
# of seminar positions available	338	
# of seminar positions filled	153	69
# of positions available in simulation courses	318	
# of simulation positions filled	125	158
# of positions available in faculty supervised clinical courses	141	
# of fac. sup. clin. positions filled	96	45
# involved in field placements	260	109
# involved in law journals	89	47
# in moot court or trial competitions	156	82
# of credit hrs required to graduate	90	

J.D. Enrollment & Ethnicity

	Men		Women		Fl-Time		Pt-Time		1st Yr		2nd Yr		3rd Yr		4th Yr		Total		JD Degrees Awarded
	#	%	#	%	#	%	#	%	#	%	#	%	#	%	#	%	#	%	
African-American	8	1.5	7	1.4	11	1.4	4	1.5	4	1.2	6	1.8	4	1.2	1	1.4	15	1.4	6
American Indian	3	0.6	5	1.0	6	0.8	2	0.7	2	0.6	2	0.6	4	1.2	0	0.0	8	0.8	4
Asian American	27	5.0	20	3.9	37	4.7	10	3.7	11	3.3	7	2.1	27	8.3	2	2.9	47	4.5	15
Mexican American	0	0.0	0	0.0	0	0.0	0	0.0	0	0.0	0	0.0	0	0.0	0	0.0	0	0.0	0
Puerto Rican	0	0.0	0	0.0	0	0.0	0	0.0	0	0.0	0	0.0	0	0.0	0	0.0	0	0.0	0
Hispanic American	21	3.9	29	5.6	42	5.3	8	3.0	14	4.2	14	4.3	20	6.2	2	2.9	50	4.7	21
Total Minorities	59	11.0	61	11.8	96	12.2	24	8.9	31	9.3	29	8.8	55	17.0	5	7.1	120	11.4	46
Foreign Nationals	9	1.7	7	1.4	9	1.1	7	2.6	7	2.1	9	2.7	0	0.0	0	0.0	16	1.5	0
Caucasian	470	87.4	450	86.9	682	86.7	238	88.5	295	88.6	291	88.4	269	83.0	65	92.9	920	87.1	260
Total	538	50.9	518	49.1	787	74.5	269	25.5	333	31.5	329	31.2	324	30.7	70	6.6	1056		306

GPA & LSAT Scores

	Full Time	Part Time	Total
# of apps	1,604	232	1,836
# admits	1,006	144	1,150
# of matrics	254	77	331
75% GPA	3.38	3.45	
25% GPA	2.85	2.87	
75% LSAT	157	158	
25% LSAT	151	151	

Tuition & Fees

	Resident	Non-resident
Full-Time	$17,970	$17,970
Part-Time	$13,478	$13,478

Living Expenses

Estimated living expenses for Singles		
Living on campus	Living off campus	Living at home
$11,663	$11,663	$11,663

Employment

	Total	%
Employment status known	150	50.7
Employment status unknown	146	49.3
Employed	127	84.7
Pursuing graduate degrees	3	2.0
Unemployed seeking employment	17	11.3
Unemployed not seeking employment	3	2.0
Type of Employment		
# employed in law firms	62	48.8
# employed in business & industry	26	20.5
# employed in government	17	13.4
# employed in public interest	2	1.6
# employed as judicial clerks	16	12.6
# employed in academia	1	0.8
Geographic Location		
# employed in state	105	82.7
# employed in foreign countries	0	0.0
# of states where employed	5	

Financial Aid

	Full-time		Part-time		Total	
	#	%	#	%	#	%
Total # of Students	787		269		1056	
Total # receiving grants	218	27.7	63	23.4	281	26.6
Less than 1/2 tuition	165	21.0	35	13.0	200	18.9
Half to full tuition	19	2.4	20	7.4	39	3.7
Full tuition	34	4.3	8	3.0	42	4.0
More than full tuition	0	0.0	0	0.0	0	0.0
Median Grant Amount	$6,000		$6,000			

Informational & Library Resources

# of volumes & volume equivalents	314,155	# of professional staff	10
# of titles	112,574	Hours per week with professional staff	82
# of active serial subscriptions	4,743	Hours per week without professional staff	28
Study seating capacity inside the library	624	# of student computer work stations for entire law school	93
Square feet of law library	55,000	# of additional networked connections	0
Square feet of law school (excl. Library)	126,160	Require Laptop Computer?	N

J.D. Attrition (Prior Year)

	Academic	Other	TOTALS	
	#	#	#	%
1st Year	9	24	33	9.7%
2nd Year	4	3	7	2.0%
3rd Year	0	1	1	0.3%
4th Year	0	0	0	0.0%
TOTALS	13	28	41	3.8%

Bar Passage Rates

Jurisdiction	Colorado		
Exam	Sum 96	Win 97	Total
# from school taking bar for the first time	199	50	249
School's pass rate for all first-time takers	86%	74%	84%
State's pass rate for all first-time takers	89%	82%	87%

DEPAUL UNIVERSITY

25 East Jackson Boulevard
Chicago, IL 60604-2287
(312)362-8701
http://www.law.depaul.edu

ABA Approved Since 1925

The Basics

Type of School: Private   Term: Semester
Application deadline: 04/01
Application fee: $40
Financial Aid deadline: 05/01
Can first year start other than Fall? No
Student faculty ratio: 20.7 to 1
Does the University offer:
- housing restricted to law students? No
- graduate student housing for which law students are eligible? No

Faculty & Administrators

	Total		Men		Women		Minorities	
	Fall	Spr	Fall	Spr	Fall	Spr	Fall	Spr
Full-time	39	39	27	27	12	12	5	5
Other Full-Time	6	6	1	1	5	5	0	0
Deans, librarians, & others who teach > 1/2	4	4	1	1	3	3	0	0
Part-time	58	64	35	43	21	21	3	2
Total	107	113	64	72	41	41	8	7
Deans, librarians, & others who teach < 1/2	2	2	0	0	2	2	0	0

Curriculum

	Full time	Part time
Typical first-year section size	85	80
Is there typically a "small section" of the first year class, other than Legal Writing, taught by full-time faculty?	No	No
If yes, typical size offered last year	N/A	N/A
# of classroom course titles beyond 1st year curriculum	83	83
# of upper division courses, excluding seminars, with an enrollment:		
Under 25	35	63
25 - 49	13	27
50 - 74	17	11
75 - 99	9	2
100 +	0	0
# of seminars	17	5
# of seminar positions available	396	
# of seminar positions filled	266	59
# of positions available in simulation courses	517	
# of simulation positions filled	31	486
# of positions available in faculty supervised clinical courses	60	
# of fac. sup. clin. positions filled	44	16
# involved in field placements	104	20
# involved in law journals	79	11
# in moot court or trial competitions	30	6
# of credit hrs required to graduate	86	

J.D. Enrollment & Ethnicity

	Men		Women		Fl-Time		Pt-Time		1st Yr		2nd Yr		3rd Yr		4th Yr		Total		JD Degrees Awarded
	#	%	#	%	#	%	#	%	#	%	#	%	#	%	#	%	#	%	
African-American	21	3.8	25	4.8	24	3.1	22	7.1	12	3.4	16	5.1	11	3.4	7	8.6	46	4.3	13
American Indian	2	0.4	1	0.2	2	0.3	1	0.3	1	0.3	1	0.3	1	0.3	0	0.0	3	0.3	0
Asian American	18	3.2	24	4.6	24	3.1	18	5.8	15	4.2	10	3.2	12	3.7	5	6.2	42	3.9	9
Mexican American	0	0.0	0	0.0	0	0.0	0	0.0	0	0.0	0	0.0	0	0.0	0	0.0	0	0.0	0
Puerto Rican	0	0.0	0	0.0	0	0.0	0	0.0	0	0.0	0	0.0	0	0.0	0	0.0	0	0.0	0
Hispanic American	21	3.8	33	6.4	39	5.1	15	4.9	22	6.2	12	3.8	16	4.9	4	4.9	54	5.0	13
Total Minorities	62	11.2	83	16.0	89	11.6	56	18.1	50	14.1	39	12.4	40	12.3	16	19.8	145	13.5	35
Foreign Nationals	8	1.4	1	0.2	7	0.9	2	0.6	2	0.6	2	0.6	4	1.2	1	1.2	9	0.8	0
Caucasian	485	87.4	435	83.8	669	87.5	251	81.2	302	85.3	273	86.9	281	86.5	64	79.0	920	85.7	274
Total	555	51.7	519	48.3	765	71.2	309	28.8	354	33.0	314	29.2	325	30.3	81	7.5	1074		309

GPA & LSAT Scores

	Full Time	Part Time	Total
# of apps	1,670	358	2,028
# admits	1,174	209	1,383
# of matrics	259	79	338
75% GPA	3.37	3.20	
25% GPA	2.91	2.58	
75% LSAT	156	154	
25% LSAT	151	149	

Tuition & Fees

	Resident	Non-resident
Full-Time	$18,810	$18,810
Part-Time	$12,710	$12,710

Living Expenses

Estimated living expenses for Singles		
Living on campus	Living off campus	Living at home
$12,558	$12,558	$12,558

Employment

	Total	%
Employment status known	313	90.7
Employment status unknown	32	9.3
Employed	270	86.3
Pursuing graduate degrees	6	1.9
Unemployed seeking employment	31	9.9
Unemployed not seeking employment	6	1.9
Type of Employment		
# employed in law firms	141	52.2
# employed in business & industry	63	23.3
# employed in government	40	14.8
# employed in public interest	2	0.7
# employed as judicial clerks	7	2.6
# employed in academia	5	1.9
Geographic Location		
# employed in state	228	84.4
# employed in foreign countries	3	1.1
# of states where employed	16	

Financial Aid

	Full-time		Part-time		Total	
	#	%	#	%	#	%
Total # of Students	765		309		1074	
Total # receiving grants	596	77.9	45	14.6	641	59.7
Less than 1/2 tuition	588	76.9	45	14.6	633	58.9
Half to full tuition	8	1.0	0	0.0	8	0.7
Full tuition	0	0.0	0	0.0	0	0.0
More than full tuition	0	0.0	0	0.0	0	0.0
Median Grant Amount	$1,739		$0			

Informational & Library Resources

# of volumes & volume equivalents	333,791	# of professional staff	8
# of titles	56,875	Hours per week with professional staff	76
# of active serial subscriptions	4,410	Hours per week without professional staff	19
Study seating capacity inside the library	465	# of student computer work stations for entire law school	57
Square feet of law library	36,690	# of additional networked connections	0
Square feet of law school (excl. Library)	40,063	Require Laptop Computer?	N

J.D. Attrition (Prior Year)

	Academic	Other	TOTALS	
	#	#	#	%
1st Year	5	14	19	5.4%
2nd Year	4	17	21	5.9%
3rd Year	2	3	5	1.7%
4th Year	0	0	0	0.0%
TOTALS	11	34	45	4.2%

Bar Passage Rates

Jurisdiction	Illinois		
Exam	Sum 96	Win 97	Total
# from school taking bar for the first time	256	35	291
School's pass rate for all first-time takers	88%	83%	88%
State's pass rate for all first-time takers	86%	84%	86%

DETROIT COLLEGE AT MICHIGAN STATE UNIV.

368 Law College Building
East Lansing, MI 48824-1300
(517)432-6819
http://www.dcl.edu

ABA Approved Since 1941

The Basics

Type of School: Private | Term: Semester

Application deadline: 04/15

Application fee: $50

Financial Aid deadline: 02/01

Can first year start other than Fall? No

Student faculty ratio: 26.6 to 1

Does the University offer:
- housing restricted to law students? No
- graduate student housing for which law students are eligible? Yes

Faculty & Administrators

	Total		Men		Women		Minorities	
	Fall	Spr	Fall	Spr	Fall	Spr	Fall	Spr
Full-time	21	23	12	15	9	8	2	2
Other Full-Time	5	5	3	3	2	2	0	0
Deans, librarians, & others who teach > 1/2	2	2	1	1	1	1	0	0
Part-time	30	26	26	23	4	3	4	3
Total	58	56	42	42	16	14	6	5
Deans, librarians, & others who teach < 1/2	2	2	2	2	0	0	1	1

Curriculum

	Full time	Part time
Typical first-year section size	95	40
Is there typically a "small section" of the first year class, other than Legal Writing, taught by full-time faculty?	No	Yes
If yes, typical size offered last year	N/A	40
# of classroom course titles beyond 1st year curriculum	51	74
# of upper division courses, excluding seminars, with an enrollment:		
Under 25	35	44
25 - 49	19	19
50 - 74	13	7
75 - 99	3	3
100 +	0	0
# of seminars	4	4
# of seminar positions available	151	
# of seminar positions filled	49	41
# of positions available in simulation courses	349	
# of simulation positions filled	203	83
# of positions available in faculty supervised clinical courses	0	
# of fac. sup. clin. positions filled	0	0
# involved in field placements	153	47
# involved in law journals	68	16
# in moot court or trial competitions	23	10
# of credit hrs required to graduate	85	

J.D. Enrollment & Ethnicity

	Men		Women		Fl-Time		Pt-Time		1st Yr		2nd Yr		3rd Yr		4th Yr		Total		JD Degrees Awarded
	#	%	#	%	#	%	#	%	#	%	#	%	#	%	#	%	#	%	
African-American	22	4.9	35	11.8	25	4.8	32	13.9	18	7.5	8	4.0	22	8.6	9	18.0	57	7.6	19
American Indian	2	0.4	3	1.0	4	0.8	1	0.4	1	0.4	3	1.5	1	0.4	0	0.0	5	0.7	0
Asian American	7	1.5	4	1.4	6	1.2	5	2.2	4	1.7	3	1.5	4	1.6	0	0.0	11	1.5	3
Mexican American	0	0.0	0	0.0	0	0.0	0	0.0	0	0.0	0	0.0	0	0.0	0	0.0	0	0.0	0
Puerto Rican	0	0.0	0	0.0	0	0.0	0	0.0	0	0.0	0	0.0	0	0.0	0	0.0	0	0.0	0
Hispanic American	10	2.2	8	2.7	12	2.3	6	2.6	8	3.3	8	4.0	1	0.4	1	2.0	18	2.4	6
Total Minorities	41	9.1	50	16.9	47	9.1	44	19.0	31	12.9	22	11.0	28	10.9	10	20.0	91	12.2	28
Foreign Nationals	15	3.3	12	4.1	26	5.0	1	0.4	7	2.9	13	6.5	7	2.7	0	0.0	27	3.6	4
Caucasian	396	87.6	234	79.1	444	85.9	186	80.5	203	84.2	165	82.5	222	86.4	40	80.0	630	84.2	153
Total	452	60.4	296	39.6	517	69.1	231	30.9	241	32.2	200	26.7	257	34.4	50	6.7	748		185

DETROIT COLLEGE AT MICHIGAN STATE UNIV.

GPA & LSAT Scores

	Full Time	Part Time	Total
# of apps	627	129	756
# admits	389	74	463
# of matrics	139	39	178
75% GPA	3.39	3.46	
25% GPA	2.80	2.74	
75% LSAT	155	155	
25% LSAT	147	146	

Tuition & Fees

	Resident	Non-resident
Full-Time	$14,732	$14,732
Part-Time	$11,050	$11,050

Living Expenses

Estimated living expenses for Singles		
Living on campus	Living off campus	Living at home
$9,910	$13,655	$8,680

Employment

	Total	%
Employment status known	171	85.5
Employment status unknown	29	14.5
Employed	151	88.3
Pursuing graduate degrees	2	1.2
Unemployed seeking employment	16	9.4
Unemployed not seeking employment	2	1.2
Type of Employment		
# employed in law firms	81	53.6
# employed in business & industry	32	21.2
# employed in government	15	9.9
# employed in public interest	2	1.3
# employed as judicial clerks	9	6.0
# employed in academia	2	1.3
Geographic Location		
# employed in state	139	92.1
# employed in foreign countries	5	3.3
# of states where employed	6	

Financial Aid

	Full-time		Part-time		Total	
	#	%	#	%	#	%
Total # of Students	517		231		748	
Total # receiving grants	38	7.4	15	6.5	53	7.1
Less than 1/2 tuition	0	0.0	0	0.0	0	0.0
Half to full tuition	27	5.2	7	3.0	34	4.5
Full tuition	11	2.1	8	3.5	19	2.5
More than full tuition	0	0.0	0	0.0	0	0.0
Median Grant Amount	$7,366		$11,050			

Informational & Library Resources

# of volumes & volume equivalents	230,215	# of professional staff	6
# of titles	104,231	Hours per week with professional staff	64
# of active serial subscriptions	2,920	Hours per week without professional staff	45
Study seating capacity inside the library	455	# of student computer work stations for entire law school	49
Square feet of law library	42,000	# of additional networked connections	999
Square feet of law school (excl. Library)	54,713	Require Laptop Computer?	

J.D. Attrition (Prior Year)

	Academic	Other	TOTALS	
	#	#	#	%
1st Year	4	1	5	2.8%
2nd Year	2	9	11	4.2%
3rd Year	0	0	0	0.0%
4th Year	0	0	0	0.0%
TOTALS	6	10	16	2.4%

Bar Passage Rates

Jurisdiction	Michigan		
Exam	Sum 96	Win 97	Total
# from school taking bar for the first time	115	62	177
School's pass rate for all first-time takers	82%	87%	84%
State's pass rate for all first-time takers	84%	86%	85%

DETROIT MERCY, UNIVERSITY OF

651 E. Jefferson
Detroit, MI 48226
(313)596-0200
website is currently under construction

ABA Approved Since 1933

The Basics

Type of School: Private   Term: Semester
Application deadline: 04/15
Application fee: $50
Financial Aid deadline: 04/01
Can first year start other than Fall? No
Student faculty ratio: 18.5 to 1
Does the University offer:
- housing restricted to law students? No
- graduate student housing for which law students are eligible? No

Faculty & Administrators

	Total		Men		Women		Minorities	
	Fall	Spr	Fall	Spr	Fall	Spr	Fall	Spr
Full-time	18	19	15	15	3	4	1	1
Other Full-Time	3	3	0	0	3	3	1	1
Deans, librarians, & others who teach > 1/2	5	5	4	4	1	1	0	0
Part-time	26	34	21	23	5	11	3	1
Total	52	61	40	42	12	19	5	3
Deans, librarians, & others who teach < 1/2	1	1	1	1	0	0	0	0

Curriculum

	Full time	Part time
Typical first-year section size	45	55
Is there typically a "small section" of the first year class, other than Legal Writing, taught by full-time faculty?	No	No
If yes, typical size offered last year	N/A	N/A
# of classroom course titles beyond 1st year curriculum	66	50
# of upper division courses, excluding seminars, with an enrollment:		
Under 25	33	18
25 - 49	15	14
50 - 74	4	6
75 - 99	4	1
100 +	0	1
# of seminars	13	10
# of seminar positions available	345	
# of seminar positions filled	105	127
# of positions available in simulation courses	393	
# of simulation positions filled	212	86
# of positions available in faculty supervised clinical courses	39	
# of fac. sup. clin. positions filled	27	12
# involved in field placements	49	23
# involved in law journals	116	27
# in moot court or trial competitions	31	12
# of credit hrs required to graduate	90	

J.D. Enrollment & Ethnicity

	Men		Women		Fl-Time		Pt-Time		1st Yr		2nd Yr		3rd Yr		4th Yr		Total		JD Degrees Awarded
	#	%	#	%	#	%	#	%	#	%	#	%	#	%	#	%	#	%	
African-American	22	8.3	29	12.0	12	4.5	39	16.5	17	11.8	4	3.2	16	9.4	14	20.9	51	10.1	23
American Indian	0	0.0	1	0.4	0	0.0	1	0.4	1	0.7	0	0.0	0	0.0	0	0.0	1	0.2	0
Asian American	7	2.6	2	0.8	3	1.1	6	2.5	5	3.5	3	2.4	0	0.0	1	1.5	9	1.8	11
Mexican American	2	0.8	0	0.0	2	0.7	0	0.0	0	0.0	2	1.6	0	0.0	0	0.0	2	0.4	0
Puerto Rican	0	0.0	2	0.8	1	0.4	1	0.4	2	1.4	0	0.0	0	0.0	0	0.0	2	0.4	0
Hispanic American	0	0.0	2	0.8	1	0.4	1	0.4	2	1.4	0	0.0	0	0.0	0	0.0	2	0.4	3
Total Minorities	31	11.7	36	14.9	19	7.1	48	20.3	27	18.8	9	7.2	16	9.4	15	22.4	67	13.2	37
Foreign Nationals	19	7.2	15	6.2	8	3.0	26	11.0	0	0.0	2	1.6	22	12.9	10	14.9	34	6.7	28
Caucasian	215	81.1	190	78.8	242	90.0	163	68.8	117	81.3	114	91.2	132	77.6	42	62.7	405	80.0	162
Total	265	52.4	241	47.6	269	53.2	237	46.8	144	28.5	125	24.7	170	33.6	67	13.2	506		227

DETROIT MERCY, UNIVERSITY OF

GPA & LSAT Scores

	Full Time	Part Time	Total
# of apps	552	132	684
# admits	328	90	418
# of matrics	92	55	147
75% GPA	3.30	3.32	
25% GPA	2.72	2.59	
75% LSAT	151	150	
25% LSAT	144	145	

Tuition & Fees

	Resident	Non-resident
Full-Time	$15,450	$15,450
Part-Time	$11,046	$11,046

Living Expenses

Estimated living expenses for Singles		
Living on campus	Living off campus	Living at home
N/A	$11,853	$6,976

Employment

	Total	%
Employment status known	73	31.3
Employment status unknown	160	68.7
Employed	71	97.3
Pursuing graduate degrees	1	1.4
Unemployed seeking employment	1	1.4
Unemployed not seeking employment	0	0.0
Type of Employment		
# employed in law firms	35	49.3
# employed in business & industry	14	19.7
# employed in government	14	19.7
# employed in public interest	0	0.0
# employed as judicial clerks	8	11.3
# employed in academia	0	0.0
Geographic Location		
# employed in state	67	94.4
# employed in foreign countries	1	1.4
# of states where employed	4	

Financial Aid

	Full-time		Part-time		Total	
	#	%	#	%	#	%
Total # of Students	269		237		506	
Total # receiving grants	69	25.7	24	10.1	93	18.4
Less than 1/2 tuition	21	7.8	4	1.7	25	4.9
Half to full tuition	46	17.1	17	7.2	63	12.5
Full tuition	2	0.7	2	0.8	4	0.8
More than full tuition	0	0.0	1	0.4	1	0.2
Median Grant Amount	$7,500		$5,390			

Informational & Library Resources

# of volumes & volume equivalents	296,757	# of professional staff	6
# of titles	121,389	Hours per week with professional staff	92
# of active serial subscriptions	3,495	Hours per week without professional staff	0
Study seating capacity inside the library	406	# of student computer work stations for entire law school	42
Square feet of law library	23,839	# of additional networked connections	0
Square feet of law school (excl. Library)	47,241	Require Laptop Computer?	N

J.D. Attrition (Prior Year)

	Academic	Other	TOTALS	
	#	#	#	%
1st Year	23	26	49	31%
2nd Year	2	1	3	1.7%
3rd Year	0	0	0	0.0%
4th Year	0	0	0	0.0%
TOTALS	25	27	52	8.5%

Bar Passage Rates

Jurisdiction	Michigan		
Exam	Sum 96	Win 97	Total
# from school taking bar for the first time	174	31	205
School's pass rate for all first-time takers	79%	77%	79%
State's pass rate for all first-time takers	84%	86%	85%

DRAKE UNIVERSITY

2507 University Avenue
Des Moines, IA 50311
(515)271-2824
http://www.drake.edu

ABA Approved Since 1923

The Basics

Type of School: Private Term: Semester
Application deadline: 03/01
Application fee: $35
Financial Aid deadline: 03/01
Can first year start other than Fall? Yes
Student faculty ratio: 16.8 to 1
Does the University offer:
- housing restricted to law students? No
- graduate student housing for which law students are eligible? Yes

Faculty & Administrators

	Total		Men		Women		Minorities	
	Fall	Spr	Fall	Spr	Fall	Spr	Fall	Spr
Full-time	20	22	14	15	6	7	1	1
Other Full-Time	1	1	0	0	1	1	0	0
Deans, librarians, & others who teach > 1/2	2	2	2	2	0	0	0	0
Part-time	16	15	8	9	8	6	0	0
Total	39	40	24	26	15	14	1	1
Deans, librarians, & others who teach < 1/2	1	1	1	1	0	0	0	0

Curriculum

	Full time	Part time
Typical first-year section size	79	0
Is there typically a "small section" of the first year class, other than Legal Writing, taught by full-time faculty?	No	No
If yes, typical size offered last year	N/A	N/A
# of classroom course titles beyond 1st year curriculum	150	0
# of upper division courses, excluding seminars, with an enrollment:		
Under 25	93	0
25 - 49	21	0
50 - 74	14	0
75 - 99	3	0
100 +	0	0
# of seminars	8	0
# of seminar positions available	160	
# of seminar positions filled	140	0
# of positions available in simulation courses	453	
# of simulation positions filled	381	0
# of positions available in faculty supervised clinical courses	175	
# of fac. sup. clin. positions filled	114	0
# involved in field placements	124	0
# involved in law journals	123	0
# in moot court or trial competitions	71	0
# of credit hrs required to graduate	90	

J.D. Enrollment & Ethnicity

	Men		Women		Fl-Time		Pt-Time		1st Yr		2nd Yr		3rd Yr		4th Yr		Total		JD Degrees Awarded
	#	%	#	%	#	%	#	%	#	%	#	%	#	%	#	%	#	%	
African-American	7	3.0	7	4.0	14	3.5	0	0.0	6	4.9	7	4.9	1	0.7	0	0.0	14	3.4	5
American Indian	2	0.9	3	1.7	5	1.3	0	0.0	0	0.0	3	2.1	2	1.4	0	0.0	5	1.2	0
Asian American	7	3.0	2	1.2	8	2.0	1	9.1	4	3.3	1	0.7	4	2.8	0	0.0	9	2.2	7
Mexican American	3	1.3	1	0.6	4	1.0	0	0.0	1	0.8	2	1.4	1	0.7	0	0.0	4	1.0	1
Puerto Rican	0	0.0	1	0.6	1	0.3	0	0.0	0	0.0	1	0.7	0	0.0	0	0.0	1	0.2	0
Hispanic American	4	1.7	5	2.9	8	2.0	1	9.1	4	3.3	4	2.8	1	0.7	0	0.0	9	2.2	4
Total Minorities	23	9.9	19	11.0	40	10.1	2	18.2	15	12.2	18	12.7	9	6.4	0	0.0	42	10.3	17
Foreign Nationals	3	1.3	2	1.2	4	1.0	1	9.1	1	0.8	3	2.1	1	0.7	0	0.0	5	1.2	1
Caucasian	207	88.8	152	87.9	351	88.9	8	72.7	107	87.0	121	85.2	131	92.9	0	0.0	359	88.4	132
Total	233	57.4	173	42.6	395	97.3	11	2.7	123	30.3	142	35.0	141	34.7	0	0.0	406		150

DRAKE UNIVERSITY

GPA & LSAT Scores

	Full Time	Part Time	Total
# of apps	860	28	888
# admits	391	4	395
# of matrics	120	3	123
75% GPA	3.51	0.00	
25% GPA	2.89	0.00	
75% LSAT	156	0	
25% LSAT	151	0	

Tuition & Fees

	Resident	Non-resident
Full-Time	$16,330	$16,330
Part-Time	$550	$550

Living Expenses

Estimated living expenses for Singles		
Living on campus	Living off campus	Living at home
N/A	$10,679	$5,754

Financial Aid

	Full-time		Part-time		Total	
	#	%	#	%	#	%
Total # of Students	395		11		406	
Total # receiving grants	242	61.3	0	0.0	242	59.6
Less than 1/2 tuition	171	43.3	0	0.0	171	42.1
Half to full tuition	45	11.4	0	0.0	45	11.1
Full tuition	26	6.6	0	0.0	26	6.4
More than full tuition	0	0.0	0	0.0	0	0.0
Median Grant Amount	$4,060		$0			

Informational & Library Resources

# of volumes & volume equivalents	265,170	# of professional staff	4
# of titles	33,270	Hours per week with professional staff	40
# of active serial subscriptions	3,066	Hours per week without professional staff	69
Study seating capacity inside the library	705	# of student computer work stations for entire law school	88
Square feet of law library	50,541	# of additional networked connections	5
Square feet of law school (excl. Library)	62,341	Require Laptop Computer?	N

Employment

	Total	%
Employment status known	199	100.0
Employment status unknown	0	0.0
Employed	183	92.0
Pursuing graduate degrees	2	1.0
Unemployed seeking employment	13	6.5
Unemployed not seeking employment	1	0.5
Type of Employment		
# employed in law firms	99	54.1
# employed in business & industry	33	18.0
# employed in government	28	15.3
# employed in public interest	6	3.3
# employed as judicial clerks	12	6.6
# employed in academia	3	1.6
Geographic Location		
# employed in state	79	43.2
# employed in foreign countries	0	0.0
# of states where employed	27	

J.D. Attrition (Prior Year)

	Academic	Other	TOTALS	
	#	#	#	%
1st Year	0	4	4	2.5%
2nd Year	2	1	3	2.1%
3rd Year	0	3	3	1.9%
4th Year	0	0	0	0.0%
TOTALS	2	8	10	2.2%

Bar Passage Rates

Jurisdiction	Iowa		
Exam	Sum 96	Win 97	Total
# from school taking bar for the first time	81	20	101
School's pass rate for all first-time takers	81%	80%	81%
State's pass rate for all first-time takers	78%	80%	78%

DUKE UNIVERSITY

P.O. Box 90362
Science Drive and Toweview Road
Durham, NC 27708-0362
(919)613-7000
http://www.law.duke.edu

ABA Approved Since 1931

The Basics

Type of School: Private — Term: Semester
Application deadline: 02/01
Application fee: $65
Financial Aid deadline: 06/15
Can first year start other than Fall? Yes
Student faculty ratio: 15.4 to 1
Does the University offer:
- housing restricted to law students? No
- graduate student housing for which law students are eligible? No

Curriculum

	Full time	Part time
Typical first-year section size	85	0
Is there typically a "small section" of the first year class, other than Legal Writing, taught by full-time faculty?	Yes	No
If yes, typical size offered last year	28	N/A
# of classroom course titles beyond 1st year curriculum	100	0
# of upper division courses, excluding seminars, with an enrollment:		
Under 25	20	0
25 - 49	18	0
50 - 74	9	0
75 - 99	6	0
100 +	6	0
# of seminars	44	0
# of seminar positions available	722	
# of seminar positions filled	666	0
# of positions available in simulation courses	86	
# of simulation positions filled	60	0
# of positions available in faculty supervised clinical courses	20	
# of fac. sup. clin. positions filled	20	0
# involved in field placements	80	0
# involved in law journals	140	0
# in moot court or trial competitions	60	0
# of credit hrs required to graduate	84	

Faculty & Administrators

	Total		Men		Women		Minorities	
	Fall	Spr	Fall	Spr	Fall	Spr	Fall	Spr
Full-time	33	33	23	25	10	8	4	3
Other Full-Time	1	1	0	0	1	1	0	0
Deans, librarians, & others who teach > 1/2	1	1	0	0	1	1	0	0
Part-time	24	22	17	16	7	6	0	2
Total	59	57	40	41	19	16	4	5
Deans, librarians, & others who teach < 1/2	8	8	2	2	6	6	0	0

J.D. Enrollment & Ethnicity

	Men		Women		Fl-Time		Pt-Time		1st Yr		2nd Yr		3rd Yr		4th Yr		Total		JD Degrees Awarded
	#	%	#	%	#	%	#	%	#	%	#	%	#	%	#	%	#	%	
African-American	23	6.4	30	12.0	53	8.7	0	0.0	18	8.9	21	10.4	14	6.8	0	0.0	53	8.7	13
American Indian	1	0.3	0	0.0	1	0.2	0	0.0	0	0.0	0	0.0	1	0.5	0	0.0	1	0.2	1
Asian American	15	4.1	12	4.8	27	4.4	0	0.0	12	5.9	10	5.0	5	2.4	0	0.0	27	4.4	7
Mexican American	0	0.0	0	0.0	0	0.0	0	0.0	0	0.0	0	0.0	0	0.0	0	0.0	0	0.0	0
Puerto Rican	0	0.0	0	0.0	0	0.0	0	0.0	0	0.0	0	0.0	0	0.0	0	0.0	0	0.0	0
Hispanic American	9	2.5	7	2.8	16	2.6	0	0.0	5	2.5	5	2.5	6	2.9	0	0.0	16	2.6	5
Total Minorities	48	13.3	49	19.7	97	15.9	0	0.0	35	17.2	36	17.8	26	12.6	0	0.0	97	15.9	26
Foreign Nationals	14	3.9	8	3.2	22	3.6	0	0.0	5	2.5	13	6.4	4	1.9	0	0.0	22	3.6	0
Caucasian	300	82.9	192	77.1	492	80.5	0	0.0	163	80.3	153	75.7	176	85.4	0	0.0	492	80.5	169
Total	362	59.2	249	40.8	611	100.0	0	0.0	203	33.2	202	33.1	206	33.7	0	0.0	611		195

GPA & LSAT Scores

	Full Time	Part Time	Total
# of apps	3,152	0	3,152
# admits	911	0	911
# of matrics	205	0	205
75% GPA	3.78	0.00	
25% GPA	3.29	0.00	
75% LSAT	169	0	
25% LSAT	161	0	

Tuition & Fees

	Resident	Non-resident
Full-Time	$24,537	$24,537
Part-Time	$0	$0

Living Expenses

Estimated living expenses for Singles		
Living on campus	Living off campus	Living at home
$11,610	$11,610	$11,610

Employment

	Total	%
Employment status known	185	100.0
Employment status unknown	0	0.0
Employed	182	98.4
Pursuing graduate degrees	2	1.1
Unemployed seeking employment	1	0.5
Unemployed not seeking employment	0	0.0
Type of Employment		
# employed in law firms	148	81.3
# employed in business & industry	4	2.2
# employed in government	5	2.7
# employed in public interest	2	1.1
# employed as judicial clerks	23	12.6
# employed in academia	0	0.0
Geographic Location		
# employed in state	14	7.7
# employed in foreign countries	0	0.0
# of states where employed	31	

Financial Aid

	Full-time		Part-time		Total	
	#	%	#	%	#	%
Total # of Students	611		0		611	
Total # receiving grants	353	57.8	0	0.0	353	57.8
Less than 1/2 tuition	326	53.4	0	0.0	326	53.4
Half to full tuition	27	4.4	0	0.0	27	4.4
Full tuition	0	0.0	0	0.0	0	0.0
More than full tuition	0	0.0	0	0.0	0	0.0
Median Grant Amount	$7,000		$0			

Informational & Library Resources

# of volumes & volume equivalents	509,776	# of professional staff	8
# of titles	185,327	Hours per week with professional staff	68
# of active serial subscriptions	7,090	Hours per week without professional staff	43
Study seating capacity inside the library	451	# of student computer work stations for entire law school	155
Square feet of law library	65,265	# of additional networked connections	192
Square feet of law school (excl. Library)	50,523	Require Laptop Computer?	N

J.D. Attrition (Prior Year)

	Academic	Other	TOTALS	
	#	#	#	%
1st Year	0	9	9	4.5%
2nd Year	0	4	4	1.9%
3rd Year	0	2	2	1.1%
4th Year	0	0	0	0.0%
TOTALS	0	15	15	2.5%

Bar Passage Rates

Jurisdiction	North Carolina			New York		
Exam	Sum 96	Win 97	Total	Sum 96	Win 97	Total
# from school taking bar for the first time	35	6	41	34	6	40
School's pass rate for all first-time takers	97%	83%	95%	97%	100%	98%
State's pass rate for all first-time takers	81%	76%	80%	78%	67%	77%

DUQUESNE UNIVERSITY

900 Locust Street
Pittsburgh, PA 15282
(412)396-6280
http://www.duq.edu/law

ABA Approved Since 1960

The Basics

Type of School: Private

Term: Semester

Application deadline: 04/01

Application fee: $50

Financial Aid deadline: 05/31

Can first year start other than Fall? No

Student faculty ratio: 24.3 to 1

Does the University offer:
- housing restricted to law students? No
- graduate student housing for which law students are eligible? Yes

Faculty & Administrators

	Total		Men		Women		Minorities	
	Fall	Spr	Fall	Spr	Fall	Spr	Fall	Spr
Full-time	19	19	14	14	5	5	2	2
Other Full-Time	3	3	1	1	2	2	0	0
Deans, librarians, & others who teach > 1/2	3	3	3	3	0	0	0	0
Part-time	19	29	15	26	4	3	2	2
Total	44	54	33	44	11	10	4	4
Deans, librarians, & others who teach < 1/2	1	1	1	1	0	0	0	0

Curriculum

	Full time	Part time
Typical first-year section size	57	88
Is there typically a "small section" of the first year class, other than Legal Writing, taught by full-time faculty?	Yes	No
If yes, typical size offered last year	38	N/A
# of classroom course titles beyond 1st year curriculum	55	52
# of upper division courses, excluding seminars, with an enrollment:		
Under 25	18	15
25 - 49	15	11
50 - 74	8	10
75 - 99	3	8
100 +	4	0
# of seminars	7	9
# of seminar positions available	233	
# of seminar positions filled	85	113
# of positions available in simulation courses	202	
# of simulation positions filled	78	94
# of positions available in faculty supervised clinical courses	60	
# of fac. sup. clin. positions filled	26	16
# involved in field placements	95	38
# involved in law journals	41	41
# in moot court or trial competitions	68	39
# of credit hrs required to graduate	86	

J.D. Enrollment & Ethnicity

	Men		Women		Fl-Time		Pt-Time		1st Yr		2nd Yr		3rd Yr		4th Yr		Total		JD Degrees Awarded
	#	%	#	%	#	%	#	%	#	%	#	%	#	%	#	%	#	%	
African-American	13	3.4	16	5.5	13	3.9	16	4.8	9	3.4	7	4.3	7	4.2	6	8.1	29	4.3	10
American Indian	0	0.0	0	0.0	0	0.0	0	0.0	0	0.0	0	0.0	0	0.0	0	0.0	0	0.0	0
Asian American	2	0.5	0	0.0	1	0.3	1	0.3	1	0.4	0	0.0	0	0.0	1	1.4	2	0.3	1
Mexican American	0	0.0	0	0.0	0	0.0	0	0.0	0	0.0	0	0.0	0	0.0	0	0.0	0	0.0	0
Puerto Rican	0	0.0	0	0.0	0	0.0	0	0.0	0	0.0	0	0.0	0	0.0	0	0.0	0	0.0	1
Hispanic American	4	1.1	2	0.7	4	1.2	2	0.6	2	0.8	2	1.2	1	0.6	1	1.4	6	0.9	1
Total Minorities	19	5.0	18	6.2	18	5.3	19	5.8	12	4.5	9	5.6	8	4.8	8	10.8	37	5.5	13
Foreign Nationals	1	0.3	0	0.0	0	0.0	1	0.3	0	0.0	0	0.0	0	0.0	1	1.4	1	0.1	1
Caucasian	358	94.7	271	93.8	319	94.7	310	93.9	252	95.5	153	94.4	159	95.2	65	87.8	629	94.3	155
Total	378	56.7	289	43.3	337	50.5	330	49.5	264	39.6	162	24.3	167	25.0	74	11.1	667		169

GPA & LSAT Scores

	Full Time	Part Time	Total
# of apps	488	179	667
# admits	384	114	498
# of matrics	152	87	239
75% GPA	3.41	3.33	
25% GPA	2.78	2.58	
75% LSAT	154	156	
25% LSAT	149	147	

Tuition & Fees

	Resident	Non-resident
Full-Time	$14,414	$14,414
Part-Time	$11,020	$11,020

Living Expenses

Estimated living expenses for Singles

Living on campus	Living off campus	Living at home
$8,332	$8,332	$3,000

Financial Aid

	Full-time		Part-time		Total	
	#	%	#	%	#	%
Total # of Students	337		330		667	
Total # receiving grants	135	40.1	59	17.9	194	29.1
Less than 1/2 tuition	78	23.1	34	10.3	112	16.8
Half to full tuition	45	13.4	15	4.5	60	9.0
Full tuition	12	3.6	10	3.0	22	3.3
More than full tuition	0	0.0	0	0.0	0	0.0
Median Grant Amount	$3,500		$3,000			

Informational & Library Resources

# of volumes & volume equivalents	218,158	# of professional staff	6
# of titles	59,000	Hours per week with professional staff	78
# of active serial subscriptions	4,442	Hours per week without professional staff	24
Study seating capacity inside the library	246	# of student computer work stations for entire law school	28
Square feet of law library	25,034	# of additional networked connections	0
Square feet of law school (excl. Library)	108,136	Require Laptop Computer?	N

Employment

	Total	%
Employment status known	167	98.8
Employment status unknown	2	1.2
Employed	146	87.4
Pursuing graduate degrees	0	0.0
Unemployed seeking employment	19	11.4
Unemployed not seeking employment	2	1.2
Type of Employment		
# employed in law firms	70	47.9
# employed in business & industry	38	26.0
# employed in government	15	10.3
# employed in public interest	6	4.1
# employed as judicial clerks	15	10.3
# employed in academia	2	1.4
Geographic Location		
# employed in state	130	89.0
# employed in foreign countries	0	0.0
# of states where employed	9	

J.D. Attrition (Prior Year)

	Academic	Other	TOTALS	
	#	#	#	%
1st Year	22	19	41	21%
2nd Year	7	2	9	5.1%
3rd Year	0	0	0	0.0%
4th Year	0	0	0	0.0%
TOTALS	29	21	50	7.9%

Bar Passage Rates

Jurisdiction	Pennsylvania		
Exam	Sum 96	Win 97	Total
# from school taking bar for the first time	148	14	162
School's pass rate for all first-time takers	75%	71%	75%
State's pass rate for all first-time takers	75%	76%	75%

EMORY UNIVERSITY

Gambrell Hall
1301 Clifton Road
Atlanta, GA 30322-2770
(404)727-6816
http://www.law.emory.edu

ABA Approved Since 1923

The Basics

Type of School: Private Term: Semester
Application deadline: 03/01
Application fee: $50
Financial Aid deadline: 03/01
Can first year start other than Fall? No
Student faculty ratio: 19.1 to 1
Does the University offer:
- housing restricted to law students? No
- graduate student housing for which law students are eligible? Yes

Faculty & Administrators

	Total		Men		Women		Minorities	
	Fall	Spr	Fall	Spr	Fall	Spr	Fall	Spr
Full-time	28	26	25	23	3	3	2	2
Other Full-Time	0	0	0	0	0	0	0	0
Deans, librarians, & others who teach > 1/2	7	8	4	5	3	3	0	0
Part-time	43	20	29	11	14	9	3	1
Total	78	54	58	39	20	15	5	3
Deans, librarians, & others who teach < 1/2	0	0	0	0	0	0	0	0

Curriculum

	Full time	Part time
Typical first-year section size	52	0
Is there typically a "small section" of the first year class, other than Legal Writing, taught by full-time faculty?	Yes	No
If yes, typical size offered last year	26	N/A
# of classroom course titles beyond 1st year curriculum	89	0
# of upper division courses, excluding seminars, with an enrollment:		
Under 25	46	0
25 - 49	26	0
50 - 74	20	0
75 - 99	11	0
100 +	4	0
# of seminars	15	0
# of seminar positions available	225	
# of seminar positions filled	204	0
# of positions available in simulation courses	730	
# of simulation positions filled	684	0
# of positions available in faculty supervised clinical courses	12	
# of fac. sup. clin. positions filled	2	0
# involved in field placements	283	0
# involved in law journals	148	0
# in moot court or trial competitions	132	0
# of credit hrs required to graduate	88	

J.D. Enrollment & Ethnicity

	Men		Women		Fl-Time		Pt-Time		1st Yr		2nd Yr		3rd Yr		4th Yr		Total		JD Degrees Awarded
	#	%	#	%	#	%	#	%	#	%	#	%	#	%	#	%	#	%	
African-American	17	4.9	47	15.8	64	10.0	0	0.0	30	14.6	19	9.1	15	6.6	0	0.0	64	10.0	16
American Indian	1	0.3	1	0.3	2	0.3	0	0.0	0	0.0	0	0.0	2	0.9	0	0.0	2	0.3	1
Asian American	17	4.9	18	6.0	35	5.5	0	0.0	8	3.9	13	6.2	14	6.1	0	0.0	35	5.4	17
Mexican American	0	0.0	0	0.0	0	0.0	0	0.0	0	0.0	0	0.0	0	0.0	0	0.0	0	0.0	0
Puerto Rican	0	0.0	0	0.0	0	0.0	0	0.0	0	0.0	0	0.0	0	0.0	0	0.0	0	0.0	0
Hispanic American	24	7.0	22	7.4	45	7.1	1	20.0	14	6.8	19	9.1	13	5.7	0	0.0	46	7.2	7
Total Minorities	59	17.1	88	29.5	146	22.9	1	20.0	52	25.2	51	24.4	44	19.3	0	0.0	147	22.9	41
Foreign Nationals	3	0.9	6	2.0	8	1.3	1	20.0	2	1.0	4	1.9	3	1.3	0	0.0	9	1.4	4
Caucasian	283	82.0	204	68.5	484	75.9	3	60.0	152	73.8	154	73.7	181	79.4	0	0.0	487	75.7	208
Total	345	53.7	298	46.3	638	99.2	5	0.8	206	32.0	209	32.5	228	35.5	0	0.0	643		253

EMORY UNIVERSITY

GPA & LSAT Scores

	Full Time	Part Time	Total
# of apps	2,757	0	2,757
# admits	1,049	0	1,049
# of matrics	207	0	207
75% GPA	3.60	0.00	
25% GPA	3.23	0.00	
75% LSAT	163	0	
25% LSAT	158	0	

Tuition & Fees

	Resident	Non-resident
Full-Time	$22,700	$22,700
Part-Time	$0	$0

Living Expenses

Estimated living expenses for Singles		
Living on campus	Living off campus	Living at home
$9,946	$9,946	$9,946

Employment

	Total	%
Employment status known	216	95.6
Employment status unknown	10	4.4
Employed	196	90.7
Pursuing graduate degrees	5	2.3
Unemployed seeking employment	15	6.9
Unemployed not seeking employment	0	0.0
Type of Employment		
# employed in law firms	123	62.8
# employed in business & industry	38	19.4
# employed in government	15	7.7
# employed in public interest	1	0.5
# employed as judicial clerks	17	8.7
# employed in academia	2	1.0
Geographic Location		
# employed in state	133	67.9
# employed in foreign countries	3	1.5
# of states where employed	25	

Financial Aid

	Full-time		Part-time		Total	
	#	%	#	%	#	%
Total # of Students	638		5		643	
Total # receiving grants	170	26.6	0	0.0	170	26.4
Less than 1/2 tuition	59	9.2	0	0.0	59	9.2
Half to full tuition	46	7.2	0	0.0	46	7.2
Full tuition	50	7.8	0	0.0	50	7.8
More than full tuition	15	2.4	0	0.0	15	2.3
Median Grant Amount	$13,066		$0			

Informational & Library Resources

# of volumes & volume equivalents	332,803	# of professional staff	7
# of titles	103,463	Hours per week with professional staff	60
# of active serial subscriptions	5,368	Hours per week without professional staff	54
Study seating capacity inside the library	451	# of student computer work stations for entire law school	68
Square feet of law library	70,000	# of additional networked connections	427
Square feet of law school (excl. Library)	61,000	Require Laptop Computer?	N

J.D. Attrition (Prior Year)

	Academic	Other	TOTALS	
	#	#	#	%
1st Year	0	1	1	0.5%
2nd Year	0	8	8	3.4%
3rd Year	0	1	1	0.4%
4th Year	0	0	0	0.0%
TOTALS	0	10	10	1.4%

Bar Passage Rates

Jurisdiction	Georgia		
Exam	Sum 96	Win 97	Total
# from school taking bar for the first time	54	13	67
School's pass rate for all first-time takers	93%	85%	91%
State's pass rate for all first-time takers	88%	76%	83%

FLORIDA STATE UNIVERSITY

425 W. Jefferson Street
Tallahassee, FL 32306-1601
(850)644-3400
http://www.law.fsu.edu

ABA Approved Since 1968

The Basics

Type of School: Public — Term: Semester
Application deadline: 02/15
Application fee: $20
Financial Aid deadline: 03/01
Can first year start other than Fall? No
Student faculty ratio: 20.5 to 1
Does the University offer:
- housing restricted to law students? No
- graduate student housing for which law students are eligible? Yes

Faculty & Administrators

	Total		Men		Women		Minorities	
	Fall	Spr	Fall	Spr	Fall	Spr	Fall	Spr
Full-time	26	23	19	18	7	5	4	4
Other Full-Time	7	7	4	4	3	3	1	1
Deans, librarians, & others who teach > 1/2	3	1	1	0	2	1	0	0
Part-time	11	8	8	5	3	3	1	0
Total	47	39	32	27	15	12	6	5
Deans, librarians, & others who teach < 1/2	2	2	2	2	0	0	0	0

Curriculum

	Full time	Part time
Typical first-year section size	70	0
Is there typically a "small section" of the first year class, other than Legal Writing, taught by full-time faculty?	No	No
If yes, typical size offered last year	N/A	N/A
# of classroom course titles beyond 1st year curriculum	95	0
# of upper division courses, excluding seminars, with an enrollment:		
Under 25	36	0
25 - 49	28	0
50 - 74	9	0
75 - 99	6	0
100 +	4	0
# of seminars	32	0
# of seminar positions available	532	
# of seminar positions filled	419	0
# of positions available in simulation courses	259	
# of simulation positions filled	219	0
# of positions available in faculty supervised clinical courses	40	
# of fac. sup. clin. positions filled	36	0
# involved in field placements	111	0
# involved in law journals	182	0
# in moot court or trial competitions	64	0
# of credit hrs required to graduate	88	

J.D. Enrollment & Ethnicity

	Men		Women		Fl-Time		Pt-Time		1st Yr		2nd Yr		3rd Yr		4th Yr		Total		JD Degrees Awarded
	#	%	#	%	#	%	#	%	#	%	#	%	#	%	#	%	#	%	
African-American	27	7.4	51	18.5	78	12.2	0	0.0	26	12.0	29	14.3	23	10.5	0	0.0	78	12.2	23
American Indian	5	1.4	4	1.4	9	1.4	0	0.0	4	1.8	2	1.0	3	1.4	0	0.0	9	1.4	0
Asian American	6	1.6	7	2.5	13	2.0	0	0.0	3	1.4	5	2.5	5	2.3	0	0.0	13	2.0	7
Mexican American	0	0.0	0	0.0	0	0.0	0	0.0	0	0.0	0	0.0	0	0.0	0	0.0	0	0.0	0
Puerto Rican	0	0.0	0	0.0	0	0.0	0	0.0	0	0.0	0	0.0	0	0.0	0	0.0	0	0.0	4
Hispanic American	38	10.4	24	8.7	62	9.7	0	0.0	24	11.1	19	9.4	19	8.6	0	0.0	62	9.7	17
Total Minorities	76	20.9	86	31.2	162	25.4	0	0.0	57	26.3	55	27.1	50	22.7	0	0.0	162	25.3	51
Foreign Nationals	2	0.5	4	1.4	4	0.6	2	100.0	2	0.9	3	1.5	1	0.5	0	0.0	6	0.9	0
Caucasian	286	78.6	186	67.4	472	74.0	0	0.0	158	72.8	145	71.4	169	76.8	0	0.0	472	73.8	152
Total	364	56.9	276	43.1	638	99.7	2	0.3	217	33.9	203	31.7	220	34.4	0	0.0	640		203

GPA & LSAT Scores

	Full Time	Part Time	Total
# of apps	1,896	0	1,896
# admits	643	0	643
# of matrics	221	0	221
75% GPA	3.56	0.00	
25% GPA	3.05	0.00	
75% LSAT	159	0	
25% LSAT	152	0	

Tuition & Fees

	Resident	Non-resident
Full-Time	$4,386	$13,930
Part-Time	$0	$0

Living Expenses

Estimated living expenses for Singles		
Living on campus	Living off campus	Living at home
$14,034	$14,034	$14,034

Employment

	Total	%
Employment status known	171	92.4
Employment status unknown	14	7.6
Employed	151	88.3
Pursuing graduate degrees	8	4.7
Unemployed seeking employment	10	5.8
Unemployed not seeking employment	2	1.2
Type of Employment		
# employed in law firms	82	54.3
# employed in business & industry	12	7.9
# employed in government	35	23.2
# employed in public interest	13	8.6
# employed as judicial clerks	7	4.6
# employed in academia	2	1.3
Geographic Location		
# employed in state	115	76.2
# employed in foreign countries	0	0.0
# of states where employed	7	

Financial Aid

	Full-time		Part-time		Total	
	#	%	#	%	#	%
Total # of Students	638		2		640	
Total # receiving grants	61	9.6	0	0.0	61	9.5
Less than 1/2 tuition	28	4.4	0	0.0	28	4.4
Half to full tuition	13	2.0	0	0.0	13	2.0
Full tuition	16	2.5	0	0.0	16	2.5
More than full tuition	4	0.6	0	0.0	4	0.6
Median Grant Amount	$1,200		$0			

Informational & Library Resources

# of volumes & volume equivalents	390,268	# of professional staff	6
# of titles	140,908	Hours per week with professional staff	50
# of active serial subscriptions	5,686	Hours per week without professional staff	43
Study seating capacity inside the library	429	# of student computer work stations for entire law school	63
Square feet of law library	33,237	# of additional networked connections	0
Square feet of law school (excl. Library)	57,433	Require Laptop Computer?	N

J.D. Attrition (Prior Year)

	Academic	Other	TOTALS	
	#	#	#	%
1st Year	1	4	5	2.5%
2nd Year	0	7	7	3.2%
3rd Year	1	0	1	0.5%
4th Year	0	0	0	0.0%
TOTALS	2	11	13	2.1%

Bar Passage Rates

Jurisdiction	Florida		
Exam	Sum 96	Win 97	Total
# from school taking bar for the first time	141	40	181
School's pass rate for all first-time takers	87%	88%	87%
State's pass rate for all first-time takers	84%	85%	84%

FLORIDA, UNIVERSITY OF

P.O. Box 117620
Gainesville, FL 32611
(352)392-9238
http://www.law.ufl.edu

ABA Approved Since 1925

The Basics

Type of School: Public   Term: Semester
Application deadline: 02/01
Application fee: $20
Financial Aid deadline: 03/15
Can first year start other than Fall? Yes
Student faculty ratio: 20.5 to 1
Does the University offer:
- housing restricted to law students? No
- graduate student housing for which law students are eligible? No

Faculty & Administrators

	Total		Men		Women		Minorities	
	Fall	Spr	Fall	Spr	Fall	Spr	Fall	Spr
Full-time	45	43	33	31	12	12	7	7
Other Full-Time	14	15	2	3	12	12	0	0
Deans, librarians, & others who teach > 1/2	5	5	4	4	1	1	0	0
Part-time	10	11	9	10	1	1	2	1
Total	74	74	48	48	26	26	9	8
Deans, librarians, & others who teach < 1/2	3	3	3	3	0	0	0	0

Curriculum

	Full time	Part time
Typical first-year section size	100	0
Is there typically a "small section" of the first year class, other than Legal Writing, taught by full-time faculty?	No	No
If yes, typical size offered last year	N/A	N/A
# of classroom course titles beyond 1st year curriculum	70	0
# of upper division courses, excluding seminars, with an enrollment:		
Under 25	43	0
25 - 49	43	0
50 - 74	22	0
75 - 99	26	0
100 +	14	0
# of seminars	41	0
# of seminar positions available	716	
# of seminar positions filled	520	0
# of positions available in simulation courses	312	
# of simulation positions filled	302	0
# of positions available in faculty supervised clinical courses	237	
# of fac. sup. clin. positions filled	219	0
# involved in field placements	21	0
# involved in law journals	172	0
# in moot court or trial competitions	48	0
# of credit hrs required to graduate	88	

J.D. Enrollment & Ethnicity

	Men		Women		Fl-Time		Pt-Time		1st Yr		2nd Yr		3rd Yr		4th Yr		Total		JD Degrees Awarded
	#	%	#	%	#	%	#	%	#	%	#	%	#	%	#	%	#	%	
African-American	51	7.9	84	18.1	135	12.2	0	0.0	40	9.7	38	10.2	57	17.8	0	0.0	135	12.2	40
American Indian	1	0.2	3	0.6	4	0.4	0	0.0	2	0.5	1	0.3	1	0.3	0	0.0	4	0.4	1
Asian American	18	2.8	11	2.4	29	2.6	0	0.0	7	1.7	11	3.0	11	3.4	0	0.0	29	2.6	13
Mexican American	0	0.0	0	0.0	0	0.0	0	0.0	0	0.0	0	0.0	0	0.0	0	0.0	0	0.0	0
Puerto Rican	0	0.0	0	0.0	0	0.0	0	0.0	0	0.0	0	0.0	0	0.0	0	0.0	0	0.0	1
Hispanic American	57	8.9	43	9.3	100	9.0	0	0.0	36	8.7	44	11.8	20	6.2	0	0.0	100	9.0	24
Total Minorities	127	19.7	141	30.5	268	24.2	0	0.0	85	20.5	94	25.3	89	27.7	0	0.0	268	24.2	79
Foreign Nationals	4	0.6	3	0.6	7	0.6	0	0.0	5	1.2	1	0.3	1	0.3	0	0.0	7	0.6	3
Caucasian	513	79.7	319	68.9	832	75.2	0	0.0	324	78.3	277	74.5	231	72.0	0	0.0	832	75.2	307
Total	644	58.2	463	41.8	1107	100.0	0	0.0	414	37.4	372	33.6	321	29.0	0	0.0	1107		389

GPA & LSAT Scores

	Full Time	Part Time	Total
# of apps	1,750	0	1,750
# admits	485	0	485
# of matrics	202	0	202
75% GPA	3.78	0.00	
25% GPA	3.38	0.00	
75% LSAT	162	0	
25% LSAT	154	0	

Tuition & Fees

	Resident	Non-resident
Full-Time	$4,036	$12,942
Part-Time	$0	$0

Living Expenses

Estimated living expenses for Singles		
Living on campus	Living off campus	Living at home
$7,840	$9,110	$4,370

Financial Aid

	Full-time		Part-time		Total	
	#	%	#	%	#	%
Total # of Students	1107		0		1107	
Total # receiving grants	135	12.2	0	0.0	135	12.2
Less than 1/2 tuition	73	6.6	0	0.0	73	6.6
Half to full tuition	42	3.8	0	0.0	42	3.8
Full tuition	0	0.0	0	0.0	0	0.0
More than full tuition	20	1.8	0	0.0	20	1.8
Median Grant Amount	$2,378		$0			

Informational & Library Resources

# of volumes & volume equivalents	576,741	# of professional staff	10
# of titles	156,575	Hours per week with professional staff	58
# of active serial subscriptions	7,967	Hours per week without professional staff	44
Study seating capacity inside the library	812	# of student computer work stations for entire law school	97
Square feet of law library	47,654	# of additional networked connections	0
Square feet of law school (excl. Library)	96,875	Require Laptop Computer?	N

Employment

	Total	%
Employment status known	344	95.6
Employment status unknown	16	4.4
Employed	298	86.6
Pursuing graduate degrees	6	1.7
Unemployed seeking employment	28	8.1
Unemployed not seeking employment	12	3.5
Type of Employment		
# employed in law firms	188	63.1
# employed in business & industry	18	6.0
# employed in government	51	17.1
# employed in public interest	3	1.0
# employed as judicial clerks	10	3.4
# employed in academia	0	0.0
Geographic Location		
# employed in state	240	80.5
# employed in foreign countries	3	1.0
# of states where employed	13	

J.D. Attrition (Prior Year)

	Academic	Other	TOTALS	
	#	#	#	%
1st Year	0	10	10	2.4%
2nd Year	1	7	8	2.3%
3rd Year	0	0	0	0.0%
4th Year	0	0	0	0.0%
TOTALS	1	17	18	1.6%

Bar Passage Rates

Jurisdiction	Florida		
Exam	Sum 96	Win 97	Total
# from school taking bar for the first time	196	138	334
School's pass rate for all first-time takers	91%	85%	88%
State's pass rate for all first-time takers	84%	85%	84%

FORDHAM UNIVERSITY

140 West 62nd Street
New York, NY 10023-7485
(212)636-6875
http://www.fordham.edu/law/cle/law_main

ABA Approved Since 1936

The Basics

Type of School: Private Term: Semester
Application deadline: 03/01
Application fee: $60
Financial Aid deadline: 04/30
Can first year start other than Fall? No
Student faculty ratio: 21.5 to 1
Does the University offer:
- housing restricted to law students? Yes
- graduate student housing for which law students are eligible? No

Faculty & Administrators

	Total		Men		Women		Minorities	
	Fall	Spr	Fall	Spr	Fall	Spr	Fall	Spr
Full-time	50	49	39	34	11	15	6	6
Other Full-Time	6	6	0	0	6	6	1	1
Deans, librarians, & others who teach > 1/2	2	2	1	1	1	1	0	0
Part-time	95	116	61	80	32	36	6	5
Total	153	173	101	115	50	58	13	12
Deans, librarians, & others who teach < 1/2	5	5	3	3	2	2	1	1

Curriculum

	Full time	Part time
Typical first-year section size	77	79
Is there typically a "small section" of the first year class, other than Legal Writing, taught by full-time faculty?	Yes	Yes
If yes, typical size offered last year	37	41
# of classroom course titles beyond 1st year curriculum	126	103
# of upper division courses, excluding seminars, with an enrollment:		
Under 25	29	22
25 - 49	39	16
50 - 74	18	4
75 - 99	7	4
100 +	13	6
# of seminars	36	48
# of seminar positions available	1,774	
# of seminar positions filled	583	720
# of positions available in simulation courses	629	
# of simulation positions filled	596	108
# of positions available in faculty supervised clinical courses	427	
# of fac. sup. clin. positions filled	314	19
# involved in field placements	366	6
# involved in law journals	438	4
# in moot court or trial competitions	28	2
# of credit hrs required to graduate	83	

J.D. Enrollment & Ethnicity

	Men		Women		Fl-Time		Pt-Time		1st Yr		2nd Yr		3rd Yr		4th Yr		Total		JD Degrees Awarded
	#	%	#	%	#	%	#	%	#	%	#	%	#	%	#	%	#	%	
African-American	54	6.9	76	12.2	93	8.8	37	10.4	39	8.8	36	7.9	50	11.4	5	6.9	130	9.2	31
American Indian	1	0.1	0	0.0	1	0.1	0	0.0	0	0.0	0	0.0	1	0.2	0	0.0	1	0.1	2
Asian American	48	6.1	55	8.8	89	8.4	14	3.9	32	7.2	34	7.5	35	8.0	2	2.8	103	7.3	34
Mexican American	4	0.5	2	0.3	6	0.6	0	0.0	2	0.5	1	0.2	3	0.7	0	0.0	6	0.4	0
Puerto Rican	31	3.9	27	4.3	34	3.2	24	6.8	14	3.2	21	4.6	19	4.3	4	5.6	58	4.1	14
Hispanic American	20	2.5	22	3.5	35	3.3	7	2.0	16	3.6	13	2.9	11	2.5	2	2.8	42	3.0	15
Total Minorities	158	20.1	182	29.1	258	24.5	82	23.1	103	23.3	105	23.0	119	27.0	13	18.1	340	24.1	96
Foreign Nationals	0	0.0	0	0.0	0	0.0	0	0.0	0	0.0	0	0.0	0	0.0	0	0.0	0	0.0	0
Caucasian	627	79.9	443	70.9	797	75.5	273	76.9	339	76.7	351	77.0	321	73.0	59	81.9	1070	75.9	317
Total	785	55.7	625	44.3	1055	74.8	355	25.2	442	31.3	456	32.3	440	31.2	72	5.1	1410		413

GPA & LSAT Scores

	Full Time	Part Time	Total
# of apps	3,489	611	4,100
# admits	1,085	198	1,283
# of matrics	321	121	442
75% GPA	3.62	3.55	
25% GPA	3.09	2.93	
75% LSAT	164	161	
25% LSAT	159	155	

Tuition & Fees

	Resident	Non-resident
Full-Time	$22,699	$22,699
Part-Time	$17,029	$17,029

Living Expenses

Estimated living expenses for Singles

Living on campus	Living off campus	Living at home
$16,995	$16,995	$4,995

Financial Aid

	Full-time		Part-time		Total	
	#	%	#	%	#	%
Total # of Students	1055		355		1410	
Total # receiving grants	464	44.0	48	13.5	512	36.3
Less than 1/2 tuition	449	42.6	46	13.0	495	35.1
Half to full tuition	6	0.6	1	0.3	7	0.5
Full tuition	9	0.9	1	0.3	10	0.7
More than full tuition	0	0.0	0	0.0	0	0.0
Median Grant Amount	$6,800		$3,500			

Informational & Library Resources

# of volumes & volume equivalents	506,009	# of professional staff	13
# of titles	167,964	Hours per week with professional staff	86
# of active serial subscriptions	3,904	Hours per week without professional staff	36
Study seating capacity inside the library	465	# of student computer work stations for entire law school	42
Square feet of law library	45,755	# of additional networked connections	103
Square feet of law school (excl. Library)	129,398	Require Laptop Computer?	N

Employment

	Total	%
Employment status known	469	90.2
Employment status unknown	51	9.8
Employed	435	92.8
Pursuing graduate degrees	6	1.3
Unemployed seeking employment	23	4.9
Unemployed not seeking employment	5	1.1
Type of Employment		
# employed in law firms	245	56.3
# employed in business & industry	74	17.0
# employed in government	57	13.1
# employed in public interest	3	0.7
# employed as judicial clerks	25	5.7
# employed in academia	3	0.7
Geographic Location		
# employed in state	361	83.0
# employed in foreign countries	2	0.5
# of states where employed	17	

J.D. Attrition (Prior Year)

	Academic	Other	TOTALS	
	#	#	#	%
1st Year	1	7	8	1.7%
2nd Year	0	8	8	1.8%
3rd Year	0	1	1	0.2%
4th Year	0	0	0	0.0%
TOTALS	1	16	17	1.2%

Bar Passage Rates

Jurisdiction	New York		
Exam	Sum 96	Win 97	Total
# from school taking bar for the first time	461	21	482
School's pass rate for all first-time takers	86%	86%	86%
State's pass rate for all first-time takers	78%	67%	77%

FRANKLIN PIERCE LAW CENTER

2 White Street
Concord, NH 03301
(603)228-1541
http://www.fplc.edu

ABA Approved Since 1974

The Basics

Type of School: Private   Term: Semester
Application deadline: 05/01
Application fee: $45
Financial Aid deadline: 05/15
Can first year start other than Fall? No
Student faculty ratio: 22.5 to 1
Does the University offer:
- housing restricted to law students? No
- graduate student housing for which law students are eligible? No

Faculty & Administrators

	Total		Men		Women		Minorities	
	Fall	Spr	Fall	Spr	Fall	Spr	Fall	Spr
Full-time	15	13	12	10	3	3	0	0
Other Full-Time	3	3	1	1	2	2	0	0
Deans, librarians, & others who teach > 1/2	1	1	1	1	0	0	0	0
Part-time	24	34	18	25	6	9	1	1
Total	43	51	32	37	11	14	1	1
Deans, librarians, & others who teach < 1/2	7	7	3	3	4	4	0	0

Curriculum

	Full time	Part time
Typical first-year section size	137	0
Is there typically a "small section" of the first year class, other than Legal Writing, taught by full-time faculty?	Yes	No
If yes, typical size offered last year	24	N/A
# of classroom course titles beyond 1st year curriculum	90	0
# of upper division courses, excluding seminars, with an enrollment:		
Under 25	32	0
25 - 49	24	0
50 - 74	10	0
75 - 99	4	0
100 +	5	0
# of seminars	15	0
# of seminar positions available	250	
# of seminar positions filled	223	0
# of positions available in simulation courses	224	
# of simulation positions filled	220	0
# of positions available in faculty supervised clinical courses	156	
# of fac. sup. clin. positions filled	98	0
# involved in field placements	62	0
# involved in law journals	56	0
# in moot court or trial competitions	32	0
# of credit hrs required to graduate	84	

J.D. Enrollment & Ethnicity

	Men		Women		Fl-Time		Pt-Time		1st Yr		2nd Yr		3rd Yr		4th Yr		Total		JD Degrees Awarded
	#	%	#	%	#	%	#	%	#	%	#	%	#	%	#	%	#	%	
African-American	7	2.8	3	2.0	10	2.5	0	0.0	3	2.2	3	2.1	4	3.1	0	0.0	10	2.5	2
American Indian	2	0.8	3	2.0	5	1.2	0	0.0	3	2.2	0	0.0	2	1.6	0	0.0	5	1.2	0
Asian American	16	6.3	15	10.0	31	7.7	0	0.0	17	12.4	8	5.6	6	4.7	0	0.0	31	7.7	3
Mexican American	0	0.0	0	0.0	0	0.0	0	0.0	0	0.0	0	0.0	0	0.0	0	0.0	0	0.0	0
Puerto Rican	0	0.0	0	0.0	0	0.0	0	0.0	0	0.0	0	0.0	0	0.0	0	0.0	0	0.0	0
Hispanic American	9	3.6	4	2.7	13	3.2	0	0.0	4	2.9	4	2.8	5	3.9	0	0.0	13	3.2	3
Total Minorities	34	13.4	25	16.7	59	14.6	0	0.0	27	19.7	15	10.6	17	13.3	0	0.0	59	14.6	8
Foreign Nationals	13	5.1	3	2.0	16	4.0	0	0.0	4	2.9	6	4.2	6	4.7	0	0.0	16	4.0	0
Caucasian	206	81.4	122	81.3	328	81.4	0	0.0	102	74.5	121	85.2	105	82.0	0	0.0	328	81.4	118
Total	253	62.8	150	37.2	403	100.0	0	0.0	137	34.0	142	35.2	128	31.8	0	0.0	403		126

FRANKLIN PIERCE LAW CENTER

GPA & LSAT Scores

	Full Time	Part Time	Total
# of apps	799	0	799
# admits	546	0	546
# of matrics	133	4	137
75% GPA	3.20	0.00	
25% GPA	2.66	0.00	
75% LSAT	156	0	
25% LSAT	145	0	

Tuition & Fees

	Resident	Non-resident
Full-Time	$15,857	$0
Part-Time	$0	$0

Living Expenses

Estimated living expenses for Singles		
Living on campus	Living off campus	Living at home
N/A	$11,800	$11,800

Financial Aid

	Full-time		Part-time		Total	
	#	%	#	%	#	%
Total # of Students	403		0		403	
Total # receiving grants	245	60.8	3	.3E+8	248	61.5
Less than 1/2 tuition	222	55.1	2	.2E+8	224	55.6
Half to full tuition	10	2.5	1	.1E+8	11	2.7
Full tuition	13	3.2	0	0.0	13	3.2
More than full tuition	0	0.0	0	0.0	0	0.0
Median Grant Amount	$2,191		$1,233			

Informational & Library Resources

# of volumes & volume equivalents	205,960	# of professional staff	5
# of titles	47,395	Hours per week with professional staff	45
# of active serial subscriptions	2,576	Hours per week without professional staff	59
Study seating capacity inside the library	231	# of student computer work stations for entire law school	54
Square feet of law library	20,016	# of additional networked connections	325
Square feet of law school (excl. Library)	53,984	Require Laptop Computer?	N

Employment

	Total	%
Employment status known	113	89.7
Employment status unknown	13	10.3
Employed	98	86.7
Pursuing graduate degrees	0	0.0
Unemployed seeking employment	14	12.4
Unemployed not seeking employment	1	0.9
Type of Employment		
# employed in law firms	62	63.3
# employed in business & industry	19	19.4
# employed in government	9	9.2
# employed in public interest	3	3.1
# employed as judicial clerks	2	2.0
# employed in academia	3	3.1
Geographic Location		
# employed in state	40	40.8
# employed in foreign countries	2	2.0
# of states where employed	20	

J.D. Attrition (Prior Year)

	Academic	Other	TOTALS	
	#	#	#	%
1st Year	2	16	18	12%
2nd Year	2	1	3	2.4%
3rd Year	1	2	3	2.2%
4th Year	0	0	0	0.0%
TOTALS	5	19	24	5.8%

Bar Passage Rates

Jurisdiction	New Hampshire		
Exam	Sum 96	Win 97	Total
# from school taking bar for the first time	46	7	53
School's pass rate for all first-time takers	83%	71%	81%
State's pass rate for all first-time takers	77%	77%	77%

GEORGE MASON UNIVERSITY

3401 North Fairfax Drive
Arlington, VA 22201-4498
(703)993-8000
http://www.gmu.edu/departments/law

ABA Approved Since 1980

The Basics

Type of School: Public Term: Semester
Application deadline: 03/01
Application fee: $35
Financial Aid deadline: 03/01
Can first year start other than Fall? No
Student faculty ratio: 21.7 to 1
Does the University offer:
- housing restricted to law students? No
- graduate student housing for which law students are eligible? No

Faculty & Administrators

	Total		Men		Women		Minorities	
	Fall	Spr	Fall	Spr	Fall	Spr	Fall	Spr
Full-time	23	23	19	19	4	4	2	2
Other Full-Time	1	1	1	1	0	0	0	0
Deans, librarians, & others who teach > 1/2	0	0	0	0	0	0	0	0
Part-time	34	43	29	35	5	8	2	4
Total	58	67	49	55	9	12	4	6
Deans, librarians, & others who teach < 1/2	1	1	1	1	0	0	0	0

Curriculum

	Full time	Part time
Typical first-year section size	133	88
Is there typically a "small section" of the first year class, other than Legal Writing, taught by full-time faculty?	No	No
If yes, typical size offered last year	N/A	N/A
# of classroom course titles beyond 1st year curriculum	58	79
# of upper division courses, excluding seminars, with an enrollment:		
Under 25	34	44
25 - 49	12	20
50 - 74	4	7
75 - 99	1	3
100 +	2	2
# of seminars	9	5
# of seminar positions available	220	
# of seminar positions filled	136	84
# of positions available in simulation courses	153	
# of simulation positions filled	62	91
# of positions available in faculty supervised clinical courses	23	
# of fac. sup. clin. positions filled	23	0
# involved in field placements	67	11
# involved in law journals	33	12
# in moot court or trial competitions	35	5
# of credit hrs required to graduate	90	

J.D. Enrollment & Ethnicity

	Men		Women		Fl-Time		Pt-Time		1st Yr		2nd Yr		3rd Yr		4th Yr		Total		JD Degrees Awarded
	#	%	#	%	#	%	#	%	#	%	#	%	#	%	#	%	#	%	
African-American	10	2.3	16	5.9	12	3.2	14	4.2	5	2.3	4	1.9	12	6.0	5	5.6	26	3.6	4
American Indian	0	0.0	2	0.7	0	0.0	2	0.6	0	0.0	2	0.9	0	0.0	0	0.0	2	0.3	0
Asian American	15	3.4	17	6.3	17	4.5	15	4.5	11	5.2	8	3.8	9	4.5	4	4.4	32	4.5	14
Mexican American	0	0.0	0	0.0	0	0.0	0	0.0	0	0.0	0	0.0	0	0.0	0	0.0	0	0.0	0
Puerto Rican	0	0.0	0	0.0	0	0.0	0	0.0	0	0.0	0	0.0	0	0.0	0	0.0	0	0.0	0
Hispanic American	9	2.0	3	1.1	6	1.6	6	1.8	9	4.2	3	1.4	0	0.0	0	0.0	12	1.7	0
Total Minorities	34	7.7	38	14.0	35	9.3	37	11.0	25	11.7	17	8.0	21	10.6	9	10.0	72	10.1	18
Foreign Nationals	0	0.0	0	0.0	0	0.0	0	0.0	0	0.0	0	0.0	0	0.0	0	0.0	0	0.0	0
Caucasian	409	92.3	234	86.0	343	90.7	300	89.0	188	88.3	195	92.0	179	89.9	81	90.0	643	89.9	163
Total	443	62.0	272	38.0	378	52.9	337	47.1	213	29.8	212	29.7	199	27.8	90	12.6	715		181

GEORGE MASON UNIVERSITY

GPA & LSAT Scores

	Full Time	Part Time	Total
# of apps	1,178	463	1,641
# admits	503	155	658
# of matrics	135	78	213
75% GPA	3.31	3.19	
25% GPA	2.84	2.57	
75% LSAT	159	161	
25% LSAT	155	155	

Tuition & Fees

	Resident	Non-resident
Full-Time	$7,448	$17,990
Part-Time	$5,320	$12,850

Living Expenses

Estimated living expenses for Singles		
Living on campus	Living off campus	Living at home
N/A	$14,953	$5,141

Financial Aid

	Full-time		Part-time		Total	
	#	%	#	%	#	%
Total # of Students	378		337		715	
Total # receiving grants	17	4.5	13	3.9	30	4.2
Less than 1/2 tuition	9	2.4	10	3.0	19	2.7
Half to full tuition	2	0.5	1	0.3	3	0.4
Full tuition	0	0.0	0	0.0	0	0.0
More than full tuition	6	1.6	2	0.6	8	1.1
Median Grant Amount	$5,000		$2,500			

Informational & Library Resources

# of volumes & volume equivalents	359,464	# of professional staff	3
# of titles	143,350	Hours per week with professional staff	66
# of active serial subscriptions	5,065	Hours per week without professional staff	25
Study seating capacity inside the library	250	# of student computer work stations for entire law school	27
Square feet of law library	26,277	# of additional networked connections	16
Square feet of law school (excl. Library)	25,970	Require Laptop Computer?	N

Employment

	Total	%
Employment status known	177	89.4
Employment status unknown	21	10.6
Employed	161	91.0
Pursuing graduate degrees	0	0.0
Unemployed seeking employment	6	3.4
Unemployed not seeking employment	10	5.6
Type of Employment		
# employed in law firms	61	37.9
# employed in business & industry	28	17.4
# employed in government	43	26.7
# employed in public interest	6	3.7
# employed as judicial clerks	23	14.3
# employed in academia	0	0.0
Geographic Location		
# employed in state	69	42.9
# employed in foreign countries	0	0.0
# of states where employed	14	

J.D. Attrition (Prior Year)

	Academic	Other	TOTALS	
	#	#	#	%
1st Year	2	7	9	4.1%
2nd Year	0	7	7	3.5%
3rd Year	0	1	1	0.5%
4th Year	0	0	0	0.0%
TOTALS	2	15	17	2.5%

Bar Passage Rates

Jurisdiction	Virginia		
Exam	Sum 96	Win 97	Total
# from school taking bar for the first time	107	20	127
School's pass rate for all first-time takers	86%	70%	83%
State's pass rate for all first-time takers	80%	66%	77%

GEORGE WASHINGTON UNIVERSITY

2000 H Street, N.W.
Washington, DC 20052
(202)994-7230
http://www.law.gwu.edu

ABA Approved Since 1923

The Basics

Type of School: Private   Term: Semester

Application deadline: 03/01

Application fee: $55

Financial Aid deadline: 03/01

Can first year start other than Fall? No

Student faculty ratio: 17.7 to 1

Does the University offer:
- housing restricted to law students? No
- graduate student housing for which law students are eligible? Yes

Faculty & Administrators

	Total		Men		Women		Minorities	
	Fall	Spr	Fall	Spr	Fall	Spr	Fall	Spr
Full-time	64	66	44	46	20	20	8	8
Other Full-Time	0	0	0	0	0	0	0	0
Deans, librarians, & others who teach > 1/2	1	1	1	1	0	0	0	0
Part-time	111	118	70	80	40	38	12	9
Total	176	185	115	127	60	58	20	17
Deans, librarians, & others who teach < 1/2	5	5	3	3	2	2	1	1

Curriculum

	Full time	Part time
Typical first-year section size	90	50
Is there typically a "small section" of the first year class, other than Legal Writing, taught by full-time faculty?	No	No
If yes, typical size offered last year	N/A	N/A
# of classroom course titles beyond 1st year curriculum	110	90
# of upper division courses, excluding seminars, with an enrollment:		
Under 25	53	51
25 - 49	29	27
50 - 74	26	9
75 - 99	15	4
100 +	13	3
# of seminars	21	9
# of seminar positions available	600	
# of seminar positions filled	274	119
# of positions available in simulation courses	707	
# of simulation positions filled	244	360
# of positions available in faculty supervised clinical courses	192	
# of fac. sup. clin. positions filled	169	14
# involved in field placements	255	2
# involved in law journals	379	29
# in moot court or trial competitions	256	31
# of credit hrs required to graduate	84	

J.D. Enrollment & Ethnicity

	Men		Women		Fl-Time		Pt-Time		1st Yr		2nd Yr		3rd Yr		4th Yr		Total		JD Degrees Awarded
	#	%	#	%	#	%	#	%	#	%	#	%	#	%	#	%	#	%	
African-American	68	8.4	112	18.1	139	11.4	41	18.9	55	12.0	49	11.3	68	13.8	8	16.7	180	12.6	46
American Indian	1	0.1	3	0.5	4	0.3	0	0.0	2	0.4	2	0.5	0	0.0	0	0.0	4	0.3	3
Asian American	58	7.1	60	9.7	102	8.4	16	7.4	34	7.4	39	9.0	42	8.5	3	6.3	118	8.2	35
Mexican American	0	0.0	0	0.0	0	0.0	0	0.0	0	0.0	0	0.0	0	0.0	0	0.0	0	0.0	0
Puerto Rican	0	0.0	0	0.0	0	0.0	0	0.0	0	0.0	0	0.0	0	0.0	0	0.0	0	0.0	0
Hispanic American	60	7.4	36	5.8	88	7.2	8	3.7	32	7.0	21	4.8	40	8.1	3	6.3	96	6.7	34
Total Minorities	187	23.0	211	34.1	333	27.4	65	30.0	123	26.9	111	25.5	150	30.5	14	29.2	398	27.8	118
Foreign Nationals	8	1.0	2	0.3	10	0.8	0	0.0	4	0.9	1	0.2	5	1.0	0	0.0	10	0.7	7
Caucasian	619	76.0	405	65.5	872	71.8	152	70.0	330	72.2	323	74.3	337	68.5	34	70.8	1024	71.5	347
Total	814	56.8	618	43.2	1215	84.8	217	15.2	457	31.9	435	30.4	492	34.4	48	3.4	1432		472

GEORGE WASHINGTON UNIVERSITY

GPA & LSAT Scores

	Full Time	Part Time	Total
# of apps	N/A	N/A	6,468
# admits	N/A	N/A	2,037
# of matrics	377	59	436
75% GPA	3.57	3.42	
25% GPA	3.23	3.09	
75% LSAT	163	161	
25% LSAT	159	154	

Tuition & Fees

	Resident	Non-resident
Full-Time	$22,959	$22,959
Part-Time	$16,200	$16,200

Living Expenses

Estimated living expenses for Singles		
Living on campus	Living off campus	Living at home
$13,587	$13,587	$13,587

Employment

	Total	%
Employment status known	398	85.8
Employment status unknown	66	14.2
Employed	383	96.2
Pursuing graduate degrees	4	1.0
Unemployed seeking employment	10	2.5
Unemployed not seeking employment	1	0.3
Type of Employment		
# employed in law firms	210	54.8
# employed in business & industry	37	9.7
# employed in government	60	15.7
# employed in public interest	9	2.3
# employed as judicial clerks	47	12.3
# employed in academia	2	0.5
Geographic Location		
# employed in state	152	39.7
# employed in foreign countries	2	0.5
# of states where employed	31	

Financial Aid

	Full-time		Part-time		Total	
	#	%	#	%	#	%
Total # of Students	1215		217		1432	
Total # receiving grants	479	39.4	25	11.5	504	35.2
Less than 1/2 tuition	399	32.8	22	10.1	421	29.4
Half to full tuition	80	6.6	3	1.4	83	5.8
Full tuition	0	0.0	0	0.0	0	0.0
More than full tuition	0	0.0	0	0.0	0	0.0
Median Grant Amount	$9,000		$3,600			

Informational & Library Resources

# of volumes & volume equivalents	500,013	# of professional staff	17
# of titles	96,891	Hours per week with professional staff	81
# of active serial subscriptions	5,740	Hours per week without professional staff	29
Study seating capacity inside the library	797	# of student computer work stations for entire law school	140
Square feet of law library	45,999	# of additional networked connections	0
Square feet of law school (excl. Library)	136,931	Require Laptop Computer?	N

J.D. Attrition (Prior Year)

	Academic	Other	TOTALS	
	#	#	#	%
1st Year	1	10	11	2.4%
2nd Year	1	4	5	1.0%
3rd Year	5	1	6	1.2%
4th Year	0	0	0	0.0%
TOTALS	7	15	22	1.5%

Bar Passage Rates

Jurisdiction	Maryland			New York		
Exam	Sum 96	Win 97	Total	Sum 96	Win 97	Total
# from school taking bar for the first time	117	23	140	91	10	101
School's pass rate for all first-time takers	94%	96%	94%	97%	90%	96%
State's pass rate for all first-time takers	76%	79%	76%	78%	67%	77%

GEORGETOWN UNIVERSITY

600 New Jersey Avenue N.W.
Washington, DC 20001
(202)662-9000
http://www.law.georgetown.edu/lc

ABA Approved Since 1924

The Basics

Type of School: Private   Term: Semester

Application deadline: 03/01

Application fee: $60

Financial Aid deadline: 03/01

Can first year start other than Fall? No

Student faculty ratio: 19.3 to 1

Does the University offer:
- housing restricted to law students? Yes
- graduate student housing for which law students are eligible? No

Faculty & Administrators

	Total		Men		Women		Minorities	
	Fall	Spr	Fall	Spr	Fall	Spr	Fall	Spr
Full-time	83	86	52	57	31	29	8	8
Other Full-Time	5	5	1	1	4	4	1	1
Deans, librarians, & others who teach > 1/2	2	2	1	1	1	1	1	1
Part-time	110	116	91	96	19	20	5	5
Total	200	209	145	155	55	54	15	15
Deans, librarians, & others who teach < 1/2	4	4	4	4	0	0	1	1

Curriculum

	Full time	Part time
Typical first-year section size	125	125
Is there typically a "small section" of the first year class, other than Legal Writing, taught by full-time faculty?	Yes	Yes
If yes, typical size offered last year	32	32
# of classroom course titles beyond 1st year curriculum	152	108
# of upper division courses, excluding seminars, with an enrollment:		
Under 25	70	44
25 - 49	29	28
50 - 74	25	4
75 - 99	10	6
100 +	23	4
# of seminars	75	51
# of seminar positions available	2,478	
# of seminar positions filled	1,020	751
# of positions available in simulation courses	940	
# of simulation positions filled	359	421
# of positions available in faculty supervised clinical courses	318	
# of fac. sup. clin. positions filled	306	12
# involved in field placements	0	0
# involved in law journals	745	82
# in moot court or trial competitions	275	65
# of credit hrs required to graduate	83	

J.D. Enrollment & Ethnicity

	Men		Women		Fl-Time		Pt-Time		1st Yr		2nd Yr		3rd Yr		4th Yr		Total		JD Degrees Awarded
	#	%	#	%	#	%	#	%	#	%	#	%	#	%	#	%	#	%	
African-American	88	7.9	130	13.4	165	10.3	53	10.9	76	12.0	55	8.3	73	10.9	14	11.4	218	10.4	73
American Indian	5	0.4	6	0.6	9	0.6	2	0.4	3	0.5	2	0.3	6	0.9	0	0.0	11	0.5	5
Asian American	78	7.0	107	11.0	151	9.4	34	7.0	48	7.6	68	10.3	61	9.1	8	6.5	185	8.9	44
Mexican American	2	0.2	2	0.2	3	0.2	1	0.2	3	0.5	1	0.2	0	0.0	0	0.0	4	0.2	1
Puerto Rican	2	0.2	3	0.3	4	0.2	1	0.2	1	0.2	3	0.5	1	0.1	0	0.0	5	0.2	1
Hispanic American	53	4.7	46	4.7	85	5.3	14	2.9	35	5.5	25	3.8	31	4.6	8	6.5	99	4.7	37
Total Minorities	228	20.4	294	30.2	417	26.0	105	21.6	166	26.2	154	23.3	172	25.6	30	24.4	522	25.0	161
Foreign Nationals	24	2.1	19	2.0	38	2.4	5	1.0	12	1.9	21	3.2	8	1.2	2	1.6	43	2.1	12
Caucasian	865	77.4	660	67.8	1150	71.7	375	77.3	456	71.9	487	73.6	491	73.2	91	74.0	1525	73.0	452
Total	1117	53.4	973	46.6	1605	76.8	485	23.2	634	30.3	662	31.7	671	32.1	123	5.9	2090		625

GPA & LSAT Scores

	Full Time	Part Time	Total
# of apps	6,448	656	7,104
# admits	1,884	220	2,104
# of matrics	510	125	635
75% GPA	3.75	3.62	
25% GPA	3.26	3.14	
75% LSAT	168	167	
25% LSAT	163	159	

Tuition & Fees

	Resident	Non-resident
Full-Time	$23,375	$23,375
Part-Time	$0	$16,200

Living Expenses

Estimated living expenses for Singles		
Living on campus	Living off campus	Living at home
$14,575	$14,575	$10,990

Employment

	Total	%
Employment status known	576	97.3
Employment status unknown	16	2.7
Employed	555	96.4
Pursuing graduate degrees	7	1.2
Unemployed seeking employment	11	1.9
Unemployed not seeking employment	3	0.5
Type of Employment		
# employed in law firms	350	63.1
# employed in business & industry	48	8.6
# employed in government	48	8.6
# employed in public interest	28	5.0
# employed as judicial clerks	64	11.5
# employed in academia	10	1.8
Geographic Location		
# employed in state	248	44.7
# employed in foreign countries	7	1.3
# of states where employed	41	

Financial Aid

	Full-time		Part-time		Total	
	#	%	#	%	#	%
Total # of Students	1605		485		2090	
Total # receiving grants	490	30.5	3	0.6	493	23.6
Less than 1/2 tuition	368	22.9	3	0.6	371	17.8
Half to full tuition	121	7.5	0	0.0	121	5.8
Full tuition	1	0.1	0	0.0	1	0.0
More than full tuition	0	0.0	0	0.0	0	0.0
Median Grant Amount	$8,200		$5,800			

Informational & Library Resources

# of volumes & volume equivalents	892,428	# of professional staff	22
# of titles	286,550	Hours per week with professional staff	76
# of active serial subscriptions	12,430	Hours per week without professional staff	31
Study seating capacity inside the library	1,260	# of student computer work stations for entire law school	184
Square feet of law library	119,743	# of additional networked connections	576
Square feet of law school (excl. Library)	269,906	Require Laptop Computer?	N

J.D. Attrition (Prior Year)

	Academic	Other	TOTALS	
	#	#	#	%
1st Year	0	12	12	1.7%
2nd Year	0	3	3	0.5%
3rd Year	0	1	1	0.2%
4th Year	1	1	2	1.6%
TOTALS	1	17	18	0.9%

Bar Passage Rates

Jurisdiction	New York			Maryland		
Exam	Sum 96	Win 97	Total	Sum 96	Win 97	Total
# from school taking bar for the first time	159	24	183	92	35	127
School's pass rate for all first-time takers	86%	92%	87%	86%	80%	84%
State's pass rate for all first-time takers	78%	67%	77%	76%	79%	76%

GEORGIA STATE UNIVERSITY

P.O. Box 4037
Atlanta, GA 30302-4037
(404)651-2096
http://gsulaw.gsu.edu

ABA Approved Since 1984

The Basics

Type of School: Public Term: Semester

Application deadline: 03/15

Application fee: $30

Financial Aid deadline: 04/01

Can first year start other than Fall? No

Student faculty ratio: 16.6 to 1

Does the University offer:
- housing restricted to law students? No
- graduate student housing for which law students are eligible? Yes

Faculty & Administrators

	Total		Men		Women		Minorities	
	Fall	Spr	Fall	Spr	Fall	Spr	Fall	Spr
Full-time	28	29	19	20	9	9	3	3
Other Full-Time	4	4	0	0	4	4	1	1
Deans, librarians, & others who teach > 1/2	2	2	1	1	1	1	0	0
Part-time	8	20	5	13	3	7	1	6
Total	42	55	25	34	17	21	5	10
Deans, librarians, & others who teach < 1/2	4	4	0	0	4	4	1	1

Curriculum

	Full time	Part time
Typical first-year section size	70	70
Is there typically a "small section" of the first year class, other than Legal Writing, taught by full-time faculty?	No	No
If yes, typical size offered last year	N/A	N/A
# of classroom course titles beyond 1st year curriculum	70	62
# of upper division courses, excluding seminars, with an enrollment:		
Under 25	20	29
25 - 49	19	13
50 - 74	9	5
75 - 99	1	0
100 +	0	0
# of seminars	11	6
# of seminar positions available	296	
# of seminar positions filled	133	62
# of positions available in simulation courses	168	
# of simulation positions filled	37	116
# of positions available in faculty supervised clinical courses	30	
# of fac. sup. clin. positions filled	19	0
# involved in field placements	107	0
# involved in law journals	56	0
# in moot court or trial competitions	92	0
# of credit hrs required to graduate	90	

J.D. Enrollment & Ethnicity

	Men		Women		Fl-Time		Pt-Time		1st Yr		2nd Yr		3rd Yr		4th Yr		Total		JD Degrees Awarded
	#	%	#	%	#	%	#	%	#	%	#	%	#	%	#	%	#	%	
African-American	34	10.5	57	18.0	54	13.8	37	14.9	25	12.9	26	12.7	30	17.2	10	14.5	91	14.2	34
American Indian	1	0.3	2	0.6	2	0.5	1	0.4	0	0.0	1	0.5	2	1.1	0	0.0	3	0.5	0
Asian American	17	5.2	13	4.1	23	5.9	7	2.8	6	3.1	9	4.4	12	6.9	3	4.3	30	4.7	12
Mexican American	7	2.2	7	2.2	5	1.3	9	3.6	2	1.0	2	1.0	6	3.4	4	5.8	14	2.2	6
Puerto Rican	0	0.0	0	0.0	0	0.0	0	0.0	0	0.0	0	0.0	0	0.0	0	0.0	0	0.0	0
Hispanic American	20	6.2	5	1.6	18	4.6	7	2.8	11	5.7	8	3.9	5	2.9	1	1.4	25	3.9	2
Total Minorities	79	24.3	84	26.6	102	26.0	61	24.5	44	22.7	46	22.5	55	31.6	18	26.1	163	25.4	54
Foreign Nationals	0	0.0	0	0.0	0	0.0	0	0.0	0	0.0	0	0.0	0	0.0	0	0.0	0	0.0	0
Caucasian	246	75.7	232	73.4	290	74.0	188	75.5	150	77.3	158	77.5	119	68.4	51	73.9	478	74.6	144
Total	325	50.7	316	49.3	392	61.2	249	38.8	194	30.3	204	31.8	174	27.1	69	10.8	641		198

GEORGIA STATE UNIVERSITY

GPA & LSAT Scores

	Full Time	Part Time	Total
# of apps	1,500	372	1,872
# admits	347	117	464
# of matrics	121	79	200
75% GPA	3.40	3.59	
25% GPA	2.87	2.91	
75% LSAT	160	161	
25% LSAT	154	154	

Tuition & Fees

	Resident	Non-resident
Full-Time	$3,345	$10,429
Part-Time	$2,537	$7,597

Living Expenses

Estimated living expenses for Singles		
Living on campus	Living off campus	Living at home
$11,552	$12,705	$7,170

Financial Aid

	Full-time		Part-time		Total	
	#	%	#	%	#	%
Total # of Students	392		249		641	
Total # receiving grants	20	5.1	6	2.4	26	4.1
Less than 1/2 tuition	2	0.5	0	0.0	2	0.3
Half to full tuition	3	0.8	0	0.0	3	0.5
Full tuition	14	3.6	6	2.4	20	3.1
More than full tuition	1	0.3	0	0.0	1	0.2
Median Grant Amount	$3,546		$2,480			

Informational & Library Resources

# of volumes & volume equivalents	261,697	# of professional staff	4
# of titles	48,668	Hours per week with professional staff	68
# of active serial subscriptions	3,548	Hours per week without professional staff	37
Study seating capacity inside the library	335	# of student computer work stations for entire law school	36
Square feet of law library	37,010	# of additional networked connections	0
Square feet of law school (excl. Library)	43,323	Require Laptop Computer?	N

Employment

	Total	%
Employment status known	139	95.2
Employment status unknown	7	4.8
Employed	129	92.8
Pursuing graduate degrees	0	0.0
Unemployed seeking employment	7	5.0
Unemployed not seeking employment	3	2.2
Type of Employment		
# employed in law firms	78	60.5
# employed in business & industry	22	17.1
# employed in government	16	12.4
# employed in public interest	6	4.7
# employed as judicial clerks	5	3.9
# employed in academia	2	1.6
Geographic Location		
# employed in state	123	95.3
# employed in foreign countries	1	0.8
# of states where employed	5	

J.D. Attrition (Prior Year)

	Academic	Other	TOTALS	
	#	#	#	%
1st Year	5	24	29	13%
2nd Year	0	2	2	1.3%
3rd Year	0	0	0	0.0%
4th Year	0	0	0	0.0%
TOTALS	5	26	31	4.6%

Bar Passage Rates

Jurisdiction	Georgia
Exam	
# from school taking bar for the first time	The Georgia Board of Bar Examiners now requires students to graduate prior to taking the bar. This resulted in too few graduates taking the Summer '96 and Winter '97 tests to warrant reporting.
School's pass rate for all first-time takers	
State's pass rate for all first-time takers	

GEORGIA, UNIVERSITY OF

Herty Drive
Athens, GA 30602
(706)542-7140
http://www.lawsch.uga.edu

ABA Approved Since 1930

The Basics

Type of School: Public Term: Semester

Application deadline: 03/01

Application fee: $30

Financial Aid deadline: 03/01

Can first year start other than Fall? No

Student faculty ratio: 18.7 to 1

Does the University offer:
- housing restricted to law students? No
- graduate student housing for which law students are eligible? Yes

Faculty & Administrators

	Total		Men		Women		Minorities	
	Fall	Spr	Fall	Spr	Fall	Spr	Fall	Spr
Full-time	29	31	23	25	6	6	2	3
Other Full-Time	6	6	1	1	5	5	0	0
Deans, librarians, & others who teach > 1/2	5	5	5	5	0	0	0	0
Part-time	8	16	5	13	3	3	0	1
Total	48	58	34	44	14	14	2	4
Deans, librarians, & others who teach < 1/2	5	5	1	1	4	4	0	0

Curriculum

	Full time	Part time
Typical first-year section size	78	0
Is there typically a "small section" of the first year class, other than Legal Writing, taught by full-time faculty?	No	No
If yes, typical size offered last year	N/A	N/A
# of classroom course titles beyond 1st year curriculum	132	0
# of upper division courses, excluding seminars, with an enrollment:		
Under 25	58	0
25 - 49	35	0
50 - 74	10	0
75 - 99	7	0
100 +	7	0
# of seminars	27	0
# of seminar positions available	336	
# of seminar positions filled	307	0
# of positions available in simulation courses	405	
# of simulation positions filled	288	0
# of positions available in faculty supervised clinical courses	220	
# of fac. sup. clin. positions filled	165	0
# involved in field placements	19	0
# involved in law journals	143	0
# in moot court or trial competitions	235	0
# of credit hrs required to graduate	88	

J.D. Enrollment & Ethnicity

	Men		Women		Fl-Time		Pt-Time		1st Yr		2nd Yr		3rd Yr		4th Yr		Total		JD Degrees Awarded
	#	%	#	%	#	%	#	%	#	%	#	%	#	%	#	%	#	%	
African-American	17	4.8	32	10.7	49	7.5	0	0.0	9	3.9	15	6.7	25	12.6	0	0.0	49	7.5	23
American Indian	0	0.0	2	0.7	2	0.3	0	0.0	0	0.0	2	0.9	0	0.0	0	0.0	2	0.3	0
Asian American	7	2.0	9	3.0	16	2.5	0	0.0	5	2.2	8	3.6	3	1.5	0	0.0	16	2.5	5
Mexican American	0	0.0	0	0.0	0	0.0	0	0.0	0	0.0	0	0.0	0	0.0	0	0.0	0	0.0	0
Puerto Rican	0	0.0	0	0.0	0	0.0	0	0.0	0	0.0	0	0.0	0	0.0	0	0.0	0	0.0	0
Hispanic American	4	1.1	3	1.0	7	1.1	0	0.0	5	2.2	0	0.0	2	1.0	0	0.0	7	1.1	3
Total Minorities	28	7.9	46	15.4	74	11.3	0	0.0	19	8.3	25	11.1	30	15.2	0	0.0	74	11.3	31
Foreign Nationals	1	0.3	3	1.0	4	0.6	0	0.0	4	1.7	0	0.0	0	0.0	0	0.0	4	0.6	1
Caucasian	324	91.8	250	83.6	574	88.0	0	0.0	206	90.0	200	88.9	168	84.8	0	0.0	574	88.0	169
Total	353	54.1	299	45.9	652	100.0	0	0.0	229	35.1	225	34.5	198	30.4	0	0.0	652		201

GPA & LSAT Scores

	Full Time	Part Time	Total
# of apps	1,859	0	1,859
# admits	482	0	482
# of matrics	233	0	233
75% GPA	3.73	0.00	
25% GPA	3.33	0.00	
75% LSAT	164	0	
25% LSAT	158	0	

Tuition & Fees

	Resident	Non-resident
Full-Time	$3,757	$12,357
Part-Time	$0	$0

Living Expenses

Estimated living expenses for Singles

Living on campus	Living off campus	Living at home
$7,054	$9,328	$5,353

Employment

	Total	%
Employment status known	214	96.0
Employment status unknown	9	4.0
Employed	201	93.9
Pursuing graduate degrees	4	1.9
Unemployed seeking employment	7	3.3
Unemployed not seeking employment	2	0.9
Type of Employment		
# employed in law firms	137	68.2
# employed in business & industry	15	7.5
# employed in government	18	9.0
# employed in public interest	3	1.5
# employed as judicial clerks	26	12.9
# employed in academia	0	0.0
Geographic Location		
# employed in state	161	80.1
# employed in foreign countries	2	1.0
# of states where employed	19	

Financial Aid

	Full-time		Part-time		Total	
	#	%	#	%	#	%
Total # of Students	652		0		652	
Total # receiving grants	160	24.5	0	0.0	160	24.5
Less than 1/2 tuition	55	8.4	0	0.0	55	8.4
Half to full tuition	71	10.9	0	0.0	71	10.9
Full tuition	15	2.3	0	0.0	15	2.3
More than full tuition	19	2.9	0	0.0	19	2.9
Median Grant Amount	$2,500		$0			

Informational & Library Resources

# of volumes & volume equivalents	459,513	# of professional staff	9
# of titles	121,909	Hours per week with professional staff	76
# of active serial subscriptions	6,782	Hours per week without professional staff	39
Study seating capacity inside the library	421	# of student computer work stations for entire law school	53
Square feet of law library	45,381	# of additional networked connections	0
Square feet of law school (excl. Library)	75,197	Require Laptop Computer?	N

J.D. Attrition (Prior Year)

	Academic	Other	TOTALS	
	#	#	#	%
1st Year	1	13	14	6.2%
2nd Year	0	0	0	0.0%
3rd Year	0	1	1	0.5%
4th Year	0	0	0	0.0%
TOTALS	1	14	15	2.4%

Bar Passage Rates

Jurisdiction	Georgia		
Exam	Sum 96	Win 97	Total
# from school taking bar for the first time	22	11	33
School's pass rate for all first-time takers	95%	100%	97%
State's pass rate for all first-time takers	88%	76%	83%

GOLDEN GATE UNIVERSITY

536 Mission Street
San Francisco, CA 94105-2968
(415)442-6600
http://www.ggu.edu/law/

ABA Approved Since 1956

The Basics

Type of School: Private Term: Semester
Application deadline: 04/15
Application fee: $40
Financial Aid deadline: 03/02
Can first year start other than Fall? Yes
Student faculty ratio: 16.7 to 1
Does the University offer:
- housing restricted to law students? No
- graduate student housing for which law students are eligible? No

Faculty & Administrators

	Total		Men		Women		Minorities	
	Fall	Spr	Fall	Spr	Fall	Spr	Fall	Spr
Full-time	30	28	19	17	11	11	5	5
Other Full-Time	2	2	1	1	1	1	0	0
Deans, librarians, & others who teach > 1/2	3	3	2	2	1	1	2	2
Part-time	49	43	29	25	20	18	6	4
Total	84	76	51	45	33	31	13	11
Deans, librarians, & others who teach < 1/2	5	5	2	2	3	3	0	0

Curriculum

	Full time	Part time
Typical first-year section size	60	50
Is there typically a "small section" of the first year class, other than Legal Writing, taught by full-time faculty?	Yes	No
If yes, typical size offered last year	25	N/A
# of classroom course titles beyond 1st year curriculum	94	34
# of upper division courses, excluding seminars, with an enrollment:		
Under 25	78	21
25 - 49	46	9
50 - 74	6	3
75 - 99	3	0
100 +	0	0
# of seminars	28	4
# of seminar positions available	440	
# of seminar positions filled	153	15
# of positions available in simulation courses	978	
# of simulation positions filled	786	144
# of positions available in faculty supervised clinical courses	87	
# of fac. sup. clin. positions filled	43	11
# involved in field placements	149	37
# involved in law journals	35	14
# in moot court or trial competitions	19	3
# of credit hrs required to graduate	88	

J.D. Enrollment & Ethnicity

	Men		Women		Fl-Time		Pt-Time		1st Yr		2nd Yr		3rd Yr		4th Yr		Total		JD Degrees Awarded
	#	%	#	%	#	%	#	%	#	%	#	%	#	%	#	%	#	%	
African-American	7	2.4	22	6.0	24	4.8	5	3.3	8	3.6	8	4.5	12	5.4	1	3.0	29	4.4	4
American Indian	0	0.0	0	0.0	0	0.0	0	0.0	0	0.0	0	0.0	0	0.0	0	0.0	0	0.0	0
Asian American	35	12.2	41	11.1	55	11.0	21	13.8	25	11.3	22	12.4	23	10.4	6	18.2	76	11.6	16
Mexican American	0	0.0	0	0.0	0	0.0	0	0.0	0	0.0	0	0.0	0	0.0	0	0.0	0	0.0	0
Puerto Rican	0	0.0	0	0.0	0	0.0	0	0.0	0	0.0	0	0.0	0	0.0	0	0.0	0	0.0	0
Hispanic American	24	8.4	35	9.5	48	9.6	11	7.2	16	7.2	19	10.7	21	9.5	3	9.1	59	9.0	18
Total Minorities	66	23.1	98	26.6	127	25.3	37	24.3	49	22.1	49	27.5	56	25.3	10	30.3	164	25.1	38
Foreign Nationals	0	0.0	3	0.8	3	0.6	0	0.0	1	0.5	1	0.6	1	0.5	0	0.0	3	0.5	0
Caucasian	220	76.9	267	72.6	372	74.1	115	75.7	172	77.5	128	71.9	164	74.2	23	69.7	487	74.5	134
Total	286	43.7	368	56.3	502	76.8	152	23.2	222	33.9	178	27.2	221	33.8	33	5.0	654		172

GPA & LSAT Scores

	Full Time	Part Time	Total
# of apps	1,733	230	1,963
# admits	1,029	115	1,144
# of matrics	178	52	230
75% GPA	3.27	3.21	
25% GPA	2.75	2.64	
75% LSAT	156	154	
25% LSAT	148	148	

Tuition & Fees

	Resident	Non-resident
Full-Time	$19,074	$19,074
Part-Time	$13,224	$13,224

Living Expenses

Estimated living expenses for Singles		
Living on campus	Living off campus	Living at home
N/A	$11,030	$3,605

Employment

	Total	%
Employment status known	151	86.8
Employment status unknown	23	13.2
Employed	115	76.2
Pursuing graduate degrees	7	4.6
Unemployed seeking employment	24	15.9
Unemployed not seeking employment	5	3.3
Type of Employment		
# employed in law firms	65	56.5
# employed in business & industry	25	21.7
# employed in government	10	8.7
# employed in public interest	7	6.1
# employed as judicial clerks	5	4.3
# employed in academia	1	0.9
Geographic Location		
# employed in state	108	93.9
# employed in foreign countries	0	0.0
# of states where employed	4	

Financial Aid

	Full-time		Part-time		Total	
	#	%	#	%	#	%
Total # of Students	502		152		654	
Total # receiving grants	126	25.1	32	21.1	158	24.2
Less than 1/2 tuition	83	16.5	16	10.5	99	15.1
Half to full tuition	24	4.8	8	5.3	32	4.9
Full tuition	19	3.8	8	5.3	27	4.1
More than full tuition	0	0.0	0	0.0	0	0.0
Median Grant Amount	$6,000		$6,000			

Informational & Library Resources

# of volumes & volume equivalents	234,368	# of professional staff	5
# of titles	30,499	Hours per week with professional staff	55
# of active serial subscriptions	3,917	Hours per week without professional staff	36
Study seating capacity inside the library	336	# of student computer work stations for entire law school	69
Square feet of law library	27,296	# of additional networked connections	22
Square feet of law school (excl. Library)	36,798	Require Laptop Computer?	N

J.D. Attrition (Prior Year)

	Academic	Other	TOTALS	
	#	#	#	%
1st Year	30	3	33	12%
2nd Year	2	16	18	11%
3rd Year	0	0	0	0.0%
4th Year	0	0	0	0.0%
TOTALS	32	19	51	7.2%

Bar Passage Rates

Jurisdiction	California		
Exam	Sum 96	Win 97	Total
# from school taking bar for the first time	129	51	180
School's pass rate for all first-time takers	71%	63%	69%
State's pass rate for all first-time takers	69%	62%	67%

GONZAGA UNIVERSITY

P.O. Box 3528
Spokane, WA 99220-3528
(509)328-4220
http://www.law.gonzaga.edu

ABA Approved Since 1951

The Basics

Type of School: Private   Term: Semester
Application deadline: 03/15
Application fee: $40
Financial Aid deadline: 02/01
Can first year start other than Fall? No
Student faculty ratio: 20.7 to 1
Does the University offer:
- housing restricted to law students? No
- graduate student housing for which law students are eligible? Yes

Faculty & Administrators

	Total		Men		Women		Minorities	
	Fall	Spr	Fall	Spr	Fall	Spr	Fall	Spr
Full-time	20	21	15	15	5	6	1	2
Other Full-Time	6	6	4	4	2	2	0	0
Deans, librarians, & others who teach > 1/2	1	1	1	1	0	0	0	0
Part-time	17	16	11	13	6	3	0	2
Total	44	44	31	33	13	11	1	4
Deans, librarians, & others who teach < 1/2	1	1	1	1	0	0	0	0

Curriculum

	Full time	Part time
Typical first-year section size	81	0
Is there typically a "small section" of the first year class, other than Legal Writing, taught by full-time faculty?	No	No
If yes, typical size offered last year	N/A	N/A
# of classroom course titles beyond 1st year curriculum	75	0
# of upper division courses, excluding seminars, with an enrollment:		
Under 25	62	0
25 - 49	28	0
50 - 74	16	0
75 - 99	2	0
100 +	2	0
# of seminars	4	0
# of seminar positions available	64	
# of seminar positions filled	34	0
# of positions available in simulation courses	64	
# of simulation positions filled	37	0
# of positions available in faculty supervised clinical courses	96	
# of fac. sup. clin. positions filled	76	0
# involved in field placements	107	0
# involved in law journals	45	0
# in moot court or trial competitions	23	0
# of credit hrs required to graduate	90	

J.D. Enrollment & Ethnicity

	Men		Women		Fl-Time		Pt-Time		1st Yr		2nd Yr		3rd Yr		4th Yr		Total		JD Degrees Awarded
	#	%	#	%	#	%	#	%	#	%	#	%	#	%	#	%	#	%	
African-American	9	3.0	3	1.5	11	2.3	1	5.3	7	4.1	3	2.1	1	0.6	1	11.1	12	2.4	5
American Indian	8	2.6	4	2.0	12	2.5	0	0.0	3	1.8	1	0.7	8	4.5	0	0.0	12	2.4	3
Asian American	16	5.2	15	7.6	31	6.4	0	0.0	11	6.5	7	4.8	13	7.3	0	0.0	31	6.2	9
Mexican American	16	5.2	5	2.5	21	4.3	0	0.0	10	5.9	3	2.1	8	4.5	0	0.0	21	4.2	5
Puerto Rican	0	0.0	0	0.0	0	0.0	0	0.0	0	0.0	0	0.0	0	0.0	0	0.0	0	0.0	1
Hispanic American	0	0.0	0	0.0	0	0.0	0	0.0	0	0.0	0	0.0	0	0.0	0	0.0	0	0.0	0
Total Minorities	49	16.1	27	13.6	75	15.5	1	5.3	31	18.2	14	9.7	30	16.8	1	11.1	76	15.1	23
Foreign Nationals	0	0.0	0	0.0	0	0.0	0	0.0	0	0.0	0	0.0	0	0.0	0	0.0	0	0.0	0
Caucasian	256	83.9	171	86.4	409	84.5	18	94.7	139	81.8	131	90.3	149	83.2	8	88.9	427	84.9	146
Total	305	60.6	198	39.4	484	96.2	19	3.8	170	33.8	145	28.8	179	35.6	9	1.8	503		169

GONZAGA UNIVERSITY

GPA & LSAT Scores

	Full Time	Part Time	Total
# of apps	1,005	0	1,005
# admits	752	0	752
# of matrics	168	2	170
75% GPA	3.38	0.00	
25% GPA	2.72	0.00	
75% LSAT	154	0	
25% LSAT	148	0	

Tuition & Fees

	Resident	Non-resident
Full-Time	$17,030	$17,030
Part-Time	$10,250	$10,250

Living Expenses

Estimated living expenses for Singles		
Living on campus	Living off campus	Living at home
$12,050	$12,050	$7,500

Financial Aid

	Full-time		Part-time		Total	
	#	%	#	%	#	%
Total # of Students	484		19		503	
Total # receiving grants	152	31.4	0	0.0	152	30.2
Less than 1/2 tuition	51	10.5	0	0.0	51	10.1
Half to full tuition	58	12.0	0	0.0	58	11.5
Full tuition	43	8.9	0	0.0	43	8.5
More than full tuition	0	0.0	0	0.0	0	0.0
Median Grant Amount	$5,000		$0			

Informational & Library Resources

# of volumes & volume equivalents	225,422	# of professional staff	4
# of titles	32,555	Hours per week with professional staff	52
# of active serial subscriptions	2,986	Hours per week without professional staff	56
Study seating capacity inside the library	468	# of student computer work stations for entire law school	57
Square feet of law library	23,806	# of additional networked connections	0
Square feet of law school (excl. Library)	35,305	Require Laptop Computer?	N

Employment

	Total	%
Employment status known	162	97.0
Employment status unknown	5	3.0
Employed	129	79.6
Pursuing graduate degrees	19	11.7
Unemployed seeking employment	10	6.2
Unemployed not seeking employment	4	2.5
Type of Employment		
# employed in law firms	72	55.8
# employed in business & industry	14	10.9
# employed in government	19	14.7
# employed in public interest	2	1.6
# employed as judicial clerks	13	10.1
# employed in academia	4	3.1
Geographic Location		
# employed in state	60	46.5
# employed in foreign countries	0	0.0
# of states where employed	22	

J.D. Attrition (Prior Year)

	Academic	Other	TOTALS	
	#	#	#	%
1st Year	12	12	24	14%
2nd Year	0	15	15	8.0%
3rd Year	0	0	0	0.0%
4th Year	0	0	0	0.0%
TOTALS	12	27	39	7.3%

Bar Passage Rates

Jurisdiction	Washington		
Exam	Sum 96	Win 97	Total
# from school taking bar for the first time	89	14	103
School's pass rate for all first-time takers	88%	71%	85%
State's pass rate for all first-time takers	73%	82%	76%

HAMLINE UNIVERSITY

1536 Hewitt Avenue
St. Paul, MN 55104
(612)523-2941
http://www.hamline.edu

ABA Approved Since 1975

The Basics

Type of School: Private
Term: Semester
Application deadline: 05/15
Application fee: $30
Financial Aid deadline: Rolling
Can first year start other than Fall? No
Student faculty ratio: 17.6 to 1
Does the University offer:
- housing restricted to law students? Yes
- graduate student housing for which law students are eligible? No

Faculty & Administrators

	Total		Men		Women		Minorities	
	Fall	Spr	Fall	Spr	Fall	Spr	Fall	Spr
Full-time	24	21	16	13	8	8	2	2
Other Full-Time	4	4	2	2	2	2	0	0
Deans, librarians, & others who teach > 1/2	2	2	0	0	2	2	0	0
Part-time	38	55	28	38	10	17	1	4
Total	68	82	46	53	22	29	3	6
Deans, librarians, & others who teach < 1/2	4	4	3	3	1	1	1	1

Curriculum

	Full time	Part time
Typical first-year section size	65	0
Is there typically a "small section" of the first year class, other than Legal Writing, taught by full-time faculty?	No	No
If yes, typical size offered last year	N/A	N/A
# of classroom course titles beyond 1st year curriculum	104	0
# of upper division courses, excluding seminars, with an enrollment:		
Under 25	68	0
25 - 49	38	0
50 - 74	17	0
75 - 99	7	0
100 +	0	0
# of seminars	15	0
# of seminar positions available	225	
# of seminar positions filled	188	0
# of positions available in simulation courses	1,071	
# of simulation positions filled	421	0
# of positions available in faculty supervised clinical courses	92	
# of fac. sup. clin. positions filled	83	0
# involved in field placements	79	0
# involved in law journals	111	0
# in moot court or trial competitions	45	0
# of credit hrs required to graduate	88	

J.D. Enrollment & Ethnicity

	Men		Women		Fl-Time		Pt-Time		1st Yr		2nd Yr		3rd Yr		4th Yr		Total		JD Degrees Awarded
	#	%	#	%	#	%	#	%	#	%	#	%	#	%	#	%	#	%	
African-American	12	4.6	12	4.8	23	4.7	1	5.0	5	3.8	7	4.0	12	5.8	0	0.0	24	4.7	7
American Indian	2	0.8	3	1.2	5	1.0	0	0.0	1	0.8	1	0.6	3	1.4	0	0.0	5	1.0	3
Asian American	10	3.8	6	2.4	14	2.8	2	10.0	5	3.8	5	2.9	6	2.9	0	0.0	16	3.1	2
Mexican American	0	0.0	0	0.0	0	0.0	0	0.0	0	0.0	0	0.0	0	0.0	0	0.0	0	0.0	0
Puerto Rican	0	0.0	0	0.0	0	0.0	0	0.0	0	0.0	0	0.0	0	0.0	0	0.0	0	0.0	0
Hispanic American	3	1.1	3	1.2	6	1.2	0	0.0	2	1.5	1	0.6	3	1.4	0	0.0	6	1.2	4
Total Minorities	27	10.3	24	9.6	48	9.7	3	15.0	13	9.8	14	8.1	24	11.5	0	0.0	51	9.9	16
Foreign Nationals	2	0.8	4	1.6	6	1.2	0	0.0	0	0.0	1	0.6	5	2.4	0	0.0	6	1.2	0
Caucasian	234	89.0	223	88.8	440	89.1	17	85.0	120	90.2	158	91.3	179	86.1	0	0.0	457	88.9	164
Total	263	51.2	251	48.8	494	96.1	20	3.9	133	25.9	173	33.7	208	40.5	0	0.0	514		180

GPA & LSAT Scores

	Full Time	Part Time	Total
# of apps	958	0	958
# admits	522	0	522
# of matrics	138	4	142
75% GPA	3.45	0.00	
25% GPA	2.89	0.00	
75% LSAT	152	0	
25% LSAT	150	0	

Tuition & Fees

	Resident	Non-resident
Full-Time	$15,545	$15,545
Part-Time	$11,197	$11,197

Living Expenses

Estimated living expenses for Singles		
Living on campus	Living off campus	Living at home
$7,573	$10,120	$10,120

Employment

	Total	%
Employment status known	171	95.0
Employment status unknown	9	5.0
Employed	148	86.5
Pursuing graduate degrees	4	2.3
Unemployed seeking employment	14	8.2
Unemployed not seeking employment	5	2.9
Type of Employment		
# employed in law firms	51	34.5
# employed in business & industry	43	29.1
# employed in government	14	9.5
# employed in public interest	11	7.4
# employed as judicial clerks	26	17.6
# employed in academia	3	2.0
Geographic Location		
# employed in state	110	74.3
# employed in foreign countries	1	0.7
# of states where employed	15	

Financial Aid

	Full-time		Part-time		Total	
	#	%	#	%	#	%
Total # of Students	494		20		514	
Total # receiving grants	124	25.1	1	5.0	125	24.3
Less than 1/2 tuition	88	17.8	1	5.0	89	17.3
Half to full tuition	21	4.3	0	0.0	21	4.1
Full tuition	12	2.4	0	0.0	12	2.3
More than full tuition	3	0.6	0	0.0	3	0.6
Median Grant Amount	$5,500		$0			

Informational & Library Resources

# of volumes & volume equivalents	231,885	# of professional staff	5
# of titles	125,959	Hours per week with professional staff	68
# of active serial subscriptions	2,692	Hours per week without professional staff	39
Study seating capacity inside the library	374	# of student computer work stations for entire law school	47
Square feet of law library	39,500	# of additional networked connections	180
Square feet of law school (excl. Library)	93,916	Require Laptop Computer?	N

J.D. Attrition (Prior Year)

	Academic	Other	TOTALS	
	#	#	#	%
1st Year	2	7	9	4.8%
2nd Year	0	13	13	6.3%
3rd Year	0	0	0	0.0%
4th Year	0	0	0	0.0%
TOTALS	2	20	22	3.8%

Bar Passage Rates

Jurisdiction	Minnesota		
Exam	Sum 96	Win 97	Total
# from school taking bar for the first time	132	13	145
School's pass rate for all first-time takers	87%	77%	86%
State's pass rate for all first-time takers	92%	84%	91%

HARVARD UNIVERSITY

Cambridge, MA 02138
(617)495-1000
http://www.law.harvard.edu

ABA Approved Since 1923

The Basics

Type of School: Private   Term: Semester
Application deadline: 02/02
Application fee: $65
Financial Aid deadline: 03/01
Can first year start other than Fall? No
Student faculty ratio: 21.6 to 1
Does the University offer:
- housing restricted to law students? Yes
- graduate student housing for which law students are eligible? Yes

Faculty & Administrators

	Total		Men		Women		Minorities	
	Fall	Spr	Fall	Spr	Fall	Spr	Fall	Spr
Full-time	64	64	56	52	8	12	8	6
Other Full-Time	19	19	6	6	13	13	11	11
Deans, librarians, & others who teach > 1/2	1	1	0	0	1	1	1	1
Part-time	19	19	14	15	5	4	4	5
Total	103	103	76	73	27	30	24	23
Deans, librarians, & others who teach < 1/2	10	10	7	7	3	3	0	0

Curriculum

	Full time	Part time
Typical first-year section size	138	0
Is there typically a "small section" of the first year class, other than Legal Writing, taught by full-time faculty?	Yes	No
If yes, typical size offered last year	45	N/A
# of classroom course titles beyond 1st year curriculum	218	0
# of upper division courses, excluding seminars, with an enrollment:		
Under 25	49	0
25 - 49	51	0
50 - 74	30	0
75 - 99	18	0
100 +	25	0
# of seminars	77	0
# of seminar positions available	1,540	
# of seminar positions filled	924	0
# of positions available in simulation courses	415	
# of simulation positions filled	415	0
# of positions available in faculty supervised clinical courses	650	
# of fac. sup. clin. positions filled	571	0
# involved in field placements	571	0
# involved in law journals	900	0
# in moot court or trial competitions	551	0
# of credit hrs required to graduate	80	

J.D. Enrollment & Ethnicity

	Men		Women		Fl-Time		Pt-Time		1st Yr		2nd Yr		3rd Yr		4th Yr		Total		JD Degrees Awarded
	#	%	#	%	#	%	#	%	#	%	#	%	#	%	#	%	#	%	
African-American	71	7.4	82	11.8	153	9.2	0	0.0	43	7.7	59	10.5	51	9.5	0	0.0	153	9.2	59
American Indian	2	0.2	7	1.0	9	0.5	0	0.0	4	0.7	2	0.4	3	0.6	0	0.0	9	0.5	3
Asian American	87	9.0	94	13.5	181	10.9	0	0.0	52	9.3	73	13.0	56	10.4	0	0.0	181	10.9	65
Mexican American	21	2.2	9	1.3	30	1.8	0	0.0	7	1.3	18	3.2	5	0.9	0	0.0	30	1.8	14
Puerto Rican	3	0.3	3	0.4	6	0.4	0	0.0	4	0.7	1	0.2	1	0.2	0	0.0	6	0.4	7
Hispanic American	26	2.7	18	2.6	44	2.7	0	0.0	15	2.7	14	2.5	15	2.8	0	0.0	44	2.7	10
Total Minorities	210	21.8	213	30.7	423	25.5	0	0.0	125	22.4	167	29.7	131	24.3	0	0.0	423	25.5	158
Foreign Nationals	40	4.1	19	2.7	59	3.6	0	0.0	21	3.8	21	3.7	17	3.2	0	0.0	59	3.6	22
Caucasian	714	74.1	462	66.6	1176	70.9	0	0.0	411	73.8	374	66.5	391	72.5	0	0.0	1176	70.9	368
Total	964	58.1	694	41.9	1658	100.0	0	0.0	557	33.6	562	33.9	539	32.5	0	0.0	1658		548

GPA & LSAT Scores

	Full Time	Part Time	Total
# of apps	5,869	0	5,869
# admits	843	0	843
# of matrics	556	0	556
75% GPA	3.93	0.00	
25% GPA	3.73	0.00	
75% LSAT	173	0	
25% LSAT	166	0	

Tuition & Fees

	Resident	Non-resident
Full-Time	$23,466	$23,466
Part-Time	$0	$0

Living Expenses

Estimated living expenses for Singles

Living on campus	Living off campus	Living at home
$12,695	$12,695	N/A

Employment

	Total	%
Employment status known	544	99.6
Employment status unknown	2	0.4
Employed	524	96.3
Pursuing graduate degrees	7	1.3
Unemployed seeking employment	12	2.2
Unemployed not seeking employment	1	0.2
Type of Employment		
# employed in law firms	332	63.4
# employed in business & industry	19	3.6
# employed in government	4	0.8
# employed in public interest	18	3.4
# employed as judicial clerks	149	28.4
# employed in academia	2	0.4
Geographic Location		
# employed in state	45	8.6
# employed in foreign countries	7	1.3
# of states where employed	43	

Financial Aid

	Full-time		Part-time		Total	
	#	%	#	%	#	%
Total # of Students	1658		0		1658	
Total # receiving grants	517	31.2	0	0.0	517	31.2
Less than 1/2 tuition	377	22.7	0	0.0	377	22.7
Half to full tuition	129	7.8	0	0.0	129	7.8
Full tuition	11	0.7	0	0.0	11	0.7
More than full tuition	0	0.0	0	0.0	0	0.0
Median Grant Amount	$8,655		$0			

Informational & Library Resources

# of volumes & volume equivalents	1,920,648	# of professional staff	28
# of titles	739,964	Hours per week with professional staff	69
# of active serial subscriptions	14,560	Hours per week without professional staff	30
Study seating capacity inside the library	300	# of student computer work stations for entire law school	167
Square feet of law library	60,500	# of additional networked connections	54
Square feet of law school (excl. Library)	294,105	Require Laptop Computer?	N

J.D. Attrition (Prior Year)

	Academic	Other	TOTALS	
	#	#	#	%
1st Year	0	1	1	0.2%
2nd Year	1	2	3	0.5%
3rd Year	0	2	2	0.4%
4th Year	0	0	0	0.0%
TOTALS	1	5	6	0.4%

Bar Passage Rates

Jurisdiction	New York			Massachusetts		
Exam	Sum 96	Win 97	Total	Sum 96	Win 97	Total
# from school taking bar for the first time	199	0	199	68	0	68
School's pass rate for all first-time takers	92%		92%	100%		100%
State's pass rate for all first-time takers	78%	67%	77%	83%	76%	81%

HAWAII, UNIVERSITY OF

William S. Richardson School of Law
2515 Dole Street
Honolulu, HI 96822
(808)956-8636
gopher://gopher.hawaii.edu/11/student/ca

ABA Approved Since 1974

The Basics

Type of School: Public Term: Semester
Application deadline: 03/01
Application fee: $30
Financial Aid deadline: 03/01
Can first year start other than Fall? No
Student faculty ratio: 11.8 to 1
Does the University offer:
- housing restricted to law students? No
- graduate student housing for which law students are eligible? Yes

Faculty & Administrators

	Total		Men		Women		Minorities	
	Fall	Spr	Fall	Spr	Fall	Spr	Fall	Spr
Full-time	16	16	10	9	6	7	3	4
Other Full-Time	1	1	0	0	1	1	0	0
Deans, librarians, & others who teach > 1/2	0	0	0	0	0	0	0	0
Part-time	12	23	9	18	3	5	5	14
Total	29	40	19	27	10	13	8	18
Deans, librarians, & others who teach < 1/2	3	3	1	1	2	2	2	2

Curriculum

	Full time	Part time
Typical first-year section size	69	0
Is there typically a "small section" of the first year class, other than Legal Writing, taught by full-time faculty?	Yes	No
If yes, typical size offered last year	19	N/A
# of classroom course titles beyond 1st year curriculum	51	0
# of upper division courses, excluding seminars, with an enrollment:		
Under 25	45	0
25 - 49	9	0
50 - 74	6	0
75 - 99	1	0
100 +	0	0
# of seminars	7	0
# of seminar positions available	93	
# of seminar positions filled	87	0
# of positions available in simulation courses	100	
# of simulation positions filled	77	0
# of positions available in faculty supervised clinical courses	62	
# of fac. sup. clin. positions filled	55	0
# involved in field placements	86	0
# involved in law journals	28	0
# in moot court or trial competitions	19	0
# of credit hrs required to graduate	89	

J.D. Enrollment & Ethnicity

	Men		Women		Fl-Time		Pt-Time		1st Yr		2nd Yr		3rd Yr		4th Yr		Total		JD Degrees Awarded
	#	%	#	%	#	%	#	%	#	%	#	%	#	%	#	%	#	%	
African-American	0	0.0	1	0.9	1	0.4	0	0.0	0	0.0	0	0.0	1	1.3	0	0.0	1	0.4	1
American Indian	1	0.9	1	0.9	2	0.9	0	0.0	0	0.0	1	1.4	1	1.3	0	0.0	2	0.9	0
Asian American	69	61.6	77	67.5	146	64.6	0	0.0	49	63.6	47	67.1	50	63.3	0	0.0	146	64.6	47
Mexican American	0	0.0	0	0.0	0	0.0	0	0.0	0	0.0	0	0.0	0	0.0	0	0.0	0	0.0	0
Puerto Rican	0	0.0	1	0.9	1	0.4	0	0.0	0	0.0	0	0.0	1	1.3	0	0.0	1	0.4	0
Hispanic American	0	0.0	0	0.0	0	0.0	0	0.0	0	0.0	0	0.0	0	0.0	0	0.0	0	0.0	1
Total Minorities	70	62.5	80	70.2	150	66.4	0	0.0	49	63.6	48	68.6	53	67.1	0	0.0	150	66.4	49
Foreign Nationals	1	0.9	4	3.5	5	2.2	0	0.0	1	1.3	2	2.9	2	2.5	0	0.0	5	2.2	2
Caucasian	41	36.6	30	26.3	71	31.4	0	0.0	27	35.1	20	28.6	24	30.4	0	0.0	71	31.4	24
Total	112	49.6	114	50.4	226	100.0	0	0.0	77	34.1	70	31.0	79	35.0	0	0.0	226		75

GPA & LSAT Scores

	Full Time	Part Time	Total
# of apps	431	0	431
# admits	158	0	158
# of matrics	77	0	77
75% GPA	3.53	0.00	
25% GPA	3.07	0.00	
75% LSAT	160	0	
25% LSAT	154	0	

Tuition & Fees

	Resident	Non-resident
Full-Time	$7,115	$13,547
Part-Time	$0	$0

Living Expenses

Estimated living expenses for Singles		
Living on campus	Living off campus	Living at home
$7,200	$9,700	$4,700

Financial Aid

	Full-time		Part-time		Total	
	#	%	#	%	#	%
Total # of Students	226		0		226	
Total # receiving grants	116	51.3	0	0.0	116	51.3
Less than 1/2 tuition	16	7.1	0	0.0	16	7.1
Half to full tuition	51	22.6	0	0.0	51	22.6
Full tuition	21	9.3	0	0.0	21	9.3
More than full tuition	28	12.4	0	0.0	28	12.4
Median Grant Amount	$5,280		$0			

Informational & Library Resources

# of volumes & volume equivalents	248,829	# of professional staff	5
# of titles	29,293	Hours per week with professional staff	70
# of active serial subscriptions	2,736	Hours per week without professional staff	4
Study seating capacity inside the library	392	# of student computer work stations for entire law school	21
Square feet of law library	32,126	# of additional networked connections	1
Square feet of law school (excl. Library)	36,233	Require Laptop Computer?	N

Employment

	Total	%
Employment status known	73	100.0
Employment status unknown	0	0.0
Employed	65	89.0
Pursuing graduate degrees	1	1.4
Unemployed seeking employment	4	5.5
Unemployed not seeking employment	3	4.1
Type of Employment		
# employed in law firms	24	36.9
# employed in business & industry	7	10.8
# employed in government	8	12.3
# employed in public interest	2	3.1
# employed as judicial clerks	24	36.9
# employed in academia	0	0.0
Geographic Location		
# employed in state	56	86.2
# employed in foreign countries	6	9.2
# of states where employed	3	

J.D. Attrition (Prior Year)

	Academic	Other	TOTALS	
	#	#	#	%
1st Year	4	2	6	8.8%
2nd Year	1	1	2	2.6%
3rd Year	0	0	0	0.0%
4th Year	0	0	0	0.0%
TOTALS	5	3	8	3.5%

Bar Passage Rates

Jurisdiction	Hawaii		
Exam	Sum 96	Win 97	Total
# from school taking bar for the first time	56	6	62
School's pass rate for all first-time takers	91%	83%	90%
State's pass rate for all first-time takers	76%	57%	70%

HOFSTRA UNIVERSITY

121 Hofstra University
Hempstead, NY 11549-1210
(516)463-5858
http://www.hofstra.edu

ABA Approved Since 1971

The Basics

Type of School: Private   Term: Semester
Application deadline: 04/15
Application fee: $60
Financial Aid deadline: 06/01
Can first year start other than Fall? No
Student faculty ratio: 23.4 to 1
Does the University offer:
- housing restricted to law students? No
- graduate student housing for which law students are eligible? Yes

Faculty & Administrators

	Total		Men		Women		Minorities	
	Fall	Spr	Fall	Spr	Fall	Spr	Fall	Spr
Full-time	29	30	25	25	4	5	4	4
Other Full-Time	5	5	1	1	4	4	0	0
Deans, librarians, & others who teach > 1/2	1	1	0	0	1	1	1	1
Part-time	15	27	12	24	3	3	0	0
Total	50	63	38	50	12	13	5	5
Deans, librarians, & others who teach < 1/2	4	4	1	1	3	3	0	0

Curriculum

	Full time	Part time
Typical first-year section size	102	0
Is there typically a "small section" of the first year class, other than Legal Writing, taught by full-time faculty?	Yes	No
If yes, typical size offered last year	25	N/A
# of classroom course titles beyond 1st year curriculum	100	0
# of upper division courses, excluding seminars, with an enrollment:		
Under 25	43	0
25 - 49	31	0
50 - 74	12	0
75 - 99	5	0
100 +	16	0
# of seminars	26	0
# of seminar positions available	565	
# of seminar positions filled	432	0
# of positions available in simulation courses	673	
# of simulation positions filled	657	0
# of positions available in faculty supervised clinical courses	77	
# of fac. sup. clin. positions filled	68	0
# involved in field placements	54	0
# involved in law journals	135	0
# in moot court or trial competitions	45	0
# of credit hrs required to graduate	87	

J.D. Enrollment & Ethnicity

	Men		Women		Fl-Time		Pt-Time		1st Yr		2nd Yr		3rd Yr		4th Yr		Total		JD Degrees Awarded
	#	%	#	%	#	%	#	%	#	%	#	%	#	%	#	%	#	%	
African-American	13	2.9	40	10.8	53	6.5	0	0.0	18	6.2	18	7.4	17	6.0	0	0.0	53	6.5	23
American Indian	0	0.0	0	0.0	0	0.0	0	0.0	0	0.0	0	0.0	0	0.0	0	0.0	0	0.0	0
Asian American	21	4.7	20	5.4	41	5.0	0	0.0	19	6.5	11	4.5	11	3.9	0	0.0	41	5.0	8
Mexican American	0	0.0	1	0.3	1	0.1	0	0.0	0	0.0	1	0.4	0	0.0	0	0.0	1	0.1	0
Puerto Rican	2	0.5	2	0.5	4	0.5	0	0.0	4	1.4	0	0.0	0	0.0	0	0.0	4	0.5	2
Hispanic American	27	6.1	23	6.2	49	6.0	1	50.0	13	4.5	14	5.8	23	8.2	0	0.0	50	6.1	10
Total Minorities	63	14.2	86	23.1	148	18.2	1	50.0	54	18.6	44	18.1	51	18.1	0	0.0	149	18.3	43
Foreign Nationals	1	0.2	0	0.0	1	0.1	0	0.0	0	0.0	0	0.0	1	0.4	0	0.0	1	0.1	0
Caucasian	380	85.6	286	76.9	665	81.7	1	50.0	237	81.4	199	81.9	230	81.6	0	0.0	666	81.6	232
Total	444	54.4	372	45.6	814	99.8	2	0.2	291	35.7	243	29.8	282	34.6	0	0.0	816		275

GPA & LSAT Scores

	Full Time	Part Time	Total
# of apps	1,689	0	1,689
# admits	823	0	823
# of matrics	291	0	291
75% GPA	3.50	0.00	
25% GPA	2.95	0.00	
75% LSAT	157	0	
25% LSAT	149	0	

Tuition & Fees

	Resident	Non-resident
Full-Time	$21,182	$21,182
Part-Time	$0	$0

Living Expenses

Estimated living expenses for Singles		
Living on campus	Living off campus	Living at home
$13,280	$16,788	$7,518

Financial Aid

	Full-time		Part-time		Total	
	#	%	#	%	#	%
Total # of Students	814		2		816	
Total # receiving grants	415	51.0	0	0.0	415	50.9
Less than 1/2 tuition	394	48.4	0	0.0	394	48.3
Half to full tuition	9	1.1	0	0.0	9	1.1
Full tuition	7	0.9	0	0.0	7	0.9
More than full tuition	5	0.6	0	0.0	5	0.6
Median Grant Amount	$3,716		$0			

Informational & Library Resources

# of volumes & volume equivalents	488,617	# of professional staff	8
# of titles	115,947	Hours per week with professional staff	92
# of active serial subscriptions	6,136	Hours per week without professional staff	6
Study seating capacity inside the library	595	# of student computer work stations for entire law school	106
Square feet of law library	50,665	# of additional networked connections	50
Square feet of law school (excl. Library)	56,499	Require Laptop Computer?	N

Employment

	Total	%
Employment status known	247	89.8
Employment status unknown	28	10.2
Employed	224	90.7
Pursuing graduate degrees	7	2.8
Unemployed seeking employment	10	4.0
Unemployed not seeking employment	6	2.4
Type of Employment		
# employed in law firms	146	65.2
# employed in business & industry	33	14.7
# employed in government	24	10.7
# employed in public interest	7	3.1
# employed as judicial clerks	14	6.2
# employed in academia	0	0.0
Geographic Location		
# employed in state	168	75.0
# employed in foreign countries	2	0.9
# of states where employed	15	

J.D. Attrition (Prior Year)

	Academic	Other	TOTALS	
	#	#	#	%
1st Year	0	2	2	0.8%
2nd Year	1	14	15	5.5%
3rd Year	0	4	4	1.4%
4th Year	0	0	0	0.0%
TOTALS	1	20	21	2.6%

Bar Passage Rates

Jurisdiction	New York		
Exam	Sum 96	Win 97	Total
# from school taking bar for the first time	243	15	258
School's pass rate for all first-time takers	79%	33%	77%
State's pass rate for all first-time takers	78%	67%	77%

HOUSTON, UNIVERSITY OF

4800 Calhoun
Entrance 19
Houston, TX 77004-6371
(713)743-2100
http://www.law.uh.edu

ABA Approved Since 1950

The Basics

Type of School: Public   Term: Semester
Application deadline: 02/01
Application fee: $50
Financial Aid deadline: 04/01
Can first year start other than Fall? Yes
Student faculty ratio: 21.0 to 1
Does the University offer:
- housing restricted to law students? No
- graduate student housing for which law students are eligible? No

Faculty & Administrators

	Total		Men		Women		Minorities	
	Fall	Spr	Fall	Spr	Fall	Spr	Fall	Spr
Full-time	35	38	30	32	5	6	1	3
Other Full-Time	0	0	0	0	0	0	0	0
Deans, librarians, & others who teach > 1/2	11	11	7	7	4	4	1	1
Part-time	38	55	31	44	7	11	3	4
Total	84	104	68	83	16	21	5	8
Deans, librarians, & others who teach < 1/2	1	1	1	1	0	0	0	0

Curriculum

	Full time	Part time
Typical first-year section size	85	65
Is there typically a "small section" of the first year class, other than Legal Writing, taught by full-time faculty?	No	No
If yes, typical size offered last year	N/A	N/A
# of classroom course titles beyond 1st year curriculum	168	0
# of upper division courses, excluding seminars, with an enrollment:		
Under 25	125	0
25 - 49	69	0
50 - 74	23	0
75 - 99	8	0
100 +	4	0
# of seminars	30	0
# of seminar positions available	514	
# of seminar positions filled	399	27
# of positions available in simulation courses	856	
# of simulation positions filled	483	57
# of positions available in faculty supervised clinical courses	86	
# of fac. sup. clin. positions filled	67	3
# involved in field placements	134	5
# involved in law journals	130	7
# in moot court or trial competitions	581	71
# of credit hrs required to graduate	90	

J.D. Enrollment & Ethnicity

	Men		Women		Fl-Time		Pt-Time		1st Yr		2nd Yr		3rd Yr		4th Yr		Total		JD Degrees Awarded
	#	%	#	%	#	%	#	%	#	%	#	%	#	%	#	%	#	%	
African-American	21	3.8	23	5.7	25	3.4	19	8.9	9	2.9	10	3.4	18	6.3	7	11.3	44	4.6	12
American Indian	7	1.3	2	0.5	9	1.2	0	0.0	2	0.6	2	0.7	5	1.7	0	0.0	9	0.9	0
Asian American	36	6.5	29	7.2	54	7.3	11	5.2	20	6.5	26	8.8	19	6.6	0	0.0	65	6.8	28
Mexican American	35	6.4	21	5.2	47	6.3	9	4.2	20	6.5	16	5.4	15	5.2	5	8.1	56	5.9	14
Puerto Rican	0	0.0	0	0.0	0	0.0	0	0.0	0	0.0	0	0.0	0	0.0	0	0.0	0	0.0	0
Hispanic American	15	2.7	15	3.7	24	3.2	6	2.8	10	3.2	13	4.4	7	2.4	0	0.0	30	3.1	10
Total Minorities	114	20.7	90	22.3	159	21.5	45	21.1	61	19.8	67	22.6	64	22.2	12	19.4	204	21.4	64
Foreign Nationals	1	0.2	0	0.0	1	0.1	0	0.0	1	0.3	0	0.0	0	0.0	0	0.0	1	0.1	0
Caucasian	435	79.1	314	77.7	581	78.4	168	78.9	246	79.9	229	77.4	224	77.8	50	80.6	749	78.5	293
Total	550	57.7	404	42.3	741	77.7	213	22.3	308	32.3	296	31.0	288	30.2	62	6.5	954		357

GPA & LSAT Scores

	Full Time	Part Time	Total
# of apps	1,800	269	2,069
# admits	770	91	861
# of matrics	254	70	324
75% GPA	3.57	3.58	
25% GPA	3.05	2.98	
75% LSAT	161	161	
25% LSAT	154	155	

Tuition & Fees

	Resident	Non-resident
Full-Time	$5,505	$9,705
Part-Time	$4,049	$7,049

Living Expenses

Estimated living expenses for Singles		
Living on campus	Living off campus	Living at home
$7,680	$9,670	$6,240

Employment

	Total	%
Employment status known	256	88.0
Employment status unknown	35	12.0
Employed	227	88.7
Pursuing graduate degrees	5	2.0
Unemployed seeking employment	13	5.1
Unemployed not seeking employment	11	4.3
Type of Employment		
# employed in law firms	148	65.2
# employed in business & industry	42	18.5
# employed in government	19	8.4
# employed in public interest	2	0.9
# employed as judicial clerks	13	5.7
# employed in academia	3	1.3
Geographic Location		
# employed in state	211	93.0
# employed in foreign countries	0	0.0
# of states where employed	11	

Financial Aid

	Full-time		Part-time		Total	
	#	%	#	%	#	%
Total # of Students	741		213		954	
Total # receiving grants	425	57.4	121	56.8	546	57.2
Less than 1/2 tuition	280	37.8	75	35.2	355	37.2
Half to full tuition	145	19.6	46	21.6	191	20.0
Full tuition	0	0.0	0	0.0	0	0.0
More than full tuition	0	0.0	0	0.0	0	0.0
Median Grant Amount	$1,250		$1,000			

Informational & Library Resources

# of volumes & volume equivalents	451,569	# of professional staff	9
# of titles	88,293	Hours per week with professional staff	62
# of active serial subscriptions	2,750	Hours per week without professional staff	43
Study seating capacity inside the library	936	# of student computer work stations for entire law school	100
Square feet of law library	87,528	# of additional networked connections	450
Square feet of law school (excl. Library)	75,585	Require Laptop Computer?	N

J.D. Attrition (Prior Year)

	Academic	Other	TOTALS	
	#	#	#	%
1st Year	0	9	9	3.1%
2nd Year	0	16	16	5.8%
3rd Year	0	14	14	3.7%
4th Year	0	4	4	8.3%
TOTALS	0	43	43	4.3%

Bar Passage Rates

Jurisdiction	Texas		
Exam	Sum 96	Win 97	Total
# from school taking bar for the first time	208	74	282
School's pass rate for all first-time takers	92%	88%	91%
State's pass rate for all first-time takers	84%	81%	84%

HOWARD UNIVERSITY

2900 Van Ness Street
Washington, DC 20008
(202)806-8000
http://www.law.howard.edu

ABA Approved Since 1931

The Basics

Type of School: Private   Term: Semester
Application deadline: 04/30
Application fee: $60
Financial Aid deadline: 04/01
Can first year start other than Fall? No
Student faculty ratio: 16.6 to 1
Does the University offer:
- housing restricted to law students? No
- graduate student housing for which law students are eligible? No

Faculty & Administrators

	Total		Men		Women		Minorities	
	Fall	Spr	Fall	Spr	Fall	Spr	Fall	Spr
Full-time	21	21	15	15	6	6	17	18
Other Full-Time	0	0	0	0	0	0	0	0
Deans, librarians, & others who teach > 1/2	0	0	0	0	0	0	0	0
Part-time	19	12	15	9	4	3	13	9
Total	40	33	30	24	10	9	30	27
Deans, librarians, & others who teach < 1/2	3	3	1	1	2	2	3	3

Curriculum

	Full time	Part time
Typical first-year section size	70	0
Is there typically a "small section" of the first year class, other than Legal Writing, taught by full-time faculty?	No	No
If yes, typical size offered last year	N/A	N/A
# of classroom course titles beyond 1st year curriculum	65	0
# of upper division courses, excluding seminars, with an enrollment:		
Under 25	38	0
25 - 49	19	0
50 - 74	10	0
75 - 99	5	0
100 +	0	0
# of seminars	22	0
# of seminar positions available	352	
# of seminar positions filled	313	0
# of positions available in simulation courses	405	
# of simulation positions filled	329	0
# of positions available in faculty supervised clinical courses	70	
# of fac. sup. clin. positions filled	52	0
# involved in field placements	33	0
# involved in law journals	57	0
# in moot court or trial competitions	54	0
# of credit hrs required to graduate	88	

J.D. Enrollment & Ethnicity

	Men		Women		Fl-Time		Pt-Time		1st Yr		2nd Yr		3rd Yr		4th Yr		Total		JD Degrees Awarded
	#	%	#	%	#	%	#	%	#	%	#	%	#	%	#	%	#	%	
African-American	155	81.6	207	90.4	362	86.4	0	0.0	121	87.1	104	90.4	137	83.0	0	0.0	362	86.4	94
American Indian	1	0.5	0	0.0	1	0.2	0	0.0	0	0.0	1	0.9	0	0.0	0	0.0	1	0.2	0
Asian American	7	3.7	6	2.6	13	3.1	0	0.0	5	3.6	3	2.6	5	3.0	0	0.0	13	3.1	4
Mexican American	0	0.0	0	0.0	0	0.0	0	0.0	0	0.0	0	0.0	0	0.0	0	0.0	0	0.0	0
Puerto Rican	0	0.0	0	0.0	0	0.0	0	0.0	0	0.0	0	0.0	0	0.0	0	0.0	0	0.0	0
Hispanic American	7	3.7	5	2.2	12	2.9	0	0.0	3	2.2	1	0.9	8	4.8	0	0.0	12	2.9	6
Total Minorities	170	89.5	218	95.2	388	92.6	0	0.0	129	92.8	109	94.8	150	90.9	0	0.0	388	92.6	104
Foreign Nationals	0	0.0	0	0.0	0	0.0	0	0.0	0	0.0	0	0.0	0	0.0	0	0.0	0	0.0	0
Caucasian	20	10.5	11	4.8	31	7.4	0	0.0	10	7.2	6	5.2	15	9.1	0	0.0	31	7.4	15
Total	190	45.3	229	54.7	419	100.0	0	0.0	139	33.2	115	27.4	165	39.4	0	0.0	419		119

GPA & LSAT Scores

	Full Time	Part Time	Total
# of apps	1,078	0	1,078
# admits	391	0	391
# of matrics	127	0	127
75% GPA	3.30	0.00	
25% GPA	2.71	0.00	
75% LSAT	154	0	
25% LSAT	148	0	

Tuition & Fees

	Resident	Non-resident
Full-Time	$12,425	$12,425
Part-Time	$0	$0

Living Expenses

Estimated living expenses for Singles		
Living on campus	Living off campus	Living at home
$10,957	$13,198	$13,198

Financial Aid

	Full-time		Part-time		Total	
	#	%	#	%	#	%
Total # of Students	419		0		419	
Total # receiving grants	228	54.4	0	0.0	228	54.4
Less than 1/2 tuition	88	21.0	0	0.0	88	21.0
Half to full tuition	91	21.7	0	0.0	91	21.7
Full tuition	20	4.8	0	0.0	20	4.8
More than full tuition	29	6.9	0	0.0	29	6.9
Median Grant Amount	$8,700		$0			

Informational & Library Resources

# of volumes & volume equivalents	246,364	# of professional staff	8
# of titles	25,253	Hours per week with professional staff	72
# of active serial subscriptions	2,687	Hours per week without professional staff	39
Study seating capacity inside the library	173	# of student computer work stations for entire law school	70
Square feet of law library	29,110	# of additional networked connections	0
Square feet of law school (excl. Library)	125,610	Require Laptop Computer?	N

Employment

	Total	%
Employment status known	108	78.3
Employment status unknown	30	21.7
Employed	95	88.0
Pursuing graduate degrees	2	1.9
Unemployed seeking employment	11	10.2
Unemployed not seeking employment	0	0.0
Type of Employment		
# employed in law firms	27	28.4
# employed in business & industry	19	20.0
# employed in government	28	29.5
# employed in public interest	5	5.3
# employed as judicial clerks	14	14.7
# employed in academia	1	1.1
Geographic Location		
# employed in state	32	33.7
# employed in foreign countries	2	2.1
# of states where employed	21	

J.D. Attrition (Prior Year)

	Academic	Other	TOTALS	
	#	#	#	%
1st Year	2	15	17	13%
2nd Year	2	6	8	4.9%
3rd Year	2	1	3	2.3%
4th Year	0	0	0	0.0%
TOTALS	6	22	28	6.7%

Bar Passage Rates

Jurisdiction	Maryland		
Exam	Sum 96	Win 97	Total
# from school taking bar for the first time	35	16	51
School's pass rate for all first-time takers	46%	31%	41%
State's pass rate for all first-time takers	76%	79%	76%

IDAHO, UNIVERSITY OF

6th & Rayburn
Moscow, ID 83844-2321
(208)885-6422
http://www.uidaho.edu/law

ABA Approved Since 1925

The Basics

Type of School: Public   Term: Semester
Application deadline: 02/01
Application fee: $30
Financial Aid deadline: 02/15
Can first year start other than Fall? No
Student faculty ratio: 14.5 to 1
Does the University offer:
- housing restricted to law students? No
- graduate student housing for which law students are eligible? Yes

Faculty & Administrators

	Total		Men		Women		Minorities	
	Fall	Spr	Fall	Spr	Fall	Spr	Fall	Spr
Full-time	17	18	11	12	6	6	0	0
Other Full-Time	3	3	1	1	2	2	0	0
Deans, librarians, & others who teach > 1/2	1	0	1	0	0	0	0	0
Part-time	7	1	4	0	3	1	0	0
Total	28	22	17	13	11	9	0	0
Deans, librarians, & others who teach < 1/2	1	1	1	1	0	0	0	0

Curriculum

	Full time	Part time
Typical first-year section size	60	0
Is there typically a "small section" of the first year class, other than Legal Writing, taught by full-time faculty?	No	No
If yes, typical size offered last year	N/A	N/A
# of classroom course titles beyond 1st year curriculum	49	0
# of upper division courses, excluding seminars, with an enrollment:		
Under 25	31	0
25 - 49	14	0
50 - 74	6	0
75 - 99	6	0
100 +	0	0
# of seminars	4	0
# of seminar positions available	75	
# of seminar positions filled	72	0
# of positions available in simulation courses	150	
# of simulation positions filled	149	0
# of positions available in faculty supervised clinical courses	41	
# of fac. sup. clin. positions filled	41	0
# involved in field placements	74	0
# involved in law journals	18	0
# in moot court or trial competitions	10	0
# of credit hrs required to graduate	88	

J.D. Enrollment & Ethnicity

	Men		Women		Fl-Time		Pt-Time		1st Yr		2nd Yr		3rd Yr		4th Yr		Total		JD Degrees Awarded
	#	%	#	%	#	%	#	%	#	%	#	%	#	%	#	%	#	%	
African-American	1	0.5	0	0.0	1	0.3	0	0.0	1	0.8	0	0.0	0	0.0	0	0.0	1	0.3	0
American Indian	3	1.5	0	0.0	3	1.0	0	0.0	2	1.6	1	1.2	0	0.0	0	0.0	3	1.0	2
Asian American	3	1.5	7	6.9	10	3.4	0	0.0	2	1.6	3	3.6	5	6.0	0	0.0	10	3.4	0
Mexican American	1	0.5	0	0.0	1	0.3	0	0.0	1	0.8	0	0.0	0	0.0	0	0.0	1	0.3	3
Puerto Rican	0	0.0	0	0.0	0	0.0	0	0.0	0	0.0	0	0.0	0	0.0	0	0.0	0	0.0	0
Hispanic American	4	2.1	5	5.0	9	3.0	0	0.0	1	0.8	5	6.0	3	3.6	0	0.0	9	3.0	5
Total Minorities	12	6.2	12	11.9	24	8.1	0	0.0	7	5.5	9	10.7	8	9.5	0	0.0	24	8.1	10
Foreign Nationals	0	0.0	0	0.0	0	0.0	0	0.0	0	0.0	0	0.0	0	0.0	0	0.0	0	0.0	0
Caucasian	183	93.8	89	88.1	272	91.9	0	0.0	121	94.5	75	89.3	76	90.5	0	0.0	272	91.9	65
Total	195	65.9	101	34.1	296	100.0	0	0.0	128	43.2	84	28.4	84	28.4	0	0.0	296		75

GPA & LSAT Scores

	Full Time	Part Time	Total
# of apps	428	0	428
# admits	296	0	296
# of matrics	128	0	128
75% GPA	3.42	0.00	
25% GPA	2.90	0.00	
75% LSAT	155	0	
25% LSAT	152	0	

Tuition & Fees

	Resident	Non-resident
Full-Time	$3,882	$9,682
Part-Time	$0	$0

Living Expenses

Estimated living expenses for Singles		
Living on campus	Living off campus	Living at home
$10,106	$10,106	$5,328

Financial Aid

	Full-time		Part-time		Total	
	#	%	#	%	#	%
Total # of Students	296		0		296	
Total # receiving grants	166	56.1	0	0.0	166	56.1
Less than 1/2 tuition	137	46.3	0	0.0	137	46.3
Half to full tuition	19	6.4	0	0.0	19	6.4
Full tuition	10	3.4	0	0.0	10	3.4
More than full tuition	0	0.0	0	0.0	0	0.0
Median Grant Amount	$500		$0			

Informational & Library Resources

# of volumes & volume equivalents	169,770	# of professional staff	3
# of titles	25,146	Hours per week with professional staff	45
# of active serial subscriptions	2,726	Hours per week without professional staff	51
Study seating capacity inside the library	369	# of student computer work stations for entire law school	9
Square feet of law library	24,822	# of additional networked connections	174
Square feet of law school (excl. Library)	24,150	Require Laptop Computer?	N

Employment

	Total	%
Employment status known	69	94.5
Employment status unknown	4	5.5
Employed	63	91.3
Pursuing graduate degrees	3	4.3
Unemployed seeking employment	1	1.4
Unemployed not seeking employment	2	2.9
Type of Employment		
# employed in law firms	23	36.5
# employed in business & industry	8	12.7
# employed in government	13	20.6
# employed in public interest	1	1.6
# employed as judicial clerks	16	25.4
# employed in academia	0	0.0
Geographic Location		
# employed in state	48	76.2
# employed in foreign countries	1	1.6
# of states where employed	9	

J.D. Attrition (Prior Year)

	Academic	Other	TOTALS	
	#	#	#	%
1st Year	0	2	2	2.4%
2nd Year	8	4	12	14%
3rd Year	5	6	11	11%
4th Year	0	0	0	0.0%
TOTALS	13	12	25	9.4%

Bar Passage Rates

Jurisdiction	Idaho		
Exam	Sum 96	Win 97	Total
# from school taking bar for the first time	47	9	56
School's pass rate for all first-time takers	91%	78%	89%
State's pass rate for all first-time takers	81%	68%	76%

ILLINOIS INSTITUTE OF TECHNOLOGY

Chicago-Kent College of Law
565 West Adams Street
Chicago, IL 60661
(312)906-5000
http://www.kentlaw.edu

ABA Approved Since 1936

The Basics

Type of School: Private   Term: Semester
Application deadline: 04/01
Application fee: $40
Financial Aid deadline: 04/15
Can first year start other than Fall? No
Student faculty ratio: 21.4 to 1
Does the University offer:
- housing restricted to law students? No
- graduate student housing for which law students are eligible? No

Faculty & Administrators

	Total		Men		Women		Minorities	
	Fall	Spr	Fall	Spr	Fall	Spr	Fall	Spr
Full-time	42	38	28	26	14	12	5	5
Other Full-Time	15	15	8	8	7	7	0	0
Deans, librarians, & others who teach > 1/2	5	5	4	4	1	1	0	0
Part-time	77	81	61	64	15	17	3	3
Total	139	139	101	102	37	37	8	8
Deans, librarians, & others who teach < 1/2	1	1	1	1	0	0	0	0

Curriculum

	Full time	Part time
Typical first-year section size	100	100
Is there typically a "small section" of the first year class, other than Legal Writing, taught by full-time faculty?	Yes	Yes
If yes, typical size offered last year	50	50
# of classroom course titles beyond 1st year curriculum	114	65
# of upper division courses, excluding seminars, with an enrollment:		
Under 25	95	43
25 - 49	37	18
50 - 74	10	3
75 - 99	9	6
100 +	2	0
# of seminars	25	11
# of seminar positions available	540	
# of seminar positions filled	254	119
# of positions available in simulation courses	782	
# of simulation positions filled	320	179
# of positions available in faculty supervised clinical courses	183	
# of fac. sup. clin. positions filled	170	9
# involved in field placements	120	3
# involved in law journals	46	7
# in moot court or trial competitions	36	16
# of credit hrs required to graduate	87	

J.D. Enrollment & Ethnicity

	Men		Women		Fl-Time		Pt-Time		1st Yr		2nd Yr		3rd Yr		4th Yr		Total		JD Degrees Awarded
	#	%	#	%	#	%	#	%	#	%	#	%	#	%	#	%	#	%	
African-American	19	3.1	35	6.1	31	3.6	23	7.1	24	6.0	12	3.1	10	3.1	8	11.1	54	4.5	14
American Indian	3	0.5	2	0.3	4	0.5	1	0.3	3	0.7	1	0.3	1	0.3	0	0.0	5	0.4	0
Asian American	57	9.3	48	8.4	89	10.3	16	4.9	32	8.0	40	10.3	28	8.6	5	6.9	105	8.8	33
Mexican American	5	0.8	12	2.1	14	1.6	3	0.9	7	1.7	3	0.8	6	1.8	1	1.4	17	1.4	3
Puerto Rican	2	0.3	6	1.0	7	0.8	1	0.3	5	1.2	2	0.5	1	0.3	0	0.0	8	0.7	4
Hispanic American	7	1.1	14	2.4	11	1.3	10	3.1	12	3.0	5	1.3	3	0.9	1	1.4	21	1.8	5
Total Minorities	93	15.1	117	20.4	156	18.1	54	16.6	83	20.6	63	16.2	49	15.1	15	20.8	210	17.7	59
Foreign Nationals	2	0.3	1	0.2	2	0.2	1	0.3	0	0.0	0	0.0	2	0.6	1	1.4	3	0.3	5
Caucasian	519	84.5	455	79.4	704	81.7	270	83.1	319	79.4	325	83.8	274	84.3	56	77.8	974	82.1	271
Total	614	51.7	573	48.3	862	72.6	325	27.4	402	33.9	388	32.7	325	27.4	72	6.1	1187		335

ILLINOIS INSTITUTE OF TECHNOLOGY

GPA & LSAT Scores

	Full Time	Part Time	Total
# of apps	1,518	346	1,864
# admits	1,009	191	1,200
# of matrics	282	102	384
75% GPA	3.43	3.38	
25% GPA	2.92	2.76	
75% LSAT	156	157	
25% LSAT	150	148	

Tuition & Fees

	Resident	Non-resident
Full-Time	$19,930	$19,930
Part-Time	$14,400	$14,400

Living Expenses

Estimated living expenses for Singles		
Living on campus	Living off campus	Living at home
N/A	$15,670	$9,685

Employment

	Total	%
Employment status known	379	97.4
Employment status unknown	10	2.6
Employed	313	82.6
Pursuing graduate degrees	5	1.3
Unemployed seeking employment	27	7.1
Unemployed not seeking employment	34	9.0
Type of Employment		
# employed in law firms	163	52.1
# employed in business & industry	94	30.0
# employed in government	31	9.9
# employed in public interest	8	2.6
# employed as judicial clerks	14	4.5
# employed in academia	3	1.0
Geographic Location		
# employed in state	259	82.7
# employed in foreign countries	1	0.3
# of states where employed	28	

Financial Aid

	Full-time		Part-time		Total	
	#	%	#	%	#	%
Total # of Students	862		325		1187	
Total # receiving grants	306	35.5	121	37.2	427	36.0
Less than 1/2 tuition	235	27.3	96	29.5	331	27.9
Half to full tuition	47	5.5	25	7.7	72	6.1
Full tuition	21	2.4	0	0.0	21	1.8
More than full tuition	3	0.3	0	0.0	3	0.3
Median Grant Amount	$6,000		$3,000			

Informational & Library Resources

# of volumes & volume equivalents	535,375	# of professional staff	9
# of titles	132,780	Hours per week with professional staff	95
# of active serial subscriptions	7,846	Hours per week without professional staff	9
Study seating capacity inside the library	689	# of student computer work stations for entire law school	135
Square feet of law library	60,916	# of additional networked connections	1860
Square feet of law school (excl. Library)	190,720	Require Laptop Computer?	N

J.D. Attrition (Prior Year)

	Academic	Other	TOTALS	
	#	#	#	%
1st Year	2	20	22	5.2%
2nd Year	0	31	31	8.4%
3rd Year	0	11	11	3.4%
4th Year	0	1	1	1.5%
TOTALS	2	63	65	5.5%

Bar Passage Rates

Jurisdiction	Illinois		
Exam	Sum 96	Win 97	Total
# from school taking bar for the first time	285	47	332
School's pass rate for all first-time takers	87%	83%	86%
State's pass rate for all first-time takers	86%	84%	86%

ILLINOIS, UNIVERSITY OF

504 East Pennsylvania Avenue
Champaign, IL 61820
(217)333-0931
http://www.law.uiuc.edu

ABA Approved Since 1923

The Basics

Type of School: Public — Term: Semester

Application deadline: 03/15

Application fee: $40

Financial Aid deadline: 03/15

Can first year start other than Fall? Yes

Student faculty ratio: 15.8 to 1

Does the University offer:
- housing restricted to law students? No
- graduate student housing for which law students are eligible? Yes

Faculty & Administrators

	Total		Men		Women		Minorities	
	Fall	Spr	Fall	Spr	Fall	Spr	Fall	Spr
Full-time	32	33	22	22	10	11	5	5
Other Full-Time	6	6	4	4	2	2	1	1
Deans, librarians, & others who teach > 1/2	1	1	1	1	0	0	0	0
Part-time	19	15	17	10	2	5	1	1
Total	58	55	44	37	14	18	7	7
Deans, librarians, & others who teach < 1/2	1	1	1	1	0	0	0	0

Curriculum

	Full time	Part time
Typical first-year section size	70	0
Is there typically a "small section" of the first year class, other than Legal Writing, taught by full-time faculty?	No	No
If yes, typical size offered last year	N/A	N/A
# of classroom course titles beyond 1st year curriculum	93	0
# of upper division courses, excluding seminars, with an enrollment:		
Under 25	37	0
25 - 49	22	0
50 - 74	14	0
75 - 99	10	0
100 +	5	0
# of seminars	15	0
# of seminar positions available	213	
# of seminar positions filled	188	0
# of positions available in simulation courses	196	
# of simulation positions filled	196	0
# of positions available in faculty supervised clinical courses	60	
# of fac. sup. clin. positions filled	50	0
# involved in field placements	84	0
# involved in law journals	99	0
# in moot court or trial competitions	147	0
# of credit hrs required to graduate	90	

J.D. Enrollment & Ethnicity

	Men		Women		Fl-Time		Pt-Time		1st Yr		2nd Yr		3rd Yr		4th Yr		Total		JD Degrees Awarded
	#	%	#	%	#	%	#	%	#	%	#	%	#	%	#	%	#	%	
African-American	30	8.3	45	18.4	75	12.4	0	0.0	23	11.5	19	10.2	33	15.1	0	0.0	75	12.4	22
American Indian	0	0.0	0	0.0	0	0.0	0	0.0	0	0.0	0	0.0	0	0.0	0	0.0	0	0.0	0
Asian American	31	8.6	22	9.0	53	8.8	0	0.0	17	8.5	14	7.5	22	10.0	0	0.0	53	8.8	14
Mexican American	0	0.0	0	0.0	0	0.0	0	0.0	0	0.0	0	0.0	0	0.0	0	0.0	0	0.0	0
Puerto Rican	0	0.0	0	0.0	0	0.0	0	0.0	0	0.0	0	0.0	0	0.0	0	0.0	0	0.0	0
Hispanic American	29	8.1	17	6.9	46	7.6	0	0.0	16	8.0	11	5.9	19	8.7	0	0.0	46	7.6	11
Total Minorities	90	25.0	84	34.3	174	28.8	0	0.0	56	28.0	44	23.7	74	33.8	0	0.0	174	28.8	47
Foreign Nationals	1	0.3	0	0.0	1	0.2	0	0.0	0	0.0	1	0.5	0	0.0	0	0.0	1	0.2	0
Caucasian	269	74.7	161	65.7	430	71.1	0	0.0	144	72.0	141	75.8	145	66.2	0	0.0	430	71.1	192
Total	360	59.5	245	40.5	605	100.0	0	0.0	200	33.1	186	30.7	219	36.2	0	0.0	605		239

GPA & LSAT Scores

	Full Time	Part Time	Total
# of apps	1,635	0	1,635
# admits	558	0	558
# of matrics	200	0	200
75% GPA	3.75	0.00	
25% GPA	3.20	0.00	
75% LSAT	164	0	
25% LSAT	157	0	

Tuition & Fees

	Resident	Non-resident
Full-Time	$7,646	$17,718
Part-Time	$0	$0

Living Expenses

Estimated living expenses for Singles		
Living on campus	Living off campus	Living at home
$9,632	$9,632	$9,632

Financial Aid

	Full-time		Part-time		Total	
	#	%	#	%	#	%
Total # of Students	605		0		605	
Total # receiving grants	237	39.2	0	0.0	237	39.2
Less than 1/2 tuition	106	17.5	0	0.0	106	17.5
Half to full tuition	33	5.5	0	0.0	33	5.5
Full tuition	14	2.3	0	0.0	14	2.3
More than full tuition	84	13.9	0	0.0	84	13.9
Median Grant Amount	$5,469		$0			

Informational & Library Resources

# of volumes & volume equivalents	677,635	# of professional staff	5
# of titles	240,968	Hours per week with professional staff	52
# of active serial subscriptions	8,190	Hours per week without professional staff	48
Study seating capacity inside the library	429	# of student computer work stations for entire law school	268
Square feet of law library	59,617	# of additional networked connections	93
Square feet of law school (excl. Library)	65,283	Require Laptop Computer?	N

Employment

	Total	%
Employment status known	185	99.5
Employment status unknown	1	0.5
Employed	169	91.4
Pursuing graduate degrees	6	3.2
Unemployed seeking employment	9	4.9
Unemployed not seeking employment	1	0.5
Type of Employment		
# employed in law firms	115	68.0
# employed in business & industry	22	13.0
# employed in government	9	5.3
# employed in public interest	2	1.2
# employed as judicial clerks	14	8.3
# employed in academia	7	4.1
Geographic Location		
# employed in state	110	65.1
# employed in foreign countries	1	0.6
# of states where employed	23	

J.D. Attrition (Prior Year)

	Academic	Other	TOTALS	
	#	#	#	%
1st Year	0	13	13	7.1%
2nd Year	0	0	0	0.0%
3rd Year	0	0	0	0.0%
4th Year	0	0	0	0.0%
TOTALS	0	13	13	2.1%

Bar Passage Rates

Jurisdiction	Illinois		
Exam	Sum 96	Win 97	Total
# from school taking bar for the first time	122	13	135
School's pass rate for all first-time takers	97%	85%	96%
State's pass rate for all first-time takers	86%	84%	86%

INDIANA UNIVERSITY - BLOOMINGTON

211 S. Indiana Avenue
Bloomington, IN 47405
(812)855-7995
http://www.law.indiana.edu

ABA Approved Since 1923

The Basics

Type of School: Public Term: Semester
Application deadline: 03/01 (Preferred)
Application fee: $35
Financial Aid deadline: 04/01
Can first year start other than Fall? Yes
Student faculty ratio: 16.8 to 1
Does the University offer:
- housing restricted to law students? No
- graduate student housing for which law students are eligible? Yes

Faculty & Administrators

	Total		Men		Women		Minorities	
	Fall	Spr	Fall	Spr	Fall	Spr	Fall	Spr
Full-time	32	33	26	26	6	7	2	2
Other Full-Time	6	6	1	1	5	5	0	0
Deans, librarians, & others who teach > 1/2	2	1	1	0	1	1	0	0
Part-time	13	6	8	3	5	3	0	0
Total	53	46	36	30	17	16	2	2
Deans, librarians, & others who teach < 1/2	2	2	1	1	1	1	0	0

Curriculum

	Full time	Part time
Typical first-year section size	80	0
Is there typically a "small section" of the first year class, other than Legal Writing, taught by full-time faculty?	No	No
If yes, typical size offered last year	N/A	N/A
# of classroom course titles beyond 1st year curriculum	91	0
# of upper division courses, excluding seminars, with an enrollment:		
Under 25	35	0
25 - 49	18	0
50 - 74	13	0
75 - 99	7	0
100 +	6	0
# of seminars	12	0
# of seminar positions available	240	
# of seminar positions filled	166	0
# of positions available in simulation courses	260	
# of simulation positions filled	230	0
# of positions available in faculty supervised clinical courses	72	
# of fac. sup. clin. positions filled	60	0
# involved in field placements	152	0
# involved in law journals	178	0
# in moot court or trial competitions	142	0
# of credit hrs required to graduate	86	

J.D. Enrollment & Ethnicity

	Men		Women		Fl-Time		Pt-Time		1st Yr		2nd Yr		3rd Yr		4th Yr		Total		JD Degrees Awarded
	#	%	#	%	#	%	#	%	#	%	#	%	#	%	#	%	#	%	
African-American	24	6.5	30	10.8	54	8.4	0	0.0	14	6.9	20	8.7	20	9.3	0	0.0	54	8.3	25
American Indian	1	0.3	1	0.4	2	0.3	0	0.0	1	0.5	0	0.0	1	0.5	0	0.0	2	0.3	1
Asian American	13	3.5	18	6.5	31	4.8	0	0.0	8	3.9	15	6.5	8	3.7	0	0.0	31	4.8	5
Mexican American	20	5.4	9	3.2	29	4.5	0	0.0	7	3.4	7	3.0	15	7.0	0	0.0	29	4.5	13
Puerto Rican	0	0.0	0	0.0	0	0.0	0	0.0	0	0.0	0	0.0	0	0.0	0	0.0	0	0.0	0
Hispanic American	0	0.0	0	0.0	0	0.0	0	0.0	0	0.0	0	0.0	0	0.0	0	0.0	0	0.0	0
Total Minorities	58	15.6	58	20.9	116	18.1	0	0.0	30	14.7	42	18.2	44	20.6	0	0.0	116	17.9	44
Foreign Nationals	3	0.8	3	1.1	6	0.9	0	0.0	1	0.5	2	0.9	3	1.4	0	0.0	6	0.9	5
Caucasian	311	83.6	216	78.0	518	80.9	9	100.0	173	84.8	187	81.0	167	78.0	0	0.0	527	81.2	171
Total	372	57.3	277	42.7	640	98.6	9	1.4	204	31.4	231	35.6	214	33.0	0	0.0	649		220

INDIANA UNIVERSITY - BLOOMINGTON

GPA & LSAT Scores

	Full Time	Part Time	Total
# of apps	1,319	2	1,321
# admits	545	2	547
# of matrics	203	2	205
75% GPA	3.68	0.00	
25% GPA	3.03	0.00	
75% LSAT	162	0	
25% LSAT	155	0	

Tuition & Fees

	Resident	Non-resident
Full-Time	$6,162	$15,268
Part-Time	$0	$0

Living Expenses

Estimated living expenses for Singles		
Living on campus	Living off campus	Living at home
$6,298	$6,562	$2,514

Financial Aid

	Full-time		Part-time		Total	
	#	%	#	%	#	%
Total # of Students	640		9		649	
Total # receiving grants	260	40.6	0	0.0	260	40.1
Less than 1/2 tuition	190	29.7	0	0.0	190	29.3
Half to full tuition	55	8.6	0	0.0	55	8.5
Full tuition	4	0.6	0	0.0	4	0.6
More than full tuition	11	1.7	0	0.0	11	1.7
Median Grant Amount	$2,500		$0			

Informational & Library Resources

# of volumes & volume equivalents	591,504	# of professional staff	9
# of titles	182,579	Hours per week with professional staff	65
# of active serial subscriptions	7,584	Hours per week without professional staff	50
Study seating capacity inside the library	723	# of student computer work stations for entire law school	86
Square feet of law library	65,526	# of additional networked connections	11
Square feet of law school (excl. Library)	42,787	Require Laptop Computer?	N

Employment

	Total	%
Employment status known	178	97.8
Employment status unknown	4	2.2
Employed	160	89.9
Pursuing graduate degrees	8	4.5
Unemployed seeking employment	8	4.5
Unemployed not seeking employment	2	1.1
Type of Employment		
# employed in law firms	80	50.0
# employed in business & industry	28	17.5
# employed in government	21	13.1
# employed in public interest	5	3.1
# employed as judicial clerks	21	13.1
# employed in academia	5	3.1
Geographic Location		
# employed in state	79	49.4
# employed in foreign countries	6	3.7
# of states where employed	27	

J.D. Attrition (Prior Year)

	Academic	Other	TOTALS	
	#	#	#	%
1st Year	0	7	7	3.1%
2nd Year	0	6	6	3.0%
3rd Year	0	2	2	0.9%
4th Year	0	0	0	0.0%
TOTALS	0	15	15	2.3%

Bar Passage Rates

Jurisdiction	Indiana		
Exam	Sum 96	Win 97	Total
# from school taking bar for the first time	87	20	107
School's pass rate for all first-time takers	86%	90%	87%
State's pass rate for all first-time takers	78%	88%	80%

INDIANA UNIVERSITY - INDIANAPOLIS

735 West New York Street
Indianapolis, IN 46202-5194
(317)274-8523
http://www.iulaw.indy.indiana.edu

ABA Approved Since 1936

The Basics

Type of School: Public Term: Semester

Application deadline: 03/01

Application fee: $35

Financial Aid deadline: 03/01

Can first year start other than Fall? Yes

Student faculty ratio: 18.5 to 1

Does the University offer:
- housing restricted to law students? No
- graduate student housing for which law students are eligible? No

Faculty & Administrators

	Total		Men		Women		Minorities	
	Fall	Spr	Fall	Spr	Fall	Spr	Fall	Spr
Full-time	34	34	24	24	10	10	2	2
Other Full-Time	5	5	1	1	4	4	0	0
Deans, librarians, & others who teach > 1/2	0	0	0	0	0	0	0	0
Part-time	16	10	12	8	4	2	1	0
Total	55	49	37	33	18	16	3	2
Deans, librarians, & others who teach < 1/2	3	3	2	2	1	1	0	0

Curriculum

	Full time	Part time
Typical first-year section size	88	77
Is there typically a "small section" of the first year class, other than Legal Writing, taught by full-time faculty?	Yes	Yes
If yes, typical size offered last year	N/A	N/A
# of classroom course titles beyond 1st year curriculum	62	48
# of upper division courses, excluding seminars, with an enrollment:		
Under 25	15	18
25 - 49	29	16
50 - 74	10	10
75 - 99	10	2
100 +	2	0
# of seminars	10	3
# of seminar positions available	289	
# of seminar positions filled	151	47
# of positions available in simulation courses	299	
# of simulation positions filled	198	56
# of positions available in faculty supervised clinical courses	116	
# of fac. sup. clin. positions filled	49	14
# involved in field placements	79	13
# involved in law journals	75	21
# in moot court or trial competitions	128	35
# of credit hrs required to graduate	90	

J.D. Enrollment & Ethnicity

	Men		Women		Fl-Time		Pt-Time		1st Yr		2nd Yr		3rd Yr		4th Yr		Total		JD Degrees Awarded
	#	%	#	%	#	%	#	%	#	%	#	%	#	%	#	%	#	%	
African-American	22	4.8	36	9.1	41	7.3	17	5.8	26	7.4	11	4.6	21	8.0	0	0.0	58	6.8	13
American Indian	2	0.4	2	0.5	3	0.5	1	0.3	2	0.6	1	0.4	1	0.4	0	0.0	4	0.5	0
Asian American	5	1.1	10	2.5	13	2.3	2	0.7	8	2.3	4	1.7	3	1.1	0	0.0	15	1.8	4
Mexican American	8	1.7	9	2.3	13	2.3	4	1.4	5	1.4	9	3.8	3	1.1	0	0.0	17	2.0	6
Puerto Rican	0	0.0	0	0.0	0	0.0	0	0.0	0	0.0	0	0.0	0	0.0	0	0.0	0	0.0	0
Hispanic American	0	0.0	0	0.0	0	0.0	0	0.0	0	0.0	0	0.0	0	0.0	0	0.0	0	0.0	0
Total Minorities	37	8.0	57	14.4	70	12.4	24	8.2	41	11.6	25	10.5	28	10.6	0	0.0	94	11.0	23
Foreign Nationals	9	2.0	5	1.3	11	2.0	3	1.0	6	1.7	5	2.1	3	1.1	0	0.0	14	1.6	3
Caucasian	414	90.0	333	84.3	482	85.6	265	90.8	306	86.7	208	87.4	233	88.3	0	0.0	747	87.4	192
Total	460	53.8	395	46.2	563	65.8	292	34.2	353	41.3	238	27.8	264	30.9	0	0.0	855		218

INDIANA UNIVERSITY - INDIANAPOLIS

GPA & LSAT Scores

	Full Time	Part Time	Total
# of apps	670	275	945
# admits	396	110	506
# of matrics	186	82	268
75% GPA	3.49	3.55	
25% GPA	2.96	2.94	
75% LSAT	157	158	
25% LSAT	151	151	

Tuition & Fees

	Resident	Non-resident
Full-Time	$5,612	$13,380
Part-Time	$4,059	$9,608

Living Expenses

Estimated living expenses for Singles		
Living on campus	Living off campus	Living at home
$8,106	$11,576	$7,476

Financial Aid

	Full-time		Part-time		Total	
	#	%	#	%	#	%
Total # of Students	563		292		855	
Total # receiving grants	76	13.5	19	6.5	95	11.1
Less than 1/2 tuition	49	8.7	10	3.4	59	6.9
Half to full tuition	15	2.7	5	1.7	20	2.3
Full tuition	5	0.9	0	0.0	5	0.6
More than full tuition	7	1.2	4	1.4	11	1.3
Median Grant Amount	$1,500		$1,000			

Informational & Library Resources

# of volumes & volume equivalents	491,716	# of professional staff	7
# of titles	174,839	Hours per week with professional staff	60
# of active serial subscriptions	6,994	Hours per week without professional staff	39
Study seating capacity inside the library	452	# of student computer work stations for entire law school	70
Square feet of law library	32,016	# of additional networked connections	0
Square feet of law school (excl. Library)	40,150	Require Laptop Computer?	N

Employment

	Total	%
Employment status known	238	95.2
Employment status unknown	12	4.8
Employed	217	91.2
Pursuing graduate degrees	2	0.8
Unemployed seeking employment	11	4.6
Unemployed not seeking employment	8	3.4
Type of Employment		
# employed in law firms	134	61.8
# employed in business & industry	35	16.1
# employed in government	29	13.4
# employed in public interest	6	2.8
# employed as judicial clerks	9	4.1
# employed in academia	4	1.8
Geographic Location		
# employed in state	192	88.5
# employed in foreign countries	1	0.5
# of states where employed	13	

J.D. Attrition (Prior Year)

	Academic	Other	TOTALS	
	#	#	#	%
1st Year	2	16	18	5.4%
2nd Year	4	9	13	5.1%
3rd Year	0	4	4	1.7%
4th Year	0	0	0	0.0%
TOTALS	6	29	35	4.2%

Bar Passage Rates

Jurisdiction	Indiana		
Exam	Sum 96	Win 97	Total
# from school taking bar for the first time	183	33	216
School's pass rate for all first-time takers	82%	94%	84%
State's pass rate for all first-time takers	78%	88%	80%

INTER AMERICAN UNIVERSITY OF PUERTO RICO

P.O. Box 70351
San Juan, PR 00936-8351
(787)751-1912
http://www.derecho.inter.edu

ABA Approved Since 1969

The Basics

Type of School: Private   Term: Semester
Application deadline: 03/31
Application fee: $63
Financial Aid deadline: 09/30
Can first year start other than Fall? No
Student faculty ratio: 23.9 to 1
Does the University offer:
- housing restricted to law students? No
- graduate student housing for which law students are eligible? No

Faculty & Administrators

	Total		Men		Women		Minorities	
	Fall	Spr	Fall	Spr	Fall	Spr	Fall	Spr
Full-time	20	20	12	12	8	8	20	20
Other Full-Time	1	1	0	0	1	1	1	1
Deans, librarians, & others who teach > 1/2	0	0	0	0	0	0	0	0
Part-time	24	28	17	20	7	8	23	27
Total	45	49	29	32	16	17	44	48
Deans, librarians, & others who teach < 1/2	4	4	4	4	0	0	4	4

Curriculum

	Full time	Part time
Typical first-year section size	60	50
Is there typically a "small section" of the first year class, other than Legal Writing, taught by full-time faculty?	No	No
If yes, typical size offered last year	N/A	N/A
# of classroom course titles beyond 1st year curriculum	40	39
# of upper division courses, excluding seminars, with an enrollment:		
Under 25	34	18
25 - 49	17	22
50 - 74	7	9
75 - 99	0	0
100 +	0	0
# of seminars	11	7
# of seminar positions available	270	
# of seminar positions filled	103	72
# of positions available in simulation courses	250	
# of simulation positions filled	73	100
# of positions available in faculty supervised clinical courses	165	
# of fac. sup. clin. positions filled	80	0
# involved in field placements	3	0
# involved in law journals	42	9
# in moot court or trial competitions	2	0
# of credit hrs required to graduate	92	

J.D. Enrollment & Ethnicity

	Men		Women		Fl-Time		Pt-Time		1st Yr		2nd Yr		3rd Yr		4th Yr		Total		JD Degrees Awarded
	#	%	#	%	#	%	#	%	#	%	#	%	#	%	#	%	#	%	
African-American	0	0.0	0	0.0	0	0.0	0	0.0	0	0.0	0	0.0	0	0.0	0	0.0	0	0.0	0
American Indian	0	0.0	0	0.0	0	0.0	0	0.0	0	0.0	0	0.0	0	0.0	0	0.0	0	0.0	0
Asian American	0	0.0	0	0.0	0	0.0	0	0.0	0	0.0	0	0.0	0	0.0	0	0.0	0	0.0	0
Mexican American	0	0.0	0	0.0	0	0.0	0	0.0	0	0.0	0	0.0	0	0.0	0	0.0	0	0.0	0
Puerto Rican	302	99.7	371	99.7	373	99.5	300	100.0	218	99.5	204	99.5	196	100.0	55	100.0	673	99.7	160
Hispanic American	1	0.3	1	0.3	2	0.5	0	0.0	1	0.5	1	0.5	0	0.0	0	0.0	2	0.3	1
Total Minorities	303	100.0	372	100.0	375	100.0	300	100.0	219	100.0	205	100.0	196	100.0	55	100.0	675	100.0	161
Foreign Nationals	0	0.0	0	0.0	0	0.0	0	0.0	0	0.0	0	0.0	0	0.0	0	0.0	0	0.0	0
Caucasian	0	0.0	0	0.0	0	0.0	0	0.0	0	0.0	0	0.0	0	0.0	0	0.0	0	0.0	0
Total	303	44.9	372	55.1	375	55.6	300	44.4	219	32.4	205	30.4	196	29.0	55	8.1	675		161

INTER AMERICAN UNIVERSITY OF PUERTO RICO

GPA & LSAT Scores

	Full Time	Part Time	Total
# of apps	468	481	949
# admits	179	159	338
# of matrics	122	104	226
75% GPA	3.26	3.31	
25% GPA	2.82	2.70	
75% LSAT	144	142	
25% LSAT	137	136	

Tuition & Fees

	Resident	Non-resident
Full-Time	$10,495	$10,495
Part-Time	$7,895	$0

Living Expenses

Estimated living expenses for Singles		
Living on campus	Living off campus	Living at home
N/A	$8,900	$5,400

Financial Aid

	Full-time		Part-time		Total	
	#	%	#	%	#	%
Total # of Students	375		300		675	
Total # receiving grants	44	11.7	1	0.3	45	6.7
Less than 1/2 tuition	2	0.5	1	0.3	3	0.4
Half to full tuition	42	11.2	0	0.0	42	6.2
Full tuition	0	0.0	0	0.0	0	0.0
More than full tuition	0	0.0	0	0.0	0	0.0
Median Grant Amount	$2,125		$420			

Informational & Library Resources

# of volumes & volume equivalents	172,236	# of professional staff	14
# of titles	22,243	Hours per week with professional staff	87
# of active serial subscriptions	3,925	Hours per week without professional staff	16
Study seating capacity inside the library	329	# of student computer work stations for entire law school	35
Square feet of law library	35,136	# of additional networked connections	3
Square feet of law school (excl. Library)	174,864	Require Laptop Computer?	N

Employment

	Total	%
Employment status known	171	97.2
Employment status unknown	5	2.8
Employed	149	87.1
Pursuing graduate degrees	5	2.9
Unemployed seeking employment	14	8.2
Unemployed not seeking employment	3	1.8
Type of Employment		
# employed in law firms	86	57.7
# employed in business & industry	27	18.1
# employed in government	23	15.4
# employed in public interest	13	8.7
# employed as judicial clerks	20	13.4
# employed in academia	2	1.3
Geographic Location		
# employed in state	147	98.7
# employed in foreign countries	1	0.7
# of states where employed	2	

J.D. Attrition (Prior Year)

	Academic	Other	TOTALS	
	#	#	#	%
1st Year	9	19	28	13%
2nd Year	2	7	9	4.9%
3rd Year	2	1	3	1.5%
4th Year	0	0	0	0.0%
TOTALS	13	27	40	6.2%

Bar Passage Rates

Jurisdiction	Puerto Rico		
Exam	Sum 96	Win 97	Total
# from school taking bar for the first time	139	32	171
School's pass rate for all first-time takers	61%	47%	58%
State's pass rate for all first-time takers	71%	53%	68%

IOWA, UNIVERSITY OF

Melrose and Byington
Iowa City, IA 52242
(319)335-9034
http://www.uiowa.edu/~/lawcoll

ABA Approved Since 1923

The Basics

Type of School: Public Term: Semester
Application deadline: 03/01
Application fee: $20
Financial Aid deadline: 01/01
Can first year start other than Fall? Yes
Student faculty ratio: 13.3 to 1
Does the University offer:
- housing restricted to law students? No
- graduate student housing for which law students are eligible? No

Faculty & Administrators

	Total		Men		Women		Minorities	
	Fall	Spr	Fall	Spr	Fall	Spr	Fall	Spr
Full-time	44	43	31	31	13	12	4	4
Other Full-Time	0	0	0	0	0	0	0	0
Deans, librarians, & others who teach > 1/2	4	4	3	3	1	1	0	0
Part-time	16	15	15	10	1	5	0	0
Total	64	62	49	44	15	18	4	4
Deans, librarians, & others who teach < 1/2	1	1	0	0	1	1	0	0

Curriculum

	Full time	Part time
Typical first-year section size	75	0
Is there typically a "small section" of the first year class, other than Legal Writing, taught by full-time faculty?	Yes	No
If yes, typical size offered last year	30	N/A
# of classroom course titles beyond 1st year curriculum	127	0
# of upper division courses, excluding seminars, with an enrollment:		
Under 25	54	0
25 - 49	27	0
50 - 74	11	0
75 - 99	9	0
100 +	2	0
# of seminars	24	0
# of seminar positions available	240	
# of seminar positions filled	200	0
# of positions available in simulation courses	232	
# of simulation positions filled	232	0
# of positions available in faculty supervised clinical courses	84	
# of fac. sup. clin. positions filled	84	0
# involved in field placements	30	0
# involved in law journals	200	0
# in moot court or trial competitions	180	0
# of credit hrs required to graduate	90	

J.D. Enrollment & Ethnicity

	Men		Women		Fl-Time		Pt-Time		1st Yr		2nd Yr		3rd Yr		4th Yr		Total		JD Degrees Awarded
	#	%	#	%	#	%	#	%	#	%	#	%	#	%	#	%	#	%	
African-American	25	6.6	22	7.9	47	7.2	0	0.0	18	8.0	11	5.8	18	7.5	0	0.0	47	7.2	16
American Indian	6	1.6	10	3.6	16	2.4	0	0.0	5	2.2	6	3.1	5	2.1	0	0.0	16	2.4	2
Asian American	22	5.8	14	5.1	36	5.5	0	0.0	6	2.7	15	7.9	15	6.3	0	0.0	36	5.5	16
Mexican American	15	3.9	21	7.6	36	5.5	0	0.0	11	4.9	12	6.3	13	5.4	0	0.0	36	5.5	11
Puerto Rican	0	0.0	0	0.0	0	0.0	0	0.0	0	0.0	0	0.0	0	0.0	0	0.0	0	0.0	0
Hispanic American	0	0.0	0	0.0	0	0.0	0	0.0	0	0.0	0	0.0	0	0.0	0	0.0	0	0.0	0
Total Minorities	68	17.9	67	24.2	135	20.5	0	0.0	40	17.7	44	23.0	51	21.3	0	0.0	135	20.5	45
Foreign Nationals	4	1.1	1	0.4	5	0.8	0	0.0	1	0.4	2	1.0	2	0.8	0	0.0	5	0.8	0
Caucasian	308	81.1	209	75.5	517	78.7	0	0.0	185	81.9	145	75.9	187	77.9	0	0.0	517	78.7	190
Total	380	57.8	277	42.2	657	100.0	0	0.0	226	34.4	191	29.1	240	36.5	0	0.0	657		235

GPA & LSAT Scores

	Full Time	Part Time	Total
# of apps	1,006	0	1,006
# admits	470	0	470
# of matrics	231	0	231
75% GPA	3.73	0.00	
25% GPA	3.09	0.00	
75% LSAT	163	0	
25% LSAT	154	0	

Tuition & Fees

	Resident	Non-resident
Full-Time	$5,974	$15,324
Part-Time	$0	$0

Living Expenses

Estimated living expenses for Singles		
Living on campus	Living off campus	Living at home
$7,998	$9,320	$5,684

Financial Aid

	Full-time		Part-time		Total	
	#	%	#	%	#	%
Total # of Students	657		0		657	
Total # receiving grants	258	39.3	0	0.0	258	39.3
Less than 1/2 tuition	108	16.4	0	0.0	108	16.4
Half to full tuition	25	3.8	0	0.0	25	3.8
Full tuition	30	4.6	0	0.0	30	4.6
More than full tuition	95	14.5	0	0.0	95	14.5
Median Grant Amount	$5,166		$0			

Informational & Library Resources

# of volumes & volume equivalents	864,882	# of professional staff	13
# of titles	343,059	Hours per week with professional staff	104
# of active serial subscriptions	8,261	Hours per week without professional staff	0
Study seating capacity inside the library	672	# of student computer work stations for entire law school	75
Square feet of law library	76,571	# of additional networked connections	15
Square feet of law school (excl. Library)	68,429	Require Laptop Computer?	N

Employment

	Total	%
Employment status known	211	98.1
Employment status unknown	4	1.9
Employed	191	90.5
Pursuing graduate degrees	3	1.4
Unemployed seeking employment	11	5.2
Unemployed not seeking employment	6	2.8
Type of Employment		
# employed in law firms	113	59.2
# employed in business & industry	23	12.0
# employed in government	20	10.5
# employed in public interest	8	4.2
# employed as judicial clerks	24	12.6
# employed in academia	3	1.6
Geographic Location		
# employed in state	70	36.6
# employed in foreign countries	1	0.5
# of states where employed	30	

J.D. Attrition (Prior Year)

	Academic	Other	TOTALS	
	#	#	#	%
1st Year	0	15	15	7.0%
2nd Year	1	8	9	4.8%
3rd Year	0	3	3	1.2%
4th Year	0	0	0	0.0%
TOTALS	1	26	27	4.1%

Bar Passage Rates

Jurisdiction	Iowa		
Exam	Sum 96	Win 97	Total
# from school taking bar for the first time	90	20	110
School's pass rate for all first-time takers	78%	80%	78%
State's pass rate for all first-time takers	78%	80%	78%

JOHN MARSHALL LAW SCHOOL

315 S. Plymouth Ct.
Chicago, IL 60604
(312)427-2737
http://www.jmls.edu

ABA Approved Since 1951

The Basics

Type of School: Private   Term: Semester

Application deadline: 03/01

Application fee: $50

Financial Aid deadline: 06/01

Can first year start other than Fall? Yes

Student faculty ratio: 14.7 to 1

Does the University offer:
- housing restricted to law students? No
- graduate student housing for which law students are eligible? No

Faculty & Administrators

	Total		Men		Women		Minorities	
	Fall	Spr	Fall	Spr	Fall	Spr	Fall	Spr
Full-time	54	48	40	35	14	13	4	4
Other Full-Time	0	0	0	0	0	0	0	0
Deans, librarians, & others who teach > 1/2	2	2	1	1	1	1	0	0
Part-time	96	101	74	80	22	21	4	7
Total	152	151	115	116	37	35	8	11
Deans, librarians, & others who teach < 1/2	1	1	1	1	0	0	0	0

Curriculum

	Full time	Part time
Typical first-year section size	60	60
Is there typically a "small section" of the first year class, other than Legal Writing, taught by full-time faculty?	No	No
If yes, typical size offered last year	N/A	N/A
# of classroom course titles beyond 1st year curriculum	63	115
# of upper division courses, excluding seminars, with an enrollment:		
Under 25	80	99
25 - 49	24	24
50 - 74	19	14
75 - 99	6	3
100 +	0	0
# of seminars	10	27
# of seminar positions available	555	
# of seminar positions filled	94	235
# of positions available in simulation courses	1,308	
# of simulation positions filled	473	445
# of positions available in faculty supervised clinical courses	105	
# of fac. sup. clin. positions filled	21	9
# involved in field placements	137	23
# involved in law journals	122	35
# in moot court or trial competitions	57	13
# of credit hrs required to graduate	90	

J.D. Enrollment & Ethnicity

	Men		Women		Fl-Time		Pt-Time		1st Yr		2nd Yr		3rd Yr		4th Yr		Total		JD Degrees Awarded
	#	%	#	%	#	%	#	%	#	%	#	%	#	%	#	%	#	%	
African-American	20	3.2	49	10.6	31	4.4	38	9.9	26	7.4	21	6.3	17	5.4	5	5.7	69	6.4	9
American Indian	5	0.8	3	0.6	5	0.7	3	0.8	3	0.9	2	0.6	3	1.0	0	0.0	8	0.7	0
Asian American	33	5.3	25	5.4	39	5.6	19	4.9	15	4.3	26	7.8	14	4.5	3	3.4	58	5.3	11
Mexican American	13	2.1	6	1.3	11	1.6	8	2.1	8	2.3	6	1.8	4	1.3	1	1.1	19	1.8	4
Puerto Rican	6	1.0	3	0.6	6	0.9	3	0.8	4	1.1	3	0.9	1	0.3	1	1.1	9	0.8	2
Hispanic American	12	1.9	13	2.8	11	1.6	14	3.6	7	2.0	7	2.1	10	3.2	1	1.1	25	2.3	4
Total Minorities	89	14.3	99	21.4	103	14.7	85	22.1	63	17.9	65	19.5	49	15.7	11	12.5	188	17.3	30
Foreign Nationals	5	0.8	4	0.9	5	0.7	4	1.0	5	1.4	3	0.9	1	0.3	0	0.0	9	0.8	1
Caucasian	528	84.9	360	77.8	592	84.6	296	76.9	284	80.7	265	79.6	262	84.0	77	87.5	888	81.8	297
Total	622	57.3	463	42.7	700	64.5	385	35.5	352	32.4	333	30.7	312	28.8	88	8.1	1085		328

GPA & LSAT Scores

	Full Time	Part Time	Total
# of apps	1,423	432	1,855
# admits	897	219	1,116
# of matrics	232	135	367
75% GPA	3.23	3.08	
25% GPA	2.67	2.42	
75% LSAT	152	154	
25% LSAT	145	146	

Tuition & Fees

	Resident	Non-resident
Full-Time	$16,600	$16,600
Part-Time	$11,880	$11,880

Living Expenses

Estimated living expenses for Singles		
Living on campus	Living off campus	Living at home
N/A	$12,924	$12,924

Employment

	Total	%
Employment status known	333	95.4
Employment status unknown	16	4.6
Employed	281	84.4
Pursuing graduate degrees	11	3.3
Unemployed seeking employment	39	11.7
Unemployed not seeking employment	2	0.6
Type of Employment		
# employed in law firms	153	54.4
# employed in business & industry	50	17.8
# employed in government	55	19.6
# employed in public interest	3	1.1
# employed as judicial clerks	13	4.6
# employed in academia	3	1.1
Geographic Location		
# employed in state	230	81.9
# employed in foreign countries	0	0.0
# of states where employed	12	

Financial Aid

	Full-time		Part-time		Total	
	#	%	#	%	#	%
Total # of Students	700		385		1085	
Total # receiving grants	95	13.6	47	12.2	142	13.1
Less than 1/2 tuition	65	9.3	40	10.4	105	9.7
Half to full tuition	23	3.3	7	1.8	30	2.8
Full tuition	1	0.1	0	0.0	1	0.1
More than full tuition	6	0.9	0	0.0	6	0.6
Median Grant Amount	$10,700		$6,240			

Informational & Library Resources

# of volumes & volume equivalents	353,737	# of professional staff	9
# of titles	91,968	Hours per week with professional staff	67
# of active serial subscriptions	5,011	Hours per week without professional staff	33
Study seating capacity inside the library	624	# of student computer work stations for entire law school	80
Square feet of law library	50,000	# of additional networked connections	42
Square feet of law school (excl. Library)	76,729	Require Laptop Computer?	N

J.D. Attrition (Prior Year)

	Academic	Other	TOTALS	
	#	#	#	%
1st Year	25	28	53	14%
2nd Year	8	22	30	10%
3rd Year	1	4	5	1.4%
4th Year	0	1	1	1.1%
TOTALS	34	55	89	8.0%

Bar Passage Rates

Jurisdiction	Illinois		
Exam	Sum 96	Win 97	Total
# from school taking bar for the first time	186	110	296
School's pass rate for all first-time takers	78%	77%	78%
State's pass rate for all first-time takers	86%	84%	86%

KANSAS, UNIVERSITY OF

Green Hall
Lawrence, KS 66045
(785)864-4550
http://www.law.ukans.edu

ABA Approved Since 1923

The Basics

Type of School: Public Term: Semester
Application deadline: 03/15
Application fee: $40
Financial Aid deadline: 03/01
Can first year start other than Fall? Yes
Student faculty ratio: 17.5 to 1
Does the University offer:
- housing restricted to law students? No
- graduate student housing for which law students are eligible? Yes

Faculty & Administrators

	Total		Men		Women		Minorities	
	Fall	Spr	Fall	Spr	Fall	Spr	Fall	Spr
Full-time	26	28	20	22	6	6	3	3
Other Full-Time	0	0	0	0	0	0	0	0
Deans, librarians, & others who teach > 1/2	5	5	2	2	3	3	0	0
Part-time	13	17	9	14	4	3	0	0
Total	44	50	31	38	13	12	3	3
Deans, librarians, & others who teach < 1/2	0	0	0	0	0	0	0	0

Curriculum

	Full time	Part time
Typical first-year section size	90	0
Is there typically a "small section" of the first year class, other than Legal Writing, taught by full-time faculty?	Yes	No
If yes, typical size offered last year	20	N/A
# of classroom course titles beyond 1st year curriculum	82	0
# of upper division courses, excluding seminars, with an enrollment:		
Under 25	45	0
25 - 49	21	0
50 - 74	8	0
75 - 99	2	0
100 +	8	0
# of seminars	14	0
# of seminar positions available	264	
# of seminar positions filled	146	0
# of positions available in simulation courses	312	
# of simulation positions filled	255	0
# of positions available in faculty supervised clinical courses	166	
# of fac. sup. clin. positions filled	129	0
# involved in field placements	0	0
# involved in law journals	96	0
# in moot court or trial competitions	46	0
# of credit hrs required to graduate	90	

J.D. Enrollment & Ethnicity

	Men		Women		Fl-Time		Pt-Time		1st Yr		2nd Yr		3rd Yr		4th Yr		Total		JD Degrees Awarded
	#	%	#	%	#	%	#	%	#	%	#	%	#	%	#	%	#	%	
African-American	10	3.1	8	3.9	18	3.4	0	0.0	3	1.7	10	5.2	5	3.0	0	0.0	18	3.4	2
American Indian	7	2.1	5	2.4	12	2.3	0	0.0	5	2.8	5	2.6	2	1.2	0	0.0	12	2.3	5
Asian American	5	1.5	2	1.0	7	1.3	0	0.0	2	1.1	4	2.1	1	0.6	0	0.0	7	1.3	2
Mexican American	0	0.0	0	0.0	0	0.0	0	0.0	0	0.0	0	0.0	0	0.0	0	0.0	0	0.0	0
Puerto Rican	0	0.0	0	0.0	0	0.0	0	0.0	0	0.0	0	0.0	0	0.0	0	0.0	0	0.0	0
Hispanic American	14	4.3	6	2.9	20	3.8	0	0.0	4	2.2	8	4.2	8	4.9	0	0.0	20	3.8	13
Total Minorities	36	11.0	21	10.2	57	10.7	0	0.0	14	7.9	27	14.1	16	9.8	0	0.0	57	10.7	22
Foreign Nationals	3	0.9	2	1.0	5	0.9	0	0.0	2	1.1	1	0.5	2	1.2	0	0.0	5	0.9	0
Caucasian	288	88.1	183	88.8	471	88.4	0	0.0	162	91.0	163	85.3	146	89.0	0	0.0	471	88.4	127
Total	327	61.4	206	38.6	533	100.0	0	0.0	178	33.4	191	35.8	164	30.8	0	0.0	533		149

GPA & LSAT Scores

	Full Time	Part Time	Total
# of apps	813	0	813
# admits	403	0	403
# of matrics	180	0	180
75% GPA	3.63	0.00	
25% GPA	3.12	0.00	
75% LSAT	158	0	
25% LSAT	152	0	

Tuition & Fees

	Resident	Non-resident
Full-Time	$4,553	$11,260
Part-Time	$0	$0

Living Expenses

Estimated living expenses for Singles

Living on campus	Living off campus	Living at home
$10,391	$10,391	$6,581

Financial Aid

	Full-time		Part-time		Total	
	#	%	#	%	#	%
Total # of Students	533		0		533	
Total # receiving grants	198	37.1	0	0.0	198	37.1
Less than 1/2 tuition	140	26.3	0	0.0	140	26.3
Half to full tuition	42	7.9	0	0.0	42	7.9
Full tuition	16	3.0	0	0.0	16	3.0
More than full tuition	0	0.0	0	0.0	0	0.0
Median Grant Amount	$2,000		$0			

Informational & Library Resources

# of volumes & volume equivalents	331,393	# of professional staff	5
# of titles	116,075	Hours per week with professional staff	65
# of active serial subscriptions	4,345	Hours per week without professional staff	38
Study seating capacity inside the library	276	# of student computer work stations for entire law school	66
Square feet of law library	34,655	# of additional networked connections	0
Square feet of law school (excl. Library)	30,009	Require Laptop Computer?	N

Employment

	Total	%
Employment status known	148	91.4
Employment status unknown	14	8.6
Employed	132	89.2
Pursuing graduate degrees	6	4.1
Unemployed seeking employment	6	4.1
Unemployed not seeking employment	4	2.7
Type of Employment		
# employed in law firms	64	48.5
# employed in business & industry	36	27.3
# employed in government	17	12.9
# employed in public interest	3	2.3
# employed as judicial clerks	9	6.8
# employed in academia	2	1.5
Geographic Location		
# employed in state	65	49.2
# employed in foreign countries	1	0.8
# of states where employed	17	

J.D. Attrition (Prior Year)

	Academic	Other	TOTALS	
	#	#	#	%
1st Year	0	2	2	1.1%
2nd Year	0	8	8	4.8%
3rd Year	0	2	2	1.5%
4th Year	0	0	0	0.0%
TOTALS	0	12	12	2.5%

Bar Passage Rates

Jurisdiction	Kansas		
Exam	Sum 96	Win 97	Total
# from school taking bar for the first time	84	42	126
School's pass rate for all first-time takers	88%	93%	90%
State's pass rate for all first-time takers	87%	93%	90%

KENTUCKY, UNIVERSITY OF

209 Law Building
Lexington, KY 40506-0048
(606)257-1678
http://www.uky.edu/law

ABA Approved Since 1925

The Basics

Type of School: Public — Term: Semester
Application deadline: 03/01
Application fee: $25
Financial Aid deadline: 04/01
Can first year start other than Fall? No
Student faculty ratio: 16.8 to 1
Does the University offer:
- housing restricted to law students? No
- graduate student housing for which law students are eligible? Yes

Faculty & Administrators

	Total		Men		Women		Minorities	
	Fall	Spr	Fall	Spr	Fall	Spr	Fall	Spr
Full-time	21	20	17	15	4	5	1	1
Other Full-Time	0	0	0	0	0	0	0	0
Deans, librarians, & others who teach > 1/2	3	3	1	1	2	2	0	0
Part-time	17	16	11	10	5	6	1	0
Total	41	39	29	26	11	13	2	1
Deans, librarians, & others who teach < 1/2	1	1	1	1	0	0	0	0

Curriculum

	Full time	Part time
Typical first-year section size	72	0
Is there typically a "small section" of the first year class, other than Legal Writing, taught by full-time faculty?	Yes	No
If yes, typical size offered last year	45	N/A
# of classroom course titles beyond 1st year curriculum	57	0
# of upper division courses, excluding seminars, with an enrollment:		
Under 25	33	0
25 - 49	13	0
50 - 74	17	0
75 - 99	3	0
100 +	0	0
# of seminars	11	0
# of seminar positions available	176	
# of seminar positions filled	162	0
# of positions available in simulation courses	158	
# of simulation positions filled	135	0
# of positions available in faculty supervised clinical courses	0	
# of fac. sup. clin. positions filled	0	0
# involved in field placements	58	0
# involved in law journals	41	0
# in moot court or trial competitions	99	0
# of credit hrs required to graduate	90	

J.D. Enrollment & Ethnicity

	Men		Women		Fl-Time		Pt-Time		1st Yr		2nd Yr		3rd Yr		4th Yr		Total		JD Degrees Awarded
	#	%	#	%	#	%	#	%	#	%	#	%	#	%	#	%	#	%	
African-American	10	4.0	10	5.7	20	4.7	0	0.0	9	6.4	2	1.5	9	5.9	0	0.0	20	4.7	8
American Indian	0	0.0	0	0.0	0	0.0	0	0.0	0	0.0	0	0.0	0	0.0	0	0.0	0	0.0	0
Asian American	3	1.2	1	0.6	4	0.9	0	0.0	1	0.7	1	0.8	2	1.3	0	0.0	4	0.9	1
Mexican American	0	0.0	0	0.0	0	0.0	0	0.0	0	0.0	0	0.0	0	0.0	0	0.0	0	0.0	0
Puerto Rican	0	0.0	0	0.0	0	0.0	0	0.0	0	0.0	0	0.0	0	0.0	0	0.0	0	0.0	0
Hispanic American	0	0.0	0	0.0	0	0.0	0	0.0	0	0.0	0	0.0	0	0.0	0	0.0	0	0.0	0
Total Minorities	13	5.2	11	6.3	24	5.7	0	0.0	10	7.1	3	2.3	11	7.2	0	0.0	24	5.7	9
Foreign Nationals	0	0.0	0	0.0	0	0.0	0	0.0	0	0.0	0	0.0	0	0.0	0	0.0	0	0.0	0
Caucasian	235	94.8	164	93.7	399	94.3	0	0.0	130	92.9	128	97.7	141	92.8	0	0.0	399	94.3	133
Total	248	58.6	175	41.4	423	100.0	0	0.0	140	33.1	131	31.0	152	35.9	0	0.0	423		142

GPA & LSAT Scores

	Full Time	Part Time	Total
# of apps	741	0	741
# admits	323	0	323
# of matrics	142	0	142
75% GPA	3.70	0.00	
25% GPA	3.14	0.00	
75% LSAT	160	0	
25% LSAT	154	0	

Tuition & Fees

	Resident	Non-resident
Full-Time	$4,956	$12,796
Part-Time	$0	$0

Living Expenses

Estimated living expenses for Singles

Living on campus	Living off campus	Living at home
$9,898	$9,898	$4,648

Financial Aid

	Full-time		Part-time		Total	
	#	%	#	%	#	%
Total # of Students	423		0		423	
Total # receiving grants	124	29.3	0	0.0	124	29.3
Less than 1/2 tuition	68	16.1	0	0.0	68	16.1
Half to full tuition	11	2.6	0	0.0	11	2.6
Full tuition	30	7.1	0	0.0	30	7.1
More than full tuition	15	3.5	0	0.0	15	3.5
Median Grant Amount	$2,000		$0			

Informational & Library Resources

# of volumes & volume equivalents	385,250	# of professional staff	8
# of titles	49,841	Hours per week with professional staff	67
# of active serial subscriptions	3,833	Hours per week without professional staff	39
Study seating capacity inside the library	279	# of student computer work stations for entire law school	48
Square feet of law library	36,843	# of additional networked connections	45
Square feet of law school (excl. Library)	28,071	Require Laptop Computer?	N

Employment

	Total	%
Employment status known	139	100.0
Employment status unknown	0	0.0
Employed	135	97.1
Pursuing graduate degrees	3	2.2
Unemployed seeking employment	0	0.0
Unemployed not seeking employment	1	0.7
Type of Employment		
# employed in law firms	78	57.8
# employed in business & industry	16	11.9
# employed in government	16	11.9
# employed in public interest	2	1.5
# employed as judicial clerks	22	16.3
# employed in academia	1	0.7
Geographic Location		
# employed in state	106	78.5
# employed in foreign countries	2	1.5
# of states where employed	13	

J.D. Attrition (Prior Year)

	Academic	Other	TOTALS	
	#	#	#	%
1st Year	4	4	8	6.1%
2nd Year	0	3	3	2.0%
3rd Year	0	0	0	0.0%
4th Year	0	0	0	0.0%
TOTALS	4	7	11	2.6%

Bar Passage Rates

Jurisdiction	Kentucky		
Exam	Sum 96	Win 97	Total
# from school taking bar for the first time	106	10	116
School's pass rate for all first-time takers	85%	100%	86%
State's pass rate for all first-time takers	84%	82%	83%

LEWIS AND CLARK COLLEGE

10015 S.W. Terwilliger Blvd.
Portland, OR 97219-7799
(503)768-6600
http://lclark.edu/law/index.htm

ABA Approved Since 1970

The Basics

Type of School: Private Term: Semester
Application deadline: 03/15
Application fee: $50
Financial Aid deadline: 03/01
Can first year start other than Fall? Yes
Student faculty ratio: 13.5 to 1
Does the University offer:
- housing restricted to law students? No
- graduate student housing for which law students are eligible? No

Faculty & Administrators

	Total		Men		Women		Minorities	
	Fall	Spr	Fall	Spr	Fall	Spr	Fall	Spr
Full-time	36	37	25	26	11	11	1	1
Other Full-Time	0	0	0	0	0	0	0	0
Deans, librarians, & others who teach > 1/2	1	1	0	0	1	1	0	0
Part-time	31	31	21	23	10	8	1	0
Total	68	69	46	49	22	20	2	1
Deans, librarians, & others who teach < 1/2	0	0	0	0	0	0	0	0

Curriculum

	Full time	Part time
Typical first-year section size	55	55
Is there typically a "small section" of the first year class, other than Legal Writing, taught by full-time faculty?	Yes	Yes
If yes, typical size offered last year	27	28
# of classroom course titles beyond 1st year curriculum	59	48
# of upper division courses, excluding seminars, with an enrollment:		
Under 25	33	16
25 - 49	20	15
50 - 74	6	7
75 - 99	9	2
100 +	0	0
# of seminars	18	13
# of seminar positions available	598	
# of seminar positions filled	306	136
# of positions available in simulation courses	282	
# of simulation positions filled	174	57
# of positions available in faculty supervised clinical courses	98	
# of fac. sup. clin. positions filled	60	26
# involved in field placements	42	13
# involved in law journals	58	17
# in moot court or trial competitions	89	34
# of credit hrs required to graduate	86	

J.D. Enrollment & Ethnicity

	Men		Women		Fl-Time		Pt-Time		1st Yr		2nd Yr		3rd Yr		4th Yr		Total		JD Degrees Awarded
	#	%	#	%	#	%	#	%	#	%	#	%	#	%	#	%	#	%	
African-American	11	3.2	4	1.4	7	1.5	8	4.9	1	0.5	7	4.2	3	1.4	4	12.9	15	2.4	2
American Indian	3	0.9	1	0.4	0	0.0	4	2.5	2	0.9	0	0.0	1	0.5	1	3.2	4	0.6	4
Asian American	21	6.1	29	10.2	42	9.1	8	4.9	8	3.7	17	10.1	23	10.9	2	6.5	50	8.0	10
Mexican American	6	1.8	3	1.1	5	1.1	4	2.5	1	0.5	1	0.6	7	3.3	0	0.0	9	1.4	3
Puerto Rican	2	0.6	0	0.0	1	0.2	1	0.6	1	0.5	0	0.0	1	0.5	0	0.0	2	0.3	0
Hispanic American	2	0.6	9	3.2	3	0.6	8	4.9	1	0.5	4	2.4	6	2.8	0	0.0	11	1.8	5
Total Minorities	45	13.2	46	16.1	58	12.5	33	20.2	14	6.5	29	17.3	41	19.4	7	22.6	91	14.5	24
Foreign Nationals	10	2.9	8	2.8	10	2.2	8	4.9	7	3.2	3	1.8	7	3.3	1	3.2	18	2.9	8
Caucasian	287	83.9	231	81.1	396	85.3	122	74.8	196	90.3	136	81.0	163	77.3	23	74.2	518	82.6	185
Total	342	54.5	285	45.5	464	74.0	163	26.0	217	34.6	168	26.8	211	33.7	31	4.9	627		217

LEWIS AND CLARK COLLEGE

GPA & LSAT Scores

	Full Time	Part Time	Total
# of apps	1,541	146	1,687
# admits	854	76	930
# of matrics	179	41	220
75% GPA	3.47	3.46	
25% GPA	2.99	2.95	
75% LSAT	163	160	
25% LSAT	157	154	

Tuition & Fees

	Resident	Non-resident
Full-Time	$17,395	$17,395
Part-Time	$13,045	$13,045

Living Expenses

Estimated living expenses for Singles		
Living on campus	Living off campus	Living at home
N/A	$11,200	$11,200

Employment

	Total	%
Employment status known	215	97.3
Employment status unknown	6	2.7
Employed	181	84.2
Pursuing graduate degrees	1	0.5
Unemployed seeking employment	27	12.6
Unemployed not seeking employment	6	2.8
Type of Employment		
# employed in law firms	93	51.4
# employed in business & industry	23	12.7
# employed in government	34	18.8
# employed in public interest	12	6.6
# employed as judicial clerks	17	9.4
# employed in academia	2	1.1
Geographic Location		
# employed in state	111	61.3
# employed in foreign countries	9	5.0
# of states where employed	21	

Financial Aid

	Full-time		Part-time		Total	
	#	%	#	%	#	%
Total # of Students	464		163		627	
Total # receiving grants	145	31.3	45	27.6	190	30.3
Less than 1/2 tuition	131	28.2	27	16.6	158	25.2
Half to full tuition	13	2.8	18	11.0	31	4.9
Full tuition	1	0.2	0	0.0	1	0.2
More than full tuition	0	0.0	0	0.0	0	0.0
Median Grant Amount	$6,000		$5,000			

Informational & Library Resources

# of volumes & volume equivalents	429,167	# of professional staff	8
# of titles	74,875	Hours per week with professional staff	69
# of active serial subscriptions	4,887	Hours per week without professional staff	44
Study seating capacity inside the library	194	# of student computer work stations for entire law school	63
Square feet of law library	27,939	# of additional networked connections	112
Square feet of law school (excl. Library)	59,361	Require Laptop Computer?	N

J.D. Attrition (Prior Year)

	Academic	Other	TOTALS	
	#	#	#	%
1st Year	0	12	12	7.2%
2nd Year	1	9	10	4.6%
3rd Year	1	2	3	1.4%
4th Year	1	1	2	6.7%
TOTALS	3	24	27	4.3%

Bar Passage Rates

Jurisdiction	Oregon			Washington		
Exam	Sum 96	Win 97	Total	Sum 96	Win 97	Total
# from school taking bar for the first time	120	20	140	27	13	40
School's pass rate for all first-time takers	86%	60%	82%	85%	77%	83%
State's pass rate for all first-time takers	77%	74%	77%	73%	82%	76%

LOUISIANA STATE UNIVERSITY

210 Law Center
Baton Rouge, LA 70803
(504)388-8491
http://www.lsu.edu/guests/lsulaw/index

ABA Approved Since 1926

The Basics

Type of School: Public   Term: Semester

Application deadline: 02/01

Application fee: $25

Financial Aid deadline: 04/01

Can first year start other than Fall? Yes

Student faculty ratio: 19.6 to 1

Does the University offer:
- housing restricted to law students? No
- graduate student housing for which law students are eligible? No

Faculty & Administrators

	Total		Men		Women		Minorities	
	Fall	Spr	Fall	Spr	Fall	Spr	Fall	Spr
Full-time	26	27	23	24	3	3	2	2
Other Full-Time	3	3	1	1	2	2	0	0
Deans, librarians, & others who teach > 1/2	3	2	3	2	0	0	0	0
Part-time	14	11	13	10	1	1	1	1
Total	46	43	40	37	6	6	3	3
Deans, librarians, & others who teach < 1/2	1	1	0	0	1	1	0	0

Curriculum

	Full time	Part time
Typical first-year section size	60	0
Is there typically a "small section" of the first year class, other than Legal Writing, taught by full-time faculty?	Yes	No
If yes, typical size offered last year	30	N/A
# of classroom course titles beyond 1st year curriculum	62	0
# of upper division courses, excluding seminars, with an enrollment:		
Under 25	5	0
25 - 49	14	0
50 - 74	5	0
75 - 99	6	0
100 +	16	0
# of seminars	9	0
# of seminar positions available	180	
# of seminar positions filled	168	0
# of positions available in simulation courses	738	
# of simulation positions filled	729	0
# of positions available in faculty supervised clinical courses	0	
# of fac. sup. clin. positions filled	0	0
# involved in field placements	0	0
# involved in law journals	43	0
# in moot court or trial competitions	24	0
# of credit hrs required to graduate	97	

J.D. Enrollment & Ethnicity

	Men		Women		Fl-Time		Pt-Time		1st Yr		2nd Yr		3rd Yr		4th Yr		Total		JD Degrees Awarded
	#	%	#	%	#	%	#	%	#	%	#	%	#	%	#	%	#	%	
African-American	21	6.3	33	11.9	54	8.9	0	0.0	32	13.6	12	6.7	10	5.1	0	0.0	54	8.9	4
American Indian	1	0.3	1	0.4	2	0.3	0	0.0	1	0.4	0	0.0	1	0.5	0	0.0	2	0.3	0
Asian American	1	0.3	1	0.4	2	0.3	0	0.0	0	0.0	2	1.1	0	0.0	0	0.0	2	0.3	3
Mexican American	0	0.0	0	0.0	0	0.0	0	0.0	0	0.0	0	0.0	0	0.0	0	0.0	0	0.0	0
Puerto Rican	0	0.0	0	0.0	0	0.0	0	0.0	0	0.0	0	0.0	0	0.0	0	0.0	0	0.0	0
Hispanic American	3	0.9	1	0.4	4	0.7	0	0.0	1	0.4	2	1.1	1	0.5	0	0.0	4	0.7	4
Total Minorities	26	7.8	36	12.9	62	10.2	0	0.0	34	14.5	16	8.9	12	6.1	0	0.0	62	10.2	11
Foreign Nationals	4	1.2	2	0.7	6	1.0	0	0.0	3	1.3	1	0.6	2	1.0	0	0.0	6	1.0	2
Caucasian	302	91.0	240	86.3	542	88.9	0	0.0	198	84.3	162	90.5	182	92.9	0	0.0	542	88.9	180
Total	332	54.4	278	45.6	610	100.0	0	0.0	235	38.5	179	29.3	196	32.1	0	0.0	610		193

LOUISIANA STATE UNIVERSITY

GPA & LSAT Scores

	Full Time	Part Time	Total
# of apps	986	0	986
# admits	531	0	531
# of matrics	244	0	244
75% GPA	3.53	0.00	
25% GPA	3.06	0.00	
75% LSAT	157	0	
25% LSAT	148	0	

Tuition & Fees

	Resident	Non-resident
Full-Time	$3,936	$8,923
Part-Time	$2,643	$6,011

Living Expenses

Estimated living expenses for Singles		
Living on campus	Living off campus	Living at home
$10,550	$18,950	$9,110

Employment

	Total	%
Employment status known	182	94.8
Employment status unknown	10	5.2
Employed	176	96.7
Pursuing graduate degrees	3	1.6
Unemployed seeking employment	3	1.6
Unemployed not seeking employment	0	0.0
Type of Employment		
# employed in law firms	109	61.9
# employed in business & industry	18	10.2
# employed in government	14	8.0
# employed in public interest	0	0.0
# employed as judicial clerks	35	19.9
# employed in academia	0	0.0
Geographic Location		
# employed in state	151	85.8
# employed in foreign countries	0	0.0
# of states where employed	7	

Financial Aid

	Full-time		Part-time		Total	
	#	%	#	%	#	%
Total # of Students	610		0		610	
Total # receiving grants	133	21.8	0	0.0	133	21.8
Less than 1/2 tuition	48	7.9	0	0.0	48	7.9
Half to full tuition	47	7.7	0	0.0	47	7.7
Full tuition	0	0.0	0	0.0	0	0.0
More than full tuition	38	6.2	0	0.0	38	6.2
Median Grant Amount	$3,500		$0			

Informational & Library Resources

# of volumes & volume equivalents	568,350	# of professional staff	18
# of titles	141,294	Hours per week with professional staff	65
# of active serial subscriptions	2,928	Hours per week without professional staff	34
Study seating capacity inside the library	464	# of student computer work stations for entire law school	44
Square feet of law library	71,056	# of additional networked connections	33
Square feet of law school (excl. Library)	112,947	Require Laptop Computer?	N

J.D. Attrition (Prior Year)

	Academic	Other	TOTALS	
	#	#	#	%
1st Year	44	39	83	33%
2nd Year	0	5	5	2.6%
3rd Year	0	0	0	0.0%
4th Year	0	0	0	0.0%
TOTALS	44	44	88	14%

Bar Passage Rates

Jurisdiction	Louisiana		
Exam	Sum 96	Win 97	Total
# from school taking bar for the first time	169	7	176
School's pass rate for all first-time takers	79%	86%	80%
State's pass rate for all first-time takers	69%	54%	66%

LOUISVILLE, UNIVERSITY OF

Louis D. Brandeis School of Law
Louisville, KY 40292
(502)852-6879
http://www.louisville.edu/law/

ABA Approved Since 1931

The Basics

Type of School: Public   Term: Semester

Application deadline: 02/15

Application fee: $30

Financial Aid deadline: 04/15

Can first year start other than Fall? No

Student faculty ratio: 14.4 to 1

Does the University offer:
- housing restricted to law students? No
- graduate student housing for which law students are eligible? Yes

Faculty & Administrators

	Total		Men		Women		Minorities	
	Fall	Spr	Fall	Spr	Fall	Spr	Fall	Spr
Full-time	25	22	18	15	7	7	3	3
Other Full-Time	1	1	1	1	0	0	0	0
Deans, librarians, & others who teach > 1/2	4	4	3	3	1	1	0	0
Part-time	12	9	9	6	3	3	0	0
Total	42	36	31	25	11	11	3	3
Deans, librarians, & others who teach < 1/2	0	0	0	0	0	0	0	0

Curriculum

	Full time	Part time
Typical first-year section size	62	43
Is there typically a "small section" of the first year class, other than Legal Writing, taught by full-time faculty?	No	No
If yes, typical size offered last year	N/A	N/A
# of classroom course titles beyond 1st year curriculum	63	26
# of upper division courses, excluding seminars, with an enrollment:		
Under 25	29	4
25 - 49	20	11
50 - 74	15	5
75 - 99	5	0
100 +	0	0
# of seminars	21	7
# of seminar positions available	504	
# of seminar positions filled	378	118
# of positions available in simulation courses	1,400	
# of simulation positions filled	924	264
# of positions available in faculty supervised clinical courses	0	
# of fac. sup. clin. positions filled	0	0
# involved in field placements	277	10
# involved in law journals	77	1
# in moot court or trial competitions	70	3
# of credit hrs required to graduate	90	

J.D. Enrollment & Ethnicity

	Men		Women		Fl-Time		Pt-Time		1st Yr		2nd Yr		3rd Yr		4th Yr		Total		JD Degrees Awarded
	#	%	#	%	#	%	#	%	#	%	#	%	#	%	#	%	#	%	
African-American	7	2.8	12	6.0	16	4.4	3	3.3	15	12.3	2	1.3	2	1.3	0	0.0	19	4.2	5
American Indian	0	0.0	1	0.5	1	0.3	0	0.0	1	0.8	0	0.0	0	0.0	0	0.0	1	0.2	0
Asian American	6	2.4	6	3.0	9	2.5	3	3.3	3	2.5	5	3.1	4	2.5	0	0.0	12	2.6	9
Mexican American	2	0.8	1	0.5	3	0.8	0	0.0	3	2.5	0	0.0	0	0.0	0	0.0	3	0.7	1
Puerto Rican	0	0.0	1	0.5	0	0.0	1	1.1	1	0.8	0	0.0	0	0.0	0	0.0	1	0.2	0
Hispanic American	1	0.4	0	0.0	1	0.3	0	0.0	1	0.8	0	0.0	0	0.0	0	0.0	1	0.2	0
Total Minorities	16	6.3	21	10.4	30	8.2	7	7.8	24	19.7	7	4.4	6	3.8	0	0.0	37	8.1	15
Foreign Nationals	1	0.4	2	1.0	3	0.8	0	0.0	0	0.0	2	1.3	1	0.6	0	0.0	3	0.7	0
Caucasian	237	93.3	178	88.6	332	91.0	83	92.2	98	80.3	151	94.4	152	95.6	14	100.0	415	91.2	139
Total	254	55.8	201	44.2	365	80.2	90	19.8	122	26.8	160	35.2	159	34.9	14	3.1	455		154

LOUISVILLE, UNIVERSITY OF

GPA & LSAT Scores

	Full Time	Part Time	Total
# of apps	750	120	870
# admits	256	47	303
# of matrics	91	33	124
75% GPA	3.46	3.66	
25% GPA	2.82	3.07	
75% LSAT	160	159	
25% LSAT	152	152	

Tuition & Fees

	Resident	Non-resident
Full-Time	$4,850	$12,690
Part-Time	$4,060	$10,590

Living Expenses

Estimated living expenses for Singles		
Living on campus	Living off campus	Living at home
$7,646	$9,090	$4,282

Financial Aid

	Full-time		Part-time		Total	
	#	%	#	%	#	%
Total # of Students	365		90		455	
Total # receiving grants	76	20.8	16	17.8	92	20.2
Less than 1/2 tuition	22	6.0	4	4.4	26	5.7
Half to full tuition	7	1.9	1	1.1	8	1.8
Full tuition	32	8.8	7	7.8	39	8.6
More than full tuition	15	4.1	4	4.4	19	4.2
Median Grant Amount	$4,850		$4,850			

Informational & Library Resources

# of volumes & volume equivalents	281,633	# of professional staff	4
# of titles	38,146	Hours per week with professional staff	82
# of active serial subscriptions	5,048	Hours per week without professional staff	6
Study seating capacity inside the library	391	# of student computer work stations for entire law school	46
Square feet of law library	53,060	# of additional networked connections	6
Square feet of law school (excl. Library)	62,850	Require Laptop Computer?	N

Employment

	Total	%
Employment status known	97	98.0
Employment status unknown	2	2.0
Employed	89	91.8
Pursuing graduate degrees	0	0.0
Unemployed seeking employment	5	5.2
Unemployed not seeking employment	3	3.1
Type of Employment		
# employed in law firms	53	59.6
# employed in business & industry	16	18.0
# employed in government	10	11.2
# employed in public interest	3	3.4
# employed as judicial clerks	5	5.6
# employed in academia	2	2.2
Geographic Location		
# employed in state	71	79.8
# employed in foreign countries	0	0.0
# of states where employed	8	

J.D. Attrition (Prior Year)

	Academic	Other	TOTALS	
	#	#	#	%
1st Year	6	6	12	7.3%
2nd Year	3	3	6	3.7%
3rd Year	0	0	0	0.0%
4th Year	0	0	0	0.0%
TOTALS	9	9	18	3.6%

Bar Passage Rates

Jurisdiction	Kentucky		
Exam	Sum 96	Win 97	Total
# from school taking bar for the first time	83	15	98
School's pass rate for all first-time takers	89%	80%	88%
State's pass rate for all first-time takers	84%	82%	83%

LOYOLA MARYMOUNT UNIVERSITY-LOS ANGELES

919 South Albany Street
Los Angeles, CA 90015
(213)736-1000
http://www.law.lmu.edu

ABA Approved Since 1935

The Basics

Type of School: Private Term: Semester

Application deadline: 02/01

Application fee: $50

Financial Aid deadline: 03/02

Can first year start other than Fall? No

Student faculty ratio: 22.0 to 1

Does the University offer:
- housing restricted to law students? No
- graduate student housing for which law students are eligible? No

Faculty & Administrators

	Total		Men		Women		Minorities	
	Fall	Spr	Fall	Spr	Fall	Spr	Fall	Spr
Full-time	45	48	29	29	16	19	11	11
Other Full-Time	6	6	2	2	4	4	0	0
Deans, librarians, & others who teach > 1/2	3	3	1	1	2	2	1	1
Part-time	32	28	26	21	6	7	3	3
Total	86	85	58	53	28	32	15	15
Deans, librarians, & others who teach < 1/2	3	3	3	3	0	0	0	0

Curriculum

	Full time	Part time
Typical first-year section size	77	115
Is there typically a "small section" of the first year class, other than Legal Writing, taught by full-time faculty?	No	No
If yes, typical size offered last year	N/A	N/A
# of classroom course titles beyond 1st year curriculum	76	80
# of upper division courses, excluding seminars, with an enrollment:		
Under 25	39	39
25 - 49	28	25
50 - 74	6	6
75 - 99	3	1
100 +	5	1
# of seminars	8	6
# of seminar positions available	257	
# of seminar positions filled	118	75
# of positions available in simulation courses	658	
# of simulation positions filled	486	121
# of positions available in faculty supervised clinical courses	103	
# of fac. sup. clin. positions filled	91	10
# involved in field placements	315	35
# involved in law journals	398	75
# in moot court or trial competitions	140	30
# of credit hrs required to graduate	87	

J.D. Enrollment & Ethnicity

	Men		Women		Fl-Time		Pt-Time		1st Yr		2nd Yr		3rd Yr		4th Yr		Total		JD Degrees Awarded
	#	%	#	%	#	%	#	%	#	%	#	%	#	%	#	%	#	%	
African-American	26	3.7	41	6.7	41	4.4	26	6.6	18	4.3	19	4.6	21	5.3	9	8.9	67	5.1	21
American Indian	12	1.7	7	1.1	14	1.5	5	1.3	8	1.9	6	1.5	3	0.8	2	2.0	19	1.4	4
Asian American	133	18.7	132	21.6	203	21.9	62	15.8	85	20.5	82	20.0	83	21.0	15	14.9	265	20.1	79
Mexican American	58	8.2	61	10.0	86	9.3	33	8.4	44	10.6	31	7.6	35	8.9	9	8.9	119	9.0	29
Puerto Rican	0	0.0	0	0.0	0	0.0	0	0.0	0	0.0	0	0.0	0	0.0	0	0.0	0	0.0	0
Hispanic American	29	4.1	30	4.9	43	4.6	16	4.1	18	4.3	22	5.4	17	4.3	2	2.0	59	4.5	15
Total Minorities	258	36.3	271	44.4	387	41.7	142	36.1	173	41.8	160	39.0	159	40.3	37	36.6	529	40.1	148
Foreign Nationals	3	0.4	1	0.2	3	0.3	1	0.3	2	0.5	1	0.2	1	0.3	0	0.0	4	0.3	2
Caucasian	449	63.2	338	55.4	537	57.9	250	63.6	239	57.7	249	60.7	235	59.5	64	63.4	787	59.6	258
Total	710	53.8	610	46.2	927	70.2	393	29.8	414	31.4	410	31.1	395	29.9	101	7.7	1320		408

LOYOLA MARYMOUNT UNIVERSITY-LOS ANGELES

GPA & LSAT Scores

	Full Time	Part Time	Total
# of apps	2,228	410	2,638
# admits	893	171	1,064
# of matrics	365	119	484
75% GPA	3.47	3.44	
25% GPA	3.01	2.99	
75% LSAT	160	158	
25% LSAT	153	152	

Tuition & Fees

	Resident	Non-resident
Full-Time	$20,734	$0
Part-Time	$13,922	$0

Living Expenses

Estimated living expenses for Singles		
Living on campus	Living off campus	Living at home
N/A	$13,445	$7,960

Financial Aid

	Full-time		Part-time		Total	
	#	%	#	%	#	%
Total # of Students	927		393		1320	
Total # receiving grants	127	13.7	44	11.2	171	13.0
Less than 1/2 tuition	27	2.9	10	2.5	37	2.8
Half to full tuition	57	6.1	27	6.9	84	6.4
Full tuition	23	2.5	5	1.3	28	2.1
More than full tuition	20	2.2	2	0.5	22	1.7
Median Grant Amount	$17,500		$10,000			

Informational & Library Resources

# of volumes & volume equivalents	436,836	# of professional staff	11
# of titles	202,283	Hours per week with professional staff	84
# of active serial subscriptions	6,628	Hours per week without professional staff	24
Study seating capacity inside the library	683	# of student computer work stations for entire law school	53
Square feet of law library	46,802	# of additional networked connections	63
Square feet of law school (excl. Library)	65,615	Require Laptop Computer?	N

Employment

	Total	%
Employment status known	392	97.8
Employment status unknown	9	2.2
Employed	347	88.5
Pursuing graduate degrees	3	0.8
Unemployed seeking employment	39	9.9
Unemployed not seeking employment	3	0.8
Type of Employment		
# employed in law firms	225	64.8
# employed in business & industry	70	20.2
# employed in government	27	7.8
# employed in public interest	11	3.2
# employed as judicial clerks	12	3.5
# employed in academia	2	0.6
Geographic Location		
# employed in state	237	68.3
# employed in foreign countries	0	0.0
# of states where employed	8	

J.D. Attrition (Prior Year)

	Academic	Other	TOTALS	
	#	#	#	%
1st Year	11	18	29	6.9%
2nd Year	6	11	17	4.2%
3rd Year	7	6	13	3.1%
4th Year	4	3	7	6.4%
TOTALS	28	38	66	4.9%

Bar Passage Rates

Jurisdiction	California		
Exam	Sum 96	Win 97	Total
# from school taking bar for the first time	361	21	382
School's pass rate for all first-time takers	77%	52%	76%
State's pass rate for all first-time takers	69%	62%	67%

LOYOLA UNIVERSITY-CHICAGO

One East Pearson Street
Chicago, IL 60611
(312)915-7120
gopher://gopher.luc.edu/11/loyola/colleg

ABA Approved Since 1925

The Basics

Type of School: Private Term: Semester
Application deadline: 04/01
Application fee: $45
Financial Aid deadline: 04/01
Can first year start other than Fall? Yes
Student faculty ratio: 20.9 to 1
Does the University offer:
- housing restricted to law students? No
- graduate student housing for which law students are eligible? Yes

Faculty & Administrators

	Total		Men		Women		Minorities	
	Fall	Spr	Fall	Spr	Fall	Spr	Fall	Spr
Full-time	26	27	18	19	8	8	4	4
Other Full-Time	2	2	0	0	2	2	0	0
Deans, librarians, & others who teach > 1/2	0	0	0	0	0	0	0	0
Part-time	64	51	38	33	26	18	4	2
Total	92	80	56	52	36	28	8	6
Deans, librarians, & others who teach < 1/2	4	4	3	3	1	1	0	0

Curriculum

	Full time	Part time
Typical first-year section size	55	60
Is there typically a "small section" of the first year class, other than Legal Writing, taught by full-time faculty?	No	No
If yes, typical size offered last year	N/A	N/A
# of classroom course titles beyond 1st year curriculum	93	62
# of upper division courses, excluding seminars, with an enrollment:		
Under 25	99	12
25 - 49	2	6
50 - 74	9	2
75 - 99	2	0
100 +	2	0
# of seminars	29	5
# of seminar positions available	565	
# of seminar positions filled	393	71
# of positions available in simulation courses	646	
# of simulation positions filled	433	173
# of positions available in faculty supervised clinical courses	130	
# of fac. sup. clin. positions filled	93	15
# involved in field placements	102	28
# involved in law journals	170	27
# in moot court or trial competitions	106	23
# of credit hrs required to graduate	86	

J.D. Enrollment & Ethnicity

	Men		Women		Fl-Time		Pt-Time		1st Yr		2nd Yr		3rd Yr		4th Yr		Total		JD Degrees Awarded
	#	%	#	%	#	%	#	%	#	%	#	%	#	%	#	%	#	%	
African-American	22	7.0	27	6.6	26	5.0	23	11.1	16	6.6	19	8.3	9	4.2	5	12.5	49	6.8	16
American Indian	1	0.3	3	0.7	4	0.8	0	0.0	1	0.4	3	1.3	0	0.0	0	0.0	4	0.6	2
Asian American	21	6.7	31	7.6	42	8.1	10	4.8	19	7.9	20	8.7	11	5.2	2	5.0	52	7.2	29
Mexican American	4	1.3	2	0.5	5	1.0	1	0.5	3	1.2	2	0.9	1	0.5	0	0.0	6	0.8	4
Puerto Rican	3	1.0	2	0.5	4	0.8	1	0.5	3	1.2	2	0.9	0	0.0	0	0.0	5	0.7	1
Hispanic American	3	1.0	12	2.9	13	2.5	2	1.0	8	3.3	3	1.3	3	1.4	1	2.5	15	2.1	6
Total Minorities	54	17.1	77	18.9	94	18.2	37	17.9	50	20.7	49	21.3	24	11.3	8	20.0	131	18.1	58
Foreign Nationals	17	5.4	15	3.7	24	4.7	8	3.9	8	3.3	15	6.5	7	3.3	2	5.0	32	4.4	4
Caucasian	244	77.5	316	77.5	398	77.1	162	78.3	183	75.9	166	72.2	181	85.4	30	75.0	560	77.5	195
Total	315	43.6	408	56.4	516	71.4	207	28.6	241	33.3	230	31.8	212	29.3	40	5.5	723		257

GPA & LSAT Scores

	Full Time	Part Time	Total
# of apps	1,955	276	2,231
# admits	713	148	861
# of matrics	169	72	241
75% GPA	3.56	3.39	
25% GPA	2.97	2.75	
75% LSAT	161	157	
25% LSAT	155	150	

Tuition & Fees

	Resident	Non-resident
Full-Time	$20,856	$20,856
Part-Time	$15,668	$15,668

Living Expenses

Estimated living expenses for Singles		
Living on campus	Living off campus	Living at home
N/A	$13,250	$9,250

Financial Aid

	Full-time		Part-time		Total	
	#	%	#	%	#	%
Total # of Students	516		207		723	
Total # receiving grants	426	82.6	52	25.1	478	66.1
Less than 1/2 tuition	413	80.0	48	23.2	461	63.8
Half to full tuition	11	2.1	4	1.9	15	2.1
Full tuition	2	0.4	0	0.0	2	0.3
More than full tuition	0	0.0	0	0.0	0	0.0
Median Grant Amount	$2,400		$1,910			

Informational & Library Resources

# of volumes & volume equivalents	335,970	# of professional staff	9
# of titles	51,424	Hours per week with professional staff	90
# of active serial subscriptions	3,499	Hours per week without professional staff	9
Study seating capacity inside the library	380	# of student computer work stations for entire law school	77
Square feet of law library	43,900	# of additional networked connections	0
Square feet of law school (excl. Library)	39,202	Require Laptop Computer?	N

Employment

	Total	%
Employment status known	227	100.0
Employment status unknown	0	0.0
Employed	220	96.9
Pursuing graduate degrees	2	0.9
Unemployed seeking employment	2	0.9
Unemployed not seeking employment	3	1.3
Type of Employment		
# employed in law firms	124	56.4
# employed in business & industry	40	18.2
# employed in government	41	18.6
# employed in public interest	4	1.8
# employed as judicial clerks	6	2.7
# employed in academia	5	2.3
Geographic Location		
# employed in state	186	84.5
# employed in foreign countries	2	0.9
# of states where employed	16	

J.D. Attrition (Prior Year)

	Academic	Other	TOTALS	
	#	#	#	%
1st Year	6	23	29	12%
2nd Year	0	13	13	5.9%
3rd Year	0	1	1	0.4%
4th Year	0	0	0	0.0%
TOTALS	6	37	43	5.7%

Bar Passage Rates

Jurisdiction	Illinois		
Exam	Sum 96	Win 97	Total
# from school taking bar for the first time	176	25	201
School's pass rate for all first-time takers	85%	72%	84%
State's pass rate for all first-time takers	86%	84%	86%

LOYOLA UNIVERSITY-NEW ORLEANS

7214 St. Charles Avenue
New Orleans, LA 70118
(504)861-5550
www.loyno.edu/SchoolofLaw

ABA Approved Since 1931

The Basics

Type of School: Private Term: Semester
Application deadline: 08/20
Application fee: $20
Financial Aid deadline: Rolling
Can first year start other than Fall? No
Student faculty ratio: 17.7 to 1
Does the University offer:
- housing restricted to law students? No
- graduate student housing for which law students are eligible? No

Faculty & Administrators

	Total		Men		Women		Minorities	
	Fall	Spr	Fall	Spr	Fall	Spr	Fall	Spr
Full-time	30	30	20	20	10	10	8	8
Other Full-Time	0	0	0	0	0	0	0	0
Deans, librarians, & others who teach > 1/2	0	0	0	0	0	0	0	0
Part-time	18	20	16	17	2	3	0	0
Total	48	50	36	37	12	13	8	8
Deans, librarians, & others who teach < 1/2	4	4	4	4	0	0	0	0

Curriculum

	Full time	Part time
Typical first-year section size	73	49
Is there typically a "small section" of the first year class, other than Legal Writing, taught by full-time faculty?	Yes	No
If yes, typical size offered last year	N/A	N/A
# of classroom course titles beyond 1st year curriculum	62	35
# of upper division courses, excluding seminars, with an enrollment:		
Under 25	25	13
25 - 49	8	12
50 - 74	10	4
75 - 99	13	5
100 +	1	0
# of seminars	11	7
# of seminar positions available	359	
# of seminar positions filled	140	92
# of positions available in simulation courses	393	
# of simulation positions filled	242	97
# of positions available in faculty supervised clinical courses	100	
# of fac. sup. clin. positions filled	87	7
# involved in field placements	61	8
# involved in law journals	43	21
# in moot court or trial competitions	14	1
# of credit hrs required to graduate	90	

J.D. Enrollment & Ethnicity

	Men		Women		Fl-Time		Pt-Time		1st Yr		2nd Yr		3rd Yr		4th Yr		Total		JD Degrees Awarded
	#	%	#	%	#	%	#	%	#	%	#	%	#	%	#	%	#	%	
African-American	25	7.0	51	16.0	65	12.6	11	7.0	27	13.4	24	12.4	23	9.6	2	5.4	76	11.3	32
American Indian	3	0.8	2	0.6	5	1.0	0	0.0	3	1.5	0	0.0	2	0.8	0	0.0	5	0.7	0
Asian American	11	3.1	6	1.9	16	3.1	1	0.6	4	2.0	4	2.1	9	3.8	0	0.0	17	2.5	10
Mexican American	0	0.0	0	0.0	0	0.0	0	0.0	0	0.0	0	0.0	0	0.0	0	0.0	0	0.0	0
Puerto Rican	0	0.0	0	0.0	0	0.0	0	0.0	0	0.0	0	0.0	0	0.0	0	0.0	0	0.0	1
Hispanic American	20	5.6	35	11.0	45	8.7	10	6.4	16	7.9	14	7.2	23	9.6	2	5.4	55	8.2	13
Total Minorities	59	16.6	94	29.6	131	25.4	22	14.0	50	24.8	42	21.6	57	23.8	4	10.8	153	22.7	56
Foreign Nationals	2	0.6	1	0.3	3	0.6	0	0.0	2	1.0	1	0.5	0	0.0	0	0.0	3	0.4	2
Caucasian	294	82.8	223	70.1	382	74.0	135	86.0	150	74.3	151	77.8	183	76.3	33	89.2	517	76.8	145
Total	355	52.7	318	47.3	516	76.7	157	23.3	202	30.0	194	28.8	240	35.7	37	5.5	673		203

LOYOLA UNIVERSITY-NEW ORLEANS

GPA & LSAT Scores

	Full Time	Part Time	Total
# of apps	1,188	123	1,311
# admits	641	65	706
# of matrics	172	44	216
75% GPA	3.25	3.33	
25% GPA	2.70	2.64	
75% LSAT	154	157	
25% LSAT	149	150	

Tuition & Fees

	Resident	Non-resident
Full-Time	$16,870	$16,870
Part-Time	$12,166	$12,166

Living Expenses

Estimated living expenses for Singles		
Living on campus	Living off campus	Living at home
$11,200	$11,200	$4,400

Financial Aid

	Full-time		Part-time		Total	
	#	%	#	%	#	%
Total # of Students	516		157		673	
Total # receiving grants	143	27.7	6	3.8	149	22.1
Less than 1/2 tuition	73	14.1	4	2.5	77	11.4
Half to full tuition	61	11.8	2	1.3	63	9.4
Full tuition	9	1.7	0	0.0	9	1.3
More than full tuition	0	0.0	0	0.0	0	0.0
Median Grant Amount	$5,500		$3,056			

Informational & Library Resources

# of volumes & volume equivalents	265,089	# of professional staff	8
# of titles	84,360	Hours per week with professional staff	77
# of active serial subscriptions	2,789	Hours per week without professional staff	27
Study seating capacity inside the library	525	# of student computer work stations for entire law school	34
Square feet of law library	52,168	# of additional networked connections	0
Square feet of law school (excl. Library)	45,477	Require Laptop Computer?	N

Employment

	Total	%
Employment status known	184	81.8
Employment status unknown	41	18.2
Employed	155	84.2
Pursuing graduate degrees	4	2.2
Unemployed seeking employment	18	9.8
Unemployed not seeking employment	7	3.8
Type of Employment		
# employed in law firms	56	36.1
# employed in business & industry	15	9.7
# employed in government	6	3.9
# employed in public interest	0	0.0
# employed as judicial clerks	8	5.2
# employed in academia	1	0.6
Geographic Location		
# employed in state	67	43.2
# employed in foreign countries	0	0.0
# of states where employed	12	

J.D. Attrition (Prior Year)

	Academic	Other	TOTALS	
	#	#	#	%
1st Year	7	18	25	12%
2nd Year	1	1	2	0.8%
3rd Year	0	1	1	0.5%
4th Year	0	0	0	0.0%
TOTALS	8	20	28	4.1%

Bar Passage Rates

Jurisdiction	Louisiana		
Exam	Sum 96	Win 97	Total
# from school taking bar for the first time	134	38	172
School's pass rate for all first-time takers	66%	63%	66%
State's pass rate for all first-time takers	69%	54%	66%

MAINE, UNIVERSITY OF

246 Deering Avenue
Portland, ME 04102
(207)780-4355
http://www.law.usm.maine.edu

ABA Approved Since 1962

The Basics

Type of School: Public
Term: Semester
Application deadline: 02/15
Application fee: $25
Financial Aid deadline: 02/01
Can first year start other than Fall? No
Student faculty ratio: 20.4 to 1
Does the University offer:
- housing restricted to law students? No
- graduate student housing for which law students are eligible? No

Faculty & Administrators

	Total		Men		Women		Minorities	
	Fall	Spr	Fall	Spr	Fall	Spr	Fall	Spr
Full-time	12	12	8	8	4	4	0	0
Other Full-Time	1	1	0	0	1	1	0	0
Deans, librarians, & others who teach > 1/2	2	2	1	1	1	1	0	0
Part-time	9	9	5	5	4	4	0	0
Total	24	24	14	14	10	10	0	0
Deans, librarians, & others who teach < 1/2	1	1	1	1	0	0	0	0

Curriculum

	Full time	Part time
Typical first-year section size	94	0
Is there typically a "small section" of the first year class, other than Legal Writing, taught by full-time faculty?	No	No
If yes, typical size offered last year	N/A	N/A
# of classroom course titles beyond 1st year curriculum	49	0
# of upper division courses, excluding seminars, with an enrollment:		
Under 25	42	0
25 - 49	14	0
50 - 74	1	0
75 - 99	4	0
100 +	0	0
# of seminars	2	0
# of seminar positions available	34	
# of seminar positions filled	27	0
# of positions available in simulation courses	96	
# of simulation positions filled	81	0
# of positions available in faculty supervised clinical courses	55	
# of fac. sup. clin. positions filled	53	0
# involved in field placements	0	0
# involved in law journals	40	0
# in moot court or trial competitions	15	0
# of credit hrs required to graduate	89	

J.D. Enrollment & Ethnicity

	Men		Women		Fl-Time		Pt-Time		1st Yr		2nd Yr		3rd Yr		4th Yr		Total		JD Degrees Awarded
	#	%	#	%	#	%	#	%	#	%	#	%	#	%	#	%	#	%	
African-American	2	1.2	4	3.2	6	2.0	0	0.0	2	2.1	3	3.0	1	1.0	0	0.0	6	2.0	2
American Indian	1	0.6	4	3.2	5	1.7	0	0.0	2	2.1	0	0.0	3	3.0	0	0.0	5	1.7	1
Asian American	1	0.6	2	1.6	3	1.0	0	0.0	2	2.1	0	0.0	1	1.0	0	0.0	3	1.0	0
Mexican American	0	0.0	0	0.0	0	0.0	0	0.0	0	0.0	0	0.0	0	0.0	0	0.0	0	0.0	0
Puerto Rican	0	0.0	0	0.0	0	0.0	0	0.0	0	0.0	0	0.0	0	0.0	0	0.0	0	0.0	0
Hispanic American	2	1.2	0	0.0	2	0.7	0	0.0	1	1.1	0	0.0	1	1.0	0	0.0	2	0.7	3
Total Minorities	6	3.5	10	8.1	16	5.4	0	0.0	7	7.4	3	3.0	6	6.1	0	0.0	16	5.4	6
Foreign Nationals	6	3.5	1	0.8	7	2.4	0	0.0	2	2.1	3	3.0	2	2.0	0	0.0	7	2.4	2
Caucasian	158	92.9	113	91.1	271	92.2	0	0.0	85	90.4	95	94.1	91	91.9	0	0.0	271	92.2	83
Total	170	57.8	124	42.2	294	100.0	0	0.0	94	32.0	101	34.4	99	33.7	0	0.0	294		91

GPA & LSAT Scores

	Full Time	Part Time	Total
# of apps	569	0	569
# admits	288	0	288
# of matrics	97	0	97
75% GPA	3.49	0.00	
25% GPA	3.03	0.00	
75% LSAT	159	0	
25% LSAT	150	0	

Tuition & Fees

	Resident	Non-resident
Full-Time	$8,378	$15,994
Part-Time	$6,010	$11,450

Living Expenses

Estimated living expenses for Singles		
Living on campus	Living off campus	Living at home
$7,900	$7,900	$4,875

Financial Aid

	Full-time		Part-time		Total	
	#	%	#	%	#	%
Total # of Students	294		0		294	
Total # receiving grants	85	28.9	0	0.0	85	28.9
Less than 1/2 tuition	74	25.2	0	0.0	74	25.2
Half to full tuition	1	0.3	0	0.0	1	0.3
Full tuition	10	3.4	0	0.0	10	3.4
More than full tuition	0	0.0	0	0.0	0	0.0
Median Grant Amount	$1,500		$0			

Informational & Library Resources

# of volumes & volume equivalents	304,684	# of professional staff	6
# of titles	51,139	Hours per week with professional staff	59
# of active serial subscriptions	3,605	Hours per week without professional staff	38
Study seating capacity inside the library	172	# of student computer work stations for entire law school	20
Square feet of law library	32,800	# of additional networked connections	0
Square feet of law school (excl. Library)	30,115	Require Laptop Computer?	N

Employment

	Total	%
Employment status known	86	97.7
Employment status unknown	2	2.3
Employed	66	76.7
Pursuing graduate degrees	1	1.2
Unemployed seeking employment	14	16.3
Unemployed not seeking employment	5	5.8
Type of Employment		
# employed in law firms	44	66.7
# employed in business & industry	11	16.7
# employed in government	6	9.1
# employed in public interest	4	6.1
# employed as judicial clerks	18	27.3
# employed in academia	3	4.5
Geographic Location		
# employed in state	49	74.2
# employed in foreign countries	0	0.0
# of states where employed	14	

J.D. Attrition (Prior Year)

	Academic	Other	TOTALS	
	#	#	#	%
1st Year	0	8	8	7.7%
2nd Year	0	2	2	2.2%
3rd Year	0	2	2	2.1%
4th Year	0	0	0	0.0%
TOTALS	0	12	12	4.2%

Bar Passage Rates

Jurisdiction	Maine			Massachusetts		
Exam	Sum 96	Win 97	Total	Sum 96	Win 97	Total
# from school taking bar for the first time	65	7	72	16	3	19
School's pass rate for all first-time takers	85%	86%	85%	94%	67%	89%
State's pass rate for all first-time takers	81%	84%	82%	83%	76%	81%

MARQUETTE UNIVERSITY

Sensenbrenner Hall
P.O. Box 1881
Milwaukee, WI 53201-1881
(414)288-7090
http://www.mu.edu/dept/law

ABA Approved Since 1925

The Basics

Type of School: Private   Term: Semester
Application deadline: 04/01
Application fee: $35
Financial Aid deadline: 03/01
Can first year start other than Fall? No
Student faculty ratio: 14.5 to 1
Does the University offer:
- housing restricted to law students? No
- graduate student housing for which law students are eligible? Yes

Faculty & Administrators

	Total		Men		Women		Minorities	
	Fall	Spr	Fall	Spr	Fall	Spr	Fall	Spr
Full-time	26	23	17	15	9	8	3	3
Other Full-Time	0	0	0	0	0	0	0	0
Deans, librarians, & others who teach > 1/2	5	5	4	4	1	1	0	0
Part-time	22	32	16	26	6	6	3	3
Total	53	60	37	45	16	15	6	6
Deans, librarians, & others who teach < 1/2	1	1	1	1	0	0	0	0

Curriculum

	Full time	Part time
Typical first-year section size	75	40
Is there typically a "small section" of the first year class, other than Legal Writing, taught by full-time faculty?	Yes	Yes
If yes, typical size offered last year	39	N/A
# of classroom course titles beyond 1st year curriculum	72	0
# of upper division courses, excluding seminars, with an enrollment:		
Under 25	37	0
25 - 49	38	0
50 - 74	8	0
75 - 99	2	0
100 +	0	0
# of seminars	20	0
# of seminar positions available	300	
# of seminar positions filled	225	0
# of positions available in simulation courses	389	
# of simulation positions filled	298	0
# of positions available in faculty supervised clinical courses	111	
# of fac. sup. clin. positions filled	90	0
# involved in field placements	40	0
# involved in law journals	80	0
# in moot court or trial competitions	13	0
# of credit hrs required to graduate	90	

J.D. Enrollment & Ethnicity

	Men		Women		Fl-Time		Pt-Time		1st Yr		2nd Yr		3rd Yr		4th Yr		Total		JD Degrees Awarded
	#	%	#	%	#	%	#	%	#	%	#	%	#	%	#	%	#	%	
African-American	4	1.5	7	3.5	10	2.4	1	1.7	6	3.3	2	1.3	3	2.2	0	0.0	11	2.3	6
American Indian	0	0.0	3	1.5	3	0.7	0	0.0	0	0.0	0	0.0	3	2.2	0	0.0	3	0.6	0
Asian American	8	2.9	6	3.0	13	3.1	1	1.7	5	2.8	2	1.3	7	5.1	0	0.0	14	3.0	11
Mexican American	1	0.4	6	3.0	6	1.4	1	1.7	2	1.1	0	0.0	5	3.7	0	0.0	7	1.5	5
Puerto Rican	2	0.7	2	1.0	4	1.0	0	0.0	2	1.1	0	0.0	2	1.5	0	0.0	4	0.8	3
Hispanic American	4	1.5	8	4.0	11	2.7	1	1.7	4	2.2	6	3.8	2	1.5	0	0.0	12	2.5	4
Total Minorities	19	7.0	32	15.9	47	11.3	4	6.8	19	10.5	10	6.4	22	16.2	0	0.0	51	10.8	29
Foreign Nationals	0	0.0	0	0.0	0	0.0	0	0.0	0	0.0	0	0.0	0	0.0	0	0.0	0	0.0	0
Caucasian	254	93.0	169	84.1	368	88.7	55	93.2	162	89.5	147	93.6	114	83.8	0	0.0	423	89.2	128
Total	273	57.6	201	42.4	415	87.6	59	12.4	181	38.2	157	33.1	136	28.7	0	0.0	474		157

GPA & LSAT Scores

	Full Time	Part Time	Total
# of apps	813	148	961
# admits	443	64	507
# of matrics	141	46	187
75% GPA	3.33	3.33	
25% GPA	2.80	2.70	
75% LSAT	157	157	
25% LSAT	151	152	

Tuition & Fees

	Resident	Non-resident
Full-Time	$17,830	$17,830
Part-Time	$14,800	$14,800

Living Expenses

Estimated living expenses for Singles		
Living on campus	Living off campus	Living at home
$11,990	$11,990	$11,990

Employment

	Total	%
Employment status known	158	98.7
Employment status unknown	2	1.2
Employed	141	89.2
Pursuing graduate degrees	2	1.3
Unemployed seeking employment	12	7.6
Unemployed not seeking employment	3	1.9
Type of Employment		
# employed in law firms	83	58.9
# employed in business & industry	22	15.6
# employed in government	23	16.3
# employed in public interest	2	1.4
# employed as judicial clerks	7	5.0
# employed in academia	0	0.0
Geographic Location		
# employed in state	102	72.3
# employed in foreign countries	1	0.7
# of states where employed	17	

Financial Aid

	Full-time		Part-time		Total	
	#	%	#	%	#	%
Total # of Students	415		59		474	
Total # receiving grants	107	25.8	2	3.4	109	23.0
Less than 1/2 tuition	96	23.1	2	3.4	98	20.7
Half to full tuition	8	1.9	0	0.0	8	1.7
Full tuition	3	0.7	0	0.0	3	0.6
More than full tuition	0	0.0	0	0.0	0	0.0
Median Grant Amount	$4,261		$959			

Informational & Library Resources

# of volumes & volume equivalents	255,349	# of professional staff	8
# of titles	123,427	Hours per week with professional staff	77
# of active serial subscriptions	3,193	Hours per week without professional staff	29
Study seating capacity inside the library	315	# of student computer work stations for entire law school	35
Square feet of law library	32,911	# of additional networked connections	0
Square feet of law school (excl. Library)	30,198	Require Laptop Computer?	N

J.D. Attrition (Prior Year)

	Academic	Other	TOTALS	
	#	#	#	%
1st Year	0	0	0	0.0%
2nd Year	2	5	7	4.9%
3rd Year	0	1	1	0.6%
4th Year	0	0	0	0.0%
TOTALS	2	6	8	1.7%

Bar Passage Rates

Jurisdiction	Wisconsin		
Exam	Sum 96	Win 97	Total
# from school taking bar for the first time	All graduates were admitted to the Wisconsin bar via the diploma privilege.		
School's pass rate for all first-time takers			
State's pass rate for all first-time takers			

MARYLAND, UNIVERSITY OF

500 West Baltimore Street
Baltimore, MD 21201-1786
(410)706-3492
http://www.law.umaryland.edu

ABA Approved Since 1930

The Basics

Type of School: Public   Term: Semester
Application deadline: 03/01
Application fee: $42
Financial Aid deadline: 03/15
Can first year start other than Fall? No
Student faculty ratio: 14.2 to 1
Does the University offer:
- housing restricted to law students? No
- graduate student housing for which law students are eligible? No

Faculty & Administrators

	Total		Men		Women		Minorities	
	Fall	Spr	Fall	Spr	Fall	Spr	Fall	Spr
Full-time	47	44	30	28	17	16	6	6
Other Full-Time	0	0	0	0	0	0	0	0
Deans, librarians, & others who teach > 1/2	1	1	1	1	0	0	0	0
Part-time	36	44	27	32	9	12	2	5
Total	84	89	58	61	26	28	8	11
Deans, librarians, & others who teach < 1/2	2	2	1	1	1	1	0	0

Curriculum

	Full time	Part time
Typical first-year section size	68	63
Is there typically a "small section" of the first year class, other than Legal Writing, taught by full-time faculty?	Yes	Yes
If yes, typical size offered last year	23	30
# of classroom course titles beyond 1st year curriculum	113	37
# of upper division courses, excluding seminars, with an enrollment:		
Under 25	66	15
25 - 49	31	12
50 - 74	16	11
75 - 99	4	3
100 +	4	1
# of seminars	30	9
# of seminar positions available	579	
# of seminar positions filled	339	131
# of positions available in simulation courses	399	
# of simulation positions filled	228	147
# of positions available in faculty supervised clinical courses	277	
# of fac. sup. clin. positions filled	243	30
# involved in field placements	121	20
# involved in law journals	156	17
# in moot court or trial competitions	134	18
# of credit hrs required to graduate	85	

J.D. Enrollment & Ethnicity

	Men		Women		Fl-Time		Pt-Time		1st Yr		2nd Yr		3rd Yr		4th Yr		Total		JD Degrees Awarded
	#	%	#	%	#	%	#	%	#	%	#	%	#	%	#	%	#	%	
African-American	48	11.5	71	15.4	78	12.7	41	15.6	29	10.5	26	9.8	54	20.4	10	13.9	119	13.6	54
American Indian	3	0.7	0	0.0	2	0.3	1	0.4	2	0.7	0	0.0	1	0.4	0	0.0	3	0.3	0
Asian American	38	9.1	48	10.4	70	11.4	16	6.1	30	10.9	28	10.6	23	8.7	5	6.9	86	9.8	18
Mexican American	0	0.0	0	0.0	0	0.0	0	0.0	0	0.0	0	0.0	0	0.0	0	0.0	0	0.0	0
Puerto Rican	0	0.0	0	0.0	0	0.0	0	0.0	0	0.0	0	0.0	0	0.0	0	0.0	0	0.0	0
Hispanic American	12	2.9	15	3.3	19	3.1	8	3.1	11	4.0	8	3.0	6	2.3	2	2.8	27	3.1	8
Total Minorities	101	24.3	134	29.1	169	27.5	66	25.2	72	26.2	62	23.5	84	31.7	17	23.6	235	26.8	80
Foreign Nationals	1	0.2	8	1.7	6	1.0	3	1.1	2	0.7	4	1.5	2	0.8	1	1.4	9	1.0	1
Caucasian	314	75.5	318	69.1	439	71.5	193	73.7	201	73.1	198	75.0	179	67.5	54	75.0	632	72.1	160
Total	416	47.5	460	52.5	614	70.1	262	29.9	275	31.4	264	30.1	265	30.3	72	8.2	876		241

GPA & LSAT Scores

	Full Time	Part Time	Total
# of apps	2,057	359	2,416
# admits	812	119	931
# of matrics	212	62	274
75% GPA	3.60	3.53	
25% GPA	3.06	2.96	
75% LSAT	159	161	
25% LSAT	151	152	

Tuition & Fees

	Resident	Non-resident
Full-Time	$9,219	$16,603
Part-Time	$6,919	$12,455

Living Expenses

Estimated living expenses for Singles		
Living on campus	Living off campus	Living at home
$9,741	$12,630	$6,159

Financial Aid

	Full-time		Part-time		Total	
	#	%	#	%	#	%
Total # of Students	614		262		876	
Total # receiving grants	300	48.9	65	24.8	365	41.7
Less than 1/2 tuition	300	48.9	65	24.8	365	41.7
Half to full tuition	0	0.0	0	0.0	0	0.0
Full tuition	0	0.0	0	0.0	0	0.0
More than full tuition	0	0.0	0	0.0	0	0.0
Median Grant Amount	$2,657		$2,324			

Informational & Library Resources

# of volumes & volume equivalents	371,550	# of professional staff	7
# of titles	89,340	Hours per week with professional staff	55
# of active serial subscriptions	4,127	Hours per week without professional staff	43
Study seating capacity inside the library	372	# of student computer work stations for entire law school	58
Square feet of law library	45,921	# of additional networked connections	0
Square feet of law school (excl. Library)	45,695	Require Laptop Computer?	N

Employment

	Total	%
Employment status known	238	92.6
Employment status unknown	19	7.4
Employed	208	87.4
Pursuing graduate degrees	5	2.1
Unemployed seeking employment	20	8.4
Unemployed not seeking employment	5	2.1
Type of Employment		
# employed in law firms	88	42.3
# employed in business & industry	38	18.3
# employed in government	24	11.5
# employed in public interest	12	5.8
# employed as judicial clerks	43	20.7
# employed in academia	3	1.4
Geographic Location		
# employed in state	164	78.8
# employed in foreign countries	0	0.0
# of states where employed	17	

J.D. Attrition (Prior Year)

	Academic	Other	TOTALS	
	#	#	#	%
1st Year	1	11	12	4.5%
2nd Year	2	3	5	1.8%
3rd Year	1	3	4	1.6%
4th Year	0	0	0	0.0%
TOTALS	4	17	21	2.5%

Bar Passage Rates

Jurisdiction	Maryland		
Exam	Sum 96	Win 97	Total
# from school taking bar for the first time	198	30	228
School's pass rate for all first-time takers	83%	83%	83%
State's pass rate for all first-time takers	76%	79%	76%

MCGEORGE SCHOOL OF LAW

University of the Pacific
5200 Fifth Avenue
Sacramento, CA 95817
(916)739-7105
http://www.mcgeorge.edu

ABA Approved Since 1969

The Basics

Type of School: Private   Term: Semester
Application deadline: 05/15
Application fee: $40
Financial Aid deadline: Rolling
Can first year start other than Fall? No
Student faculty ratio: 23.4 to 1
Does the University offer:
- housing restricted to law students? Yes
- graduate student housing for which law students are eligible? Yes

Faculty & Administrators

	Total		Men		Women		Minorities	
	Fall	Spr	Fall	Spr	Fall	Spr	Fall	Spr
Full-time	36	34	29	27	7	7	3	3
Other Full-Time	5	5	2	2	3	3	0	0
Deans, librarians, & others who teach > 1/2	5	5	2	2	3	3	0	0
Part-time	34	37	28	33	6	4	2	2
Total	80	81	61	64	19	17	5	5
Deans, librarians, & others who teach < 1/2	2	2	1	1	1	1	0	0

Curriculum

	Full time	Part time
Typical first-year section size	100	100
Is there typically a "small section" of the first year class, other than Legal Writing, taught by full-time faculty?	No	No
If yes, typical size offered last year	N/A	N/A
# of classroom course titles beyond 1st year curriculum	81	52
# of upper division courses, excluding seminars, with an enrollment:		
Under 25	37	20
25 - 49	25	24
50 - 74	8	13
75 - 99	13	4
100 +	15	3
# of seminars	18	5
# of seminar positions available	599	
# of seminar positions filled	293	77
# of positions available in simulation courses	893	
# of simulation positions filled	640	215
# of positions available in faculty supervised clinical courses	175	
# of fac. sup. clin. positions filled	113	18
# involved in field placements	172	29
# involved in law journals	60	20
# in moot court or trial competitions	240	80
# of credit hrs required to graduate	88	

J.D. Enrollment & Ethnicity

	Men		Women		Fl-Time		Pt-Time		1st Yr		2nd Yr		3rd Yr		4th Yr		Total		JD Degrees Awarded
	#	%	#	%	#	%	#	%	#	%	#	%	#	%	#	%	#	%	
African-American	11	1.8	18	3.4	12	1.5	17	5.3	11	2.9	6	1.7	9	2.6	3	4.4	29	2.5	4
American Indian	12	2.0	9	1.7	14	1.7	7	2.2	4	1.1	6	1.7	9	2.6	2	2.9	21	1.8	5
Asian American	67	11.1	64	11.9	111	13.6	20	6.2	46	12.2	39	11.1	40	11.6	6	8.8	131	11.5	41
Mexican American	28	4.6	23	4.3	32	3.9	19	5.9	17	4.5	16	4.6	13	3.8	5	7.4	51	4.5	8
Puerto Rican	1	0.2	1	0.2	2	0.2	0	0.0	1	0.3	1	0.3	0	0.0	0	0.0	2	0.2	1
Hispanic American	15	2.5	14	2.6	19	2.3	10	3.1	6	1.6	8	2.3	14	4.1	1	1.5	29	2.5	13
Total Minorities	134	22.2	129	24.1	190	23.3	73	22.7	85	22.6	76	21.7	85	24.6	17	25.0	263	23.1	72
Foreign Nationals	0	0.0	0	0.0	0	0.0	0	0.0	0	0.0	0	0.0	0	0.0	0	0.0	0	0.0	0
Caucasian	469	77.8	407	75.9	627	76.7	249	77.3	291	77.4	274	78.3	260	75.4	51	75.0	876	76.9	283
Total	603	52.9	536	47.1	817	71.7	322	28.3	376	33.0	350	30.7	345	30.3	68	6.0	1139		355

MCGEORGE SCHOOL OF LAW

GPA & LSAT Scores

	Full Time	Part Time	Total
# of apps	1,592	219	1,811
# admits	1,100	140	1,240
# of matrics	291	96	387
75% GPA	3.31	3.18	
25% GPA	2.82	2.71	
75% LSAT	155	157	
25% LSAT	149	149	

Tuition & Fees

	Resident	Non-resident
Full-Time	$18,378	$18,378
Part-Time	$11,326	$11,326

Living Expenses

Estimated living expenses for Singles		
Living on campus	Living off campus	Living at home
$13,910	$13,910	$6,311

Employment

	Total	%
Employment status known	296	79.1
Employment status unknown	78	20.9
Employed	233	78.7
Pursuing graduate degrees	10	3.4
Unemployed seeking employment	53	17.9
Unemployed not seeking employment	0	0.0
Type of Employment		
# employed in law firms	139	59.7
# employed in business & industry	30	12.9
# employed in government	55	23.6
# employed in public interest	1	0.4
# employed as judicial clerks	6	2.6
# employed in academia	2	0.9
Geographic Location		
# employed in state	196	84.1
# employed in foreign countries	4	1.7
# of states where employed	14	

Financial Aid

	Full-time		Part-time		Total	
	#	%	#	%	#	%
Total # of Students	817		322		1139	
Total # receiving grants	311	38.1	109	33.9	420	36.9
Less than 1/2 tuition	278	34.0	89	27.6	367	32.2
Half to full tuition	27	3.3	18	5.6	45	4.0
Full tuition	6	0.7	2	0.6	8	0.7
More than full tuition	0	0.0	0	0.0	0	0.0
Median Grant Amount	$3,351		$2,257			

Informational & Library Resources

# of volumes & volume equivalents	430,207	# of professional staff	7
# of titles	92,711	Hours per week with professional staff	86
# of active serial subscriptions	4,509	Hours per week without professional staff	24
Study seating capacity inside the library	615	# of student computer work stations for entire law school	76
Square feet of law library	48,161	# of additional networked connections	0
Square feet of law school (excl. Library)	143,377	Require Laptop Computer?	N

J.D. Attrition (Prior Year)

	Academic	Other	TOTALS	
	#	#	#	%
1st Year	27	21	48	12%
2nd Year	7	33	40	11%
3rd Year	0	10	10	3.2%
4th Year	0	0	0	0.0%
TOTALS	34	64	98	8.2%

Bar Passage Rates

Jurisdiction	California		
Exam	Sum 96	Win 97	Total
# from school taking bar for the first time	298	37	335
School's pass rate for all first-time takers	74%	76%	75%
State's pass rate for all first-time takers	69%	62%	67%

MEMPHIS, UNIVERSITY OF

The University of Memphis
School of Law
Memphis, TN 39152-6513
(901)678-2421
http://www.people.memphis.edu/~law

ABA Approved Since 1965

The Basics

Type of School: Public   Term: Semester
Application deadline: 02/15
Application fee: $15
Financial Aid deadline: 04/01
Can first year start other than Fall? No
Student faculty ratio: 20.8 to 1
Does the University offer:
- housing restricted to law students? No
- graduate student housing for which law students are eligible? Yes

Faculty & Administrators

	Total		Men		Women		Minorities	
	Fall	Spr	Fall	Spr	Fall	Spr	Fall	Spr
Full-time	20	19	14	13	6	6	1	1
Other Full-Time	3	3	1	1	2	2	0	0
Deans, librarians, & others who teach > 1/2	1	1	1	1	0	0	0	0
Part-time	25	28	13	16	12	12	2	3
Total	49	51	29	31	20	20	3	4
Deans, librarians, & others who teach < 1/2	1	1	1	1	0	0	0	0

Curriculum

	Full time	Part time
Typical first-year section size	74	74
Is there typically a "small section" of the first year class, other than Legal Writing, taught by full-time faculty?	No	No
If yes, typical size offered last year	N/A	N/A
# of classroom course titles beyond 1st year curriculum	62	62
# of upper division courses, excluding seminars, with an enrollment:		
Under 25	46	46
25 - 49	16	16
50 - 74	12	12
75 - 99	11	11
100 +	1	1
# of seminars	11	11
# of seminar positions available	140	
# of seminar positions filled	133	133
# of positions available in simulation courses	274	
# of simulation positions filled	242	242
# of positions available in faculty supervised clinical courses	86	
# of fac. sup. clin. positions filled	67	67
# involved in field placements	15	15
# involved in law journals	30	30
# in moot court or trial competitions	37	37
# of credit hrs required to graduate	90	

J.D. Enrollment & Ethnicity

	Men		Women		Fl-Time		Pt-Time		1st Yr		2nd Yr		3rd Yr		4th Yr		Total		JD Degrees Awarded
	#	%	#	%	#	%	#	%	#	%	#	%	#	%	#	%	#	%	
African-American	15	5.2	33	14.9	39	8.1	9	29.0	18	8.9	16	11.9	14	8.2	0	0.0	48	9.4	13
American Indian	1	0.3	1	0.5	2	0.4	0	0.0	1	0.5	1	0.7	0	0.0	0	0.0	2	0.4	0
Asian American	0	0.0	1	0.5	1	0.2	0	0.0	0	0.0	0	0.0	1	0.6	0	0.0	1	0.2	1
Mexican American	1	0.3	0	0.0	1	0.2	0	0.0	1	0.5	0	0.0	0	0.0	0	0.0	1	0.2	0
Puerto Rican	0	0.0	0	0.0	0	0.0	0	0.0	0	0.0	0	0.0	0	0.0	0	0.0	0	0.0	0
Hispanic American	1	0.3	1	0.5	2	0.4	0	0.0	1	0.5	0	0.0	1	0.6	0	0.0	2	0.4	1
Total Minorities	18	6.2	36	16.3	45	9.4	9	29.0	21	10.4	17	12.6	16	9.4	0	0.0	54	10.6	15
Foreign Nationals	0	0.0	0	0.0	0	0.0	0	0.0	0	0.0	0	0.0	0	0.0	0	0.0	0	0.0	0
Caucasian	271	93.8	185	83.7	434	90.6	22	71.0	181	89.6	118	87.4	154	90.6	3	100.0	456	89.4	121
Total	289	56.7	221	43.3	479	93.9	31	6.1	202	39.6	135	26.5	170	33.3	3	0.6	510		136

GPA & LSAT Scores

	Full Time	Part Time	Total
# of apps	808	26	834
# admits	456	18	474
# of matrics	188	17	205
75% GPA	3.38	3.10	
25% GPA	2.66	2.86	
75% LSAT	160	157	
25% LSAT	147	143	

Tuition & Fees

	Resident	Non-resident
Full-Time	$4,182	$10,360
Part-Time	$3,320	$8,144

Living Expenses

Estimated living expenses for Singles		
Living on campus	Living off campus	Living at home
$11,090	$11,090	$11,090

Employment

	Total	%
Employment status known	93	74.4
Employment status unknown	32	25.6
Employed	89	95.7
Pursuing graduate degrees	1	1.1
Unemployed seeking employment	1	1.1
Unemployed not seeking employment	2	2.2
Type of Employment		
# employed in law firms	53	59.6
# employed in business & industry	18	20.2
# employed in government	8	9.0
# employed in public interest	0	0.0
# employed as judicial clerks	4	4.5
# employed in academia	2	2.2
Geographic Location		
# employed in state	66	74.2
# employed in foreign countries	2	2.2
# of states where employed	10	

Financial Aid

	Full-time		Part-time		Total	
	#	%	#	%	#	%
Total # of Students	479		31		510	
Total # receiving grants	106	22.1	9	29.0	115	22.5
Less than 1/2 tuition	12	2.5	0	0.0	12	2.4
Half to full tuition	4	0.8	0	0.0	4	0.8
Full tuition	0	0.0	0	0.0	0	0.0
More than full tuition	90	18.8	9	29.0	99	19.4
Median Grant Amount	$3,850		$3,524			

Informational & Library Resources

# of volumes & volume equivalents	267,566	# of professional staff	5
# of titles	41,892	Hours per week with professional staff	66
# of active serial subscriptions	3,015	Hours per week without professional staff	41
Study seating capacity inside the library	299	# of student computer work stations for entire law school	56
Square feet of law library	29,465	# of additional networked connections	4
Square feet of law school (excl. Library)	55,298	Require Laptop Computer?	N

J.D. Attrition (Prior Year)

	Academic	Other	TOTALS	
	#	#	#	%
1st Year	10	16	26	18%
2nd Year	5	3	8	4.6%
3rd Year	1	0	1	0.7%
4th Year	0	0	0	0.0%
TOTALS	16	19	35	7.4%

Bar Passage Rates

Jurisdiction	Tennessee		
Exam	Sum 96	Win 97	Total
# from school taking bar for the first time	107	10	117
School's pass rate for all first-time takers	91%	90%	91%
State's pass rate for all first-time takers	81%	72%	79%

MERCER UNIVERSITY

1021 Georgia Avenue
Macon, GA 31207
(912)752-2601
http://www.mercer.edu/~law

ABA Approved Since 1925

The Basics

Type of School: Private Term: Semester

Application deadline: 03/15

Application fee: $45

Financial Aid deadline: 04/01

Can first year start other than Fall? No

Student faculty ratio: 16.9 to 1

Does the University offer:
- housing restricted to law students? Yes
- graduate student housing for which law students are eligible? Yes

Faculty & Administrators

	Total		Men		Women		Minorities	
	Fall	Spr	Fall	Spr	Fall	Spr	Fall	Spr
Full-time	20	21	16	16	4	5	2	2
Other Full-Time	3	3	3	3	0	0	0	0
Deans, librarians, & others who teach > 1/2	2	2	1	1	1	1	0	0
Part-time	5	21	5	16	0	5	0	1
Total	30	47	25	36	5	11	2	3
Deans, librarians, & others who teach < 1/2	2	2	1	1	1	1	0	0

Curriculum

	Full time	Part time
Typical first-year section size	70	70
Is there typically a "small section" of the first year class, other than Legal Writing, taught by full-time faculty?	Yes	Yes
If yes, typical size offered last year	24	24
# of classroom course titles beyond 1st year curriculum	85	85
# of upper division courses, excluding seminars, with an enrollment:		
Under 25	55	0
25 - 49	25	0
50 - 74	9	0
75 - 99	3	0
100 +	1	0
# of seminars	14	0
# of seminar positions available	210	
# of seminar positions filled	153	0
# of positions available in simulation courses	768	
# of simulation positions filled	664	0
# of positions available in faculty supervised clinical courses	26	
# of fac. sup. clin. positions filled	21	0
# involved in field placements	40	0
# involved in law journals	46	0
# in moot court or trial competitions	38	0
# of credit hrs required to graduate	90	

J.D. Enrollment & Ethnicity

	Men		Women		Fl-Time		Pt-Time		1st Yr		2nd Yr		3rd Yr		4th Yr		Total		JD Degrees Awarded
	#	%	#	%	#	%	#	%	#	%	#	%	#	%	#	%	#	%	
African-American	5	2.1	20	12.3	25	6.2	0	0.0	9	6.0	7	5.2	9	7.5	0	0.0	25	6.2	12
American Indian	1	0.4	1	0.6	2	0.5	0	0.0	0	0.0	2	1.5	0	0.0	0	0.0	2	0.5	1
Asian American	9	3.7	1	0.6	10	2.5	0	0.0	1	0.7	6	4.5	3	2.5	0	0.0	10	2.5	0
Mexican American	3	1.2	1	0.6	4	1.0	0	0.0	2	1.3	1	0.7	1	0.8	0	0.0	4	1.0	2
Puerto Rican	1	0.4	0	0.0	1	0.2	0	0.0	1	0.7	0	0.0	0	0.0	0	0.0	1	0.2	1
Hispanic American	3	1.2	3	1.8	6	1.5	0	0.0	4	2.6	1	0.7	1	0.8	0	0.0	6	1.5	3
Total Minorities	22	9.1	26	16.0	48	11.9	0	0.0	17	11.3	17	12.7	14	11.7	0	0.0	48	11.9	19
Foreign Nationals	0	0.0	0	0.0	0	0.0	0	0.0	0	0.0	0	0.0	0	0.0	0	0.0	0	0.0	0
Caucasian	220	90.9	137	84.0	357	88.1	0	0.0	134	88.7	117	87.3	106	88.3	0	0.0	357	88.1	121
Total	242	59.8	163	40.2	405	100.0	0	0.0	151	37.3	134	33.1	120	29.6	0	0.0	405		140

GPA & LSAT Scores

	Full Time	Part Time	Total
# of apps	1,071	0	1,071
# admits	483	0	483
# of matrics	151	0	151
75% GPA	3.51	0.00	
25% GPA	2.82	0.00	
75% LSAT	157	0	
25% LSAT	151	0	

Tuition & Fees

	Resident	Non-resident
Full-Time	$17,990	$17,990
Part-Time	$8,995	$8,995

Living Expenses

Estimated living expenses for Singles

Living on campus	Living off campus	Living at home
N/A	$11,000	N/A

Financial Aid

	Full-time		Part-time		Total	
	#	%	#	%	#	%
Total # of Students	405		0		405	
Total # receiving grants	95	23.5	0	0.0	95	23.5
Less than 1/2 tuition	48	11.9	0	0.0	48	11.9
Half to full tuition	16	4.0	0	0.0	16	4.0
Full tuition	21	5.2	0	0.0	21	5.2
More than full tuition	10	2.5	0	0.0	10	2.5
Median Grant Amount	$8,222		$0			

Informational & Library Resources

# of volumes & volume equivalents	278,853	# of professional staff	6
# of titles	35,510	Hours per week with professional staff	73
# of active serial subscriptions	2,770	Hours per week without professional staff	2
Study seating capacity inside the library	326	# of student computer work stations for entire law school	56
Square feet of law library	35,000	# of additional networked connections	59
Square feet of law school (excl. Library)	48,800	Require Laptop Computer?	N

Employment

	Total	%
Employment status known	138	97.9
Employment status unknown	3	2.1
Employed	123	89.1
Pursuing graduate degrees	4	2.9
Unemployed seeking employment	11	8.0
Unemployed not seeking employment	0	0.0
Type of Employment		
# employed in law firms	81	65.9
# employed in business & industry	8	6.5
# employed in government	20	16.3
# employed in public interest	0	0.0
# employed as judicial clerks	12	9.8
# employed in academia	2	1.6
Geographic Location		
# employed in state	87	70.7
# employed in foreign countries	0	0.0
# of states where employed	13	

J.D. Attrition (Prior Year)

	Academic	Other	TOTALS	
	#	#	#	%
1st Year	6	11	17	12%
2nd Year	0	1	1	0.8%
3rd Year	0	0	0	0.0%
4th Year	0	0	0	0.0%
TOTALS	6	12	18	4.5%

Bar Passage Rates

Jurisdiction	
Exam	
# from school taking bar for the first time	The Georgia Board of Bar Examiners now requires students to graduate prior to taking the bar. This resulted in too few graduates taking the Summer '96 and Winter '97 tests to warrant reporting.
School's pass rate for all first-time takers	
State's pass rate for all first-time takers	

MIAMI, UNIVERSITY OF

P.O. Box 248087
Coral Gables, FL 33124
(305)284-2394
http://www.law.miami.edu

ABA Approved Since 1941

The Basics

Type of School: Private Term: Semester
Application deadline: 07/31
Application fee: $45
Financial Aid deadline: 03/01
Can first year start other than Fall? No
Student faculty ratio: 24.4 to 1
Does the University offer:
- housing restricted to law students? No
- graduate student housing for which law students are eligible? Yes

Faculty & Administrators

	Total		Men		Women		Minorities	
	Fall	Spr	Fall	Spr	Fall	Spr	Fall	Spr
Full-time	45	44	34	34	11	10	7	6
Other Full-Time	6	6	2	2	4	4	0	0
Deans, librarians, & others who teach > 1/2	3	3	2	2	1	1	1	1
Part-time	113	137	87	106	26	31	9	10
Total	167	190	125	144	42	46	17	17
Deans, librarians, & others who teach < 1/2	1	1	0	0	1	1	1	1

Curriculum

	Full time	Part time
Typical first-year section size	125	120
Is there typically a "small section" of the first year class, other than Legal Writing, taught by full-time faculty?	Yes	Yes
If yes, typical size offered last year	42	60
# of classroom course titles beyond 1st year curriculum	84	24
# of upper division courses, excluding seminars, with an enrollment:		
Under 25	29	4
25 - 49	49	10
50 - 74	13	4
75 - 99	6	0
100 +	9	6
# of seminars	68	9
# of seminar positions available	1,925	
# of seminar positions filled	1,294	198
# of positions available in simulation courses	444	
# of simulation positions filled	385	36
# of positions available in faculty supervised clinical courses	12	
# of fac. sup. clin. positions filled	12	0
# involved in field placements	230	0
# involved in law journals	119	29
# in moot court or trial competitions	52	0
# of credit hrs required to graduate	88	

J.D. Enrollment & Ethnicity

	Men		Women		Fl-Time		Pt-Time		1st Yr		2nd Yr		3rd Yr		4th Yr		Total		JD Degrees Awarded
	#	%	#	%	#	%	#	%	#	%	#	%	#	%	#	%	#	%	
African-American	47	5.9	72	11.8	88	7.8	31	11.2	35	7.4	41	8.6	42	9.4	1	7.7	119	8.4	60
American Indian	3	0.4	3	0.5	4	0.4	2	0.7	3	0.6	0	0.0	3	0.7	0	0.0	6	0.4	1
Asian American	21	2.6	19	3.1	25	2.2	15	5.4	17	3.6	11	2.3	12	2.7	0	0.0	40	2.8	7
Mexican American	0	0.0	0	0.0	0	0.0	0	0.0	0	0.0	0	0.0	0	0.0	0	0.0	0	0.0	0
Puerto Rican	0	0.0	0	0.0	0	0.0	0	0.0	0	0.0	0	0.0	0	0.0	0	0.0	0	0.0	0
Hispanic American	104	13.0	137	22.4	172	15.2	69	24.9	86	18.1	89	18.7	64	14.3	2	15.4	241	17.1	74
Total Minorities	175	21.9	231	37.8	289	25.5	117	42.2	141	29.7	141	29.6	121	27.1	3	23.1	406	28.8	142
Foreign Nationals	44	5.5	45	7.4	63	5.6	26	9.4	35	7.4	28	5.9	25	5.6	1	7.7	89	6.3	22
Caucasian	580	72.6	335	54.8	781	68.9	134	48.4	298	62.9	308	64.6	300	67.3	9	69.2	915	64.9	246
Total	799	56.7	611	43.3	1133	80.4	277	19.6	474	33.6	477	33.8	446	31.6	13	0.9	1410		410

GPA & LSAT Scores

	Full Time	Part Time	Total
# of apps	2,080	351	2,431
# admits	1,335	251	1,586
# of matrics	354	128	482
75% GPA	3.45	3.29	
25% GPA	2.91	2.67	
75% LSAT	157	152	
25% LSAT	151	146	

Tuition & Fees

	Resident	Non-resident
Full-Time	$21,458	$21,458
Part-Time	$15,450	$15,450

Living Expenses

Estimated living expenses for Singles		
Living on campus	Living off campus	Living at home
$14,665	$14,665	$9,490

Financial Aid

	Full-time		Part-time		Total	
	#	%	#	%	#	%
Total # of Students	1133		277		1410	
Total # receiving grants	379	33.5	11	4.0	390	27.7
Less than 1/2 tuition	156	13.8	4	1.4	160	11.3
Half to full tuition	144	12.7	7	2.5	151	10.7
Full tuition	62	5.5	0	0.0	62	4.4
More than full tuition	17	1.5	0	0.0	17	1.2
Median Grant Amount	$11,213		$5,000			

Informational & Library Resources

# of volumes & volume equivalents	456,418	# of professional staff	11
# of titles	77,553	Hours per week with professional staff	84
# of active serial subscriptions	7,485	Hours per week without professional staff	35
Study seating capacity inside the library	663	# of student computer work stations for entire law school	152
Square feet of law library	77,446	# of additional networked connections	145
Square feet of law school (excl. Library)	119,486	Require Laptop Computer?	N

Employment

	Total	%
Employment status known	366	94.1
Employment status unknown	23	5.9
Employed	253	69.1
Pursuing graduate degrees	12	3.3
Unemployed seeking employment	97	26.5
Unemployed not seeking employment	4	1.1
Type of Employment		
# employed in law firms	147	58.1
# employed in business & industry	21	8.3
# employed in government	34	13.4
# employed in public interest	2	0.8
# employed as judicial clerks	13	5.1
# employed in academia	5	2.0
Geographic Location		
# employed in state	195	77.1
# employed in foreign countries	0	0.0
# of states where employed	27	

J.D. Attrition (Prior Year)

	Academic	Other	TOTALS	
	#	#	#	%
1st Year	0	8	8	1.6%
2nd Year	13	18	31	6.4%
3rd Year	4	1	5	1.3%
4th Year	0	0	0	0.0%
TOTALS	17	27	44	3.1%

Bar Passage Rates

Jurisdiction	Florida		
Exam	Sum 96	Win 97	Total
# from school taking bar for the first time	252	70	322
School's pass rate for all first-time takers	88%	70%	84%
State's pass rate for all first-time takers	84%	85%	84%

MICHIGAN, UNIVERSITY OF

Hutchins Hall
625 South State Street
Ann Arbor, MI 48109-1215
(313)764-1358
http://www.law.umich.edu

ABA Approved Since 1923

The Basics

Type of School: Public Term: Semester
Application deadline: 02/15
Application fee: $70
Financial Aid deadline: Rolling
Can first year start other than Fall? Yes
Student faculty ratio: 15.9 to 1
Does the University offer:
- housing restricted to law students? Yes
- graduate student housing for which law students are eligible? Yes

Faculty & Administrators

	Total		Men		Women		Minorities	
	Fall	Spr	Fall	Spr	Fall	Spr	Fall	Spr
Full-time	54	43	44	35	10	8	5	5
Other Full-Time	14	14	7	7	7	7	4	4
Deans, librarians, & others who teach > 1/2	3	3	0	0	3	3	0	0
Part-time	15	23	11	20	4	3	1	0
Total	86	83	62	62	24	21	10	9
Deans, librarians, & others who teach < 1/2	1	1	1	1	0	0	0	0

Curriculum

	Full time	Part time
Typical first-year section size	80	0
Is there typically a "small section" of the first year class, other than Legal Writing, taught by full-time faculty?	Yes	No
If yes, typical size offered last year	40	N/A
# of classroom course titles beyond 1st year curriculum	142	0
# of upper division courses, excluding seminars, with an enrollment:		
Under 25	33	0
25 - 49	31	0
50 - 74	17	0
75 - 99	14	0
100 +	17	0
# of seminars	54	0
# of seminar positions available	800	
# of seminar positions filled	631	0
# of positions available in simulation courses	127	
# of simulation positions filled	127	0
# of positions available in faculty supervised clinical courses	169	
# of fac. sup. clin. positions filled	158	0
# involved in field placements	57	0
# involved in law journals	396	0
# in moot court or trial competitions	204	0
# of credit hrs required to graduate	86	

J.D. Enrollment & Ethnicity

	Men		Women		Fl-Time		Pt-Time		1st Yr		2nd Yr		3rd Yr		4th Yr		Total		JD Degrees Awarded
	#	%	#	%	#	%	#	%	#	%	#	%	#	%	#	%	#	%	
African-American	37	6.1	39	9.1	76	7.3	0	0.0	25	7.4	25	7.5	26	7.2	0	0.0	76	7.3	39
American Indian	8	1.3	7	1.6	15	1.4	0	0.0	7	2.1	3	0.9	5	1.4	0	0.0	15	1.4	12
Asian American	36	5.9	41	9.6	77	7.4	0	0.0	31	9.1	21	6.3	25	6.9	0	0.0	77	7.4	15
Mexican American	19	3.1	8	1.9	27	2.6	0	0.0	7	2.1	12	3.6	8	2.2	0	0.0	27	2.6	17
Puerto Rican	6	1.0	4	0.9	10	1.0	0	0.0	3	0.9	4	1.2	3	0.8	0	0.0	10	1.0	4
Hispanic American	6	1.0	4	0.9	10	1.0	0	0.0	4	1.2	3	0.9	3	0.8	0	0.0	10	1.0	4
Total Minorities	112	18.5	103	24.1	215	20.8	0	0.0	77	22.7	68	20.4	70	19.3	0	0.0	215	20.8	91
Foreign Nationals	8	1.3	5	1.2	13	1.3	0	0.0	5	1.5	6	1.8	2	0.6	0	0.0	13	1.3	3
Caucasian	487	80.2	320	74.8	807	78.0	0	0.0	257	75.8	260	77.8	290	80.1	0	0.0	807	78.0	298
Total	607	58.6	428	41.4	1035	100.0	0	0.0	339	32.8	334	32.3	362	35.0	0	0.0	1035		392

GPA & LSAT Scores

	Full Time	Part Time	Total
# of apps	3,373	0	3,373
# admits	1,163	0	1,163
# of matrics	339	0	339
75% GPA	3.69	0.00	
25% GPA	3.33	0.00	
75% LSAT	169	0	
25% LSAT	163	0	

Tuition & Fees

	Resident	Non-resident
Full-Time	$17,332	$23,332
Part-Time	$0	$0

Living Expenses

Estimated living expenses for Singles		
Living on campus	Living off campus	Living at home
$12,900	$12,250	$6,250

Employment

	Total	%
Employment status known	371	96.6
Employment status unknown	13	3.4
Employed	345	93.0
Pursuing graduate degrees	2	0.5
Unemployed seeking employment	22	5.9
Unemployed not seeking employment	2	0.5
Type of Employment		
# employed in law firms	227	65.8
# employed in business & industry	22	6.4
# employed in government	14	4.1
# employed in public interest	8	2.3
# employed as judicial clerks	71	20.6
# employed in academia	2	0.6
Geographic Location		
# employed in state	75	21.7
# employed in foreign countries	4	1.2
# of states where employed	32	

Financial Aid

	Full-time		Part-time		Total	
	#	%	#	%	#	%
Total # of Students	1035		0		1035	
Total # receiving grants	340	32.9	0	0.0	340	32.9
Less than 1/2 tuition	247	23.9	0	0.0	247	23.9
Half to full tuition	46	4.4	0	0.0	46	4.4
Full tuition	0	0.0	0	0.0	0	0.0
More than full tuition	47	4.5	0	0.0	47	4.5
Median Grant Amount	$8,688		$0			

Informational & Library Resources

# of volumes & volume equivalents	811,774	# of professional staff	10
# of titles	264,490	Hours per week with professional staff	71
# of active serial subscriptions	9,835	Hours per week without professional staff	41
Study seating capacity inside the library	843	# of student computer work stations for entire law school	92
Square feet of law library	101,876	# of additional networked connections	27
Square feet of law school (excl. Library)	81,793	Require Laptop Computer?	N

J.D. Attrition (Prior Year)

	Academic	Other	TOTALS	
	#	#	#	%
1st Year	0	2	2	0.6%
2nd Year	0	2	2	0.6%
3rd Year	0	0	0	0.0%
4th Year	0	0	0	0.0%
TOTALS	0	4	4	0.4%

Bar Passage Rates

Jurisdiction	Michigan			New York		
Exam	Sum 96	Win 97	Total	Sum 96	Win 97	Total
# from school taking bar for the first time	65	31	96	47	15	62
School's pass rate for all first-time takers	86%	84%	85%	74%	80%	76%
State's pass rate for all first-time takers	84%	86%	85%	78%	67%	77%

MINNESOTA, UNIVERSITY OF

229 19 Ave S.
Minneapolis, MN 55455
(612)625-1000
http://www.law.umn.edu/

ABA Approved Since 1923

The Basics

Type of School: Public   Term: Semester

Application deadline: 03/01

Application fee: $40

Financial Aid deadline: 03/01

Can first year start other than Fall? No

Student faculty ratio: 16.3 to 1

Does the University offer:
- housing restricted to law students? No
- graduate student housing for which law students are eligible? No

Faculty & Administrators

	Total		Men		Women		Minorities	
	Fall	Spr	Fall	Spr	Fall	Spr	Fall	Spr
Full-time	39	40	29	28	10	12	3	3
Other Full-Time	3	3	2	2	1	1	0	0
Deans, librarians, & others who teach > 1/2	1	1	0	0	1	1	1	1
Part-time	54	81	37	50	17	31	2	3
Total	97	125	68	80	29	45	6	7
Deans, librarians, & others who teach < 1/2	7	7	3	3	4	4	1	1

Curriculum

	Full time	Part time
Typical first-year section size	110	0
Is there typically a "small section" of the first year class, other than Legal Writing, taught by full-time faculty?	Yes	No
If yes, typical size offered last year	55	N/A
# of classroom course titles beyond 1st year curriculum	142	0
# of upper division courses, excluding seminars, with an enrollment:		
Under 25	38	0
25 - 49	19	0
50 - 74	16	0
75 - 99	6	0
100 +	16	0
# of seminars	47	0
# of seminar positions available	780	
# of seminar positions filled	752	0
# of positions available in simulation courses	156	
# of simulation positions filled	153	0
# of positions available in faculty supervised clinical courses	184	
# of fac. sup. clin. positions filled	184	0
# involved in field placements	50	0
# involved in law journals	145	0
# in moot court or trial competitions	236	0
# of credit hrs required to graduate	88	

J.D. Enrollment & Ethnicity

	Men		Women		Fl-Time		Pt-Time		1st Yr		2nd Yr		3rd Yr		4th Yr		Total		JD Degrees Awarded
	#	%	#	%	#	%	#	%	#	%	#	%	#	%	#	%	#	%	
African-American	10	2.3	13	4.0	23	3.0	0	0.0	8	3.3	7	2.7	8	3.1	0	0.0	23	3.0	15
American Indian	3	0.7	6	1.9	9	1.2	0	0.0	4	1.7	3	1.2	2	0.8	0	0.0	9	1.2	6
Asian American	34	7.7	34	10.6	68	8.9	0	0.0	32	13.3	20	7.7	16	6.1	0	0.0	68	8.9	27
Mexican American	5	1.1	9	2.8	14	1.8	0	0.0	5	2.1	7	2.7	2	0.8	0	0.0	14	1.8	3
Puerto Rican	3	0.7	1	0.3	4	0.5	0	0.0	1	0.4	2	0.8	1	0.4	0	0.0	4	0.5	0
Hispanic American	6	1.4	7	2.2	13	1.7	0	0.0	8	3.3	5	1.9	0	0.0	0	0.0	13	1.7	3
Total Minorities	61	13.8	70	21.8	131	17.2	0	0.0	58	24.1	44	16.9	29	11.1	0	0.0	131	17.2	54
Foreign Nationals	9	2.0	7	2.2	16	2.1	0	0.0	9	3.7	3	1.2	4	1.5	0	0.0	16	2.1	0
Caucasian	371	84.1	244	76.0	615	80.7	0	0.0	174	72.2	210	80.8	231	88.5	0	0.0	615	80.7	210
Total	441	57.9	321	42.1	762	100.0	0	0.0	241	31.6	260	34.1	261	34.3	0	0.0	762		264

GPA & LSAT Scores

	Full Time	Part Time	Total
# of apps	1,513	0	1,513
# admits	644	0	644
# of matrics	245	0	245
75% GPA	3.77	0.00	
25% GPA	3.28	0.00	
75% LSAT	164	0	
25% LSAT	158	0	

Tuition & Fees

	Resident	Non-resident
Full-Time	$9,230	$15,274
Part-Time	$0	$0

Living Expenses

Estimated living expenses for Singles

Living on campus	Living off campus	Living at home
$8,849	$8,849	$5,900

Employment

	Total	%
Employment status known	270	99.6
Employment status unknown	1	0.4
Employed	246	91.1
Pursuing graduate degrees	4	1.5
Unemployed seeking employment	7	2.6
Unemployed not seeking employment	13	4.8
Type of Employment		
# employed in law firms	97	39.4
# employed in business & industry	38	15.4
# employed in government	30	12.2
# employed in public interest	10	4.1
# employed as judicial clerks	64	26.0
# employed in academia	3	1.2
Geographic Location		
# employed in state	156	63.4
# employed in foreign countries	1	0.4
# of states where employed	30	

Financial Aid

	Full-time		Part-time		Total	
	#	%	#	%	#	%
Total # of Students	762		0		762	
Total # receiving grants	300	39.4	0	0.0	300	39.4
Less than 1/2 tuition	159	20.9	0	0.0	159	20.9
Half to full tuition	82	10.8	0	0.0	82	10.8
Full tuition	59	7.7	0	0.0	59	7.7
More than full tuition	0	0.0	0	0.0	0	0.0
Median Grant Amount	$6,044		$0			

Informational & Library Resources

# of volumes & volume equivalents	830,290	# of professional staff	12
# of titles	220,612	Hours per week with professional staff	67
# of active serial subscriptions	9,661	Hours per week without professional staff	14
Study seating capacity inside the library	934	# of student computer work stations for entire law school	76
Square feet of law library	95,000	# of additional networked connections	0
Square feet of law school (excl. Library)	265,000	Require Laptop Computer?	Y

J.D. Attrition (Prior Year)

	Academic	Other	TOTALS	
	#	#	#	%
1st Year	0	10	10	4.0%
2nd Year	0	0	0	0.0%
3rd Year	0	0	0	0.0%
4th Year	0	0	0	0.0%
TOTALS	0	10	10	1.3%

Bar Passage Rates

Jurisdiction	Minnesota		
Exam	Sum 96	Win 97	Total
# from school taking bar for the first time	174	8	182
School's pass rate for all first-time takers	98%	100%	98%
State's pass rate for all first-time takers	92%	84%	91%

MISSISSIPPI COLLEGE

151 East Griffith Street
Jackson, MS 39201
(601)925-7100
http://www.mc.edu

ABA Approved Since 1980

The Basics

Type of School: Private Term: Semester
Application deadline: 05/01
Application fee: $25
Financial Aid deadline: 06/01
Can first year start other than Fall? Yes
Student faculty ratio: 21.8 to 1
Does the University offer:
- housing restricted to law students? No
- graduate student housing for which law students are eligible? No

Faculty & Administrators

	Total		Men		Women		Minorities	
	Fall	Spr	Fall	Spr	Fall	Spr	Fall	Spr
Full-time	16	17	10	11	6	6	2	2
Other Full-Time	1	1	0	0	1	1	0	0
Deans, librarians, & others who teach > 1/2	1	1	1	1	0	0	0	0
Part-time	8	10	6	10	2	0	0	1
Total	26	29	17	22	9	7	2	3
Deans, librarians, & others who teach < 1/2	2	2	1	1	1	1	0	0

Curriculum

	Full time	Part time
Typical first-year section size	70	0
Is there typically a "small section" of the first year class, other than Legal Writing, taught by full-time faculty?	Yes	No
If yes, typical size offered last year	25	N/A
# of classroom course titles beyond 1st year curriculum	62	0
# of upper division courses, excluding seminars, with an enrollment:		
Under 25	28	0
25 - 49	9	0
50 - 74	20	0
75 - 99	1	0
100 +	1	0
# of seminars	6	0
# of seminar positions available	90	
# of seminar positions filled	74	0
# of positions available in simulation courses	238	
# of simulation positions filled	206	0
# of positions available in faculty supervised clinical courses	0	
# of fac. sup. clin. positions filled	0	0
# involved in field placements	25	0
# involved in law journals	34	0
# in moot court or trial competitions	47	0
# of credit hrs required to graduate	88	

J.D. Enrollment & Ethnicity

	Men		Women		Fl-Time		Pt-Time		1st Yr		2nd Yr		3rd Yr		4th Yr		Total		JD Degrees Awarded
	#	%	#	%	#	%	#	%	#	%	#	%	#	%	#	%	#	%	
African-American	11	4.2	23	14.6	34	8.1	0	0.0	12	8.5	11	7.7	11	8.2	0	0.0	34	8.1	4
American Indian	2	0.8	2	1.3	4	1.0	0	0.0	1	0.7	2	1.4	1	0.7	0	0.0	4	1.0	0
Asian American	6	2.3	1	0.6	7	1.7	0	0.0	0	0.0	3	2.1	4	3.0	0	0.0	7	1.7	1
Mexican American	0	0.0	0	0.0	0	0.0	0	0.0	0	0.0	0	0.0	0	0.0	0	0.0	0	0.0	0
Puerto Rican	0	0.0	0	0.0	0	0.0	0	0.0	0	0.0	0	0.0	0	0.0	0	0.0	0	0.0	0
Hispanic American	1	0.4	1	0.6	2	0.5	0	0.0	1	0.7	1	0.7	0	0.0	0	0.0	2	0.5	1
Total Minorities	20	7.7	27	17.2	47	11.2	0	0.0	14	9.9	17	12.0	16	11.9	0	0.0	47	11.2	6
Foreign Nationals	0	0.0	0	0.0	0	0.0	0	0.0	0	0.0	0	0.0	0	0.0	0	0.0	0	0.0	0
Caucasian	241	92.3	130	82.8	371	88.8	0	0.0	128	90.1	125	88.0	118	88.1	0	0.0	371	88.8	113
Total	261	62.4	157	37.6	418	100.0	0	0.0	142	34.0	142	34.0	134	32.1	0	0.0	418		119

GPA & LSAT Scores

	Full Time	Part Time	Total
# of apps	699	0	699
# admits	483	0	483
# of matrics	142	0	142
75% GPA	3.27	0.00	
25% GPA	2.67	0.00	
75% LSAT	152	0	
25% LSAT	145	0	

Tuition & Fees

	Resident	Non-resident
Full-Time	$12,610	$0
Part-Time	$0	$0

Living Expenses

Estimated living expenses for Singles		
Living on campus	Living off campus	Living at home
$10,186	$13,816	$13,816

Employment

	Total	%
Employment status known	104	92.0
Employment status unknown	9	8.0
Employed	90	86.5
Pursuing graduate degrees	5	4.8
Unemployed seeking employment	3	2.9
Unemployed not seeking employment	6	5.8
Type of Employment		
# employed in law firms	63	70.0
# employed in business & industry	0	0.0
# employed in government	8	8.9
# employed in public interest	2	2.2
# employed as judicial clerks	16	17.8
# employed in academia	1	1.1
Geographic Location		
# employed in state	53	58.9
# employed in foreign countries	0	0.0
# of states where employed	14	

Financial Aid

	Full-time		Part-time		Total	
	#	%	#	%	#	%
Total # of Students	418		0		418	
Total # receiving grants	104	24.9	0	0.0	104	24.9
Less than 1/2 tuition	32	7.7	0	0.0	32	7.7
Half to full tuition	32	7.7	0	0.0	32	7.7
Full tuition	37	8.9	0	0.0	37	8.9
More than full tuition	3	0.7	0	0.0	3	0.7
Median Grant Amount	$8,181		$0			

Informational & Library Resources

# of volumes & volume equivalents	253,272	# of professional staff	5
# of titles	87,808	Hours per week with professional staff	62
# of active serial subscriptions	3,438	Hours per week without professional staff	36
Study seating capacity inside the library	275	# of student computer work stations for entire law school	34
Square feet of law library	22,305	# of additional networked connections	3
Square feet of law school (excl. Library)	50,997	Require Laptop Computer?	N

J.D. Attrition (Prior Year)

	Academic	Other	TOTALS	
	#	#	#	%
1st Year	0	1	1	0.6%
2nd Year	0	12	12	8.8%
3rd Year	0	0	0	0.0%
4th Year	0	0	0	0.0%
TOTALS	0	13	13	3.1%

Bar Passage Rates

Jurisdiction	Mississippi		
Exam	Sum 96	Win 97	Total
# from school taking bar for the first time	57	9	66
School's pass rate for all first-time takers	86%	78%	85%
State's pass rate for all first-time takers	94%	84%	91%

MISSISSIPPI, UNIVERSITY OF

Office of the Dean
Law Center
University, MS 38677
(601)232-6900
http://www.olemiss.edu/depts/law_school

ABA Approved Since 1930

The Basics

Type of School: Public Term: Semester
Application deadline: 03/01
Application fee: $20
Financial Aid deadline: 03/15
Can first year start other than Fall? Yes
Student faculty ratio: 21.8 to 1
Does the University offer:
- housing restricted to law students? No
- graduate student housing for which law students are eligible? Yes

Curriculum

	Full time	Part time
Typical first-year section size	74	0
Is there typically a "small section" of the first year class, other than Legal Writing, taught by full-time faculty?	No	No
If yes, typical size offered last year	N/A	N/A
# of classroom course titles beyond 1st year curriculum	56	0
# of upper division courses, excluding seminars, with an enrollment:		
Under 25	19	0
25 - 49	18	0
50 - 74	11	0
75 - 99	3	0
100 +	1	0
# of seminars	20	0
# of seminar positions available	246	
# of seminar positions filled	191	0
# of positions available in simulation courses	177	
# of simulation positions filled	168	0
# of positions available in faculty supervised clinical courses	0	
# of fac. sup. clin. positions filled	0	0
# involved in field placements	78	0
# involved in law journals	63	0
# in moot court or trial competitions	151	0
# of credit hrs required to graduate	90	

Faculty & Administrators

	Total		Men		Women		Minorities	
	Fall	Spr	Fall	Spr	Fall	Spr	Fall	Spr
Full-time	19	20	16	16	3	4	4	4
Other Full-Time	2	2	1	1	1	1	0	0
Deans, librarians, & others who teach > 1/2	3	3	2	2	1	1	0	0
Part-time	5	4	4	3	1	1	1	1
Total	29	29	23	22	6	7	5	5
Deans, librarians, & others who teach < 1/2	1	1	1	1	0	0	0	0

J.D. Enrollment & Ethnicity

	Men		Women		Fl-Time		Pt-Time		1st Yr		2nd Yr		3rd Yr		4th Yr		Total		JD Degrees Awarded
	#	%	#	%	#	%	#	%	#	%	#	%	#	%	#	%	#	%	
African-American	15	5.1	35	17.3	50	10.1	0	0.0	11	6.5	22	11.9	17	11.7	0	0.0	50	10.0	11
American Indian	2	0.7	2	1.0	4	0.8	0	0.0	2	1.2	2	1.1	0	0.0	0	0.0	4	0.8	4
Asian American	1	0.3	3	1.5	4	0.8	0	0.0	2	1.2	0	0.0	2	1.4	0	0.0	4	0.8	1
Mexican American	4	1.3	0	0.0	4	0.8	0	0.0	2	1.2	1	0.5	1	0.7	0	0.0	4	0.8	1
Puerto Rican	0	0.0	0	0.0	0	0.0	0	0.0	0	0.0	0	0.0	0	0.0	0	0.0	0	0.0	0
Hispanic American	0	0.0	0	0.0	0	0.0	0	0.0	0	0.0	0	0.0	0	0.0	0	0.0	0	0.0	0
Total Minorities	22	7.4	40	19.8	62	12.5	0	0.0	17	10.1	25	13.5	20	13.8	0	0.0	62	12.4	17
Foreign Nationals	0	0.0	0	0.0	0	0.0	0	0.0	0	0.0	0	0.0	0	0.0	0	0.0	0	0.0	0
Caucasian	275	92.6	162	80.2	434	87.5	3	100.0	152	89.9	160	86.5	125	86.2	0	0.0	437	87.6	122
Total	297	59.5	202	40.5	496	99.4	3	0.6	169	33.9	185	37.1	145	29.1	0	0.0	499		139

GPA & LSAT Scores

	Full Time	Part Time	Total
# of apps	1,244	0	1,244
# admits	441	0	441
# of matrics	170	0	170
75% GPA	3.63	0.00	
25% GPA	3.02	0.00	
75% LSAT	157	0	
25% LSAT	150	0	

Tuition & Fees

	Resident	Non-resident
Full-Time	$3,181	$7,103
Part-Time	$118	$314

Living Expenses

Estimated living expenses for Singles		
Living on campus	Living off campus	Living at home
$9,600	$9,600	$9,600

Financial Aid

	Full-time		Part-time		Total	
	#	%	#	%	#	%
Total # of Students	496		3		499	
Total # receiving grants	55	11.1	0	0.0	55	11.0
Less than 1/2 tuition	0	0.0	0	0.0	0	0.0
Half to full tuition	0	0.0	0	0.0	0	0.0
Full tuition	55	11.1	0	0.0	55	11.0
More than full tuition	0	0.0	0	0.0	0	0.0
Median Grant Amount	$2,346		$0			

Informational & Library Resources

# of volumes & volume equivalents	286,902	# of professional staff	6
# of titles	62,349	Hours per week with professional staff	60
# of active serial subscriptions	2,891	Hours per week without professional staff	55
Study seating capacity inside the library	332	# of student computer work stations for entire law school	60
Square feet of law library	29,908	# of additional networked connections	0
Square feet of law school (excl. Library)	39,441	Require Laptop Computer?	N

Employment

	Total	%
Employment status known	139	99.3
Employment status unknown	1	0.7
Employed	126	90.6
Pursuing graduate degrees	6	4.3
Unemployed seeking employment	3	2.2
Unemployed not seeking employment	4	2.9
Type of Employment		
# employed in law firms	80	63.5
# employed in business & industry	12	9.5
# employed in government	12	9.5
# employed in public interest	1	0.8
# employed as judicial clerks	20	15.9
# employed in academia	0	0.0
Geographic Location		
# employed in state	90	71.4
# employed in foreign countries	0	0.0
# of states where employed	18	

J.D. Attrition (Prior Year)

	Academic	Other	TOTALS	
	#	#	#	%
1st Year	25	16	41	18%
2nd Year	3	0	3	2.0%
3rd Year	0	0	0	0.0%
4th Year	0	0	0	0.0%
TOTALS	28	16	44	8.5%

Bar Passage Rates

Jurisdiction	Mississippi		
Exam	Sum 96	Win 97	Total
# from school taking bar for the first time	97	34	131
School's pass rate for all first-time takers	98%	88%	95%
State's pass rate for all first-time takers	94%	84%	91%

MISSOURI-COLUMBIA, UNIVERSITY OF

203 Hulston Hall
University of Missouri-Columbia
Columbia, MO 65211
(573)882-6487
http://www.law.missouri.edu

ABA Approved Since 1923

The Basics

Type of School: Public   Term: Semester
Application deadline: 03/01
Application fee: $40
Financial Aid deadline: 03/01
Can first year start other than Fall? No
Student faculty ratio: 17.9 to 1
Does the University offer:
- housing restricted to law students? No
- graduate student housing for which law students are eligible? Yes

Faculty & Administrators

	Total		Men		Women		Minorities	
	Fall	Spr	Fall	Spr	Fall	Spr	Fall	Spr
Full-time	25	23	19	18	6	5	1	1
Other Full-Time	2	2	1	1	1	1	0	0
Deans, librarians, & others who teach > 1/2	3	3	3	3	0	0	0	0
Part-time	8	6	5	3	3	3	0	0
Total	38	34	28	25	10	9	1	1
Deans, librarians, & others who teach < 1/2	5	5	3	3	2	2	0	0

Curriculum

	Full time	Part time
Typical first-year section size	65	0
Is there typically a "small section" of the first year class, other than Legal Writing, taught by full-time faculty?	No	No
If yes, typical size offered last year	N/A	N/A
# of classroom course titles beyond 1st year curriculum	81	0
# of upper division courses, excluding seminars, with an enrollment:		
Under 25	66	0
25 - 49	15	0
50 - 74	8	0
75 - 99	5	0
100 +	1	0
# of seminars	7	0
# of seminar positions available	98	
# of seminar positions filled	64	0
# of positions available in simulation courses	257	
# of simulation positions filled	203	0
# of positions available in faculty supervised clinical courses	52	
# of fac. sup. clin. positions filled	44	0
# involved in field placements	44	0
# involved in law journals	94	0
# in moot court or trial competitions	200	0
# of credit hrs required to graduate	89	

J.D. Enrollment & Ethnicity

	Men		Women		Fl-Time		Pt-Time		1st Yr		2nd Yr		3rd Yr		4th Yr		Total		JD Degrees Awarded
	#	%	#	%	#	%	#	%	#	%	#	%	#	%	#	%	#	%	
African-American	12	3.6	10	4.9	22	4.1	0	0.0	11	5.4	4	2.0	7	5.1	0	0.0	22	4.1	9
American Indian	3	0.9	1	0.5	4	0.7	0	0.0	0	0.0	2	1.0	2	1.5	0	0.0	4	0.7	2
Asian American	5	1.5	7	3.4	12	2.2	0	0.0	4	2.0	5	2.5	3	2.2	0	0.0	12	2.2	3
Mexican American	5	1.5	5	2.4	10	1.9	0	0.0	5	2.5	2	1.0	3	2.2	0	0.0	10	1.9	1
Puerto Rican	0	0.0	0	0.0	0	0.0	0	0.0	0	0.0	0	0.0	0	0.0	0	0.0	0	0.0	0
Hispanic American	0	0.0	0	0.0	0	0.0	0	0.0	0	0.0	0	0.0	0	0.0	0	0.0	0	0.0	0
Total Minorities	25	7.5	23	11.2	48	8.9	0	0.0	20	9.9	13	6.5	15	11.0	0	0.0	48	8.9	15
Foreign Nationals	0	0.0	0	0.0	0	0.0	0	0.0	0	0.0	0	0.0	0	0.0	0	0.0	0	0.0	0
Caucasian	307	92.5	183	88.8	490	91.1	0	0.0	183	90.1	186	93.5	121	89.0	0	0.0	490	91.1	116
Total	332	61.7	206	38.3	538	100.0	0	0.0	203	37.7	199	37.0	136	25.3	0	0.0	538		131

MISSOURI-COLUMBIA, UNIVERSITY OF

GPA & LSAT Scores

	Full Time	Part Time	Total
# of apps	727	0	727
# admits	413	0	413
# of matrics	192	0	192
75% GPA	3.58	0.00	
25% GPA	3.04	0.00	
75% LSAT	158	0	
25% LSAT	152	0	

Tuition & Fees

	Resident	Non-resident
Full-Time	$8,555	$16,588
Part-Time	$0	$0

Living Expenses

Estimated living expenses for Singles		
Living on campus	Living off campus	Living at home
$9,072	$11,675	$11,675

Employment

	Total	%
Employment status known	104	67.5
Employment status unknown	50	32.5
Employed	94	90.4
Pursuing graduate degrees	1	1.0
Unemployed seeking employment	9	8.7
Unemployed not seeking employment	0	0.0
Type of Employment		
# employed in law firms	49	52.1
# employed in business & industry	5	5.3
# employed in government	19	20.2
# employed in public interest	1	1.1
# employed as judicial clerks	20	21.3
# employed in academia	0	0.0
Geographic Location		
# employed in state	82	87.2
# employed in foreign countries	0	0.0
# of states where employed	9	

Financial Aid

	Full-time		Part-time		Total	
	#	%	#	%	#	%
Total # of Students	538		0		538	
Total # receiving grants	188	34.9	0	0.0	188	34.9
Less than 1/2 tuition	168	31.2	0	0.0	168	31.2
Half to full tuition	9	1.7	0	0.0	9	1.7
Full tuition	0	0.0	0	0.0	0	0.0
More than full tuition	11	2.0	0	0.0	11	2.0
Median Grant Amount	$2,100		$0			

Informational & Library Resources

# of volumes & volume equivalents	311,976	# of professional staff	7
# of titles	164,904	Hours per week with professional staff	66
# of active serial subscriptions	5,074	Hours per week without professional staff	23
Study seating capacity inside the library	376	# of student computer work stations for entire law school	31
Square feet of law library	61,851	# of additional networked connections	6
Square feet of law school (excl. Library)	30,699	Require Laptop Computer?	N

J.D. Attrition (Prior Year)

	Academic	Other	TOTALS	
	#	#	#	%
1st Year	3	8	11	5.2%
2nd Year	0	5	5	3.5%
3rd Year	1	0	1	0.8%
4th Year	0	0	0	0.0%
TOTALS	4	13	17	3.5%

Bar Passage Rates

Jurisdiction	Missouri		
Exam	Sum 96	Win 97	Total
# from school taking bar for the first time	119	10	129
School's pass rate for all first-time takers	88%	80%	88%
State's pass rate for all first-time takers	83%	81%	82%

MISSOURI-KANSAS CITY, UNIVERSITY OF

5100 Rockhill Road
Kansas City, MO 64110
(816)235-1644
http://www.law.umkc.edu

ABA Approved Since 1936

The Basics

Type of School: Public Term: Semester

Application deadline: Rolling

Application fee: $25

Financial Aid deadline: 03/01

Can first year start other than Fall? No

Student faculty ratio: 17.1 to 1

Does the University offer:
- housing restricted to law students? No
- graduate student housing for which law students are eligible? No

Faculty & Administrators

	Total		Men		Women		Minorities	
	Fall	Spr	Fall	Spr	Fall	Spr	Fall	Spr
Full-time	24	21	16	14	8	7	1	1
Other Full-Time	1	1	0	0	1	1	0	0
Deans, librarians, & others who teach > 1/2	4	4	2	2	2	2	1	1
Part-time	11	33	10	26	1	7	1	1
Total	40	59	28	42	12	17	3	3
Deans, librarians, & others who teach < 1/2	0	0	0	0	0	0	0	0

Curriculum

	Full time	Part time
Typical first-year section size	56	0
Is there typically a "small section" of the first year class, other than Legal Writing, taught by full-time faculty?	No	No
If yes, typical size offered last year	N/A	N/A
# of classroom course titles beyond 1st year curriculum	83	83
# of upper division courses, excluding seminars, with an enrollment:		
Under 25	47	47
25 - 49	24	24
50 - 74	14	14
75 - 99	8	8
100 +	0	0
# of seminars	18	18
# of seminar positions available	316	
# of seminar positions filled	270	0
# of positions available in simulation courses	510	
# of simulation positions filled	358	0
# of positions available in faculty supervised clinical courses	0	
# of fac. sup. clin. positions filled	0	0
# involved in field placements	39	0
# involved in law journals	97	0
# in moot court or trial competitions	70	0
# of credit hrs required to graduate	91	

J.D. Enrollment & Ethnicity

	Men		Women		Fl-Time		Pt-Time		1st Yr		2nd Yr		3rd Yr		4th Yr		Total		JD Degrees Awarded
	#	%	#	%	#	%	#	%	#	%	#	%	#	%	#	%	#	%	
African-American	9	3.3	11	4.9	19	4.1	1	3.1	7	4.1	8	4.8	5	3.2	0	0.0	20	4.0	6
American Indian	1	0.4	0	0.0	1	0.2	0	0.0	0	0.0	0	0.0	1	0.6	0	0.0	1	0.2	0
Asian American	10	3.7	8	3.5	16	3.5	2	6.3	5	2.9	5	3.0	8	5.1	0	0.0	18	3.6	1
Mexican American	6	2.2	3	1.3	9	1.9	0	0.0	6	3.5	1	0.6	2	1.3	0	0.0	9	1.8	4
Puerto Rican	0	0.0	0	0.0	0	0.0	0	0.0	0	0.0	0	0.0	0	0.0	0	0.0	0	0.0	0
Hispanic American	5	1.9	0	0.0	5	1.1	0	0.0	0	0.0	4	2.4	1	0.6	0	0.0	5	1.0	0
Total Minorities	31	11.5	22	9.7	50	10.8	3	9.4	18	10.5	18	10.8	17	10.8	0	0.0	53	10.7	11
Foreign Nationals	0	0.0	0	0.0	0	0.0	0	0.0	0	0.0	0	0.0	0	0.0	0	0.0	0	0.0	0
Caucasian	238	88.5	204	90.3	413	89.2	29	90.6	153	89.5	149	89.2	140	89.2	0	0.0	442	89.3	125
Total	269	54.3	226	45.7	463	93.5	32	6.5	171	34.5	167	33.7	157	31.7	0	0.0	495		136

GPA & LSAT Scores

	Full Time	Part Time	Total
# of apps	726	52	778
# admits	443	24	467
# of matrics	156	15	171
75% GPA	3.40	3.61	
25% GPA	2.81	3.22	
75% LSAT	156	156	
25% LSAT	150	151	

Tuition & Fees

	Resident	Non-resident
Full-Time	$8,548	$16,581
Part-Time	$6,154	$11,892

Living Expenses

Estimated living expenses for Singles		
Living on campus	Living off campus	Living at home
$10,130	$12,460	$7,410

Financial Aid

	Full-time		Part-time		Total	
	#	%	#	%	#	%
Total # of Students	463		32		495	
Total # receiving grants	97	21.0	0	0.0	97	19.6
Less than 1/2 tuition	73	15.8	0	0.0	73	14.7
Half to full tuition	21	4.5	0	0.0	21	4.2
Full tuition	3	0.6	0	0.0	3	0.6
More than full tuition	0	0.0	0	0.0	0	0.0
Median Grant Amount	$3,902		$0			

Informational & Library Resources

# of volumes & volume equivalents	268,633	# of professional staff	5
# of titles	47,943	Hours per week with professional staff	45
# of active serial subscriptions	3,878	Hours per week without professional staff	47
Study seating capacity inside the library	311	# of student computer work stations for entire law school	50
Square feet of law library	33,456	# of additional networked connections	0
Square feet of law school (excl. Library)	84,921	Require Laptop Computer?	N

Employment

	Total	%
Employment status known	136	97.8
Employment status unknown	3	2.2
Employed	126	92.6
Pursuing graduate degrees	0	0.0
Unemployed seeking employment	7	5.1
Unemployed not seeking employment	3	2.2
Type of Employment		
# employed in law firms	70	55.6
# employed in business & industry	20	15.9
# employed in government	21	16.7
# employed in public interest	1	0.8
# employed as judicial clerks	11	8.7
# employed in academia	3	2.4
Geographic Location		
# employed in state	98	77.8
# employed in foreign countries	0	0.0
# of states where employed	11	

J.D. Attrition (Prior Year)

	Academic	Other	TOTALS	
	#	#	#	%
1st Year	4	2	6	3.4%
2nd Year	2	10	12	7.1%
3rd Year	0	18	18	11%
4th Year	0	0	0	0.0%
TOTALS	6	30	36	7.2%

Bar Passage Rates

Jurisdiction	Missouri			Kansas		
Exam	Sum 96	Win 97	Total	Sum 96	Win 97	Total
# from school taking bar for the first time	102	19	121	35	54	89
School's pass rate for all first-time takers	70%	63%	69%	80%	91%	87%
State's pass rate for all first-time takers	83%	81%	82%	87%	93%	90%

MONTANA, UNIVERSITY OF

Missoula, MT 59812
(406)243-4311
http://www.umt.edu/law

ABA Approved Since 1923

The Basics

Type of School: Public   Term: Semester
Application deadline: 03/01
Application fee: $60
Financial Aid deadline: 03/01
Can first year start other than Fall? No
Student faculty ratio: 15.1 to 1
Does the University offer:
- housing restricted to law students? No
- graduate student housing for which law students are eligible? No

Faculty & Administrators

	Total		Men		Women		Minorities	
	Fall	Spr	Fall	Spr	Fall	Spr	Fall	Spr
Full-time	13	14	8	9	5	5	1	1
Other Full-Time	2	2	1	1	1	1	0	0
Deans, librarians, & others who teach > 1/2	2	2	1	1	1	1	0	0
Part-time	10	9	7	7	3	2	0	0
Total	27	27	17	18	10	9	1	1
Deans, librarians, & others who teach < 1/2	1	1	1	1	0	0	0	0

Curriculum

	Full time	Part time
Typical first-year section size	40	0
Is there typically a "small section" of the first year class, other than Legal Writing, taught by full-time faculty?	No	No
If yes, typical size offered last year	N/A	N/A
# of classroom course titles beyond 1st year curriculum	56	0
# of upper division courses, excluding seminars, with an enrollment:		
Under 25	16	0
25 - 49	10	0
50 - 74	12	0
75 - 99	0	0
100 +	0	0
# of seminars	19	0
# of seminar positions available	250	
# of seminar positions filled	252	0
# of positions available in simulation courses	226	
# of simulation positions filled	226	0
# of positions available in faculty supervised clinical courses	76	
# of fac. sup. clin. positions filled	76	0
# involved in field placements	6	0
# involved in law journals	27	0
# in moot court or trial competitions	33	0
# of credit hrs required to graduate	90	

J.D. Enrollment & Ethnicity

	Men		Women		Fl-Time		Pt-Time		1st Yr		2nd Yr		3rd Yr		4th Yr		Total		JD Degrees Awarded
	#	%	#	%	#	%	#	%	#	%	#	%	#	%	#	%	#	%	
African-American	2	1.5	0	0.0	2	0.9	0	0.0	0	0.0	1	1.3	1	1.4	0	0.0	2	0.9	0
American Indian	5	3.7	4	4.0	9	3.8	0	0.0	3	3.7	5	6.3	1	1.4	0	0.0	9	3.8	2
Asian American	0	0.0	2	2.0	2	0.9	0	0.0	1	1.2	1	1.3	0	0.0	0	0.0	2	0.9	0
Mexican American	0	0.0	0	0.0	0	0.0	0	0.0	0	0.0	0	0.0	0	0.0	0	0.0	0	0.0	0
Puerto Rican	0	0.0	0	0.0	0	0.0	0	0.0	0	0.0	0	0.0	0	0.0	0	0.0	0	0.0	0
Hispanic American	2	1.5	3	3.0	5	2.1	0	0.0	2	2.5	2	2.5	1	1.4	0	0.0	5	2.1	0
Total Minorities	9	6.7	9	9.0	18	7.7	0	0.0	6	7.4	9	11.3	3	4.1	0	0.0	18	7.7	2
Foreign Nationals	1	0.7	2	2.0	3	1.3	0	0.0	0	0.0	2	2.5	1	1.4	0	0.0	3	1.3	0
Caucasian	125	92.6	89	89.0	214	91.1	0	0.0	75	92.6	69	86.3	70	94.6	0	0.0	214	91.1	73
Total	135	57.4	100	42.6	235	100.0	0	0.0	81	34.5	80	34.0	74	31.5	0	0.0	235		75

GPA & LSAT Scores

	Full Time	Part Time	Total
# of apps	413	0	413
# admits	221	0	221
# of matrics	82	0	82
75% GPA	3.63	0.00	
25% GPA	3.01	0.00	
75% LSAT	160	0	
25% LSAT	153	0	

Tuition & Fees

	Resident	Non-resident
Full-Time	$6,046	$11,048
Part-Time	$0	$0

Living Expenses

Estimated living expenses for Singles		
Living on campus	Living off campus	Living at home
$7,540	$7,540	$5,540

Employment

	Total	%
Employment status known	71	95.9
Employment status unknown	3	4.1
Employed	66	93.0
Pursuing graduate degrees	2	2.8
Unemployed seeking employment	2	2.8
Unemployed not seeking employment	1	1.4
Type of Employment		
# employed in law firms	39	59.1
# employed in business & industry	2	3.0
# employed in government	10	15.2
# employed in public interest	0	0.0
# employed as judicial clerks	13	19.7
# employed in academia	2	3.0
Geographic Location		
# employed in state	58	87.9
# employed in foreign countries	1	1.5
# of states where employed	8	

Financial Aid

	Full-time		Part-time		Total	
	#	%	#	%	#	%
Total # of Students	235		0		235	
Total # receiving grants	100	42.6	0	0.0	100	42.6
Less than 1/2 tuition	96	40.9	0	0.0	96	40.9
Half to full tuition	4	1.7	0	0.0	4	1.7
Full tuition	0	0.0	0	0.0	0	0.0
More than full tuition	0	0.0	0	0.0	0	0.0
Median Grant Amount	$1,160		$0			

Informational & Library Resources

# of volumes & volume equivalents	101,990	# of professional staff	3
# of titles	18,520	Hours per week with professional staff	40
# of active serial subscriptions	1,717	Hours per week without professional staff	53
Study seating capacity inside the library	212	# of student computer work stations for entire law school	25
Square feet of law library	18,716	# of additional networked connections	20
Square feet of law school (excl. Library)	40,034	Require Laptop Computer?	N

J.D. Attrition (Prior Year)

	Academic	Other	TOTALS	
	#	#	#	%
1st Year	0	1	1	1.2%
2nd Year	1	1	2	2.7%
3rd Year	0	0	0	0.0%
4th Year	0	0	0	0.0%
TOTALS	1	2	3	1.3%

Bar Passage Rates

Jurisdiction	Montana		
Exam	Sum 96	Win 97	Total
# from school taking bar for the first time	68	0	68
School's pass rate for all first-time takers	96%		96%
State's pass rate for all first-time takers	94%	0%	94%

NEBRASKA, UNIVERSITY OF

P.O. Box 830902
Lincoln, NE 68583-0902
(402)472-2161
http://www.unl.edu/lawcoll

ABA Approved Since 1923

The Basics

Type of School: Public Term: Semester
Application deadline: 03/01
Application fee: $25
Financial Aid deadline: 05/01
Can first year start other than Fall? No
Student faculty ratio: 14.1 to 1
Does the University offer:
- housing restricted to law students? No
- graduate student housing for which law students are eligible? No

Faculty & Administrators

	Total		Men		Women		Minorities	
	Fall	Spr	Fall	Spr	Fall	Spr	Fall	Spr
Full-time	22	22	19	19	3	3	2	2
Other Full-Time	1	1	0	0	1	1	0	0
Deans, librarians, & others who teach > 1/2	1	1	1	1	0	0	0	0
Part-time	14	18	7	11	7	7	2	2
Total	38	42	27	31	11	11	4	4
Deans, librarians, & others who teach < 1/2	2	2	0	0	2	2	0	0

Curriculum

	Full time	Part time
Typical first-year section size	70	0
Is there typically a "small section" of the first year class, other than Legal Writing, taught by full-time faculty?	No	No
If yes, typical size offered last year	N/A	N/A
# of classroom course titles beyond 1st year curriculum	78	0
# of upper division courses, excluding seminars, with an enrollment:		
Under 25	42	0
25 - 49	27	0
50 - 74	7	0
75 - 99	1	0
100 +	1	0
# of seminars	11	0
# of seminar positions available	132	
# of seminar positions filled	131	0
# of positions available in simulation courses	298	
# of simulation positions filled	274	0
# of positions available in faculty supervised clinical courses	82	
# of fac. sup. clin. positions filled	73	0
# involved in field placements	0	0
# involved in law journals	33	0
# in moot court or trial competitions	58	0
# of credit hrs required to graduate	96	

J.D. Enrollment & Ethnicity

	Men		Women		Fl-Time		Pt-Time		1st Yr		2nd Yr		3rd Yr		4th Yr		Total		JD Degrees Awarded
	#	%	#	%	#	%	#	%	#	%	#	%	#	%	#	%	#	%	
African-American	4	1.9	3	1.9	7	1.9	0	0.0	3	2.1	4	3.3	0	0.0	0	0.0	7	1.9	4
American Indian	2	0.9	0	0.0	2	0.5	0	0.0	1	0.7	0	0.0	1	0.9	0	0.0	2	0.5	0
Asian American	4	1.9	6	3.8	10	2.7	0	0.0	3	2.1	3	2.5	4	3.6	0	0.0	10	2.7	1
Mexican American	1	0.5	3	1.9	4	1.1	0	0.0	1	0.7	2	1.6	1	0.9	0	0.0	4	1.1	6
Puerto Rican	2	0.9	1	0.6	3	0.8	0	0.0	2	1.4	0	0.0	1	0.9	0	0.0	3	0.8	0
Hispanic American	1	0.5	1	0.6	2	0.5	0	0.0	1	0.7	1	0.8	0	0.0	0	0.0	2	0.5	2
Total Minorities	14	6.6	14	8.8	28	7.5	0	0.0	11	7.9	10	8.2	7	6.3	0	0.0	28	7.5	13
Foreign Nationals	9	4.2	0	0.0	9	2.4	0	0.0	4	2.9	2	1.6	3	2.7	0	0.0	9	2.4	1
Caucasian	190	89.2	146	91.3	335	90.1	1	100.0	125	89.3	110	90.2	101	91.0	0	0.0	336	90.1	116
Total	213	57.1	160	42.9	372	99.7	1	0.3	140	37.5	122	32.7	111	29.8	0	0.0	373		130

GPA & LSAT Scores

	Full Time	Part Time	Total
# of apps	670	0	670
# admits	351	0	351
# of matrics	142	0	142
75% GPA	3.67	0.00	
25% GPA	3.13	0.00	
75% LSAT	158	0	
25% LSAT	150	0	

Tuition & Fees

	Resident	Non-resident
Full-Time	$3,920	$8,386
Part-Time	$0	$0

Living Expenses

Estimated living expenses for Singles		
Living on campus	Living off campus	Living at home
$6,885	$9,005	$4,920

Financial Aid

	Full-time		Part-time		Total	
	#	%	#	%	#	%
Total # of Students	372		1		373	
Total # receiving grants	215	57.8	0	0.0	215	57.6
Less than 1/2 tuition	151	40.6	0	0.0	151	40.5
Half to full tuition	21	5.6	0	0.0	21	5.6
Full tuition	25	6.7	0	0.0	25	6.7
More than full tuition	18	4.8	0	0.0	18	4.8
Median Grant Amount	$2,538		$0			

Informational & Library Resources

# of volumes & volume equivalents	341,070	# of professional staff	6
# of titles	49,353	Hours per week with professional staff	65
# of active serial subscriptions	2,858	Hours per week without professional staff	44
Study seating capacity inside the library	339	# of student computer work stations for entire law school	47
Square feet of law library	30,872	# of additional networked connections	0
Square feet of law school (excl. Library)	77,628	Require Laptop Computer?	N

Employment

	Total	%
Employment status known	146	98.6
Employment status unknown	2	1.4
Employed	135	92.5
Pursuing graduate degrees	4	2.7
Unemployed seeking employment	5	3.4
Unemployed not seeking employment	2	1.4
Type of Employment		
# employed in law firms	72	53.3
# employed in business & industry	25	18.5
# employed in government	28	20.7
# employed in public interest	4	3.0
# employed as judicial clerks	9	6.7
# employed in academia	1	0.7
Geographic Location		
# employed in state	87	64.4
# employed in foreign countries	2	1.5
# of states where employed	23	

J.D. Attrition (Prior Year)

	Academic	Other	TOTALS	
	#	#	#	%
1st Year	12	7	19	13%
2nd Year	0	7	7	6.3%
3rd Year	1	0	1	0.8%
4th Year	0	0	0	0.0%
TOTALS	13	14	27	7.0%

Bar Passage Rates

Jurisdiction	Nebraska		
Exam	Sum 96	Win 97	Total
# from school taking bar for the first time	87	12	99
School's pass rate for all first-time takers	99%	92%	98%
State's pass rate for all first-time takers	97%	87%	95%

NEW ENGLAND SCHOOL OF LAW

154 Stuart Street
Boston, MA 02116
(617)451-0010
http://www.nesl.edu

ABA Approved Since 1969

The Basics

Type of School: Private Term: Semester
Application deadline: 06/01
Application fee: $50
Financial Aid deadline: 04/15
Can first year start other than Fall? No
Student faculty ratio: 19.8 to 1
Does the University offer:
- housing restricted to law students? No
- graduate student housing for which law students are eligible? No

Faculty & Administrators

	Total		Men		Women		Minorities	
	Fall	Spr	Fall	Spr	Fall	Spr	Fall	Spr
Full-time	34	34	25	25	9	9	3	2
Other Full-Time	0	0	0	0	0	0	0	0
Deans, librarians, & others who teach > 1/2	0	0	0	0	0	0	0	0
Part-time	44	53	30	39	14	14	1	2
Total	78	87	55	64	23	23	4	4
Deans, librarians, & others who teach < 1/2	3	3	3	3	0	0	1	1

Curriculum

	Full time	Part time
Typical first-year section size	88	77
Is there typically a "small section" of the first year class, other than Legal Writing, taught by full-time faculty?	No	No
If yes, typical size offered last year	N/A	N/A
# of classroom course titles beyond 1st year curriculum	75	71
# of upper division courses, excluding seminars, with an enrollment:		
Under 25	20	30
25 - 49	17	10
50 - 74	13	11
75 - 99	7	5
100 +	3	4
# of seminars	15	14
# of seminar positions available	625	
# of seminar positions filled	208	243
# of positions available in simulation courses	442	
# of simulation positions filled	232	105
# of positions available in faculty supervised clinical courses	46	
# of fac. sup. clin. positions filled	27	19
# involved in field placements	152	27
# involved in law journals	83	28
# in moot court or trial competitions	11	5
# of credit hrs required to graduate	84	

J.D. Enrollment & Ethnicity

	Men		Women		Fl-Time		Pt-Time		1st Yr		2nd Yr		3rd Yr		4th Yr		Total		JD Degrees Awarded
	#	%	#	%	#	%	#	%	#	%	#	%	#	%	#	%	#	%	
African-American	23	4.7	24	5.3	36	6.6	11	2.8	18	6.1	10	4.3	17	5.5	2	1.8	47	5.0	8
American Indian	6	1.2	4	0.9	3	0.5	7	1.8	3	1.0	3	1.3	3	1.0	1	0.9	10	1.1	2
Asian American	19	3.9	29	6.4	38	6.9	10	2.6	21	7.1	13	5.6	10	3.3	4	3.7	48	5.1	10
Mexican American	3	0.6	3	0.7	4	0.7	2	0.5	2	0.7	1	0.4	3	1.0	0	0.0	6	0.6	1
Puerto Rican	1	0.2	4	0.9	2	0.4	3	0.8	3	1.0	1	0.4	0	0.0	1	0.9	5	0.5	1
Hispanic American	20	4.1	16	3.5	32	5.8	4	1.0	17	5.8	8	3.5	10	3.3	1	0.9	36	3.8	10
Total Minorities	72	14.8	80	17.5	115	20.9	37	9.4	64	21.8	36	15.6	43	14.0	9	8.3	152	16.2	32
Foreign Nationals	7	1.4	3	0.7	10	1.8	0	0.0	2	0.7	4	1.7	4	1.3	0	0.0	10	1.1	1
Caucasian	406	83.7	373	81.8	424	77.2	355	90.6	228	77.6	191	82.7	260	84.7	100	91.7	779	82.8	261
Total	485	51.5	456	48.5	549	58.3	392	41.7	294	31.2	231	24.5	307	32.6	109	11.6	941		294

NEW ENGLAND SCHOOL OF LAW

GPA & LSAT Scores

	Full Time	Part Time	Total
# of apps	1,867	351	2,218
# admits	1,254	259	1,513
# of matrics	187	99	286
75% GPA	3.29	3.32	
25% GPA	2.59	2.52	
75% LSAT	153	154	
25% LSAT	145	145	

Tuition & Fees

	Resident	Non-resident
Full-Time	$14,450	$14,450
Part-Time	$10,880	$10,880

Living Expenses

Estimated living expenses for Singles		
Living on campus	Living off campus	Living at home
N/A	$13,450	$9,290

Employment

	Total	%
Employment status known	257	80.3
Employment status unknown	63	19.7
Employed	224	87.2
Pursuing graduate degrees	5	1.9
Unemployed seeking employment	25	9.7
Unemployed not seeking employment	3	1.2
Type of Employment		
# employed in law firms	109	48.7
# employed in business & industry	52	23.2
# employed in government	36	16.1
# employed in public interest	1	0.4
# employed as judicial clerks	20	8.9
# employed in academia	6	2.7
Geographic Location		
# employed in state	137	61.2
# employed in foreign countries	0	0.0
# of states where employed	20	

Financial Aid

	Full-time		Part-time		Total	
	#	%	#	%	#	%
Total # of Students	549		392		941	
Total # receiving grants	291	53.0	78	19.9	369	39.2
Less than 1/2 tuition	252	45.9	48	12.2	300	31.9
Half to full tuition	13	2.4	13	3.3	26	2.8
Full tuition	26	4.7	17	4.3	43	4.6
More than full tuition	0	0.0	0	0.0	0	0.0
Median Grant Amount	$3,349		$4,355			

Informational & Library Resources

# of volumes & volume equivalents	281,606	# of professional staff	9
# of titles	40,858	Hours per week with professional staff	80
# of active serial subscriptions	3,023	Hours per week without professional staff	21
Study seating capacity inside the library	392	# of student computer work stations for entire law school	85
Square feet of law library	28,087	# of additional networked connections	0
Square feet of law school (excl. Library)	45,264	Require Laptop Computer?	N

J.D. Attrition (Prior Year)

	Academic	Other	TOTALS	
	#	#	#	%
1st Year	4	14	18	7.3%
2nd Year	1	3	4	1.3%
3rd Year	0	3	3	1.0%
4th Year	0	0	0	0.0%
TOTALS	5	20	25	2.6%

Bar Passage Rates

Jurisdiction	Massachusetts		
Exam	Sum 96	Win 97	Total
# from school taking bar for the first time	233	33	266
School's pass rate for all first-time takers	82%	73%	81%
State's pass rate for all first-time takers	83%	76%	81%

NEW MEXICO, UNIVERSITY OF

1117 Stanford, N.E.
Albuquerque, NM 87131-1431
(505)277-2146
http://www.unm.edu/~unmlaw

ABA Approved Since 1948

The Basics

Type of School: Public Term: Semester
Application deadline: 02/16
Application fee: $40
Financial Aid deadline: 03/01
Can first year start other than Fall? No
Student faculty ratio: 11.3 to 1
Does the University offer:
- housing restricted to law students? No
- graduate student housing for which law students are eligible? No

Faculty & Administrators

	Total		Men		Women		Minorities	
	Fall	Spr	Fall	Spr	Fall	Spr	Fall	Spr
Full-time	25	25	13	12	12	13	6	5
Other Full-Time	1	0	0	0	1	0	1	0
Deans, librarians, & others who teach > 1/2	4	4	3	3	1	1	2	2
Part-time	12	14	7	8	5	6	1	2
Total	42	43	23	23	19	20	10	9
Deans, librarians, & others who teach < 1/2	1	1	1	1	0	0	0	0

Curriculum

	Full time	Part time
Typical first-year section size	54	0
Is there typically a "small section" of the first year class, other than Legal Writing, taught by full-time faculty?	Yes	No
If yes, typical size offered last year	18	N/A
# of classroom course titles beyond 1st year curriculum	92	0
# of upper division courses, excluding seminars, with an enrollment:		
Under 25	50	0
25 - 49	11	0
50 - 74	9	0
75 - 99	2	0
100 +	0	0
# of seminars	20	0
# of seminar positions available	249	
# of seminar positions filled	162	0
# of positions available in simulation courses	136	
# of simulation positions filled	128	0
# of positions available in faculty supervised clinical courses	80	
# of fac. sup. clin. positions filled	75	0
# involved in field placements	40	0
# involved in law journals	80	0
# in moot court or trial competitions	34	0
# of credit hrs required to graduate	86	

J.D. Enrollment & Ethnicity

	Men		Women		Fl-Time		Pt-Time		1st Yr		2nd Yr		3rd Yr		4th Yr		Total		JD Degrees Awarded
	#	%	#	%	#	%	#	%	#	%	#	%	#	%	#	%	#	%	
African-American	3	1.8	7	4.0	10	2.9	0	0.0	3	2.6	3	2.7	4	3.5	0	0.0	10	2.9	2
American Indian	6	3.6	19	11.0	25	7.3	0	0.0	10	8.7	5	4.5	10	8.7	0	0.0	25	7.3	11
Asian American	2	1.2	6	3.5	8	2.3	0	0.0	1	0.9	3	2.7	4	3.5	0	0.0	8	2.3	4
Mexican American	54	32.1	38	22.0	92	27.0	0	0.0	32	27.8	29	26.1	31	27.0	0	0.0	92	27.0	23
Puerto Rican	0	0.0	0	0.0	0	0.0	0	0.0	0	0.0	0	0.0	0	0.0	0	0.0	0	0.0	0
Hispanic American	0	0.0	0	0.0	0	0.0	0	0.0	0	0.0	0	0.0	0	0.0	0	0.0	0	0.0	0
Total Minorities	65	38.7	70	40.5	135	39.6	0	0.0	46	40.0	40	36.0	49	42.6	0	0.0	135	39.6	40
Foreign Nationals	0	0.0	0	0.0	0	0.0	0	0.0	0	0.0	0	0.0	0	0.0	0	0.0	0	0.0	0
Caucasian	103	61.3	103	59.5	206	60.4	0	0.0	69	60.0	71	64.0	66	57.4	0	0.0	206	60.4	63
Total	168	49.3	173	50.7	341	100.0	0	0.0	115	33.7	111	32.6	115	33.7	0	0.0	341		103

GPA & LSAT Scores

	Full Time	Part Time	Total
# of apps	734	0	734
# admits	251	0	251
# of matrics	118	0	118
75% GPA	3.52	0.00	
25% GPA	2.80	0.00	
75% LSAT	160	0	
25% LSAT	151	0	

Tuition & Fees

	Resident	Non-resident
Full-Time	$3,612	$12,116
Part-Time	$0	$0

Living Expenses

Estimated living expenses for Singles		
Living on campus	Living off campus	Living at home
$7,895	$10,304	$5,280

Financial Aid

	Full-time		Part-time		Total	
	#	%	#	%	#	%
Total # of Students	341		0		341	
Total # receiving grants	46	13.5	0	0.0	46	13.5
Less than 1/2 tuition	8	2.3	0	0.0	8	2.3
Half to full tuition	5	1.5	0	0.0	5	1.5
Full tuition	21	6.2	0	0.0	21	6.2
More than full tuition	12	3.5	0	0.0	12	3.5
Median Grant Amount	$3,612		$0			

Informational & Library Resources

# of volumes & volume equivalents	357,354	# of professional staff	4
# of titles	75,194	Hours per week with professional staff	56
# of active serial subscriptions	3,168	Hours per week without professional staff	49
Study seating capacity inside the library	329	# of student computer work stations for entire law school	70
Square feet of law library	32,443	# of additional networked connections	8
Square feet of law school (excl. Library)	36,005	Require Laptop Computer?	N

Employment

	Total	%
Employment status known	96	82.1
Employment status unknown	21	17.9
Employed	83	86.5
Pursuing graduate degrees	3	3.1
Unemployed seeking employment	9	9.4
Unemployed not seeking employment	1	1.0
Type of Employment		
# employed in law firms	39	47.0
# employed in business & industry	4	4.8
# employed in government	26	31.3
# employed in public interest	4	4.8
# employed as judicial clerks	9	10.8
# employed in academia	1	1.2
Geographic Location		
# employed in state	69	83.1
# employed in foreign countries	0	0.0
# of states where employed	9	

J.D. Attrition (Prior Year)

	Academic	Other	TOTALS	
	#	#	#	%
1st Year	1	7	8	7.3%
2nd Year	0	3	3	2.6%
3rd Year	1	1	2	1.7%
4th Year	0	0	0	0.0%
TOTALS	2	11	13	3.8%

Bar Passage Rates

Jurisdiction	New Mexico		
Exam	Sum 96	Win 97	Total
# from school taking bar for the first time	91	21	112
School's pass rate for all first-time takers	86%	90%	87%
State's pass rate for all first-time takers	89%	94%	91%

NEW YORK LAW SCHOOL

57 Worth Street
New York, NY 10013-2960
(212)431-2100
http://www.nyls.edu

ABA Approved Since 1954

The Basics

Type of School: Private Term: Semester
Application deadline: 04/01
Application fee: $50
Financial Aid deadline: 04/15
Can first year start other than Fall? No
Student faculty ratio: 23.3 to 1
Does the University offer:
- housing restricted to law students? No
- graduate student housing for which law students are eligible? Yes

Faculty & Administrators

	Total		Men		Women		Minorities	
	Fall	Spr	Fall	Spr	Fall	Spr	Fall	Spr
Full-time	43	46	30	31	13	15	5	5
Other Full-Time	1	1	0	0	1	1	0	0
Deans, librarians, & others who teach > 1/2	0	0	0	0	0	0	0	0
Part-time	66	60	44	37	22	23	2	2
Total	110	107	74	68	36	39	7	7
Deans, librarians, & others who teach < 1/2	4	4	2	2	2	2	0	0

Curriculum

	Full time	Part time
Typical first-year section size	110	120
Is there typically a "small section" of the first year class, other than Legal Writing, taught by full-time faculty?	Yes	Yes
If yes, typical size offered last year	35	42
# of classroom course titles beyond 1st year curriculum	82	80
# of upper division courses, excluding seminars, with an enrollment:		
Under 25	13	19
25 - 49	15	24
50 - 74	12	12
75 - 99	15	6
100 +	9	3
# of seminars	43	29
# of seminar positions available	1,213	
# of seminar positions filled	549	363
# of positions available in simulation courses	252	
# of simulation positions filled	144	96
# of positions available in faculty supervised clinical courses	50	
# of fac. sup. clin. positions filled	44	0
# involved in field placements	244	48
# involved in law journals	149	37
# in moot court or trial competitions	55	6
# of credit hrs required to graduate	86	

J.D. Enrollment & Ethnicity

	Men		Women		Fl-Time		Pt-Time		1st Yr		2nd Yr		3rd Yr		4th Yr		Total		JD Degrees Awarded
	#	%	#	%	#	%	#	%	#	%	#	%	#	%	#	%	#	%	
African-American	51	6.9	55	8.7	37	4.2	69	14.1	44	9.7	24	6.1	26	6.4	12	10.4	106	7.7	37
American Indian	3	0.4	3	0.5	3	0.3	3	0.6	2	0.4	1	0.3	1	0.2	2	1.7	6	0.4	2
Asian American	31	4.2	46	7.3	57	6.5	20	4.1	33	7.3	15	3.8	22	5.4	7	6.1	77	5.6	26
Mexican American	8	1.1	1	0.2	4	0.5	5	1.0	0	0.0	8	2.0	1	0.2	0	0.0	9	0.7	0
Puerto Rican	6	0.8	14	2.2	7	0.8	13	2.7	6	1.3	7	1.8	3	0.7	4	3.5	20	1.5	0
Hispanic American	31	4.2	37	5.8	44	5.0	24	4.9	24	5.3	17	4.3	20	4.9	7	6.1	68	5.0	40
Total Minorities	130	17.7	156	24.6	152	17.3	134	27.5	109	24.0	72	18.4	73	17.9	32	27.8	286	20.9	105
Foreign Nationals	4	0.5	4	0.6	8	0.9	0	0.0	4	0.9	1	0.3	3	0.7	0	0.0	8	0.6	0
Caucasian	601	81.8	473	74.7	720	81.8	354	72.5	342	75.2	318	81.3	331	81.3	83	72.2	1074	78.5	325
Total	735	53.7	633	46.3	880	64.3	488	35.7	455	33.3	391	28.6	407	29.8	115	8.4	1368		430

NEW YORK LAW SCHOOL

GPA & LSAT Scores

	Full Time	Part Time	Total
# of apps	3,171	1,006	4,177
# admits	1,639	351	1,990
# of matrics	332	127	459
75% GPA	3.33	3.43	
25% GPA	2.85	2.72	
75% LSAT	154	154	
25% LSAT	148	146	

Tuition & Fees

	Resident	Non-resident
Full-Time	$21,060	$21,060
Part-Time	$15,793	$15,793

Living Expenses

Estimated living expenses for Singles		
Living on campus	Living off campus	Living at home
$13,945	$13,945	$7,520

Employment

	Total	%
Employment status known	319	85.3
Employment status unknown	55	14.7
Employed	292	91.5
Pursuing graduate degrees	1	0.3
Unemployed seeking employment	17	5.3
Unemployed not seeking employment	9	2.8
Type of Employment		
# employed in law firms	140	47.9
# employed in business & industry	70	24.0
# employed in government	44	15.1
# employed in public interest	4	1.4
# employed as judicial clerks	12	4.1
# employed in academia	2	0.7
Geographic Location		
# employed in state	184	63.0
# employed in foreign countries	2	0.7
# of states where employed	15	

Financial Aid

	Full-time		Part-time		Total	
	#	%	#	%	#	%
Total # of Students	880		488		1368	
Total # receiving grants	333	37.8	111	22.7	444	32.5
Less than 1/2 tuition	250	28.4	76	15.6	326	23.8
Half to full tuition	65	7.4	0	0.0	65	4.8
Full tuition	0	0.0	35	7.2	35	2.6
More than full tuition	18	2.0	0	0.0	18	1.3
Median Grant Amount	$7,475		$6,770			

Informational & Library Resources

# of volumes & volume equivalents	435,223	# of professional staff	13
# of titles	129,043	Hours per week with professional staff	81
# of active serial subscriptions	4,921	Hours per week without professional staff	17
Study seating capacity inside the library	616	# of student computer work stations for entire law school	110
Square feet of law library	48,464	# of additional networked connections	70
Square feet of law school (excl. Library)	101,036	Require Laptop Computer?	N

J.D. Attrition (Prior Year)

	Academic	Other	TOTALS	
	#	#	#	%
1st Year	10	14	24	5.5%
2nd Year	19	20	39	9.4%
3rd Year	3	3	6	1.4%
4th Year	1	1	2	1.7%
TOTALS	33	38	71	5.1%

Bar Passage Rates

Jurisdiction	New York		
Exam	Sum 96	Win 97	Total
# from school taking bar for the first time	279	49	328
School's pass rate for all first-time takers	67%	65%	67%
State's pass rate for all first-time takers	78%	67%	77%

NEW YORK UNIVERSITY

40 Washington Square South
New York, NY 10012
(212)998-6100
http://www.nyu.edu/law

ABA Approved Since 1930

The Basics

Type of School: Private   Term: Semester
Application deadline: 02/01
Application fee: $65
Financial Aid deadline: 04/15
Can first year start other than Fall? No
Student faculty ratio: 14.8 to 1
Does the University offer:
- housing restricted to law students? No
- graduate student housing for which law students are eligible? Yes

Faculty & Administrators

	Total		Men		Women		Minorities	
	Fall	Spr	Fall	Spr	Fall	Spr	Fall	Spr
Full-time	74	73	54	52	20	21	9	7
Other Full-Time	22	22	7	6	15	16	9	8
Deans, librarians, & others who teach > 1/2	4	4	4	4	0	0	0	0
Part-time	68	82	55	58	13	24	7	4
Total	168	181	120	120	48	61	25	19
Deans, librarians, & others who teach < 1/2	0	0	0	0	0	0	0	0

Curriculum

	Full time	Part time
Typical first-year section size	100	0
Is there typically a "small section" of the first year class, other than Legal Writing, taught by full-time faculty?	Yes	No
If yes, typical size offered last year	20	N/A
# of classroom course titles beyond 1st year curriculum	247	0
# of upper division courses, excluding seminars, with an enrollment:		
Under 25	23	0
25 - 49	33	0
50 - 74	17	0
75 - 99	18	0
100 +	32	0
# of seminars	100	0
# of seminar positions available	2,500	
# of seminar positions filled	1,626	0
# of positions available in simulation courses	88	
# of simulation positions filled	88	0
# of positions available in faculty supervised clinical courses	214	
# of fac. sup. clin. positions filled	200	0
# involved in field placements	325	0
# involved in law journals	470	0
# in moot court or trial competitions	140	0
# of credit hrs required to graduate	82	

J.D. Enrollment & Ethnicity

	Men		Women		Fl-Time		Pt-Time		1st Yr		2nd Yr		3rd Yr		4th Yr		Total		JD Degrees Awarded
	#	%	#	%	#	%	#	%	#	%	#	%	#	%	#	%	#	%	
African-American	30	4.3	44	7.2	74	5.6	0	0.0	21	5.4	32	6.9	21	4.5	0	0.0	74	5.6	28
American Indian	1	0.1	0	0.0	1	0.1	0	0.0	0	0.0	0	0.0	1	0.2	0	0.0	1	0.1	0
Asian American	50	7.1	69	11.3	119	9.0	0	0.0	27	7.0	42	9.1	50	10.7	0	0.0	119	9.0	48
Mexican American	7	1.0	1	0.2	8	0.6	0	0.0	1	0.3	2	0.4	5	1.1	0	0.0	8	0.6	0
Puerto Rican	8	1.1	8	1.3	16	1.2	0	0.0	9	2.3	3	0.7	4	0.9	0	0.0	16	1.2	7
Hispanic American	23	3.3	15	2.4	38	2.9	0	0.0	12	3.1	15	3.3	11	2.4	0	0.0	38	2.9	30
Total Minorities	119	16.9	137	22.3	256	19.4	0	0.0	70	18.0	94	20.4	92	19.7	0	0.0	256	19.4	113
Foreign Nationals	27	3.8	24	3.9	51	3.9	0	0.0	11	2.8	21	4.6	19	4.1	0	0.0	51	3.9	13
Caucasian	558	79.3	452	73.7	1010	76.7	0	0.0	307	79.1	346	75.1	357	76.3	0	0.0	1010	76.7	311
Total	704	53.5	613	46.5	1317	100.0	0	0.0	388	29.5	461	35.0	468	35.5	0	0.0	1317		437

GPA & LSAT Scores

	Full Time	Part Time	Total
# of apps	6,185	0	6,185
# admits	1,493	0	1,493
# of matrics	393	0	393
75% GPA	3.81	0.00	
25% GPA	3.55	0.00	
75% LSAT	170	0	
25% LSAT	166	0	

Tuition & Fees

	Resident	Non-resident
Full-Time	$25,685	$25,685
Part-Time	$0	$0

Living Expenses

Estimated living expenses for Singles		
Living on campus	Living off campus	Living at home
$16,225	$16,225	$8,260

Financial Aid

	Full-time		Part-time		Total	
	#	%	#	%	#	%
Total # of Students	1317		0		1317	
Total # receiving grants	303	23.0	0	0.0	303	23.0
Less than 1/2 tuition	132	10.0	0	0.0	132	10.0
Half to full tuition	144	10.9	0	0.0	144	10.9
Full tuition	27	2.1	0	0.0	27	2.1
More than full tuition	0	0.0	0	0.0	0	0.0
Median Grant Amount	$12,735		$0			

Informational & Library Resources

# of volumes & volume equivalents	963,754	# of professional staff	13
# of titles	159,917	Hours per week with professional staff	65
# of active serial subscriptions	5,799	Hours per week without professional staff	36
Study seating capacity inside the library	897	# of student computer work stations for entire law school	125
Square feet of law library	82,000	# of additional networked connections	1000
Square feet of law school (excl. Library)	197,100	Require Laptop Computer?	N

Employment

	Total	%
Employment status known	437	99.3
Employment status unknown	3	0.7
Employed	435	99.5
Pursuing graduate degrees	2	0.5
Unemployed seeking employment	0	0.0
Unemployed not seeking employment	0	0.0
Type of Employment		
# employed in law firms	308	70.8
# employed in business & industry	20	4.6
# employed in government	13	3.0
# employed in public interest	20	4.6
# employed as judicial clerks	70	16.1
# employed in academia	1	0.2
Geographic Location		
# employed in state	294	67.6
# employed in foreign countries	0	0.0
# of states where employed	28	

J.D. Attrition (Prior Year)

	Academic	Other	TOTALS	
	#	#	#	%
1st Year	0	6	6	1.4%
2nd Year	0	4	4	0.9%
3rd Year	0	0	0	0.0%
4th Year	0	0	0	0.0%
TOTALS	0	10	10	0.7%

Bar Passage Rates

Jurisdiction	New York			New Jersey		
Exam	Sum 96	Win 97	Total	Sum 96	Win 97	Total
# from school taking bar for the first time	354	7	361	71	2	73
School's pass rate for all first-time takers	94%	86%	94%	94%	100%	95%
State's pass rate for all first-time takers	78%	67%	77%	78%	68%	77%

NORTH CAROLINA CENTRAL UNIVERSITY

1512 South Alston Avenue
Durham, NC 27707
(919)560-6333
http://www.nccu.edu/law

ABA Approved Since 1950

The Basics

Type of School: Public   Term: Semester

Application deadline: 04/15

Application fee: $30

Financial Aid deadline: 06/01

Can first year start other than Fall? No

Student faculty ratio: 25.1 to 1

Does the University offer:
- housing restricted to law students? No
- graduate student housing for which law students are eligible? No

Faculty & Administrators

	Total		Men		Women		Minorities	
	Fall	Spr	Fall	Spr	Fall	Spr	Fall	Spr
Full-time	11	11	4	4	7	7	7	7
Other Full-Time	3	3	1	1	2	2	0	0
Deans, librarians, & others who teach > 1/2	6	6	3	3	3	3	3	3
Part-time	6	7	3	6	3	1	1	2
Total	26	27	11	14	15	13	11	12
Deans, librarians, & others who teach < 1/2	0	0	0	0	0	0	0	0

Curriculum

	Full time	Part time
Typical first-year section size	56	30
Is there typically a "small section" of the first year class, other than Legal Writing, taught by full-time faculty?	No	No
If yes, typical size offered last year	N/A	N/A
# of classroom course titles beyond 1st year curriculum	45	17
# of upper division courses, excluding seminars, with an enrollment:		
Under 25	20	6
25 - 49	8	7
50 - 74	8	3
75 - 99	3	0
100 +	0	0
# of seminars	6	1
# of seminar positions available	87	
# of seminar positions filled	73	14
# of positions available in simulation courses	163	
# of simulation positions filled	119	44
# of positions available in faculty supervised clinical courses	64	
# of fac. sup. clin. positions filled	64	0
# involved in field placements	55	0
# involved in law journals	19	0
# in moot court or trial competitions	27	1
# of credit hrs required to graduate	88	

J.D. Enrollment & Ethnicity

	Men		Women		Fl-Time		Pt-Time		1st Yr		2nd Yr		3rd Yr		4th Yr		Total		JD Degrees Awarded
	#	%	#	%	#	%	#	%	#	%	#	%	#	%	#	%	#	%	
African-American	67	40.9	106	51.2	137	54.2	36	30.5	63	48.1	56	47.5	46	46.9	8	33.3	173	46.6	47
American Indian	2	1.2	2	1.0	3	1.2	1	0.8	2	1.5	2	1.7	0	0.0	0	0.0	4	1.1	0
Asian American	1	0.6	3	1.4	4	1.6	0	0.0	3	2.3	1	0.8	0	0.0	0	0.0	4	1.1	0
Mexican American	0	0.0	0	0.0	0	0.0	0	0.0	0	0.0	0	0.0	0	0.0	0	0.0	0	0.0	0
Puerto Rican	0	0.0	1	0.5	1	0.4	0	0.0	0	0.0	1	0.8	0	0.0	0	0.0	1	0.3	0
Hispanic American	1	0.6	2	1.0	3	1.2	0	0.0	2	1.5	1	0.8	0	0.0	0	0.0	3	0.8	0
Total Minorities	71	43.3	114	55.1	148	58.5	37	31.4	70	53.4	61	51.7	46	46.9	8	33.3	185	49.9	47
Foreign Nationals	2	1.2	4	1.9	4	1.6	2	1.7	0	0.0	3	2.5	3	3.1	0	0.0	6	1.6	0
Caucasian	91	55.5	89	43.0	101	39.9	79	66.9	61	46.6	54	45.8	49	50.0	16	66.7	180	48.5	38
Total	164	44.2	207	55.8	253	68.2	118	31.8	131	35.3	118	31.8	98	26.4	24	6.5	371		85

NORTH CAROLINA CENTRAL UNIVERSITY

GPA & LSAT Scores

	Full Time	Part Time	Total
# of apps	835	223	1,058
# admits	169	49	218
# of matrics	99	34	133
75% GPA	3.30	3.30	
25% GPA	2.60	2.80	
75% LSAT	152	160	
25% LSAT	146	152	

Tuition & Fees

	Resident	Non-resident
Full-Time	$2,072	$11,034
Part-Time	$2,072	$11,034

Living Expenses

Estimated living expenses for Singles		
Living on campus	Living off campus	Living at home
$7,783	$10,650	$2,250

Financial Aid

	Full-time		Part-time		Total	
	#	%	#	%	#	%
Total # of Students	253		118		371	
Total # receiving grants	75	29.6	1	0.8	76	20.5
Less than 1/2 tuition	57	22.5	0	0.0	57	15.4
Half to full tuition	0	0.0	0	0.0	0	0.0
Full tuition	0	0.0	0	0.0	0	0.0
More than full tuition	18	7.1	1	0.8	19	5.1
Median Grant Amount	$400		$0			

Informational & Library Resources

# of volumes & volume equivalents	284,115	# of professional staff	4
# of titles	57,052	Hours per week with professional staff	50
# of active serial subscriptions	3,328	Hours per week without professional staff	47
Study seating capacity inside the library	334	# of student computer work stations for entire law school	46
Square feet of law library	28,674	# of additional networked connections	0
Square feet of law school (excl. Library)	47,660	Require Laptop Computer?	N

Employment

	Total	%
Employment status known	68	80.0
Employment status unknown	17	20.0
Employed	54	79.4
Pursuing graduate degrees	3	4.4
Unemployed seeking employment	11	16.2
Unemployed not seeking employment	0	0.0
Type of Employment		
# employed in law firms	20	37.0
# employed in business & industry	16	29.6
# employed in government	10	18.5
# employed in public interest	7	13.0
# employed as judicial clerks	0	0.0
# employed in academia	1	1.9
Geographic Location		
# employed in state	40	74.1
# employed in foreign countries	0	0.0
# of states where employed	10	

J.D. Attrition (Prior Year)

	Academic	Other	TOTALS	
	#	#	#	%
1st Year	6	9	15	11%
2nd Year	2	1	3	2.9%
3rd Year	0	1	1	1.1%
4th Year	0	0	0	0.0%
TOTALS	8	11	19	5.5%

Bar Passage Rates

Jurisdiction	North Carolina			Maryland		
Exam	Sum 96	Win 97	Total	Sum 96	Win 97	Total
# from school taking bar for the first time	72	4	76	4	0	4
School's pass rate for all first-time takers	65%	50%	64%	75%		75%
State's pass rate for all first-time takers	81%	76%	80%	76%	79%	76%

NORTH CAROLINA, UNIVERSITY OF

Campus Box 3380
Van Hecke-Wettach Hall
Chapel Hill, NC 27599-3380
(919)962-5106
http://www.law.unc.edu

ABA Approved Since 1923

The Basics

Type of School: Public Term: Semester

Application deadline: 02/01

Application fee: $60

Financial Aid deadline: 03/01

Can first year start other than Fall? No

Student faculty ratio: 19.5 to 1

Does the University offer:
- housing restricted to law students? No
- graduate student housing for which law students are eligible? Yes

Faculty & Administrators

	Total		Men		Women		Minorities	
	Fall	Spr	Fall	Spr	Fall	Spr	Fall	Spr
Full-time	30	33	21	22	9	11	2	3
Other Full-Time	2	2	1	1	1	1	0	0
Deans, librarians, & others who teach > 1/2	4	4	2	2	2	2	0	0
Part-time	11	31	7	21	4	10	2	4
Total	47	70	31	46	16	24	4	7
Deans, librarians, & others who teach < 1/2	1	1	0	0	1	1	0	0

Curriculum

	Full time	Part time
Typical first-year section size	77	0
Is there typically a "small section" of the first year class, other than Legal Writing, taught by full-time faculty?	Yes	No
If yes, typical size offered last year	26	N/A
# of classroom course titles beyond 1st year curriculum	89	0
# of upper division courses, excluding seminars, with an enrollment:		
Under 25	46	0
25 - 49	34	0
50 - 74	7	0
75 - 99	6	0
100 +	5	0
# of seminars	24	0
# of seminar positions available	346	
# of seminar positions filled	313	0
# of positions available in simulation courses	513	
# of simulation positions filled	420	0
# of positions available in faculty supervised clinical courses	60	
# of fac. sup. clin. positions filled	54	0
# involved in field placements	0	0
# involved in law journals	142	0
# in moot court or trial competitions	48	0
# of credit hrs required to graduate	86	

J.D. Enrollment & Ethnicity

	Men		Women		Fl-Time		Pt-Time		1st Yr		2nd Yr		3rd Yr		4th Yr		Total		JD Degrees Awarded
	#	%	#	%	#	%	#	%	#	%	#	%	#	%	#	%	#	%	
African-American	30	8.5	58	17.4	88	12.8	0	0.0	27	11.7	37	15.9	24	10.7	0	0.0	88	12.8	22
American Indian	2	0.6	8	2.4	10	1.5	0	0.0	1	0.4	4	1.7	5	2.2	0	0.0	10	1.5	1
Asian American	11	3.1	19	5.7	30	4.4	0	0.0	12	5.2	7	3.0	11	4.9	0	0.0	30	4.4	8
Mexican American	0	0.0	0	0.0	0	0.0	0	0.0	0	0.0	0	0.0	0	0.0	0	0.0	0	0.0	0
Puerto Rican	0	0.0	0	0.0	0	0.0	0	0.0	0	0.0	0	0.0	0	0.0	0	0.0	0	0.0	0
Hispanic American	8	2.3	6	1.8	14	2.0	0	0.0	2	0.9	5	2.1	7	3.1	0	0.0	14	2.0	4
Total Minorities	51	14.4	91	27.2	142	20.7	0	0.0	42	18.3	53	22.7	47	21.0	0	0.0	142	20.7	35
Foreign Nationals	2	0.6	3	0.9	5	0.7	0	0.0	3	1.3	2	0.9	0	0.0	0	0.0	5	0.7	2
Caucasian	300	85.0	240	71.9	540	78.6	0	0.0	185	80.4	178	76.4	177	79.0	0	0.0	540	78.6	186
Total	353	51.4	334	48.6	687	100.0	0	0.0	230	33.5	233	33.9	224	32.6	0	0.0	687		223

GPA & LSAT Scores

	Full Time	Part Time	Total
# of apps	1,720	0	1,720
# admits	582	0	582
# of matrics	230	0	230
75% GPA	3.73	0.00	
25% GPA	3.23	0.00	
75% LSAT	164	0	
25% LSAT	156	0	

Tuition & Fees

	Resident	Non-resident
Full-Time	$2,881	$14,743
Part-Time	$0	$0

Living Expenses

Estimated living expenses for Singles		
Living on campus	Living off campus	Living at home
$8,950	$8,950	$4,173

Financial Aid

	Full-time		Part-time		Total	
	#	%	#	%	#	%
Total # of Students	687		0		687	
Total # receiving grants	115	16.7	0	0.0	115	16.7
Less than 1/2 tuition	18	2.6	0	0.0	18	2.6
Half to full tuition	57	8.3	0	0.0	57	8.3
Full tuition	0	0.0	0	0.0	0	0.0
More than full tuition	40	5.8	0	0.0	40	5.8
Median Grant Amount	$2,500		$0			

Informational & Library Resources

# of volumes & volume equivalents	447,320	# of professional staff	9
# of titles	79,378	Hours per week with professional staff	66
# of active serial subscriptions	5,926	Hours per week without professional staff	43
Study seating capacity inside the library	407	# of student computer work stations for entire law school	48
Square feet of law library	41,081	# of additional networked connections	110
Square feet of law school (excl. Library)	32,937	Require Laptop Computer?	N

Employment

	Total	%
Employment status known	233	97.5
Employment status unknown	6	2.5
Employed	220	94.4
Pursuing graduate degrees	5	2.1
Unemployed seeking employment	7	3.0
Unemployed not seeking employment	1	0.4
Type of Employment		
# employed in law firms	125	56.8
# employed in business & industry	28	12.7
# employed in government	29	13.2
# employed in public interest	7	3.2
# employed as judicial clerks	27	12.3
# employed in academia	4	1.8
Geographic Location		
# employed in state	140	63.6
# employed in foreign countries	4	1.8
# of states where employed	24	

J.D. Attrition (Prior Year)

	Academic	Other	TOTALS	
	#	#	#	%
1st Year	0	5	5	2.1%
2nd Year	0	0	0	0.0%
3rd Year	0	0	0	0.0%
4th Year	0	0	0	0.0%
TOTALS	0	5	5	0.7%

Bar Passage Rates

Jurisdiction	North Carolina		
Exam	Sum 96	Win 97	Total
# from school taking bar for the first time	165	15	180
School's pass rate for all first-time takers	89%	93%	89%
State's pass rate for all first-time takers	81%	76%	80%

NORTH DAKOTA, UNIVERSITY OF

Centennial Drive
P.O. Box 9003
Grand Forks, ND 58202
(701)777-2104
http://www.law.und.nodak.edu

ABA Approved Since 1923

The Basics

Type of School: Public Term: Semester

Application deadline: 04/01

Application fee: $35

Financial Aid deadline: 04/15

Can first year start other than Fall? No

Student faculty ratio: 14.5 to 1

Does the University offer:
- housing restricted to law students? No
- graduate student housing for which law students are eligible? No

Faculty & Administrators

	Total		Men		Women		Minorities	
	Fall	Spr	Fall	Spr	Fall	Spr	Fall	Spr
Full-time	11	9	6	5	5	4	0	0
Other Full-Time	1	1	0	0	1	1	0	0
Deans, librarians, & others who teach > 1/2	1	1	1	1	0	0	0	0
Part-time	5	5	3	3	2	2	0	0
Total	18	16	10	9	8	7	0	0
Deans, librarians, & others who teach < 1/2	3	3	2	2	1	1	0	0

Curriculum

	Full time	Part time
Typical first-year section size	72	0
Is there typically a "small section" of the first year class, other than Legal Writing, taught by full-time faculty?	No	No
If yes, typical size offered last year	N/A	N/A
# of classroom course titles beyond 1st year curriculum	59	0
# of upper division courses, excluding seminars, with an enrollment:		
Under 25	28	0
25 - 49	11	0
50 - 74	7	0
75 - 99	2	0
100 +	0	0
# of seminars	3	0
# of seminar positions available	36	
# of seminar positions filled	37	0
# of positions available in simulation courses	74	
# of simulation positions filled	67	0
# of positions available in faculty supervised clinical courses	0	
# of fac. sup. clin. positions filled	42	0
# involved in field placements	27	0
# involved in law journals	43	0
# in moot court or trial competitions	41	0
# of credit hrs required to graduate	90	

J.D. Enrollment & Ethnicity

	Men		Women		Fl-Time		Pt-Time		1st Yr		2nd Yr		3rd Yr		4th Yr		Total		JD Degrees Awarded
	#	%	#	%	#	%	#	%	#	%	#	%	#	%	#	%	#	%	
African-American	1	0.9	0	0.0	1	0.5	0	0.0	0	0.0	1	1.4	0	0.0	0	0.0	1	0.5	0
American Indian	3	2.6	3	4.0	6	3.1	0	0.0	1	1.5	4	5.7	1	1.8	0	0.0	6	3.1	2
Asian American	0	0.0	2	2.7	2	1.0	0	0.0	1	1.5	1	1.4	0	0.0	0	0.0	2	1.0	1
Mexican American	1	0.9	0	0.0	1	0.5	0	0.0	0	0.0	1	1.4	0	0.0	0	0.0	1	0.5	0
Puerto Rican	0	0.0	0	0.0	0	0.0	0	0.0	0	0.0	0	0.0	0	0.0	0	0.0	0	0.0	0
Hispanic American	0	0.0	0	0.0	0	0.0	0	0.0	0	0.0	0	0.0	0	0.0	0	0.0	0	0.0	0
Total Minorities	5	4.3	5	6.7	10	5.2	0	0.0	2	3.1	7	10.0	1	1.8	0	0.0	10	5.2	3
Foreign Nationals	5	4.3	3	4.0	8	4.2	0	0.0	4	6.2	2	2.9	2	3.5	0	0.0	8	4.2	6
Caucasian	107	91.5	67	89.3	174	90.6	0	0.0	59	90.8	61	87.1	54	94.7	0	0.0	174	90.6	66
Total	117	60.9	75	39.1	192	100.0	0	0.0	65	33.9	70	36.5	57	29.7	0	0.0	192		75

GPA & LSAT Scores

	Full Time	Part Time	Total
# of apps	236	0	236
# admits	157	0	157
# of matrics	65	0	65
75% GPA	3.52	0.00	
25% GPA	2.97	0.00	
75% LSAT	154	0	
25% LSAT	147	0	

Tuition & Fees

	Resident	Non-resident
Full-Time	$4,097	$8,533
Part-Time	$0	$0

Living Expenses

Estimated living expenses for Singles		
Living on campus	Living off campus	Living at home
$7,300	$7,300	$7,300

Financial Aid

	Full-time		Part-time		Total	
	#	%	#	%	#	%
Total # of Students	192		0		192	
Total # receiving grants	67	34.9	0	0.0	67	34.9
Less than 1/2 tuition	27	14.1	0	0.0	27	14.1
Half to full tuition	3	1.6	0	0.0	3	1.6
Full tuition	37	19.3	0	0.0	37	19.3
More than full tuition	0	0.0	0	0.0	0	0.0
Median Grant Amount	$2,656		$0			

Informational & Library Resources

# of volumes & volume equivalents	251,320	# of professional staff	2
# of titles	71,479	Hours per week with professional staff	45
# of active serial subscriptions	2,710	Hours per week without professional staff	61
Study seating capacity inside the library	279	# of student computer work stations for entire law school	68
Square feet of law library	21,582	# of additional networked connections	120
Square feet of law school (excl. Library)	19,409	Require Laptop Computer?	N

Employment

	Total	%
Employment status known	64	92.8
Employment status unknown	5	7.2
Employed	54	84.4
Pursuing graduate degrees	4	6.2
Unemployed seeking employment	3	4.7
Unemployed not seeking employment	3	4.7
Type of Employment		
# employed in law firms	28	51.9
# employed in business & industry	6	11.1
# employed in government	2	3.7
# employed in public interest	3	5.6
# employed as judicial clerks	15	27.8
# employed in academia	0	0.0
Geographic Location		
# employed in state	37	68.5
# employed in foreign countries	1	1.9
# of states where employed	11	

J.D. Attrition (Prior Year)

	Academic	Other	TOTALS	
	#	#	#	%
1st Year	0	3	3	4.5%
2nd Year	0	1	1	1.6%
3rd Year	0	1	1	1.4%
4th Year	0	0	0	0.0%
TOTALS	0	5	5	2.5%

Bar Passage Rates

Jurisdiction	North Dakota			Minnesota		
Exam	Sum 96	Win 97	Total	Sum 96	Win 97	Total
# from school taking bar for the first time	46	0	46	31	3	34
School's pass rate for all first-time takers	89%		89%	87%	67%	85%
State's pass rate for all first-time takers	85%	0%	85%	92%	84%	91%

NORTHEASTERN UNIVERSITY

400 Huntington Avenue
Boston, MA 02115
(617)373-5149
http://www.slaw.neu.edu

ABA Approved Since 1969

The Basics

Type of School: Private   Term: Quarter
Application deadline: 03/01
Application fee: $55
Financial Aid deadline: 03/01
Can first year start other than Fall? No
Student faculty ratio: 21.2 to 1
Does the University offer:
- housing restricted to law students? No
- graduate student housing for which law students are eligible? Yes

Faculty & Administrators

	Total		Men		Women		Minorities	
	Fall	Spr	Fall	Spr	Fall	Spr	Fall	Spr
Full-time	23	21	13	12	10	9	5	5
Other Full-Time	0	0	0	0	0	0	0	0
Deans, librarians, & others who teach > 1/2	4	4	0	0	4	4	1	1
Part-time	17	15	11	9	6	6	1	4
Total	44	40	24	21	20	19	7	10
Deans, librarians, & others who teach < 1/2	3	3	2	2	1	1	1	1

Curriculum

	Full time	Part time
Typical first-year section size	70	0
Is there typically a "small section" of the first year class, other than Legal Writing, taught by full-time faculty?	No	No
If yes, typical size offered last year	N/A	N/A
# of classroom course titles beyond 1st year curriculum	75	0
# of upper division courses, excluding seminars, with an enrollment:		
Under 25	70	0
25 - 49	26	0
50 - 74	13	0
75 - 99	6	0
100 +	1	0
# of seminars	13	0
# of seminar positions available	212	
# of seminar positions filled	190	0
# of positions available in simulation courses	232	
# of simulation positions filled	230	0
# of positions available in faculty supervised clinical courses	132	
# of fac. sup. clin. positions filled	99	0
# involved in field placements	377	0
# involved in law journals	50	0
# in moot court or trial competitions	57	0
# of credit hrs required to graduate	99	

J.D. Enrollment & Ethnicity

	Men		Women		Fl-Time		Pt-Time		1st Yr		2nd Yr		3rd Yr		4th Yr		Total		JD Degrees Awarded
	#	%	#	%	#	%	#	%	#	%	#	%	#	%	#	%	#	%	
African-American	20	10.6	35	8.8	55	9.4	0	0.0	15	8.6	21	10.0	19	9.5	0	0.0	55	9.4	18
American Indian	0	0.0	2	0.5	2	0.3	0	0.0	0	0.0	2	0.9	0	0.0	0	0.0	2	0.3	0
Asian American	17	9.0	42	10.6	59	10.1	0	0.0	14	8.0	23	10.9	22	11.0	0	0.0	59	10.1	13
Mexican American	2	1.1	5	1.3	7	1.2	0	0.0	4	2.3	3	1.4	0	0.0	0	0.0	7	1.2	2
Puerto Rican	2	1.1	6	1.5	8	1.4	0	0.0	4	2.3	4	1.9	0	0.0	0	0.0	8	1.4	4
Hispanic American	6	3.2	17	4.3	23	3.9	0	0.0	8	4.6	3	1.4	12	6.0	0	0.0	23	3.9	8
Total Minorities	47	24.9	107	27.0	154	26.3	0	0.0	45	25.9	56	26.5	53	26.5	0	0.0	154	26.3	45
Foreign Nationals	1	0.5	1	0.3	2	0.3	0	0.0	1	0.6	1	0.5	0	0.0	0	0.0	2	0.3	0
Caucasian	141	74.6	288	72.7	429	73.3	0	0.0	128	73.6	154	73.0	147	73.5	0	0.0	429	73.3	148
Total	189	32.3	396	67.7	585	100.0	0	0.0	174	29.7	211	36.1	200	34.2	0	0.0	585		193

NORTHEASTERN UNIVERSITY

GPA & LSAT Scores

	Full Time	Part Time	Total
# of apps	2,167	0	2,167
# admits	773	0	773
# of matrics	176	0	176
75% GPA	3.50	0.00	
25% GPA	3.04	0.00	
75% LSAT	158	0	
25% LSAT	151	0	

Tuition & Fees

	Resident	Non-resident
Full-Time	$21,300	$21,300
Part-Time	$0	$0

Living Expenses

Estimated living expenses for Singles		
Living on campus	Living off campus	Living at home
$12,700	$12,700	$6,850

Financial Aid

	Full-time		Part-time		Total	
	#	%	#	%	#	%
Total # of Students	585		0		585	
Total # receiving grants	322	55.0	0	0.0	322	55.0
Less than 1/2 tuition	273	46.7	0	0.0	273	46.7
Half to full tuition	39	6.7	0	0.0	39	6.7
Full tuition	10	1.7	0	0.0	10	1.7
More than full tuition	0	0.0	0	0.0	0	0.0
Median Grant Amount	$3,800		$0			

Informational & Library Resources

# of volumes & volume equivalents	227,479	# of professional staff	8
# of titles	31,931	Hours per week with professional staff	73
# of active serial subscriptions	2,778	Hours per week without professional staff	22
Study seating capacity inside the library	388	# of student computer work stations for entire law school	85
Square feet of law library	23,845	# of additional networked connections	0
Square feet of law school (excl. Library)	59,077	Require Laptop Computer?	N

Employment

	Total	%
Employment status known	169	86.7
Employment status unknown	26	13.3
Employed	148	87.6
Pursuing graduate degrees	3	1.8
Unemployed seeking employment	15	8.9
Unemployed not seeking employment	3	1.8
Type of Employment		
# employed in law firms	68	45.9
# employed in business & industry	12	8.1
# employed in government	10	6.8
# employed in public interest	26	17.6
# employed as judicial clerks	32	21.6
# employed in academia	0	0.0
Geographic Location		
# employed in state	87	58.8
# employed in foreign countries	3	2.0
# of states where employed	23	

J.D. Attrition (Prior Year)

	Academic	Other	TOTALS	
	#	#	#	%
1st Year	1	6	7	3.2%
2nd Year	1	3	4	2.1%
3rd Year	0	0	0	0.0%
4th Year	0	0	0	0.0%
TOTALS	2	9	11	1.8%

Bar Passage Rates

Jurisdiction	Massachusetts		
Exam	Sum 96	Win 97	Total
# from school taking bar for the first time	120	15	135
School's pass rate for all first-time takers	88%	87%	88%
State's pass rate for all first-time takers	83%	76%	81%

NORTHERN ILLINOIS UNIVERSITY

College of Law
DeKalb, IL 60115
(815)753-1420
http://www.niu.edu/claw

ABA Approved Since 1978

The Basics

Type of School: Public Term: Semester
Application deadline: 05/15
Application fee: $35
Financial Aid deadline: 03/01
Can first year start other than Fall? No
Student faculty ratio: 14.4 to 1
Does the University offer:
- housing restricted to law students? Yes
- graduate student housing for which law students are eligible? No

Faculty & Administrators

	Total		Men		Women		Minorities	
	Fall	Spr	Fall	Spr	Fall	Spr	Fall	Spr
Full-time	16	17	13	14	3	3	2	2
Other Full-Time	2	2	0	0	2	2	0	0
Deans, librarians, & others who teach > 1/2	1	1	1	1	0	0	0	0
Part-time	8	7	6	5	2	2	1	0
Total	27	27	20	20	7	7	3	2
Deans, librarians, & others who teach < 1/2	4	4	4	4	0	0	1	1

Curriculum

	Full time	Part time
Typical first-year section size	44	0
Is there typically a "small section" of the first year class, other than Legal Writing, taught by full-time faculty?	No	No
If yes, typical size offered last year	N/A	N/A
# of classroom course titles beyond 1st year curriculum	64	0
# of upper division courses, excluding seminars, with an enrollment:		
Under 25	50	0
25 - 49	9	0
50 - 74	10	0
75 - 99	3	0
100 +	0	0
# of seminars	8	0
# of seminar positions available	96	
# of seminar positions filled	91	0
# of positions available in simulation courses	185	
# of simulation positions filled	161	0
# of positions available in faculty supervised clinical courses	0	
# of fac. sup. clin. positions filled	0	0
# involved in field placements	37	0
# involved in law journals	33	0
# in moot court or trial competitions	64	0
# of credit hrs required to graduate	90	

J.D. Enrollment & Ethnicity

	Men		Women		Fl-Time		Pt-Time		1st Yr		2nd Yr		3rd Yr		4th Yr		Total		JD Degrees Awarded
	#	%	#	%	#	%	#	%	#	%	#	%	#	%	#	%	#	%	
African-American	12	6.7	11	10.6	21	8.1	2	8.3	7	8.0	6	6.1	10	10.1	0	0.0	23	8.1	8
American Indian	0	0.0	0	0.0	0	0.0	0	0.0	0	0.0	0	0.0	0	0.0	0	0.0	0	0.0	0
Asian American	12	6.7	7	6.7	18	6.9	1	4.2	4	4.6	9	9.2	5	5.1	1	****	19	6.7	0
Mexican American	12	6.7	3	2.9	15	5.8	0	0.0	4	4.6	4	4.1	7	7.1	0	0.0	15	5.3	5
Puerto Rican	0	0.0	0	0.0	0	0.0	0	0.0	0	0.0	0	0.0	0	0.0	0	0.0	0	0.0	0
Hispanic American	0	0.0	0	0.0	0	0.0	0	0.0	0	0.0	0	0.0	0	0.0	0	0.0	0	0.0	0
Total Minorities	36	20.0	21	20.2	54	20.8	3	12.5	15	17.2	19	19.4	22	22.2	1	****	57	20.1	13
Foreign Nationals	0	0.0	0	0.0	0	0.0	0	0.0	0	0.0	0	0.0	0	0.0	0	0.0	0	0.0	0
Caucasian	144	80.0	83	79.8	206	79.2	21	87.5	72	82.8	79	80.6	74	74.7	2	****	227	79.9	78
Total	180	63.4	104	36.6	260	91.5	24	8.5	87	30.6	98	34.5	99	34.9	0	0.0	284		91

NORTHERN ILLINOIS UNIVERSITY

GPA & LSAT Scores

	Full Time	Part Time	Total
# of apps	782	23	805
# admits	327	11	338
# of matrics	82	5	87
75% GPA	3.27	2.90	
25% GPA	2.71	2.65	
75% LSAT	157	156	
25% LSAT	152	151	

Tuition & Fees

	Resident	Non-resident
Full-Time	$5,938	$10,976
Part-Time	$0	$0

Living Expenses

Estimated living expenses for Singles		
Living on campus	Living off campus	Living at home
$7,662	$8,462	$8,462

Financial Aid

	Full-time		Part-time		Total	
	#	%	#	%	#	%
Total # of Students	260		24		284	
Total # receiving grants	49	18.8	0	0.0	49	17.3
Less than 1/2 tuition	19	7.3	0	0.0	19	6.7
Half to full tuition	18	6.9	0	0.0	18	6.3
Full tuition	3	1.2	0	0.0	3	1.1
More than full tuition	9	3.5	0	0.0	9	3.2
Median Grant Amount	$2,316		$0			

Informational & Library Resources

# of volumes & volume equivalents	201,875	# of professional staff	4
# of titles	31,933	Hours per week with professional staff	53
# of active serial subscriptions	3,212	Hours per week without professional staff	44
Study seating capacity inside the library	210	# of student computer work stations for entire law school	26
Square feet of law library	24,700	# of additional networked connections	0
Square feet of law school (excl. Library)	18,600	Require Laptop Computer?	N

Employment

	Total	%
Employment status known	83	96.5
Employment status unknown	3	3.5
Employed	73	88.0
Pursuing graduate degrees	2	2.4
Unemployed seeking employment	7	8.4
Unemployed not seeking employment	1	1.2
Type of Employment		
# employed in law firms	42	57.5
# employed in business & industry	9	12.3
# employed in government	19	26.0
# employed in public interest	1	1.4
# employed as judicial clerks	2	2.7
# employed in academia	0	0.0
Geographic Location		
# employed in state	58	79.5
# employed in foreign countries	0	0.0
# of states where employed	11	

J.D. Attrition (Prior Year)

	Academic	Other	TOTALS	
	#	#	#	%
1st Year	0	10	10	9.6%
2nd Year	6	1	7	7.2%
3rd Year	0	1	1	1.1%
4th Year	0	0	0	0.0%
TOTALS	6	12	18	6.1%

Bar Passage Rates

Jurisdiction	Illinois			Wisconsin		
Exam	Sum 96	Win 97	Total	Sum 96	Win 97	Total
# from school taking bar for the first time	89	4	93	3	1	4
School's pass rate for all first-time takers	75%	75%	75%	67%	100%	75%
State's pass rate for all first-time takers	86%	84%	86%	93%	90%	92%

NORTHERN KENTUCKY UNIVERSITY

Nunn Drive
Highland Heights, KY 41099
(606)572-5340
http://www.eku.edu/~chase

ABA Approved Since 1954

The Basics

Type of School: Public
Term: Semester
Application deadline: 05/15
Application fee: $35
Financial Aid deadline: 04/01
Can first year start other than Fall? No
Student faculty ratio: 13.2 to 1
Does the University offer:
- housing restricted to law students? No
- graduate student housing for which law students are eligible? Yes

Faculty & Administrators

	Total		Men		Women		Minorities	
	Fall	Spr	Fall	Spr	Fall	Spr	Fall	Spr
Full-time	21	22	17	17	4	5	1	1
Other Full-Time	3	3	1	1	2	2	0	0
Deans, librarians, & others who teach > 1/2	1	1	0	0	1	1	0	0
Part-time	33	27	26	20	7	7	1	1
Total	58	53	44	38	14	15	2	2
Deans, librarians, & others who teach < 1/2	0	0	0	0	0	0	0	0

Curriculum

	Full time	Part time
Typical first-year section size	70	54
Is there typically a "small section" of the first year class, other than Legal Writing, taught by full-time faculty?	Yes	Yes
If yes, typical size offered last year	25	25
# of classroom course titles beyond 1st year curriculum	40	72
# of upper division courses, excluding seminars, with an enrollment:		
Under 25	26	42
25 - 49	9	22
50 - 74	3	4
75 - 99	0	0
100 +	0	0
# of seminars	3	3
# of seminar positions available	0	
# of seminar positions filled	45	58
# of positions available in simulation courses	242	
# of simulation positions filled	48	157
# of positions available in faculty supervised clinical courses	50	
# of fac. sup. clin. positions filled	31	7
# involved in field placements	9	1
# involved in law journals	21	8
# in moot court or trial competitions	20	16
# of credit hrs required to graduate	90	

J.D. Enrollment & Ethnicity

	Men		Women		Fl-Time		Pt-Time		1st Yr		2nd Yr		3rd Yr		4th Yr		Total		JD Degrees Awarded
	#	%	#	%	#	%	#	%	#	%	#	%	#	%	#	%	#	%	
African-American	14	5.4	7	4.9	4	2.0	17	8.3	5	4.2	8	6.7	6	5.2	2	4.3	21	5.2	10
American Indian	1	0.4	0	0.0	0	0.0	1	0.5	1	0.8	0	0.0	0	0.0	0	0.0	1	0.2	0
Asian American	1	0.4	0	0.0	1	0.5	0	0.0	0	0.0	0	0.0	1	0.9	0	0.0	1	0.2	3
Mexican American	0	0.0	0	0.0	0	0.0	0	0.0	0	0.0	0	0.0	0	0.0	0	0.0	0	0.0	0
Puerto Rican	0	0.0	0	0.0	0	0.0	0	0.0	0	0.0	0	0.0	0	0.0	0	0.0	0	0.0	0
Hispanic American	3	1.2	1	0.7	1	0.5	3	1.5	2	1.7	2	1.7	0	0.0	0	0.0	4	1.0	2
Total Minorities	19	7.3	8	5.6	6	3.0	21	10.3	8	6.7	10	8.3	7	6.0	2	4.3	27	6.7	15
Foreign Nationals	0	0.0	0	0.0	0	0.0	0	0.0	0	0.0	0	0.0	0	0.0	0	0.0	0	0.0	0
Caucasian	240	92.7	136	94.4	193	97.0	183	89.7	112	93.3	110	91.7	109	94.0	45	95.7	376	93.3	92
Total	259	64.3	144	35.7	199	49.4	204	50.6	120	29.8	120	29.8	116	28.8	47	11.7	403		107

NORTHERN KENTUCKY UNIVERSITY

GPA & LSAT Scores

	Full Time	Part Time	Total
# of apps	529	170	699
# admits	195	80	275
# of matrics	68	56	124
75% GPA	3.26	3.65	
25% GPA	2.76	2.99	
75% LSAT	155	159	
25% LSAT	151	151	

Tuition & Fees

	Resident	Non-resident
Full-Time	$5,200	$13,040
Part-Time	$4,340	$10,880

Living Expenses

Estimated living expenses for Singles		
Living on campus	Living off campus	Living at home
$6,304	$10,500	$10,500

Financial Aid

	Full-time		Part-time		Total	
	#	%	#	%	#	%
Total # of Students	199		204		403	
Total # receiving grants	133	66.8	0	0.0	133	33.0
Less than 1/2 tuition	65	32.7	0	0.0	65	16.1
Half to full tuition	0	0.0	0	0.0	0	0.0
Full tuition	68	34.2	0	0.0	68	16.9
More than full tuition	0	0.0	0	0.0	0	0.0
Median Grant Amount	$0		$0			

Informational & Library Resources

# of volumes & volume equivalents	245,351	# of professional staff	6
# of titles	32,733	Hours per week with professional staff	67
# of active serial subscriptions	2,138	Hours per week without professional staff	33
Study seating capacity inside the library	200	# of student computer work stations for entire law school	37
Square feet of law library	25,897	# of additional networked connections	0
Square feet of law school (excl. Library)	56,492	Require Laptop Computer?	N

Employment

	Total	%
Employment status known	111	87.4
Employment status unknown	16	12.6
Employed	105	94.6
Pursuing graduate degrees	2	1.8
Unemployed seeking employment	2	1.8
Unemployed not seeking employment	2	1.8
Type of Employment		
# employed in law firms	65	61.9
# employed in business & industry	20	19.0
# employed in government	9	8.6
# employed in public interest	1	1.0
# employed as judicial clerks	3	2.9
# employed in academia	1	1.0
Geographic Location		
# employed in state	50	47.6
# employed in foreign countries	0	0.0
# of states where employed	7	

J.D. Attrition (Prior Year)

	Academic	Other	TOTALS	
	#	#	#	%
1st Year	5	7	12	9.4%
2nd Year	0	3	3	2.7%
3rd Year	0	0	0	0.0%
4th Year	0	0	0	0.0%
TOTALS	5	10	15	3.7%

Bar Passage Rates

Jurisdiction	Kentucky			Ohio		
Exam	Sum 96	Win 97	Total	Sum 96	Win 97	Total
# from school taking bar for the first time	55	18	73	52	16	68
School's pass rate for all first-time takers	73%	61%	70%	92%	94%	93%
State's pass rate for all first-time takers	84%	82%	83%	90%	90%	90%

NORTHWESTERN UNIVERSITY

357 East Chicago Avenue
Chicago, IL 60611
(312)503-8462
http://www.law1.nwu.edu/

ABA Approved Since 1923

The Basics

Type of School: Private   Term: Semester

Application deadline: 02/16

Application fee: $80

Financial Aid deadline: 03/15

Can first year start other than Fall? No

Student faculty ratio: 14.6 to 1

Does the University offer:
- housing restricted to law students? No
- graduate student housing for which law students are eligible? Yes

Faculty & Administrators

	Total		Men		Women		Minorities	
	Fall	Spr	Fall	Spr	Fall	Spr	Fall	Spr
Full-time	36	37	29	28	7	9	2	1
Other Full-Time	13	13	5	5	8	8	0	0
Deans, librarians, & others who teach > 1/2	1	1	1	1	0	0	0	0
Part-time	111	33	81	25	29	8	8	2
Total	161	84	116	59	44	25	10	3
Deans, librarians, & others who teach < 1/2	3	3	3	3	0	0	0	0

Curriculum

	Full time	Part time
Typical first-year section size	100	0
Is there typically a "small section" of the first year class, other than Legal Writing, taught by full-time faculty?	Yes	No
If yes, typical size offered last year	50	N/A
# of classroom course titles beyond 1st year curriculum	142	0
# of upper division courses, excluding seminars, with an enrollment:		
Under 25	38	0
25 - 49	25	0
50 - 74	15	0
75 - 99	7	0
100 +	4	0
# of seminars	53	0
# of seminar positions available	1,300	
# of seminar positions filled	445	0
# of positions available in simulation courses	340	
# of simulation positions filled	319	0
# of positions available in faculty supervised clinical courses	90	
# of fac. sup. clin. positions filled	65	0
# involved in field placements	24	0
# involved in law journals	165	0
# in moot court or trial competitions	44	0
# of credit hrs required to graduate	86	

J.D. Enrollment & Ethnicity

	Men		Women		Fl-Time		Pt-Time		1st Yr		2nd Yr		3rd Yr		4th Yr		Total		JD Degrees Awarded
	#	%	#	%	#	%	#	%	#	%	#	%	#	%	#	%	#	%	
African-American	22	6.1	25	9.4	47	7.5	0	0.0	16	7.8	13	6.0	18	8.7	0	0.0	47	7.5	14
American Indian	2	0.6	2	0.7	4	0.6	0	0.0	1	0.5	2	0.9	1	0.5	0	0.0	4	0.6	1
Asian American	28	7.7	20	7.5	48	7.6	0	0.0	22	10.8	16	7.3	10	4.8	0	0.0	48	7.6	18
Mexican American	4	1.1	3	1.1	7	1.1	0	0.0	1	0.5	6	2.8	0	0.0	0	0.0	7	1.1	2
Puerto Rican	1	0.3	2	0.7	3	0.5	0	0.0	3	1.5	0	0.0	0	0.0	0	0.0	3	0.5	4
Hispanic American	18	5.0	11	4.1	29	4.6	0	0.0	11	5.4	14	6.4	4	1.9	0	0.0	29	4.6	7
Total Minorities	75	20.7	63	23.6	138	21.9	0	0.0	54	26.5	51	23.4	33	15.9	0	0.0	138	21.9	46
Foreign Nationals	6	1.7	6	2.2	12	1.9	0	0.0	4	2.0	4	1.8	4	1.9	0	0.0	12	1.9	3
Caucasian	281	77.6	198	74.2	479	76.2	0	0.0	146	71.6	163	74.8	170	82.1	0	0.0	479	76.2	159
Total	362	57.6	267	42.4	629	100.0	0	0.0	204	32.4	218	34.7	207	32.9	0	0.0	629		208

NORTHWESTERN UNIVERSITY

GPA & LSAT Scores

	Full Time	Part Time	Total
# of apps	3,537	0	3,537
# admits	749	0	749
# of matrics	206	0	206
75% GPA	3.68	0.00	
25% GPA	3.33	0.00	
75% LSAT	166	0	
25% LSAT	161	0	

Tuition & Fees

	Resident	Non-resident
Full-Time	$22,638	$0
Part-Time	$0	$0

Living Expenses

Estimated living expenses for Singles		
Living on campus	Living off campus	Living at home
$14,178	$14,808	$8,508

Employment

	Total	%
Employment status known	194	97.0
Employment status unknown	6	3.0
Employed	188	96.9
Pursuing graduate degrees	0	0.0
Unemployed seeking employment	1	0.5
Unemployed not seeking employment	5	2.6
Type of Employment		
# employed in law firms	137	72.9
# employed in business & industry	15	8.0
# employed in government	11	5.9
# employed in public interest	2	1.1
# employed as judicial clerks	22	11.7
# employed in academia	1	0.5
Geographic Location		
# employed in state	106	56.4
# employed in foreign countries	2	1.1
# of states where employed	23	

Financial Aid

	Full-time		Part-time		Total	
	#	%	#	%	#	%
Total # of Students	629		0		629	
Total # receiving grants	241	38.3	0	0.0	241	38.3
Less than 1/2 tuition	128	20.3	0	0.0	128	20.3
Half to full tuition	97	15.4	0	0.0	97	15.4
Full tuition	12	1.9	0	0.0	12	1.9
More than full tuition	4	0.6	0	0.0	4	0.6
Median Grant Amount	$10,862		$0			

Informational & Library Resources

# of volumes & volume equivalents	634,272	# of professional staff	11
# of titles	188,293	Hours per week with professional staff	77
# of active serial subscriptions	8,257	Hours per week without professional staff	28
Study seating capacity inside the library	718	# of student computer work stations for entire law school	70
Square feet of law library	93,900	# of additional networked connections	84
Square feet of law school (excl. Library)	83,254	Require Laptop Computer?	N

J.D. Attrition (Prior Year)

	Academic	Other	TOTALS	
	#	#	#	%
1st Year	0	10	10	5.0%
2nd Year	0	0	0	0.0%
3rd Year	0	0	0	0.0%
4th Year	0	0	0	0.0%
TOTALS	0	10	10	1.6%

Bar Passage Rates

Jurisdiction	Illinois			New York		
Exam	Sum 96	Win 97	Total	Sum 96	Win 97	Total
# from school taking bar for the first time	117	9	126	19	2	21
School's pass rate for all first-time takers	92%	100%	93%	63%	100%	67%
State's pass rate for all first-time takers	86%	84%	86%	78%	67%	77%

NOTRE DAME, UNIVERSITY OF

103 Law Building
Notre Dame, IN 46556
(219)631-6627
http://www.nd.edu/~ndlaw

ABA Approved Since 1925

The Basics

Type of School: Private — Term: Semester
Application deadline: 03/01
Application fee: $65
Financial Aid deadline: 03/01
Can first year start other than Fall? No
Student faculty ratio: 17.3 to 1
Does the University offer:
- housing restricted to law students? No
- graduate student housing for which law students are eligible? Yes

Faculty & Administrators

	Total		Men		Women		Minorities	
	Fall	Spr	Fall	Spr	Fall	Spr	Fall	Spr
Full-time	24	25	21	23	3	2	3	3
Other Full-Time	5	5	1	1	4	4	0	0
Deans, librarians, & others who teach > 1/2	6	6	4	4	2	2	0	0
Part-time	21	21	17	17	4	4	0	0
Total	56	57	43	45	13	12	3	3
Deans, librarians, & others who teach < 1/2	12	12	7	7	5	5	1	1

Curriculum

	Full time	Part time
Typical first-year section size	90	0
Is there typically a "small section" of the first year class, other than Legal Writing, taught by full-time faculty?	No	No
If yes, typical size offered last year	N/A	N/A
# of classroom course titles beyond 1st year curriculum	76	76
# of upper division courses, excluding seminars, with an enrollment:		
Under 25	70	0
25 - 49	18	0
50 - 74	9	0
75 - 99	4	0
100 +	3	0
# of seminars	7	0
# of seminar positions available	200	
# of seminar positions filled	181	0
# of positions available in simulation courses	220	
# of simulation positions filled	195	0
# of positions available in faculty supervised clinical courses	120	
# of fac. sup. clin. positions filled	79	0
# involved in field placements	115	0
# involved in law journals	123	0
# in moot court or trial competitions	118	0
# of credit hrs required to graduate	90	

J.D. Enrollment & Ethnicity

	Men		Women		Fl-Time		Pt-Time		1st Yr		2nd Yr		3rd Yr		4th Yr		Total		JD Degrees Awarded
	#	%	#	%	#	%	#	%	#	%	#	%	#	%	#	%	#	%	
African-American	4	1.2	10	5.2	14	2.7	0	0.0	7	3.9	5	2.9	2	1.2	0	0.0	14	2.7	6
American Indian	6	1.8	3	1.6	9	1.7	0	0.0	5	2.8	3	1.8	1	0.6	0	0.0	9	1.7	1
Asian American	18	5.5	17	8.8	35	6.7	0	0.0	12	6.7	10	5.8	13	7.6	0	0.0	35	6.7	9
Mexican American	0	0.0	0	0.0	0	0.0	0	0.0	0	0.0	0	0.0	0	0.0	0	0.0	0	0.0	0
Puerto Rican	0	0.0	0	0.0	0	0.0	0	0.0	0	0.0	0	0.0	0	0.0	0	0.0	0	0.0	0
Hispanic American	23	7.0	17	8.8	40	7.7	0	0.0	15	8.4	14	8.2	11	6.4	0	0.0	40	7.7	12
Total Minorities	51	15.5	47	24.4	98	18.8	0	0.0	39	21.8	32	18.7	27	15.7	0	0.0	98	18.8	28
Foreign Nationals	0	0.0	0	0.0	0	0.0	0	0.0	0	0.0	0	0.0	0	0.0	0	0.0	0	0.0	4
Caucasian	278	84.5	146	75.6	424	81.2	0	0.0	140	78.2	139	81.3	145	84.3	0	0.0	424	81.2	154
Total	329	63.0	193	37.0	522	100.0	0	0.0	179	34.3	171	32.8	172	33.0	0	0.0	522		186

NOTRE DAME, UNIVERSITY OF

GPA & LSAT Scores

	Full Time	Part Time	Total
# of apps	1,845	0	1,845
# admits	514	0	514
# of matrics	180	0	180
75% GPA	3.66	0.00	
25% GPA	3.15	0.00	
75% LSAT	165	0	
25% LSAT	160	0	

Tuition & Fees

	Resident	Non-resident
Full-Time	$20,427	$20,427
Part-Time	$0	$0

Living Expenses

Estimated living expenses for Singles		
Living on campus	Living off campus	Living at home
$5,150	$5,150	$5,150

Financial Aid

	Full-time		Part-time		Total	
	#	%	#	%	#	%
Total # of Students	522		0		522	
Total # receiving grants	180	34.5	0	0.0	180	34.5
Less than 1/2 tuition	113	21.6	0	0.0	113	21.6
Half to full tuition	48	9.2	0	0.0	48	9.2
Full tuition	16	3.1	0	0.0	16	3.1
More than full tuition	3	0.6	0	0.0	3	0.6
Median Grant Amount	$7,500		$0			

Informational & Library Resources

# of volumes & volume equivalents	454,082	# of professional staff	10
# of titles	82,002	Hours per week with professional staff	74
# of active serial subscriptions	5,276	Hours per week without professional staff	12
Study seating capacity inside the library	509	# of student computer work stations for entire law school	47
Square feet of law library	37,222	# of additional networked connections	48
Square feet of law school (excl. Library)	43,057	Require Laptop Computer?	N

Employment

	Total	%
Employment status known	169	96.0
Employment status unknown	7	4.0
Employed	154	91.1
Pursuing graduate degrees	5	3.0
Unemployed seeking employment	6	3.6
Unemployed not seeking employment	4	2.4
Type of Employment		
# employed in law firms	94	61.0
# employed in business & industry	15	9.7
# employed in government	15	9.7
# employed in public interest	3	1.9
# employed as judicial clerks	24	15.6
# employed in academia	3	1.9
Geographic Location		
# employed in state	18	11.7
# employed in foreign countries	3	1.9
# of states where employed	30	

J.D. Attrition (Prior Year)

	Academic	Other	TOTALS	
	#	#	#	%
1st Year	1	4	5	2.9%
2nd Year	1	0	1	0.6%
3rd Year	0	0	0	0.0%
4th Year	0	0	0	0.0%
TOTALS	2	4	6	1.1%

Bar Passage Rates

Jurisdiction	Illinois		
Exam	Sum 96	Win 97	Total
# from school taking bar for the first time	37	5	42
School's pass rate for all first-time takers	97%	80%	95%
State's pass rate for all first-time takers	86%	84%	86%

NOVA SOUTHEASTERN UNIVERSITY

3305 College Avenue
Fort Lauderdale, FL 33314-7721
(954)262-6100
http://www.nsulaw.nova.edu

ABA Approved Since 1975

The Basics

Type of School: Private Term: Semester
Application deadline: 03/01
Application fee: $50
Financial Aid deadline: 03/01
Can first year start other than Fall? No
Student faculty ratio: 18.2 to 1
Does the University offer:
- housing restricted to law students? No
- graduate student housing for which law students are eligible? Yes

Faculty & Administrators

	Total		Men		Women		Minorities	
	Fall	Spr	Fall	Spr	Fall	Spr	Fall	Spr
Full-time	40	39	25	24	15	15	7	7
Other Full-Time	5	5	4	4	1	1	0	0
Deans, librarians, & others who teach > 1/2	1	1	0	0	1	1	0	0
Part-time	27	36	19	25	8	11	2	2
Total	73	81	48	53	25	28	9	9
Deans, librarians, & others who teach < 1/2	4	4	2	2	2	2	0	0

Curriculum

	Full time	Part time
Typical first-year section size	62	63
Is there typically a "small section" of the first year class, other than Legal Writing, taught by full-time faculty?	No	No
If yes, typical size offered last year	N/A	N/A
# of classroom course titles beyond 1st year curriculum	93	0
# of upper division courses, excluding seminars, with an enrollment:		
Under 25	67	0
25 - 49	34	0
50 - 74	18	0
75 - 99	13	0
100 +	0	0
# of seminars	19	0
# of seminar positions available	384	
# of seminar positions filled	335	0
# of positions available in simulation courses	775	
# of simulation positions filled	662	0
# of positions available in faculty supervised clinical courses	53	
# of fac. sup. clin. positions filled	35	0
# involved in field placements	226	0
# involved in law journals	93	0
# in moot court or trial competitions	108	0
# of credit hrs required to graduate	90	

J.D. Enrollment & Ethnicity

	Men		Women		Fl-Time		Pt-Time		1st Yr		2nd Yr		3rd Yr		4th Yr		Total		JD Degrees Awarded
	#	%	#	%	#	%	#	%	#	%	#	%	#	%	#	%	#	%	
African-American	25	4.6	39	10.3	58	7.4	6	4.3	27	8.8	17	4.7	20	8.1	0	0.0	64	7.0	29
American Indian	3	0.6	2	0.5	4	0.5	1	0.7	1	0.3	3	0.8	1	0.4	0	0.0	5	0.5	1
Asian American	5	0.9	8	2.1	8	1.0	5	3.6	3	1.0	10	2.7	0	0.0	0	0.0	13	1.4	2
Mexican American	0	0.0	2	0.5	2	0.3	0	0.0	2	0.7	0	0.0	0	0.0	0	0.0	2	0.2	1
Puerto Rican	6	1.1	6	1.6	10	1.3	2	1.4	3	1.0	7	1.9	2	0.8	0	0.0	12	1.3	2
Hispanic American	66	12.2	64	16.9	107	13.7	23	16.4	45	14.7	50	13.7	34	13.8	1	33.3	130	14.1	42
Total Minorities	105	19.4	121	31.9	189	24.2	37	26.4	81	26.4	87	23.9	57	23.2	1	33.3	226	24.6	77
Foreign Nationals	4	0.7	8	2.1	11	1.4	1	0.7	6	2.0	2	0.5	4	1.6	0	0.0	12	1.3	0
Caucasian	432	79.9	250	66.0	580	74.4	102	72.9	220	71.7	275	75.5	185	75.2	2	66.7	682	74.1	237
Total	541	58.8	379	41.2	780	84.8	140	15.2	307	33.4	364	39.6	246	26.7	3	0.3	920		314

NOVA SOUTHEASTERN UNIVERSITY

GPA & LSAT Scores

	Full Time	Part Time	Total
# of apps	1,234	214	1,448
# admits	679	118	797
# of matrics	248	67	315
75% GPA	3.15	3.20	
25% GPA	2.57	2.45	
75% LSAT	151	151	
25% LSAT	143	145	

Tuition & Fees

	Resident	Non-resident
Full-Time	$19,400	$19,400
Part-Time	$14,550	$14,550

Living Expenses

Estimated living expenses for Singles		
Living on campus	Living off campus	Living at home
$11,659	$12,664	$7,724

Financial Aid

	Full-time		Part-time		Total	
	#	%	#	%	#	%
Total # of Students	780		140		920	
Total # receiving grants	167	21.4	3	2.1	170	18.5
Less than 1/2 tuition	128	16.4	2	1.4	130	14.1
Half to full tuition	20	2.6	0	0.0	20	2.2
Full tuition	19	2.4	1	0.7	20	2.2
More than full tuition	0	0.0	0	0.0	0	0.0
Median Grant Amount	$6,600		$3,638			

Informational & Library Resources

# of volumes & volume equivalents	294,698	# of professional staff	11
# of titles	120,042	Hours per week with professional staff	78
# of active serial subscriptions	5,477	Hours per week without professional staff	27
Study seating capacity inside the library	559	# of student computer work stations for entire law school	56
Square feet of law library	43,062	# of additional networked connections	172
Square feet of law school (excl. Library)	76,525	Require Laptop Computer?	Y

Employment

	Total	%
Employment status known	208	74.8
Employment status unknown	70	25.2
Employed	172	82.7
Pursuing graduate degrees	5	2.4
Unemployed seeking employment	28	13.5
Unemployed not seeking employment	3	1.4
Type of Employment		
# employed in law firms	98	57.0
# employed in business & industry	17	9.9
# employed in government	36	20.9
# employed in public interest	3	1.7
# employed as judicial clerks	1	0.6
# employed in academia	4	2.3
Geographic Location		
# employed in state	147	85.5
# employed in foreign countries	1	0.6
# of states where employed	10	

J.D. Attrition (Prior Year)

	Academic	Other	TOTALS	
	#	#	#	%
1st Year	14	37	51	13%
2nd Year	4	1	5	1.9%
3rd Year	1	1	2	0.6%
4th Year	0	0	0	0.0%
TOTALS	19	39	58	6.0%

Bar Passage Rates

Jurisdiction	Florida			New York		
Exam	Sum 96	Win 97	Total	Sum 96	Win 97	Total
# from school taking bar for the first time	225	51	276	4	5	9
School's pass rate for all first-time takers	82%	73%	80%	100%	40%	67%
State's pass rate for all first-time takers	84%	85%	84%	78%	67%	77%

OHIO NORTHERN UNIVERSITY

525 S. Main Street
Ada, OH 45810-1599
(419)772-2205
http://www.law.onu.edu

ABA Approved Since 1948

The Basics

Type of School: Private
Term: Semester
Application deadline: Rolling
Application fee: $40
Financial Aid deadline: 06/01
Can first year start other than Fall? No
Student faculty ratio: 16.8 to 1
Does the University offer:
- housing restricted to law students? Yes
- graduate student housing for which law students are eligible? No

Faculty & Administrators

	Total		Men		Women		Minorities	
	Fall	Spr	Fall	Spr	Fall	Spr	Fall	Spr
Full-time	17	17	13	13	4	4	1	1
Other Full-Time	0	0	0	0	0	0	0	0
Deans, librarians, & others who teach > 1/2	3	3	3	3	0	0	0	0
Part-time	6	13	3	11	3	2	0	1
Total	26	33	19	27	7	6	1	2
Deans, librarians, & others who teach < 1/2	1	1	1	1	0	0	0	0

Curriculum

	Full time	Part time
Typical first-year section size	42	0
Is there typically a "small section" of the first year class, other than Legal Writing, taught by full-time faculty?	No	No
If yes, typical size offered last year	N/A	N/A
# of classroom course titles beyond 1st year curriculum	68	0
# of upper division courses, excluding seminars, with an enrollment:		
Under 25	28	0
25 - 49	18	0
50 - 74	10	0
75 - 99	0	0
100 +	0	0
# of seminars	12	0
# of seminar positions available	185	
# of seminar positions filled	174	0
# of positions available in simulation courses	125	
# of simulation positions filled	124	0
# of positions available in faculty supervised clinical courses	17	
# of fac. sup. clin. positions filled	17	0
# involved in field placements	41	0
# involved in law journals	61	0
# in moot court or trial competitions	44	0
# of credit hrs required to graduate	87	

J.D. Enrollment & Ethnicity

	Men		Women		Fl-Time		Pt-Time		1st Yr		2nd Yr		3rd Yr		4th Yr		Total		JD Degrees Awarded
	#	%	#	%	#	%	#	%	#	%	#	%	#	%	#	%	#	%	
African-American	14	6.5	12	10.7	26	7.9	0	0.0	12	9.4	7	6.9	7	7.1	0	0.0	26	7.9	5
American Indian	2	0.9	0	0.0	2	0.6	0	0.0	1	0.8	0	0.0	1	1.0	0	0.0	2	0.6	0
Asian American	7	3.2	4	3.6	11	3.3	0	0.0	5	3.9	4	3.9	2	2.0	0	0.0	11	3.3	0
Mexican American	1	0.5	1	0.9	2	0.6	0	0.0	1	0.8	0	0.0	1	1.0	0	0.0	2	0.6	1
Puerto Rican	0	0.0	0	0.0	0	0.0	0	0.0	0	0.0	0	0.0	0	0.0	0	0.0	0	0.0	0
Hispanic American	4	1.8	2	1.8	6	1.8	0	0.0	4	3.1	2	2.0	0	0.0	0	0.0	6	1.8	0
Total Minorities	28	12.9	19	17.0	47	14.3	0	0.0	23	18.0	13	12.7	11	11.1	0	0.0	47	14.3	6
Foreign Nationals	0	0.0	0	0.0	0	0.0	0	0.0	0	0.0	0	0.0	0	0.0	0	0.0	0	0.0	1
Caucasian	189	87.1	93	83.0	282	85.7	0	0.0	105	82.0	89	87.3	88	88.9	0	0.0	282	85.7	97
Total	217	66.0	112	34.0	329	100.0	0	0.0	128	38.9	102	31.0	99	30.1	0	0.0	329		104

OHIO NORTHERN UNIVERSITY

GPA & LSAT Scores

	Full Time	Part Time	Total
# of apps	865	0	865
# admits	662	0	662
# of matrics	131	0	131
75% GPA	3.19	0.00	
25% GPA	2.47	0.00	
75% LSAT	152	0	
25% LSAT	143	0	

Tuition & Fees

	Resident	Non-resident
Full-Time	$18,980	$18,980
Part-Time	$0	$0

Living Expenses

Estimated living expenses for Singles		
Living on campus	Living off campus	Living at home
$7,450	$8,700	$4,020

Financial Aid

	Full-time		Part-time		Total	
	#	%	#	%	#	%
Total # of Students	329		0		329	
Total # receiving grants	122	37.1	0	0.0	122	37.1
Less than 1/2 tuition	80	24.3	0	0.0	80	24.3
Half to full tuition	42	12.8	0	0.0	42	12.8
Full tuition	0	0.0	0	0.0	0	0.0
More than full tuition	0	0.0	0	0.0	0	0.0
Median Grant Amount	$10,400		$0			

Informational & Library Resources

# of volumes & volume equivalents	263,747	# of professional staff	4
# of titles	72,794	Hours per week with professional staff	59
# of active serial subscriptions	3,245	Hours per week without professional staff	49
Study seating capacity inside the library	261	# of student computer work stations for entire law school	35
Square feet of law library	27,027	# of additional networked connections	0
Square feet of law school (excl. Library)	15,935	Require Laptop Computer?	N

Employment

	Total	%
Employment status known	91	81.2
Employment status unknown	21	18.7
Employed	69	75.8
Pursuing graduate degrees	6	6.6
Unemployed seeking employment	14	15.4
Unemployed not seeking employment	2	2.2
Type of Employment		
# employed in law firms	39	56.5
# employed in business & industry	6	8.7
# employed in government	12	17.4
# employed in public interest	3	4.3
# employed as judicial clerks	5	7.2
# employed in academia	1	1.4
Geographic Location		
# employed in state	25	36.2
# employed in foreign countries	0	0.0
# of states where employed	24	

J.D. Attrition (Prior Year)

	Academic	Other	TOTALS	
	#	#	#	%
1st Year	5	20	25	20%
2nd Year	3	1	4	3.6%
3rd Year	0	0	0	0.0%
4th Year	0	0	0	0.0%
TOTALS	8	21	29	8.5%

Bar Passage Rates

Jurisdiction	Ohio			Pennsylvania		
Exam	Sum 96	Win 97	Total	Sum 96	Win 97	Total
# from school taking bar for the first time	40	7	47	7	1	8
School's pass rate for all first-time takers	78%	57%	74%	86%	100%	88%
State's pass rate for all first-time takers	90%	90%	90%	75%	76%	75%

OHIO STATE UNIVERSITY

55 W. 12th Avenue
Columbus, OH 43210
(614)292-2631
http://www.acs.ohio-state.edu/units/law

ABA Approved Since 1923

The Basics

Type of School: Public   Term: Semester
Application deadline: 03/15
Application fee: $30
Financial Aid deadline: 03/01
Can first year start other than Fall? No
Student faculty ratio: 16.9 to 1
Does the University offer:
- housing restricted to law students? No
- graduate student housing for which law students are eligible? Yes

Faculty & Administrators

	Total		Men		Women		Minorities	
	Fall	Spr	Fall	Spr	Fall	Spr	Fall	Spr
Full-time	33	34	26	25	7	9	3	4
Other Full-Time	1	1	0	0	1	1	0	0
Deans, librarians, & others who teach > 1/2	2	2	0	0	2	2	0	0
Part-time	30	17	21	14	9	3	5	2
Total	66	54	47	39	19	15	8	6
Deans, librarians, & others who teach < 1/2	8	8	4	4	4	4	3	3

Curriculum

	Full time	Part time
Typical first-year section size	75	0
Is there typically a "small section" of the first year class, other than Legal Writing, taught by full-time faculty?	Yes	No
If yes, typical size offered last year	34	N/A
# of classroom course titles beyond 1st year curriculum	69	0
# of upper division courses, excluding seminars, with an enrollment:		
Under 25	37	0
25 - 49	17	0
50 - 74	26	0
75 - 99	5	0
100 +	3	0
# of seminars	30	0
# of seminar positions available	600	
# of seminar positions filled	371	0
# of positions available in simulation courses	180	
# of simulation positions filled	149	0
# of positions available in faculty supervised clinical courses	80	
# of fac. sup. clin. positions filled	73	0
# involved in field placements	69	0
# involved in law journals	134	0
# in moot court or trial competitions	175	0
# of credit hrs required to graduate	88	

J.D. Enrollment & Ethnicity

	Men		Women		Fl-Time		Pt-Time		1st Yr		2nd Yr		3rd Yr		4th Yr		Total		JD Degrees Awarded
	#	%	#	%	#	%	#	%	#	%	#	%	#	%	#	%	#	%	
African-American	20	5.3	32	10.8	50	7.5	2	50.0	12	5.7	20	8.7	20	8.7	0	0.0	52	7.7	18
American Indian	0	0.0	1	0.3	1	0.1	0	0.0	0	0.0	1	0.4	0	0.0	0	0.0	1	0.1	1
Asian American	21	5.6	19	6.4	40	6.0	0	0.0	17	8.1	15	6.5	8	3.5	0	0.0	40	6.0	11
Mexican American	0	0.0	0	0.0	0	0.0	0	0.0	0	0.0	0	0.0	0	0.0	0	0.0	0	0.0	0
Puerto Rican	0	0.0	0	0.0	0	0.0	0	0.0	0	0.0	0	0.0	0	0.0	0	0.0	0	0.0	0
Hispanic American	12	3.2	5	1.7	17	2.5	0	0.0	6	2.8	7	3.0	4	1.7	0	0.0	17	2.5	5
Total Minorities	53	14.1	57	19.2	108	16.2	2	50.0	35	16.6	43	18.7	32	13.9	0	0.0	110	16.4	35
Foreign Nationals	0	0.0	1	0.3	1	0.1	0	0.0	0	0.0	0	0.0	1	0.4	0	0.0	1	0.1	0
Caucasian	322	85.9	239	80.5	559	83.7	2	50.0	176	83.4	187	81.3	198	85.7	0	0.0	561	83.5	175
Total	375	55.8	297	44.2	668	99.4	4	0.6	211	31.4	230	34.2	231	34.4	0	0.0	672		210

OHIO STATE UNIVERSITY

GPA & LSAT Scores

	Full Time	Part Time	Total
# of apps	1,364	0	1,364
# admits	581	0	581
# of matrics	213	0	213
75% GPA	3.69	0.00	
25% GPA	3.23	0.00	
75% LSAT	161	0	
25% LSAT	153	0	

Tuition & Fees

	Resident	Non-resident
Full-Time	$7,022	$15,968
Part-Time	$0	$0

Living Expenses

Estimated living expenses for Singles		
Living on campus	Living off campus	Living at home
$9,569	$9,569	$6,380

Financial Aid

	Full-time		Part-time		Total	
	#	%	#	%	#	%
Total # of Students	668		4		672	
Total # receiving grants	431	64.5	0	0.0	431	64.1
Less than 1/2 tuition	421	63.0	0	0.0	421	62.6
Half to full tuition	3	0.4	0	0.0	3	0.4
Full tuition	4	0.6	0	0.0	4	0.6
More than full tuition	3	0.4	0	0.0	3	0.4
Median Grant Amount	$1,500		$0			

Informational & Library Resources

# of volumes & volume equivalents	653,399	# of professional staff	8
# of titles	153,771	Hours per week with professional staff	68
# of active serial subscriptions	7,722	Hours per week without professional staff	39
Study seating capacity inside the library	660	# of student computer work stations for entire law school	79
Square feet of law library	81,340	# of additional networked connections	0
Square feet of law school (excl. Library)	78,009	Require Laptop Computer?	N

Employment

	Total	%
Employment status known	213	97.3
Employment status unknown	6	2.7
Employed	191	89.7
Pursuing graduate degrees	3	1.4
Unemployed seeking employment	17	8.0
Unemployed not seeking employment	2	0.9
Type of Employment		
# employed in law firms	102	53.4
# employed in business & industry	20	10.5
# employed in government	33	17.3
# employed in public interest	6	3.1
# employed as judicial clerks	21	11.0
# employed in academia	4	2.1
Geographic Location		
# employed in state	139	72.8
# employed in foreign countries	1	0.5
# of states where employed	23	

J.D. Attrition (Prior Year)

	Academic	Other	TOTALS	
	#	#	#	%
1st Year	0	9	9	3.7%
2nd Year	0	2	2	0.9%
3rd Year	0	0	0	0.0%
4th Year	0	0	0	0.0%
TOTALS	0	11	11	1.6%

Bar Passage Rates

Jurisdiction	Ohio		
Exam	Sum 96	Win 97	Total
# from school taking bar for the first time	153	15	168
School's pass rate for all first-time takers	93%	93%	93%
State's pass rate for all first-time takers	90%	90%	90%

OKLAHOMA CITY UNIVERSITY

2501 North Blackwelder
Oklahoma City, OK 73106
(405)521-5354
http://www.okcu.edu/~law/home.htm

ABA
Approved
Since
1960

The Basics

Type of School: Private   Term: Semester
Application deadline: 07/15
Application fee: $35
Financial Aid deadline: 03/01
Can first year start other than Fall? No
Student faculty ratio: 18.2 to 1
Does the University offer:
- housing restricted to law students? No
- graduate student housing for which law students are eligible? No

Curriculum

	Full time	Part time
Typical first-year section size	75	50
Is there typically a "small section" of the first year class, other than Legal Writing, taught by full-time faculty?	No	No
If yes, typical size offered last year	N/A	N/A
# of classroom course titles beyond 1st year curriculum	68	53
# of upper division courses, excluding seminars, with an enrollment:		
Under 25	39	34
25 - 49	10	15
50 - 74	16	4
75 - 99	3	0
100 +	0	0
# of seminars	6	5
# of seminar positions available	187	
# of seminar positions filled	70	63
# of positions available in simulation courses	346	
# of simulation positions filled	162	112
# of positions available in faculty supervised clinical courses	58	
# of fac. sup. clin. positions filled	43	0
# involved in field placements	11	0
# involved in law journals	26	10
# in moot court or trial competitions	14	0
# of credit hrs required to graduate	90	

Faculty & Administrators

	Total		Men		Women		Minorities	
	Fall	Spr	Fall	Spr	Fall	Spr	Fall	Spr
Full-time	23	23	18	18	5	5	2	2
Other Full-Time	3	3	1	1	2	2	0	0
Deans, librarians, & others who teach > 1/2	5	5	2	2	3	3	1	1
Part-time	12	14	11	11	1	3	1	1
Total	43	45	32	32	11	13	4	4
Deans, librarians, & others who teach < 1/2	1	1	1	1	0	0	0	0

J.D. Enrollment & Ethnicity

	Men		Women		Fl-Time		Pt-Time		1st Yr		2nd Yr		3rd Yr		4th Yr		Total		JD Degrees Awarded
	#	%	#	%	#	%	#	%	#	%	#	%	#	%	#	%	#	%	
African-American	9	2.6	7	3.2	10	2.6	6	3.5	6	3.1	5	3.6	3	1.6	2	5.3	16	2.9	1
American Indian	16	4.7	18	8.3	25	6.4	9	5.3	10	5.2	11	8.0	10	5.3	3	7.9	34	6.1	9
Asian American	7	2.0	6	2.8	7	1.8	6	3.5	3	1.5	6	4.3	2	1.1	2	5.3	13	2.3	4
Mexican American	0	0.0	0	0.0	0	0.0	0	0.0	0	0.0	0	0.0	0	0.0	0	0.0	0	0.0	0
Puerto Rican	0	0.0	0	0.0	0	0.0	0	0.0	0	0.0	0	0.0	0	0.0	0	0.0	0	0.0	0
Hispanic American	11	3.2	8	3.7	17	4.4	2	1.2	10	5.2	3	2.2	5	2.6	1	2.6	19	3.4	1
Total Minorities	43	12.5	39	18.1	59	15.2	23	13.5	29	14.9	25	18.1	20	10.5	8	21.1	82	14.6	15
Foreign Nationals	1	0.3	0	0.0	1	0.3	0	0.0	0	0.0	1	0.7	0	0.0	0	0.0	1	0.2	0
Caucasian	300	87.2	177	81.9	329	84.6	148	86.5	165	85.1	112	81.2	170	89.5	30	78.9	477	85.2	155
Total	344	61.4	216	38.6	389	69.5	171	30.5	194	34.6	138	24.6	190	33.9	38	6.8	560		170

GPA & LSAT Scores

	Full Time	Part Time	Total
# of apps	757	136	893
# admits	513	102	615
# of matrics	149	41	190
75% GPA	3.23	3.28	
25% GPA	2.53	2.49	
75% LSAT	150	150	
25% LSAT	143	143	

Tuition & Fees

	Resident	Non-resident
Full-Time	$13,488	$13,488
Part-Time	$9,680	$9,680

Living Expenses

Estimated living expenses for Singles		
Living on campus	Living off campus	Living at home
$6,741	$9,094	$6,150

Financial Aid

	Full-time		Part-time		Total	
	#	%	#	%	#	%
Total # of Students	389		171		560	
Total # receiving grants	52	13.4	18	10.5	70	12.5
Less than 1/2 tuition	33	8.5	18	10.5	51	9.1
Half to full tuition	0	0.0	0	0.0	0	0.0
Full tuition	7	1.8	0	0.0	7	1.3
More than full tuition	12	3.1	0	0.0	12	2.1
Median Grant Amount	$5,000		$3,000			

Informational & Library Resources

# of volumes & volume equivalents	252,368	# of professional staff	7
# of titles	57,294	Hours per week with professional staff	96
# of active serial subscriptions	3,941	Hours per week without professional staff	6
Study seating capacity inside the library	364	# of student computer work stations for entire law school	8
Square feet of law library	36,802	# of additional networked connections	44
Square feet of law school (excl. Library)	67,650	Require Laptop Computer?	N

Employment

	Total	%
Employment status known	148	83.6
Employment status unknown	29	16.4
Employed	115	77.7
Pursuing graduate degrees	4	2.7
Unemployed seeking employment	29	19.6
Unemployed not seeking employment	0	0.0
Type of Employment		
# employed in law firms	89	77.4
# employed in business & industry	23	20.0
# employed in government	17	14.8
# employed in public interest	0	0.0
# employed as judicial clerks	1	0.9
# employed in academia	2	1.7
Geographic Location		
# employed in state	67	58.3
# employed in foreign countries	0	0.0
# of states where employed	21	

J.D. Attrition (Prior Year)

	Academic	Other	TOTALS	
	#	#	#	%
1st Year	19	19	38	21%
2nd Year	2	5	7	3.6%
3rd Year	0	2	2	0.9%
4th Year	0	0	0	0.0%
TOTALS	21	26	47	8.0%

Bar Passage Rates

Jurisdiction	Oklahoma			Texas		
Exam	Sum 96	Win 97	Total	Sum 96	Win 97	Total
# from school taking bar for the first time	73	23	96	19	3	22
School's pass rate for all first-time takers	86%	78%	84%	79%	100%	82%
State's pass rate for all first-time takers	84%	88%	85%	84%	81%	84%

OKLAHOMA, UNIVERSITY OF

300 Timberdell Road
Norman, OK 73019-5081
(405)325-4699
http://www.law.ou.edu

ABA Approved Since 1923

The Basics

Type of School: Public Term: Semester
Application deadline: 04/15
Application fee: $50
Financial Aid deadline: 03/01
Can first year start other than Fall? No
Student faculty ratio: 18.8 to 1
Does the University offer:
- housing restricted to law students? No
- graduate student housing for which law students are eligible? No

Faculty & Administrators

	Total		Men		Women		Minorities	
	Fall	Spr	Fall	Spr	Fall	Spr	Fall	Spr
Full-time	24	24	18	20	6	4	2	1
Other Full-Time	3	3	0	0	3	3	0	0
Deans, librarians, & others who teach > 1/2	4	4	3	3	1	1	0	0
Part-time	14	22	8	17	6	5	0	1
Total	45	53	29	40	16	13	2	2
Deans, librarians, & others who teach < 1/2	1	1	1	1	0	0	0	0

Curriculum

	Full time	Part time
Typical first-year section size	41	0
Is there typically a "small section" of the first year class, other than Legal Writing, taught by full-time faculty?	Yes	No
If yes, typical size offered last year	18	N/A
# of classroom course titles beyond 1st year curriculum	155	0
# of upper division courses, excluding seminars, with an enrollment:		
Under 25	81	0
25 - 49	35	0
50 - 74	22	0
75 - 99	3	0
100 +	0	0
# of seminars	14	0
# of seminar positions available	252	
# of seminar positions filled	232	0
# of positions available in simulation courses	190	
# of simulation positions filled	185	0
# of positions available in faculty supervised clinical courses	100	
# of fac. sup. clin. positions filled	70	0
# involved in field placements	129	0
# involved in law journals	65	0
# in moot court or trial competitions	25	0
# of credit hrs required to graduate	90	

J.D. Enrollment & Ethnicity

	Men		Women		Fl-Time		Pt-Time		1st Yr		2nd Yr		3rd Yr		4th Yr		Total		JD Degrees Awarded
	#	%	#	%	#	%	#	%	#	%	#	%	#	%	#	%	#	%	
African-American	4	1.4	11	4.2	15	2.8	0	0.0	9	4.3	1	0.6	5	2.9	0	0.0	15	2.8	3
American Indian	18	6.4	10	3.9	28	5.2	0	0.0	13	6.2	10	6.2	5	2.9	0	0.0	28	5.2	9
Asian American	8	2.8	10	3.9	18	3.3	0	0.0	7	3.3	6	3.7	5	2.9	0	0.0	18	3.3	9
Mexican American	2	0.7	9	3.5	11	2.0	0	0.0	0	0.0	5	3.1	6	3.5	0	0.0	11	2.0	5
Puerto Rican	0	0.0	0	0.0	0	0.0	0	0.0	0	0.0	0	0.0	0	0.0	0	0.0	0	0.0	0
Hispanic American	7	2.5	2	0.8	9	1.7	0	0.0	8	3.8	0	0.0	1	0.6	0	0.0	9	1.7	0
Total Minorities	39	13.8	42	16.2	81	14.9	0	0.0	37	17.7	22	13.6	22	12.9	0	0.0	81	14.9	26
Foreign Nationals	1	0.4	0	0.0	1	0.2	0	0.0	0	0.0	0	0.0	1	0.6	0	0.0	1	0.2	0
Caucasian	243	85.9	217	83.8	460	84.9	0	0.0	172	82.3	140	86.4	148	86.5	0	0.0	460	84.9	175
Total	283	52.2	259	47.8	542	100.0	0	0.0	209	38.6	162	29.9	171	31.5	0	0.0	542		201

GPA & LSAT Scores

	Full Time	Part Time	Total
# of apps	640	0	640
# admits	377	0	377
# of matrics	210	0	210
75% GPA	3.51	0.00	
25% GPA	3.01	0.00	
75% LSAT	156	0	
25% LSAT	149	0	

Tuition & Fees

	Resident	Non-resident
Full-Time	$4,492	$13,260
Part-Time	$0	$0

Living Expenses

Estimated living expenses for Singles		
Living on campus	Living off campus	Living at home
$9,294	$10,932	$7,494

Employment

	Total	%
Employment status known	220	98.7
Employment status unknown	3	1.3
Employed	185	84.1
Pursuing graduate degrees	0	0.0
Unemployed seeking employment	35	15.9
Unemployed not seeking employment	0	0.0
Type of Employment		
# employed in law firms	152	82.2
# employed in business & industry	9	4.9
# employed in government	17	9.2
# employed in public interest	1	0.5
# employed as judicial clerks	4	2.2
# employed in academia	0	0.0
Geographic Location		
# employed in state	132	71.4
# employed in foreign countries	1	0.5
# of states where employed	9	

Financial Aid

	Full-time		Part-time		Total	
	#	%	#	%	#	%
Total # of Students	542		0		542	
Total # receiving grants	271	50.0	0	0.0	271	50.0
Less than 1/2 tuition	203	37.5	0	0.0	203	37.5
Half to full tuition	60	11.1	0	0.0	60	11.1
Full tuition	0	0.0	0	0.0	0	0.0
More than full tuition	8	1.5	0	0.0	8	1.5
Median Grant Amount	$3,775		$0			

Informational & Library Resources

# of volumes & volume equivalents	302,738	# of professional staff	7
# of titles	133,017	Hours per week with professional staff	54
# of active serial subscriptions	3,977	Hours per week without professional staff	44
Study seating capacity inside the library	375	# of student computer work stations for entire law school	49
Square feet of law library	28,733	# of additional networked connections	0
Square feet of law school (excl. Library)	58,063	Require Laptop Computer?	N

J.D. Attrition (Prior Year)

	Academic	Other	TOTALS	
	#	#	#	%
1st Year	0	6	6	3.6%
2nd Year	2	12	14	8.5%
3rd Year	1	0	1	0.5%
4th Year	0	0	0	0.0%
TOTALS	3	18	21	3.9%

Bar Passage Rates

Jurisdiction	Oklahoma		
Exam	Sum 96	Win 97	Total
# from school taking bar for the first time	130	25	155
School's pass rate for all first-time takers	90%	88%	90%
State's pass rate for all first-time takers	84%	88%	85%

OREGON, UNIVERSITY OF

1221 University of Oregon
Eugene, OR 97403-1221
(541)346-3852
http://www.law.uoregon.edu

ABA Approved Since 1923

The Basics

Type of School: Public Term: Semester

Application deadline: 04/01

Application fee: $50

Financial Aid deadline: 03/01

Can first year start other than Fall? No

Student faculty ratio: 16.8 to 1

Does the University offer:
- housing restricted to law students? No
- graduate student housing for which law students are eligible? No

Faculty & Administrators

	Total		Men		Women		Minorities	
	Fall	Spr	Fall	Spr	Fall	Spr	Fall	Spr
Full-time	26	24	16	14	10	10	4	4
Other Full-Time	4	4	2	2	2	2	0	0
Deans, librarians, & others who teach > 1/2	1	1	1	1	0	0	1	1
Part-time	7	9	6	7	1	2	0	1
Total	38	38	25	24	13	14	5	6
Deans, librarians, & others who teach < 1/2	1	0	1	0	0	0	1	0

Curriculum

	Full time	Part time
Typical first-year section size	53	0
Is there typically a "small section" of the first year class, other than Legal Writing, taught by full-time faculty?	No	No
If yes, typical size offered last year	N/A	N/A
# of classroom course titles beyond 1st year curriculum	85	0
# of upper division courses, excluding seminars, with an enrollment:		
Under 25	23	0
25 - 49	19	0
50 - 74	15	0
75 - 99	5	0
100 +	1	0
# of seminars	10	0
# of seminar positions available	191	
# of seminar positions filled	140	0
# of positions available in simulation courses	221	
# of simulation positions filled	113	0
# of positions available in faculty supervised clinical courses	169	
# of fac. sup. clin. positions filled	123	0
# involved in field placements	16	0
# involved in law journals	118	0
# in moot court or trial competitions	124	0
# of credit hrs required to graduate	85	

J.D. Enrollment & Ethnicity

	Men		Women		Fl-Time		Pt-Time		1st Yr		2nd Yr		3rd Yr		4th Yr		Total		JD Degrees Awarded
	#	%	#	%	#	%	#	%	#	%	#	%	#	%	#	%	#	%	
African-American	9	3.3	4	1.6	13	2.5	0	0.0	3	1.5	5	3.2	5	2.9	0	0.0	13	2.5	4
American Indian	1	0.4	2	0.8	3	0.6	0	0.0	0	0.0	2	1.3	1	0.6	0	0.0	3	0.6	1
Asian American	17	6.3	18	7.1	35	6.7	0	0.0	11	5.7	7	4.5	17	9.8	0	0.0	35	6.7	11
Mexican American	5	1.8	6	2.4	11	2.1	0	0.0	3	1.5	5	3.2	3	1.7	0	0.0	11	2.1	1
Puerto Rican	1	0.4	2	0.8	3	0.6	0	0.0	0	0.0	1	0.6	2	1.2	0	0.0	3	0.6	1
Hispanic American	4	1.5	5	2.0	9	1.7	0	0.0	4	2.1	2	1.3	3	1.7	0	0.0	9	1.7	2
Total Minorities	37	13.7	37	14.6	74	14.1	0	0.0	21	10.8	22	14.0	31	17.9	0	0.0	74	14.1	20
Foreign Nationals	5	1.8	4	1.6	9	1.7	0	0.0	1	0.5	4	2.5	4	2.3	0	0.0	9	1.7	3
Caucasian	229	84.5	212	83.8	441	84.2	0	0.0	172	88.7	131	83.4	138	79.8	0	0.0	441	84.2	134
Total	271	51.7	253	48.3	524	100.0	0	0.0	194	37.0	157	30.0	173	33.0	0	0.0	524		157

GPA & LSAT Scores

	Full Time	Part Time	Total
# of apps	1,035	0	1,035
# admits	602	0	602
# of matrics	194	0	194
75% GPA	3.58	0.00	
25% GPA	3.16	0.00	
75% LSAT	159	0	
25% LSAT	152	0	

Tuition & Fees

	Resident	Non-resident
Full-Time	$10,004	$13,642
Part-Time	$0	$0

Living Expenses

Estimated living expenses for Singles		
Living on campus	Living off campus	Living at home
$7,032	$7,515	$4,185

Financial Aid

	Full-time		Part-time		Total	
	#	%	#	%	#	%
Total # of Students	524		0		524	
Total # receiving grants	220	42.0	0	0.0	220	42.0
Less than 1/2 tuition	205	39.1	0	0.0	205	39.1
Half to full tuition	15	2.9	0	0.0	15	2.9
Full tuition	0	0.0	0	0.0	0	0.0
More than full tuition	0	0.0	0	0.0	0	0.0
Median Grant Amount	$2,231		$0			

Informational & Library Resources

# of volumes & volume equivalents	346,596	# of professional staff	6
# of titles	45,198	Hours per week with professional staff	67
# of active serial subscriptions	3,314	Hours per week without professional staff	43
Study seating capacity inside the library	227	# of student computer work stations for entire law school	53
Square feet of law library	24,714	# of additional networked connections	92
Square feet of law school (excl. Library)	32,685	Require Laptop Computer?	Y

Employment

	Total	%
Employment status known	127	94.8
Employment status unknown	7	5.2
Employed	109	85.8
Pursuing graduate degrees	6	4.7
Unemployed seeking employment	7	5.5
Unemployed not seeking employment	5	3.9
Type of Employment		
# employed in law firms	54	49.5
# employed in business & industry	8	7.3
# employed in government	13	11.9
# employed in public interest	6	5.5
# employed as judicial clerks	24	22.0
# employed in academia	4	3.7
Geographic Location		
# employed in state	73	67.0
# employed in foreign countries	2	1.8
# of states where employed	14	

J.D. Attrition (Prior Year)

	Academic	Other	TOTALS	
	#	#	#	%
1st Year	0	2	2	1.2%
2nd Year	0	7	7	3.9%
3rd Year	0	0	0	0.0%
4th Year	0	0	0	0.0%
TOTALS	0	9	9	1.8%

Bar Passage Rates

Jurisdiction	Oregon		
Exam	Sum 96	Win 97	Total
# from school taking bar for the first time	81	9	90
School's pass rate for all first-time takers	74%	67%	73%
State's pass rate for all first-time takers	77%	74%	77%

PACE UNIVERSITY

78 North Broadway
White Plains, NY 10603
(914)422-4210
http://www.law.pace.edu

ABA Approved Since 1978

The Basics

Type of School: Private
Term: Semester
Application deadline: 02/15
Application fee: $55
Financial Aid deadline: 02/01
Can first year start other than Fall? No
Student faculty ratio: 16.2 to 1
Does the University offer:
- housing restricted to law students? No
- graduate student housing for which law students are eligible? Yes

Faculty & Administrators

	Total		Men		Women		Minorities	
	Fall	Spr	Fall	Spr	Fall	Spr	Fall	Spr
Full-time	36	34	23	22	13	12	3	3
Other Full-Time	0	0	0	0	0	0	0	0
Deans, librarians, & others who teach > 1/2	2	2	1	1	1	1	0	0
Part-time	36	48	20	35	16	13	1	1
Total	74	84	44	58	30	26	4	4
Deans, librarians, & others who teach < 1/2	4	4	3	3	1	1	0	0

Curriculum

	Full time	Part time
Typical first-year section size	80	78
Is there typically a "small section" of the first year class, other than Legal Writing, taught by full-time faculty?	Yes	Yes
If yes, typical size offered last year	20	20
# of classroom course titles beyond 1st year curriculum	94	95
# of upper division courses, excluding seminars, with an enrollment:		
Under 25	53	50
25 - 49	18	23
50 - 74	8	10
75 - 99	6	1
100 +	1	2
# of seminars	19	11
# of seminar positions available	347	
# of seminar positions filled	144	139
# of positions available in simulation courses	214	
# of simulation positions filled	63	130
# of positions available in faculty supervised clinical courses	60	
# of fac. sup. clin. positions filled	41	9
# involved in field placements	61	40
# involved in law journals	134	27
# in moot court or trial competitions	118	40
# of credit hrs required to graduate	90	

J.D. Enrollment & Ethnicity

	Men		Women		Fl-Time		Pt-Time		1st Yr		2nd Yr		3rd Yr		4th Yr		Total		JD Degrees Awarded
	#	%	#	%	#	%	#	%	#	%	#	%	#	%	#	%	#	%	
African-American	21	5.4	27	6.6	18	3.6	30	9.7	21	8.1	12	5.5	8	3.4	7	7.6	48	6.0	14
American Indian	0	0.0	1	0.2	1	0.2	0	0.0	0	0.0	0	0.0	1	0.4	0	0.0	1	0.1	1
Asian American	13	3.3	21	5.1	28	5.7	6	1.9	13	5.0	8	3.7	12	5.1	1	1.1	34	4.2	10
Mexican American	1	0.3	0	0.0	1	0.2	0	0.0	1	0.4	0	0.0	0	0.0	0	0.0	1	0.1	0
Puerto Rican	9	2.3	11	2.7	13	2.6	7	2.3	9	3.5	2	0.9	6	2.6	3	3.3	20	2.5	4
Hispanic American	14	3.6	17	4.1	19	3.8	12	3.9	12	4.6	8	3.7	8	3.4	3	3.3	31	3.9	6
Total Minorities	58	14.8	77	18.7	80	16.2	55	17.7	56	21.6	30	13.8	35	14.9	14	15.2	135	16.8	35
Foreign Nationals	4	1.0	3	0.7	7	1.4	0	0.0	0	0.0	5	2.3	2	0.9	0	0.0	7	0.9	0
Caucasian	330	84.2	332	80.6	407	82.4	255	82.3	203	78.4	183	83.9	198	84.3	78	84.8	662	82.3	187
Total	392	48.8	412	51.2	494	61.4	310	38.6	259	32.2	218	27.1	235	29.2	92	11.4	804		222

GPA & LSAT Scores

	Full Time	Part Time	Total
# of apps	1,333	374	1,707
# admits	672	184	856
# of matrics	181	103	284
75% GPA	3.36	3.15	
25% GPA	2.83	2.65	
75% LSAT	155	154	
25% LSAT	147	147	

Tuition & Fees

	Resident	Non-resident
Full-Time	$20,640	$20,640
Part-Time	$15,490	$15,490

Living Expenses

Estimated living expenses for Singles		
Living on campus	Living off campus	Living at home
$9,760	$13,210	$5,480

Employment

	Total	%
Employment status known	184	83.3
Employment status unknown	37	16.7
Employed	164	89.1
Pursuing graduate degrees	1	0.5
Unemployed seeking employment	14	7.6
Unemployed not seeking employment	5	2.7
Type of Employment		
# employed in law firms	92	56.1
# employed in business & industry	37	22.6
# employed in government	20	12.2
# employed in public interest	1	0.6
# employed as judicial clerks	7	4.3
# employed in academia	1	0.6
Geographic Location		
# employed in state	97	59.1
# employed in foreign countries	1	0.6
# of states where employed	14	

Financial Aid

	Full-time		Part-time		Total	
	#	%	#	%	#	%
Total # of Students	494		310		804	
Total # receiving grants	165	33.4	68	21.9	233	29.0
Less than 1/2 tuition	135	27.3	50	16.1	185	23.0
Half to full tuition	24	4.9	18	5.8	42	5.2
Full tuition	1	0.2	0	0.0	1	0.1
More than full tuition	5	1.0	0	0.0	5	0.6
Median Grant Amount	$3,000		$5,000			

Informational & Library Resources

# of volumes & volume equivalents	323,237	# of professional staff	11
# of titles	124,147	Hours per week with professional staff	76
# of active serial subscriptions	3,773	Hours per week without professional staff	26
Study seating capacity inside the library	346	# of student computer work stations for entire law school	88
Square feet of law library	34,646	# of additional networked connections	220
Square feet of law school (excl. Library)	114,697	Require Laptop Computer?	N

J.D. Attrition (Prior Year)

	Academic	Other	TOTALS	
	#	#	#	%
1st Year	3	17	20	8.5%
2nd Year	2	13	15	5.6%
3rd Year	0	4	4	1.8%
4th Year	0	0	0	0.0%
TOTALS	5	34	39	4.9%

Bar Passage Rates

Jurisdiction	New York		
Exam	Sum 96	Win 97	Total
# from school taking bar for the first time	150	20	170
School's pass rate for all first-time takers	70%	70%	70%
State's pass rate for all first-time takers	78%	67%	77%

PENNSYLVANIA STATE UNIVERSITY

Dickinson School of Law
150 S. College Street
Carlisle, PA 17013-2899
(717)240-5000
http://www.dsl.edu

ABA Approved Since 1931

The Basics

Type of School: Public Term: Semester
Application deadline: 03/01
Application fee: $50
Financial Aid deadline: 02/15
Can first year start other than Fall? No
Student faculty ratio: 26.3 to 1
Does the University offer:
- housing restricted to law students? Yes
- graduate student housing for which law students are eligible? No

Faculty & Administrators

	Total		Men		Women		Minorities	
	Fall	Spr	Fall	Spr	Fall	Spr	Fall	Spr
Full-time	16	15	12	11	4	4	1	1
Other Full-Time	4	4	3	3	1	1	0	0
Deans, librarians, & others who teach > 1/2	6	6	5	5	1	1	1	1
Part-time	43	24	37	18	6	6	0	0
Total	69	49	57	37	12	12	2	2
Deans, librarians, & others who teach < 1/2	0	0	0	0	0	0	0	0

Curriculum

	Full time	Part time
Typical first-year section size	60	0
Is there typically a "small section" of the first year class, other than Legal Writing, taught by full-time faculty?	Yes	No
If yes, typical size offered last year	42	N/A
# of classroom course titles beyond 1st year curriculum	101	0
# of upper division courses, excluding seminars, with an enrollment:		
Under 25	49	0
25 - 49	39	0
50 - 74	11	0
75 - 99	11	0
100 +	0	0
# of seminars	20	0
# of seminar positions available	408	
# of seminar positions filled	319	0
# of positions available in simulation courses	627	
# of simulation positions filled	519	0
# of positions available in faculty supervised clinical courses	57	
# of fac. sup. clin. positions filled	57	0
# involved in field placements	84	0
# involved in law journals	117	0
# in moot court or trial competitions	42	0
# of credit hrs required to graduate	88	

J.D. Enrollment & Ethnicity

	Men		Women		Fl-Time		Pt-Time		1st Yr		2nd Yr		3rd Yr		4th Yr		Total		JD Degrees Awarded
	#	%	#	%	#	%	#	%	#	%	#	%	#	%	#	%	#	%	
African-American	5	1.7	11	5.3	16	3.2	0	0.0	7	4.0	8	4.7	1	0.6	0	0.0	16	3.2	5
American Indian	1	0.3	2	1.0	3	0.6	0	0.0	0	0.0	2	1.2	1	0.6	0	0.0	3	0.6	0
Asian American	5	1.7	8	3.8	13	2.6	0	0.0	6	3.4	2	1.2	5	3.1	0	0.0	13	2.6	5
Mexican American	0	0.0	0	0.0	0	0.0	0	0.0	0	0.0	0	0.0	0	0.0	0	0.0	0	0.0	0
Puerto Rican	0	0.0	0	0.0	0	0.0	0	0.0	0	0.0	0	0.0	0	0.0	0	0.0	0	0.0	0
Hispanic American	6	2.0	5	2.4	11	2.2	0	0.0	3	1.7	5	2.9	3	1.9	0	0.0	11	2.2	8
Total Minorities	17	5.7	26	12.4	43	8.5	0	0.0	16	9.0	17	9.9	10	6.3	0	0.0	43	8.5	18
Foreign Nationals	0	0.0	0	0.0	0	0.0	0	0.0	0	0.0	0	0.0	0	0.0	0	0.0	0	0.0	0
Caucasian	281	94.3	183	87.6	460	91.5	4	100.0	161	91.0	154	90.1	149	93.7	0	0.0	464	91.5	164
Total	298	58.8	209	41.2	503	99.2	4	0.8	177	34.9	171	33.7	159	31.4	0	0.0	507		182

PENNSYLVANIA STATE UNIVERSITY

GPA & LSAT Scores

	Full Time	Part Time	Total
# of apps	1,054	0	1,054
# admits	560	0	560
# of matrics	176	0	176
75% GPA	3.45	0.00	
25% GPA	2.86	0.00	
75% LSAT	157	0	
25% LSAT	152	0	

Tuition & Fees

	Resident	Non-resident
Full-Time	$14,600	$14,600
Part-Time	$0	$0

Living Expenses

Estimated living expenses for Singles		
Living on campus	Living off campus	Living at home
$9,955	$12,155	$10,055

Employment

	Total	%
Employment status known	153	94.4
Employment status unknown	9	5.6
Employed	140	91.5
Pursuing graduate degrees	3	2.0
Unemployed seeking employment	8	5.2
Unemployed not seeking employment	2	1.3
Type of Employment		
# employed in law firms	68	48.6
# employed in business & industry	3	2.1
# employed in government	23	16.4
# employed in public interest	2	1.4
# employed as judicial clerks	28	20.0
# employed in academia	0	0.0
Geographic Location		
# employed in state	93	66.4
# employed in foreign countries	0	0.0
# of states where employed	13	

Financial Aid

	Full-time		Part-time		Total	
	#	%	#	%	#	%
Total # of Students	503		4		507	
Total # receiving grants	169	33.6	1	25.0	170	33.5
Less than 1/2 tuition	137	27.2	1	25.0	138	27.2
Half to full tuition	22	4.4	0	0.0	22	4.3
Full tuition	9	1.8	0	0.0	9	1.8
More than full tuition	1	0.2	0	0.0	1	0.2
Median Grant Amount	$4,528		$7,653			

Informational & Library Resources

# of volumes & volume equivalents	394,228	# of professional staff	7
# of titles	80,808	Hours per week with professional staff	81
# of active serial subscriptions	3,578	Hours per week without professional staff	5
Study seating capacity inside the library	444	# of student computer work stations for entire law school	59
Square feet of law library	33,134	# of additional networked connections	82
Square feet of law school (excl. Library)	41,550	Require Laptop Computer?	N

J.D. Attrition (Prior Year)

	Academic	Other	TOTALS	
	#	#	#	%
1st Year	4	6	10	5.7%
2nd Year	2	1	3	1.8%
3rd Year	0	1	1	0.6%
4th Year	0	0	0	0.0%
TOTALS	6	8	14	2.7%

Bar Passage Rates

Jurisdiction	Pennsylvania		
Exam	Sum 96	Win 97	Total
# from school taking bar for the first time	124	8	132
School's pass rate for all first-time takers	89%	75%	88%
State's pass rate for all first-time takers	75%	76%	75%

PENNSYLVANIA, UNIVERSITY OF

3400 Chestnut Street
Philadelphia, PA 19104-6204
(215)898-7483
http://www.law.upenn.edu

ABA Approved Since 1923

The Basics

Type of School: Private — Term: Semester
Application deadline: 03/01
Application fee: $65
Financial Aid deadline: 03/01
Can first year start other than Fall? No
Student faculty ratio: 17.7 to 1
Does the University offer:
- housing restricted to law students? Yes
- graduate student housing for which law students are eligible? Yes

Faculty & Administrators

	Total		Men		Women		Minorities	
	Fall	Spr	Fall	Spr	Fall	Spr	Fall	Spr
Full-time	34	36	28	29	6	7	3	3
Other Full-Time	4	4	0	0	4	4	0	0
Deans, librarians, & others who teach > 1/2	2	2	2	2	0	0	0	0
Part-time	32	36	24	25	8	11	6	8
Total	72	78	54	56	18	22	9	11
Deans, librarians, & others who teach < 1/2	0	0	0	0	0	0	0	0

Curriculum

	Full time	Part time
Typical first-year section size	116	0
Is there typically a "small section" of the first year class, other than Legal Writing, taught by full-time faculty?	Yes	No
If yes, typical size offered last year	58	N/A
# of classroom course titles beyond 1st year curriculum	73	0
# of upper division courses, excluding seminars, with an enrollment:		
Under 25	30	0
25 - 49	34	0
50 - 74	14	0
75 - 99	7	0
100 +	8	0
# of seminars	33	0
# of seminar positions available	579	
# of seminar positions filled	516	0
# of positions available in simulation courses	304	
# of simulation positions filled	286	0
# of positions available in faculty supervised clinical courses	120	
# of fac. sup. clin. positions filled	95	0
# involved in field placements	15	0
# involved in law journals	184	0
# in moot court or trial competitions	143	0
# of credit hrs required to graduate	89	

J.D. Enrollment & Ethnicity

	Men		Women		Fl-Time		Pt-Time		1st Yr		2nd Yr		3rd Yr		4th Yr		Total		JD Degrees Awarded
	#	%	#	%	#	%	#	%	#	%	#	%	#	%	#	%	#	%	
African-American	34	8.1	31	10.3	65	9.0	0	0.0	26	11.2	24	8.8	15	6.9	0	0.0	65	9.0	32
American Indian	2	0.5	1	0.3	3	0.4	0	0.0	0	0.0	3	1.1	0	0.0	0	0.0	3	0.4	1
Asian American	21	5.0	37	12.3	58	8.0	0	0.0	16	6.9	24	8.8	18	8.3	0	0.0	58	8.0	20
Mexican American	4	1.0	2	0.7	6	0.8	0	0.0	0	0.0	2	0.7	4	1.9	0	0.0	6	0.8	2
Puerto Rican	8	1.9	4	1.3	12	1.7	0	0.0	4	1.7	5	1.8	3	1.4	0	0.0	12	1.7	5
Hispanic American	23	5.5	15	5.0	38	5.3	0	0.0	11	4.7	13	4.8	14	6.5	0	0.0	38	5.3	13
Total Minorities	92	21.9	90	29.9	182	25.2	0	0.0	57	24.5	71	26.1	54	25.0	0	0.0	182	25.2	73
Foreign Nationals	9	2.1	12	4.0	21	2.9	0	0.0	6	2.6	11	4.0	4	1.9	0	0.0	21	2.9	7
Caucasian	319	76.0	199	66.1	518	71.8	0	0.0	170	73.0	190	69.9	158	73.1	0	0.0	518	71.8	212
Total	420	58.3	301	41.7	721	100.0	0	0.0	233	32.3	272	37.7	216	30.0	0	0.0	721		292

GPA & LSAT Scores

	Full Time	Part Time	Total
# of apps	3,844	0	3,844
# admits	1,141	0	1,141
# of matrics	230	0	230
75% GPA	3.73	0.00	
25% GPA	3.39	0.00	
75% LSAT	167	0	
25% LSAT	163	0	

Tuition & Fees

	Resident	Non-resident
Full-Time	$24,530	$24,530
Part-Time	$0	$0

Living Expenses

Estimated living expenses for Singles		
Living on campus	Living off campus	Living at home
$12,000	$12,000	$6,770

Financial Aid

	Full-time		Part-time		Total	
	#	%	#	%	#	%
Total # of Students	721		0		721	
Total # receiving grants	240	33.3	0	0.0	240	33.3
Less than 1/2 tuition	180	25.0	0	0.0	180	25.0
Half to full tuition	52	7.2	0	0.0	52	7.2
Full tuition	6	0.8	0	0.0	6	0.8
More than full tuition	2	0.3	0	0.0	2	0.3
Median Grant Amount	$7,850		$0			

Informational & Library Resources

# of volumes & volume equivalents	639,660	# of professional staff	12
# of titles	166,071	Hours per week with professional staff	76
# of active serial subscriptions	7,311	Hours per week without professional staff	35
Study seating capacity inside the library	550	# of student computer work stations for entire law school	130
Square feet of law library	72,000	# of additional networked connections	1006
Square feet of law school (excl. Library)	76,800	Require Laptop Computer?	N

Employment

	Total	%
Employment status known	214	98.2
Employment status unknown	4	1.8
Employed	206	96.3
Pursuing graduate degrees	2	0.9
Unemployed seeking employment	3	1.4
Unemployed not seeking employment	3	1.4
Type of Employment		
# employed in law firms	149	72.3
# employed in business & industry	12	5.8
# employed in government	3	1.5
# employed in public interest	5	2.4
# employed as judicial clerks	34	16.5
# employed in academia	0	0.0
Geographic Location		
# employed in state	52	25.2
# employed in foreign countries	2	1.0
# of states where employed	20	

J.D. Attrition (Prior Year)

	Academic	Other	TOTALS	
	#	#	#	%
1st Year	0	0	0	0.0%
2nd Year	0	16	16	7.2%
3rd Year	0	0	0	0.0%
4th Year	0	0	0	0.0%
TOTALS	0	16	16	2.0%

Bar Passage Rates

Jurisdiction	New York			Pennsylvania		
Exam	Sum 96	Win 97	Total	Sum 96	Win 97	Total
# from school taking bar for the first time	89	8	97	67	3	70
School's pass rate for all first-time takers	93%	88%	93%	93%	100%	93%
State's pass rate for all first-time takers	78%	67%	77%	75%	76%	75%

PEPPERDINE UNIVERSITY

24255 Pacific Coast Highway
Malibu, CA 90263
(310)456-4611
http://law.pepperdine.edu

ABA Approved Since 1972

The Basics

Type of School: Private   Term: Semester
Application deadline: 03/01
Application fee: $50
Financial Aid deadline: 05/01
Can first year start other than Fall? No
Student faculty ratio: 18.8 to 1
Does the University offer:
- housing restricted to law students? No
- graduate student housing for which law students are eligible? Yes

Faculty & Administrators

	Total		Men		Women		Minorities	
	Fall	Spr	Fall	Spr	Fall	Spr	Fall	Spr
Full-time	28	28	23	23	5	5	4	4
Other Full-Time	0	0	0	0	0	0	0	0
Deans, librarians, & others who teach > 1/2	1	1	1	1	0	0	0	0
Part-time	22	24	14	18	8	6	0	2
Total	51	53	38	42	13	11	4	6
Deans, librarians, & others who teach < 1/2	8	8	5	5	3	3	1	1

Curriculum

	Full time	Part time
Typical first-year section size	80	0
Is there typically a "small section" of the first year class, other than Legal Writing, taught by full-time faculty?	No	No
If yes, typical size offered last year	N/A	N/A
# of classroom course titles beyond 1st year curriculum	94	0
# of upper division courses, excluding seminars, with an enrollment:		
Under 25	75	0
25 - 49	21	0
50 - 74	14	0
75 - 99	9	0
100 +	10	0
# of seminars	29	0
# of seminar positions available	604	
# of seminar positions filled	469	0
# of positions available in simulation courses	852	
# of simulation positions filled	745	0
# of positions available in faculty supervised clinical courses	33	
# of fac. sup. clin. positions filled	27	0
# involved in field placements	244	0
# involved in law journals	79	0
# in moot court or trial competitions	281	0
# of credit hrs required to graduate	88	

J.D. Enrollment & Ethnicity

	Men		Women		Fl-Time		Pt-Time		1st Yr		2nd Yr		3rd Yr		4th Yr		Total		JD Degrees Awarded
	#	%	#	%	#	%	#	%	#	%	#	%	#	%	#	%	#	%	
African-American	13	3.6	15	5.1	28	4.3	0	0.0	15	6.3	8	4.0	5	2.3	0	0.0	28	4.3	4
American Indian	5	1.4	2	0.7	7	1.1	0	0.0	1	0.4	2	1.0	4	1.8	0	0.0	7	1.1	2
Asian American	25	6.9	24	8.2	49	7.5	0	0.0	9	3.8	20	10.1	20	9.1	0	0.0	49	7.5	11
Mexican American	14	3.9	11	3.7	25	3.8	0	0.0	7	2.9	10	5.1	8	3.7	0	0.0	25	3.8	5
Puerto Rican	0	0.0	0	0.0	0	0.0	0	0.0	0	0.0	0	0.0	0	0.0	0	0.0	0	0.0	0
Hispanic American	0	0.0	0	0.0	0	0.0	0	0.0	0	0.0	0	0.0	0	0.0	0	0.0	0	0.0	0
Total Minorities	57	15.7	52	17.7	109	16.6	0	0.0	32	13.3	40	20.2	37	16.9	0	0.0	109	16.6	22
Foreign Nationals	0	0.0	0	0.0	0	0.0	0	0.0	0	0.0	0	0.0	0	0.0	0	0.0	0	0.0	0
Caucasian	306	84.3	242	82.3	548	83.4	0	0.0	208	86.7	158	79.8	182	83.1	0	0.0	548	83.4	234
Total	363	55.3	294	44.7	657	100.0	0	0.0	240	36.5	198	30.1	219	33.3	0	0.0	657		256

GPA & LSAT Scores

	Full Time	Part Time	Total
# of apps	2,265	0	2,265
# admits	1,043	0	1,043
# of matrics	243	0	243
75% GPA	3.51	0.00	
25% GPA	3.02	0.00	
75% LSAT	159	0	
25% LSAT	153	0	

Tuition & Fees

	Resident	Non-resident
Full-Time	$21,900	$21,900
Part-Time	$0	$0

Living Expenses

Estimated living expenses for Singles

Living on campus	Living off campus	Living at home
$15,234	$15,234	$15,234

Financial Aid

	Full-time		Part-time		Total	
	#	%	#	%	#	%
Total # of Students	657		0		657	
Total # receiving grants	525	79.9	0	0.0	525	79.9
Less than 1/2 tuition	405	61.6	0	0.0	405	61.6
Half to full tuition	85	12.9	0	0.0	85	12.9
Full tuition	2	0.3	0	0.0	2	0.3
More than full tuition	33	5.0	0	0.0	33	5.0
Median Grant Amount	$8,450		$0			

Informational & Library Resources

# of volumes & volume equivalents	264,673	# of professional staff	6
# of titles	110,220	Hours per week with professional staff	74
# of active serial subscriptions	3,551	Hours per week without professional staff	35
Study seating capacity inside the library	500	# of student computer work stations for entire law school	52
Square feet of law library	40,915	# of additional networked connections	0
Square feet of law school (excl. Library)	81,190	Require Laptop Computer?	N

Employment

	Total	%
Employment status known	142	67.6
Employment status unknown	68	32.4
Employed	104	73.2
Pursuing graduate degrees	6	4.2
Unemployed seeking employment	32	22.5
Unemployed not seeking employment	0	0.0
Type of Employment		
# employed in law firms	61	58.7
# employed in business & industry	24	23.1
# employed in government	14	13.5
# employed in public interest	0	0.0
# employed as judicial clerks	5	4.8
# employed in academia	0	0.0
Geographic Location		
# employed in state	70	67.3
# employed in foreign countries	0	0.0
# of states where employed	17	

J.D. Attrition (Prior Year)

	Academic	Other	TOTALS	
	#	#	#	%
1st Year	6	4	10	4.9%
2nd Year	0	0	0	0.0%
3rd Year	0	0	0	0.0%
4th Year	0	0	0	0.0%
TOTALS	6	4	10	1.5%

Bar Passage Rates

Jurisdiction	California		
Exam	Sum 96	Win 97	Total
# from school taking bar for the first time	146	17	163
School's pass rate for all first-time takers	73%	59%	72%
State's pass rate for all first-time takers	69%	62%	67%

PITTSBURGH, UNIVERSITY OF

3900 Forbes Avenue
Pittsburgh, PA 15260
(412)648-1400
http://www.law.pitt.edu

ABA Approved Since 1923

The Basics

Type of School: Public   Term: Semester

Application deadline: 03/01

Application fee: $40

Financial Aid deadline: 03/01

Can first year start other than Fall? No

Student faculty ratio: 22.2 to 1

Does the University offer:
- housing restricted to law students? No
- graduate student housing for which law students are eligible? No

Faculty & Administrators

	Total		Men		Women		Minorities	
	Fall	Spr	Fall	Spr	Fall	Spr	Fall	Spr
Full-time	26	23	16	14	10	9	4	4
Other Full-Time	8	8	3	3	5	5	0	0
Deans, librarians, & others who teach > 1/2	4	3	4	3	0	0	0	0
Part-time	21	30	14	24	7	6	2	2
Total	59	64	37	44	22	20	6	6
Deans, librarians, & others who teach < 1/2	3	3	2	2	1	1	0	0

Curriculum

	Full time	Part time
Typical first-year section size	88	0
Is there typically a "small section" of the first year class, other than Legal Writing, taught by full-time faculty?	Yes	No
If yes, typical size offered last year	30	N/A
# of classroom course titles beyond 1st year curriculum	122	0
# of upper division courses, excluding seminars, with an enrollment:		
Under 25	69	0
25 - 49	22	0
50 - 74	17	0
75 - 99	7	0
100 +	6	0
# of seminars	21	0
# of seminar positions available	252	
# of seminar positions filled	211	0
# of positions available in simulation courses	446	
# of simulation positions filled	296	0
# of positions available in faculty supervised clinical courses	104	
# of fac. sup. clin. positions filled	77	0
# involved in field placements	248	0
# involved in law journals	86	0
# in moot court or trial competitions	119	0
# of credit hrs required to graduate	88	

J.D. Enrollment & Ethnicity

	Men		Women		Fl-Time		Pt-Time		1st Yr		2nd Yr		3rd Yr		4th Yr		Total		JD Degrees Awarded
	#	%	#	%	#	%	#	%	#	%	#	%	#	%	#	%	#	%	
African-American	11	2.7	29	10.0	40	5.8	0	0.0	11	5.0	13	5.3	16	7.0	0	0.0	40	5.8	16
American Indian	1	0.2	1	0.3	2	0.3	0	0.0	2	0.9	0	0.0	0	0.0	0	0.0	2	0.3	1
Asian American	6	1.5	8	2.8	14	2.0	0	0.0	5	2.3	4	1.6	5	2.2	0	0.0	14	2.0	5
Mexican American	0	0.0	0	0.0	0	0.0	0	0.0	0	0.0	0	0.0	0	0.0	0	0.0	0	0.0	0
Puerto Rican	1	0.2	3	1.0	4	0.6	0	0.0	0	0.0	4	1.6	0	0.0	0	0.0	4	0.6	1
Hispanic American	5	1.2	1	0.3	6	0.9	0	0.0	2	0.9	4	1.6	0	0.0	0	0.0	6	0.9	2
Total Minorities	24	5.9	42	14.5	66	9.5	0	0.0	20	9.0	25	10.2	21	9.3	0	0.0	66	9.5	25
Foreign Nationals	1	0.2	1	0.3	2	0.3	0	0.0	0	0.0	2	0.8	0	0.0	0	0.0	2	0.3	2
Caucasian	379	93.8	246	85.1	625	90.2	0	0.0	201	91.0	218	89.0	206	90.7	0	0.0	625	90.2	206
Total	404	58.3	289	41.7	693	100.0	0	0.0	221	31.9	245	35.4	227	32.8	0	0.0	693		233

GPA & LSAT Scores

	Full Time	Part Time	Total
# of apps	1,183	0	1,183
# admits	801	0	801
# of matrics	222	0	222
75% GPA	3.50	0.00	
25% GPA	2.90	0.00	
75% LSAT	158	0	
25% LSAT	152	0	

Tuition & Fees

	Resident	Non-resident
Full-Time	$11,898	$18,346
Part-Time	$0	$0

Living Expenses

Estimated living expenses for Singles		
Living on campus	Living off campus	Living at home
N/A	$10,180	$9,000

Employment

	Total	%
Employment status known	189	90.4
Employment status unknown	20	9.6
Employed	154	81.5
Pursuing graduate degrees	7	3.7
Unemployed seeking employment	24	12.7
Unemployed not seeking employment	4	2.1
Type of Employment		
# employed in law firms	79	51.3
# employed in business & industry	20	13.0
# employed in government	13	8.4
# employed in public interest	6	3.9
# employed as judicial clerks	23	14.9
# employed in academia	1	0.6
Geographic Location		
# employed in state	94	61.0
# employed in foreign countries	0	0.0
# of states where employed	17	

Financial Aid

	Full-time		Part-time		Total	
	#	%	#	%	#	%
Total # of Students	693		0		693	
Total # receiving grants	240	34.6	0	0.0	240	34.6
Less than 1/2 tuition	233	33.6	0	0.0	233	33.6
Half to full tuition	4	0.6	0	0.0	4	0.6
Full tuition	3	0.4	0	0.0	3	0.4
More than full tuition	0	0.0	0	0.0	0	0.0
Median Grant Amount	$4,050		$0			

Informational & Library Resources

# of volumes & volume equivalents	367,265	# of professional staff	5
# of titles	148,510	Hours per week with professional staff	61
# of active serial subscriptions	4,964	Hours per week without professional staff	41
Study seating capacity inside the library	446	# of student computer work stations for entire law school	42
Square feet of law library	43,050	# of additional networked connections	0
Square feet of law school (excl. Library)	41,455	Require Laptop Computer?	N

J.D. Attrition (Prior Year)

	Academic	Other	TOTALS	
	#	#	#	%
1st Year	0	1	1	0.4%
2nd Year	0	13	13	5.6%
3rd Year	0	1	1	0.4%
4th Year	0	0	0	0.0%
TOTALS	0	15	15	2.0%

Bar Passage Rates

Jurisdiction	Pennsylvania		
Exam	Sum 96	Win 97	Total
# from school taking bar for the first time	132	13	145
School's pass rate for all first-time takers	87%	77%	86%
State's pass rate for all first-time takers	75%	76%	75%

PONTIFICAL CATHOLIC UNIVERSITY OF P.R.

2250 Las Americas Avenue Suite 543
Ponce, PR 00731-6382
(787)841-2000

ABA Approved Since 1967

The Basics

Type of School: Private Term: Semester

Application deadline: 04/15

Application fee: $25

Financial Aid deadline: 05/22

Can first year start other than Fall? No

Student faculty ratio: 21.4 to 1

Does the University offer:
- housing restricted to law students? No
- graduate student housing for which law students are eligible? No

Faculty & Administrators

	Total		Men		Women		Minorities	
	Fall	Spr	Fall	Spr	Fall	Spr	Fall	Spr
Full-time	17	17	10	10	7	7	17	17
Other Full-Time	0	0	0	0	0	0	0	0
Deans, librarians, & others who teach > 1/2	0	0	0	0	0	0	0	0
Part-time	13	11	11	9	2	2	13	11
Total	30	28	21	19	9	9	30	28
Deans, librarians, & others who teach < 1/2	3	3	1	1	2	2	3	3

Curriculum

	Full time	Part time
Typical first-year section size	60	50
Is there typically a "small section" of the first year class, other than Legal Writing, taught by full-time faculty?	Yes	Yes
If yes, typical size offered last year	20	20
# of classroom course titles beyond 1st year curriculum	26	31
# of upper division courses, excluding seminars, with an enrollment:		
Under 25	3	5
25 - 49	10	7
50 - 74	9	4
75 - 99	0	0
100 +	0	0
# of seminars	2	1
# of seminar positions available	61	
# of seminar positions filled	31	19
# of positions available in simulation courses	40	
# of simulation positions filled	0	33
# of positions available in faculty supervised clinical courses	6	
# of fac. sup. clin. positions filled	6	0
# involved in field placements	46	0
# involved in law journals	49	10
# in moot court or trial competitions	0	0
# of credit hrs required to graduate	94	

J.D. Enrollment & Ethnicity

	Men		Women		Fl-Time		Pt-Time		1st Yr		2nd Yr		3rd Yr		4th Yr		Total		JD Degrees Awarded
	#	%	#	%	#	%	#	%	#	%	#	%	#	%	#	%	#	%	
African-American	0	0.0	0	0.0	0	0.0	0	0.0	0	0.0	0	0.0	0	0.0	0	0.0	0	0.0	0
American Indian	0	0.0	0	0.0	0	0.0	0	0.0	0	0.0	0	0.0	0	0.0	0	0.0	0	0.0	0
Asian American	0	0.0	0	0.0	0	0.0	0	0.0	0	0.0	0	0.0	0	0.0	0	0.0	0	0.0	0
Mexican American	0	0.0	0	0.0	0	0.0	0	0.0	0	0.0	0	0.0	0	0.0	0	0.0	0	0.0	0
Puerto Rican	240	100.0	253	100.0	319	100.0	174	100.0	168	100.0	148	100.0	138	100.0	39	100.0	493	100.0	135
Hispanic American	0	0.0	0	0.0	0	0.0	0	0.0	0	0.0	0	0.0	0	0.0	0	0.0	0	0.0	0
Total Minorities	240	100.0	253	100.0	319	100.0	174	100.0	168	100.0	148	100.0	138	100.0	39	100.0	493	100.0	135
Foreign Nationals	0	0.0	0	0.0	0	0.0	0	0.0	0	0.0	0	0.0	0	0.0	0	0.0	0	0.0	0
Caucasian	0	0.0	0	0.0	0	0.0	0	0.0	0	0.0	0	0.0	0	0.0	0	0.0	0	0.0	0
Total	240	48.7	253	51.3	319	64.7	174	35.3	168	34.1	148	30.0	138	28.0	39	7.9	493		135

PONTIFICAL CATHOLIC UNIVERSITY OF P.R.

GPA & LSAT Scores

	Full Time	Part Time	Total
# of apps	325	164	489
# admits	147	65	212
# of matrics	110	58	168
75% GPA	3.33	3.20	
25% GPA	2.87	2.72	
75% LSAT	141	142	
25% LSAT	134	133	

Tuition & Fees

	Resident	Non-resident
Full-Time	$8,768	$8,768
Part-Time	$6,256	$0

Living Expenses

Estimated living expenses for Singles		
Living on campus	Living off campus	Living at home
$6,811	$8,927	$6,227

Employment

	Total	%
Employment status known	34	33.0
Employment status unknown	69	67.0
Employed	17	50.0
Pursuing graduate degrees	4	11.8
Unemployed seeking employment	13	38.2
Unemployed not seeking employment	0	0.0
Type of Employment		
# employed in law firms	7	41.2
# employed in business & industry	0	0.0
# employed in government	3	17.6
# employed in public interest	0	0.0
# employed as judicial clerks	6	35.3
# employed in academia	1	5.9
Geographic Location		
# employed in state	17	100.0
# employed in foreign countries	0	0.0
# of states where employed	0	

Financial Aid

	Full-time		Part-time		Total	
	#	%	#	%	#	%
Total # of Students	319		174		493	
Total # receiving grants	0	0.0	0	0.0	0	0.0
Less than 1/2 tuition	0	0.0	0	0.0	0	0.0
Half to full tuition	0	0.0	0	0.0	0	0.0
Full tuition	0	0.0	0	0.0	0	0.0
More than full tuition	0	0.0	0	0.0	0	0.0
Median Grant Amount	$0		$0			

Informational & Library Resources

# of volumes & volume equivalents	176,914	# of professional staff	4
# of titles	22,329	Hours per week with professional staff	80
# of active serial subscriptions	2,225	Hours per week without professional staff	12
Study seating capacity inside the library	169	# of student computer work stations for entire law school	2
Square feet of law library	20,393	# of additional networked connections	33
Square feet of law school (excl. Library)	25,612	Require Laptop Computer?	N

J.D. Attrition (Prior Year)

	Academic	Other	TOTALS	
	#	#	#	%
1st Year	9	23	32	19%
2nd Year	6	3	9	7.0%
3rd Year	0	3	3	2.0%
4th Year	0	0	0	0.0%
TOTALS	15	29	44	9.0%

Bar Passage Rates

Jurisdiction	Puerto Rico		
Exam	Sum 96	Win 97	Total
# from school taking bar for the first time	84	34	118
School's pass rate for all first-time takers	60%	50%	57%
State's pass rate for all first-time takers	71%	53%	68%

PUERTO RICO, UNIVERSITY OF

P.O. Box 23349
San Juan, PR 00931-3349
(787)764-2680

ABA Approved Since 1945

The Basics

Type of School: Public | Term: Semester
Application deadline: 02/16
Application fee: $15
Financial Aid deadline: 05/01
Can first year start other than Fall? No
Student faculty ratio: 24.5 to 1
Does the University offer:
- housing restricted to law students? No
- graduate student housing for which law students are eligible? No

Faculty & Administrators

	Total		Men		Women		Minorities	
	Fall	Spr	Fall	Spr	Fall	Spr	Fall	Spr
Full-time	16	18	13	15	3	3	16	18
Other Full-Time	0	0	0	0	0	0	0	0
Deans, librarians, & others who teach > 1/2	4	4	3	3	1	1	4	4
Part-time	33	22	15	12	18	10	32	14
Total	53	44	31	30	22	14	52	36
Deans, librarians, & others who teach < 1/2	3	3	3	3	0	0	2	2

Curriculum

	Full time	Part time
Typical first-year section size	50	50
Is there typically a "small section" of the first year class, other than Legal Writing, taught by full-time faculty?	No	No
If yes, typical size offered last year	N/A	N/A
# of classroom course titles beyond 1st year curriculum	60	38
# of upper division courses, excluding seminars, with an enrollment:		
Under 25	29	19
25 - 49	26	9
50 - 74	12	3
75 - 99	0	0
100 +	0	0
# of seminars	0	0
# of seminar positions available	135	
# of seminar positions filled	40	36
# of positions available in simulation courses	30	
# of simulation positions filled	15	8
# of positions available in faculty supervised clinical courses	130	
# of fac. sup. clin. positions filled	88	30
# involved in field placements	88	30
# involved in law journals	10	2
# in moot court or trial competitions	3	0
# of credit hrs required to graduate	92	

J.D. Enrollment & Ethnicity

	Men		Women		Fl-Time		Pt-Time		1st Yr		2nd Yr		3rd Yr		4th Yr		Total		JD Degrees Awarded
	#	%	#	%	#	%	#	%	#	%	#	%	#	%	#	%	#	%	
African-American	0	0.0	0	0.0	0	0.0	0	0.0	0	0.0	0	0.0	0	0.0	0	0.0	0	0.0	0
American Indian	0	0.0	0	0.0	0	0.0	0	0.0	0	0.0	0	0.0	0	0.0	0	0.0	0	0.0	0
Asian American	0	0.0	0	0.0	0	0.0	0	0.0	0	0.0	0	0.0	0	0.0	0	0.0	0	0.0	0
Mexican American	0	0.0	0	0.0	0	0.0	0	0.0	0	0.0	0	0.0	0	0.0	0	0.0	0	0.0	0
Puerto Rican	237	100.0	299	98.0	326	98.2	210	100.0	148	98.7	184	100.0	149	97.4	55	100.0	536	98.9	120
Hispanic American	0	0.0	6	2.0	6	1.8	0	0.0	2	1.3	0	0.0	4	2.6	0	0.0	6	1.1	0
Total Minorities	237	100.0	305	100.0	332	100.0	210	100.0	150	100.0	184	100.0	153	100.0	55	100.0	542	100.0	120
Foreign Nationals	0	0.0	0	0.0	0	0.0	0	0.0	0	0.0	0	0.0	0	0.0	0	0.0	0	0.0	0
Caucasian	0	0.0	0	0.0	0	0.0	0	0.0	0	0.0	0	0.0	0	0.0	0	0.0	0	0.0	0
Total	237	43.7	305	56.3	332	61.3	210	38.7	150	27.7	184	33.9	153	28.2	55	10.1	542		120

GPA & LSAT Scores

	Full Time	Part Time	Total
# of apps	468	357	825
# admits	128	49	177
# of matrics	100	50	150
75% GPA	3.84	3.51	
25% GPA	3.30	3.10	
75% LSAT	151	150	
25% LSAT	143	142	

Tuition & Fees

	Resident	Non-resident
Full-Time	$2,320	$3,570
Part-Time	$1,570	$3,500

Living Expenses

Estimated living expenses for Singles		
Living on campus	Living off campus	Living at home
$7,544	$6,044	$5,144

Employment

	Total	%
Employment status known	70	61.4
Employment status unknown	44	38.6
Employed	64	91.4
Pursuing graduate degrees	4	5.7
Unemployed seeking employment	2	2.9
Unemployed not seeking employment	0	0.0
Type of Employment		
# employed in law firms	31	48.4
# employed in business & industry	18	28.1
# employed in government	4	6.2
# employed in public interest	3	4.7
# employed as judicial clerks	6	9.4
# employed in academia	2	3.1
Geographic Location		
# employed in state	64	100.0
# employed in foreign countries	0	0.0
# of states where employed	1	

Financial Aid

	Full-time		Part-time		Total	
	#	%	#	%	#	%
Total # of Students	332		210		542	
Total # receiving grants	188	56.6	18	8.6	206	38.0
Less than 1/2 tuition	0	0.0	0	0.0	0	0.0
Half to full tuition	0	0.0	0	0.0	0	0.0
Full tuition	14	4.2	0	0.0	14	2.6
More than full tuition	174	52.4	18	8.6	192	35.4
Median Grant Amount	$2,000		$1,000			

Informational & Library Resources

# of volumes & volume equivalents	308,751	# of professional staff	10
# of titles	63,159	Hours per week with professional staff	95
# of active serial subscriptions	4,363	Hours per week without professional staff	17
Study seating capacity inside the library	360	# of student computer work stations for entire law school	26
Square feet of law library	44,275	# of additional networked connections	0
Square feet of law school (excl. Library)	36,657	Require Laptop Computer?	N

J.D. Attrition (Prior Year)

	Academic	Other	TOTALS	
	#	#	#	%
1st Year	5	7	12	7.5%
2nd Year	2	4	6	3.2%
3rd Year	0	0	0	0.0%
4th Year	0	0	0	0.0%
TOTALS	7	11	18	3.4%

Bar Passage Rates

Jurisdiction	Puerto Rico		
Exam	Sum 96	Win 97	Total
# from school taking bar for the first time	15	101	116
School's pass rate for all first-time takers	53%	77%	74%
State's pass rate for all first-time takers	71%	53%	68%

QUINNIPIAC COLLEGE

275 Mount Carmel Avenue
Hamden, CT 06518-1950
(203)287-3200
http://www.quinnipiac.edu/law

ABA Approved Since 1992

The Basics

Type of School: Private   Term: Semester
Application deadline: Rolling
Application fee: $40
Financial Aid deadline: 05/01
Can first year start other than Fall? Yes
Student faculty ratio: 18.7 to 1
Does the University offer:
- housing restricted to law students? No
- graduate student housing for which law students are eligible? No

Faculty & Administrators

	Total		Men		Women		Minorities	
	Fall	Spr	Fall	Spr	Fall	Spr	Fall	Spr
Full-time	31	32	21	22	10	10	4	4
Other Full-Time	6	6	2	2	4	4	0	0
Deans, librarians, & others who teach > 1/2	1	1	1	1	0	0	0	0
Part-time	23	29	19	23	4	6	1	1
Total	61	68	43	48	18	20	5	5
Deans, librarians, & others who teach < 1/2	2	2	1	1	1	1	0	0

Curriculum

	Full time	Part time
Typical first-year section size	85	60
Is there typically a "small section" of the first year class, other than Legal Writing, taught by full-time faculty?	Yes	Yes
If yes, typical size offered last year	25	40
# of classroom course titles beyond 1st year curriculum	51	47
# of upper division courses, excluding seminars, with an enrollment:		
Under 25	40	33
25 - 49	15	14
50 - 74	6	4
75 - 99	10	5
100 +	0	0
# of seminars	8	4
# of seminar positions available	178	
# of seminar positions filled	95	38
# of positions available in simulation courses	304	
# of simulation positions filled	85	190
# of positions available in faculty supervised clinical courses	76	
# of fac. sup. clin. positions filled	74	0
# involved in field placements	110	0
# involved in law journals	80	40
# in moot court or trial competitions	20	10
# of credit hrs required to graduate	86	

J.D. Enrollment & Ethnicity

	Men		Women		Fl-Time		Pt-Time		1st Yr		2nd Yr		3rd Yr		4th Yr		Total		JD Degrees Awarded
	#	%	#	%	#	%	#	%	#	%	#	%	#	%	#	%	#	%	
African-American	13	2.7	24	8.0	25	4.6	12	5.0	7	2.8	14	5.7	13	5.6	3	6.4	37	4.8	5
American Indian	4	0.8	2	0.7	4	0.7	2	0.8	3	1.2	2	0.8	0	0.0	1	2.1	6	0.8	3
Asian American	6	1.3	9	3.0	14	2.6	1	0.4	4	1.6	5	2.0	6	2.6	0	0.0	15	1.9	11
Mexican American	0	0.0	0	0.0	0	0.0	0	0.0	0	0.0	0	0.0	0	0.0	0	0.0	0	0.0	0
Puerto Rican	11	2.3	6	2.0	17	3.1	0	0.0	8	3.2	5	2.0	4	1.7	0	0.0	17	2.2	0
Hispanic American	2	0.4	7	2.3	0	0.0	9	3.8	5	2.0	2	0.8	1	0.4	1	2.1	9	1.2	14
Total Minorities	36	7.5	48	16.1	60	11.1	24	10.1	27	10.7	28	11.3	24	10.3	5	10.6	84	10.8	33
Foreign Nationals	8	1.7	1	0.3	9	1.7	0	0.0	5	2.0	3	1.2	1	0.4	0	0.0	9	1.2	0
Caucasian	435	90.8	250	83.6	471	87.2	214	89.9	219	86.9	218	88.3	206	88.8	42	89.4	685	88.0	211
Total	479	61.6	299	38.4	540	69.4	238	30.6	252	32.4	247	31.7	232	29.8	47	6.0	778		244

GPA & LSAT Scores

	Full Time	Part Time	Total
# of apps	1,661	304	1,965
# admits	962	123	1,085
# of matrics	197	101	298
75% GPA	3.15	3.18	
25% GPA	2.47	2.55	
75% LSAT	152	151	
25% LSAT	145	145	

Tuition & Fees

	Resident	Non-resident
Full-Time	$19,323	$19,323
Part-Time	$16,175	$16,175

Living Expenses

Estimated living expenses for Singles		
Living on campus	Living off campus	Living at home
N/A	$13,075	$8,695

Financial Aid

	Full-time		Part-time		Total	
	#	%	#	%	#	%
Total # of Students	540		238		778	
Total # receiving grants	200	37.0	120	50.4	320	41.1
Less than 1/2 tuition	164	30.4	86	36.1	250	32.1
Half to full tuition	27	5.0	29	12.2	56	7.2
Full tuition	7	1.3	4	1.7	11	1.4
More than full tuition	2	0.4	1	0.4	3	0.4
Median Grant Amount	$6,050		$5,000			

Informational & Library Resources

# of volumes & volume equivalents	308,759	# of professional staff	7
# of titles	36,596	Hours per week with professional staff	65
# of active serial subscriptions	3,054	Hours per week without professional staff	31
Study seating capacity inside the library	400	# of student computer work stations for entire law school	121
Square feet of law library	46,000	# of additional networked connections	750
Square feet of law school (excl. Library)	84,000	Require Laptop Computer?	N

Employment

	Total	%
Employment status known	186	84.5
Employment status unknown	34	15.5
Employed	164	88.2
Pursuing graduate degrees	4	2.2
Unemployed seeking employment	17	9.1
Unemployed not seeking employment	1	0.5
Type of Employment		
# employed in law firms	84	51.2
# employed in business & industry	30	18.3
# employed in government	27	16.5
# employed in public interest	1	0.6
# employed as judicial clerks	15	9.1
# employed in academia	3	1.8
Geographic Location		
# employed in state	82	50.0
# employed in foreign countries	1	0.6
# of states where employed	16	

J.D. Attrition (Prior Year)

	Academic	Other	TOTALS	
	#	#	#	%
1st Year	18	2	20	8.8%
2nd Year	1	16	17	7.4%
3rd Year	0	2	2	0.8%
4th Year	0	0	0	0.0%
TOTALS	19	20	39	5.1%

Bar Passage Rates

Jurisdiction	Connecticut		
Exam	Sum 96	Win 97	Total
# from school taking bar for the first time	105	35	140
School's pass rate for all first-time takers	82%	83%	82%
State's pass rate for all first-time takers	84%	84%	84%

REGENT UNIVERSITY

1000 Regent University Drive
Virginia Beach, VA 23464
(757)579-4040
http://www.regent.edu/acad/schlaw

ABA Approved Since 1989

The Basics

Type of School: Private   Term: Semester
Application deadline: 04/01
Application fee: $40
Financial Aid deadline: 04/01
Can first year start other than Fall? No
Student faculty ratio: 19.5 to 1
Does the University offer:
- housing restricted to law students? No
- graduate student housing for which law students are eligible? Yes

Faculty & Administrators

	Total		Men		Women		Minorities	
	Fall	Spr	Fall	Spr	Fall	Spr	Fall	Spr
Full-time	17	17	14	14	3	3	3	4
Other Full-Time	0	0	0	0	0	0	0	0
Deans, librarians, & others who teach > 1/2	3	3	3	3	0	0	0	0
Part-time	23	23	17	18	6	5	0	0
Total	43	43	34	35	9	8	3	4
Deans, librarians, & others who teach < 1/2	0	0	0	0	0	0	0	0

Curriculum

	Full time	Part time
Typical first-year section size	70	0
Is there typically a "small section" of the first year class, other than Legal Writing, taught by full-time faculty?	No	No
If yes, typical size offered last year	N/A	N/A
# of classroom course titles beyond 1st year curriculum	57	0
# of upper division courses, excluding seminars, with an enrollment:		
Under 25	39	0
25 - 49	25	0
50 - 74	12	0
75 - 99	0	0
100 +	0	0
# of seminars	4	0
# of seminar positions available	80	
# of seminar positions filled	34	0
# of positions available in simulation courses	311	
# of simulation positions filled	299	0
# of positions available in faculty supervised clinical courses	0	
# of fac. sup. clin. positions filled	0	0
# involved in field placements	48	0
# involved in law journals	28	0
# in moot court or trial competitions	22	0
# of credit hrs required to graduate	90	

J.D. Enrollment & Ethnicity

	Men		Women		Fl-Time		Pt-Time		1st Yr		2nd Yr		3rd Yr		4th Yr		Total		JD Degrees Awarded
	#	%	#	%	#	%	#	%	#	%	#	%	#	%	#	%	#	%	
African-American	6	2.4	11	7.7	17	4.3	0	0.0	10	7.0	4	3.0	3	2.5	0	0.0	17	4.3	1
American Indian	1	0.4	0	0.0	1	0.3	0	0.0	1	0.7	0	0.0	0	0.0	0	0.0	1	0.3	0
Asian American	6	2.4	3	2.1	9	2.3	0	0.0	5	3.5	2	1.5	2	1.6	0	0.0	9	2.3	1
Mexican American	0	0.0	0	0.0	0	0.0	0	0.0	0	0.0	0	0.0	0	0.0	0	0.0	0	0.0	0
Puerto Rican	1	0.4	0	0.0	1	0.3	0	0.0	0	0.0	0	0.0	1	0.8	0	0.0	1	0.3	0
Hispanic American	3	1.2	3	2.1	6	1.5	0	0.0	1	0.7	5	3.8	0	0.0	0	0.0	6	1.5	0
Total Minorities	17	6.7	17	11.9	34	8.5	0	0.0	17	11.9	11	8.3	6	4.9	0	0.0	34	8.5	2
Foreign Nationals	1	0.4	5	3.5	6	1.5	0	0.0	4	2.8	0	0.0	2	1.6	0	0.0	6	1.5	0
Caucasian	237	92.9	121	84.6	358	89.9	0	0.0	122	85.3	122	91.7	114	93.4	0	0.0	358	89.9	100
Total	255	64.1	143	35.9	398	100.0	0	0.0	143	35.9	133	33.4	122	30.7	0	0.0	398		102

GPA & LSAT Scores

	Full Time	Part Time	Total
# of apps	419	0	419
# admits	237	0	237
# of matrics	143	0	143
75% GPA	3.41	0.00	
25% GPA	2.70	0.00	
75% LSAT	155	0	
25% LSAT	147	0	

Tuition & Fees

	Resident	Non-resident
Full-Time	$13,872	$13,872
Part-Time	$0	$0

Living Expenses

Estimated living expenses for Singles		
Living on campus	Living off campus	Living at home
$10,793	$10,793	$10,793

Financial Aid

	Full-time		Part-time		Total	
	#	%	#	%	#	%
Total # of Students	398		0		398	
Total # receiving grants	328	82.4	0	0.0	328	82.4
Less than 1/2 tuition	284	71.4	0	0.0	284	71.4
Half to full tuition	34	8.5	0	0.0	34	8.5
Full tuition	6	1.5	0	0.0	6	1.5
More than full tuition	4	1.0	0	0.0	4	1.0
Median Grant Amount	$2,955		$0			

Informational & Library Resources

# of volumes & volume equivalents	302,613	# of professional staff	5
# of titles	40,807	Hours per week with professional staff	40
# of active serial subscriptions	4,394	Hours per week without professional staff	58
Study seating capacity inside the library	269	# of student computer work stations for entire law school	27
Square feet of law library	38,730	# of additional networked connections	18
Square feet of law school (excl. Library)	71,970	Require Laptop Computer?	N

Employment

	Total	%
Employment status known	83	79.0
Employment status unknown	22	21.0
Employed	76	91.6
Pursuing graduate degrees	1	1.2
Unemployed seeking employment	4	4.8
Unemployed not seeking employment	2	2.4
Type of Employment		
# employed in law firms	39	51.3
# employed in business & industry	11	14.5
# employed in government	16	21.1
# employed in public interest	5	6.6
# employed as judicial clerks	4	5.3
# employed in academia	1	1.3
Geographic Location		
# employed in state	25	32.9
# employed in foreign countries	0	0.0
# of states where employed	26	

J.D. Attrition (Prior Year)

	Academic	Other	TOTALS	
	#	#	#	%
1st Year	3	13	16	11%
2nd Year	0	0	0	0.0%
3rd Year	0	0	0	0.0%
4th Year	0	0	0	0.0%
TOTALS	3	13	16	4.4%

Bar Passage Rates

Jurisdiction	Virginia			Pennsylvania		
Exam	Sum 96	Win 97	Total	Sum 96	Win 97	Total
# from school taking bar for the first time	21	5	26	5	2	7
School's pass rate for all first-time takers	71%	60%	69%	80%	100%	86%
State's pass rate for all first-time takers	80%	66%	77%	75%	76%	75%

RICHMOND, UNIVERSITY OF

Law School
University of Richmond
Richmond, VA 23173
(804)289-8189
http://law.richmond.edu

ABA Approved Since 1928

The Basics

Type of School: Private   Term: Semester

Application deadline: 02/01

Application fee: $35

Financial Aid deadline: 02/25

Can first year start other than Fall? Yes

Student faculty ratio: 16.4 to 1

Does the University offer:
- housing restricted to law students? Yes
- graduate student housing for which law students are eligible? Yes

Faculty & Administrators

	Total		Men		Women		Minorities	
	Fall	Spr	Fall	Spr	Fall	Spr	Fall	Spr
Full-time	24	21	17	14	7	7	2	2
Other Full-Time	0	0	0	0	0	0	0	0
Deans, librarians, & others who teach > 1/2	2	2	2	2	0	0	0	0
Part-time	40	47	20	26	20	21	3	4
Total	66	70	39	42	27	28	5	6
Deans, librarians, & others who teach < 1/2	1	1	0	0	1	1	0	0

Curriculum

	Full time	Part time
Typical first-year section size	70	0
Is there typically a "small section" of the first year class, other than Legal Writing, taught by full-time faculty?	Yes	No
If yes, typical size offered last year	40	N/A
# of classroom course titles beyond 1st year curriculum	97	0
# of upper division courses, excluding seminars, with an enrollment:		
Under 25	46	0
25 - 49	19	0
50 - 74	12	0
75 - 99	6	0
100 +	0	0
# of seminars	13	0
# of seminar positions available	208	
# of seminar positions filled	131	0
# of positions available in simulation courses	485	
# of simulation positions filled	478	0
# of positions available in faculty supervised clinical courses	52	
# of fac. sup. clin. positions filled	27	0
# involved in field placements	66	0
# involved in law journals	97	0
# in moot court or trial competitions	374	0
# of credit hrs required to graduate	86	

J.D. Enrollment & Ethnicity

	Men		Women		Fl-Time		Pt-Time		1st Yr		2nd Yr		3rd Yr		4th Yr		Total		JD Degrees Awarded
	#	%	#	%	#	%	#	%	#	%	#	%	#	%	#	%	#	%	
African-American	13	5.1	28	13.0	41	8.7	0	0.0	17	10.2	7	4.7	17	11.0	0	0.0	41	8.7	14
American Indian	2	0.8	1	0.5	3	0.6	0	0.0	0	0.0	1	0.7	2	1.3	0	0.0	3	0.6	1
Asian American	10	3.9	12	5.6	22	4.7	0	0.0	6	3.6	8	5.3	8	5.2	0	0.0	22	4.7	10
Mexican American	0	0.0	0	0.0	0	0.0	0	0.0	0	0.0	0	0.0	0	0.0	0	0.0	0	0.0	0
Puerto Rican	0	0.0	0	0.0	0	0.0	0	0.0	0	0.0	0	0.0	0	0.0	0	0.0	0	0.0	1
Hispanic American	7	2.7	3	1.4	10	2.1	0	0.0	2	1.2	3	2.0	5	3.2	0	0.0	10	2.1	5
Total Minorities	32	12.5	44	20.4	76	16.1	0	0.0	25	15.0	19	12.7	32	20.6	0	0.0	76	16.1	31
Foreign Nationals	3	1.2	2	0.9	5	1.1	0	0.0	1	0.6	2	1.3	2	1.3	0	0.0	5	1.1	0
Caucasian	221	86.3	170	78.7	390	82.8	1	100.0	141	84.4	129	86.0	121	78.1	0	0.0	391	82.8	131
Total	256	54.2	216	45.8	471	99.8	1	0.2	167	35.4	150	31.8	155	32.8	0	0.0	472		162

GPA & LSAT Scores

	Full Time	Part Time	Total
# of apps	1,314	0	1,314
# admits	554	0	554
# of matrics	167	0	167
75% GPA	3.31	0.00	
25% GPA	2.77	0.00	
75% LSAT	159	0	
25% LSAT	154	0	

Tuition & Fees

	Resident	Non-resident
Full-Time	$18,170	$18,170
Part-Time	$0	$0

Living Expenses

Estimated living expenses for Singles		
Living on campus	Living off campus	Living at home
$7,920	$10,170	$5,280

Financial Aid

	Full-time		Part-time		Total	
	#	%	#	%	#	%
Total # of Students	471		1		472	
Total # receiving grants	229	48.6	0	0.0	229	48.5
Less than 1/2 tuition	205	43.5	0	0.0	205	43.4
Half to full tuition	17	3.6	0	0.0	17	3.6
Full tuition	7	1.5	0	0.0	7	1.5
More than full tuition	0	0.0	0	0.0	0	0.0
Median Grant Amount	$1,730		$0			

Informational & Library Resources

# of volumes & volume equivalents	257,857	# of professional staff	6
# of titles	115,790	Hours per week with professional staff	77
# of active serial subscriptions	4,170	Hours per week without professional staff	29
Study seating capacity inside the library	602	# of student computer work stations for entire law school	10
Square feet of law library	49,000	# of additional networked connections	563
Square feet of law school (excl. Library)	41,745	Require Laptop Computer?	Y

Employment

	Total	%
Employment status known	148	96.1
Employment status unknown	6	3.9
Employed	127	85.8
Pursuing graduate degrees	2	1.4
Unemployed seeking employment	10	6.8
Unemployed not seeking employment	9	6.1
Type of Employment		
# employed in law firms	71	55.9
# employed in business & industry	17	13.4
# employed in government	14	11.0
# employed in public interest	4	3.1
# employed as judicial clerks	20	15.7
# employed in academia	1	0.8
Geographic Location		
# employed in state	92	72.4
# employed in foreign countries	1	0.8
# of states where employed	16	

J.D. Attrition (Prior Year)

	Academic	Other	TOTALS	
	#	#	#	%
1st Year	3	16	19	13%
2nd Year	0	2	2	1.2%
3rd Year	0	1	1	0.6%
4th Year	0	0	0	0.0%
TOTALS	3	19	22	4.6%

Bar Passage Rates

Jurisdiction	Virginia		
Exam	Sum 96	Win 97	Total
# from school taking bar for the first time	94	32	126
School's pass rate for all first-time takers	79%	75%	78%
State's pass rate for all first-time takers	80%	66%	77%

ROGER WILLIAMS UNIVERSITY

Ten Metacom Avenue
Bristol, RI 02809
(401)254-4500
www.rwu.edu/law

ABA Approved Since 1995

The Basics

Type of School: Private   Term: Semester

Application deadline: 05/15

Application fee: $60

Financial Aid deadline: 05/01

Can first year start other than Fall? No

Student faculty ratio: 14.4 to 1

Does the University offer:

- housing restricted to law students? Yes
- graduate student housing for which law students are eligible? No

Faculty & Administrators

	Total		Men		Women		Minorities	
	Fall	Spr	Fall	Spr	Fall	Spr	Fall	Spr
Full-time	22	22	13	14	9	8	3	3
Other Full-Time	1	1	0	0	1	1	0	0
Deans, librarians, & others who teach > 1/2	1	1	1	1	0	0	0	0
Part-time	20	19	16	16	4	3	1	0
Total	44	43	30	31	14	12	4	3
Deans, librarians, & others who teach < 1/2	1	1	1	1	0	0	0	0

Curriculum

	Full time	Part time
Typical first-year section size	91	46
Is there typically a "small section" of the first year class, other than Legal Writing, taught by full-time faculty?	Yes	Yes
If yes, typical size offered last year	45	46
# of classroom course titles beyond 1st year curriculum	45	28
# of upper division courses, excluding seminars, with an enrollment:		
Under 25	19	9
25 - 49	8	14
50 - 74	6	4
75 - 99	5	0
100 +	0	0
# of seminars	6	3
# of seminar positions available	150	
# of seminar positions filled	72	56
# of positions available in simulation courses	200	
# of simulation positions filled	125	53
# of positions available in faculty supervised clinical courses	44	
# of fac. sup. clin. positions filled	42	0
# involved in field placements	42	8
# involved in law journals	18	9
# in moot court or trial competitions	10	7
# of credit hrs required to graduate	90	

J.D. Enrollment & Ethnicity

	Men		Women		Fl-Time		Pt-Time		1st Yr		2nd Yr		3rd Yr		4th Yr		Total		JD Degrees Awarded
	#	%	#	%	#	%	#	%	#	%	#	%	#	%	#	%	#	%	
African-American	6	2.3	10	5.3	8	3.3	8	4.0	9	6.5	2	1.7	2	1.4	3	6.3	16	3.6	2
American Indian	0	0.0	0	0.0	0	0.0	0	0.0	0	0.0	0	0.0	0	0.0	0	0.0	0	0.0	0
Asian American	2	0.8	2	1.1	4	1.6	0	0.0	3	2.2	0	0.0	1	0.7	0	0.0	4	0.9	1
Mexican American	0	0.0	0	0.0	0	0.0	0	0.0	0	0.0	0	0.0	0	0.0	0	0.0	0	0.0	0
Puerto Rican	0	0.0	0	0.0	0	0.0	0	0.0	0	0.0	0	0.0	0	0.0	0	0.0	0	0.0	0
Hispanic American	6	2.3	6	3.2	5	2.0	7	3.5	6	4.3	4	3.3	2	1.4	0	0.0	12	2.7	2
Total Minorities	14	5.4	18	9.6	17	6.9	15	7.4	18	13.0	6	5.0	5	3.5	3	6.3	32	7.1	5
Foreign Nationals	0	0.0	0	0.0	0	0.0	0	0.0	0	0.0	0	0.0	0	0.0	0	0.0	0	0.0	0
Caucasian	246	94.6	170	90.4	229	93.1	187	92.6	121	87.7	113	94.2	137	96.5	45	93.8	416	92.9	142
Total	260	58.0	188	42.0	246	54.9	202	45.1	138	30.8	120	26.8	142	31.7	48	10.7	448		147

GPA & LSAT Scores

	Full Time	Part Time	Total
# of apps	584	122	706
# admits	364	84	448
# of matrics	91	48	139
75% GPA	3.33	3.29	
25% GPA	2.79	2.61	
75% LSAT	151	151	
25% LSAT	144	142	

Tuition & Fees

	Resident	Non-resident
Full-Time	$18,080	$18,080
Part-Time	$13,873	$13,873

Living Expenses

Estimated living expenses for Singles		
Living on campus	Living off campus	Living at home
$12,704	$13,610	$13,610

Employment

	Total	%
Employment status known	62	72.9
Employment status unknown	23	27.1
Employed	60	96.8
Pursuing graduate degrees	0	0.0
Unemployed seeking employment	2	3.2
Unemployed not seeking employment	0	0.0
Type of Employment		
# employed in law firms	34	56.7
# employed in business & industry	16	26.7
# employed in government	5	8.3
# employed in public interest	0	0.0
# employed as judicial clerks	5	8.3
# employed in academia	0	0.0
Geographic Location		
# employed in state	34	56.7
# employed in foreign countries	0	0.0
# of states where employed	8	

Financial Aid

	Full-time		Part-time		Total	
	#	%	#	%	#	%
Total # of Students	246		202		448	
Total # receiving grants	33	13.4	10	5.0	43	9.6
Less than 1/2 tuition	33	13.4	10	5.0	43	9.6
Half to full tuition	0	0.0	0	0.0	0	0.0
Full tuition	0	0.0	0	0.0	0	0.0
More than full tuition	0	0.0	0	0.0	0	0.0
Median Grant Amount	$3,000		$2,000			

Informational & Library Resources

# of volumes & volume equivalents	199,273	# of professional staff	6
# of titles	85,659	Hours per week with professional staff	61
# of active serial subscriptions	3,171	Hours per week without professional staff	49
Study seating capacity inside the library	383	# of student computer work stations for entire law school	77
Square feet of law library	30,083	# of additional networked connections	109
Square feet of law school (excl. Library)	91,617	Require Laptop Computer?	N

J.D. Attrition (Prior Year)

	Academic	Other	TOTALS	
	#	#	#	%
1st Year	23	25	48	29%
2nd Year	0	4	4	2.8%
3rd Year	0	4	4	2.5%
4th Year	0	0	0	0.0%
TOTALS	23	33	56	11%

Bar Passage Rates

Jurisdiction	Rhode Island			Massachusetts		
Exam	Sum 96	Win 97	Total	Sum 96	Win 97	Total
# from school taking bar for the first time	53	6	59	5	11	16
School's pass rate for all first-time takers	53%	67%	54%	80%	73%	75%
State's pass rate for all first-time takers	67%	88%	72%	83%	76%	81%

RUTGERS UNIVERSITY-CAMDEN

217 North Fifth Street
Camden, NJ 08102-1203
(609)225-6102
http://www-camlaw.rutgers.edu

ABA Approved Since 1951

The Basics

Type of School: Public Term: Semester
Application deadline: 03/01
Application fee: $40
Financial Aid deadline: 03/01
Can first year start other than Fall? No
Student faculty ratio: 21.8 to 1
Does the University offer:
- housing restricted to law students? No
- graduate student housing for which law students are eligible? Yes

Faculty & Administrators

	Total		Men		Women		Minorities	
	Fall	Spr	Fall	Spr	Fall	Spr	Fall	Spr
Full-time	25	24	19	19	6	5	3	2
Other Full-Time	0	0	0	0	0	0	0	0
Deans, librarians, & others who teach > 1/2	4	4	1	1	3	3	0	0
Part-time	27	34	19	31	8	3	1	2
Total	56	62	39	51	17	11	4	4
Deans, librarians, & others who teach < 1/2	3	3	2	2	1	1	0	0

Curriculum

	Full time	Part time
Typical first-year section size	96	42
Is there typically a "small section" of the first year class, other than Legal Writing, taught by full-time faculty?	No	No
If yes, typical size offered last year	N/A	N/A
# of classroom course titles beyond 1st year curriculum	58	41
# of upper division courses, excluding seminars, with an enrollment:		
Under 25	29	44
25 - 49	19	11
50 - 74	10	2
75 - 99	8	2
100 +	0	1
# of seminars	19	2
# of seminar positions available	294	
# of seminar positions filled	205	36
# of positions available in simulation courses	785	
# of simulation positions filled	565	120
# of positions available in faculty supervised clinical courses	32	
# of fac. sup. clin. positions filled	27	3
# involved in field placements	84	4
# involved in law journals	57	4
# in moot court or trial competitions	144	18
# of credit hrs required to graduate	84	

J.D. Enrollment & Ethnicity

	Men		Women		Fl-Time		Pt-Time		1st Yr		2nd Yr		3rd Yr		4th Yr		Total		JD Degrees Awarded
	#	%	#	%	#	%	#	%	#	%	#	%	#	%	#	%	#	%	
African-American	31	8.1	33	10.1	46	8.4	18	11.3	17	7.2	22	10.5	22	9.8	3	8.1	64	9.1	14
American Indian	0	0.0	1	0.3	0	0.0	1	0.6	0	0.0	1	0.5	0	0.0	0	0.0	1	0.1	0
Asian American	20	5.2	18	5.5	33	6.0	5	3.1	8	3.4	12	5.7	16	7.1	2	5.4	38	5.4	15
Mexican American	1	0.3	1	0.3	2	0.4	0	0.0	1	0.4	1	0.5	0	0.0	0	0.0	2	0.3	3
Puerto Rican	3	0.8	7	2.1	10	1.8	0	0.0	2	0.9	2	1.0	6	2.7	0	0.0	10	1.4	4
Hispanic American	12	3.1	5	1.5	16	2.9	1	0.6	2	0.9	7	3.3	8	3.6	0	0.0	17	2.4	5
Total Minorities	67	17.6	65	19.9	107	19.5	25	15.7	30	12.8	45	21.4	52	23.1	5	13.5	132	18.7	41
Foreign Nationals	6	1.6	9	2.8	12	2.2	3	1.9	7	3.0	5	2.4	3	1.3	0	0.0	15	2.1	0
Caucasian	308	80.8	252	77.3	429	78.3	131	82.4	198	84.3	160	76.2	170	75.6	32	86.5	560	79.2	230
Total	381	53.9	326	46.1	548	77.5	159	22.5	235	33.2	210	29.7	225	31.8	37	5.2	707		271

RUTGERS UNIVERSITY-CAMDEN

GPA & LSAT Scores

	Full Time	Part Time	Total
# of apps	1,503	0	1,503
# admits	754	0	754
# of matrics	191	45	236
75% GPA	3.49	3.35	
25% GPA	3.04	2.64	
75% LSAT	155	158	
25% LSAT	150	149	

Tuition & Fees

	Resident	Non-resident
Full-Time	$10,062	$14,288
Part-Time	$7,940	$11,500

Living Expenses

Estimated living expenses for Singles

Living on campus	Living off campus	Living at home
$8,995	$11,295	$5,445

Employment

	Total	%
Employment status known	201	93.9
Employment status unknown	13	6.1
Employed	186	92.5
Pursuing graduate degrees	0	0.0
Unemployed seeking employment	8	4.0
Unemployed not seeking employment	7	3.5
Type of Employment		
# employed in law firms	74	39.8
# employed in business & industry	24	12.9
# employed in government	20	10.8
# employed in public interest	6	3.2
# employed as judicial clerks	57	30.6
# employed in academia	5	2.7
Geographic Location		
# employed in state	115	61.8
# employed in foreign countries	3	1.6
# of states where employed	15	

Financial Aid

	Full-time		Part-time		Total	
	#	%	#	%	#	%
Total # of Students	548		159		707	
Total # receiving grants	31	5.7	5	3.1	36	5.1
Less than 1/2 tuition	29	5.3	5	3.1	34	4.8
Half to full tuition	1	0.2	0	0.0	1	0.1
Full tuition	1	0.2	0	0.0	1	0.1
More than full tuition	0	0.0	0	0.0	0	0.0
Median Grant Amount	$2,250		$1,500			

Informational & Library Resources

# of volumes & volume equivalents	399,018	# of professional staff	7
# of titles	75,165	Hours per week with professional staff	48
# of active serial subscriptions	3,152	Hours per week without professional staff	52
Study seating capacity inside the library	402	# of student computer work stations for entire law school	50
Square feet of law library	46,856	# of additional networked connections	50
Square feet of law school (excl. Library)	48,852	Require Laptop Computer?	N

J.D. Attrition (Prior Year)

	Academic	Other	TOTALS	
	#	#	#	%
1st Year	0	25	25	10%
2nd Year	0	4	4	1.9%
3rd Year	0	2	2	0.7%
4th Year	0	0	0	0.0%
TOTALS	0	31	31	4.0%

Bar Passage Rates

Jurisdiction	New Jersey		
Exam	Sum 96	Win 97	Total
# from school taking bar for the first time	153	29	182
School's pass rate for all first-time takers	80%	69%	78%
State's pass rate for all first-time takers	78%	68%	77%

RUTGERS UNIVERSITY-NEWARK

15 Washington Street
Newark, NJ 07102-3192
(973)353-5561
http://www.rutgers.edu/rusln

ABA Approved Since 1941

The Basics

Type of School: Public | Term: Semester

Application deadline: 03/15

Application fee: $40

Financial Aid deadline: 03/01

Can first year start other than Fall? No

Student faculty ratio: 15.9 to 1

Does the University offer:
- housing restricted to law students? No
- graduate student housing for which law students are eligible? Yes

Faculty & Administrators

	Total		Men		Women		Minorities	
	Fall	Spr	Fall	Spr	Fall	Spr	Fall	Spr
Full-time	34	37	21	26	13	11	7	8
Other Full-Time	2	2	2	2	0	0	0	0
Deans, librarians, & others who teach > 1/2	2	2	2	2	0	0	1	1
Part-time	30	19	20	14	10	5	3	4
Total	68	60	45	44	23	16	11	13
Deans, librarians, & others who teach < 1/2	4	4	2	2	2	2	0	0

Curriculum

	Full time	Part time
Typical first-year section size	80	55
Is there typically a "small section" of the first year class, other than Legal Writing, taught by full-time faculty?	Yes	Yes
If yes, typical size offered last year	28	25
# of classroom course titles beyond 1st year curriculum	78	41
# of upper division courses, excluding seminars, with an enrollment:		
Under 25	41	16
25 - 49	18	15
50 - 74	6	1
75 - 99	2	4
100 +	4	0
# of seminars	24	8
# of seminar positions available	576	
# of seminar positions filled	279	73
# of positions available in simulation courses	210	
# of simulation positions filled	104	79
# of positions available in faculty supervised clinical courses	224	
# of fac. sup. clin. positions filled	182	23
# involved in field placements	111	5
# involved in law journals	137	11
# in moot court or trial competitions	55	16
# of credit hrs required to graduate	84	

J.D. Enrollment & Ethnicity

	Men		Women		Fl-Time		Pt-Time		1st Yr		2nd Yr		3rd Yr		4th Yr		Total		JD Degrees Awarded
	#	%	#	%	#	%	#	%	#	%	#	%	#	%	#	%	#	%	
African-American	48	12.2	46	13.9	54	10.8	40	18.1	26	12.5	29	13.2	32	13.1	7	14.0	94	13.0	25
American Indian	0	0.0	0	0.0	0	0.0	0	0.0	0	0.0	0	0.0	0	0.0	0	0.0	0	0.0	0
Asian American	27	6.9	31	9.4	48	9.6	10	4.5	15	7.2	28	12.7	13	5.3	2	4.0	58	8.0	20
Mexican American	2	0.5	0	0.0	2	0.4	0	0.0	1	0.5	1	0.5	0	0.0	0	0.0	2	0.3	0
Puerto Rican	21	5.3	15	4.5	27	5.4	9	4.1	12	5.8	9	4.1	13	5.3	2	4.0	36	5.0	10
Hispanic American	17	4.3	21	6.4	25	5.0	13	5.9	14	6.7	14	6.4	9	3.7	1	2.0	38	5.3	5
Total Minorities	115	29.3	113	34.2	156	31.1	72	32.6	68	32.7	81	36.8	67	27.3	12	24.0	228	31.5	60
Foreign Nationals	21	5.3	14	4.2	24	4.8	11	5.0	8	3.8	9	4.1	16	6.5	2	4.0	35	4.8	11
Caucasian	257	65.4	203	61.5	322	64.1	138	62.4	132	63.5	130	59.1	162	66.1	36	72.0	460	63.6	176
Total	393	54.4	330	45.6	502	69.4	221	30.6	208	28.8	220	30.4	245	33.9	50	6.9	723		247

GPA & LSAT Scores

	Full Time	Part Time	Total
# of apps	1,873	454	2,327
# admits	646	112	758
# of matrics	152	59	211
75% GPA	3.50	3.55	
25% GPA	3.06	2.66	
75% LSAT	159	159	
25% LSAT	153	150	

Tuition & Fees

	Resident	Non-resident
Full-Time	$10,037	$14,263
Part-Time	$6,436	$9,284

Living Expenses

Estimated living expenses for Singles

Living on campus	Living off campus	Living at home
$9,375	$11,675	$5,475

Financial Aid

	Full-time		Part-time		Total	
	#	%	#	%	#	%
Total # of Students	502		221		723	
Total # receiving grants	85	16.9	7	3.2	92	12.7
Less than 1/2 tuition	72	14.3	6	2.7	78	10.8
Half to full tuition	8	1.6	1	0.5	9	1.2
Full tuition	3	0.6	0	0.0	3	0.4
More than full tuition	2	0.4	0	0.0	2	0.3
Median Grant Amount	$1,500		$1,500			

Informational & Library Resources

# of volumes & volume equivalents	412,542	# of professional staff	10
# of titles	113,962	Hours per week with professional staff	56
# of active serial subscriptions	3,073	Hours per week without professional staff	51
Study seating capacity inside the library	397	# of student computer work stations for entire law school	89
Square feet of law library	44,523	# of additional networked connections	0
Square feet of law school (excl. Library)	77,367	Require Laptop Computer?	N

Employment

	Total	%
Employment status known	203	91.0
Employment status unknown	20	9.0
Employed	186	91.6
Pursuing graduate degrees	2	1.0
Unemployed seeking employment	12	5.9
Unemployed not seeking employment	3	1.5
Type of Employment		
# employed in law firms	71	38.2
# employed in business & industry	37	19.9
# employed in government	16	8.6
# employed in public interest	11	5.9
# employed as judicial clerks	45	24.2
# employed in academia	3	1.6
Geographic Location		
# employed in state	137	73.7
# employed in foreign countries	1	0.5
# of states where employed	10	

J.D. Attrition (Prior Year)

	Academic	Other	TOTALS	
	#	#	#	%
1st Year	4	25	29	13%
2nd Year	2	6	8	3.4%
3rd Year	0	4	4	1.5%
4th Year	0	0	0	0.0%
TOTALS	6	35	41	5.2%

Bar Passage Rates

Jurisdiction	New Jersey			New York		
Exam	Sum 96	Win 97	Total	Sum 96	Win 97	Total
# from school taking bar for the first time	172	32	204	130	19	149
School's pass rate for all first-time takers	75%	69%	74%	78%	68%	77%
State's pass rate for all first-time takers	78%	68%	77%	78%	67%	77%

SAMFORD UNIVERSITY

800 Lakeshore Drive
Birmingham, AL 35229
(205)870-2701
http://www.samford.edu/schools/law

ABA Approved Since 1949

The Basics

Type of School: Private Term: Semester
Application deadline: 05/01
Application fee: $40
Financial Aid deadline: 03/01
Can first year start other than Fall? No
Student faculty ratio: 20.3 to 1
Does the University offer:
- housing restricted to law students? No
- graduate student housing for which law students are eligible? No

Faculty & Administrators

	Total		Men		Women		Minorities	
	Fall	Spr	Fall	Spr	Fall	Spr	Fall	Spr
Full-time	26	26	21	21	5	5	3	3
Other Full-Time	0	0	0	0	0	0	0	0
Deans, librarians, & others who teach > 1/2	2	2	1	1	1	1	1	1
Part-time	14	20	11	18	3	2	2	3
Total	42	48	33	40	9	8	6	7
Deans, librarians, & others who teach < 1/2	1	1	1	1	0	0	0	0

Curriculum

	Full time	Part time
Typical first-year section size	70	0
Is there typically a "small section" of the first year class, other than Legal Writing, taught by full-time faculty?	No	No
If yes, typical size offered last year	N/A	N/A
# of classroom course titles beyond 1st year curriculum	68	0
# of upper division courses, excluding seminars, with an enrollment:		
Under 25	11	0
25 - 49	31	0
50 - 74	37	0
75 - 99	5	0
100 +	0	0
# of seminars	25	0
# of seminar positions available	500	
# of seminar positions filled	415	0
# of positions available in simulation courses	417	
# of simulation positions filled	417	0
# of positions available in faculty supervised clinical courses	332	
# of fac. sup. clin. positions filled	288	0
# involved in field placements	152	0
# involved in law journals	105	0
# in moot court or trial competitions	19	0
# of credit hrs required to graduate	90	

J.D. Enrollment & Ethnicity

	Men		Women		Fl-Time		Pt-Time		1st Yr		2nd Yr		3rd Yr		4th Yr		Total		JD Degrees Awarded
	#	%	#	%	#	%	#	%	#	%	#	%	#	%	#	%	#	%	
African-American	17	4.2	23	11.0	40	6.5	0	0.0	6	2.9	15	7.5	19	9.1	0	0.0	40	6.5	14
American Indian	0	0.0	0	0.0	0	0.0	0	0.0	0	0.0	0	0.0	0	0.0	0	0.0	0	0.0	0
Asian American	1	0.2	2	1.0	3	0.5	0	0.0	1	0.5	1	0.5	1	0.5	0	0.0	3	0.5	1
Mexican American	0	0.0	0	0.0	0	0.0	0	0.0	0	0.0	0	0.0	0	0.0	0	0.0	0	0.0	0
Puerto Rican	0	0.0	0	0.0	0	0.0	0	0.0	0	0.0	0	0.0	0	0.0	0	0.0	0	0.0	0
Hispanic American	2	0.5	3	1.4	5	0.8	0	0.0	3	1.4	1	0.5	1	0.5	0	0.0	5	0.8	2
Total Minorities	20	4.9	28	13.3	48	7.8	0	0.0	10	4.8	17	8.5	21	10.0	0	0.0	48	7.8	17
Foreign Nationals	0	0.0	0	0.0	0	0.0	0	0.0	0	0.0	0	0.0	0	0.0	0	0.0	0	0.0	0
Caucasian	386	95.1	182	86.7	568	92.2	0	0.0	198	95.2	182	91.5	188	90.0	0	0.0	568	92.2	195
Total	406	65.9	210	34.1	616	100.0	0	0.0	208	33.8	199	32.3	209	33.9	0	0.0	616		212

GPA & LSAT Scores

	Full Time	Part Time	Total
# of apps	1,003	0	1,003
# admits	580	0	580
# of matrics	212	0	212
75% GPA	3.28	0.00	
25% GPA	2.75	0.00	
75% LSAT	154	0	
25% LSAT	148	0	

Tuition & Fees

	Resident	Non-resident
Full-Time	$17,700	$17,700
Part-Time	$0	$0

Living Expenses

Estimated living expenses for Singles		
Living on campus	Living off campus	Living at home
N/A	$11,089	$5,143

Financial Aid

	Full-time		Part-time		Total	
	#	%	#	%	#	%
Total # of Students	616		0		616	
Total # receiving grants	170	27.6	0	0.0	170	27.6
Less than 1/2 tuition	94	15.3	0	0.0	94	15.3
Half to full tuition	18	2.9	0	0.0	18	2.9
Full tuition	31	5.0	0	0.0	31	5.0
More than full tuition	27	4.4	0	0.0	27	4.4
Median Grant Amount	$7,000		$0			

Informational & Library Resources

# of volumes & volume equivalents	240,329	# of professional staff	7
# of titles	33,061	Hours per week with professional staff	54
# of active serial subscriptions	2,703	Hours per week without professional staff	53
Study seating capacity inside the library	474	# of student computer work stations for entire law school	55
Square feet of law library	42,500	# of additional networked connections	170
Square feet of law school (excl. Library)	72,900	Require Laptop Computer?	N

Employment

	Total	%
Employment status known	206	97.2
Employment status unknown	6	2.8
Employed	186	90.3
Pursuing graduate degrees	5	2.4
Unemployed seeking employment	8	3.9
Unemployed not seeking employment	7	3.4
Type of Employment		
# employed in law firms	125	67.2
# employed in business & industry	16	8.6
# employed in government	18	9.7
# employed in public interest	2	1.1
# employed as judicial clerks	22	11.8
# employed in academia	1	0.5
Geographic Location		
# employed in state	99	53.2
# employed in foreign countries	0	0.0
# of states where employed	15	

J.D. Attrition (Prior Year)

	Academic	Other	TOTALS	
	#	#	#	%
1st Year	1	11	12	5.7%
2nd Year	1	0	1	0.5%
3rd Year	0	0	0	0.0%
4th Year	0	0	0	0.0%
TOTALS	2	11	13	2.1%

Bar Passage Rates

Jurisdiction	Alabama		
Exam	Sum 96	Win 97	Total
# from school taking bar for the first time	117	12	129
School's pass rate for all first-time takers	89%	92%	89%
State's pass rate for all first-time takers	78%	66%	74%

SAN DIEGO, UNIVERSITY OF

5998 Alcala Park
San Diego, CA 92110-2492
(619)260-4527
http://www.acusd.edu/~usdlaw

ABA Approved Since 1961

The Basics

Type of School: Private — Term: Semester
Application deadline: 02/01
Application fee: $40
Financial Aid deadline: 03/01
Can first year start other than Fall? No
Student faculty ratio: 15.9 to 1
Does the University offer:
- housing restricted to law students? No
- graduate student housing for which law students are eligible? Yes

Faculty & Administrators

	Total		Men		Women		Minorities	
	Fall	Spr	Fall	Spr	Fall	Spr	Fall	Spr
Full-time	46	46	35	36	11	10	7	7
Other Full-Time	9	9	2	2	7	7	1	1
Deans, librarians, & others who teach > 1/2	1	1	0	0	1	1	0	0
Part-time	33	32	27	27	6	5	4	3
Total	89	88	64	65	25	23	12	11
Deans, librarians, & others who teach < 1/2	5	5	0	0	5	5	0	0

Curriculum

	Full time	Part time
Typical first-year section size	80	80
Is there typically a "small section" of the first year class, other than Legal Writing, taught by full-time faculty?	Yes	Yes
If yes, typical size offered last year	40	40
# of classroom course titles beyond 1st year curriculum	75	50
# of upper division courses, excluding seminars, with an enrollment:		
Under 25	45	34
25 - 49	27	12
50 - 74	13	6
75 - 99	15	6
100 +	1	0
# of seminars	22	9
# of seminar positions available	687	
# of seminar positions filled	340	181
# of positions available in simulation courses	605	
# of simulation positions filled	395	173
# of positions available in faculty supervised clinical courses	78	
# of fac. sup. clin. positions filled	56	12
# involved in field placements	121	12
# involved in law journals	86	24
# in moot court or trial competitions	121	13
# of credit hrs required to graduate	85	

J.D. Enrollment & Ethnicity

	Men		Women		Fl-Time		Pt-Time		1st Yr		2nd Yr		3rd Yr		4th Yr		Total		JD Degrees Awarded
	#	%	#	%	#	%	#	%	#	%	#	%	#	%	#	%	#	%	
African-American	3	0.5	10	2.5	5	0.7	8	2.9	4	1.2	2	0.7	5	1.6	2	5.0	13	1.3	6
American Indian	10	1.7	7	1.8	15	2.2	2	0.7	5	1.6	7	2.4	5	1.6	0	0.0	17	1.7	6
Asian American	59	10.3	66	16.5	91	13.1	34	12.2	47	14.6	35	11.9	39	12.2	4	10.0	125	12.8	29
Mexican American	19	3.3	13	3.3	26	3.7	6	2.2	12	3.7	4	1.4	15	4.7	1	2.5	32	3.3	21
Puerto Rican	0	0.0	1	0.3	1	0.1	0	0.0	1	0.3	0	0.0	0	0.0	0	0.0	1	0.1	0
Hispanic American	18	3.1	6	1.5	20	2.9	4	1.4	12	3.7	12	4.1	0	0.0	0	0.0	24	2.5	1
Total Minorities	109	19.0	103	25.8	158	22.7	54	19.4	81	25.2	60	20.5	64	20.0	7	17.5	212	21.8	63
Foreign Nationals	5	0.9	1	0.3	6	0.9	0	0.0	0	0.0	2	0.7	4	1.3	0	0.0	6	0.6	0
Caucasian	460	80.1	296	74.0	531	76.4	225	80.6	240	74.8	231	78.8	252	78.8	33	82.5	756	77.6	242
Total	574	58.9	400	41.1	695	71.4	279	28.6	321	33.0	293	30.1	320	32.9	40	4.1	974		305

SAN DIEGO, UNIVERSITY OF

GPA & LSAT Scores

	Full Time	Part Time	Total
# of apps	2,481	240	2,721
# admits	1,068	208	1,276
# of matrics	243	91	334
75% GPA	3.36	3.24	
25% GPA	2.79	2.73	
75% LSAT	161	157	
25% LSAT	157	154	

Tuition & Fees

	Resident	Non-resident
Full-Time	$19,980	$19,980
Part-Time	$14,180	$14,180

Living Expenses

Estimated living expenses for Singles		
Living on campus	Living off campus	Living at home
$12,538	$12,538	$6,940

Employment

	Total	%
Employment status known	277	88.2
Employment status unknown	37	11.8
Employed	239	86.3
Pursuing graduate degrees	10	3.6
Unemployed seeking employment	19	6.9
Unemployed not seeking employment	9	3.2
Type of Employment		
# employed in law firms	155	64.9
# employed in business & industry	36	15.1
# employed in government	35	14.6
# employed in public interest	2	0.8
# employed as judicial clerks	11	4.6
# employed in academia	0	0.0
Geographic Location		
# employed in state	186	77.8
# employed in foreign countries	0	0.0
# of states where employed	16	

Financial Aid

	Full-time		Part-time		Total	
	#	%	#	%	#	%
Total # of Students	695		279		974	
Total # receiving grants	271	39.0	76	27.2	347	35.6
Less than 1/2 tuition	71	10.2	18	6.5	89	9.1
Half to full tuition	176	25.3	54	19.4	230	23.6
Full tuition	11	1.6	3	1.1	14	1.4
More than full tuition	13	1.9	1	0.4	14	1.4
Median Grant Amount	$11,497		$6,671			

Informational & Library Resources

# of volumes & volume equivalents	422,270	# of professional staff	9
# of titles	184,861	Hours per week with professional staff	70
# of active serial subscriptions	5,187	Hours per week without professional staff	38
Study seating capacity inside the library	600	# of student computer work stations for entire law school	37
Square feet of law library	53,800	# of additional networked connections	83
Square feet of law school (excl. Library)	62,040	Require Laptop Computer?	N

J.D. Attrition (Prior Year)

	Academic	Other	TOTALS	
	#	#	#	%
1st Year	18	25	43	14%
2nd Year	1	4	5	1.6%
3rd Year	0	2	2	0.6%
4th Year	0	0	0	0.0%
TOTALS	19	31	50	5.2%

Bar Passage Rates

Jurisdiction	California		
Exam	Sum 96	Win 97	Total
# from school taking bar for the first time	248	38	286
School's pass rate for all first-time takers	79%	74%	79%
State's pass rate for all first-time takers	69%	62%	67%

SAN FRANCISCO, UNIVERSITY OF

2130 Fulton Street
San Francisco, CA 94117-1080
(415)422-6586
http://www.usfca.edu

ABA Approved Since 1935

The Basics

Type of School: Private Term: Semester
Application deadline: 04/01
Application fee: $40
Financial Aid deadline: 02/15
Can first year start other than Fall? No
Student faculty ratio: 20.2 to 1
Does the University offer:
- housing restricted to law students? No
- graduate student housing for which law students are eligible? Yes

Faculty & Administrators

	Total		Men		Women		Minorities	
	Fall	Spr	Fall	Spr	Fall	Spr	Fall	Spr
Full-time	25	25	18	19	7	6	5	4
Other Full-Time	0	0	0	0	0	0	0	0
Deans, librarians, & others who teach > 1/2	1	1	1	1	0	0	0	0
Part-time	31	36	21	27	10	9	5	3
Total	57	62	40	47	17	15	10	7
Deans, librarians, & others who teach < 1/2	1	1	1	1	0	0	0	0

Curriculum

	Full time	Part time
Typical first-year section size	89	50
Is there typically a "small section" of the first year class, other than Legal Writing, taught by full-time faculty?	No	No
If yes, typical size offered last year	N/A	N/A
# of classroom course titles beyond 1st year curriculum	57	44
# of upper division courses, excluding seminars, with an enrollment:		
Under 25	39	17
25 - 49	11	12
50 - 74	11	5
75 - 99	3	3
100 +	0	4
# of seminars	10	3
# of seminar positions available	401	
# of seminar positions filled	255	99
# of positions available in simulation courses	588	
# of simulation positions filled	246	206
# of positions available in faculty supervised clinical courses	111	
# of fac. sup. clin. positions filled	87	5
# involved in field placements	145	13
# involved in law journals	125	0
# in moot court or trial competitions	68	3
# of credit hrs required to graduate	86	

J.D. Enrollment & Ethnicity

	Men		Women		Fl-Time		Pt-Time		1st Yr		2nd Yr		3rd Yr		4th Yr		Total		JD Degrees Awarded
	#	%	#	%	#	%	#	%	#	%	#	%	#	%	#	%	#	%	
African-American	9	2.9	14	4.1	18	3.4	5	4.0	10	4.6	7	3.6	6	2.9	0	0.0	23	3.5	10
American Indian	2	0.6	3	0.9	3	0.6	2	1.6	1	0.5	1	0.5	3	1.5	0	0.0	5	0.8	1
Asian American	46	14.9	53	15.5	81	15.4	18	14.4	25	11.5	28	14.2	40	19.4	6	20.0	99	15.2	31
Mexican American	21	6.8	23	6.7	36	6.9	8	6.4	17	7.8	12	6.1	13	6.3	2	6.7	44	6.8	8
Puerto Rican	0	0.0	0	0.0	0	0.0	0	0.0	0	0.0	0	0.0	0	0.0	0	0.0	0	0.0	0
Hispanic American	0	0.0	0	0.0	0	0.0	0	0.0	0	0.0	0	0.0	0	0.0	0	0.0	0	0.0	0
Total Minorities	78	25.2	93	27.3	138	26.3	33	26.4	53	24.4	48	24.4	62	30.1	8	26.7	171	26.3	50
Foreign Nationals	2	0.6	3	0.9	5	1.0	0	0.0	2	0.9	2	1.0	1	0.5	0	0.0	5	0.8	0
Caucasian	229	74.1	245	71.8	382	72.8	92	73.6	162	74.7	147	74.6	143	69.4	22	73.3	474	72.9	170
Total	309	47.5	341	52.5	525	80.8	125	19.2	217	33.4	197	30.3	206	31.7	30	4.6	650		220

SAN FRANCISCO, UNIVERSITY OF

GPA & LSAT Scores

	Full Time	Part Time	Total
# of apps	2,171	235	2,406
# admits	927	111	1,038
# of matrics	172	46	218
75% GPA	3.32	3.24	
25% GPA	2.79	2.67	
75% LSAT	159	156	
25% LSAT	152	150	

Tuition & Fees

	Resident	Non-resident
Full-Time	$20,000	$20,000
Part-Time	$14,275	$14,275

Living Expenses

Estimated living expenses for Singles		
Living on campus	Living off campus	Living at home
$10,910	$12,850	$5,750

Employment

	Total	%
Employment status known	175	87.1
Employment status unknown	26	12.9
Employed	142	81.1
Pursuing graduate degrees	4	2.3
Unemployed seeking employment	17	9.7
Unemployed not seeking employment	12	6.9
Type of Employment		
# employed in law firms	82	57.7
# employed in business & industry	26	18.3
# employed in government	18	12.7
# employed in public interest	3	2.1
# employed as judicial clerks	8	5.6
# employed in academia	2	1.4
Geographic Location		
# employed in state	129	90.8
# employed in foreign countries	0	0.0
# of states where employed	10	

Financial Aid

	Full-time		Part-time		Total	
	#	%	#	%	#	%
Total # of Students	525		125		650	
Total # receiving grants	312	59.4	43	34.4	355	54.6
Less than 1/2 tuition	296	56.4	40	32.0	336	51.7
Half to full tuition	16	3.0	3	2.4	19	2.9
Full tuition	0	0.0	0	0.0	0	0.0
More than full tuition	0	0.0	0	0.0	0	0.0
Median Grant Amount	$1,400		$3,000			

Informational & Library Resources

# of volumes & volume equivalents	281,939	# of professional staff	6
# of titles	28,273	Hours per week with professional staff	63
# of active serial subscriptions	2,488	Hours per week without professional staff	37
Study seating capacity inside the library	293	# of student computer work stations for entire law school	58
Square feet of law library	21,708	# of additional networked connections	4
Square feet of law school (excl. Library)	30,792	Require Laptop Computer?	N

J.D. Attrition (Prior Year)

	Academic	Other	TOTALS	
	#	#	#	%
1st Year	20	8	28	12%
2nd Year	2	13	15	7.5%
3rd Year	1	4	5	2.1%
4th Year	1	0	1	3.6%
TOTALS	24	25	49	7.1%

Bar Passage Rates

Jurisdiction	California		
Exam	Sum 96	Win 97	Total
# from school taking bar for the first time	174	20	194
School's pass rate for all first-time takers	82%	85%	82%
State's pass rate for all first-time takers	69%	62%	67%

SANTA CLARA UNIVERSITY

500 El Camino Real
Santa Clara, CA 95053
(408)554-4767
http://www.scu.edu/law

ABA Approved Since 1937

The Basics

Type of School: Private   Term: Semester
Application deadline: 03/01
Application fee: $40
Financial Aid deadline: 02/01
Can first year start other than Fall? No
Student faculty ratio: 25.3 to 1
Does the University offer:
- housing restricted to law students? Yes
- graduate student housing for which law students are eligible? No

Faculty & Administrators

	Total		Men		Women		Minorities	
	Fall	Spr	Fall	Spr	Fall	Spr	Fall	Spr
Full-time	28	30	18	19	10	11	6	6
Other Full-Time	7	7	0	0	7	7	0	0
Deans, librarians, & others who teach > 1/2	4	4	1	1	3	3	1	1
Part-time	23	30	19	24	4	6	4	4
Total	62	71	38	44	24	27	11	11
Deans, librarians, & others who teach < 1/2	4	4	2	2	2	2	1	1

Curriculum

	Full time	Part time
Typical first-year section size	74	53
Is there typically a "small section" of the first year class, other than Legal Writing, taught by full-time faculty?	Yes	No
If yes, typical size offered last year	40	N/A
# of classroom course titles beyond 1st year curriculum	134	0
# of upper division courses, excluding seminars, with an enrollment:		
Under 25	89	0
25 - 49	32	0
50 - 74	19	0
75 - 99	8	0
100 +	6	0
# of seminars	35	0
# of seminar positions available	782	
# of seminar positions filled	519	0
# of positions available in simulation courses	754	
# of simulation positions filled	340	0
# of positions available in faculty supervised clinical courses	344	
# of fac. sup. clin. positions filled	150	0
# involved in field placements	220	0
# involved in law journals	79	0
# in moot court or trial competitions	94	0
# of credit hrs required to graduate	86	

J.D. Enrollment & Ethnicity

	Men		Women		Fl-Time		Pt-Time		1st Yr		2nd Yr		3rd Yr		4th Yr		Total		JD Degrees Awarded
	#	%	#	%	#	%	#	%	#	%	#	%	#	%	#	%	#	%	
African-American	19	3.9	21	4.8	28	4.0	12	5.2	8	2.7	12	3.9	15	5.6	5	8.2	40	4.3	12
American Indian	6	1.2	3	0.7	6	0.9	3	1.3	3	1.0	2	0.7	4	1.5	0	0.0	9	1.0	1
Asian American	77	15.8	101	22.9	136	19.5	42	18.2	49	16.8	64	20.8	51	19.0	14	23.0	178	19.2	48
Mexican American	0	0.0	0	0.0	0	0.0	0	0.0	0	0.0	0	0.0	0	0.0	0	0.0	0	0.0	0
Puerto Rican	0	0.0	0	0.0	0	0.0	0	0.0	0	0.0	0	0.0	0	0.0	0	0.0	0	0.0	0
Hispanic American	50	10.3	43	9.7	74	10.6	19	8.2	28	9.6	34	11.1	26	9.7	5	8.2	93	10.0	32
Total Minorities	152	31.3	168	38.0	244	35.0	76	32.9	88	30.1	112	36.5	96	35.8	24	39.3	320	34.5	93
Foreign Nationals	0	0.0	0	0.0	0	0.0	0	0.0	0	0.0	0	0.0	0	0.0	0	0.0	0	0.0	0
Caucasian	334	68.7	274	62.0	453	65.0	155	67.1	204	69.9	195	63.5	172	64.2	37	60.7	608	65.5	166
Total	486	52.4	442	47.6	697	75.1	231	24.9	292	31.5	307	33.1	268	28.9	61	6.6	928		259

GPA & LSAT Scores

	Full Time	Part Time	Total
# of apps	2,351	208	2,559
# admits	1,174	101	1,275
# of matrics	242	56	298
75% GPA	3.42	3.35	
25% GPA	2.96	2.82	
75% LSAT	160	161	
25% LSAT	153	153	

Tuition & Fees

	Resident	Non-resident
Full-Time	$19,810	$19,810
Part-Time	$13,800	$13,800

Living Expenses

Estimated living expenses for Singles		
Living on campus	Living off campus	Living at home
N/A	$15,164	N/A

Financial Aid

	Full-time		Part-time		Total	
	#	%	#	%	#	%
Total # of Students	697		231		928	
Total # receiving grants	303	43.5	30	13.0	333	35.9
Less than 1/2 tuition	244	35.0	22	9.5	266	28.7
Half to full tuition	50	7.2	4	1.7	54	5.8
Full tuition	9	1.3	4	1.7	13	1.4
More than full tuition	0	0.0	0	0.0	0	0.0
Median Grant Amount	$9,000		$7,000			

Informational & Library Resources

# of volumes & volume equivalents	262,447	# of professional staff	7
# of titles	108,104	Hours per week with professional staff	76
# of active serial subscriptions	3,544	Hours per week without professional staff	29
Study seating capacity inside the library	448	# of student computer work stations for entire law school	60
Square feet of law library	39,554	# of additional networked connections	470
Square feet of law school (excl. Library)	98,647	Require Laptop Computer?	N

Employment

	Total	%
Employment status known	194	79.8
Employment status unknown	49	20.2
Employed	165	85.1
Pursuing graduate degrees	4	2.1
Unemployed seeking employment	18	9.3
Unemployed not seeking employment	7	3.6
Type of Employment		
# employed in law firms	107	64.8
# employed in business & industry	39	23.6
# employed in government	14	8.5
# employed in public interest	2	1.2
# employed as judicial clerks	3	1.8
# employed in academia	0	0.0
Geographic Location		
# employed in state	140	84.8
# employed in foreign countries	2	1.2
# of states where employed	7	

J.D. Attrition (Prior Year)

	Academic	Other	TOTALS	
	#	#	#	%
1st Year	15	23	38	13%
2nd Year	0	5	5	1.8%
3rd Year	1	0	1	0.4%
4th Year	0	0	0	0.0%
TOTALS	16	28	44	4.9%

Bar Passage Rates

Jurisdiction	California		
Exam	Sum 96	Win 97	Total
# from school taking bar for the first time	200	28	228
School's pass rate for all first-time takers	71%	75%	71%
State's pass rate for all first-time takers	69%	62%	67%

SEATTLE UNIVERSITY

950 Broadway Plaza
Tacoma, WA 98402
(206)591-2275
http://www.law.seattleu.edu

ABA Approved Since 1994

The Basics

Type of School: Private Term: Semester

Application deadline: 04/01

Application fee: $50

Financial Aid deadline: 04/01

Can first year start other than Fall? Yes

Student faculty ratio: 22.8 to 1

Does the University offer:
- housing restricted to law students? No
- graduate student housing for which law students are eligible? No

Faculty & Administrators

	Total		Men		Women		Minorities	
	Fall	Spr	Fall	Spr	Fall	Spr	Fall	Spr
Full-time	28	29	18	19	10	10	3	3
Other Full-Time	6	6	2	2	4	4	1	1
Deans, librarians, & others who teach > 1/2	1	1	0	0	1	1	0	0
Part-time	21	23	14	17	7	6	4	3
Total	56	59	34	38	22	21	8	7
Deans, librarians, & others who teach < 1/2	2	2	1	1	1	1	0	0

Curriculum

	Full time	Part time
Typical first-year section size	70	50
Is there typically a "small section" of the first year class, other than Legal Writing, taught by full-time faculty?	No	No
If yes, typical size offered last year	N/A	N/A
# of classroom course titles beyond 1st year curriculum	99	0
# of upper division courses, excluding seminars, with an enrollment:		
Under 25	48	0
25 - 49	32	0
50 - 74	21	0
75 - 99	10	0
100 +	3	0
# of seminars	8	0
# of seminar positions available	160	
# of seminar positions filled	154	0
# of positions available in simulation courses	626	
# of simulation positions filled	664	0
# of positions available in faculty supervised clinical courses	130	
# of fac. sup. clin. positions filled	135	0
# involved in field placements	42	0
# involved in law journals	62	0
# in moot court or trial competitions	15	0
# of credit hrs required to graduate	90	

J.D. Enrollment & Ethnicity

	Men		Women		Fl-Time		Pt-Time		1st Yr		2nd Yr		3rd Yr		4th Yr		Total		JD Degrees Awarded
	#	%	#	%	#	%	#	%	#	%	#	%	#	%	#	%	#	%	
African-American	10	2.4	26	6.3	22	3.4	14	7.4	16	6.3	8	3.1	6	1.9	6	****	36	4.3	14
American Indian	16	3.8	9	2.2	18	2.8	7	3.7	4	1.6	7	2.7	11	3.5	3	****	25	3.0	9
Asian American	33	7.9	41	9.9	57	8.9	17	9.0	28	10.9	23	8.8	19	6.1	4	****	74	8.9	23
Mexican American	0	0.0	2	0.5	2	0.3	0	0.0	2	0.8	0	0.0	0	0.0	0	0.0	2	0.2	0
Puerto Rican	1	0.2	1	0.2	2	0.3	0	0.0	1	0.4	1	0.4	0	0.0	0	0.0	2	0.2	0
Hispanic American	11	2.6	8	1.9	14	2.2	5	2.6	9	3.5	4	1.5	5	1.6	1	****	19	2.3	11
Total Minorities	71	17.1	87	21.0	115	17.9	43	22.8	60	23.4	43	16.5	41	13.1	14	****	158	19.0	57
Foreign Nationals	0	0.0	0	0.0	0	0.0	0	0.0	0	0.0	0	0.0	0	0.0	0	0.0	0	0.0	0
Caucasian	345	82.9	327	79.0	526	82.1	146	77.2	196	76.6	217	83.5	236	75.2	23	****	672	81.0	215
Total	416	50.1	414	49.9	641	77.2	189	22.8	256	30.8	260	31.3	314	37.8	0	0.0	830		272

GPA & LSAT Scores

	Full Time	Part Time	Total
# of apps	987	171	1,158
# admits	666	124	790
# of matrics	173	89	262
75% GPA	3.61	3.40	
25% GPA	3.06	2.64	
75% LSAT	159	152	
25% LSAT	151	145	

Tuition & Fees

	Resident	Non-resident
Full-Time	$17,086	$17,086
Part-Time	$14,232	$14,232

Living Expenses

Estimated living expenses for Singles		
Living on campus	Living off campus	Living at home
N/A	$11,008	$6,112

Financial Aid

	Full-time		Part-time		Total	
	#	%	#	%	#	%
Total # of Students	641		189		830	
Total # receiving grants	256	39.9	41	21.7	297	35.8
Less than 1/2 tuition	222	34.6	41	21.7	263	31.7
Half to full tuition	34	5.3	0	0.0	34	4.1
Full tuition	0	0.0	0	0.0	0	0.0
More than full tuition	0	0.0	0	0.0	0	0.0
Median Grant Amount	$4,813		$3,163			

Informational & Library Resources

# of volumes & volume equivalents	341,306	# of professional staff	8
# of titles	138,062	Hours per week with professional staff	61
# of active serial subscriptions	3,778	Hours per week without professional staff	58
Study seating capacity inside the library	589	# of student computer work stations for entire law school	105
Square feet of law library	40,397	# of additional networked connections	0
Square feet of law school (excl. Library)	59,290	Require Laptop Computer?	N

Employment

	Total	%
Employment status known	252	93.0
Employment status unknown	19	7.0
Employed	206	81.7
Pursuing graduate degrees	2	0.8
Unemployed seeking employment	37	14.7
Unemployed not seeking employment	7	2.8
Type of Employment		
# employed in law firms	113	54.9
# employed in business & industry	33	16.0
# employed in government	40	19.4
# employed in public interest	1	0.5
# employed as judicial clerks	10	4.9
# employed in academia	2	1.0
Geographic Location		
# employed in state	176	85.4
# employed in foreign countries	0	0.0
# of states where employed	20	

J.D. Attrition (Prior Year)

	Academic	Other	TOTALS	
	#	#	#	%
1st Year	11	19	30	11%
2nd Year	3	15	18	6.7%
3rd Year	0	2	2	0.7%
4th Year	0	0	0	0.0%
TOTALS	14	36	50	5.6%

Bar Passage Rates

Jurisdiction	Washington		
Exam	Sum 96	Win 97	Total
# from school taking bar for the first time	191	46	237
School's pass rate for all first-time takers	82%	76%	81%
State's pass rate for all first-time takers	73%	82%	76%

SETON HALL UNIVERSITY

One Newark Center
Newark, NJ 07102
(973)642-8500
http://www.shu.edu/law

ABA Approved Since 1951

The Basics

Type of School: Private Term: Semester

Application deadline: 04/15

Application fee: $50

Financial Aid deadline: 04/15

Can first year start other than Fall? No

Student faculty ratio: 26.0 to 1

Does the University offer:
- housing restricted to law students? No
- graduate student housing for which law students are eligible? No

Faculty & Administrators

	Total		Men		Women		Minorities	
	Fall	Spr	Fall	Spr	Fall	Spr	Fall	Spr
Full-time	36	37	25	25	11	12	7	7
Other Full-Time	4	4	1	1	3	3	0	0
Deans, librarians, & others who teach > 1/2	3	3	3	3	0	0	0	0
Part-time	74	88	55	70	19	18	5	5
Total	117	132	84	99	33	33	12	12
Deans, librarians, & others who teach < 1/2	0	0	0	0	0	0	0	0

Curriculum

	Full time	Part time
Typical first-year section size	80	65
Is there typically a "small section" of the first year class, other than Legal Writing, taught by full-time faculty?	No	No
If yes, typical size offered last year	N/A	N/A
# of classroom course titles beyond 1st year curriculum	100	76
# of upper division courses, excluding seminars, with an enrollment:		
Under 25	45	26
25 - 49	32	24
50 - 74	19	9
75 - 99	19	7
100 +	0	0
# of seminars	34	24
# of seminar positions available	975	
# of seminar positions filled	457	326
# of positions available in simulation courses	434	
# of simulation positions filled	176	216
# of positions available in faculty supervised clinical courses	130	
# of fac. sup. clin. positions filled	96	17
# involved in field placements	78	10
# involved in law journals	106	12
# in moot court or trial competitions	40	1
# of credit hrs required to graduate	85	

J.D. Enrollment & Ethnicity

	Men		Women		Fl-Time		Pt-Time		1st Yr		2nd Yr		3rd Yr		4th Yr		Total		JD Degrees Awarded
	#	%	#	%	#	%	#	%	#	%	#	%	#	%	#	%	#	%	
African-American	31	4.4	32	6.0	41	4.5	22	6.9	22	5.7	12	3.4	23	5.6	6	7.1	63	5.1	25
American Indian	1	0.1	4	0.7	1	0.1	4	1.3	0	0.0	3	0.8	0	0.0	2	2.4	5	0.4	1
Asian American	39	5.6	25	4.7	55	6.0	9	2.8	24	6.2	19	5.4	18	4.4	3	3.6	64	5.2	16
Mexican American	1	0.1	0	0.0	1	0.1	0	0.0	1	0.3	0	0.0	0	0.0	0	0.0	1	0.1	0
Puerto Rican	8	1.1	8	1.5	11	1.2	5	1.6	3	0.8	4	1.1	7	1.7	2	2.4	16	1.3	4
Hispanic American	21	3.0	29	5.4	39	4.3	11	3.4	17	4.4	11	3.1	22	5.4	0	0.0	50	4.1	17
Total Minorities	101	14.4	98	18.3	148	16.2	51	15.9	67	17.4	49	13.8	70	17.1	13	15.5	199	16.1	63
Foreign Nationals	0	0.0	0	0.0	0	0.0	0	0.0	0	0.0	0	0.0	0	0.0	0	0.0	0	0.0	0
Caucasian	598	85.6	437	81.7	766	83.8	269	84.1	318	82.6	306	86.2	340	82.9	71	84.5	1035	83.9	304
Total	699	56.6	535	43.4	914	74.1	320	25.9	385	31.2	355	28.8	410	33.2	84	6.8	1234		367

GPA & LSAT Scores

	Full Time	Part Time	Total
# of apps	1,990	412	2,402
# admits	1,001	133	1,134
# of matrics	321	64	385
75% GPA	3.36	3.41	
25% GPA	2.81	2.67	
75% LSAT	157	157	
25% LSAT	151	150	

Tuition & Fees

	Resident	Non-resident
Full-Time	$18,631	$18,631
Part-Time	$0	$13,285

Living Expenses

Estimated living expenses for Singles		
Living on campus	Living off campus	Living at home
N/A	$16,565	N/A

Financial Aid

	Full-time		Part-time		Total	
	#	%	#	%	#	%
Total # of Students	914		320		1234	
Total # receiving grants	586	64.1	79	24.7	665	53.9
Less than 1/2 tuition	585	64.0	78	24.4	663	53.7
Half to full tuition	1	0.1	1	0.3	2	0.2
Full tuition	0	0.0	0	0.0	0	0.0
More than full tuition	0	0.0	0	0.0	0	0.0
Median Grant Amount	$1,800		$442			

Informational & Library Resources

# of volumes & volume equivalents	374,067	# of professional staff	10
# of titles	60,918	Hours per week with professional staff	81
# of active serial subscriptions	3,320	Hours per week without professional staff	17
Study seating capacity inside the library	600	# of student computer work stations for entire law school	125
Square feet of law library	55,250	# of additional networked connections	40
Square feet of law school (excl. Library)	154,750	Require Laptop Computer?	N

Employment

	Total	%
Employment status known	399	95.0
Employment status unknown	21	5.0
Employed	364	91.2
Pursuing graduate degrees	2	0.5
Unemployed seeking employment	28	7.0
Unemployed not seeking employment	5	1.3
Type of Employment		
# employed in law firms	148	40.7
# employed in business & industry	52	14.3
# employed in government	28	7.7
# employed in public interest	3	0.8
# employed as judicial clerks	126	34.6
# employed in academia	0	0.0
Geographic Location		
# employed in state	254	69.8
# employed in foreign countries	0	0.0
# of states where employed	25	

J.D. Attrition (Prior Year)

	Academic	Other	TOTALS	
	#	#	#	%
1st Year	13	9	22	6.3%
2nd Year	7	7	14	3.3%
3rd Year	1	2	3	0.8%
4th Year	0	0	0	0.0%
TOTALS	21	18	39	3.2%

Bar Passage Rates

Jurisdiction	New Jersey		
Exam	Sum 96	Win 97	Total
# from school taking bar for the first time	365	43	408
School's pass rate for all first-time takers	79%	53%	76%
State's pass rate for all first-time takers	78%	68%	77%

SOUTH CAROLINA, UNIVERSITY OF

Main and Greene Streets
Columbia, SC 29208
(803)777-6857
http://www.law.sc.edu

ABA Approved Since 1925

The Basics

Type of School: Public Term: Semester
Application deadline: 02/15
Application fee: $35
Financial Aid deadline: 04/15
Can first year start other than Fall? No
Student faculty ratio: 20.9 to 1
Does the University offer:
- housing restricted to law students? No
- graduate student housing for which law students are eligible? No

Faculty & Administrators

	Total		Men		Women		Minorities	
	Fall	Spr	Fall	Spr	Fall	Spr	Fall	Spr
Full-time	35	34	31	31	4	3	10	10
Other Full-Time	0	0	0	0	0	0	0	0
Deans, librarians, & others who teach > 1/2	3	3	3	3	0	0	1	1
Part-time	0	0	0	0	0	0	0	0
Total	38	37	34	34	4	3	11	11
Deans, librarians, & others who teach < 1/2	0	0	0	0	0	0	0	0

Curriculum

	Full time	Part time
Typical first-year section size	85	0
Is there typically a "small section" of the first year class, other than Legal Writing, taught by full-time faculty?	No	No
If yes, typical size offered last year	N/A	N/A
# of classroom course titles beyond 1st year curriculum	108	0
# of upper division courses, excluding seminars, with an enrollment:		
Under 25	32	0
25 - 49	27	0
50 - 74	20	0
75 - 99	18	0
100 +	3	0
# of seminars	28	0
# of seminar positions available	528	
# of seminar positions filled	331	0
# of positions available in simulation courses	368	
# of simulation positions filled	335	0
# of positions available in faculty supervised clinical courses	54	
# of fac. sup. clin. positions filled	53	0
# involved in field placements	0	0
# involved in law journals	164	0
# in moot court or trial competitions	18	0
# of credit hrs required to graduate	90	

J.D. Enrollment & Ethnicity

	Men		Women		Fl-Time		Pt-Time		1st Yr		2nd Yr		3rd Yr		4th Yr		Total		JD Degrees Awarded
	#	%	#	%	#	%	#	%	#	%	#	%	#	%	#	%	#	%	
African-American	19	4.3	37	11.7	56	7.3	0	0.0	22	9.1	18	7.1	16	6.0	0	0.0	56	7.3	20
American Indian	1	0.2	1	0.3	2	0.3	0	0.0	0	0.0	1	0.4	1	0.4	0	0.0	2	0.3	1
Asian American	3	0.7	4	1.3	7	0.9	0	0.0	3	1.2	2	0.8	2	0.8	0	0.0	7	0.9	5
Mexican American	0	0.0	0	0.0	0	0.0	0	0.0	0	0.0	0	0.0	0	0.0	0	0.0	0	0.0	0
Puerto Rican	0	0.0	0	0.0	0	0.0	0	0.0	0	0.0	0	0.0	0	0.0	0	0.0	0	0.0	0
Hispanic American	1	0.2	3	0.9	4	0.5	0	0.0	1	0.4	0	0.0	3	1.1	0	0.0	4	0.5	5
Total Minorities	24	5.4	45	14.2	69	9.0	0	0.0	26	10.7	21	8.2	22	8.3	0	0.0	69	9.0	31
Foreign Nationals	2	0.4	0	0.0	2	0.3	0	0.0	1	0.4	1	0.4	0	0.0	0	0.0	2	0.3	1
Caucasian	421	94.2	272	85.8	693	90.7	0	0.0	216	88.9	233	91.4	244	91.7	0	0.0	693	90.7	203
Total	447	58.5	317	41.5	764	100.0	0	0.0	243	31.8	255	33.4	266	34.8	0	0.0	764		235

GPA & LSAT Scores

	Full Time	Part Time	Total
# of apps	1,158	0	1,158
# admits	461	0	461
# of matrics	242	0	242
75% GPA	3.49	0.00	
25% GPA	2.93	0.00	
75% LSAT	159	0	
25% LSAT	152	0	

Tuition & Fees

	Resident	Non-resident
Full-Time	$6,964	$13,706
Part-Time	$0	$0

Living Expenses

Estimated living expenses for Singles		
Living on campus	Living off campus	Living at home
$11,009	$11,009	$6,687

Financial Aid

	Full-time		Part-time		Total	
	#	%	#	%	#	%
Total # of Students	764		0		764	
Total # receiving grants	271	35.5	0	0.0	271	35.5
Less than 1/2 tuition	243	31.8	0	0.0	243	31.8
Half to full tuition	11	1.4	0	0.0	11	1.4
Full tuition	4	0.5	0	0.0	4	0.5
More than full tuition	13	1.7	0	0.0	13	1.7
Median Grant Amount	$1,300		$0			

Informational & Library Resources

# of volumes & volume equivalents	412,406	# of professional staff	3
# of titles	68,876	Hours per week with professional staff	65
# of active serial subscriptions	3,043	Hours per week without professional staff	46
Study seating capacity inside the library	642	# of student computer work stations for entire law school	72
Square feet of law library	51,915	# of additional networked connections	40
Square feet of law school (excl. Library)	83,170	Require Laptop Computer?	N

Employment

	Total	%
Employment status known	249	96.9
Employment status unknown	8	3.1
Employed	221	88.8
Pursuing graduate degrees	10	4.0
Unemployed seeking employment	13	5.2
Unemployed not seeking employment	5	2.0
Type of Employment		
# employed in law firms	113	51.1
# employed in business & industry	20	9.0
# employed in government	35	15.8
# employed in public interest	3	1.4
# employed as judicial clerks	48	21.7
# employed in academia	2	0.9
Geographic Location		
# employed in state	191	86.4
# employed in foreign countries	2	0.9
# of states where employed	12	

J.D. Attrition (Prior Year)

	Academic	Other	TOTALS	
	#	#	#	%
1st Year	3	7	10	4.0%
2nd Year	1	2	3	1.1%
3rd Year	0	2	2	0.8%
4th Year	0	0	0	0.0%
TOTALS	4	11	15	2.0%

Bar Passage Rates

Jurisdiction	South Carolina		
Exam	Sum 96	Win 97	Total
# from school taking bar for the first time	219	14	233
School's pass rate for all first-time takers	91%	93%	91%
State's pass rate for all first-time takers	90%	82%	88%

SOUTH DAKOTA, UNIVERSITY OF

414 E. Clark Street
Vermillion, SD 57069-2390
(605)677-5443
http://www.usd.edu/law

ABA Approved Since 1923

The Basics

Type of School: Public   Term: Semester

Application deadline: 03/01 (Preferred)

Application fee: $15

Financial Aid deadline: 05/01

Can first year start other than Fall? No

Student faculty ratio: 15.2 to 1

Does the University offer:
- housing restricted to law students? No
- graduate student housing for which law students are eligible? Yes

Faculty & Administrators

	Total		Men		Women		Minorities	
	Fall	Spr	Fall	Spr	Fall	Spr	Fall	Spr
Full-time	12	12	10	10	2	2	1	1
Other Full-Time	2	2	1	1	1	1	0	0
Deans, librarians, & others who teach > 1/2	1	1	1	1	0	0	0	0
Part-time	1	2	1	2	0	0	0	0
Total	16	17	13	14	3	3	1	1
Deans, librarians, & others who teach < 1/2	2	2	1	1	1	1	0	0

Curriculum

	Full time	Part time
Typical first-year section size	73	0
Is there typically a "small section" of the first year class, other than Legal Writing, taught by full-time faculty?	No	No
If yes, typical size offered last year	N/A	N/A
# of classroom course titles beyond 1st year curriculum	46	0
# of upper division courses, excluding seminars, with an enrollment:		
Under 25	27	0
25 - 49	14	0
50 - 74	4	0
75 - 99	0	0
100 +	0	0
# of seminars	1	0
# of seminar positions available	18	
# of seminar positions filled	6	0
# of positions available in simulation courses	145	
# of simulation positions filled	138	0
# of positions available in faculty supervised clinical courses	0	
# of fac. sup. clin. positions filled	0	0
# involved in field placements	16	0
# involved in law journals	36	0
# in moot court or trial competitions	34	0
# of credit hrs required to graduate	90	

J.D. Enrollment & Ethnicity

	Men		Women		Fl-Time		Pt-Time		1st Yr		2nd Yr		3rd Yr		4th Yr		Total		JD Degrees Awarded
	#	%	#	%	#	%	#	%	#	%	#	%	#	%	#	%	#	%	
African-American	5	3.7	0	0.0	5	2.3	0	0.0	2	2.3	2	2.8	1	1.7	0	0.0	5	2.3	0
American Indian	3	2.2	2	2.4	5	2.3	0	0.0	2	2.3	3	4.2	0	0.0	0	0.0	5	2.3	1
Asian American	1	0.7	1	1.2	2	0.9	0	0.0	0	0.0	2	2.8	0	0.0	0	0.0	2	0.9	0
Mexican American	0	0.0	0	0.0	0	0.0	0	0.0	0	0.0	0	0.0	0	0.0	0	0.0	0	0.0	0
Puerto Rican	0	0.0	0	0.0	0	0.0	0	0.0	0	0.0	0	0.0	0	0.0	0	0.0	0	0.0	0
Hispanic American	0	0.0	0	0.0	0	0.0	0	0.0	0	0.0	0	0.0	0	0.0	0	0.0	0	0.0	1
Total Minorities	9	6.7	3	3.5	12	5.5	0	0.0	4	4.5	7	9.7	1	1.7	0	0.0	12	5.5	2
Foreign Nationals	0	0.0	0	0.0	0	0.0	0	0.0	0	0.0	0	0.0	0	0.0	0	0.0	0	0.0	0
Caucasian	125	93.3	82	96.5	207	94.5	0	0.0	84	95.5	65	90.3	58	98.3	0	0.0	207	94.5	73
Total	134	61.2	85	38.8	219	100.0	0	0.0	88	40.2	72	32.9	59	26.9	0	0.0	219		75

GPA & LSAT Scores

	Full Time	Part Time	Total
# of apps	292	0	292
# admits	182	0	182
# of matrics	90	0	90
75% GPA	3.54	0.00	
25% GPA	2.78	0.00	
75% LSAT	154	0	
25% LSAT	149	0	

Tuition & Fees

	Resident	Non-resident
Full-Time	$4,715	$9,979
Part-Time	$0	$0

Living Expenses

Estimated living expenses for Singles		
Living on campus	Living off campus	Living at home
$6,233	$8,429	$8,429

Financial Aid

	Full-time		Part-time		Total	
	#	%	#	%	#	%
Total # of Students	219		0		219	
Total # receiving grants	143	65.3	0	0.0	143	65.3
Less than 1/2 tuition	112	51.1	0	0.0	112	51.1
Half to full tuition	9	4.1	0	0.0	9	4.1
Full tuition	6	2.7	0	0.0	6	2.7
More than full tuition	16	7.3	0	0.0	16	7.3
Median Grant Amount	$900		$0			

Informational & Library Resources

# of volumes & volume equivalents	179,082	# of professional staff	6
# of titles	36,868	Hours per week with professional staff	53
# of active serial subscriptions	2,074	Hours per week without professional staff	43
Study seating capacity inside the library	227	# of student computer work stations for entire law school	33
Square feet of law library	23,469	# of additional networked connections	12
Square feet of law school (excl. Library)	36,763	Require Laptop Computer?	N

Employment

	Total	%
Employment status known	72	100.0
Employment status unknown	0	0.0
Employed	68	94.4
Pursuing graduate degrees	2	2.8
Unemployed seeking employment	2	2.8
Unemployed not seeking employment	0	0.0
Type of Employment		
# employed in law firms	25	36.8
# employed in business & industry	10	14.7
# employed in government	14	20.6
# employed in public interest	0	0.0
# employed as judicial clerks	18	26.5
# employed in academia	1	1.5
Geographic Location		
# employed in state	41	60.3
# employed in foreign countries	0	0.0
# of states where employed	17	

J.D. Attrition (Prior Year)

	Academic	Other	TOTALS	
	#	#	#	%
1st Year	1	3	4	5.5%
2nd Year	1	0	1	1.5%
3rd Year	0	0	0	0.0%
4th Year	0	0	0	0.0%
TOTALS	2	3	5	2.3%

Bar Passage Rates

Jurisdiction	South Dakota		
Exam	Sum 96	Win 97	Total
# from school taking bar for the first time	43	4	47
School's pass rate for all first-time takers	84%	50%	81%
State's pass rate for all first-time takers	86%	88%	86%

SOUTH TEXAS COLLEGE OF LAW

1303 San Jacinto
Houston, TX 77002-7000
(713)659-8040
http://www.stcl.edu

ABA Approved Since 1959

The Basics

Type of School: Private Term: Semester
Application deadline: 03/01
Application fee: $40
Financial Aid deadline: 05/01
Can first year start other than Fall? Yes
Student faculty ratio: 20.3 to 1
Does the University offer:
- housing restricted to law students? No
- graduate student housing for which law students are eligible? No

Faculty & Administrators

	Total		Men		Women		Minorities	
	Fall	Spr	Fall	Spr	Fall	Spr	Fall	Spr
Full-time	45	43	33	33	12	10	6	6
Other Full-Time	0	0	0	0	0	0	0	0
Deans, librarians, & others who teach > 1/2	6	6	3	3	3	3	0	0
Part-time	23	30	19	24	4	6	1	0
Total	74	79	55	60	19	19	7	6
Deans, librarians, & others who teach < 1/2	2	2	1	1	1	1	0	0

Curriculum

	Full time	Part time
Typical first-year section size	90	70
Is there typically a "small section" of the first year class, other than Legal Writing, taught by full-time faculty?	No	No
If yes, typical size offered last year	N/A	N/A
# of classroom course titles beyond 1st year curriculum	76	58
# of upper division courses, excluding seminars, with an enrollment:		
Under 25	42	35
25 - 49	29	15
50 - 74	20	15
75 - 99	14	4
100 +	0	0
# of seminars	9	14
# of seminar positions available	460	
# of seminar positions filled	116	194
# of positions available in simulation courses	810	
# of simulation positions filled	376	381
# of positions available in faculty supervised clinical courses	52	
# of fac. sup. clin. positions filled	30	7
# involved in field placements	110	27
# involved in law journals	150	37
# in moot court or trial competitions	54	13
# of credit hrs required to graduate	90	

J.D. Enrollment & Ethnicity

	Men		Women		Fl-Time		Pt-Time		1st Yr		2nd Yr		3rd Yr		4th Yr		Total		JD Degrees Awarded
	#	%	#	%	#	%	#	%	#	%	#	%	#	%	#	%	#	%	
African-American	27	3.9	38	7.4	27	3.4	38	9.0	31	5.0	16	4.8	13	5.7	5	17.9	65	5.4	29
American Indian	9	1.3	5	1.0	10	1.3	4	0.9	8	1.3	3	0.9	3	1.3	0	0.0	14	1.2	3
Asian American	28	4.0	28	5.4	33	4.2	23	5.4	27	4.3	15	4.5	14	6.1	0	0.0	56	4.6	18
Mexican American	32	4.6	25	4.9	46	5.8	11	2.6	33	5.3	15	4.5	7	3.1	2	7.1	57	4.7	13
Puerto Rican	1	0.1	4	0.8	5	0.6	0	0.0	4	0.6	1	0.3	0	0.0	0	0.0	5	0.4	1
Hispanic American	27	3.9	29	5.6	42	5.3	14	3.3	37	6.0	12	3.6	6	2.6	1	3.6	56	4.6	10
Total Minorities	124	17.8	129	25.0	163	20.6	90	21.3	140	22.5	62	18.5	43	18.8	8	28.6	253	20.9	74
Foreign Nationals	1	0.1	0	0.0	0	0.0	1	0.2	0	0.0	1	0.3	0	0.0	0	0.0	1	0.1	0
Caucasian	573	82.1	386	75.0	627	79.4	332	78.5	481	77.5	272	81.2	186	81.2	20	71.4	959	79.1	254
Total	698	57.5	515	42.5	790	65.1	423	34.9	621	51.2	335	27.6	229	18.9	28	2.3	1213		328

GPA & LSAT Scores

	Full Time	Part Time	Total
# of apps	1,198	488	1,686
# admits	715	322	1,037
# of matrics	292	146	438
75% GPA	3.21	3.26	
25% GPA	2.66	2.74	
75% LSAT	155	157	
25% LSAT	151	152	

Tuition & Fees

	Resident	Non-resident
Full-Time	$14,700	$14,700
Part-Time	$10,000	$10,000

Living Expenses

Estimated living expenses for Singles		
Living on campus	Living off campus	Living at home
N/A	$12,024	$8,376

Employment

	Total	%
Employment status known	220	52.9
Employment status unknown	196	47.1
Employed	170	77.3
Pursuing graduate degrees	4	1.8
Unemployed seeking employment	45	20.5
Unemployed not seeking employment	1	0.5
Type of Employment		
# employed in law firms	97	57.1
# employed in business & industry	22	12.9
# employed in government	10	5.9
# employed in public interest	0	0.0
# employed as judicial clerks	13	7.6
# employed in academia	3	1.8
Geographic Location		
# employed in state	122	71.8
# employed in foreign countries	0	0.0
# of states where employed	5	

Financial Aid

	Full-time		Part-time		Total	
	#	%	#	%	#	%
Total # of Students	790		423		1213	
Total # receiving grants	344	43.5	127	30.0	471	38.8
Less than 1/2 tuition	334	42.3	122	28.8	456	37.6
Half to full tuition	9	1.1	5	1.2	14	1.2
Full tuition	0	0.0	0	0.0	0	0.0
More than full tuition	1	0.1	0	0.0	1	0.1
Median Grant Amount	$1,143		$1,154			

Informational & Library Resources

# of volumes & volume equivalents	347,220	# of professional staff	9
# of titles	55,435	Hours per week with professional staff	83
# of active serial subscriptions	4,083	Hours per week without professional staff	20
Study seating capacity inside the library	582	# of student computer work stations for entire law school	71
Square feet of law library	43,767	# of additional networked connections	12
Square feet of law school (excl. Library)	101,984	Require Laptop Computer?	N

J.D. Attrition (Prior Year)

	Academic	Other	TOTALS	
	#	#	#	%
1st Year	39	56	95	15%
2nd Year	10	4	14	4.3%
3rd Year	3	0	3	1.5%
4th Year	0	0	0	0.0%
TOTALS	52	60	112	9.2%

Bar Passage Rates

Jurisdiction	Texas		
Exam	Sum 96	Win 97	Total
# from school taking bar for the first time	260	97	357
School's pass rate for all first-time takers	83%	85%	83%
State's pass rate for all first-time takers	84%	81%	84%

SOUTHERN CALIFORNIA, UNIVERSITY OF

University Park
Los Angeles, CA 90089-0071
(213)740-7331
http://www.usc.edu/dept/law

ABA Approved Since 1924

The Basics

Type of School: Private — Term: Semester
Application deadline: 02/01
Application fee: $60
Financial Aid deadline: 02/15
Can first year start other than Fall? No
Student faculty ratio: 15.5 to 1
Does the University offer:
- housing restricted to law students? Yes
- graduate student housing for which law students are eligible? Yes

Faculty & Administrators

	Total		Men		Women		Minorities	
	Fall	Spr	Fall	Spr	Fall	Spr	Fall	Spr
Full-time	34	30	24	21	10	9	5	4
Other Full-Time	1	1	0	0	1	1	0	0
Deans, librarians, & others who teach > 1/2	3	3	3	3	0	0	0	0
Part-time	15	36	13	31	2	5	1	7
Total	53	70	40	55	13	15	6	11
Deans, librarians, & others who teach < 1/2	2	2	0	0	2	2	0	0

Curriculum

	Full time	Part time
Typical first-year section size	70	0
Is there typically a "small section" of the first year class, other than Legal Writing, taught by full-time faculty?	No	No
If yes, typical size offered last year	N/A	N/A
# of classroom course titles beyond 1st year curriculum	95	0
# of upper division courses, excluding seminars, with an enrollment:		
Under 25	32	0
25 - 49	29	0
50 - 74	13	0
75 - 99	8	0
100 +	5	0
# of seminars	8	0
# of seminar positions available	160	
# of seminar positions filled	142	0
# of positions available in simulation courses	228	
# of simulation positions filled	202	0
# of positions available in faculty supervised clinical courses	40	
# of fac. sup. clin. positions filled	35	0
# involved in field placements	106	0
# involved in law journals	148	0
# in moot court or trial competitions	45	0
# of credit hrs required to graduate	88	

J.D. Enrollment & Ethnicity

	Men		Women		Fl-Time		Pt-Time		1st Yr		2nd Yr		3rd Yr		4th Yr		Total		JD Degrees Awarded
	#	%	#	%	#	%	#	%	#	%	#	%	#	%	#	%	#	%	
African-American	30	8.6	45	16.5	75	12.1	0	0.0	23	11.5	22	11.1	30	13.6	0	0.0	75	12.1	16
American Indian	2	0.6	1	0.4	3	0.5	0	0.0	0	0.0	2	1.0	1	0.5	0	0.0	3	0.5	0
Asian American	47	13.5	34	12.5	81	13.1	0	0.0	27	13.5	28	14.1	26	11.8	0	0.0	81	13.1	29
Mexican American	35	10.1	32	11.8	67	10.8	0	0.0	24	12.0	18	9.0	25	11.4	0	0.0	67	10.8	15
Puerto Rican	0	0.0	0	0.0	0	0.0	0	0.0	0	0.0	0	0.0	0	0.0	0	0.0	0	0.0	2
Hispanic American	10	2.9	12	4.4	22	3.6	0	0.0	6	3.0	7	3.5	9	4.1	0	0.0	22	3.6	9
Total Minorities	124	35.7	124	45.6	248	40.1	0	0.0	80	40.0	77	38.7	91	41.4	0	0.0	248	40.1	71
Foreign Nationals	1	0.3	0	0.0	1	0.2	0	0.0	0	0.0	1	0.5	0	0.0	0	0.0	1	0.2	0
Caucasian	222	64.0	148	54.4	370	59.8	0	0.0	120	60.0	121	60.8	129	58.6	0	0.0	370	59.8	137
Total	347	56.1	272	43.9	619	100.0	0	0.0	200	32.3	199	32.1	220	35.5	0	0.0	619		208

SOUTHERN CALIFORNIA, UNIVERSITY OF

GPA & LSAT Scores

	Full Time	Part Time	Total
# of apps	3,297	0	3,297
# admits	899	0	899
# of matrics	200	0	200
75% GPA	3.60	0.00	
25% GPA	3.20	0.00	
75% LSAT	166	0	
25% LSAT	159	0	

Tuition & Fees

	Resident	Non-resident
Full-Time	$23,862	$23,862
Part-Time	$0	$0

Living Expenses

Estimated living expenses for Singles		
Living on campus	Living off campus	Living at home
$11,098	$12,024	$5,984

Financial Aid

	Full-time		Part-time		Total	
	#	%	#	%	#	%
Total # of Students	619		0		619	
Total # receiving grants	308	49.8	0	0.0	308	49.8
Less than 1/2 tuition	199	32.1	0	0.0	199	32.1
Half to full tuition	78	12.6	0	0.0	78	12.6
Full tuition	28	4.5	0	0.0	28	4.5
More than full tuition	3	0.5	0	0.0	3	0.5
Median Grant Amount	$10,000		$0			

Informational & Library Resources

# of volumes & volume equivalents	352,143	# of professional staff	9
# of titles	151,186	Hours per week with professional staff	52
# of active serial subscriptions	4,142	Hours per week without professional staff	49
Study seating capacity inside the library	294	# of student computer work stations for entire law school	88
Square feet of law library	40,000	# of additional networked connections	68
Square feet of law school (excl. Library)	121,447	Require Laptop Computer?	N

Employment

	Total	%
Employment status known	206	95.8
Employment status unknown	9	4.2
Employed	194	94.2
Pursuing graduate degrees	3	1.5
Unemployed seeking employment	4	1.9
Unemployed not seeking employment	5	2.4
Type of Employment		
# employed in law firms	135	69.6
# employed in business & industry	19	9.8
# employed in government	10	5.2
# employed in public interest	11	5.7
# employed as judicial clerks	19	9.8
# employed in academia	0	0.0
Geographic Location		
# employed in state	155	79.9
# employed in foreign countries	4	2.1
# of states where employed	12	

J.D. Attrition (Prior Year)

	Academic	Other	TOTALS	
	#	#	#	%
1st Year	0	5	5	2.4%
2nd Year	0	1	1	0.5%
3rd Year	0	0	0	0.0%
4th Year	0	0	0	0.0%
TOTALS	0	6	6	1.0%

Bar Passage Rates

Jurisdiction	California		
Exam	Sum 96	Win 97	Total
# from school taking bar for the first time	183	8	191
School's pass rate for all first-time takers	83%	75%	82%
State's pass rate for all first-time takers	69%	62%	67%

SOUTHERN ILLINOIS UNIVERSITY-CARBONDALE

Lesar Law Building
Carbondale, IL 62901-6804
(618)536-7711
http://www.siu.edu/~lawsch

ABA Approved Since 1974

The Basics

Type of School: Public
Term: Semester
Application deadline: 03/01
Application fee: $25
Financial Aid deadline: 04/01
Can first year start other than Fall? No
Student faculty ratio: 13.3 to 1
Does the University offer:
- housing restricted to law students? No
- graduate student housing for which law students are eligible? Yes

Faculty & Administrators

	Total		Men		Women		Minorities	
	Fall	Spr	Fall	Spr	Fall	Spr	Fall	Spr
Full-time	23	23	16	16	7	7	3	3
Other Full-Time	0	0	0	0	0	0	0	0
Deans, librarians, & others who teach > 1/2	7	7	3	3	4	4	0	0
Part-time	5	7	2	5	3	2	0	0
Total	35	37	21	24	14	13	3	3
Deans, librarians, & others who teach < 1/2	1	1	1	1	0	0	0	0

Curriculum

	Full time	Part time
Typical first-year section size	62	0
Is there typically a "small section" of the first year class, other than Legal Writing, taught by full-time faculty?	No	No
If yes, typical size offered last year	N/A	N/A
# of classroom course titles beyond 1st year curriculum	52	0
# of upper division courses, excluding seminars, with an enrollment:		
Under 25	32	0
25 - 49	18	0
50 - 74	15	0
75 - 99	0	0
100 +	0	0
# of seminars	7	0
# of seminar positions available	81	
# of seminar positions filled	78	0
# of positions available in simulation courses	328	
# of simulation positions filled	271	0
# of positions available in faculty supervised clinical courses	72	
# of fac. sup. clin. positions filled	42	0
# involved in field placements	52	0
# involved in law journals	60	0
# in moot court or trial competitions	50	0
# of credit hrs required to graduate	90	

J.D. Enrollment & Ethnicity

	Men		Women		Fl-Time		Pt-Time		1st Yr		2nd Yr		3rd Yr		4th Yr		Total		JD Degrees Awarded
	#	%	#	%	#	%	#	%	#	%	#	%	#	%	#	%	#	%	
African-American	10	4.6	13	9.7	23	6.5	0	0.0	6	5.0	11	9.2	6	5.3	0	0.0	23	6.5	8
American Indian	3	1.4	3	2.2	6	1.7	0	0.0	1	0.8	3	2.5	2	1.8	0	0.0	6	1.7	1
Asian American	11	5.0	8	6.0	19	5.4	0	0.0	4	3.3	7	5.9	8	7.0	0	0.0	19	5.4	4
Mexican American	2	0.9	1	0.7	3	0.8	0	0.0	0	0.0	1	0.8	2	1.8	0	0.0	3	0.8	1
Puerto Rican	2	0.9	0	0.0	2	0.6	0	0.0	0	0.0	0	0.0	2	1.8	0	0.0	2	0.6	1
Hispanic American	4	1.8	1	0.7	5	1.4	0	0.0	1	0.8	2	1.7	2	1.8	0	0.0	5	1.4	1
Total Minorities	32	14.6	26	19.4	58	16.4	0	0.0	12	10.0	24	20.2	22	19.3	0	0.0	58	16.4	16
Foreign Nationals	4	1.8	1	0.7	5	1.4	0	0.0	1	0.8	1	0.8	3	2.6	0	0.0	5	1.4	3
Caucasian	183	83.6	107	79.9	290	82.2	0	0.0	107	89.2	94	79.0	89	78.1	0	0.0	290	82.2	96
Total	219	62.0	134	38.0	353	100.0	0	0.0	120	34.0	119	33.7	114	32.3	0	0.0	353		115

SOUTHERN ILLINOIS UNIVERSITY-CARBONDALE

GPA & LSAT Scores

	Full Time	Part Time	Total
# of apps	680	0	680
# admits	388	0	388
# of matrics	120	0	120
75% GPA	3.53	0.00	
25% GPA	2.77	0.00	
75% LSAT	157	0	
25% LSAT	150	0	

Tuition & Fees

	Resident	Non-resident
Full-Time	$5,300	$13,924
Part-Time	$0	$0

Living Expenses

Estimated living expenses for Singles		
Living on campus	Living off campus	Living at home
$8,060	$8,060	$5,240

Financial Aid

	Full-time		Part-time		Total	
	#	%	#	%	#	%
Total # of Students	353		0		353	
Total # receiving grants	132	37.4	0	0.0	132	37.4
Less than 1/2 tuition	73	20.7	0	0.0	73	20.7
Half to full tuition	50	14.2	0	0.0	50	14.2
Full tuition	0	0.0	0	0.0	0	0.0
More than full tuition	9	2.5	0	0.0	9	2.5
Median Grant Amount	$2,000		$0			

Informational & Library Resources

# of volumes & volume equivalents	335,626	# of professional staff	6
# of titles	65,697	Hours per week with professional staff	52
# of active serial subscriptions	4,198	Hours per week without professional staff	34
Study seating capacity inside the library	364	# of student computer work stations for entire law school	44
Square feet of law library	34,613	# of additional networked connections	0
Square feet of law school (excl. Library)	36,833	Require Laptop Computer?	N

Employment

	Total	%
Employment status known	101	92.7
Employment status unknown	8	7.3
Employed	89	88.1
Pursuing graduate degrees	0	0.0
Unemployed seeking employment	12	11.9
Unemployed not seeking employment	0	0.0
Type of Employment		
# employed in law firms	55	61.8
# employed in business & industry	7	7.9
# employed in government	12	13.5
# employed in public interest	4	4.5
# employed as judicial clerks	4	4.5
# employed in academia	1	1.1
Geographic Location		
# employed in state	55	61.8
# employed in foreign countries	0	0.0
# of states where employed	13	

J.D. Attrition (Prior Year)

	Academic	Other	TOTALS	
	#	#	#	%
1st Year	3	9	12	9.9%
2nd Year	0	1	1	0.8%
3rd Year	0	0	0	0.0%
4th Year	0	0	0	0.0%
TOTALS	3	10	13	3.6%

Bar Passage Rates

Jurisdiction	Illinois		
Exam	Sum 96	Win 97	Total
# from school taking bar for the first time	68	9	77
School's pass rate for all first-time takers	82%	89%	83%
State's pass rate for all first-time takers	86%	84%	86%

SOUTHERN METHODIST UNIVERSITY

P.O. Box 750116
Dallas, TX 75275-0116
(214)768-2618
http://www.smu.edu/~law

ABA Approved Since 1927

The Basics

Type of School: Private — Term: Semester
Application deadline: 02/01
Application fee: $50
Financial Aid deadline: 05/01
Can first year start other than Fall? No
Student faculty ratio: 26.7 to 1
Does the University offer:
- housing restricted to law students? No
- graduate student housing for which law students are eligible? Yes

Faculty & Administrators

	Total		Men		Women		Minorities	
	Fall	Spr	Fall	Spr	Fall	Spr	Fall	Spr
Full-time	24	30	20	25	4	5	7	8
Other Full-Time	0	0	0	0	0	0	0	0
Deans, librarians, & others who teach > 1/2	3	3	1	1	2	2	0	0
Part-time	59	72	43	50	16	22	3	1
Total	86	105	64	76	22	29	10	9
Deans, librarians, & others who teach < 1/2	7	7	5	5	2	2	1	1

Curriculum

	Full time	Part time
Typical first-year section size	87	0
Is there typically a "small section" of the first year class, other than Legal Writing, taught by full-time faculty?	No	No
If yes, typical size offered last year	N/A	N/A
# of classroom course titles beyond 1st year curriculum	116	0
# of upper division courses, excluding seminars, with an enrollment:		
Under 25	29	0
25 - 49	14	0
50 - 74	15	0
75 - 99	3	0
100 +	1	0
# of seminars	24	0
# of seminar positions available	480	
# of seminar positions filled	480	0
# of positions available in simulation courses	395	
# of simulation positions filled	395	0
# of positions available in faculty supervised clinical courses	43	
# of fac. sup. clin. positions filled	43	0
# involved in field placements	75	0
# involved in law journals	131	0
# in moot court or trial competitions	30	0
# of credit hrs required to graduate	90	

J.D. Enrollment & Ethnicity

	Men		Women		Fl-Time		Pt-Time		1st Yr		2nd Yr		3rd Yr		4th Yr		Total		JD Degrees Awarded
	#	%	#	%	#	%	#	%	#	%	#	%	#	%	#	%	#	%	
African-American	22	5.2	29	8.2	50	6.6	1	4.5	6	2.5	22	8.6	23	8.1	0	0.0	51	6.6	10
American Indian	7	1.7	4	1.1	10	1.3	1	4.5	1	0.4	6	2.3	4	1.4	0	0.0	11	1.4	4
Asian American	14	3.3	15	4.2	29	3.8	0	0.0	6	2.5	9	3.5	14	4.9	0	0.0	29	3.7	17
Mexican American	29	6.9	28	7.9	57	7.5	0	0.0	13	5.5	25	9.8	19	6.7	0	0.0	57	7.3	19
Puerto Rican	0	0.0	0	0.0	0	0.0	0	0.0	0	0.0	0	0.0	0	0.0	0	0.0	0	0.0	0
Hispanic American	0	0.0	0	0.0	0	0.0	0	0.0	0	0.0	0	0.0	0	0.0	0	0.0	0	0.0	0
Total Minorities	72	17.1	76	21.4	146	19.3	2	9.1	26	10.9	62	24.2	60	21.2	0	0.0	148	19.0	50
Foreign Nationals	1	0.2	1	0.3	2	0.3	0	0.0	1	0.4	0	0.0	1	0.4	0	0.0	2	0.3	1
Caucasian	349	82.7	278	78.3	607	80.4	20	90.9	211	88.7	194	75.8	222	78.4	0	0.0	627	80.7	170
Total	422	54.3	355	45.7	755	97.2	22	2.8	238	30.6	256	32.9	283	36.4	0	0.0	777		221

SOUTHERN METHODIST UNIVERSITY

GPA & LSAT Scores

	Full Time	Part Time	Total
# of apps	1,698	18	1,716
# admits	661	3	664
# of matrics	235	2	237
75% GPA	3.48	2.95	
25% GPA	2.94	2.90	
75% LSAT	160	164	
25% LSAT	155	156	

Tuition & Fees

	Resident	Non-resident
Full-Time	$19,534	$19,534
Part-Time	$14,200	$14,200

Living Expenses

Estimated living expenses for Singles

Living on campus	Living off campus	Living at home
$6,573	$4,965	$1,965

Employment

	Total	%
Employment status known	228	93.4
Employment status unknown	16	6.6
Employed	194	85.1
Pursuing graduate degrees	12	5.3
Unemployed seeking employment	16	7.0
Unemployed not seeking employment	6	2.6
Type of Employment		
# employed in law firms	144	74.2
# employed in business & industry	27	13.9
# employed in government	14	7.2
# employed in public interest	1	0.5
# employed as judicial clerks	7	3.6
# employed in academia	1	0.5
Geographic Location		
# employed in state	132	68.0
# employed in foreign countries	0	0.0
# of states where employed	26	

Financial Aid

	Full-time		Part-time		Total	
	#	%	#	%	#	%
Total # of Students	755		22		777	
Total # receiving grants	305	40.4	0	0.0	305	39.3
Less than 1/2 tuition	198	26.2	0	0.0	198	25.5
Half to full tuition	91	12.1	0	0.0	91	11.7
Full tuition	0	0.0	0	0.0	0	0.0
More than full tuition	16	2.1	0	0.0	16	2.1
Median Grant Amount	$6,000		$0			

Informational & Library Resources

# of volumes & volume equivalents	497,265	# of professional staff	9
# of titles	177,938	Hours per week with professional staff	62
# of active serial subscriptions	5,119	Hours per week without professional staff	40
Study seating capacity inside the library	716	# of student computer work stations for entire law school	93
Square feet of law library	100,000	# of additional networked connections	13
Square feet of law school (excl. Library)	87,000	Require Laptop Computer?	N

J.D. Attrition (Prior Year)

	Academic	Other	TOTALS	
	#	#	#	%
1st Year	1	12	13	4.7%
2nd Year	1	2	3	1.1%
3rd Year	0	0	0	0.0%
4th Year	0	0	0	0.0%
TOTALS	2	14	16	2.1%

Bar Passage Rates

Jurisdiction	Texas		
Exam	Sum 96	Win 97	Total
# from school taking bar for the first time	178	15	193
School's pass rate for all first-time takers	87%	80%	86%
State's pass rate for all first-time takers	84%	81%	84%

SOUTHERN UNIVERSITY

P. O. Box 9294
Baton Rouge, LA 70813
(504)771-2552
website is currently under construction

ABA Approved Since 1953

The Basics

Type of School: Public Term: Semester
Application deadline: 03/31
Application fee: $0
Financial Aid deadline: 04/15
Can first year start other than Fall? Yes
Student faculty ratio: 12.3 to 1
Does the University offer:
- housing restricted to law students? No
- graduate student housing for which law students are eligible? No

Faculty & Administrators

	Total		Men		Women		Minorities	
	Fall	Spr	Fall	Spr	Fall	Spr	Fall	Spr
Full-time	24	24	14	14	10	10	14	14
Other Full-Time	0	0	0	0	0	0	0	0
Deans, librarians, & others who teach > 1/2	3	3	3	3	0	0	3	3
Part-time	7	7	6	6	1	1	5	5
Total	34	34	23	23	11	11	22	22
Deans, librarians, & others who teach < 1/2	0	0	0	0	0	0	0	0

Curriculum

	Full time	Part time
Typical first-year section size	42	0
Is there typically a "small section" of the first year class, other than Legal Writing, taught by full-time faculty?	No	No
If yes, typical size offered last year	N/A	N/A
# of classroom course titles beyond 1st year curriculum	61	0
# of upper division courses, excluding seminars, with an enrollment:		
Under 25	42	0
25 - 49	40	0
50 - 74	6	0
75 - 99	0	0
100 +	0	0
# of seminars	12	0
# of seminar positions available	250	
# of seminar positions filled	139	0
# of positions available in simulation courses	160	
# of simulation positions filled	122	0
# of positions available in faculty supervised clinical courses	66	
# of fac. sup. clin. positions filled	53	0
# involved in field placements	8	0
# involved in law journals	22	0
# in moot court or trial competitions	63	0
# of credit hrs required to graduate	96	

J.D. Enrollment & Ethnicity

	Men		Women		Fl-Time		Pt-Time		1st Yr		2nd Yr		3rd Yr		4th Yr		Total		JD Degrees Awarded
	#	%	#	%	#	%	#	%	#	%	#	%	#	%	#	%	#	%	
African-American	92	51.1	118	80.8	210	64.4	0	0.0	77	64.7	59	58.4	74	69.8	0	0.0	210	64.4	62
American Indian	0	0.0	0	0.0	0	0.0	0	0.0	0	0.0	0	0.0	0	0.0	0	0.0	0	0.0	0
Asian American	0	0.0	0	0.0	0	0.0	0	0.0	0	0.0	0	0.0	0	0.0	0	0.0	0	0.0	1
Mexican American	0	0.0	0	0.0	0	0.0	0	0.0	0	0.0	0	0.0	0	0.0	0	0.0	0	0.0	0
Puerto Rican	0	0.0	0	0.0	0	0.0	0	0.0	0	0.0	0	0.0	0	0.0	0	0.0	0	0.0	0
Hispanic American	0	0.0	0	0.0	0	0.0	0	0.0	0	0.0	0	0.0	0	0.0	0	0.0	0	0.0	0
Total Minorities	92	51.1	118	80.8	210	64.4	0	0.0	77	64.7	59	58.4	74	69.8	0	0.0	210	64.4	63
Foreign Nationals	0	0.0	0	0.0	0	0.0	0	0.0	0	0.0	0	0.0	0	0.0	0	0.0	0	0.0	0
Caucasian	88	48.9	28	19.2	116	35.6	0	0.0	42	35.3	42	41.6	32	30.2	0	0.0	116	35.6	35
Total	180	55.2	146	44.8	326	100.0	0	0.0	119	36.5	101	31.0	106	32.5	0	0.0	326		98

GPA & LSAT Scores

	Full Time	Part Time	Total
# of apps	700	0	700
# admits	186	0	186
# of matrics	119	0	119
75% GPA	3.00	0.00	
25% GPA	2.42	0.00	
75% LSAT	147	0	
25% LSAT	141	0	

Tuition & Fees

	Resident	Non-resident
Full-Time	$3,128	$7,728
Part-Time	$0	$0

Living Expenses

Estimated living expenses for Singles		
Living on campus	Living off campus	Living at home
$8,314	$9,504	$9,504

Employment

	Total	%
Employment status known	77	88.5
Employment status unknown	10	11.5
Employed	62	80.5
Pursuing graduate degrees	9	11.7
Unemployed seeking employment	6	7.8
Unemployed not seeking employment	0	0.0
Type of Employment		
# employed in law firms	27	43.5
# employed in business & industry	7	11.3
# employed in government	17	27.4
# employed in public interest	0	0.0
# employed as judicial clerks	9	14.5
# employed in academia	2	3.2
Geographic Location		
# employed in state	56	90.3
# employed in foreign countries	0	0.0
# of states where employed	5	

Financial Aid

	Full-time		Part-time		Total	
	#	%	#	%	#	%
Total # of Students	326		0		326	
Total # receiving grants	65	19.9	0	0.0	65	19.9
Less than 1/2 tuition	0	0.0	0	0.0	0	0.0
Half to full tuition	0	0.0	0	0.0	0	0.0
Full tuition	0	0.0	0	0.0	0	0.0
More than full tuition	65	19.9	0	0.0	65	19.9
Median Grant Amount	$4,658		$0			

Informational & Library Resources

# of volumes & volume equivalents	388,614	# of professional staff	7
# of titles	56,134	Hours per week with professional staff	86
# of active serial subscriptions	4,357	Hours per week without professional staff	8
Study seating capacity inside the library	284	# of student computer work stations for entire law school	52
Square feet of law library	28,940	# of additional networked connections	0
Square feet of law school (excl. Library)	50,768	Require Laptop Computer?	N

J.D. Attrition (Prior Year)

	Academic	Other	TOTALS	
	#	#	#	%
1st Year	10	12	22	18%
2nd Year	2	4	6	5.4%
3rd Year	0	2	2	1.9%
4th Year	0	0	0	0.0%
TOTALS	12	18	30	9.0%

Bar Passage Rates

Jurisdiction	Louisiana		
Exam	Sum 96	Win 97	Total
# from school taking bar for the first time	79	5	84
School's pass rate for all first-time takers	37%	20%	36%
State's pass rate for all first-time takers	69%	54%	66%

SOUTHWESTERN UNIVERSITY

675 South Westmoreland Avenue
Los Angeles, CA 90005-3992
(213)738-6717
http://www.swlaw.edu

ABA Approved Since 1970

The Basics

Type of School: Private — Term: Semester

Application deadline: 06/30

Application fee: $50

Financial Aid deadline: 06/01

Can first year start other than Fall? No

Student faculty ratio: 19.2 to 1

Does the University offer:

- housing restricted to law students? No
- graduate student housing for which law students are eligible? No

Faculty & Administrators

	Total		Men		Women		Minorities	
	Fall	Spr	Fall	Spr	Fall	Spr	Fall	Spr
Full-time	40	41	28	29	12	12	6	6
Other Full-Time	3	3	1	1	2	2	1	1
Deans, librarians, & others who teach > 1/2	1	1	0	0	1	1	0	0
Part-time	23	22	16	20	7	2	4	5
Total	67	67	45	50	22	17	11	12
Deans, librarians, & others who teach < 1/2	1	1	1	1	0	0	0	0

Curriculum

	Full time	Part time
Typical first-year section size	89	82
Is there typically a "small section" of the first year class, other than Legal Writing, taught by full-time faculty?	No	No
If yes, typical size offered last year	N/A	N/A
# of classroom course titles beyond 1st year curriculum	77	56
# of upper division courses, excluding seminars, with an enrollment:		
Under 25	35	26
25 - 49	17	10
50 - 74	7	11
75 - 99	3	7
100 +	13	0
# of seminars	15	6
# of seminar positions available	420	
# of seminar positions filled	210	53
# of positions available in simulation courses	508	
# of simulation positions filled	340	114
# of positions available in faculty supervised clinical courses	0	
# of fac. sup. clin. positions filled	0	0
# involved in field placements	340	43
# involved in law journals	77	14
# in moot court or trial competitions	57	16
# of credit hrs required to graduate	87	

J.D. Enrollment & Ethnicity

	Men		Women		Fl-Time		Pt-Time		1st Yr		2nd Yr		3rd Yr		4th Yr		Total		JD Degrees Awarded
	#	%	#	%	#	%	#	%	#	%	#	%	#	%	#	%	#	%	
African-American	33	6.4	31	6.0	29	4.1	35	10.7	20	6.1	18	6.4	17	5.0	9	11.3	64	6.2	12
American Indian	5	1.0	3	0.6	7	1.0	1	0.3	3	0.9	3	1.1	2	0.6	0	0.0	8	0.8	4
Asian American	92	18.0	95	18.4	136	19.3	51	15.6	62	18.9	60	21.4	54	15.9	11	13.8	187	18.2	62
Mexican American	24	4.7	33	6.4	38	5.4	19	5.8	20	6.1	12	4.3	22	6.5	3	3.8	57	5.5	9
Puerto Rican	0	0.0	1	0.2	1	0.1	0	0.0	0	0.0	0	0.0	1	0.3	0	0.0	1	0.1	1
Hispanic American	23	4.5	25	4.8	38	5.4	10	3.1	19	5.8	15	5.3	11	3.2	3	3.8	48	4.7	7
Total Minorities	177	34.6	188	36.4	249	35.4	116	35.6	124	37.8	108	38.4	107	31.5	26	32.5	365	35.5	95
Foreign Nationals	3	0.6	3	0.6	6	0.9	0	0.0	2	0.6	3	1.1	1	0.3	0	0.0	6	0.6	1
Caucasian	332	64.8	326	63.1	448	63.7	210	64.4	202	61.6	170	60.5	232	68.2	54	67.5	658	63.9	256
Total	512	49.8	517	50.2	703	68.3	326	31.7	328	31.9	281	27.3	340	33.0	80	7.8	1029		352

SOUTHWESTERN UNIVERSITY

GPA & LSAT Scores

	Full Time	Part Time	Total
# of apps	1,831	362	2,193
# admits	1,011	160	1,171
# of matrics	256	78	334
75% GPA	3.24	3.31	
25% GPA	2.67	2.57	
75% LSAT	154	153	
25% LSAT	150	149	

Tuition & Fees

	Resident	Non-resident
Full-Time	$20,050	$20,050
Part-Time	$12,735	$12,735

Living Expenses

Estimated living expenses for Singles		
Living on campus	Living off campus	Living at home
N/A	$11,430	$5,040

Financial Aid

	Full-time		Part-time		Total	
	#	%	#	%	#	%
Total # of Students	703		326		1029	
Total # receiving grants	150	21.3	58	17.8	208	20.2
Less than 1/2 tuition	136	19.3	45	13.8	181	17.6
Half to full tuition	11	1.6	9	2.8	20	1.9
Full tuition	3	0.4	4	1.2	7	0.7
More than full tuition	0	0.0	0	0.0	0	0.0
Median Grant Amount	$4,712		$4,232			

Informational & Library Resources

# of volumes & volume equivalents	381,889	# of professional staff	10
# of titles	102,531	Hours per week with professional staff	85
# of active serial subscriptions	4,984	Hours per week without professional staff	18
Study seating capacity inside the library	610	# of student computer work stations for entire law school	93
Square feet of law library	83,000	# of additional networked connections	80
Square feet of law school (excl. Library)	89,240	Require Laptop Computer?	N

Employment

	Total	%
Employment status known	319	94.7
Employment status unknown	18	5.3
Employed	254	79.6
Pursuing graduate degrees	2	0.6
Unemployed seeking employment	23	7.2
Unemployed not seeking employment	40	12.5
Type of Employment		
# employed in law firms	142	55.9
# employed in business & industry	73	28.7
# employed in government	27	10.6
# employed in public interest	6	2.4
# employed as judicial clerks	3	1.2
# employed in academia	3	1.2
Geographic Location		
# employed in state	235	92.5
# employed in foreign countries	2	0.8
# of states where employed	13	

J.D. Attrition (Prior Year)

	Academic	Other	TOTALS	
	#	#	#	%
1st Year	47	29	76	19%
2nd Year	8	7	15	4.8%
3rd Year	6	2	8	2.1%
4th Year	0	0	0	0.0%
TOTALS	61	38	99	8.5%

Bar Passage Rates

Jurisdiction	California		
Exam	Sum 96	Win 97	Total
# from school taking bar for the first time	278	32	310
School's pass rate for all first-time takers	63%	66%	63%
State's pass rate for all first-time takers	69%	62%	67%

ST. JOHN'S UNIVERSITY

8000 Utopia Parkway
Jamaica, NY 11439
(718)990-6600
http://www.stjohns.edu/law

ABA Approved Since 1937

The Basics

Type of School: Private Term: Semester

Application deadline: 03/01

Application fee: $50

Financial Aid deadline: 04/01

Can first year start other than Fall? Yes

Student faculty ratio: 17.3 to 1

Does the University offer:
- housing restricted to law students? No
- graduate student housing for which law students are eligible? No

Faculty & Administrators

	Total		Men		Women		Minorities	
	Fall	Spr	Fall	Spr	Fall	Spr	Fall	Spr
Full-time	48	48	33	31	15	17	5	6
Other Full-Time	2	2	1	1	1	1	1	1
Deans, librarians, & others who teach > 1/2	0	0	0	0	0	0	0	0
Part-time	26	27	22	21	4	6	6	4
Total	76	77	56	53	20	24	12	11
Deans, librarians, & others who teach < 1/2	2	2	2	2	0	0	0	0

Curriculum

	Full time	Part time
Typical first-year section size	75	75
Is there typically a "small section" of the first year class, other than Legal Writing, taught by full-time faculty?	No	No
If yes, typical size offered last year	N/A	N/A
# of classroom course titles beyond 1st year curriculum	73	48
# of upper division courses, excluding seminars, with an enrollment:		
Under 25	33	30
25 - 49	25	12
50 - 74	27	10
75 - 99	7	6
100 +	6	0
# of seminars	25	15
# of seminar positions available	1,649	
# of seminar positions filled	558	290
# of positions available in simulation courses	1,102	
# of simulation positions filled	314	286
# of positions available in faculty supervised clinical courses	333	
# of fac. sup. clin. positions filled	230	0
# involved in field placements	213	0
# involved in law journals	57	4
# in moot court or trial competitions	29	2
# of credit hrs required to graduate	85	

J.D. Enrollment & Ethnicity

	Men		Women		Fl-Time		Pt-Time		1st Yr		2nd Yr		3rd Yr		4th Yr		Total		JD Degrees Awarded
	#	%	#	%	#	%	#	%	#	%	#	%	#	%	#	%	#	%	
African-American	41	6.3	35	8.5	46	6.0	30	10.4	19	7.0	25	6.1	22	7.4	10	12.8	76	7.2	24
American Indian	3	0.5	2	0.5	4	0.5	1	0.3	2	0.7	1	0.2	2	0.7	0	0.0	5	0.5	0
Asian American	40	6.2	42	10.2	71	9.2	11	3.8	28	10.3	29	7.0	23	7.7	2	2.6	82	7.7	38
Mexican American	4	0.6	2	0.5	5	0.6	1	0.3	5	1.8	1	0.2	0	0.0	0	0.0	6	0.6	0
Puerto Rican	21	3.2	15	3.7	24	3.1	12	4.2	7	2.6	13	3.2	13	4.4	3	3.8	36	3.4	7
Hispanic American	32	4.9	19	4.6	34	4.4	17	5.9	9	3.3	20	4.9	16	5.4	6	7.7	51	4.8	18
Total Minorities	141	21.7	115	28.0	184	23.9	72	24.9	70	25.7	89	21.6	76	25.6	21	26.9	256	24.2	87
Foreign Nationals	2	0.3	5	1.2	6	0.8	1	0.3	3	1.1	2	0.5	2	0.7	0	0.0	7	0.7	10
Caucasian	506	78.0	290	70.7	580	75.3	216	74.7	199	73.2	321	77.9	219	73.7	57	73.1	796	75.2	296
Total	649	61.3	410	38.7	770	72.7	289	27.3	272	25.7	412	38.9	297	28.0	78	7.4	1059		393

GPA & LSAT Scores

	Full Time	Part Time	Total
# of apps	1,927	471	2,398
# admits	913	171	1,084
# of matrics	235	67	302
75% GPA	3.29	3.41	
25% GPA	2.68	2.58	
75% LSAT	160	158	
25% LSAT	151	151	

Tuition & Fees

	Resident	Non-resident
Full-Time	$21,000	$21,000
Part-Time	$15,750	$15,750

Living Expenses

Estimated living expenses for Singles		
Living on campus	Living off campus	Living at home
N/A	$12,740	$8,240

Employment

	Total	%
Employment status known	294	83.1
Employment status unknown	60	16.9
Employed	273	92.9
Pursuing graduate degrees	4	1.4
Unemployed seeking employment	10	3.4
Unemployed not seeking employment	7	2.4
Type of Employment		
# employed in law firms	144	52.7
# employed in business & industry	44	16.1
# employed in government	64	23.4
# employed in public interest	1	0.4
# employed as judicial clerks	17	6.2
# employed in academia	0	0.0
Geographic Location		
# employed in state	232	85.0
# employed in foreign countries	0	0.0
# of states where employed	11	

Financial Aid

	Full-time		Part-time		Total	
	#	%	#	%	#	%
Total # of Students	770		289		1059	
Total # receiving grants	285	37.0	72	24.9	357	33.7
Less than 1/2 tuition	211	27.4	58	20.1	269	25.4
Half to full tuition	30	3.9	3	1.0	33	3.1
Full tuition	42	5.5	7	2.4	49	4.6
More than full tuition	2	0.3	4	1.4	6	0.6
Median Grant Amount	$5,000		$4,000			

Informational & Library Resources

# of volumes & volume equivalents	432,804	# of professional staff	5
# of titles	60,069	Hours per week with professional staff	77
# of active serial subscriptions	5,500	Hours per week without professional staff	34
Study seating capacity inside the library	601	# of student computer work stations for entire law school	68
Square feet of law library	56,000	# of additional networked connections	62
Square feet of law school (excl. Library)	96,100	Require Laptop Computer?	N

J.D. Attrition (Prior Year)

	Academic	Other	TOTALS	
	#	#	#	%
1st Year	1	6	7	1.9%
2nd Year	0	7	7	2.4%
3rd Year	0	1	1	0.2%
4th Year	0	1	1	1.4%
TOTALS	1	15	16	1.4%

Bar Passage Rates

Jurisdiction	New York			Connecticut		
Exam	Sum 96	Win 97	Total	Sum 96	Win 97	Total
# from school taking bar for the first time	320	22	342	40	5	45
School's pass rate for all first-time takers	88%	68%	87%	85%	80%	84%
State's pass rate for all first-time takers	78%	67%	77%	84%	84%	84%

ST. LOUIS UNIVERSITY

3700 Lindell Blvd.
St. Louis, MO 63108
(314)977-2766
http://lawlib.slu.edu

ABA Approved Since 1924

The Basics

Type of School: Private   Term: Semester
Application deadline: 03/01
Application fee: $40
Financial Aid deadline: Rolling
Can first year start other than Fall? No
Student faculty ratio: 17.6 to 1
Does the University offer:
- housing restricted to law students? No
- graduate student housing for which law students are eligible? No

Faculty & Administrators

	Total		Men		Women		Minorities	
	Fall	Spr	Fall	Spr	Fall	Spr	Fall	Spr
Full-time	34	29	26	22	8	7	3	3
Other Full-Time	5	5	2	2	3	3	0	0
Deans, librarians, & others who teach > 1/2	1	1	1	1	0	0	0	0
Part-time	16	23	15	20	1	3	0	0
Total	56	58	44	45	12	13	3	3
Deans, librarians, & others who teach < 1/2	1	1	1	1	0	0	0	0

Curriculum

	Full time	Part time
Typical first-year section size	90	75
Is there typically a "small section" of the first year class, other than Legal Writing, taught by full-time faculty?	No	No
If yes, typical size offered last year	N/A	N/A
# of classroom course titles beyond 1st year curriculum	100	28
# of upper division courses, excluding seminars, with an enrollment:		
Under 25	31	4
25 - 49	25	4
50 - 74	12	7
75 - 99	5	1
100 +	2	3
# of seminars	27	6
# of seminar positions available	396	
# of seminar positions filled	278	61
# of positions available in simulation courses	685	
# of simulation positions filled	324	48
# of positions available in faculty supervised clinical courses	48	
# of fac. sup. clin. positions filled	41	5
# involved in field placements	82	0
# involved in law journals	105	8
# in moot court or trial competitions	99	0
# of credit hrs required to graduate	88	

J.D. Enrollment & Ethnicity

	Men		Women		Fl-Time		Pt-Time		1st Yr		2nd Yr		3rd Yr		4th Yr		Total		JD Degrees Awarded
	#	%	#	%	#	%	#	%	#	%	#	%	#	%	#	%	#	%	
African-American	36	7.9	36	10.2	40	7.3	32	12.2	23	9.1	16	6.9	26	10.4	7	10.0	72	8.9	32
American Indian	3	0.7	3	0.9	3	0.6	3	1.1	2	0.8	1	0.4	2	0.8	1	1.4	6	0.7	1
Asian American	27	5.9	12	3.4	31	5.7	8	3.1	11	4.3	10	4.3	15	6.0	3	4.3	39	4.8	8
Mexican American	2	0.4	2	0.6	4	0.7	0	0.0	2	0.8	1	0.4	1	0.4	0	0.0	4	0.5	1
Puerto Rican	0	0.0	1	0.3	0	0.0	1	0.4	0	0.0	0	0.0	0	0.0	1	1.4	1	0.1	0
Hispanic American	6	1.3	8	2.3	9	1.7	5	1.9	6	2.4	4	1.7	3	1.2	1	1.4	14	1.7	9
Total Minorities	74	16.3	62	17.6	87	16.0	49	18.7	44	17.4	32	13.7	47	18.7	13	18.6	136	16.9	51
Foreign Nationals	0	0.0	0	0.0	0	0.0	0	0.0	0	0.0	0	0.0	0	0.0	0	0.0	0	0.0	0
Caucasian	381	83.7	290	82.4	458	84.0	213	81.3	209	82.6	201	86.3	204	81.3	57	81.4	671	83.1	168
Total	455	56.4	352	43.6	545	67.5	262	32.5	253	31.4	233	28.9	251	31.1	70	8.7	807		219

GPA & LSAT Scores

	Full Time	Part Time	Total
# of apps	898	169	1,067
# admits	569	106	675
# of matrics	182	72	254
75% GPA	3.51	3.26	
25% GPA	3.01	2.66	
75% LSAT	157	156	
25% LSAT	148	147	

Tuition & Fees

	Resident	Non-resident
Full-Time	$18,205	$18,205
Part-Time	$13,580	$13,580

Living Expenses

Estimated living expenses for Singles		
Living on campus	Living off campus	Living at home
$8,900	$9,700	$8,500

Financial Aid

	Full-time		Part-time		Total	
	#	%	#	%	#	%
Total # of Students	545		262		807	
Total # receiving grants	328	60.2	75	28.6	403	49.9
Less than 1/2 tuition	282	51.7	75	28.6	357	44.2
Half to full tuition	46	8.4	0	0.0	46	5.7
Full tuition	0	0.0	0	0.0	0	0.0
More than full tuition	0	0.0	0	0.0	0	0.0
Median Grant Amount	$4,500		$3,000			

Informational & Library Resources

# of volumes & volume equivalents	511,162	# of professional staff	8
# of titles	185,883	Hours per week with professional staff	85
# of active serial subscriptions	6,365	Hours per week without professional staff	19
Study seating capacity inside the library	404	# of student computer work stations for entire law school	90
Square feet of law library	39,000	# of additional networked connections	0
Square feet of law school (excl. Library)	79,057	Require Laptop Computer?	N

Employment

	Total	%
Employment status known	220	91.7
Employment status unknown	20	8.3
Employed	203	92.3
Pursuing graduate degrees	3	1.4
Unemployed seeking employment	10	4.5
Unemployed not seeking employment	4	1.8
Type of Employment		
# employed in law firms	104	51.2
# employed in business & industry	40	19.7
# employed in government	29	14.3
# employed in public interest	2	1.0
# employed as judicial clerks	19	9.4
# employed in academia	2	1.0
Geographic Location		
# employed in state	147	72.4
# employed in foreign countries	0	0.0
# of states where employed	18	

J.D. Attrition (Prior Year)

	Academic	Other	TOTALS	
	#	#	#	%
1st Year	0	0	0	0.0%
2nd Year	6	12	18	7.2%
3rd Year	3	9	12	4.9%
4th Year	0	2	2	3.2%
TOTALS	9	23	32	3.9%

Bar Passage Rates

Jurisdiction	Missouri			Illinois		
Exam	Sum 96	Win 97	Total	Sum 96	Win 97	Total
# from school taking bar for the first time	146	25	171	36	66	102
School's pass rate for all first-time takers	79%	88%	80%	81%	92%	88%
State's pass rate for all first-time takers	83%	81%	82%	86%	84%	86%

ST. MARY'S UNIVERSITY

One Camino Santa Maria
San Antonio, TX 78228-8602
(210)436-3424
http://www.stmarylaw.edu

ABA Approved Since 1948

The Basics

Type of School: Private   Term: Semester
Application deadline: 03/01
Application fee: $45
Financial Aid deadline: 04/01
Can first year start other than Fall? No
Student faculty ratio: 22.1 to 1
Does the University offer:
- housing restricted to law students? No
- graduate student housing for which law students are eligible? Yes

Faculty & Administrators

	Total		Men		Women		Minorities	
	Fall	Spr	Fall	Spr	Fall	Spr	Fall	Spr
Full-time	29	28	21	20	8	8	5	6
Other Full-Time	0	0	0	0	0	0	0	0
Deans, librarians, & others who teach > 1/2	2	1	1	0	1	1	1	0
Part-time	34	32	22	21	12	11	4	4
Total	65	61	44	41	21	20	10	10
Deans, librarians, & others who teach < 1/2	0	0	0	0	0	0	0	0

Curriculum

	Full time	Part time
Typical first-year section size	88	0
Is there typically a "small section" of the first year class, other than Legal Writing, taught by full-time faculty?	No	No
If yes, typical size offered last year	N/A	N/A
# of classroom course titles beyond 1st year curriculum	159	0
# of upper division courses, excluding seminars, with an enrollment:		
Under 25	54	0
25 - 49	23	0
50 - 74	19	0
75 - 99	15	0
100 +	0	0
# of seminars	20	0
# of seminar positions available	254	
# of seminar positions filled	254	0
# of positions available in simulation courses	124	
# of simulation positions filled	124	0
# of positions available in faculty supervised clinical courses	44	
# of fac. sup. clin. positions filled	44	0
# involved in field placements	37	0
# involved in law journals	52	0
# in moot court or trial competitions	62	0
# of credit hrs required to graduate	90	

J.D. Enrollment & Ethnicity

	Men		Women		Fl-Time		Pt-Time		1st Yr		2nd Yr		3rd Yr		4th Yr		Total		JD Degrees Awarded
	#	%	#	%	#	%	#	%	#	%	#	%	#	%	#	%	#	%	
African-American	9	2.2	31	8.5	40	5.2	0	0.0	14	5.3	15	6.3	11	4.2	0	0.0	40	5.2	7
American Indian	4	1.0	2	0.6	6	0.8	0	0.0	1	0.4	0	0.0	5	1.9	0	0.0	6	0.8	4
Asian American	10	2.5	17	4.7	27	3.5	0	0.0	5	1.9	11	4.6	11	4.2	0	0.0	27	3.5	6
Mexican American	108	26.7	90	24.8	198	25.8	0	0.0	74	28.0	63	26.3	61	23.1	0	0.0	198	25.8	48
Puerto Rican	4	1.0	2	0.6	6	0.8	0	0.0	2	0.8	2	0.8	2	0.8	0	0.0	6	0.8	2
Hispanic American	11	2.7	12	3.3	23	3.0	0	0.0	12	4.5	7	2.9	4	1.5	0	0.0	23	3.0	10
Total Minorities	146	36.0	154	42.4	300	39.1	0	0.0	108	40.9	98	40.8	94	35.6	0	0.0	300	39.1	77
Foreign Nationals	0	0.0	0	0.0	0	0.0	0	0.0	0	0.0	0	0.0	0	0.0	0	0.0	0	0.0	0
Caucasian	259	64.0	209	57.6	468	60.9	0	0.0	156	59.1	142	59.2	170	64.4	0	0.0	468	60.9	165
Total	405	52.7	363	47.3	768	100.0	0	0.0	264	34.4	240	31.3	264	34.4	0	0.0	768		242

ST. MARY'S UNIVERSITY

GPA & LSAT Scores

	Full Time	Part Time	Total
# of apps	1,270	0	1,270
# admits	733	0	733
# of matrics	276	0	276
75% GPA	3.11	0.00	
25% GPA	2.58	0.00	
75% LSAT	153	0	
25% LSAT	147	0	

Tuition & Fees

	Resident	Non-resident
Full-Time	$14,916	$14,916
Part-Time	$0	$0

Living Expenses

Estimated living expenses for Singles		
Living on campus	Living off campus	Living at home
$9,492	$12,296	$12,296

Financial Aid

	Full-time		Part-time		Total	
	#	%	#	%	#	%
Total # of Students	768		0		768	
Total # receiving grants	241	31.4	0	0.0	241	31.4
Less than 1/2 tuition	229	29.8	0	0.0	229	29.8
Half to full tuition	11	1.4	0	0.0	11	1.4
Full tuition	0	0.0	0	0.0	0	0.0
More than full tuition	1	0.1	0	0.0	1	0.1
Median Grant Amount	$700		$0			

Informational & Library Resources

# of volumes & volume equivalents	323,943	# of professional staff	9
# of titles	32,845	Hours per week with professional staff	87
# of active serial subscriptions	3,529	Hours per week without professional staff	23
Study seating capacity inside the library	446	# of student computer work stations for entire law school	37
Square feet of law library	65,000	# of additional networked connections	124
Square feet of law school (excl. Library)	87,207	Require Laptop Computer?	N

Employment

	Total	%
Employment status known	204	82.3
Employment status unknown	44	17.7
Employed	178	87.3
Pursuing graduate degrees	1	0.5
Unemployed seeking employment	24	11.8
Unemployed not seeking employment	1	0.5
Type of Employment		
# employed in law firms	107	60.1
# employed in business & industry	22	12.4
# employed in government	25	14.0
# employed in public interest	3	1.7
# employed as judicial clerks	17	9.6
# employed in academia	4	2.2
Geographic Location		
# employed in state	166	93.3
# employed in foreign countries	0	0.0
# of states where employed	0	

J.D. Attrition (Prior Year)

	Academic	Other	TOTALS	
	#	#	#	%
1st Year	4	5	9	3.4%
2nd Year	0	19	19	7.4%
3rd Year	0	0	0	0.0%
4th Year	0	0	0	0.0%
TOTALS	4	24	28	3.6%

Bar Passage Rates

Jurisdiction	Texas		
Exam	Sum 96	Win 97	Total
# from school taking bar for the first time	170	63	233
School's pass rate for all first-time takers	71%	83%	74%
State's pass rate for all first-time takers	84%	81%	84%

ST. THOMAS UNIVERSITY

16400 N.W. 32 Avenue
Miami, FL 33054
(305)623-2320
http://www.stu.edu/law/lawmain.htm

ABA Approved Since 1988

The Basics

Type of School: Private   Term: Semester
Application deadline: 04/30
Application fee: $40
Financial Aid deadline: 04/01
Can first year start other than Fall? No
Student faculty ratio: 25.9 to 1
Does the University offer:
- housing restricted to law students? Yes
- graduate student housing for which law students are eligible? No

Faculty & Administrators

	Total		Men		Women		Minorities	
	Fall	Spr	Fall	Spr	Fall	Spr	Fall	Spr
Full-time	17	17	13	13	4	4	5	5
Other Full-Time	6	6	1	1	5	5	1	1
Deans, librarians, & others who teach > 1/2	2	2	2	2	0	0	0	0
Part-time	16	13	13	11	3	2	2	2
Total	41	38	29	27	12	11	8	8
Deans, librarians, & others who teach < 1/2	1	1	1	1	0	0	0	0

Curriculum

	Full time	Part time
Typical first-year section size	65	0
Is there typically a "small section" of the first year class, other than Legal Writing, taught by full-time faculty?	No	No
If yes, typical size offered last year	N/A	N/A
# of classroom course titles beyond 1st year curriculum	101	0
# of upper division courses, excluding seminars, with an enrollment:		
Under 25	30	0
25 - 49	17	0
50 - 74	23	0
75 - 99	1	0
100 +	0	0
# of seminars	10	0
# of seminar positions available	160	
# of seminar positions filled	123	0
# of positions available in simulation courses	248	
# of simulation positions filled	248	0
# of positions available in faculty supervised clinical courses	124	
# of fac. sup. clin. positions filled	53	0
# involved in field placements	55	0
# involved in law journals	25	0
# in moot court or trial competitions	58	0
# of credit hrs required to graduate	90	

J.D. Enrollment & Ethnicity

	Men		Women		Fl-Time		Pt-Time		1st Yr		2nd Yr		3rd Yr		4th Yr		Total		JD Degrees Awarded
	#	%	#	%	#	%	#	%	#	%	#	%	#	%	#	%	#	%	
African-American	18	5.6	36	17.3	54	10.2	0	0.0	13	6.8	17	9.8	24	14.7	0	0.0	54	10.2	11
American Indian	2	0.6	3	1.4	5	0.9	0	0.0	2	1.0	1	0.6	2	1.2	0	0.0	5	0.9	0
Asian American	6	1.9	3	1.4	9	1.7	0	0.0	4	2.1	4	2.3	1	0.6	0	0.0	9	1.7	3
Mexican American	2	0.6	1	0.5	3	0.6	0	0.0	1	0.5	2	1.1	0	0.0	0	0.0	3	0.6	0
Puerto Rican	4	1.3	7	3.4	11	2.1	0	0.0	1	0.5	5	2.9	5	3.1	0	0.0	11	2.1	8
Hispanic American	56	17.5	34	16.3	90	17.0	0	0.0	41	21.5	31	17.8	18	11.0	0	0.0	90	17.0	25
Total Minorities	88	27.5	84	40.4	172	32.6	0	0.0	62	32.5	60	34.5	50	30.7	0	0.0	172	32.6	47
Foreign Nationals	0	0.0	1	0.5	1	0.2	0	0.0	0	0.0	1	0.6	0	0.0	0	0.0	1	0.2	0
Caucasian	232	72.5	123	59.1	355	67.2	0	0.0	129	67.5	113	64.9	113	69.3	0	0.0	355	67.2	110
Total	320	60.6	208	39.4	528	100.0	0	0.0	191	36.2	174	33.0	163	30.9	0	0.0	528		157

GPA & LSAT Scores

	Full Time	Part Time	Total
# of apps	1,489	0	1,489
# admits	834	0	834
# of matrics	205	0	205
75% GPA	3.04	0.00	
25% GPA	2.46	0.00	
75% LSAT	152	0	
25% LSAT	147	0	

Tuition & Fees

	Resident	Non-resident
Full-Time	$18,985	$18,985
Part-Time	$0	$0

Living Expenses

Estimated living expenses for Singles		
Living on campus	Living off campus	Living at home
$12,015	$14,120	$6,305

Employment

	Total	%
Employment status known	131	84.5
Employment status unknown	24	15.5
Employed	114	87.0
Pursuing graduate degrees	7	5.3
Unemployed seeking employment	5	3.8
Unemployed not seeking employment	5	3.8
Type of Employment		
# employed in law firms	65	57.0
# employed in business & industry	13	11.4
# employed in government	31	27.2
# employed in public interest	2	1.8
# employed as judicial clerks	0	0.0
# employed in academia	3	2.6
Geographic Location		
# employed in state	107	93.9
# employed in foreign countries	0	0.0
# of states where employed	15	

Financial Aid

	Full-time		Part-time		Total	
	#	%	#	%	#	%
Total # of Students	528		0		528	
Total # receiving grants	163	30.9	0	0.0	163	30.9
Less than 1/2 tuition	126	23.9	0	0.0	126	23.9
Half to full tuition	36	6.8	0	0.0	36	6.8
Full tuition	1	0.2	0	0.0	1	0.2
More than full tuition	0	0.0	0	0.0	0	0.0
Median Grant Amount	$5,000		$0			

Informational & Library Resources

# of volumes & volume equivalents	272,745	# of professional staff	7
# of titles	39,416	Hours per week with professional staff	96
# of active serial subscriptions	1,485	Hours per week without professional staff	9
Study seating capacity inside the library	314	# of student computer work stations for entire law school	63
Square feet of law library	25,116	# of additional networked connections	0
Square feet of law school (excl. Library)	36,884	Require Laptop Computer?	N

J.D. Attrition (Prior Year)

	Academic	Other	TOTALS	
	#	#	#	%
1st Year	16	32	48	22%
2nd Year	5	0	5	3.1%
3rd Year	0	0	0	0.0%
4th Year	0	0	0	0.0%
TOTALS	21	32	53	10%

Bar Passage Rates

Jurisdiction	Florida		
Exam	Sum 96	Win 97	Total
# from school taking bar for the first time	118	17	135
School's pass rate for all first-time takers	78%	88%	79%
State's pass rate for all first-time takers	84%	85%	84%

STANFORD UNIVERSITY

Crown Quadrangle
Stanford, CA 94305-8610
(650)723-4985
http://www-leland.stanford.edu/group/law

ABA Approved Since 1923

The Basics

Type of School: Private | Term: Semester

Application deadline: 02/01

Application fee: $65

Financial Aid deadline: 03/15

Can first year start other than Fall? No

Student faculty ratio: 18.3 to 1

Does the University offer:
- housing restricted to law students? No
- graduate student housing for which law students are eligible? Yes

Faculty & Administrators

	Total		Men		Women		Minorities	
	Fall	Spr	Fall	Spr	Fall	Spr	Fall	Spr
Full-time	25	27	19	20	6	7	2	3
Other Full-Time	0	0	0	0	0	0	0	0
Deans, librarians, & others who teach > 1/2	2	2	2	2	0	0	0	0
Part-time	32	44	20	29	12	15	5	3
Total	59	73	41	51	18	22	7	6
Deans, librarians, & others who teach < 1/2	1	1	1	1	0	0	0	0

Curriculum

	Full time	Part time
Typical first-year section size	60	0
Is there typically a "small section" of the first year class, other than Legal Writing, taught by full-time faculty?	Yes	No
If yes, typical size offered last year	30	N/A
# of classroom course titles beyond 1st year curriculum	21	0
# of upper division courses, excluding seminars, with an enrollment:		
Under 25	24	0
25 - 49	25	0
50 - 74	9	0
75 - 99	5	0
100 +	6	0
# of seminars	66	0
# of seminar positions available	1,016	
# of seminar positions filled	821	0
# of positions available in simulation courses	469	
# of simulation positions filled	427	0
# of positions available in faculty supervised clinical courses	198	
# of fac. sup. clin. positions filled	150	0
# involved in field placements	20	0
# involved in law journals	400	0
# in moot court or trial competitions	42	0
# of credit hrs required to graduate	86	

J.D. Enrollment & Ethnicity

	Men		Women		Fl-Time		Pt-Time		1st Yr		2nd Yr		3rd Yr		4th Yr		Total		JD Degrees Awarded
	#	%	#	%	#	%	#	%	#	%	#	%	#	%	#	%	#	%	
African-American	23	7.2	22	9.5	45	8.2	0	0.0	12	6.8	16	8.8	17	8.9	0	0.0	45	8.2	9
American Indian	7	2.2	5	2.2	12	2.2	0	0.0	6	3.4	4	2.2	2	1.0	0	0.0	12	2.2	9
Asian American	17	5.3	24	10.4	41	7.5	0	0.0	14	7.9	15	8.3	12	6.3	0	0.0	41	7.5	19
Mexican American	25	7.8	25	10.8	50	9.1	0	0.0	17	9.6	12	6.6	21	10.9	0	0.0	50	9.1	22
Puerto Rican	5	1.6	1	0.4	6	1.1	0	0.0	2	1.1	2	1.1	2	1.0	0	0.0	6	1.1	2
Hispanic American	0	0.0	1	0.4	1	0.2	0	0.0	0	0.0	1	0.6	0	0.0	0	0.0	1	0.2	1
Total Minorities	77	24.1	78	33.8	155	28.2	0	0.0	51	28.8	50	27.6	54	28.1	0	0.0	155	28.2	62
Foreign Nationals	18	5.6	9	3.9	27	4.9	0	0.0	8	4.5	6	3.3	13	6.8	0	0.0	27	4.9	2
Caucasian	224	70.2	144	62.3	368	66.9	0	0.0	118	66.7	125	69.1	125	65.1	0	0.0	368	66.9	120
Total	319	58.0	231	42.0	550	100.0	0	0.0	177	32.2	181	32.9	192	34.9	0	0.0	550		184

GPA & LSAT Scores

	Full Time	Part Time	Total
# of apps	3,611	0	3,611
# admits	443	0	443
# of matrics	177	0	177
75% GPA	3.87	0.00	
25% GPA	3.60	0.00	
75% LSAT	171	0	
25% LSAT	165	0	

Tuition & Fees

	Resident	Non-resident
Full-Time	$24,276	$24,276
Part-Time	$0	$0

Living Expenses

Estimated living expenses for Singles		
Living on campus	Living off campus	Living at home
$11,136	$15,369	N/A

Financial Aid

	Full-time		Part-time		Total	
	#	%	#	%	#	%
Total # of Students	550		0		550	
Total # receiving grants	202	36.7	0	0.0	202	36.7
Less than 1/2 tuition	144	26.2	0	0.0	144	26.2
Half to full tuition	50	9.1	0	0.0	50	9.1
Full tuition	8	1.5	0	0.0	8	1.5
More than full tuition	0	0.0	0	0.0	0	0.0
Median Grant Amount	$9,116		$0			

Informational & Library Resources

# of volumes & volume equivalents	458,973	# of professional staff	7
# of titles	168,068	Hours per week with professional staff	56
# of active serial subscriptions	7,112	Hours per week without professional staff	40
Study seating capacity inside the library	555	# of student computer work stations for entire law school	35
Square feet of law library	56,617	# of additional networked connections	20
Square feet of law school (excl. Library)	96,513	Require Laptop Computer?	N

Employment

	Total	%
Employment status known	193	98.0
Employment status unknown	4	2.0
Employed	186	96.4
Pursuing graduate degrees	6	3.1
Unemployed seeking employment	1	0.5
Unemployed not seeking employment	0	0.0
Type of Employment		
# employed in law firms	101	54.3
# employed in business & industry	22	11.8
# employed in government	10	5.4
# employed in public interest	4	2.2
# employed as judicial clerks	48	25.8
# employed in academia	1	0.5
Geographic Location		
# employed in state	106	57.0
# employed in foreign countries	5	2.7
# of states where employed	23	

J.D. Attrition (Prior Year)

	Academic	Other	TOTALS	
	#	#	#	%
1st Year	0	1	1	0.6%
2nd Year	0	3	3	1.6%
3rd Year	0	0	0	0.0%
4th Year	0	0	0	0.0%
TOTALS	0	4	4	0.7%

Bar Passage Rates

Jurisdiction	California		
Exam	Sum 96	Win 97	Total
# from school taking bar for the first time	102	12	114
School's pass rate for all first-time takers	88%	83%	88%
State's pass rate for all first-time takers	69%	62%	67%

STATE UNIVERSITY OF NEW YORK AT BUFFALO

319 O'Brian Hall
North Campus
Buffalo, NY 14260
(716)645-2053
http://www.buffalo.edu/law/js.html

ABA Approved Since 1936

The Basics

Type of School: Public   Term: Semester
Application deadline: 02/01
Application fee: $50
Financial Aid deadline: 03/19
Can first year start other than Fall? No
Student faculty ratio: 18.4 to 1
Does the University offer:
- housing restricted to law students? No
- graduate student housing for which law students are eligible? No

Faculty & Administrators

	Total		Men		Women		Minorities	
	Fall	Spr	Fall	Spr	Fall	Spr	Fall	Spr
Full-time	32	35	22	23	10	12	4	5
Other Full-Time	4	4	3	3	1	1	0	0
Deans, librarians, & others who teach > 1/2	5	5	3	3	2	2	1	1
Part-time	31	60	22	38	9	22	3	4
Total	72	104	50	67	22	37	8	10
Deans, librarians, & others who teach < 1/2	0	0	0	0	0	0	0	0

Curriculum

	Full time	Part time
Typical first-year section size	110	0
Is there typically a "small section" of the first year class, other than Legal Writing, taught by full-time faculty?	Yes	No
If yes, typical size offered last year	15	N/A
# of classroom course titles beyond 1st year curriculum	151	0
# of upper division courses, excluding seminars, with an enrollment:		
Under 25	82	0
25 - 49	43	0
50 - 74	15	0
75 - 99	8	0
100 +	2	0
# of seminars	32	0
# of seminar positions available	605	
# of seminar positions filled	551	0
# of positions available in simulation courses	151	
# of simulation positions filled	145	0
# of positions available in faculty supervised clinical courses	130	
# of fac. sup. clin. positions filled	130	0
# involved in field placements	120	0
# involved in law journals	219	0
# in moot court or trial competitions	78	0
# of credit hrs required to graduate	87	

J.D. Enrollment & Ethnicity

	Men		Women		Fl-Time		Pt-Time		1st Yr		2nd Yr		3rd Yr		4th Yr		Total		JD Degrees Awarded
	#	%	#	%	#	%	#	%	#	%	#	%	#	%	#	%	#	%	
African-American	20	5.5	29	8.5	49	6.9	0	0.0	14	6.5	15	7.4	20	6.9	0	0.0	49	6.9	19
American Indian	3	0.8	1	0.3	4	0.6	0	0.0	2	0.9	1	0.5	1	0.3	0	0.0	4	0.6	2
Asian American	16	4.4	17	5.0	33	4.7	0	0.0	14	6.5	9	4.4	10	3.4	0	0.0	33	4.7	13
Mexican American	0	0.0	0	0.0	0	0.0	0	0.0	0	0.0	0	0.0	0	0.0	0	0.0	0	0.0	1
Puerto Rican	4	1.1	4	1.2	8	1.1	0	0.0	2	0.9	5	2.5	1	0.3	0	0.0	8	1.1	4
Hispanic American	14	3.8	16	4.7	30	4.2	0	0.0	10	4.7	9	4.4	11	3.8	0	0.0	30	4.2	5
Total Minorities	57	15.6	67	19.6	124	17.5	0	0.0	42	19.6	39	19.1	43	14.8	0	0.0	124	17.5	44
Foreign Nationals	0	0.0	0	0.0	0	0.0	0	0.0	0	0.0	0	0.0	0	0.0	0	0.0	0	0.0	0
Caucasian	309	84.4	275	80.4	584	82.5	0	0.0	172	80.4	165	80.9	247	85.2	0	0.0	584	82.5	208
Total	366	51.7	342	48.3	708	100.0	0	0.0	214	30.2	204	28.8	290	41.0	0	0.0	708		252

STATE UNIVERSITY OF NEW YORK AT BUFFALO

GPA & LSAT Scores

	Full Time	Part Time	Total
# of apps	951	0	951
# admits	499	0	499
# of matrics	214	0	214
75% GPA	3.55	0.00	
25% GPA	2.99	0.00	
75% LSAT	158	0	
25% LSAT	152	0	

Tuition & Fees

	Resident	Non-resident
Full-Time	$8,075	$12,725
Part-Time	$0	$0

Living Expenses

Estimated living expenses for Singles		
Living on campus	Living off campus	Living at home
$9,855	$9,855	$9,855

Financial Aid

	Full-time		Part-time		Total	
	#	%	#	%	#	%
Total # of Students	708		0		708	
Total # receiving grants	0	0.0	0	0.0	0	0.0
Less than 1/2 tuition	0	0.0	0	0.0	0	0.0
Half to full tuition	0	0.0	0	0.0	0	0.0
Full tuition	0	0.0	0	0.0	0	0.0
More than full tuition	0	0.0	0	0.0	0	0.0
Median Grant Amount	$0		$0			

Informational & Library Resources

# of volumes & volume equivalents	506,447	# of professional staff	9
# of titles	102,959	Hours per week with professional staff	74
# of active serial subscriptions	6,659	Hours per week without professional staff	19
Study seating capacity inside the library	508	# of student computer work stations for entire law school	83
Square feet of law library	52,385	# of additional networked connections	0
Square feet of law school (excl. Library)	60,080	Require Laptop Computer?	N

Employment

	Total	%
Employment status known	261	98.9
Employment status unknown	3	1.1
Employed	221	84.7
Pursuing graduate degrees	15	5.7
Unemployed seeking employment	11	4.2
Unemployed not seeking employment	14	5.4
Type of Employment		
# employed in law firms	126	57.0
# employed in business & industry	26	11.8
# employed in government	30	13.6
# employed in public interest	17	7.7
# employed as judicial clerks	10	4.5
# employed in academia	11	5.0
Geographic Location		
# employed in state	178	80.5
# employed in foreign countries	4	1.8
# of states where employed	18	

J.D. Attrition (Prior Year)

	Academic	Other	TOTALS	
	#	#	#	%
1st Year	0	14	14	6.7%
2nd Year	0	9	9	3.3%
3rd Year	1	5	6	2.3%
4th Year	0	0	0	0.0%
TOTALS	1	28	29	3.9%

Bar Passage Rates

Jurisdiction	New York		
Exam	Sum 96	Win 97	Total
# from school taking bar for the first time	210	21	231
School's pass rate for all first-time takers	74%	62%	73%
State's pass rate for all first-time takers	78%	67%	77%

STETSON UNIVERSITY

1401 61st Street South
St. Petersburg, FL 33707
(813)562-7800
http://www.law.stetson.edu

ABA Approved Since 1930

The Basics

Type of School: Private   Term: Semester
Application deadline: 03/01
Application fee: $45
Financial Aid deadline: 03/01
Can first year start other than Fall? Yes
Student faculty ratio: 17.7 to 1
Does the University offer:
- housing restricted to law students? Yes
- graduate student housing for which law students are eligible? No

Faculty & Administrators

	Total		Men		Women		Minorities	
	Fall	Spr	Fall	Spr	Fall	Spr	Fall	Spr
Full-time	30	31	21	22	9	9	3	3
Other Full-Time	2	2	1	1	1	1	0	0
Deans, librarians, & others who teach > 1/2	2	3	1	2	1	1	0	0
Part-time	24	27	24	21	0	6	1	3
Total	58	63	47	46	11	17	4	6
Deans, librarians, & others who teach < 1/2	2	2	1	1	1	1	1	1

Curriculum

	Full time	Part time
Typical first-year section size	58	0
Is there typically a "small section" of the first year class, other than Legal Writing, taught by full-time faculty?	No	No
If yes, typical size offered last year	N/A	N/A
# of classroom course titles beyond 1st year curriculum	77	0
# of upper division courses, excluding seminars, with an enrollment:		
Under 25	203	0
25 - 49	38	0
50 - 74	9	0
75 - 99	0	0
100 +	0	0
# of seminars	13	0
# of seminar positions available	260	
# of seminar positions filled	207	0
# of positions available in simulation courses	778	
# of simulation positions filled	683	0
# of positions available in faculty supervised clinical courses	198	
# of fac. sup. clin. positions filled	149	0
# involved in field placements	229	0
# involved in law journals	60	0
# in moot court or trial competitions	87	0
# of credit hrs required to graduate	88	

J.D. Enrollment & Ethnicity

	Men		Women		Fl-Time		Pt-Time		1st Yr		2nd Yr		3rd Yr		4th Yr		Total		JD Degrees Awarded
	#	%	#	%	#	%	#	%	#	%	#	%	#	%	#	%	#	%	
African-American	19	6.2	19	5.7	38	6.0	0	0.0	17	7.7	11	6.8	10	3.9	0	0.0	38	5.9	10
American Indian	1	0.3	5	1.5	6	0.9	0	0.0	2	0.9	1	0.6	3	1.2	0	0.0	6	0.9	1
Asian American	7	2.3	5	1.5	12	1.9	0	0.0	4	1.8	2	1.2	6	2.4	0	0.0	12	1.9	4
Mexican American	0	0.0	1	0.3	1	0.2	0	0.0	0	0.0	0	0.0	1	0.4	0	0.0	1	0.2	2
Puerto Rican	4	1.3	4	1.2	8	1.3	0	0.0	6	2.7	2	1.2	0	0.0	0	0.0	8	1.3	0
Hispanic American	23	7.5	22	6.6	45	7.1	0	0.0	15	6.8	10	6.2	20	7.8	0	0.0	45	7.0	8
Total Minorities	54	17.6	56	16.9	110	17.4	0	0.0	44	19.8	26	16.0	40	15.7	0	0.0	110	17.2	25
Foreign Nationals	10	3.3	6	1.8	15	2.4	1	20.0	6	2.7	3	1.9	7	2.7	0	0.0	16	2.5	0
Caucasian	243	79.2	270	81.3	509	80.3	4	80.0	172	77.5	133	82.1	208	81.6	0	0.0	513	80.3	210
Total	307	48.0	332	52.0	634	99.2	5	0.8	222	34.7	162	25.4	255	39.9	0	0.0	639		235

GPA & LSAT Scores

	Full Time	Part Time	Total
# of apps	1,564	0	1,564
# admits	737	0	737
# of matrics	237	0	237
75% GPA	3.40	0.00	
25% GPA	2.90	0.00	
75% LSAT	155	0	
25% LSAT	148	0	

Tuition & Fees

	Resident	Non-resident
Full-Time	$19,110	$19,110
Part-Time	$0	$0

Living Expenses

Estimated living expenses for Singles		
Living on campus	Living off campus	Living at home
$10,690	$12,470	$6,270

Employment

	Total	%
Employment status known	182	87.5
Employment status unknown	26	12.5
Employed	166	91.2
Pursuing graduate degrees	5	2.7
Unemployed seeking employment	11	6.0
Unemployed not seeking employment	0	0.0
Type of Employment		
# employed in law firms	95	57.2
# employed in business & industry	12	7.2
# employed in government	32	19.3
# employed in public interest	3	1.8
# employed as judicial clerks	19	11.4
# employed in academia	5	3.0
Geographic Location		
# employed in state	140	84.3
# employed in foreign countries	0	0.0
# of states where employed	13	

Financial Aid

	Full-time		Part-time		Total	
	#	%	#	%	#	%
Total # of Students	634		5		639	
Total # receiving grants	302	47.6	0	0.0	302	47.3
Less than 1/2 tuition	249	39.3	0	0.0	249	39.0
Half to full tuition	16	2.5	0	0.0	16	2.5
Full tuition	35	5.5	0	0.0	35	5.5
More than full tuition	2	0.3	0	0.0	2	0.3
Median Grant Amount	$4,550		$0			

Informational & Library Resources

# of volumes & volume equivalents	346,498	# of professional staff	8
# of titles	98,009	Hours per week with professional staff	80
# of active serial subscriptions	5,105	Hours per week without professional staff	31
Study seating capacity inside the library	375	# of student computer work stations for entire law school	61
Square feet of law library	31,886	# of additional networked connections	51
Square feet of law school (excl. Library)	99,614	Require Laptop Computer?	N

J.D. Attrition (Prior Year)

	Academic	Other	TOTALS	
	#	#	#	%
1st Year	7	11	18	8.1%
2nd Year	1	10	11	5.2%
3rd Year	0	1	1	0.4%
4th Year	0	0	0	0.0%
TOTALS	8	22	30	4.5%

Bar Passage Rates

Jurisdiction	Florida		
Exam	Sum 96	Win 97	Total
# from school taking bar for the first time	127	55	182
School's pass rate for all first-time takers	91%	93%	91%
State's pass rate for all first-time takers	84%	85%	84%

SUFFOLK UNIVERSITY

41 Temple Street
Boston, MA 02114-4280
(617)573-8155
http://www.suffolk.edu/law

ABA Approved Since 1953

The Basics

Type of School: Private   Term: Semester
Application deadline: 03/03
Application fee: $50
Financial Aid deadline: 04/01
Can first year start other than Fall? No
Student faculty ratio: 23.8 to 1
Does the University offer:
- housing restricted to law students? No
- graduate student housing for which law students are eligible? No

Faculty & Administrators

	Total		Men		Women		Minorities	
	Fall	Spr	Fall	Spr	Fall	Spr	Fall	Spr
Full-time	52	51	43	42	9	9	4	4
Other Full-Time	12	12	7	7	5	5	1	1
Deans, librarians, & others who teach > 1/2	7	7	3	3	4	4	0	0
Part-time	54	64	39	46	15	18	5	2
Total	125	134	92	98	33	36	10	7
Deans, librarians, & others who teach < 1/2	2	2	1	1	1	1	0	0

Curriculum

	Full time	Part time
Typical first-year section size	91	103
Is there typically a "small section" of the first year class, other than Legal Writing, taught by full-time faculty?	Yes	No
If yes, typical size offered last year	44	N/A
# of classroom course titles beyond 1st year curriculum	133	139
# of upper division courses, excluding seminars, with an enrollment:		
Under 25	27	52
25 - 49	39	30
50 - 74	12	8
75 - 99	10	6
100 +	10	3
# of seminars	35	39
# of seminar positions available	1,076	
# of seminar positions filled	504	434
# of positions available in simulation courses	518	
# of simulation positions filled	270	195
# of positions available in faculty supervised clinical courses	133	
# of fac. sup. clin. positions filled	125	8
# involved in field placements	135	21
# involved in law journals	93	29
# in moot court or trial competitions	188	40
# of credit hrs required to graduate	84	

J.D. Enrollment & Ethnicity

	Men		Women		Fl-Time		Pt-Time		1st Yr		2nd Yr		3rd Yr		4th Yr		Total		JD Degrees Awarded
	#	%	#	%	#	%	#	%	#	%	#	%	#	%	#	%	#	%	
African-American	17	1.9	45	5.2	36	3.6	26	3.5	23	4.3	9	1.8	21	4.0	9	5.5	62	3.6	19
American Indian	1	0.1	5	0.6	4	0.4	2	0.3	1	0.2	1	0.2	3	0.6	1	0.6	6	0.3	1
Asian American	22	2.5	38	4.4	42	4.2	18	2.4	26	4.9	17	3.3	14	2.7	3	1.8	60	3.5	11
Mexican American	0	0.0	0	0.0	0	0.0	0	0.0	0	0.0	0	0.0	0	0.0	0	0.0	0	0.0	0
Puerto Rican	0	0.0	0	0.0	0	0.0	0	0.0	0	0.0	0	0.0	0	0.0	0	0.0	0	0.0	0
Hispanic American	17	1.9	27	3.1	23	2.3	21	2.8	16	3.0	8	1.6	14	2.7	6	3.6	44	2.5	12
Total Minorities	57	6.5	115	13.3	105	10.5	67	9.1	66	12.3	35	6.8	52	9.9	19	11.5	172	9.9	43
Foreign Nationals	0	0.0	0	0.0	0	0.0	0	0.0	0	0.0	0	0.0	0	0.0	0	0.0	0	0.0	0
Caucasian	819	93.5	748	86.7	895	89.5	672	90.9	470	87.7	478	93.2	473	90.1	146	88.5	1567	90.1	434
Total	876	50.4	863	49.6	1000	57.5	739	42.5	536	30.8	513	29.5	525	30.2	165	9.5	1739		477

GPA & LSAT Scores

	Full Time	Part Time	Total
# of apps	1,501	432	1,933
# admits	1,108	306	1,414
# of matrics	348	190	538
75% GPA	3.42	3.41	
25% GPA	2.90	2.86	
75% LSAT	154	156	
25% LSAT	147	147	

Tuition & Fees

	Resident	Non-resident
Full-Time	$19,036	$19,036
Part-Time	$14,278	$14,278

Living Expenses

Estimated living expenses for Singles		
Living on campus	Living off campus	Living at home
N/A	$14,581	$7,877

Financial Aid

	Full-time		Part-time		Total	
	#	%	#	%	#	%
Total # of Students	1000		739		1739	
Total # receiving grants	350	35.0	158	21.4	508	29.2
Less than 1/2 tuition	347	34.7	153	20.7	500	28.8
Half to full tuition	3	0.3	4	0.5	7	0.4
Full tuition	0	0.0	1	0.1	1	0.1
More than full tuition	0	0.0	0	0.0	0	0.0
Median Grant Amount	$2,500		$1,500			

Informational & Library Resources

# of volumes & volume equivalents	309,420	# of professional staff	11
# of titles	112,197	Hours per week with professional staff	78
# of active serial subscriptions	5,840	Hours per week without professional staff	25
Study seating capacity inside the library	602	# of student computer work stations for entire law school	96
Square feet of law library	35,524	# of additional networked connections	10
Square feet of law school (excl. Library)	57,292	Require Laptop Computer?	N

Employment

	Total	%
Employment status known	381	75.9
Employment status unknown	121	24.1
Employed	333	87.4
Pursuing graduate degrees	3	0.8
Unemployed seeking employment	35	9.2
Unemployed not seeking employment	10	2.6
Type of Employment		
# employed in law firms	146	43.8
# employed in business & industry	90	27.0
# employed in government	57	17.1
# employed in public interest	7	2.1
# employed as judicial clerks	23	6.9
# employed in academia	7	2.1
Geographic Location		
# employed in state	286	85.9
# employed in foreign countries	0	0.0
# of states where employed	19	

J.D. Attrition (Prior Year)

	Academic	Other	TOTALS	
	#	#	#	%
1st Year	21	8	29	5.1%
2nd Year	3	31	34	6.2%
3rd Year	0	8	8	1.7%
4th Year	0	1	1	0.6%
TOTALS	24	48	72	4.1%

Bar Passage Rates

Jurisdiction	Massachusetts		
Exam	Sum 96	Win 97	Total
# from school taking bar for the first time	411	55	466
School's pass rate for all first-time takers	81%	78%	80%
State's pass rate for all first-time takers	83%	76%	81%

SYRACUSE UNIVERSITY

Syracuse, NY 13244-1030
(315)443-1962
http://www.law.syr.edu

ABA Approved Since 1923

The Basics

Type of School: Private   Term: Semester
Application deadline: 04/01
Application fee: $50
Financial Aid deadline: 03/01
Can first year start other than Fall? No
Student faculty ratio: 16.9 to 1
Does the University offer:
- housing restricted to law students? Yes
- graduate student housing for which law students are eligible? Yes

Faculty & Administrators

	Total		Men		Women		Minorities	
	Fall	Spr	Fall	Spr	Fall	Spr	Fall	Spr
Full-time	36	34	21	20	15	14	4	2
Other Full-Time	1	1	1	1	0	0	0	0
Deans, librarians, & others who teach > 1/2	2	2	0	0	2	2	0	0
Part-time	26	27	22	19	4	8	3	3
Total	65	64	44	40	21	24	7	5
Deans, librarians, & others who teach < 1/2	2	2	1	1	1	1	0	0

Curriculum

	Full time	Part time
Typical first-year section size	90	0
Is there typically a "small section" of the first year class, other than Legal Writing, taught by full-time faculty?	Yes	No
If yes, typical size offered last year	40	N/A
# of classroom course titles beyond 1st year curriculum	188	0
# of upper division courses, excluding seminars, with an enrollment:		
Under 25	89	0
25 - 49	32	0
50 - 74	13	0
75 - 99	6	0
100 +	10	0
# of seminars	10	0
# of seminar positions available	160	
# of seminar positions filled	79	0
# of positions available in simulation courses	324	
# of simulation positions filled	307	0
# of positions available in faculty supervised clinical courses	40	
# of fac. sup. clin. positions filled	34	0
# involved in field placements	58	0
# involved in law journals	180	0
# in moot court or trial competitions	179	0
# of credit hrs required to graduate	87	

J.D. Enrollment & Ethnicity

	Men		Women		Fl-Time		Pt-Time		1st Yr		2nd Yr		3rd Yr		4th Yr		Total		JD Degrees Awarded
	#	%	#	%	#	%	#	%	#	%	#	%	#	%	#	%	#	%	
African-American	18	4.4	31	9.4	48	6.7	1	4.2	13	5.1	19	8.5	17	6.5	0	0.0	49	6.6	17
American Indian	1	0.2	0	0.0	1	0.1	0	0.0	1	0.4	0	0.0	0	0.0	0	0.0	1	0.1	2
Asian American	34	8.3	28	8.5	61	8.5	1	4.2	23	9.0	19	8.5	20	7.7	0	0.0	62	8.4	11
Mexican American	0	0.0	0	0.0	0	0.0	0	0.0	0	0.0	0	0.0	0	0.0	0	0.0	0	0.0	0
Puerto Rican	2	0.5	6	1.8	7	1.0	1	4.2	6	2.4	2	0.9	0	0.0	0	0.0	8	1.1	2
Hispanic American	15	3.7	15	4.5	29	4.1	1	4.2	6	2.4	13	5.8	11	4.2	0	0.0	30	4.1	5
Total Minorities	70	17.1	80	24.2	146	20.4	4	16.7	49	19.2	53	23.7	48	18.4	0	0.0	150	20.3	37
Foreign Nationals	20	4.9	3	0.9	23	3.2	0	0.0	12	4.7	6	2.7	5	1.9	0	0.0	23	3.1	6
Caucasian	320	78.0	247	74.8	547	76.4	20	83.3	194	76.1	165	73.7	208	79.7	0	0.0	567	76.6	195
Total	410	55.4	330	44.6	716	96.8	24	3.2	255	34.5	224	30.3	261	35.3	0	0.0	740		238

GPA & LSAT Scores

	Full Time	Part Time	Total
# of apps	1,676	25	1,701
# admits	1,113	11	1,124
# of matrics	247	6	253
75% GPA	3.43	3.02	
25% GPA	2.94	2.87	
75% LSAT	154	153	
25% LSAT	148	147	

Tuition & Fees

	Resident	Non-resident
Full-Time	$21,136	$21,136
Part-Time	$18,249	$0

Living Expenses

Estimated living expenses for Singles		
Living on campus	Living off campus	Living at home
$12,094	$12,094	$12,094

Employment

	Total	%
Employment status known	268	98.2
Employment status unknown	5	1.8
Employed	242	90.3
Pursuing graduate degrees	8	3.0
Unemployed seeking employment	15	5.6
Unemployed not seeking employment	3	1.1
Type of Employment		
# employed in law firms	131	54.1
# employed in business & industry	55	22.7
# employed in government	28	11.6
# employed in public interest	4	1.7
# employed as judicial clerks	18	7.4
# employed in academia	6	2.5
Geographic Location		
# employed in state	103	42.6
# employed in foreign countries	7	2.9
# of states where employed	27	

Financial Aid

	Full-time		Part-time		Total	
	#	%	#	%	#	%
Total # of Students	716		24		740	
Total # receiving grants	517	72.2	0	0.0	517	69.9
Less than 1/2 tuition	457	63.8	0	0.0	457	61.8
Half to full tuition	32	4.5	0	0.0	32	4.3
Full tuition	23	3.2	0	0.0	23	3.1
More than full tuition	5	0.7	0	0.0	5	0.7
Median Grant Amount	$6,300		$0			

Informational & Library Resources

# of volumes & volume equivalents	368,407	# of professional staff	10
# of titles	68,328	Hours per week with professional staff	45
# of active serial subscriptions	5,958	Hours per week without professional staff	60
Study seating capacity inside the library	475	# of student computer work stations for entire law school	91
Square feet of law library	31,005	# of additional networked connections	0
Square feet of law school (excl. Library)	35,102	Require Laptop Computer?	N

J.D. Attrition (Prior Year)

	Academic	Other	TOTALS	
	#	#	#	%
1st Year	0	3	3	1.2%
2nd Year	2	15	17	6.6%
3rd Year	0	6	6	2.5%
4th Year	0	0	0	0.0%
TOTALS	2	24	26	3.5%

Bar Passage Rates

Jurisdiction	New York		
Exam	Sum 96	Win 97	Total
# from school taking bar for the first time	147	22	169
School's pass rate for all first-time takers	70%	59%	69%
State's pass rate for all first-time takers	78%	67%	77%

TEMPLE UNIVERSITY

1719 North Broad Street
Philadelphia, PA 19122
(215)204-7861
http://www.temple.edu/lawschool

ABA Approved Since 1933

The Basics

Type of School: Public — Term: Semester

Application deadline: 03/01

Application fee: $50

Financial Aid deadline: 03/01

Can first year start other than Fall? No

Student faculty ratio: 18.4 to 1

Does the University offer:
- housing restricted to law students? Yes
- graduate student housing for which law students are eligible? Yes

Faculty & Administrators

	Total		Men		Women		Minorities	
	Fall	Spr	Fall	Spr	Fall	Spr	Fall	Spr
Full-time	44	43	32	32	12	11	10	9
Other Full-Time	4	4	1	1	3	3	0	0
Deans, librarians, & others who teach > 1/2	13	13	7	7	6	6	2	2
Part-time	74	97	48	67	26	30	5	11
Total	135	157	88	107	47	50	17	22
Deans, librarians, & others who teach < 1/2	5	5	3	3	2	2	1	1

Curriculum

	Full time	Part time
Typical first-year section size	64	84
Is there typically a "small section" of the first year class, other than Legal Writing, taught by full-time faculty?	No	No
If yes, typical size offered last year	N/A	N/A
# of classroom course titles beyond 1st year curriculum	130	57
# of upper division courses, excluding seminars, with an enrollment:		
Under 25	89	24
25 - 49	36	23
50 - 74	17	3
75 - 99	11	2
100 +	0	3
# of seminars	44	8
# of seminar positions available	771	
# of seminar positions filled	495	176
# of positions available in simulation courses	751	
# of simulation positions filled	562	110
# of positions available in faculty supervised clinical courses	10	
# of fac. sup. clin. positions filled	5	0
# involved in field placements	301	31
# involved in law journals	156	9
# in moot court or trial competitions	64	1
# of credit hrs required to graduate	86	

J.D. Enrollment & Ethnicity

	Men		Women		Fl-Time		Pt-Time		1st Yr		2nd Yr		3rd Yr		4th Yr		Total		JD Degrees Awarded
	#	%	#	%	#	%	#	%	#	%	#	%	#	%	#	%	#	%	
African-American	44	7.7	110	20.4	113	14.7	41	12.1	42	11.5	53	16.4	50	14.7	9	11.1	154	13.9	52
American Indian	5	0.9	3	0.6	3	0.4	5	1.5	1	0.3	2	0.6	3	0.9	2	2.5	8	0.7	0
Asian American	44	7.7	54	10.0	86	11.2	12	3.5	36	9.8	33	10.2	25	7.4	4	4.9	98	8.8	21
Mexican American	7	1.2	4	0.7	10	1.3	1	0.3	2	0.5	5	1.5	4	1.2	0	0.0	11	1.0	2
Puerto Rican	12	2.1	6	1.1	13	1.7	5	1.5	2	0.5	5	1.5	10	2.9	1	1.2	18	1.6	6
Hispanic American	10	1.8	7	1.3	12	1.6	5	1.5	7	1.9	4	1.2	4	1.2	2	2.5	17	1.5	5
Total Minorities	122	21.4	184	34.1	237	30.8	69	20.4	90	24.6	102	31.6	96	28.3	18	22.2	306	27.6	86
Foreign Nationals	4	0.7	6	1.1	9	1.2	1	0.3	10	2.7	0	0.0	0	0.0	0	0.0	10	0.9	0
Caucasian	443	77.9	350	64.8	524	68.1	269	79.4	266	72.7	221	68.4	243	71.7	63	77.8	793	71.5	280
Total	569	51.3	540	48.7	770	69.4	339	30.6	366	33.0	323	29.1	339	30.6	81	7.3	1109		366

GPA & LSAT Scores

	Full Time	Part Time	Total
# of apps	2,330	338	2,668
# admits	935	130	1,065
# of matrics	287	83	370
75% GPA	3.49	3.37	
25% GPA	3.00	2.75	
75% LSAT	159	159	
25% LSAT	151	151	

Tuition & Fees

	Resident	Non-resident
Full-Time	$8,900	$15,414
Part-Time	$7,182	$12,392

Living Expenses

Estimated living expenses for Singles

Living on campus	Living off campus	Living at home
$12,984	$12,984	$11,395

Financial Aid

	Full-time		Part-time		Total	
	#	%	#	%	#	%
Total # of Students	770		339		1109	
Total # receiving grants	529	68.7	23	6.8	552	49.8
Less than 1/2 tuition	459	59.6	18	5.3	477	43.0
Half to full tuition	29	3.8	3	0.9	32	2.9
Full tuition	36	4.7	2	0.6	38	3.4
More than full tuition	5	0.6	0	0.0	5	0.5
Median Grant Amount	$1,957		$2,318			

Informational & Library Resources

# of volumes & volume equivalents	481,649	# of professional staff	10
# of titles	85,548	Hours per week with professional staff	78
# of active serial subscriptions	2,550	Hours per week without professional staff	18
Study seating capacity inside the library	644	# of student computer work stations for entire law school	106
Square feet of law library	45,462	# of additional networked connections	152
Square feet of law school (excl. Library)	63,478	Require Laptop Computer?	N

Employment

	Total	%
Employment status known	341	97.2
Employment status unknown	10	2.8
Employed	319	93.5
Pursuing graduate degrees	4	1.2
Unemployed seeking employment	12	3.5
Unemployed not seeking employment	6	1.8
Type of Employment		
# employed in law firms	169	53.0
# employed in business & industry	56	17.6
# employed in government	37	11.6
# employed in public interest	14	4.4
# employed as judicial clerks	41	12.9
# employed in academia	2	0.6
Geographic Location		
# employed in state	195	61.1
# employed in foreign countries	0	0.0
# of states where employed	23	

J.D. Attrition (Prior Year)

	Academic	Other	TOTALS	
	#	#	#	%
1st Year	0	13	13	3.8%
2nd Year	0	16	16	4.7%
3rd Year	0	4	4	1.1%
4th Year	0	0	0	0.0%
TOTALS	0	33	33	2.9%

Bar Passage Rates

Jurisdiction	Pennsylvania		
Exam	Sum 96	Win 97	Total
# from school taking bar for the first time	243	39	282
School's pass rate for all first-time takers	71%	74%	72%
State's pass rate for all first-time takers	75%	76%	75%

TENNESSEE, UNIVERSITY OF

1505 W. Cumberland Ave.
Knoxville, TN 37996-1810
(423)974-4241
http://www.law.utk.edu

ABA Approved Since 1925

The Basics

Type of School: Public Term: Semester
Application deadline: 02/01
Application fee: $15
Financial Aid deadline: 02/14
Can first year start other than Fall? No
Student faculty ratio: 16.5 to 1
Does the University offer:
- housing restricted to law students? No
- graduate student housing for which law students are eligible? Yes

Faculty & Administrators

	Total		Men		Women		Minorities	
	Fall	Spr	Fall	Spr	Fall	Spr	Fall	Spr
Full-time	25	26	17	18	8	8	2	2
Other Full-Time	0	0	0	0	0	0	0	0
Deans, librarians, & others who teach > 1/2	3	3	3	3	0	0	0	0
Part-time	24	25	18	17	6	8	0	0
Total	52	54	38	38	14	16	2	2
Deans, librarians, & others who teach < 1/2	1	1	1	1	0	0	0	0

Curriculum

	Full time	Part time
Typical first-year section size	60	0
Is there typically a "small section" of the first year class, other than Legal Writing, taught by full-time faculty?	No	No
If yes, typical size offered last year	N/A	N/A
# of classroom course titles beyond 1st year curriculum	77	0
# of upper division courses, excluding seminars, with an enrollment:		
Under 25	60	0
25 - 49	21	0
50 - 74	12	0
75 - 99	3	0
100 +	0	0
# of seminars	10	0
# of seminar positions available	176	
# of seminar positions filled	105	0
# of positions available in simulation courses	496	
# of simulation positions filled	402	0
# of positions available in faculty supervised clinical courses	88	
# of fac. sup. clin. positions filled	75	0
# involved in field placements	3	0
# involved in law journals	66	0
# in moot court or trial competitions	35	0
# of credit hrs required to graduate	89	

J.D. Enrollment & Ethnicity

	Men		Women		Fl-Time		Pt-Time		1st Yr		2nd Yr		3rd Yr		4th Yr		Total		JD Degrees Awarded
	#	%	#	%	#	%	#	%	#	%	#	%	#	%	#	%	#	%	
African-American	10	3.7	30	13.4	40	8.1	0	0.0	14	7.8	12	7.7	14	8.8	0	0.0	40	8.1	10
American Indian	3	1.1	3	1.3	6	1.2	0	0.0	2	1.1	2	1.3	2	1.3	0	0.0	6	1.2	0
Asian American	2	0.7	0	0.0	2	0.4	0	0.0	1	0.6	1	0.6	0	0.0	0	0.0	2	0.4	1
Mexican American	0	0.0	0	0.0	0	0.0	0	0.0	0	0.0	0	0.0	0	0.0	0	0.0	0	0.0	0
Puerto Rican	0	0.0	0	0.0	0	0.0	0	0.0	0	0.0	0	0.0	0	0.0	0	0.0	0	0.0	0
Hispanic American	4	1.5	0	0.0	4	0.8	0	0.0	1	0.6	1	0.6	2	1.3	0	0.0	4	0.8	0
Total Minorities	19	7.0	33	14.7	52	10.5	0	0.0	18	10.0	16	10.3	18	11.3	0	0.0	52	10.5	11
Foreign Nationals	0	0.0	0	0.0	0	0.0	0	0.0	0	0.0	0	0.0	0	0.0	0	0.0	0	0.0	0
Caucasian	251	93.0	191	85.3	442	89.5	0	0.0	165	91.7	139	89.7	138	86.8	0	0.0	442	89.5	119
Total	270	54.7	224	45.3	494	100.0	0	0.0	180	36.4	155	31.4	159	32.2	0	0.0	494		130

GPA & LSAT Scores

	Full Time	Part Time	Total
# of apps	1,144	0	1,144
# admits	394	0	394
# of matrics	182	0	182
75% GPA	3.74	0.00	
25% GPA	3.27	0.00	
75% LSAT	159	0	
25% LSAT	152	0	

Tuition & Fees

	Resident	Non-resident
Full-Time	$4,204	$10,496
Part-Time	$0	$0

Living Expenses

Estimated living expenses for Singles		
Living on campus	Living off campus	Living at home
$10,816	$10,816	$7,400

Employment

	Total	%
Employment status known	157	98.1
Employment status unknown	3	1.9
Employed	138	87.9
Pursuing graduate degrees	4	2.5
Unemployed seeking employment	8	5.1
Unemployed not seeking employment	7	4.5
Type of Employment		
# employed in law firms	87	63.0
# employed in business & industry	20	14.5
# employed in government	10	7.2
# employed in public interest	2	1.4
# employed as judicial clerks	17	12.3
# employed in academia	2	1.4
Geographic Location		
# employed in state	117	84.8
# employed in foreign countries	0	0.0
# of states where employed	11	

Financial Aid

	Full-time		Part-time		Total	
	#	%	#	%	#	%
Total # of Students	494		0		494	
Total # receiving grants	112	22.7	0	0.0	112	22.7
Less than 1/2 tuition	43	8.7	0	0.0	43	8.7
Half to full tuition	6	1.2	0	0.0	6	1.2
Full tuition	19	3.8	0	0.0	19	3.8
More than full tuition	44	8.9	0	0.0	44	8.9
Median Grant Amount	$4,200		$0			

Informational & Library Resources

# of volumes & volume equivalents	436,128	# of professional staff	7
# of titles	82,875	Hours per week with professional staff	71
# of active serial subscriptions	5,703	Hours per week without professional staff	41
Study seating capacity inside the library	455	# of student computer work stations for entire law school	88
Square feet of law library	57,400	# of additional networked connections	7
Square feet of law school (excl. Library)	46,987	Require Laptop Computer?	N

J.D. Attrition (Prior Year)

	Academic	Other	TOTALS	
	#	#	#	%
1st Year	1	10	11	6.7%
2nd Year	1	0	1	0.6%
3rd Year	0	0	0	0.0%
4th Year	0	0	0	0.0%
TOTALS	2	10	12	2.6%

Bar Passage Rates

Jurisdiction	Tennessee		
Exam	Sum 96	Win 97	Total
# from school taking bar for the first time	125	13	138
School's pass rate for all first-time takers	85%	85%	85%
State's pass rate for all first-time takers	81%	72%	79%

TEXAS AT AUSTIN, UNIVERSITY OF

727 E. Dean Keeton Street
Austin, TX 78705
(512)232-1200
http://www.utexas.edu/law

ABA Approved Since 1923

The Basics

Type of School: Public Term: Semester

Application deadline: 02/01

Application fee: $65

Financial Aid deadline: 03/31

Can first year start other than Fall? No

Student faculty ratio: 20.6 to 1

Does the University offer:
- housing restricted to law students? No
- graduate student housing for which law students are eligible? No

Faculty & Administrators

	Total		Men		Women		Minorities	
	Fall	Spr	Fall	Spr	Fall	Spr	Fall	Spr
Full-time	57	59	46	46	11	13	4	6
Other Full-Time	0	0	0	0	0	0	0	0
Deans, librarians, & others who teach > 1/2	5	5	3	3	2	2	1	1
Part-time	39	63	25	47	14	16	6	9
Total	101	127	74	96	27	31	11	16
Deans, librarians, & others who teach < 1/2	0	0	0	0	0	0	0	0

Curriculum

	Full time	Part time
Typical first-year section size	117	0
Is there typically a "small section" of the first year class, other than Legal Writing, taught by full-time faculty?	Yes	No
If yes, typical size offered last year	N/A	N/A
# of classroom course titles beyond 1st year curriculum	141	0
# of upper division courses, excluding seminars, with an enrollment:		
Under 25	150	0
25 - 49	48	0
50 - 74	29	0
75 - 99	11	0
100 +	19	0
# of seminars	62	0
# of seminar positions available	798	
# of seminar positions filled	632	0
# of positions available in simulation courses	833	
# of simulation positions filled	557	0
# of positions available in faculty supervised clinical courses	266	
# of fac. sup. clin. positions filled	197	0
# involved in field placements	102	0
# involved in law journals	578	0
# in moot court or trial competitions	300	0
# of credit hrs required to graduate	86	

J.D. Enrollment & Ethnicity

	Men		Women		Fl-Time		Pt-Time		1st Yr		2nd Yr		3rd Yr		4th Yr		Total		JD Degrees Awarded
	#	%	#	%	#	%	#	%	#	%	#	%	#	%	#	%	#	%	
African-American	22	2.7	48	7.4	70	4.8	0	0.0	4	0.9	30	6.1	36	7.0	0	0.0	70	4.8	35
American Indian	3	0.4	6	0.9	9	0.6	0	0.0	1	0.2	5	1.0	3	0.6	0	0.0	9	0.6	0
Asian American	48	5.9	49	7.5	97	6.6	0	0.0	37	8.0	29	5.9	31	6.0	0	0.0	97	6.6	35
Mexican American	82	10.1	73	11.2	155	10.6	0	0.0	30	6.5	52	10.6	73	14.2	0	0.0	155	10.6	63
Puerto Rican	0	0.0	0	0.0	0	0.0	0	0.0	0	0.0	0	0.0	0	0.0	0	0.0	0	0.0	0
Hispanic American	0	0.0	0	0.0	0	0.0	0	0.0	0	0.0	0	0.0	0	0.0	0	0.0	0	0.0	0
Total Minorities	155	19.0	176	27.1	331	22.6	0	0.0	72	15.7	116	23.6	143	27.8	0	0.0	331	22.6	133
Foreign Nationals	2	0.2	0	0.0	2	0.1	0	0.0	1	0.2	1	0.2	0	0.0	0	0.0	2	0.1	3
Caucasian	658	80.7	474	72.9	1132	77.3	0	0.0	387	84.1	374	76.2	371	72.2	0	0.0	1132	77.3	406
Total	815	55.6	650	44.4	1465	100.0	0	0.0	460	31.4	491	33.5	514	35.1	0	0.0	1465		542

GPA & LSAT Scores

	Full Time	Part Time	Total
# of apps	3,487	0	3,487
# admits	1,092	0	1,092
# of matrics	460	0	460
75% GPA	3.73	0.00	
25% GPA	3.40	0.00	
75% LSAT	165	0	
25% LSAT	159	0	

Tuition & Fees

	Resident	Non-resident
Full-Time	$6,300	$13,300
Part-Time	$0	$0

Living Expenses

Estimated living expenses for Singles

Living on campus	Living off campus	Living at home
$8,734	$10,306	$7,533

Financial Aid

	Full-time		Part-time		Total	
	#	%	#	%	#	%
Total # of Students	1465		0		1465	
Total # receiving grants	1400	95.6	0	0.0	1400	95.6
Less than 1/2 tuition	1333	91.0	0	0.0	1333	91.0
Half to full tuition	37	2.5	0	0.0	37	2.5
Full tuition	25	1.7	0	0.0	25	1.7
More than full tuition	5	0.3	0	0.0	5	0.3
Median Grant Amount	$1,650		$0			

Informational & Library Resources

# of volumes & volume equivalents	917,865	# of professional staff	17
# of titles	247,712	Hours per week with professional staff	80
# of active serial subscriptions	9,899	Hours per week without professional staff	22
Study seating capacity inside the library	1,361	# of student computer work stations for entire law school	186
Square feet of law library	172,000	# of additional networked connections	0
Square feet of law school (excl. Library)	96,053	Require Laptop Computer?	N

Employment

	Total	%
Employment status known	422	87.4
Employment status unknown	61	12.6
Employed	381	90.3
Pursuing graduate degrees	4	0.9
Unemployed seeking employment	30	7.1
Unemployed not seeking employment	7	1.7
Type of Employment		
# employed in law firms	245	64.3
# employed in business & industry	26	6.8
# employed in government	36	9.4
# employed in public interest	1	0.3
# employed as judicial clerks	40	10.5
# employed in academia	4	1.0
Geographic Location		
# employed in state	233	61.2
# employed in foreign countries	5	1.3
# of states where employed	31	

J.D. Attrition (Prior Year)

	Academic	Other	TOTALS	
	#	#	#	%
1st Year	0	17	17	3.4%
2nd Year	1	6	7	1.4%
3rd Year	0	1	1	0.2%
4th Year	0	0	0	0.0%
TOTALS	1	24	25	1.6%

Bar Passage Rates

Jurisdiction	Texas			New York		
Exam	Sum 96	Win 97	Total	Sum 96	Win 97	Total
# from school taking bar for the first time	338	43	381	25	7	32
School's pass rate for all first-time takers	97%	88%	96%	72%	100%	78%
State's pass rate for all first-time takers	84%	81%	84%	78%	67%	77%

TEXAS SOUTHERN UNIVERSITY

3100 Cleburne
Houston, TX 77004-3216
(713)313-1075
http://www.tsulaw.edu

ABA Approved Since 1949

The Basics

Type of School: Public Term: Semester
Application deadline: 04/01
Application fee: $40
Financial Aid deadline: Rolling
Can first year start other than Fall? No
Student faculty ratio: 19.1 to 1
Does the University offer:
- housing restricted to law students? Yes
- graduate student housing for which law students are eligible? No

Faculty & Administrators

	Total		Men		Women		Minorities	
	Fall	Spr	Fall	Spr	Fall	Spr	Fall	Spr
Full-time	26	25	21	20	5	5	21	20
Other Full-Time	5	5	2	2	3	3	0	0
Deans, librarians, & others who teach > 1/2	2	2	2	2	0	0	3	3
Part-time	7	14	5	12	2	2	5	13
Total	40	46	30	36	10	10	29	36
Deans, librarians, & others who teach < 1/2	1	1	0	0	1	1	1	1

Curriculum

	Full time	Part time
Typical first-year section size	65	0
Is there typically a "small section" of the first year class, other than Legal Writing, taught by full-time faculty?	Yes	No
If yes, typical size offered last year	50	N/A
# of classroom course titles beyond 1st year curriculum	68	0
# of upper division courses, excluding seminars, with an enrollment:		
Under 25	51	0
25 - 49	9	0
50 - 74	10	0
75 - 99	9	0
100 +	0	0
# of seminars	12	0
# of seminar positions available	240	
# of seminar positions filled	138	0
# of positions available in simulation courses	160	
# of simulation positions filled	160	0
# of positions available in faculty supervised clinical courses	170	
# of fac. sup. clin. positions filled	170	0
# involved in field placements	129	0
# involved in law journals	0	0
# in moot court or trial competitions	0	0
# of credit hrs required to graduate	90	

J.D. Enrollment & Ethnicity

	Men		Women		Fl-Time		Pt-Time		1st Yr		2nd Yr		3rd Yr		4th Yr		Total		JD Degrees Awarded
	#	%	#	%	#	%	#	%	#	%	#	%	#	%	#	%	#	%	
African-American	148	46.4	179	64.6	327	54.9	0	0.0	158	57.7	94	57.3	75	47.5	0	0.0	327	54.9	68
American Indian	5	1.6	1	0.4	6	1.0	0	0.0	4	1.5	2	1.2	0	0.0	0	0.0	6	1.0	1
Asian American	9	2.8	21	7.6	30	5.0	0	0.0	10	3.6	9	5.5	11	7.0	0	0.0	30	5.0	8
Mexican American	83	26.0	42	15.2	125	21.0	0	0.0	61	22.3	27	16.5	37	23.4	0	0.0	125	21.0	27
Puerto Rican	1	0.3	1	0.4	2	0.3	0	0.0	0	0.0	0	0.0	2	1.3	0	0.0	2	0.3	1
Hispanic American	9	2.8	2	0.7	11	1.8	0	0.0	0	0.0	7	4.3	4	2.5	0	0.0	11	1.8	4
Total Minorities	255	79.9	246	88.8	501	84.1	0	0.0	233	85.0	139	84.8	129	81.6	0	0.0	501	84.1	109
Foreign Nationals	7	2.2	3	1.1	10	1.7	0	0.0	1	0.4	9	5.5	0	0.0	0	0.0	10	1.7	0
Caucasian	57	17.9	28	10.1	85	14.3	0	0.0	40	14.6	16	9.8	29	18.4	0	0.0	85	14.3	29
Total	319	53.5	277	46.5	596	100.0	0	0.0	274	46.0	164	27.5	158	26.5	0	0.0	596		138

GPA & LSAT Scores

	Full Time	Part Time	Total
# of apps	1,165	0	1,165
# admits	548	0	548
# of matrics	260	0	260
75% GPA	2.89	0.00	
25% GPA	2.38	0.00	
75% LSAT	145	0	
25% LSAT	140	0	

Tuition & Fees

	Resident	Non-resident
Full-Time	$4,367	$8,007
Part-Time	$0	$0

Living Expenses

Estimated living expenses for Singles		
Living on campus	Living off campus	Living at home
$2,734	$9,872	$2,734

Financial Aid

	Full-time		Part-time		Total	
	#	%	#	%	#	%
Total # of Students	596		0		596	
Total # receiving grants	470	78.9	0	0.0	470	78.9
Less than 1/2 tuition	459	77.0	0	0.0	459	77.0
Half to full tuition	11	1.8	0	0.0	11	1.8
Full tuition	0	0.0	0	0.0	0	0.0
More than full tuition	0	0.0	0	0.0	0	0.0
Median Grant Amount	$1,800		$0			

Informational & Library Resources

# of volumes & volume equivalents	379,979	# of professional staff	3
# of titles	65,868	Hours per week with professional staff	63
# of active serial subscriptions	2,463	Hours per week without professional staff	44
Study seating capacity inside the library	348	# of student computer work stations for entire law school	41
Square feet of law library	47,883	# of additional networked connections	45
Square feet of law school (excl. Library)	49,326	Require Laptop Computer?	N

Employment

	Total	%
Employment status known	87	78.4
Employment status unknown	24	21.6
Employed	81	93.1
Pursuing graduate degrees	4	4.6
Unemployed seeking employment	0	0.0
Unemployed not seeking employment	2	2.3
Type of Employment		
# employed in law firms	35	43.2
# employed in business & industry	7	8.6
# employed in government	1	1.2
# employed in public interest	0	0.0
# employed as judicial clerks	2	2.5
# employed in academia	0	0.0
Geographic Location		
# employed in state	39	48.1
# employed in foreign countries	0	0.0
# of states where employed	6	

J.D. Attrition (Prior Year)

	Academic	Other	TOTALS	
	#	#	#	%
1st Year	90	29	119	40%
2nd Year	3	4	7	4.2%
3rd Year	0	0	0	0.0%
4th Year	0	0	0	0.0%
TOTALS	93	33	126	21%

Bar Passage Rates

Jurisdiction	Texas		
Exam	Sum 96	Win 97	Total
# from school taking bar for the first time	85	27	112
School's pass rate for all first-time takers	75%	74%	75%
State's pass rate for all first-time takers	84%	81%	84%

TEXAS TECH UNIVERSITY

1802 Hartford
Lubbock, TX 79409-0004
(806)742-3791
http://www.law.ttu.edu

ABA Approved Since 1969

The Basics

Type of School: Public Term: Semester
Application deadline: 02/01
Application fee: $50
Financial Aid deadline: 05/01
Can first year start other than Fall? No
Student faculty ratio: 24.9 to 1
Does the University offer:
- housing restricted to law students? No
- graduate student housing for which law students are eligible? No

Faculty & Administrators

	Total		Men		Women		Minorities	
	Fall	Spr	Fall	Spr	Fall	Spr	Fall	Spr
Full-time	22	22	17	17	5	5	3	3
Other Full-Time	0	0	0	0	0	0	0	0
Deans, librarians, & others who teach > 1/2	6	6	3	3	3	3	0	0
Part-time	6	5	6	5	0	0	0	0
Total	34	33	26	25	8	8	3	3
Deans, librarians, & others who teach < 1/2	0	0	0	0	0	0	0	0

Curriculum

	Full time	Part time
Typical first-year section size	75	0
Is there typically a "small section" of the first year class, other than Legal Writing, taught by full-time faculty?	No	No
If yes, typical size offered last year	N/A	N/A
# of classroom course titles beyond 1st year curriculum	82	0
# of upper division courses, excluding seminars, with an enrollment:		
Under 25	21	0
25 - 49	18	0
50 - 74	16	0
75 - 99	5	0
100 +	7	0
# of seminars	8	0
# of seminar positions available	130	
# of seminar positions filled	122	0
# of positions available in simulation courses	193	
# of simulation positions filled	176	0
# of positions available in faculty supervised clinical courses	0	
# of fac. sup. clin. positions filled	0	0
# involved in field placements	75	0
# involved in law journals	70	0
# in moot court or trial competitions	150	0
# of credit hrs required to graduate	90	

J.D. Enrollment & Ethnicity

	Men		Women		Fl-Time		Pt-Time		1st Yr		2nd Yr		3rd Yr		4th Yr		Total		JD Degrees Awarded
	#	%	#	%	#	%	#	%	#	%	#	%	#	%	#	%	#	%	
African-American	5	1.3	6	2.3	11	1.7	0	0.0	2	1.0	5	2.3	4	1.9	0	0.0	11	1.7	4
American Indian	3	0.8	7	2.6	10	1.6	0	0.0	1	0.5	2	0.9	7	3.3	0	0.0	10	1.6	4
Asian American	4	1.1	5	1.9	9	1.4	0	0.0	2	1.0	3	1.4	4	1.9	0	0.0	9	1.4	4
Mexican American	28	7.5	25	9.4	53	8.3	0	0.0	16	7.9	20	9.1	17	7.9	0	0.0	53	8.3	16
Puerto Rican	0	0.0	0	0.0	0	0.0	0	0.0	0	0.0	0	0.0	0	0.0	0	0.0	0	0.0	0
Hispanic American	0	0.0	0	0.0	0	0.0	0	0.0	0	0.0	0	0.0	0	0.0	0	0.0	0	0.0	0
Total Minorities	40	10.8	43	16.2	83	13.0	0	0.0	21	10.3	30	13.7	32	14.9	0	0.0	83	13.0	28
Foreign Nationals	4	1.1	1	0.4	5	0.8	0	0.0	3	1.5	1	0.5	1	0.5	0	0.0	5	0.8	0
Caucasian	327	88.1	222	83.5	549	86.2	0	0.0	179	88.2	188	85.8	182	84.7	0	0.0	549	86.2	165
Total	371	58.2	266	41.8	637	100.0	0	0.0	203	31.9	219	34.4	215	33.8	0	0.0	637		193

GPA & LSAT Scores

	Full Time	Part Time	Total
# of apps	1,149	0	1,149
# admits	547	0	547
# of matrics	205	0	205
75% GPA	3.62	0.00	
25% GPA	3.18	0.00	
75% LSAT	158	0	
25% LSAT	152	0	

Tuition & Fees

	Resident	Non-resident
Full-Time	$6,195	$10,335
Part-Time	$0	$0

Living Expenses

Estimated living expenses for Singles		
Living on campus	Living off campus	Living at home
$9,190	$9,190	$5,010

Employment

	Total	%
Employment status known	172	90.5
Employment status unknown	18	9.5
Employed	146	84.9
Pursuing graduate degrees	0	0.0
Unemployed seeking employment	26	15.1
Unemployed not seeking employment	0	0.0
Type of Employment		
# employed in law firms	126	86.3
# employed in business & industry	1	0.7
# employed in government	7	4.8
# employed in public interest	1	0.7
# employed as judicial clerks	11	7.5
# employed in academia	0	0.0
Geographic Location		
# employed in state	141	96.6
# employed in foreign countries	0	0.0
# of states where employed	3	

Financial Aid

	Full-time		Part-time		Total	
	#	%	#	%	#	%
Total # of Students	637		0		637	
Total # receiving grants	288	45.2	0	0.0	288	45.2
Less than 1/2 tuition	170	26.7	0	0.0	170	26.7
Half to full tuition	6	0.9	0	0.0	6	0.9
Full tuition	0	0.0	0	0.0	0	0.0
More than full tuition	112	17.6	0	0.0	112	17.6
Median Grant Amount	$3,000		$0			

Informational & Library Resources

# of volumes & volume equivalents	259,426	# of professional staff	6
# of titles	53,423	Hours per week with professional staff	40
# of active serial subscriptions	2,277	Hours per week without professional staff	53
Study seating capacity inside the library	380	# of student computer work stations for entire law school	232
Square feet of law library	49,302	# of additional networked connections	0
Square feet of law school (excl. Library)	40,436	Require Laptop Computer?	N

J.D. Attrition (Prior Year)

	Academic	Other	TOTALS	
	#	#	#	%
1st Year	4	16	20	8.8%
2nd Year	0	0	0	0.0%
3rd Year	0	1	1	0.5%
4th Year	0	0	0	0.0%
TOTALS	4	17	21	3.3%

Bar Passage Rates

Jurisdiction	Texas		
Exam	Sum 96	Win 97	Total
# from school taking bar for the first time	147	33	180
School's pass rate for all first-time takers	86%	88%	87%
State's pass rate for all first-time takers	84%	81%	84%

TEXAS WESLEYAN UNIVERSITY (Provisional)

1515 Commerce Street
Fort Worth, TX 76102
(817)212-4100
http://www.txwesleyan.edu

ABA Approved Since 1994

The Basics

Type of School: Private Term: Semester

Application deadline: 03/15 (Preferred)

Application fee: $50

Financial Aid deadline: 04/15 (Preferred)

Can first year start other than Fall? No

Student faculty ratio: 22.4 to 1

Does the University offer:

- housing restricted to law students? No
- graduate student housing for which law students are eligible? No

Faculty & Administrators

	Total		Men		Women		Minorities	
	Fall	Spr	Fall	Spr	Fall	Spr	Fall	Spr
Full-time	21	20	17	16	4	4	4	3
Other Full-Time	0	0	0	0	0	0	0	0
Deans, librarians, & others who teach > 1/2	3	3	2	2	1	1	0	0
Part-time	18	26	12	15	6	11	1	1
Total	42	49	31	33	11	16	5	4
Deans, librarians, & others who teach < 1/2	1	1	1	1	0	0	0	0

Curriculum

	Full time	Part time
Typical first-year section size	72	105
Is there typically a "small section" of the first year class, other than Legal Writing, taught by full-time faculty?	Yes	Yes
If yes, typical size offered last year	36	53
# of classroom course titles beyond 1st year curriculum	46	37
# of upper division courses, excluding seminars, with an enrollment:		
Under 25	25	20
25 - 49	12	18
50 - 74	3	5
75 - 99	3	3
100 +	2	0
# of seminars	6	6
# of seminar positions available	192	
# of seminar positions filled	62	76
# of positions available in simulation courses	317	
# of simulation positions filled	128	159
# of positions available in faculty supervised clinical courses	0	
# of fac. sup. clin. positions filled	0	0
# involved in field placements	23	8
# involved in law journals	35	10
# in moot court or trial competitions	30	8
# of credit hrs required to graduate	88	

J.D. Enrollment & Ethnicity

	Men		Women		Fl-Time		Pt-Time		1st Yr		2nd Yr		3rd Yr		4th Yr		Total		JD Degrees Awarded
	#	%	#	%	#	%	#	%	#	%	#	%	#	%	#	%	#	%	
African-American	17	4.3	24	9.0	13	3.4	28	10.1	12	6.1	8	4.1	14	7.0	7	10.9	41	6.2	6
American Indian	7	1.8	5	1.9	7	1.8	5	1.8	7	3.5	2	1.0	2	1.0	1	1.6	12	1.8	1
Asian American	7	1.8	9	3.4	10	2.6	6	2.2	6	3.0	8	4.1	1	0.5	1	1.6	16	2.4	4
Mexican American	30	7.7	28	10.5	33	8.7	25	9.0	17	8.6	17	8.7	20	10.0	4	6.3	58	8.8	12
Puerto Rican	0	0.0	0	0.0	0	0.0	0	0.0	0	0.0	0	0.0	0	0.0	0	0.0	0	0.0	0
Hispanic American	0	0.0	0	0.0	0	0.0	0	0.0	0	0.0	0	0.0	0	0.0	0	0.0	0	0.0	0
Total Minorities	61	15.6	66	24.7	63	16.5	64	23.1	42	21.2	35	17.9	37	18.4	13	20.3	127	19.3	23
Foreign Nationals	0	0.0	0	0.0	0	0.0	0	0.0	0	0.0	0	0.0	0	0.0	0	0.0	0	0.0	0
Caucasian	330	84.4	201	75.3	318	83.5	213	76.9	156	78.8	160	82.1	164	81.6	51	79.7	531	80.7	129
Total	391	59.4	267	40.6	381	57.9	277	42.1	198	30.1	195	29.6	201	30.5	64	9.7	658		152

TEXAS WESLEYAN UNIVERSITY (Provisional)

GPA & LSAT Scores

	Full Time	Part Time	Total
# of apps	729	193	922
# admits	407	104	511
# of matrics	136	75	211
75% GPA	3.14	3.09	
25% GPA	2.56	2.75	
75% LSAT	152	152	
25% LSAT	147	146	

Tuition & Fees

	Resident	Non-resident
Full-Time	$12,074	$12,074
Part-Time	$8,674	$8,674

Living Expenses

Estimated living expenses for Singles		
Living on campus	Living off campus	Living at home
$6,541	$8,506	$5,739

Employment

	Total	%
Employment status known	100	70.9
Employment status unknown	41	29.1
Employed	76	76.0
Pursuing graduate degrees	3	3.0
Unemployed seeking employment	10	10.0
Unemployed not seeking employment	11	11.0
Type of Employment		
# employed in law firms	40	52.6
# employed in business & industry	23	30.3
# employed in government	7	9.2
# employed in public interest	0	0.0
# employed as judicial clerks	2	2.6
# employed in academia	4	5.3
Geographic Location		
# employed in state	75	98.7
# employed in foreign countries	0	0.0
# of states where employed	2	

Financial Aid

	Full-time		Part-time		Total	
	#	%	#	%	#	%
Total # of Students	381		277		658	
Total # receiving grants	252	66.1	182	65.7	434	66.0
Less than 1/2 tuition	250	65.6	182	65.7	432	65.7
Half to full tuition	0	0.0	0	0.0	0	0.0
Full tuition	0	0.0	0	0.0	0	0.0
More than full tuition	2	0.5	0	0.0	2	0.3
Median Grant Amount	$2,200		$1,600			

Informational & Library Resources

# of volumes & volume equivalents	145,595	# of professional staff	7
# of titles	15,166	Hours per week with professional staff	89
# of active serial subscriptions	2,747	Hours per week without professional staff	23
Study seating capacity inside the library	254	# of student computer work stations for entire law school	30
Square feet of law library	14,222	# of additional networked connections	0
Square feet of law school (excl. Library)	60,264	Require Laptop Computer?	N

J.D. Attrition (Prior Year)

	Academic	Other	TOTALS	
	#	#	#	%
1st Year	40	11	51	20%
2nd Year	13	1	14	5.2%
3rd Year	3	0	3	2.4%
4th Year	1	1	2	3.7%
TOTALS	57	13	70	10%

Bar Passage Rates

Jurisdiction	Texas		
Exam	Sum 96	Win 97	Total
# from school taking bar for the first time	60	64	124
School's pass rate for all first-time takers	53%	61%	57%
State's pass rate for all first-time takers	84%	81%	84%

THOMAS JEFFERSON SCHOOL OF LAW (Provisional)

2121 San Diego Avenue
San Diego, CA 92110
(619)297-9700
http://www.jeffersonlaw.edu

ABA Approved Since 1996

The Basics

Type of School: Private   Term: Semester
Application deadline: Rolling
Application fee: $35
Financial Aid deadline: Rolling
Can first year start other than Fall? Yes
Student faculty ratio: 19.1 to 1
Does the University offer:
- housing restricted to law students? No
- graduate student housing for which law students are eligible? No

Faculty & Administrators

	Total		Men		Women		Minorities	
	Fall	Spr	Fall	Spr	Fall	Spr	Fall	Spr
Full-time	21	20	11	10	10	10	1	1
Other Full-Time	0	0	0	0	0	0	0	0
Deans, librarians, & others who teach > 1/2	1	2	1	1	0	1	0	0
Part-time	28	22	22	18	6	4	1	2
Total	50	44	34	29	16	15	2	3
Deans, librarians, & others who teach < 1/2	1	1	0	0	1	1	0	0

Curriculum

	Full time	Part time
Typical first-year section size	33	21
Is there typically a "small section" of the first year class, other than Legal Writing, taught by full-time faculty?	No	No
If yes, typical size offered last year	N/A	N/A
# of classroom course titles beyond 1st year curriculum	47	46
# of upper division courses, excluding seminars, with an enrollment:		
Under 25	31	22
25 - 49	12	17
50 - 74	7	12
75 - 99	0	0
100 +	0	0
# of seminars	1	7
# of seminar positions available	120	
# of seminar positions filled	10	89
# of positions available in simulation courses	408	
# of simulation positions filled	137	160
# of positions available in faculty supervised clinical courses	0	
# of fac. sup. clin. positions filled	0	0
# involved in field placements	16	12
# involved in law journals	10	14
# in moot court or trial competitions	9	12
# of credit hrs required to graduate	88	

J.D. Enrollment & Ethnicity

	Men		Women		Fl-Time		Pt-Time		1st Yr		2nd Yr		3rd Yr		4th Yr		Total		JD Degrees Awarded
	#	%	#	%	#	%	#	%	#	%	#	%	#	%	#	%	#	%	
African-American	9	2.5	13	6.0	16	5.4	6	2.1	19	6.5	0	0.0	3	2.6	0	0.0	22	3.8	3
American Indian	3	0.8	2	0.9	4	1.3	1	0.4	3	1.0	2	1.8	0	0.0	0	0.0	5	0.9	0
Asian American	24	6.6	17	7.9	24	8.1	17	6.0	25	8.6	7	6.4	7	6.0	2	3.3	41	7.1	7
Mexican American	24	6.6	14	6.5	20	6.7	18	6.4	22	7.5	6	5.5	6	5.2	4	6.7	38	6.6	8
Puerto Rican	2	0.6	0	0.0	1	0.3	1	0.4	1	0.3	0	0.0	0	0.0	1	1.7	2	0.3	0
Hispanic American	12	3.3	6	2.8	7	2.4	11	3.9	8	2.7	6	5.5	2	1.7	2	3.3	18	3.1	7
Total Minorities	74	20.4	52	24.1	72	24.2	54	19.2	78	26.7	21	19.1	18	15.5	9	15.0	126	21.8	25
Foreign Nationals	0	0.0	1	0.5	0	0.0	1	0.4	0	0.0	0	0.0	1	0.9	0	0.0	1	0.2	1
Caucasian	288	79.6	163	75.5	225	75.8	226	80.4	214	73.3	89	80.9	97	83.6	51	85.0	451	78.0	143
Total	362	62.6	216	37.4	297	51.4	281	48.6	292	50.5	110	19.0	116	20.1	60	10.4	578		169

THOMAS JEFFERSON SCHOOL OF LAW (Provisional)

GPA & LSAT Scores

	Full Time	Part Time	Total
# of apps	913	132	1,045
# admits	745	101	846
# of matrics	151	39	190
75% GPA	3.07	3.17	
25% GPA	2.37	2.41	
75% LSAT	150	152	
25% LSAT	143	144	

Tuition & Fees

	Resident	Non-resident
Full-Time	$16,256	$16,256
Part-Time	$11,640	$11,640

Living Expenses

Estimated living expenses for Singles		
Living on campus	Living off campus	Living at home
N/A	$13,973	$8,650

Financial Aid

	Full-time		Part-time		Total	
	#	%	#	%	#	%
Total # of Students	297		281		578	
Total # receiving grants	163	54.9	115	40.9	278	48.1
Less than 1/2 tuition	153	51.5	107	38.1	260	45.0
Half to full tuition	10	3.4	6	2.1	16	2.8
Full tuition	0	0.0	2	0.7	2	0.3
More than full tuition	0	0.0	0	0.0	0	0.0
Median Grant Amount	$3,702		$2,530			

Informational & Library Resources

# of volumes & volume equivalents	114,373	# of professional staff	7
# of titles	13,397	Hours per week with professional staff	76
# of active serial subscriptions	3,858	Hours per week without professional staff	19
Study seating capacity inside the library	286	# of student computer work stations for entire law school	43
Square feet of law library	17,588	# of additional networked connections	0
Square feet of law school (excl. Library)	49,412	Require Laptop Computer?	N

Employment

	Total	%
Employment status known	81	67.5
Employment status unknown	39	32.5
Employed	70	86.4
Pursuing graduate degrees	1	1.2
Unemployed seeking employment	7	8.6
Unemployed not seeking employment	3	3.7
Type of Employment		
# employed in law firms	41	58.6
# employed in business & industry	2	2.9
# employed in government	16	22.9
# employed in public interest	0	0.0
# employed as judicial clerks	0	0.0
# employed in academia	0	0.0
Geographic Location		
# employed in state	64	91.4
# employed in foreign countries	0	0.0
# of states where employed	2	

J.D. Attrition (Prior Year)

	Academic	Other	TOTALS	
	#	#	#	%
1st Year	37	28	65	33%
2nd Year	11	7	18	14%
3rd Year	2	1	3	2.9%
4th Year	0	0	0	0.0%
TOTALS	50	36	86	15%

Bar Passage Rates

Jurisdiction	California		
Exam	Sum 96	Win 97	Total
# from school taking bar for the first time	61	86	147
School's pass rate for all first-time takers	46%	62%	55%
State's pass rate for all first-time takers	69%	62%	67%

THOMAS M. COOLEY LAW SCHOOL

217 South Capitol Avenue
P.O. Box 13038
Lansing, MI 48901
(517)371-5140
http://www.cooley.edu

ABA Approved Since 1975

The Basics

Type of School: Private
Term: Semester
Application deadline: Rolling
Application fee: $50
Financial Aid deadline: Rolling
Can first year start other than Fall? Yes
Student faculty ratio: 18.6 to 1
Does the University offer:
- housing restricted to law students? No
- graduate student housing for which law students are eligible? No

Faculty & Administrators

	Total		Men		Women		Minorities	
	Fall	Spr	Fall	Spr	Fall	Spr	Fall	Spr
Full-time	50	45	35	31	15	14	5	5
Other Full-Time	2	2	1	1	1	1	0	0
Deans, librarians, & others who teach > 1/2	0	0	0	0	0	0	0	0
Part-time	83	1	60	0	23	1	8	0
Total	135	48	96	32	39	16	13	5
Deans, librarians, & others who teach < 1/2	6	6	3	3	3	3	0	0

Curriculum

	Full time	Part time
Typical first-year section size	0	71
Is there typically a "small section" of the first year class, other than Legal Writing, taught by full-time faculty?	No	No
If yes, typical size offered last year	N/A	N/A
# of classroom course titles beyond 1st year curriculum	0	92
# of upper division courses, excluding seminars, with an enrollment:		
Under 25	0	187
25 - 49	0	44
50 - 74	0	57
75 - 99	0	20
100 +	0	0
# of seminars	0	105
# of seminar positions available	1,798	
# of seminar positions filled	0	1,417
# of positions available in simulation courses	1,827	
# of simulation positions filled	0	1,599
# of positions available in faculty supervised clinical courses	64	
# of fac. sup. clin. positions filled	0	64
# involved in field placements	0	49
# involved in law journals	0	96
# in moot court or trial competitions	0	190
# of credit hrs required to graduate	90	

J.D. Enrollment & Ethnicity

	Men		Women		Fl-Time		Pt-Time		1st Yr		2nd Yr		3rd Yr		4th Yr		Total		JD Degrees Awarded
	#	%	#	%	#	%	#	%	#	%	#	%	#	%	#	%	#	%	
African-American	52	5.4	70	11.4	20	8.8	102	7.6	84	11.5	24	4.7	14	4.2	0	0.0	122	7.8	6
American Indian	7	0.7	10	1.6	1	0.4	16	1.2	6	0.8	6	1.2	5	1.5	0	0.0	17	1.1	1
Asian American	38	4.0	24	3.9	11	4.8	51	3.8	33	4.5	19	3.7	10	3.0	0	0.0	62	3.9	8
Mexican American	14	1.5	3	0.5	1	0.4	16	1.2	8	1.1	5	1.0	4	1.2	0	0.0	17	1.1	2
Puerto Rican	3	0.3	1	0.2	1	0.4	3	0.2	2	0.3	2	0.4	0	0.0	0	0.0	4	0.3	0
Hispanic American	12	1.3	18	2.9	3	1.3	27	2.0	17	2.3	7	1.4	6	1.8	0	0.0	30	1.9	6
Total Minorities	126	13.2	126	20.5	37	16.2	215	16.0	150	20.5	63	12.4	39	11.7	0	0.0	252	16.0	23
Foreign Nationals	19	2.0	16	2.6	8	3.5	27	2.0	20	2.7	10	2.0	5	1.5	0	0.0	35	2.2	2
Caucasian	813	84.9	473	76.9	183	80.3	1103	82.0	562	76.8	436	85.7	288	86.7	0	0.0	1286	81.8	361
Total	958	60.9	615	39.1	228	14.5	1345	85.5	732	46.5	509	32.4	332	21.1	0	0.0	1573		386

THOMAS M. COOLEY LAW SCHOOL

GPA & LSAT Scores

	Full Time	Part Time	Total
# of apps	727	1,391	2,118
# admits	547	1,063	1,610
# of matrics	209	550	759
75% GPA	3.15	3.12	
25% GPA	2.63	2.55	
75% LSAT	147	147	
25% LSAT	140	140	

Tuition & Fees

	Resident	Non-resident
Full-Time	$14,110	$14,110
Part-Time	$10,090	$10,090

Living Expenses

Estimated living expenses for Singles		
Living on campus	Living off campus	Living at home
N/A	$15,571	$7,431

Financial Aid

	Full-time		Part-time		Total	
	#	%	#	%	#	%
Total # of Students	228		1345		1573	
Total # receiving grants	27	11.8	393	29.2	420	26.7
Less than 1/2 tuition	19	8.3	285	21.2	304	19.3
Half to full tuition	5	2.2	83	6.2	88	5.6
Full tuition	3	1.3	25	1.9	28	1.8
More than full tuition	0	0.0	0	0.0	0	0.0
Median Grant Amount	$2,205		$1,078			

Informational & Library Resources

# of volumes & volume equivalents	361,885	# of professional staff	9
# of titles	73,426	Hours per week with professional staff	80
# of active serial subscriptions	5,259	Hours per week without professional staff	35
Study seating capacity inside the library	530	# of student computer work stations for entire law school	69
Square feet of law library	65,000	# of additional networked connections	85
Square feet of law school (excl. Library)	149,924	Require Laptop Computer?	N

Employment

	Total	%
Employment status known	270	59.5
Employment status unknown	184	40.5
Employed	223	82.6
Pursuing graduate degrees	13	4.8
Unemployed seeking employment	25	9.3
Unemployed not seeking employment	9	3.3
Type of Employment		
# employed in law firms	140	62.8
# employed in business & industry	30	13.5
# employed in government	35	15.7
# employed in public interest	2	0.9
# employed as judicial clerks	11	4.9
# employed in academia	4	1.8
Geographic Location		
# employed in state	84	37.7
# employed in foreign countries	0	0.0
# of states where employed	31	

J.D. Attrition (Prior Year)

	Academic	Other	TOTALS	
	#	#	#	%
1st Year	133	144	277	27%
2nd Year	98	132	230	50%
3rd Year	4	3	7	2.0%
4th Year	0	0	0	0.0%
TOTALS	235	279	514	28%

Bar Passage Rates

Jurisdiction	Michigan			Florida		
Exam	Sum 96	Win 97	Total	Sum 96	Win 97	Total
# from school taking bar for the first time	66	87	153	23	34	57
School's pass rate for all first-time takers	79%	90%	85%	70%	85%	79%
State's pass rate for all first-time takers	84%	86%	85%	84%	85%	84%

TOLEDO, UNIVERSITY OF

2801 West Bancroft
Toledo, OH 43606
(419)530-2882
http://www.utoledo.edu/law

ABA
Approved
Since
1939

The Basics

Type of School: Public   Term: Semester
Application deadline: 03/15
Application fee: $30
Financial Aid deadline: 04/01
Can first year start other than Fall? No
Student faculty ratio: 17.5 to 1
Does the University offer:
- housing restricted to law students? No
- graduate student housing for which law students are eligible? No

Faculty & Administrators

	Total		Men		Women		Minorities	
	Fall	Spr	Fall	Spr	Fall	Spr	Fall	Spr
Full-time	25	25	18	18	7	7	2	2
Other Full-Time	3	3	0	0	3	3	0	0
Deans, librarians, & others who teach > 1/2	1	1	1	1	0	0	0	0
Part-time	13	13	9	10	4	3	0	0
Total	42	42	28	29	14	13	2	2
Deans, librarians, & others who teach < 1/2	2	2	2	2	0	0	0	0

Curriculum

	Full time	Part time
Typical first-year section size	57	52
Is there typically a "small section" of the first year class, other than Legal Writing, taught by full-time faculty?	Yes	No
If yes, typical size offered last year	30	N/A
# of classroom course titles beyond 1st year curriculum	46	36
# of upper division courses, excluding seminars, with an enrollment:		
Under 25	19	13
25 - 49	14	13
50 - 74	9	8
75 - 99	4	2
100 +	0	0
# of seminars	10	4
# of seminar positions available	280	
# of seminar positions filled	112	24
# of positions available in simulation courses	224	
# of simulation positions filled	124	30
# of positions available in faculty supervised clinical courses	110	
# of fac. sup. clin. positions filled	115	17
# involved in field placements	32	3
# involved in law journals	54	8
# in moot court or trial competitions	52	4
# of credit hrs required to graduate	87	

J.D. Enrollment & Ethnicity

	Men		Women		Fl-Time		Pt-Time		1st Yr		2nd Yr		3rd Yr		4th Yr		Total		JD Degrees Awarded
	#	%	#	%	#	%	#	%	#	%	#	%	#	%	#	%	#	%	
African-American	17	5.4	11	4.1	20	4.8	8	4.9	13	6.5	5	2.6	10	6.3	0	0.0	28	4.8	13
American Indian	3	1.0	1	0.4	4	1.0	0	0.0	2	1.0	1	0.5	1	0.6	0	0.0	4	0.7	2
Asian American	3	1.0	6	2.3	9	2.2	0	0.0	3	1.5	2	1.1	4	2.5	0	0.0	9	1.5	1
Mexican American	3	1.0	3	1.1	3	0.7	3	1.8	3	1.5	1	0.5	2	1.3	0	0.0	6	1.0	0
Puerto Rican	1	0.3	2	0.8	3	0.7	0	0.0	1	0.5	0	0.0	2	1.3	0	0.0	3	0.5	0
Hispanic American	3	1.0	2	0.8	5	1.2	0	0.0	0	0.0	2	1.1	3	1.9	0	0.0	5	0.9	4
Total Minorities	30	9.5	25	9.4	44	10.6	11	6.7	22	11.1	11	5.8	22	13.8	0	0.0	55	9.5	20
Foreign Nationals	1	0.3	1	0.4	2	0.5	0	0.0	2	1.0	0	0.0	0	0.0	0	0.0	2	0.3	0
Caucasian	284	90.2	240	90.2	371	89.0	153	93.3	175	87.9	179	94.2	138	86.3	32	100.0	524	90.2	184
Total	315	54.2	266	45.8	417	71.8	164	28.2	199	34.3	190	32.7	160	27.5	32	5.5	581		204

GPA & LSAT Scores

	Full Time	Part Time	Total
# of apps	605	107	712
# admits	401	59	460
# of matrics	152	40	192
75% GPA	3.44	3.23	
25% GPA	2.86	2.59	
75% LSAT	155	152	
25% LSAT	148	147	

Tuition & Fees

	Resident	Non-resident
Full-Time	$6,970	$13,406
Part-Time	$5,808	$11,172

Living Expenses

Estimated living expenses for Singles		
Living on campus	Living off campus	Living at home
N/A	$9,639	$6,543

Financial Aid

	Full-time		Part-time		Total	
	#	%	#	%	#	%
Total # of Students	417		164		581	
Total # receiving grants	124	29.7	35	21.3	159	27.4
Less than 1/2 tuition	41	9.8	34	20.7	75	12.9
Half to full tuition	6	1.4	0	0.0	6	1.0
Full tuition	56	13.4	1	0.6	57	9.8
More than full tuition	21	5.0	0	0.0	21	3.6
Median Grant Amount	$3,206		$1,000			

Informational & Library Resources

# of volumes & volume equivalents	306,448	# of professional staff	5
# of titles	44,528	Hours per week with professional staff	76
# of active serial subscriptions	3,237	Hours per week without professional staff	37
Study seating capacity inside the library	430	# of student computer work stations for entire law school	62
Square feet of law library	41,900	# of additional networked connections	44
Square feet of law school (excl. Library)	59,972	Require Laptop Computer?	N

Employment

	Total	%
Employment status known	181	89.6
Employment status unknown	21	10.4
Employed	160	88.4
Pursuing graduate degrees	2	1.1
Unemployed seeking employment	17	9.4
Unemployed not seeking employment	2	1.1
Type of Employment		
# employed in law firms	87	54.4
# employed in business & industry	29	18.1
# employed in government	25	15.6
# employed in public interest	5	3.1
# employed as judicial clerks	9	5.6
# employed in academia	5	3.1
Geographic Location		
# employed in state	92	57.5
# employed in foreign countries	1	0.6
# of states where employed	19	

J.D. Attrition (Prior Year)

	Academic	Other	TOTALS	
	#	#	#	%
1st Year	13	9	22	11%
2nd Year	2	18	20	11%
3rd Year	0	0	0	0.0%
4th Year	0	1	1	2.0%
TOTALS	15	28	43	6.8%

Bar Passage Rates

Jurisdiction	Ohio			Michigan		
Exam	Sum 96	Win 97	Total	Sum 96	Win 97	Total
# from school taking bar for the first time	94	33	127	34	15	49
School's pass rate for all first-time takers	88%	94%	90%	76%	87%	80%
State's pass rate for all first-time takers	90%	90%	90%	84%	86%	85%

TOURO COLLEGE

300 Nassau Road
Huntington, NY 11743
(516)421-2244
http://www.tourolaw.edu

ABA Approved Since 1983

The Basics

Type of School: Private   Term: Semester
Application deadline: 05/01
Application fee: $50
Financial Aid deadline: 04/15
Can first year start other than Fall? No
Student faculty ratio: 17.7 to 1
Does the University offer:
- housing restricted to law students? Yes
- graduate student housing for which law students are eligible? No

Faculty & Administrators

	Total		Men		Women		Minorities	
	Fall	Spr	Fall	Spr	Fall	Spr	Fall	Spr
Full-time	29	29	18	18	11	11	2	2
Other Full-Time	1	1	1	1	0	0	0	0
Deans, librarians, & others who teach > 1/2	2	2	0	0	2	2	0	0
Part-time	20	16	16	12	4	4	2	0
Total	52	48	35	31	17	17	4	2
Deans, librarians, & others who teach < 1/2	1	1	1	1	0	0	0	0

Curriculum

	Full time	Part time
Typical first-year section size	52	75
Is there typically a "small section" of the first year class, other than Legal Writing, taught by full-time faculty?	Yes	Yes
If yes, typical size offered last year	52	40
# of classroom course titles beyond 1st year curriculum	47	37
# of upper division courses, excluding seminars, with an enrollment:		
Under 25	24	16
25 - 49	20	12
50 - 74	16	11
75 - 99	3	1
100 +	3	3
# of seminars	7	3
# of seminar positions available	200	
# of seminar positions filled	112	52
# of positions available in simulation courses	320	
# of simulation positions filled	174	129
# of positions available in faculty supervised clinical courses	160	
# of fac. sup. clin. positions filled	126	22
# involved in field placements	79	24
# involved in law journals	59	13
# in moot court or trial competitions	12	5
# of credit hrs required to graduate	87	

J.D. Enrollment & Ethnicity

	Men		Women		Fl-Time		Pt-Time		1st Yr		2nd Yr		3rd Yr		4th Yr		Total		JD Degrees Awarded
	#	%	#	%	#	%	#	%	#	%	#	%	#	%	#	%	#	%	
African-American	22	5.3	64	20.1	40	10.0	46	13.9	26	11.8	18	9.3	27	11.7	15	17.6	86	11.8	26
American Indian	1	0.2	1	0.3	0	0.0	2	0.6	0	0.0	0	0.0	2	0.9	0	0.0	2	0.3	0
Asian American	20	4.9	17	5.3	27	6.8	10	3.0	10	4.5	10	5.2	13	5.6	4	4.7	37	5.1	13
Mexican American	0	0.0	0	0.0	0	0.0	0	0.0	0	0.0	0	0.0	0	0.0	0	0.0	0	0.0	0
Puerto Rican	0	0.0	0	0.0	0	0.0	0	0.0	0	0.0	0	0.0	0	0.0	0	0.0	0	0.0	0
Hispanic American	18	4.4	22	6.9	15	3.8	25	7.6	11	5.0	10	5.2	11	4.8	8	9.4	40	5.5	25
Total Minorities	61	14.8	104	32.7	82	20.6	83	25.1	47	21.4	38	19.6	53	22.9	27	31.8	165	22.6	64
Foreign Nationals	0	0.0	0	0.0	0	0.0	0	0.0	0	0.0	0	0.0	0	0.0	0	0.0	0	0.0	0
Caucasian	351	85.2	214	67.3	317	79.4	248	74.9	173	78.6	156	80.4	178	77.1	58	68.2	565	77.4	177
Total	412	56.4	318	43.6	399	54.7	331	45.3	220	30.1	194	26.6	231	31.6	85	11.6	730		241

TOURO COLLEGE

GPA & LSAT Scores

	Full Time	Part Time	Total
# of apps	1,033	401	1,434
# admits	542	202	744
# of matrics	131	103	234
75% GPA	3.19	3.28	
25% GPA	2.49	2.57	
75% LSAT	151	151	
25% LSAT	145	145	

Tuition & Fees

	Resident	Non-resident
Full-Time	$19,600	$19,600
Part-Time	$15,300	$15,300

Living Expenses

Estimated living expenses for Singles		
Living on campus	Living off campus	Living at home
$15,545	$15,545	$8,190

Financial Aid

	Full-time		Part-time		Total	
	#	%	#	%	#	%
Total # of Students	399		331		730	
Total # receiving grants	162	40.6	107	32.3	269	36.8
Less than 1/2 tuition	134	33.6	87	26.3	221	30.3
Half to full tuition	22	5.5	16	4.8	38	5.2
Full tuition	3	0.8	4	1.2	7	1.0
More than full tuition	3	0.8	0	0.0	3	0.4
Median Grant Amount	$4,000		$2,500			

Informational & Library Resources

# of volumes & volume equivalents	361,477	# of professional staff	7
# of titles	55,080	Hours per week with professional staff	76
# of active serial subscriptions	34	Hours per week without professional staff	10
Study seating capacity inside the library	395	# of student computer work stations for entire law school	47
Square feet of law library	27,950	# of additional networked connections	0
Square feet of law school (excl. Library)	93,050	Require Laptop Computer?	N

Employment

	Total	%
Employment status known	192	88.9
Employment status unknown	24	11.1
Employed	168	87.5
Pursuing graduate degrees	0	0.0
Unemployed seeking employment	21	10.9
Unemployed not seeking employment	3	1.6
Type of Employment		
# employed in law firms	93	55.4
# employed in business & industry	40	23.8
# employed in government	22	13.1
# employed in public interest	5	3.0
# employed as judicial clerks	3	1.8
# employed in academia	5	3.0
Geographic Location		
# employed in state	153	91.1
# employed in foreign countries	0	0.0
# of states where employed	10	

J.D. Attrition (Prior Year)

	Academic	Other	TOTALS	
	#	#	#	%
1st Year	8	27	35	16%
2nd Year	5	3	8	3.7%
3rd Year	0	0	0	0.0%
4th Year	0	0	0	0.0%
TOTALS	13	30	43	5.5%

Bar Passage Rates

Jurisdiction	New York		
Exam	Sum 96	Win 97	Total
# from school taking bar for the first time	164	19	183
School's pass rate for all first-time takers	70%	63%	69%
State's pass rate for all first-time takers	78%	67%	77%

TULANE UNIVERSITY

6329 Freret Street
New Orleans, LA 70118-6231
(504)865-5939
http://www.law.tulane.edu

ABA Approved Since 1925

The Basics

Type of School: Private Term: Semester
Application deadline: Rolling
Application fee: $45
Financial Aid deadline: 03/15
Can first year start other than Fall? No
Student faculty ratio: 21.7 to 1
Does the University offer:
- housing restricted to law students? No
- graduate student housing for which law students are eligible? No

Faculty & Administrators

	Total		Men		Women		Minorities	
	Fall	Spr	Fall	Spr	Fall	Spr	Fall	Spr
Full-time	37	35	27	27	10	8	5	4
Other Full-Time	0	0	0	0	0	0	0	0
Deans, librarians, & others who teach > 1/2	1	1	1	1	0	0	0	0
Part-time	53	64	39	56	14	8	3	4
Total	91	100	67	84	24	16	8	8
Deans, librarians, & others who teach < 1/2	3	3	1	1	2	2	0	0

Curriculum

	Full time	Part time
Typical first-year section size	88	0
Is there typically a "small section" of the first year class, other than Legal Writing, taught by full-time faculty?	Yes	No
If yes, typical size offered last year	38	N/A
# of classroom course titles beyond 1st year curriculum	162	0
# of upper division courses, excluding seminars, with an enrollment:		
Under 25	36	0
25 - 49	39	0
50 - 74	20	0
75 - 99	13	0
100 +	12	0
# of seminars	24	0
# of seminar positions available	457	
# of seminar positions filled	456	0
# of positions available in simulation courses	377	
# of simulation positions filled	367	0
# of positions available in faculty supervised clinical courses	128	
# of fac. sup. clin. positions filled	111	0
# involved in field placements	24	0
# involved in law journals	240	0
# in moot court or trial competitions	85	0
# of credit hrs required to graduate	88	

J.D. Enrollment & Ethnicity

	Men		Women		Fl-Time		Pt-Time		1st Yr		2nd Yr		3rd Yr		4th Yr		Total		JD Degrees Awarded
	#	%	#	%	#	%	#	%	#	%	#	%	#	%	#	%	#	%	
African-American	27	5.4	53	11.5	80	8.3	0	0.0	32	10.5	20	6.3	28	8.1	0	0.0	80	8.3	40
American Indian	1	0.2	4	0.9	5	0.5	0	0.0	0	0.0	2	0.6	3	0.9	0	0.0	5	0.5	1
Asian American	23	4.6	25	5.4	48	5.0	0	0.0	18	5.9	12	3.8	18	5.2	0	0.0	48	5.0	17
Mexican American	5	1.0	3	0.6	8	0.8	0	0.0	1	0.3	4	1.3	3	0.9	0	0.0	8	0.8	3
Puerto Rican	2	0.4	5	1.1	7	0.7	0	0.0	2	0.7	2	0.6	3	0.9	0	0.0	7	0.7	6
Hispanic American	13	2.6	22	4.8	35	3.6	0	0.0	15	4.9	12	3.8	8	2.3	0	0.0	35	3.6	10
Total Minorities	71	14.1	112	24.2	183	19.1	0	0.0	68	22.4	52	16.5	63	18.3	0	0.0	183	19.0	77
Foreign Nationals	13	2.6	17	3.7	30	3.1	0	0.0	8	2.6	13	4.1	9	2.6	0	0.0	30	3.1	7
Caucasian	418	83.3	333	72.1	746	77.8	5	100.0	228	75.0	251	79.4	272	79.1	0	0.0	751	77.9	242
Total	502	52.1	462	47.9	959	99.5	5	0.5	304	31.5	316	32.8	344	35.7	0	0.0	964		326

GPA & LSAT Scores

	Full Time	Part Time	Total
# of apps	2,604	0	2,604
# admits	1,417	0	1,417
# of matrics	304	0	304
75% GPA	3.50	0.00	
25% GPA	3.00	0.00	
75% LSAT	162	0	
25% LSAT	155	0	

Tuition & Fees

	Resident	Non-resident
Full-Time	$22,940	$0
Part-Time	$0	$0

Living Expenses

Estimated living expenses for Singles		
Living on campus	Living off campus	Living at home
$11,200	$11,200	$5,895

Employment

	Total	%
Employment status known	336	96.0
Employment status unknown	14	4.0
Employed	264	78.6
Pursuing graduate degrees	13	3.9
Unemployed seeking employment	38	11.3
Unemployed not seeking employment	21	6.2
Type of Employment		
# employed in law firms	147	55.7
# employed in business & industry	26	9.8
# employed in government	37	14.0
# employed in public interest	9	3.4
# employed as judicial clerks	42	15.9
# employed in academia	2	0.8
Geographic Location		
# employed in state	96	36.4
# employed in foreign countries	7	2.7
# of states where employed	34	

Financial Aid

	Full-time		Part-time		Total	
	#	%	#	%	#	%
Total # of Students	959		5		964	
Total # receiving grants	376	39.2	0	0.0	376	39.0
Less than 1/2 tuition	303	31.6	0	0.0	303	31.4
Half to full tuition	69	7.2	0	0.0	69	7.2
Full tuition	3	0.3	0	0.0	3	0.3
More than full tuition	1	0.1	0	0.0	1	0.1
Median Grant Amount	$6,000		$0			

Informational & Library Resources

# of volumes & volume equivalents	293,387	# of professional staff	19
# of titles	199,667	Hours per week with professional staff	69
# of active serial subscriptions	5,517	Hours per week without professional staff	44
Study seating capacity inside the library	587	# of student computer work stations for entire law school	130
Square feet of law library	52,000	# of additional networked connections	350
Square feet of law school (excl. Library)	72,760	Require Laptop Computer?	N

J.D. Attrition (Prior Year)

	Academic	Other	TOTALS	
	#	#	#	%
1st Year	5	24	29	8.9%
2nd Year	1	5	6	1.8%
3rd Year	0	0	0	0.0%
4th Year	0	0	0	0.0%
TOTALS	6	29	35	3.5%

Bar Passage Rates

Jurisdiction	Louisiana			New York		
Exam	Sum 96	Win 97	Total	Sum 96	Win 97	Total
# from school taking bar for the first time	99	14	113	49	3	52
School's pass rate for all first-time takers	72%	43%	68%	82%	100%	83%
State's pass rate for all first-time takers	69%	54%	66%	78%	67%	77%

TULSA, UNIVERSITY OF

3120 East Fourth Place
Tulsa, OK 74104
(918)631-2401
http://www.utulsa.edu/law

ABA Approved Since 1950

The Basics

Type of School: Private   Term: Semester
Application deadline: Rolling
Application fee: $30
Financial Aid deadline: 08/01
Can first year start other than Fall? Yes
Student faculty ratio: 15.0 to 1
Does the University offer:
- housing restricted to law students? No
- graduate student housing for which law students are eligible? Yes

Faculty & Administrators

	Total		Men		Women		Minorities	
	Fall	Spr	Fall	Spr	Fall	Spr	Fall	Spr
Full-time	30	26	17	15	13	11	5	2
Other Full-Time	2	2	1	1	1	1	0	0
Deans, librarians, & others who teach > 1/2	4	4	3	3	1	1	1	1
Part-time	51	56	38	42	13	14	2	0
Total	87	88	59	61	28	27	8	3
Deans, librarians, & others who teach < 1/2	2	2	2	2	0	0	0	0

Curriculum

	Full time	Part time
Typical first-year section size	76	76
Is there typically a "small section" of the first year class, other than Legal Writing, taught by full-time faculty?	Yes	Yes
If yes, typical size offered last year	20	20
# of classroom course titles beyond 1st year curriculum	89	30
# of upper division courses, excluding seminars, with an enrollment:		
Under 25	131	14
25 - 49	31	9
50 - 74	12	3
75 - 99	0	0
100 +	0	0
# of seminars	11	3
# of seminar positions available	211	
# of seminar positions filled	133	20
# of positions available in simulation courses	334	
# of simulation positions filled	273	54
# of positions available in faculty supervised clinical courses	49	
# of fac. sup. clin. positions filled	47	2
# involved in field placements	70	4
# involved in law journals	122	5
# in moot court or trial competitions	190	30
# of credit hrs required to graduate	88	

J.D. Enrollment & Ethnicity

	Men		Women		Fl-Time		Pt-Time		1st Yr		2nd Yr		3rd Yr		4th Yr		Total		JD Degrees Awarded
	#	%	#	%	#	%	#	%	#	%	#	%	#	%	#	%	#	%	
African-American	4	1.2	17	6.7	15	3.3	6	4.5	15	7.9	3	1.5	2	1.1	1	4.5	21	3.6	2
American Indian	26	7.9	28	11.0	39	8.6	15	11.4	16	8.5	19	9.7	17	9.6	2	9.1	54	9.2	12
Asian American	9	2.7	3	1.2	9	2.0	3	2.3	4	2.1	5	2.6	3	1.7	0	0.0	12	2.1	5
Mexican American	0	0.0	0	0.0	0	0.0	0	0.0	0	0.0	0	0.0	0	0.0	0	0.0	0	0.0	0
Puerto Rican	0	0.0	0	0.0	0	0.0	0	0.0	0	0.0	0	0.0	0	0.0	0	0.0	0	0.0	0
Hispanic American	10	3.0	7	2.7	12	2.6	5	3.8	8	4.2	9	4.6	0	0.0	0	0.0	17	2.9	3
Total Minorities	49	14.8	55	21.6	75	16.6	29	22.0	43	22.8	36	18.4	22	12.4	3	13.6	104	17.8	22
Foreign Nationals	3	0.9	4	1.6	6	1.3	1	0.8	6	3.2	1	0.5	0	0.0	0	0.0	7	1.2	5
Caucasian	278	84.2	196	76.9	372	82.1	102	77.3	140	74.1	159	81.1	156	87.6	19	86.4	474	81.0	168
Total	330	56.4	255	43.6	453	77.4	132	22.6	189	32.3	196	33.5	178	30.4	22	3.8	585		195

TULSA, UNIVERSITY OF

GPA & LSAT Scores

	Full Time	Part Time	Total
# of apps	676	71	747
# admits	466	57	523
# of matrics	151	39	190
75% GPA	3.33	3.43	
25% GPA	2.75	2.61	
75% LSAT	154	154	
25% LSAT	146	145	

Tuition & Fees

	Resident	Non-resident
Full-Time	$15,314	$15,314
Part-Time	$10,264	$10,264

Living Expenses

Estimated living expenses for Singles		
Living on campus	Living off campus	Living at home
$5,610	$7,050	$1,800

Financial Aid

	Full-time		Part-time		Total	
	#	%	#	%	#	%
Total # of Students	453		132		585	
Total # receiving grants	168	37.1	41	31.1	209	35.7
Less than 1/2 tuition	103	22.7	27	20.5	130	22.2
Half to full tuition	45	9.9	10	7.6	55	9.4
Full tuition	20	4.4	4	3.0	24	4.1
More than full tuition	0	0.0	0	0.0	0	0.0
Median Grant Amount	$3,875		$2,800			

Informational & Library Resources

# of volumes & volume equivalents	266,553	# of professional staff	7
# of titles	49,470	Hours per week with professional staff	61
# of active serial subscriptions	3,743	Hours per week without professional staff	46
Study seating capacity inside the library	485	# of student computer work stations for entire law school	77
Square feet of law library	32,849	# of additional networked connections	0
Square feet of law school (excl. Library)	46,520	Require Laptop Computer?	N

Employment

	Total	%
Employment status known	197	96.6
Employment status unknown	7	3.4
Employed	158	80.2
Pursuing graduate degrees	11	5.6
Unemployed seeking employment	26	13.2
Unemployed not seeking employment	2	1.0
Type of Employment		
# employed in law firms	87	55.1
# employed in business & industry	39	24.7
# employed in government	21	13.3
# employed in public interest	6	3.8
# employed as judicial clerks	5	3.2
# employed in academia	0	0.0
Geographic Location		
# employed in state	98	62.0
# employed in foreign countries	0	0.0
# of states where employed	26	

J.D. Attrition (Prior Year)

	Academic	Other	TOTALS	
	#	#	#	%
1st Year	5	18	23	11%
2nd Year	6	11	17	7.9%
3rd Year	0	0	0	0.0%
4th Year	0	0	0	0.0%
TOTALS	11	29	40	6.6%

Bar Passage Rates

Jurisdiction	Oklahoma			Texas		
Exam	Sum 96	Win 97	Total	Sum 96	Win 97	Total
# from school taking bar for the first time	85	39	124	16	6	22
School's pass rate for all first-time takers	74%	92%	80%	75%	100%	82%
State's pass rate for all first-time takers	84%	88%	85%	84%	81%	84%

UTAH, UNIVERSITY OF

332 South 1400 East Front
Salt Lake City, UT 84112-0730
(801)581-6833
http://info.law.utah.edu

ABA Approved Since 1927

The Basics

Type of School: Public   Term: Semester
Application deadline: 02/01
Application fee: $40
Financial Aid deadline: 02/15
Can first year start other than Fall? No
Student faculty ratio: 14.3 to 1
Does the University offer:
- housing restricted to law students? No
- graduate student housing for which law students are eligible? Yes

Faculty & Administrators

	Total		Men		Women		Minorities	
	Fall	Spr	Fall	Spr	Fall	Spr	Fall	Spr
Full-time	21	21	18	17	3	4	4	4
Other Full-Time	0	0	0	0	0	0	0	0
Deans, librarians, & others who teach > 1/2	6	5	3	3	3	2	1	1
Part-time	6	13	3	7	3	6	0	0
Total	33	39	24	27	9	12	5	5
Deans, librarians, & others who teach < 1/2	5	5	2	2	3	3	0	0

Curriculum

	Full time	Part time
Typical first-year section size	0	0
Is there typically a "small section" of the first year class, other than Legal Writing, taught by full-time faculty?	No	No
If yes, typical size offered last year	N/A	N/A
# of classroom course titles beyond 1st year curriculum	81	0
# of upper division courses, excluding seminars, with an enrollment:		
Under 25	41	0
25 - 49	20	0
50 - 74	4	0
75 - 99	4	0
100 +	0	0
# of seminars	15	0
# of seminar positions available	225	
# of seminar positions filled	170	0
# of positions available in simulation courses	286	
# of simulation positions filled	286	0
# of positions available in faculty supervised clinical courses	0	
# of fac. sup. clin. positions filled	0	0
# involved in field placements	165	0
# involved in law journals	143	0
# in moot court or trial competitions	236	0
# of credit hrs required to graduate	88	

J.D. Enrollment & Ethnicity

	Men		Women		Fl-Time		Pt-Time		1st Yr		2nd Yr		3rd Yr		4th Yr		Total		JD Degrees Awarded
	#	%	#	%	#	%	#	%	#	%	#	%	#	%	#	%	#	%	
African-American	3	1.3	0	0.0	3	0.8	0	0.0	3	2.4	0	0.0	0	0.0	0	0.0	3	0.8	2
American Indian	1	0.4	4	3.2	5	1.4	0	0.0	1	0.8	2	2.0	2	1.5	0	0.0	5	1.4	2
Asian American	13	5.6	7	5.6	20	5.6	0	0.0	6	4.8	4	4.0	10	7.5	0	0.0	20	5.6	9
Mexican American	4	1.7	2	1.6	6	1.7	0	0.0	4	3.2	2	2.0	0	0.0	0	0.0	6	1.7	2
Puerto Rican	0	0.0	1	0.8	1	0.3	0	0.0	1	0.8	0	0.0	0	0.0	0	0.0	1	0.3	0
Hispanic American	5	2.2	8	6.3	13	3.6	0	0.0	5	4.0	4	4.0	4	3.0	0	0.0	13	3.6	7
Total Minorities	26	11.2	22	17.5	48	13.4	0	0.0	20	16.1	12	11.9	16	12.0	0	0.0	48	13.4	22
Foreign Nationals	0	0.0	0	0.0	0	0.0	0	0.0	0	0.0	0	0.0	0	0.0	0	0.0	0	0.0	0
Caucasian	206	88.8	104	82.5	310	86.6	0	0.0	105	84.7	88	87.1	117	88.0	0	0.0	310	86.6	105
Total	232	64.8	126	35.2	358	100.0	0	0.0	124	34.6	101	28.2	133	37.2	0	0.0	358		127

GPA & LSAT Scores

	Full Time	Part Time	Total
# of apps	717	0	717
# admits	299	0	299
# of matrics	128	0	128
75% GPA	3.74	0.00	
25% GPA	3.27	0.00	
75% LSAT	163	0	
25% LSAT	153	0	

Tuition & Fees

	Resident	Non-resident
Full-Time	$4,445	$9,946
Part-Time	$0	$0

Living Expenses

Estimated living expenses for Singles		
Living on campus	Living off campus	Living at home
$8,149	$8,149	$4,765

Employment

	Total	%
Employment status known	115	99.1
Employment status unknown	1	0.9
Employed	109	94.8
Pursuing graduate degrees	1	0.9
Unemployed seeking employment	1	0.9
Unemployed not seeking employment	4	3.5
Type of Employment		
# employed in law firms	62	56.9
# employed in business & industry	17	15.6
# employed in government	14	12.8
# employed in public interest	1	0.9
# employed as judicial clerks	15	13.8
# employed in academia	0	0.0
Geographic Location		
# employed in state	79	72.5
# employed in foreign countries	2	1.8
# of states where employed	14	

Financial Aid

	Full-time		Part-time		Total	
	#	%	#	%	#	%
Total # of Students	358		0		358	
Total # receiving grants	157	43.9	0	0.0	157	43.9
Less than 1/2 tuition	100	27.9	0	0.0	100	27.9
Half to full tuition	20	5.6	0	0.0	20	5.6
Full tuition	7	2.0	0	0.0	7	2.0
More than full tuition	30	8.4	0	0.0	30	8.4
Median Grant Amount	$3,226		$0			

Informational & Library Resources

# of volumes & volume equivalents	292,638	# of professional staff	6
# of titles	98,413	Hours per week with professional staff	58
# of active serial subscriptions	4,509	Hours per week without professional staff	42
Study seating capacity inside the library	356	# of student computer work stations for entire law school	113
Square feet of law library	38,895	# of additional networked connections	66
Square feet of law school (excl. Library)	54,095	Require Laptop Computer?	N

J.D. Attrition (Prior Year)

	Academic	Other	TOTALS	
	#	#	#	%
1st Year	0	3	3	3.1%
2nd Year	0	1	1	0.8%
3rd Year	0	0	0	0.0%
4th Year	0	0	0	0.0%
TOTALS	0	4	4	1.1%

Bar Passage Rates

Jurisdiction	Utah		
Exam	Sum 96	Win 97	Total
# from school taking bar for the first time	79	8	87
School's pass rate for all first-time takers	92%	100%	93%
State's pass rate for all first-time takers	92%	95%	93%

VALPARAISO UNIVERSITY

Valparaiso, IN 46383
(219)465-7829
http://www.valpo.edu/law/

ABA Approved Since 1929

The Basics

Type of School: Private
Term: Semester
Application deadline: 04/15
Application fee: $30
Financial Aid deadline: 03/01
Can first year start other than Fall? No
Student faculty ratio: 18.2 to 1
Does the University offer:
- housing restricted to law students? No
- graduate student housing for which law students are eligible? No

Faculty & Administrators

	Total		Men		Women		Minorities	
	Fall	Spr	Fall	Spr	Fall	Spr	Fall	Spr
Full-time	18	18	12	13	6	5	2	2
Other Full-Time	3	3	2	2	1	1	0	0
Deans, librarians, & others who teach > 1/2	3	3	2	2	1	1	0	0
Part-time	15	19	7	13	8	6	0	0
Total	39	43	23	30	16	13	2	2
Deans, librarians, & others who teach < 1/2	2	2	1	1	1	1	0	0

Curriculum

	Full time	Part time
Typical first-year section size	65	65
Is there typically a "small section" of the first year class, other than Legal Writing, taught by full-time faculty?	Yes	Yes
If yes, typical size offered last year	45	45
# of classroom course titles beyond 1st year curriculum	67	67
# of upper division courses, excluding seminars, with an enrollment:		
Under 25	64	64
25 - 49	27	27
50 - 74	10	10
75 - 99	4	4
100 +	0	0
# of seminars	12	12
# of seminar positions available	144	
# of seminar positions filled	120	7
# of positions available in simulation courses	993	
# of simulation positions filled	860	72
# of positions available in faculty supervised clinical courses	86	
# of fac. sup. clin. positions filled	80	2
# involved in field placements	69	1
# involved in law journals	39	0
# in moot court or trial competitions	49	0
# of credit hrs required to graduate	90	

J.D. Enrollment & Ethnicity

	Men		Women		Fl-Time		Pt-Time		1st Yr		2nd Yr		3rd Yr		4th Yr		Total		JD Degrees Awarded
	#	%	#	%	#	%	#	%	#	%	#	%	#	%	#	%	#	%	
African-American	22	10.1	23	12.2	36	9.8	9	23.1	17	12.3	13	9.3	15	11.7	0	0.0	45	11.1	11
American Indian	4	1.8	0	0.0	4	1.1	0	0.0	1	0.7	1	0.7	2	1.6	0	0.0	4	1.0	0
Asian American	3	1.4	5	2.6	8	2.2	0	0.0	3	2.2	3	2.1	2	1.6	0	0.0	8	2.0	5
Mexican American	5	2.3	5	2.6	9	2.5	1	2.6	6	4.3	2	1.4	2	1.6	0	0.0	10	2.5	6
Puerto Rican	2	0.9	2	1.1	4	1.1	0	0.0	0	0.0	3	2.1	1	0.8	0	0.0	4	1.0	1
Hispanic American	1	0.5	0	0.0	1	0.3	0	0.0	1	0.7	0	0.0	0	0.0	0	0.0	1	0.2	0
Total Minorities	37	17.1	35	18.5	62	16.9	10	25.6	28	20.3	22	15.7	22	17.2	0	0.0	72	17.7	23
Foreign Nationals	2	0.9	2	1.1	4	1.1	0	0.0	2	1.4	2	1.4	0	0.0	0	0.0	4	1.0	0
Caucasian	178	82.0	152	80.4	301	82.0	29	74.4	108	78.3	116	82.9	106	82.8	0	0.0	330	81.3	120
Total	217	53.4	189	46.6	367	90.4	39	9.6	138	34.0	140	34.5	128	31.5	0	0.0	406		143

VALPARAISO UNIVERSITY

GPA & LSAT Scores

	Full Time	Part Time	Total
# of apps	590	49	639
# admits	379	22	401
# of matrics	119	7	126
75% GPA	3.40	3.14	
25% GPA	2.69	2.47	
75% LSAT	154	155	
25% LSAT	147	147	

Tuition & Fees

	Resident	Non-resident
Full-Time	$16,920	$16,920
Part-Time	$12,940	$12,940

Living Expenses

Estimated living expenses for Singles		
Living on campus	Living off campus	Living at home
$10,390	$10,390	$5,290

Financial Aid

	Full-time		Part-time		Total	
	#	%	#	%	#	%
Total # of Students	367		39		406	
Total # receiving grants	181	49.3	10	25.6	191	47.0
Less than 1/2 tuition	118	32.2	8	20.5	126	31.0
Half to full tuition	19	5.2	0	0.0	19	4.7
Full tuition	35	9.5	2	5.1	37	9.1
More than full tuition	9	2.5	0	0.0	9	2.2
Median Grant Amount	$3,000		$2,000			

Informational & Library Resources

# of volumes & volume equivalents	265,689	# of professional staff	6
# of titles	91,920	Hours per week with professional staff	65
# of active serial subscriptions	2,989	Hours per week without professional staff	45
Study seating capacity inside the library	347	# of student computer work stations for entire law school	58
Square feet of law library	29,370	# of additional networked connections	61
Square feet of law school (excl. Library)	49,825	Require Laptop Computer?	N

Employment

	Total	%
Employment status known	151	91.0
Employment status unknown	15	9.0
Employed	145	96.0
Pursuing graduate degrees	3	2.0
Unemployed seeking employment	2	1.3
Unemployed not seeking employment	1	0.7
Type of Employment		
# employed in law firms	74	51.0
# employed in business & industry	23	15.9
# employed in government	20	13.8
# employed in public interest	0	0.0
# employed as judicial clerks	9	6.2
# employed in academia	4	2.8
Geographic Location		
# employed in state	67	46.2
# employed in foreign countries	0	0.0
# of states where employed	19	

J.D. Attrition (Prior Year)

	Academic	Other	TOTALS	
	#	#	#	%
1st Year	0	3	3	1.8%
2nd Year	4	21	25	18%
3rd Year	2	0	2	1.4%
4th Year	0	0	0	0.0%
TOTALS	6	24	30	6.6%

Bar Passage Rates

Jurisdiction	Indiana			Illinois		
Exam	Sum 96	Win 97	Total	Sum 96	Win 97	Total
# from school taking bar for the first time	66	3	69	41	3	44
School's pass rate for all first-time takers	73%	100%	74%	73%	100%	75%
State's pass rate for all first-time takers	78%	88%	80%	86%	84%	86%

VANDERBILT UNIVERSITY

21st Avenue South
Nashville, TN 37240
(615)322-2615
http://www.vanderbilt.edu/law

ABA Approved Since 1925

The Basics

Type of School: Private Term: Semester

Application deadline: 02/01

Application fee: $50

Financial Aid deadline: 03/01

Can first year start other than Fall? No

Student faculty ratio: 18.1 to 1

Does the University offer:
- housing restricted to law students? No
- graduate student housing for which law students are eligible? Yes

Faculty & Administrators

	Total		Men		Women		Minorities	
	Fall	Spr	Fall	Spr	Fall	Spr	Fall	Spr
Full-time	25	23	21	18	4	5	0	1
Other Full-Time	0	0	0	0	0	0	0	0
Deans, librarians, & others who teach > 1/2	3	3	2	2	1	1	1	1
Part-time	20	25	12	16	8	9	1	2
Total	48	51	35	36	13	15	2	4
Deans, librarians, & others who teach < 1/2	0	0	0	0	0	0	0	0

Curriculum

	Full time	Part time
Typical first-year section size	93	0
Is there typically a "small section" of the first year class, other than Legal Writing, taught by full-time faculty?	No	No
If yes, typical size offered last year	N/A	N/A
# of classroom course titles beyond 1st year curriculum	95	0
# of upper division courses, excluding seminars, with an enrollment:		
Under 25	18	0
25 - 49	27	0
50 - 74	6	0
75 - 99	6	0
100 +	9	0
# of seminars	18	0
# of seminar positions available	288	
# of seminar positions filled	220	0
# of positions available in simulation courses	267	
# of simulation positions filled	262	0
# of positions available in faculty supervised clinical courses	64	
# of fac. sup. clin. positions filled	58	0
# involved in field placements	108	0
# involved in law journals	120	0
# in moot court or trial competitions	146	0
# of credit hrs required to graduate	88	

J.D. Enrollment & Ethnicity

	Men		Women		Fl-Time		Pt-Time		1st Yr		2nd Yr		3rd Yr		4th Yr		Total		JD Degrees Awarded
	#	%	#	%	#	%	#	%	#	%	#	%	#	%	#	%	#	%	
African-American	20	6.1	34	15.7	54	10.0	0	0.0	22	11.7	14	7.7	18	10.5	0	0.0	54	10.0	19
American Indian	1	0.3	0	0.0	1	0.2	0	0.0	0	0.0	0	0.0	1	0.6	0	0.0	1	0.2	1
Asian American	12	3.7	15	6.9	27	5.0	0	0.0	5	2.7	14	7.7	8	4.7	0	0.0	27	5.0	10
Mexican American	0	0.0	0	0.0	0	0.0	0	0.0	0	0.0	0	0.0	0	0.0	0	0.0	0	0.0	0
Puerto Rican	0	0.0	0	0.0	0	0.0	0	0.0	0	0.0	0	0.0	0	0.0	0	0.0	0	0.0	0
Hispanic American	5	1.5	4	1.9	9	1.7	0	0.0	4	2.1	3	1.6	2	1.2	0	0.0	9	1.7	5
Total Minorities	38	11.7	53	24.5	91	16.8	0	0.0	31	16.5	31	17.0	29	16.9	0	0.0	91	16.8	35
Foreign Nationals	15	4.6	7	3.2	22	4.1	0	0.0	9	4.8	12	6.6	1	0.6	0	0.0	22	4.1	8
Caucasian	273	83.7	156	72.2	429	79.2	0	0.0	148	78.7	139	76.4	142	82.6	0	0.0	429	79.2	147
Total	326	60.1	216	39.9	542	100.0	0	0.0	188	34.7	182	33.6	172	31.7	0	0.0	542		190

VANDERBILT UNIVERSITY

GPA & LSAT Scores

	Full Time	Part Time	Total
# of apps	2,230	0	2,230
# admits	746	0	746
# of matrics	186	0	186
75% GPA	3.81	0.00	
25% GPA	3.43	0.00	
75% LSAT	165	0	
25% LSAT	158	0	

Tuition & Fees

	Resident	Non-resident
Full-Time	$21,971	$21,971
Part-Time	$0	$0

Living Expenses

Estimated living expenses for Singles		
Living on campus	Living off campus	Living at home
$11,800	$11,800	$11,800

Financial Aid

	Full-time		Part-time		Total	
	#	%	#	%	#	%
Total # of Students	542		0		542	
Total # receiving grants	311	57.4	0	0.0	311	57.4
Less than 1/2 tuition	255	47.0	0	0.0	255	47.0
Half to full tuition	45	8.3	0	0.0	45	8.3
Full tuition	9	1.7	0	0.0	9	1.7
More than full tuition	2	0.4	0	0.0	2	0.4
Median Grant Amount	$8,493		$0			

Informational & Library Resources

# of volumes & volume equivalents	510,348	# of professional staff	10
# of titles	107,514	Hours per week with professional staff	60
# of active serial subscriptions	6,139	Hours per week without professional staff	51
Study seating capacity inside the library	423	# of student computer work stations for entire law school	56
Square feet of law library	38,010	# of additional networked connections	40
Square feet of law school (excl. Library)	55,688	Require Laptop Computer?	N

Employment

	Total	%
Employment status known	178	98.9
Employment status unknown	2	1.1
Employed	169	94.9
Pursuing graduate degrees	4	2.2
Unemployed seeking employment	2	1.1
Unemployed not seeking employment	3	1.7
Type of Employment		
# employed in law firms	116	68.6
# employed in business & industry	14	8.3
# employed in government	16	9.5
# employed in public interest	4	2.4
# employed as judicial clerks	18	10.7
# employed in academia	1	0.6
Geographic Location		
# employed in state	50	29.6
# employed in foreign countries	1	0.6
# of states where employed	28	

J.D. Attrition (Prior Year)

	Academic	Other	TOTALS	
	#	#	#	%
1st Year	0	1	1	0.5%
2nd Year	0	1	1	0.6%
3rd Year	0	0	0	0.0%
4th Year	0	0	0	0.0%
TOTALS	0	2	2	0.4%

Bar Passage Rates

Jurisdiction	Tennessee			New York		
Exam	Sum 96	Win 97	Total	Sum 96	Win 97	Total
# from school taking bar for the first time	53	4	57	22	1	23
School's pass rate for all first-time takers	92%	100%	93%	91%	100%	91%
State's pass rate for all first-time takers	81%	72%	79%	78%	67%	77%

VERMONT LAW SCHOOL

Chelsea Street
P.O. Box 96
South Royalton, VT 05068-0096
(802)763-8303
http://www.vermontlaw.edu

ABA Approved Since 1975

The Basics

Type of School: Private   Term: Semester
Application deadline: 02/01
Application fee: $50
Financial Aid deadline: 02/15
Can first year start other than Fall? No
Student faculty ratio: 17.4 to 1
Does the University offer:
- housing restricted to law students? No
- graduate student housing for which law students are eligible? No

Faculty & Administrators

	Total		Men		Women		Minorities	
	Fall	Spr	Fall	Spr	Fall	Spr	Fall	Spr
Full-time	22	24	11	13	11	11	1	2
Other Full-Time	5	5	1	1	4	4	0	0
Deans, librarians, & others who teach > 1/2	4	4	2	2	2	2	0	0
Part-time	14	25	11	21	3	4	0	0
Total	45	58	25	37	20	21	1	2
Deans, librarians, & others who teach < 1/2	2	2	2	2	0	0	0	0

Curriculum

	Full time	Part time
Typical first-year section size	80	0
Is there typically a "small section" of the first year class, other than Legal Writing, taught by full-time faculty?	Yes	No
If yes, typical size offered last year	40	N/A
# of classroom course titles beyond 1st year curriculum	92	0
# of upper division courses, excluding seminars, with an enrollment:		
Under 25	41	0
25 - 49	19	0
50 - 74	7	0
75 - 99	3	0
100 +	0	0
# of seminars	22	0
# of seminar positions available	411	
# of seminar positions filled	311	0
# of positions available in simulation courses	232	
# of simulation positions filled	167	0
# of positions available in faculty supervised clinical courses	36	
# of fac. sup. clin. positions filled	22	0
# involved in field placements	110	0
# involved in law journals	60	0
# in moot court or trial competitions	163	0
# of credit hrs required to graduate	84	

J.D. Enrollment & Ethnicity

	Men		Women		Fl-Time		Pt-Time		1st Yr		2nd Yr		3rd Yr		4th Yr		Total		JD Degrees Awarded
	#	%	#	%	#	%	#	%	#	%	#	%	#	%	#	%	#	%	
African-American	0	0.0	5	2.3	5	1.1	0	0.0	2	1.4	0	0.0	3	2.0	0	0.0	5	1.1	3
American Indian	2	0.8	1	0.5	3	0.7	0	0.0	0	0.0	3	1.8	0	0.0	0	0.0	3	0.7	0
Asian American	7	2.9	5	2.3	12	2.6	0	0.0	6	4.2	3	1.8	3	2.0	0	0.0	12	2.6	2
Mexican American	0	0.0	3	1.4	3	0.7	0	0.0	0	0.0	2	1.2	1	0.7	0	0.0	3	0.7	4
Puerto Rican	1	0.4	2	0.9	3	0.7	0	0.0	2	1.4	0	0.0	1	0.7	0	0.0	3	0.7	0
Hispanic American	2	0.8	1	0.5	3	0.7	0	0.0	0	0.0	3	1.8	0	0.0	0	0.0	3	0.7	3
Total Minorities	12	5.0	17	7.7	29	6.3	0	0.0	10	6.9	11	6.6	8	5.4	0	0.0	29	6.3	12
Foreign Nationals	0	0.0	3	1.4	3	0.7	0	0.0	1	0.7	2	1.2	0	0.0	0	0.0	3	0.7	1
Caucasian	226	95.0	201	91.0	427	93.0	0	0.0	133	92.4	153	92.2	141	94.6	0	0.0	427	93.0	136
Total	238	51.9	221	48.1	459	100.0	0	0.0	144	31.4	166	36.2	149	32.5	0	0.0	459		149

VERMONT LAW SCHOOL

GPA & LSAT Scores

	Full Time	Part Time	Total
# of apps	927	0	927
# admits	597	0	597
# of matrics	146	0	146
75% GPA	3.30	0.00	
25% GPA	2.80	0.00	
75% LSAT	158	0	
25% LSAT	150	0	

Tuition & Fees

	Resident	Non-resident
Full-Time	$18,565	$18,565
Part-Time	$0	$0

Living Expenses

Estimated living expenses for Singles		
Living on campus	Living off campus	Living at home
N/A	$13,375	N/A

Employment

	Total	%
Employment status known	147	98.7
Employment status unknown	2	1.3
Employed	117	79.6
Pursuing graduate degrees	3	2.0
Unemployed seeking employment	24	16.3
Unemployed not seeking employment	3	2.0
Type of Employment		
# employed in law firms	58	49.6
# employed in business & industry	18	15.4
# employed in government	15	12.8
# employed in public interest	6	5.1
# employed as judicial clerks	15	12.8
# employed in academia	1	0.9
Geographic Location		
# employed in state	24	20.5
# employed in foreign countries	1	0.9
# of states where employed	32	

Financial Aid

	Full-time		Part-time		Total	
	#	%	#	%	#	%
Total # of Students	459		0		459	
Total # receiving grants	164	35.7	0	0.0	164	35.7
Less than 1/2 tuition	147	32.0	0	0.0	147	32.0
Half to full tuition	16	3.5	0	0.0	16	3.5
Full tuition	1	0.2	0	0.0	1	0.2
More than full tuition	0	0.0	0	0.0	0	0.0
Median Grant Amount	$5,650		$0			

Informational & Library Resources

# of volumes & volume equivalents	213,253	# of professional staff	6
# of titles	32,220	Hours per week with professional staff	48
# of active serial subscriptions	2,319	Hours per week without professional staff	62
Study seating capacity inside the library	414	# of student computer work stations for entire law school	20
Square feet of law library	35,143	# of additional networked connections	0
Square feet of law school (excl. Library)	83,152	Require Laptop Computer?	N

J.D. Attrition (Prior Year)

	Academic	Other	TOTALS	
	#	#	#	%
1st Year	0	14	14	8.0%
2nd Year	0	1	1	0.7%
3rd Year	0	0	0	0.0%
4th Year	0	0	0	0.0%
TOTALS	0	15	15	3.2%

Bar Passage Rates

Jurisdiction	Vermont		
Exam	Sum 96	Win 97	Total
# from school taking bar for the first time	25	4	29
School's pass rate for all first-time takers	84%	75%	83%
State's pass rate for all first-time takers	88%	67%	79%

VILLANOVA UNIVERSITY

299 North Spring Mill Road
Villanova, PA 19085-1682
(610)519-7000
http://www.law.vill.edu/vls

ABA Approved Since 1954

The Basics

Type of School: Private — Term: Semester

Application deadline: 01/31

Application fee: $75

Financial Aid deadline: 03/01

Can first year start other than Fall? No

Student faculty ratio: 21.0 to 1

Does the University offer:
- housing restricted to law students? No
- graduate student housing for which law students are eligible? No

Faculty & Administrators

	Total		Men		Women		Minorities	
	Fall	Spr	Fall	Spr	Fall	Spr	Fall	Spr
Full-time	27	24	23	19	4	5	3	3
Other Full-Time	6	6	2	2	4	4	2	2
Deans, librarians, & others who teach > 1/2	5	5	4	4	1	1	1	1
Part-time	27	58	16	40	11	18	0	0
Total	65	93	45	65	20	28	6	6
Deans, librarians, & others who teach < 1/2	0	0	0	0	0	0	0	0

Curriculum

	Full time	Part time
Typical first-year section size	117	0
Is there typically a "small section" of the first year class, other than Legal Writing, taught by full-time faculty?	Yes	No
If yes, typical size offered last year	31	N/A
# of classroom course titles beyond 1st year curriculum	997	0
# of upper division courses, excluding seminars, with an enrollment:		
Under 25	98	0
25 - 49	17	0
50 - 74	11	0
75 - 99	12	0
100 +	8	0
# of seminars	12	0
# of seminar positions available	171	
# of seminar positions filled	140	0
# of positions available in simulation courses	574	
# of simulation positions filled	458	0
# of positions available in faculty supervised clinical courses	73	
# of fac. sup. clin. positions filled	54	0
# involved in field placements	49	0
# involved in law journals	143	0
# in moot court or trial competitions	228	0
# of credit hrs required to graduate	87	

J.D. Enrollment & Ethnicity

	Men		Women		Fl-Time		Pt-Time		1st Yr		2nd Yr		3rd Yr		4th Yr		Total		JD Degrees Awarded
	#	%	#	%	#	%	#	%	#	%	#	%	#	%	#	%	#	%	
African-American	8	2.2	22	7.1	30	4.4	0	0.0	14	5.9	6	2.6	10	4.7	0	0.0	30	4.4	15
American Indian	1	0.3	3	1.0	4	0.6	0	0.0	1	0.4	2	0.9	1	0.5	0	0.0	4	0.6	1
Asian American	19	5.1	31	10.1	50	7.4	0	0.0	22	9.2	17	7.5	11	5.1	0	0.0	50	7.4	8
Mexican American	0	0.0	0	0.0	0	0.0	0	0.0	0	0.0	0	0.0	0	0.0	0	0.0	0	0.0	0
Puerto Rican	0	0.0	0	0.0	0	0.0	0	0.0	0	0.0	0	0.0	0	0.0	0	0.0	0	0.0	0
Hispanic American	14	3.8	10	3.2	24	3.5	0	0.0	13	5.5	5	2.2	6	2.8	0	0.0	24	3.5	9
Total Minorities	42	11.3	66	21.4	108	15.9	0	0.0	50	21.0	30	13.2	28	13.1	0	0.0	108	15.9	33
Foreign Nationals	0	0.0	0	0.0	0	0.0	0	0.0	0	0.0	0	0.0	0	0.0	0	0.0	0	0.0	0
Caucasian	330	88.7	242	78.6	572	84.1	0	0.0	188	79.0	198	86.8	186	86.9	0	0.0	572	84.1	210
Total	372	54.7	308	45.3	680	100.0	0	0.0	238	35.0	228	33.5	214	31.5	0	0.0	680		243

GPA & LSAT Scores

	Full Time	Part Time	Total
# of apps	1,282	0	1,282
# admits	714	0	714
# of matrics	242	0	242
75% GPA	3.79	0.00	
25% GPA	3.14	0.00	
75% LSAT	162	0	
25% LSAT	154	0	

Tuition & Fees

	Resident	Non-resident
Full-Time	$18,780	$18,780
Part-Time	$0	$0

Living Expenses

Estimated living expenses for Singles		
Living on campus	Living off campus	Living at home
$11,000	$13,440	$5,380

Financial Aid

	Full-time		Part-time		Total	
	#	%	#	%	#	%
Total # of Students	680		0		680	
Total # receiving grants	37	5.4	0	0.0	37	5.4
Less than 1/2 tuition	14	2.1	0	0.0	14	2.1
Half to full tuition	22	3.2	0	0.0	22	3.2
Full tuition	1	0.1	0	0.0	1	0.1
More than full tuition	0	0.0	0	0.0	0	0.0
Median Grant Amount	$9,375		$0			

Informational & Library Resources

# of volumes & volume equivalents	303,752	# of professional staff	8
# of titles	131,592	Hours per week with professional staff	72
# of active serial subscriptions	3,369	Hours per week without professional staff	38
Study seating capacity inside the library	368	# of student computer work stations for entire law school	150
Square feet of law library	31,056	# of additional networked connections	64
Square feet of law school (excl. Library)	42,898	Require Laptop Computer?	N

Employment

	Total	%
Employment status known	190	87.2
Employment status unknown	28	12.8
Employed	168	88.4
Pursuing graduate degrees	5	2.6
Unemployed seeking employment	17	8.9
Unemployed not seeking employment	0	0.0
Type of Employment		
# employed in law firms	99	58.9
# employed in business & industry	23	13.7
# employed in government	7	4.2
# employed in public interest	0	0.0
# employed as judicial clerks	39	23.2
# employed in academia	0	0.0
Geographic Location		
# employed in state	120	71.4
# employed in foreign countries	1	0.6
# of states where employed	13	

J.D. Attrition (Prior Year)

	Academic	Other	TOTALS	
	#	#	#	%
1st Year	1	6	7	3.0%
2nd Year	0	10	10	4.7%
3rd Year	0	0	0	0.0%
4th Year	0	0	0	0.0%
TOTALS	1	16	17	2.5%

Bar Passage Rates

Jurisdiction	Pennsylvania		
Exam	Sum 96	Win 97	Total
# from school taking bar for the first time	164	7	171
School's pass rate for all first-time takers	80%	57%	80%
State's pass rate for all first-time takers	75%	76%	75%

VIRGINIA, UNIVERSITY OF

580 Massie Road
Charlottesville, VA 22903-1789
(804)924-7354
http://www.law.virginia.edu/index.htm

ABA Approved Since 1923

The Basics

Type of School: Public Term: Semester
Application deadline: 01/15
Application fee: $40
Financial Aid deadline: 02/15
Can first year start other than Fall? No
Student faculty ratio: 16.0 to 1
Does the University offer:
- housing restricted to law students? No
- graduate student housing for which law students are eligible? Yes

Faculty & Administrators

	Total		Men		Women		Minorities	
	Fall	Spr	Fall	Spr	Fall	Spr	Fall	Spr
Full-time	62	61	48	47	14	14	5	5
Other Full-Time	0	0	0	0	0	0	0	0
Deans, librarians, & others who teach > 1/2	0	0	0	0	0	0	0	0
Part-time	38	43	31	32	7	11	1	1
Total	100	104	79	79	21	25	6	6
Deans, librarians, & others who teach < 1/2	2	2	2	2	0	0	0	0

Curriculum

	Full time	Part time
Typical first-year section size	64	0
Is there typically a "small section" of the first year class, other than Legal Writing, taught by full-time faculty?	Yes	No
If yes, typical size offered last year	30	N/A
# of classroom course titles beyond 1st year curriculum	148	0
# of upper division courses, excluding seminars, with an enrollment:		
Under 25	41	0
25 - 49	27	0
50 - 74	17	0
75 - 99	16	0
100 +	23	0
# of seminars	73	0
# of seminar positions available	1,281	
# of seminar positions filled	1,132	0
# of positions available in simulation courses	786	
# of simulation positions filled	685	0
# of positions available in faculty supervised clinical courses	137	
# of fac. sup. clin. positions filled	111	0
# involved in field placements	63	0
# involved in law journals	440	0
# in moot court or trial competitions	180	0
# of credit hrs required to graduate	86	

J.D. Enrollment & Ethnicity

	Men		Women		Fl-Time		Pt-Time		1st Yr		2nd Yr		3rd Yr		4th Yr		Total		JD Degrees Awarded
	#	%	#	%	#	%	#	%	#	%	#	%	#	%	#	%	#	%	
African-American	34	4.8	49	11.9	83	7.4	0	0.0	28	7.8	18	4.9	37	9.3	0	0.0	83	7.4	39
American Indian	2	0.3	2	0.5	4	0.4	0	0.0	2	0.6	1	0.3	1	0.3	0	0.0	4	0.4	1
Asian American	25	3.5	20	4.9	45	4.0	0	0.0	17	4.7	11	3.0	17	4.3	0	0.0	45	4.0	16
Mexican American	0	0.0	0	0.0	0	0.0	0	0.0	0	0.0	0	0.0	0	0.0	0	0.0	0	0.0	0
Puerto Rican	0	0.0	0	0.0	0	0.0	0	0.0	0	0.0	0	0.0	0	0.0	0	0.0	0	0.0	0
Hispanic American	5	0.7	5	1.2	10	0.9	0	0.0	3	0.8	5	1.4	2	0.5	0	0.0	10	0.9	5
Total Minorities	66	9.2	76	18.4	142	12.6	0	0.0	50	14.0	35	9.5	57	14.3	0	0.0	142	12.6	61
Foreign Nationals	0	0.0	0	0.0	0	0.0	0	0.0	0	0.0	0	0.0	0	0.0	0	0.0	0	0.0	0
Caucasian	649	90.8	336	81.6	985	87.4	0	0.0	308	86.0	335	90.5	342	85.7	0	0.0	985	87.4	333
Total	715	63.4	412	36.6	1127	100.0	0	0.0	358	31.8	370	32.8	399	35.4	0	0.0	1127		394

GPA & LSAT Scores

	Full Time	Part Time	Total
# of apps	3,091	0	3,091
# admits	921	0	921
# of matrics	362	0	362
75% GPA	3.78	0.00	
25% GPA	3.50	0.00	
75% LSAT	168	0	
25% LSAT	163	0	

Tuition & Fees

	Resident	Non-resident
Full-Time	$13,954	$19,870
Part-Time	$0	$0

Living Expenses

Estimated living expenses for Singles

Living on campus	Living off campus	Living at home
$10,760	$10,760	$10,760

Financial Aid

	Full-time		Part-time		Total	
	#	%	#	%	#	%
Total # of Students	1127		0		1127	
Total # receiving grants	383	34.0	0	0.0	383	34.0
Less than 1/2 tuition	312	27.7	0	0.0	312	27.7
Half to full tuition	38	3.4	0	0.0	38	3.4
Full tuition	4	0.4	0	0.0	4	0.4
More than full tuition	29	2.6	0	0.0	29	2.6
Median Grant Amount	$6,500		$0			

Informational & Library Resources

# of volumes & volume equivalents	769,196	# of professional staff	12
# of titles	224,010	Hours per week with professional staff	69
# of active serial subscriptions	10,638	Hours per week without professional staff	41
Study seating capacity inside the library	770	# of student computer work stations for entire law school	123
Square feet of law library	88,370	# of additional networked connections	187
Square feet of law school (excl. Library)	172,112	Require Laptop Computer?	N

Employment

	Total	%
Employment status known	373	98.9
Employment status unknown	4	1.1
Employed	364	97.6
Pursuing graduate degrees	4	1.1
Unemployed seeking employment	3	0.8
Unemployed not seeking employment	2	0.5
Type of Employment		
# employed in law firms	216	59.3
# employed in business & industry	31	8.5
# employed in government	21	5.8
# employed in public interest	14	3.8
# employed as judicial clerks	78	21.4
# employed in academia	1	0.3
Geographic Location		
# employed in state	71	19.5
# employed in foreign countries	4	1.1
# of states where employed	33	

J.D. Attrition (Prior Year)

	Academic	Other	TOTALS	
	#	#	#	%
1st Year	0	2	2	0.6%
2nd Year	0	1	1	0.3%
3rd Year	0	0	0	0.0%
4th Year	0	0	0	0.0%
TOTALS	0	3	3	0.3%

Bar Passage Rates

Jurisdiction	Virginia			New York		
Exam	Sum 96	Win 97	Total	Sum 96	Win 97	Total
# from school taking bar for the first time	109	9	118	68	7	75
School's pass rate for all first-time takers	91%	89%	91%	93%	100%	93%
State's pass rate for all first-time takers	80%	66%	77%	78%	67%	77%

WAKE FOREST UNIVERSITY

P.O. Box 7206
Reynolda Station
Winston-Salem, NC 27109-7206
(910)758-5435
http://www.wfu.edu

ABA Approved Since 1935

The Basics

Type of School: Private Term: Semester
Application deadline: 03/15
Application fee: $60
Financial Aid deadline: 04/01
Can first year start other than Fall? No
Student faculty ratio: 13.8 to 1
Does the University offer:
- housing restricted to law students? No
- graduate student housing for which law students are eligible? No

Faculty & Administrators

	Total		Men		Women		Minorities	
	Fall	Spr	Fall	Spr	Fall	Spr	Fall	Spr
Full-time	28	25	20	17	8	8	1	1
Other Full-Time	4	4	0	0	4	4	1	1
Deans, librarians, & others who teach > 1/2	4	4	2	2	2	2	0	0
Part-time	20	20	19	14	1	6	1	2
Total	56	53	41	33	15	20	3	4
Deans, librarians, & others who teach < 1/2	2	2	2	2	0	0	0	0

Curriculum

	Full time	Part time
Typical first-year section size	40	0
Is there typically a "small section" of the first year class, other than Legal Writing, taught by full-time faculty?	Yes	No
If yes, typical size offered last year	40	N/A
# of classroom course titles beyond 1st year curriculum	74	0
# of upper division courses, excluding seminars, with an enrollment:		
Under 25	56	0
25 - 49	29	0
50 - 74	7	0
75 - 99	7	0
100 +	0	0
# of seminars	19	0
# of seminar positions available	336	
# of seminar positions filled	234	0
# of positions available in simulation courses	496	
# of simulation positions filled	419	0
# of positions available in faculty supervised clinical courses	71	
# of fac. sup. clin. positions filled	46	0
# involved in field placements	13	0
# involved in law journals	60	0
# in moot court or trial competitions	42	0
# of credit hrs required to graduate	89	

J.D. Enrollment & Ethnicity

	Men		Women		Fl-Time		Pt-Time		1st Yr		2nd Yr		3rd Yr		4th Yr		Total		JD Degrees Awarded
	#	%	#	%	#	%	#	%	#	%	#	%	#	%	#	%	#	%	
African-American	14	4.8	20	11.1	34	7.5	0	0.0	12	7.4	11	6.9	11	7.5	0	0.0	34	7.2	8
American Indian	1	0.3	2	1.1	3	0.7	0	0.0	1	0.6	2	1.3	0	0.0	0	0.0	3	0.6	0
Asian American	3	1.0	3	1.7	6	1.3	0	0.0	3	1.8	2	1.3	1	0.7	0	0.0	6	1.3	2
Mexican American	0	0.0	0	0.0	0	0.0	0	0.0	0	0.0	0	0.0	0	0.0	0	0.0	0	0.0	0
Puerto Rican	0	0.0	0	0.0	0	0.0	0	0.0	0	0.0	0	0.0	0	0.0	0	0.0	0	0.0	0
Hispanic American	2	0.7	0	0.0	2	0.4	0	0.0	1	0.6	0	0.0	1	0.7	0	0.0	2	0.4	3
Total Minorities	20	6.9	25	13.9	45	9.9	0	0.0	17	10.4	15	9.4	13	8.8	0	0.0	45	9.6	13
Foreign Nationals	1	0.3	0	0.0	1	0.2	0	0.0	0	0.0	0	0.0	1	0.7	0	0.0	1	0.2	2
Caucasian	269	92.8	155	86.1	410	89.9	14	100.0	146	89.6	145	90.6	133	90.5	0	0.0	424	90.2	140
Total	290	61.7	180	38.3	456	97.0	14	3.0	163	34.7	160	34.0	147	31.3	0	0.0	470		155

GPA & LSAT Scores

	Full Time	Part Time	Total
# of apps	1,218	0	1,218
# admits	518	0	518
# of matrics	163	0	163
75% GPA	3.53	0.00	
25% GPA	2.96	0.00	
75% LSAT	162	0	
25% LSAT	157	0	

Tuition & Fees

	Resident	Non-resident
Full-Time	$19,500	$19,500
Part-Time	$0	$0

Living Expenses

Estimated living expenses for Singles		
Living on campus	Living off campus	Living at home
N/A	$11,700	N/A

Financial Aid

	Full-time		Part-time		Total	
	#	%	#	%	#	%
Total # of Students	456		14		470	
Total # receiving grants	114	25.0	0	0.0	114	24.3
Less than 1/2 tuition	61	13.4	0	0.0	61	13.0
Half to full tuition	36	7.9	0	0.0	36	7.7
Full tuition	11	2.4	0	0.0	11	2.3
More than full tuition	6	1.3	0	0.0	6	1.3
Median Grant Amount	$9,562		$0			

Informational & Library Resources

# of volumes & volume equivalents	319,077	# of professional staff	6
# of titles	73,567	Hours per week with professional staff	57
# of active serial subscriptions	5,724	Hours per week without professional staff	52
Study seating capacity inside the library	552	# of student computer work stations for entire law school	99
Square feet of law library	43,000	# of additional networked connections	360
Square feet of law school (excl. Library)	41,573	Require Laptop Computer?	N

Employment

	Total	%
Employment status known	153	96.2
Employment status unknown	6	3.8
Employed	147	96.1
Pursuing graduate degrees	0	0.0
Unemployed seeking employment	5	3.3
Unemployed not seeking employment	1	0.7
Type of Employment		
# employed in law firms	88	59.9
# employed in business & industry	19	12.9
# employed in government	25	17.0
# employed in public interest	1	0.7
# employed as judicial clerks	20	13.6
# employed in academia	0	0.0
Geographic Location		
# employed in state	96	65.3
# employed in foreign countries	0	0.0
# of states where employed	21	

J.D. Attrition (Prior Year)

	Academic	Other	TOTALS	
	#	#	#	%
1st Year	0	12	12	7.5%
2nd Year	0	4	4	2.7%
3rd Year	0	0	0	0.0%
4th Year	0	0	0	0.0%
TOTALS	0	16	16	3.5%

Bar Passage Rates

Jurisdiction	North Carolina		
Exam	Sum 96	Win 97	Total
# from school taking bar for the first time	104	6	110
School's pass rate for all first-time takers	90%	83%	90%
State's pass rate for all first-time takers	81%	76%	80%

WASHBURN UNIVERSITY

1700 College Avenue
Topeka, KS 66621
(785)231-1010
http://www.washburnlaw.wuacc.edu/school

ABA Approved Since 1923

The Basics

Type of School: Public　　Term: Semester
Application deadline: 03/15 (Preferred)
Application fee: $30
Financial Aid deadline: 03/15
Can first year start other than Fall? Yes
Student faculty ratio: 16.0 to 1
Does the University offer:
- housing restricted to law students? No
- graduate student housing for which law students are eligible? Yes

Faculty & Administrators

	Total		Men		Women		Minorities	
	Fall	Spr	Fall	Spr	Fall	Spr	Fall	Spr
Full-time	23	23	15	15	8	8	6	6
Other Full-Time	1	1	0	0	1	1	0	0
Deans, librarians, & others who teach > 1/2	0	0	0	0	0	0	0	0
Part-time	16	23	12	18	4	5	0	0
Total	40	47	27	33	13	14	6	6
Deans, librarians, & others who teach < 1/2	3	3	3	3	0	0	1	1

Curriculum

	Full time	Part time
Typical first-year section size	75	0
Is there typically a "small section" of the first year class, other than Legal Writing, taught by full-time faculty?	Yes	No
If yes, typical size offered last year	25	N/A
# of classroom course titles beyond 1st year curriculum	79	0
# of upper division courses, excluding seminars, with an enrollment:		
Under 25	43	0
25 - 49	21	0
50 - 74	13	0
75 - 99	4	0
100 +	0	0
# of seminars	27	0
# of seminar positions available	588	
# of seminar positions filled	416	0
# of positions available in simulation courses	178	
# of simulation positions filled	165	0
# of positions available in faculty supervised clinical courses	86	
# of fac. sup. clin. positions filled	69	0
# involved in field placements	10	0
# involved in law journals	72	0
# in moot court or trial competitions	119	0
# of credit hrs required to graduate	90	

J.D. Enrollment & Ethnicity

	Men		Women		Fl-Time		Pt-Time		1st Yr		2nd Yr		3rd Yr		4th Yr		Total		JD Degrees Awarded
	#	%	#	%	#	%	#	%	#	%	#	%	#	%	#	%	#	%	
African-American	7	2.8	9	4.7	16	3.6	0	0.0	5	3.5	5	3.6	6	3.7	0	0.0	16	3.6	5
American Indian	2	0.8	1	0.5	3	0.7	0	0.0	0	0.0	1	0.7	2	1.2	0	0.0	3	0.7	7
Asian American	8	3.2	6	3.1	14	3.2	0	0.0	4	2.8	4	2.9	6	3.7	0	0.0	14	3.2	3
Mexican American	1	0.4	2	1.0	3	0.7	0	0.0	2	1.4	1	0.7	0	0.0	0	0.0	3	0.7	0
Puerto Rican	0	0.0	1	0.5	1	0.2	0	0.0	1	0.7	0	0.0	0	0.0	0	0.0	1	0.2	1
Hispanic American	5	2.0	7	3.6	12	2.7	0	0.0	5	3.5	1	0.7	6	3.7	0	0.0	12	2.7	3
Total Minorities	23	9.2	26	13.5	49	11.1	0	0.0	17	12.1	12	8.7	20	12.3	0	0.0	49	11.1	19
Foreign Nationals	7	2.8	1	0.5	8	1.8	0	0.0	2	1.4	3	2.2	3	1.9	0	0.0	8	1.8	4
Caucasian	219	88.0	165	85.9	384	87.1	0	0.0	122	86.5	123	89.1	139	85.8	0	0.0	384	87.1	109
Total	249	56.5	192	43.5	441	100.0	0	0.0	141	32.0	138	31.3	162	36.7	0	0.0	441		132

GPA & LSAT Scores

	Full Time	Part Time	Total
# of apps	649	0	649
# admits	389	0	389
# of matrics	148	0	148
75% GPA	3.45	0.00	
25% GPA	2.88	0.00	
75% LSAT	154	0	
25% LSAT	147	0	

Tuition & Fees

	Resident	Non-resident
Full-Time	$6,396	$9,476
Part-Time	$0	$0

Living Expenses

Estimated living expenses for Singles		
Living on campus	Living off campus	Living at home
$11,316	$11,316	$11,316

Financial Aid

	Full-time		Part-time		Total	
	#	%	#	%	#	%
Total # of Students	441		0		441	
Total # receiving grants	146	33.1	0	0.0	146	33.1
Less than 1/2 tuition	98	22.2	0	0.0	98	22.2
Half to full tuition	22	5.0	0	0.0	22	5.0
Full tuition	22	5.0	0	0.0	22	5.0
More than full tuition	4	0.9	0	0.0	4	0.9
Median Grant Amount	$2,000		$0			

Informational & Library Resources

# of volumes & volume equivalents	303,423	# of professional staff	7
# of titles	192,270	Hours per week with professional staff	77
# of active serial subscriptions	3,737	Hours per week without professional staff	22
Study seating capacity inside the library	346	# of student computer work stations for entire law school	77
Square feet of law library	41,270	# of additional networked connections	0
Square feet of law school (excl. Library)	45,928	Require Laptop Computer?	N

Employment

	Total	%
Employment status known	142	96.6
Employment status unknown	5	3.4
Employed	122	85.9
Pursuing graduate degrees	5	3.5
Unemployed seeking employment	9	6.3
Unemployed not seeking employment	6	4.2
Type of Employment		
# employed in law firms	53	43.4
# employed in business & industry	23	18.9
# employed in government	32	26.2
# employed in public interest	7	5.7
# employed as judicial clerks	6	4.9
# employed in academia	1	0.8
Geographic Location		
# employed in state	81	66.4
# employed in foreign countries	2	1.6
# of states where employed	21	

J.D. Attrition (Prior Year)

	Academic	Other	TOTALS	
	#	#	#	%
1st Year	2	13	15	8.3%
2nd Year	2	6	8	6.2%
3rd Year	1	0	1	0.8%
4th Year	0	0	0	0.0%
TOTALS	5	19	24	5.4%

Bar Passage Rates

Jurisdiction	Kansas		
Exam	Sum 96	Win 97	Total
# from school taking bar for the first time	89	17	106
School's pass rate for all first-time takers	78%	94%	80%
State's pass rate for all first-time takers	87%	93%	90%

WASHINGTON AND LEE UNIVERSITY

Sydney Lewis Hall
Lexington, VA 24450-0303
(540)463-8400
http://www.wlu.edu

ABA Approved Since 1923

The Basics

Type of School: Private Term: Semester
Application deadline: 02/01
Application fee: $40
Financial Aid deadline: 02/15
Can first year start other than Fall? No
Student faculty ratio: 11.4 to 1
Does the University offer:
- housing restricted to law students? Yes
- graduate student housing for which law students are eligible? Yes

Faculty & Administrators

	Total		Men		Women		Minorities	
	Fall	Spr	Fall	Spr	Fall	Spr	Fall	Spr
Full-time	29	28	23	21	6	7	2	4
Other Full-Time	1	1	0	0	1	1	0	0
Deans, librarians, & others who teach > 1/2	3	3	1	1	2	2	0	0
Part-time	7	12	7	12	0	0	0	0
Total	40	44	31	34	9	10	2	4
Deans, librarians, & others who teach < 1/2	0	0	0	0	0	0	0	0

Curriculum

	Full time	Part time
Typical first-year section size	59	0
Is there typically a "small section" of the first year class, other than Legal Writing, taught by full-time faculty?	Yes	No
If yes, typical size offered last year	20	N/A
# of classroom course titles beyond 1st year curriculum	68	0
# of upper division courses, excluding seminars, with an enrollment:		
Under 25	32	0
25 - 49	16	0
50 - 74	14	0
75 - 99	1	0
100 +	0	0
# of seminars	18	0
# of seminar positions available	327	
# of seminar positions filled	198	0
# of positions available in simulation courses	344	
# of simulation positions filled	265	0
# of positions available in faculty supervised clinical courses	41	
# of fac. sup. clin. positions filled	41	0
# involved in field placements	38	0
# involved in law journals	76	0
# in moot court or trial competitions	90	0
# of credit hrs required to graduate	85	

J.D. Enrollment & Ethnicity

	Men		Women		Fl-Time		Pt-Time		1st Yr		2nd Yr		3rd Yr		4th Yr		Total		JD Degrees Awarded
	#	%	#	%	#	%	#	%	#	%	#	%	#	%	#	%	#	%	
African-American	11	5.0	4	2.7	15	4.1	0	0.0	2	1.6	5	4.2	8	6.7	0	0.0	15	4.1	9
American Indian	1	0.5	2	1.3	3	0.8	0	0.0	1	0.8	0	0.0	2	1.7	0	0.0	3	0.8	0
Asian American	3	1.4	10	6.7	13	3.5	0	0.0	3	2.3	6	5.0	4	3.3	0	0.0	13	3.5	3
Mexican American	1	0.5	0	0.0	1	0.3	0	0.0	1	0.8	0	0.0	0	0.0	0	0.0	1	0.3	0
Puerto Rican	0	0.0	0	0.0	0	0.0	0	0.0	0	0.0	0	0.0	0	0.0	0	0.0	0	0.0	0
Hispanic American	1	0.5	1	0.7	2	0.5	0	0.0	0	0.0	0	0.0	2	1.7	0	0.0	2	0.5	1
Total Minorities	17	7.8	17	11.4	34	9.3	0	0.0	7	5.5	11	9.2	16	13.3	0	0.0	34	9.3	13
Foreign Nationals	1	0.5	0	0.0	1	0.3	0	0.0	0	0.0	1	0.8	0	0.0	0	0.0	1	0.3	0
Caucasian	200	91.7	132	88.6	332	90.5	0	0.0	121	94.5	107	89.9	104	86.7	0	0.0	332	90.5	105
Total	218	59.4	149	40.6	367	100.0	0	0.0	128	34.9	119	32.4	120	32.7	0	0.0	367		118

WASHINGTON AND LEE UNIVERSITY

GPA & LSAT Scores

	Full Time	Part Time	Total
# of apps	1,389	0	1,389
# admits	500	0	500
# of matrics	128	0	128
75% GPA	3.64	0.00	
25% GPA	3.04	0.00	
75% LSAT	167	0	
25% LSAT	161	0	

Tuition & Fees

	Resident	Non-resident
Full-Time	$17,211	$17,211
Part-Time	$0	$0

Living Expenses

Estimated living expenses for Singles		
Living on campus	Living off campus	Living at home
$10,085	$10,085	$750

Financial Aid

	Full-time		Part-time		Total	
	#	%	#	%	#	%
Total # of Students	367		0		367	
Total # receiving grants	226	61.6	0	0.0	226	61.6
Less than 1/2 tuition	145	39.5	0	0.0	145	39.5
Half to full tuition	78	21.3	0	0.0	78	21.3
Full tuition	3	0.8	0	0.0	3	0.8
More than full tuition	0	0.0	0	0.0	0	0.0
Median Grant Amount	$7,000		$0			

Informational & Library Resources

# of volumes & volume equivalents	350,065	# of professional staff	7
# of titles	135,222	Hours per week with professional staff	60
# of active serial subscriptions	4,460	Hours per week without professional staff	108
Study seating capacity inside the library	551	# of student computer work stations for entire law school	78
Square feet of law library	56,650	# of additional networked connections	0
Square feet of law school (excl. Library)	46,648	Require Laptop Computer?	N

Employment

	Total	%
Employment status known	122	99.2
Employment status unknown	1	0.8
Employed	114	93.4
Pursuing graduate degrees	2	1.6
Unemployed seeking employment	6	4.9
Unemployed not seeking employment	0	0.0
Type of Employment		
# employed in law firms	64	56.1
# employed in business & industry	7	6.1
# employed in government	10	8.8
# employed in public interest	1	0.9
# employed as judicial clerks	31	27.2
# employed in academia	1	0.9
Geographic Location		
# employed in state	37	32.5
# employed in foreign countries	1	0.9
# of states where employed	26	

J.D. Attrition (Prior Year)

	Academic	Other	TOTALS	
	#	#	#	%
1st Year	2	1	3	2.5%
2nd Year	0	2	2	1.7%
3rd Year	0	0	0	0.0%
4th Year	0	0	0	0.0%
TOTALS	2	3	5	1.4%

Bar Passage Rates

Jurisdiction	Virginia			Maryland		
Exam	Sum 96	Win 97	Total	Sum 96	Win 97	Total
# from school taking bar for the first time	50	5	55	7	3	10
School's pass rate for all first-time takers	82%	40%	78%	100%	100%	100%
State's pass rate for all first-time takers	80%	66%	77%	76%	79%	76%

WASHINGTON UNIVERSITY

1 Brookings Drive
Campus Box 1120
St. Louis, MO 63130-4899
(314)935-6400
http://ls.wustl.edu

ABA Approved Since 1923

The Basics

Type of School: Private — Term: Semester
Application deadline: 03/01
Application fee: $50
Financial Aid deadline: 03/01
Can first year start other than Fall? No
Student faculty ratio: 15.3 to 1
Does the University offer:
- housing restricted to law students? No
- graduate student housing for which law students are eligible? Yes

Faculty & Administrators

	Total		Men		Women		Minorities	
	Fall	Spr	Fall	Spr	Fall	Spr	Fall	Spr
Full-time	34	34	20	21	14	13	4	3
Other Full-Time	3	4	1	1	2	3	0	0
Deans, librarians, & others who teach > 1/2	2	2	1	1	1	1	0	0
Part-time	44	47	32	32	12	15	5	5
Total	83	87	54	55	29	32	9	8
Deans, librarians, & others who teach < 1/2	1	1	1	1	0	0	0	0

Curriculum

	Full time	Part time
Typical first-year section size	70	0
Is there typically a "small section" of the first year class, other than Legal Writing, taught by full-time faculty?	No	No
If yes, typical size offered last year	N/A	N/A
# of classroom course titles beyond 1st year curriculum	99	0
# of upper division courses, excluding seminars, with an enrollment:		
Under 25	80	0
25 - 49	26	0
50 - 74	5	0
75 - 99	9	0
100 +	3	0
# of seminars	14	0
# of seminar positions available	257	
# of seminar positions filled	221	0
# of positions available in simulation courses	386	
# of simulation positions filled	367	0
# of positions available in faculty supervised clinical courses	40	
# of fac. sup. clin. positions filled	40	0
# involved in field placements	94	0
# involved in law journals	144	0
# in moot court or trial competitions	208	0
# of credit hrs required to graduate	85	

J.D. Enrollment & Ethnicity

	Men		Women		Fl-Time		Pt-Time		1st Yr		2nd Yr		3rd Yr		4th Yr		Total		JD Degrees Awarded
	#	%	#	%	#	%	#	%	#	%	#	%	#	%	#	%	#	%	
African-American	22	6.2	37	13.7	59	9.5	0	0.0	18	9.1	17	8.2	24	10.9	0	0.0	59	9.4	15
American Indian	7	2.0	4	1.5	11	1.8	0	0.0	5	2.5	4	1.9	2	0.9	0	0.0	11	1.8	0
Asian American	28	7.9	26	9.6	53	8.5	1	25.0	14	7.1	17	8.2	23	10.4	0	0.0	54	8.6	8
Mexican American	3	0.8	2	0.7	5	0.8	0	0.0	3	1.5	0	0.0	2	0.9	0	0.0	5	0.8	0
Puerto Rican	1	0.3	0	0.0	1	0.2	0	0.0	0	0.0	0	0.0	1	0.5	0	0.0	1	0.2	0
Hispanic American	3	0.8	7	2.6	10	1.6	0	0.0	6	3.0	3	1.4	1	0.5	0	0.0	10	1.6	1
Total Minorities	64	18.0	76	28.0	139	22.3	1	25.0	46	23.4	41	19.7	53	24.0	0	0.0	140	22.4	24
Foreign Nationals	1	0.3	0	0.0	1	0.2	0	0.0	0	0.0	1	0.5	0	0.0	0	0.0	1	0.2	5
Caucasian	290	81.7	195	72.0	482	77.5	3	75.0	151	76.6	166	79.8	168	76.0	0	0.0	485	77.5	178
Total	355	56.7	271	43.3	622	99.4	4	0.6	197	31.5	208	33.2	221	35.3	0	0.0	626		207

GPA & LSAT Scores

	Full Time	Part Time	Total
# of apps	1,357	0	1,357
# admits	758	0	758
# of matrics	197	0	197
75% GPA	3.57	0.00	
25% GPA	3.07	0.00	
75% LSAT	163	0	
25% LSAT	155	0	

Tuition & Fees

	Resident	Non-resident
Full-Time	$21,715	$21,715
Part-Time	$0	$0

Living Expenses

Estimated living expenses for Singles		
Living on campus	Living off campus	Living at home
N/A	$10,490	$7,674

Financial Aid

	Full-time		Part-time		Total	
	#	%	#	%	#	%
Total # of Students	622		4		626	
Total # receiving grants	320	51.4	0	0.0	320	51.1
Less than 1/2 tuition	236	37.9	0	0.0	236	37.7
Half to full tuition	44	7.1	0	0.0	44	7.0
Full tuition	32	5.1	0	0.0	32	5.1
More than full tuition	8	1.3	0	0.0	8	1.3
Median Grant Amount	$6,500		$0			

Informational & Library Resources

# of volumes & volume equivalents	563,292	# of professional staff	7
# of titles	104,366	Hours per week with professional staff	43
# of active serial subscriptions	6,488	Hours per week without professional staff	77
Study seating capacity inside the library	517	# of student computer work stations for entire law school	54
Square feet of law library	64,229	# of additional networked connections	700
Square feet of law school (excl. Library)	50,863	Require Laptop Computer?	N

Employment

	Total	%
Employment status known	182	96.8
Employment status unknown	6	3.2
Employed	163	89.6
Pursuing graduate degrees	5	2.7
Unemployed seeking employment	11	6.0
Unemployed not seeking employment	3	1.6
Type of Employment		
# employed in law firms	103	63.2
# employed in business & industry	22	13.5
# employed in government	19	11.7
# employed in public interest	6	3.7
# employed as judicial clerks	13	8.0
# employed in academia	0	0.0
Geographic Location		
# employed in state	78	47.9
# employed in foreign countries	1	0.6
# of states where employed	19	

J.D. Attrition (Prior Year)

	Academic	Other	TOTALS	
	#	#	#	%
1st Year	2	13	15	7.1%
2nd Year	0	5	5	2.3%
3rd Year	0	0	0	0.0%
4th Year	0	0	0	0.0%
TOTALS	2	18	20	3.1%

Bar Passage Rates

Jurisdiction	Missouri			Illinois		
Exam	Sum 96	Win 97	Total	Sum 96	Win 97	Total
# from school taking bar for the first time	81	9	90	28	20	48
School's pass rate for all first-time takers	86%	100%	88%	86%	95%	90%
State's pass rate for all first-time takers	83%	81%	82%	86%	84%	86%

WASHINGTON, UNIVERSITY OF

1100 NE Campus Parkway
Seattle, WA 98105-6617
(206)543-4551
http:/www2.law.washington.edu

ABA Approved Since 1924

The Basics

Type of School: Public   Term: Quarter
Application deadline: 01/15
Application fee: $50
Financial Aid deadline: 02/28
Can first year start other than Fall? No
Student faculty ratio: 12.8 to 1
Does the University offer:
- housing restricted to law students? No
- graduate student housing for which law students are eligible? No

Faculty & Administrators

	Total		Men		Women		Minorities	
	Fall	Spr	Fall	Spr	Fall	Spr	Fall	Spr
Full-time	36	37	20	20	16	17	4	5
Other Full-Time	0	0	0	0	0	0	0	0
Deans, librarians, & others who teach > 1/2	1	2	1	1	0	1	0	0
Part-time	14	37	7	20	7	17	1	3
Total	51	76	28	41	23	35	5	8
Deans, librarians, & others who teach < 1/2	1	1	1	1	0	0	0	0

Curriculum

	Full time	Part time
Typical first-year section size	97	0
Is there typically a "small section" of the first year class, other than Legal Writing, taught by full-time faculty?	Yes	No
If yes, typical size offered last year	28	N/A
# of classroom course titles beyond 1st year curriculum	152	0
# of upper division courses, excluding seminars, with an enrollment:		
Under 25	64	0
25 - 49	27	0
50 - 74	13	0
75 - 99	7	0
100 +	3	0
# of seminars	11	0
# of seminar positions available	127	
# of seminar positions filled	120	0
# of positions available in simulation courses	161	
# of simulation positions filled	149	0
# of positions available in faculty supervised clinical courses	80	
# of fac. sup. clin. positions filled	74	0
# involved in field placements	163	0
# involved in law journals	96	0
# in moot court or trial competitions	101	0
# of credit hrs required to graduate	135	

J.D. Enrollment & Ethnicity

	Men		Women		Fl-Time		Pt-Time		1st Yr		2nd Yr		3rd Yr		4th Yr		Total		JD Degrees Awarded
	#	%	#	%	#	%	#	%	#	%	#	%	#	%	#	%	#	%	
African-American	6	2.5	8	3.0	14	2.8	0	0.0	3	1.8	5	2.8	6	3.7	0	0.0	14	2.7	14
American Indian	7	2.9	10	3.7	17	3.3	0	0.0	5	3.0	4	2.2	8	5.0	0	0.0	17	3.3	8
Asian American	30	12.3	45	16.9	75	14.7	0	0.0	30	17.8	24	13.3	21	13.0	0	0.0	75	14.7	43
Mexican American	9	3.7	17	6.4	26	5.1	0	0.0	7	4.1	6	3.3	13	8.1	0	0.0	26	5.1	6
Puerto Rican	3	1.2	1	0.4	4	0.8	0	0.0	0	0.0	2	1.1	2	1.2	0	0.0	4	0.8	3
Hispanic American	7	2.9	6	2.2	13	2.6	0	0.0	8	4.7	2	1.1	3	1.9	0	0.0	13	2.5	2
Total Minorities	62	25.5	87	32.6	149	29.3	0	0.0	53	31.4	43	23.9	53	32.9	0	0.0	149	29.2	76
Foreign Nationals	1	0.4	0	0.0	1	0.2	0	0.0	0	0.0	1	0.6	0	0.0	0	0.0	1	0.2	2
Caucasian	180	74.1	180	67.4	359	70.5	1	100.0	116	68.6	136	75.6	108	67.1	0	0.0	360	70.6	99
Total	243	47.6	267	52.4	509	99.8	1	0.2	169	33.1	180	35.3	161	31.6	0	0.0	510		177

GPA & LSAT Scores

	Full Time	Part Time	Total
# of apps	1,759	0	1,759
# admits	469	0	469
# of matrics	166	0	166
75% GPA	3.78	0.00	
25% GPA	3.36	0.00	
75% LSAT	165	0	
25% LSAT	158	0	

Tuition & Fees

	Resident	Non-resident
Full-Time	$5,388	$13,293
Part-Time	$0	$0

Living Expenses

Estimated living expenses for Singles		
Living on campus	Living off campus	Living at home
$11,271	$11,271	$5,871

Financial Aid

	Full-time		Part-time		Total	
	#	%	#	%	#	%
Total # of Students	509		1		510	
Total # receiving grants	274	53.8	0	0.0	274	53.7
Less than 1/2 tuition	263	51.7	0	0.0	263	51.6
Half to full tuition	5	1.0	0	0.0	5	1.0
Full tuition	6	1.2	0	0.0	6	1.2
More than full tuition	0	0.0	0	0.0	0	0.0
Median Grant Amount	$1,300		$0			

Informational & Library Resources

# of volumes & volume equivalents	482,173	# of professional staff	14
# of titles	117,288	Hours per week with professional staff	60
# of active serial subscriptions	7,755	Hours per week without professional staff	29
Study seating capacity inside the library	372	# of student computer work stations for entire law school	22
Square feet of law library	48,950	# of additional networked connections	12
Square feet of law school (excl. Library)	40,440	Require Laptop Computer?	N

Employment

	Total	%
Employment status known	141	98.6
Employment status unknown	2	1.4
Employed	121	85.8
Pursuing graduate degrees	7	5.0
Unemployed seeking employment	13	9.2
Unemployed not seeking employment	0	0.0
Type of Employment		
# employed in law firms	67	55.4
# employed in business & industry	15	12.4
# employed in government	16	13.2
# employed in public interest	8	6.6
# employed as judicial clerks	11	9.1
# employed in academia	4	3.3
Geographic Location		
# employed in state	97	80.2
# employed in foreign countries	2	1.7
# of states where employed	11	

J.D. Attrition (Prior Year)

	Academic	Other	TOTALS	
	#	#	#	%
1st Year	0	0	0	0.0%
2nd Year	0	0	0	0.0%
3rd Year	0	0	0	0.0%
4th Year	0	0	0	0.0%
TOTALS	0	0	0	0.0%

Bar Passage Rates

Jurisdiction	Washington		
Exam	Sum 96	Win 97	Total
# from school taking bar for the first time	107	14	121
School's pass rate for all first-time takers	86%	93%	87%
State's pass rate for all first-time takers	73%	82%	76%

WAYNE STATE UNIVERSITY

468 Ferry Mall
Detroit, MI 48202
(313)577-3933
http://www.science.wayne.edu/~law

ABA Approved Since 1936

The Basics

Type of School: Public   Term: Semester
Application deadline: 03/15
Application fee: $20
Financial Aid deadline: 04/30
Can first year start other than Fall? No
Student faculty ratio: 26.4 to 1
Does the University offer:
- housing restricted to law students? No
- graduate student housing for which law students are eligible? Yes

Faculty & Administrators

	Total		Men		Women		Minorities	
	Fall	Spr	Fall	Spr	Fall	Spr	Fall	Spr
Full-time	21	24	15	18	6	6	4	4
Other Full-Time	1	1	0	0	1	1	0	0
Deans, librarians, & others who teach > 1/2	4	4	2	2	2	2	0	0
Part-time	23	25	17	20	6	5	1	2
Total	49	54	34	40	15	14	5	6
Deans, librarians, & others who teach < 1/2	1	1	0	0	1	1	0	0

Curriculum

	Full time	Part time
Typical first-year section size	95	72
Is there typically a "small section" of the first year class, other than Legal Writing, taught by full-time faculty?	No	No
If yes, typical size offered last year	N/A	N/A
# of classroom course titles beyond 1st year curriculum	49	27
# of upper division courses, excluding seminars, with an enrollment:		
Under 25	25	11
25 - 49	11	8
50 - 74	6	4
75 - 99	1	4
100 +	7	2
# of seminars	7	9
# of seminar positions available	224	
# of seminar positions filled	201	18
# of positions available in simulation courses	420	
# of simulation positions filled	171	226
# of positions available in faculty supervised clinical courses	0	
# of fac. sup. clin. positions filled	0	0
# involved in field placements	113	9
# involved in law journals	50	5
# in moot court or trial competitions	158	12
# of credit hrs required to graduate	86	

J.D. Enrollment & Ethnicity

	Men		Women		Fl-Time		Pt-Time		1st Yr		2nd Yr		3rd Yr		4th Yr		Total		JD Degrees Awarded
	#	%	#	%	#	%	#	%	#	%	#	%	#	%	#	%	#	%	
African-American	28	7.1	59	16.8	52	10.0	35	15.5	33	12.8	23	10.6	24	11.4	7	11.7	87	11.7	22
American Indian	3	0.8	1	0.3	2	0.4	2	0.9	1	0.4	2	0.9	1	0.5	0	0.0	4	0.5	2
Asian American	8	2.0	8	2.3	9	1.7	7	3.1	5	1.9	5	2.3	6	2.8	0	0.0	16	2.2	4
Mexican American	6	1.5	2	0.6	8	1.5	0	0.0	3	1.2	2	0.9	3	1.4	0	0.0	8	1.1	3
Puerto Rican	2	0.5	1	0.3	3	0.6	0	0.0	3	1.2	0	0.0	0	0.0	0	0.0	3	0.4	1
Hispanic American	2	0.5	5	1.4	5	1.0	2	0.9	2	0.8	1	0.5	3	1.4	1	1.7	7	0.9	5
Total Minorities	49	12.5	76	21.6	79	15.3	46	20.4	47	18.3	33	15.3	37	17.5	8	13.3	125	16.8	37
Foreign Nationals	0	0.0	0	0.0	0	0.0	0	0.0	0	0.0	0	0.0	0	0.0	0	0.0	0	0.0	0
Caucasian	343	87.5	276	78.4	439	84.7	180	79.6	210	81.7	183	84.7	174	82.5	52	86.7	619	83.2	199
Total	392	52.7	352	47.3	518	69.6	226	30.4	257	34.5	216	29.0	211	28.4	60	8.1	744		236

GPA & LSAT Scores

	Full Time	Part Time	Total
# of apps	759	192	951
# admits	454	88	542
# of matrics	163	64	227
75% GPA	3.46	3.45	
25% GPA	3.00	3.04	
75% LSAT	158	160	
25% LSAT	151	151	

Tuition & Fees

	Resident	Non-resident
Full-Time	$6,578	$13,802
Part-Time	$4,738	$9,898

Living Expenses

Estimated living expenses for Singles		
Living on campus	Living off campus	Living at home
$9,404	$9,404	$4,254

Financial Aid

	Full-time		Part-time		Total	
	#	%	#	%	#	%
Total # of Students	518		226		744	
Total # receiving grants	365	70.5	0	0.0	365	49.1
Less than 1/2 tuition	365	70.5	0	0.0	365	49.1
Half to full tuition	0	0.0	0	0.0	0	0.0
Full tuition	0	0.0	0	0.0	0	0.0
More than full tuition	0	0.0	0	0.0	0	0.0
Median Grant Amount	$1,500		$0			

Informational & Library Resources

# of volumes & volume equivalents	549,755	# of professional staff	6
# of titles	223,183	Hours per week with professional staff	69
# of active serial subscriptions	4,767	Hours per week without professional staff	28
Study seating capacity inside the library	506	# of student computer work stations for entire law school	52
Square feet of law library	28,257	# of additional networked connections	0
Square feet of law school (excl. Library)	41,942	Require Laptop Computer?	N

Employment

	Total	%
Employment status known	128	66.3
Employment status unknown	65	33.7
Employed	117	91.4
Pursuing graduate degrees	2	1.6
Unemployed seeking employment	8	6.2
Unemployed not seeking employment	1	0.8
Type of Employment		
# employed in law firms	68	58.1
# employed in business & industry	20	17.1
# employed in government	15	12.8
# employed in public interest	5	4.3
# employed as judicial clerks	9	7.7
# employed in academia	0	0.0
Geographic Location		
# employed in state	111	94.9
# employed in foreign countries	1	0.9
# of states where employed	5	

J.D. Attrition (Prior Year)

	Academic	Other	TOTALS	
	#	#	#	%
1st Year	5	22	27	12%
2nd Year	1	1	2	1.0%
3rd Year	0	1	1	0.4%
4th Year	0	1	1	1.4%
TOTALS	6	25	31	4.2%

Bar Passage Rates

Jurisdiction	Michigan		
Exam	Sum 96	Win 97	Total
# from school taking bar for the first time	152	30	182
School's pass rate for all first-time takers	97%	90%	96%
State's pass rate for all first-time takers	84%	86%	85%

WEST VIRGINIA UNIVERSITY

P.O. Box 6130
Morgantown, WV 26506-6130
(304)293-3199
gopher://wvnvm.wvnet.edu/11/wc/wvu

ABA Approved Since 1923

The Basics

Type of School: Public Term: Semester
Application deadline: 03/01
Application fee: $45
Financial Aid deadline: 03/01
Can first year start other than Fall? No
Student faculty ratio: 15.2 to 1
Does the University offer:
- housing restricted to law students? No
- graduate student housing for which law students are eligible? Yes

Faculty & Administrators

	Total		Men		Women		Minorities	
	Fall	Spr	Fall	Spr	Fall	Spr	Fall	Spr
Full-time	24	21	15	13	9	8	3	3
Other Full-Time	0	0	0	0	0	0	0	0
Deans, librarians, & others who teach > 1/2	2	2	1	1	1	1	0	0
Part-time	15	11	12	7	3	4	0	0
Total	41	34	28	21	13	13	3	3
Deans, librarians, & others who teach < 1/2	1	1	1	1	0	0	0	0

Curriculum

	Full time	Part time
Typical first-year section size	75	0
Is there typically a "small section" of the first year class, other than Legal Writing, taught by full-time faculty?	No	No
If yes, typical size offered last year	N/A	N/A
# of classroom course titles beyond 1st year curriculum	59	0
# of upper division courses, excluding seminars, with an enrollment:		
Under 25	27	0
25 - 49	20	0
50 - 74	16	0
75 - 99	5	0
100 +	0	0
# of seminars	10	0
# of seminar positions available	175	
# of seminar positions filled	145	0
# of positions available in simulation courses	294	
# of simulation positions filled	266	0
# of positions available in faculty supervised clinical courses	32	
# of fac. sup. clin. positions filled	32	0
# involved in field placements	0	0
# involved in law journals	50	0
# in moot court or trial competitions	111	0
# of credit hrs required to graduate	93	

J.D. Enrollment & Ethnicity

	Men		Women		Fl-Time		Pt-Time		1st Yr		2nd Yr		3rd Yr		4th Yr		Total		JD Degrees Awarded
	#	%	#	%	#	%	#	%	#	%	#	%	#	%	#	%	#	%	
African-American	3	1.3	6	3.0	9	2.1	0	0.0	3	2.0	4	2.9	2	1.4	0	0.0	9	2.1	6
American Indian	2	0.8	0	0.0	2	0.5	0	0.0	0	0.0	0	0.0	2	1.4	0	0.0	2	0.5	0
Asian American	2	0.8	2	1.0	4	0.9	0	0.0	2	1.3	2	1.4	0	0.0	0	0.0	4	0.9	2
Mexican American	0	0.0	0	0.0	0	0.0	0	0.0	0	0.0	0	0.0	0	0.0	0	0.0	0	0.0	0
Puerto Rican	0	0.0	0	0.0	0	0.0	0	0.0	0	0.0	0	0.0	0	0.0	0	0.0	0	0.0	0
Hispanic American	4	1.7	0	0.0	4	0.9	0	0.0	3	2.0	0	0.0	1	0.7	0	0.0	4	0.9	3
Total Minorities	11	4.6	8	4.0	19	4.5	0	0.0	8	5.3	6	4.3	5	3.5	0	0.0	19	4.3	11
Foreign Nationals	0	0.0	0	0.0	0	0.0	0	0.0	0	0.0	0	0.0	0	0.0	0	0.0	0	0.0	0
Caucasian	227	95.4	192	96.0	406	95.5	13	100.0	142	94.7	134	95.7	143	99.3	0	0.0	419	95.7	128
Total	238	54.3	200	45.7	425	97.0	13	3.0	150	34.2	140	32.0	144	32.9	0	0.0	438		139

GPA & LSAT Scores

	Full Time	Part Time	Total
# of apps	506	5	511
# admits	250	5	255
# of matrics	146	5	151
75% GPA	3.61	3.50	
25% GPA	3.06	2.71	
75% LSAT	156	154	
25% LSAT	150	152	

Tuition & Fees

	Resident	Non-resident
Full-Time	$5,062	$12,104
Part-Time	$0	$0

Living Expenses

Estimated living expenses for Singles		
Living on campus	Living off campus	Living at home
$8,302	$10,212	$5,247

Financial Aid

	Full-time		Part-time		Total	
	#	%	#	%	#	%
Total # of Students	425		13		438	
Total # receiving grants	88	20.7	0	0.0	88	20.1
Less than 1/2 tuition	59	13.9	0	0.0	59	13.5
Half to full tuition	3	0.7	0	0.0	3	0.7
Full tuition	13	3.1	0	0.0	13	3.0
More than full tuition	13	3.1	0	0.0	13	3.0
Median Grant Amount	$3,140		$0			

Informational & Library Resources

# of volumes & volume equivalents	246,532	# of professional staff	2
# of titles	41,900	Hours per week with professional staff	40
# of active serial subscriptions	2,940	Hours per week without professional staff	56
Study seating capacity inside the library	274	# of student computer work stations for entire law school	52
Square feet of law library	32,346	# of additional networked connections	0
Square feet of law school (excl. Library)	99,620	Require Laptop Computer?	N

Employment

	Total	%
Employment status known	130	93.5
Employment status unknown	9	6.5
Employed	118	90.8
Pursuing graduate degrees	5	3.8
Unemployed seeking employment	6	4.6
Unemployed not seeking employment	1	0.8
Type of Employment		
# employed in law firms	78	66.1
# employed in business & industry	11	9.3
# employed in government	18	15.3
# employed in public interest	4	3.4
# employed as judicial clerks	5	4.2
# employed in academia	2	1.7
Geographic Location		
# employed in state	105	89.0
# employed in foreign countries	0	0.0
# of states where employed	8	

J.D. Attrition (Prior Year)

	Academic	Other	TOTALS	
	#	#	#	%
1st Year	3	4	7	4.7%
2nd Year	0	0	0	0.0%
3rd Year	0	0	0	0.0%
4th Year	0	0	0	0.0%
TOTALS	3	4	7	1.6%

Bar Passage Rates

Jurisdiction	West Virginia		
Exam	Sum 96	Win 97	Total
# from school taking bar for the first time	116	3	119
School's pass rate for all first-time takers	79%	33%	78%
State's pass rate for all first-time takers	80%	64%	79%

WESTERN NEW ENGLAND COLLEGE

1215 Wilbraham Road
Springfield, MA 01119
(413)782-1412
http://www.law.wnec.edu

ABA Approved Since 1974

The Basics

Type of School: Private   Term: Semester
Application deadline: Rolling
Application fee: $35
Financial Aid deadline: 04/01
Can first year start other than Fall? Yes
Student faculty ratio: 18.1 to 1
Does the University offer:
- housing restricted to law students? No
- graduate student housing for which law students are eligible? No

Curriculum

	Full time	Part time
Typical first-year section size	71	65
Is there typically a "small section" of the first year class, other than Legal Writing, taught by full-time faculty?	No	No
If yes, typical size offered last year	N/A	N/A
# of classroom course titles beyond 1st year curriculum	54	57
# of upper division courses, excluding seminars, with an enrollment:		
Under 25	23	23
25 - 49	18	18
50 - 74	8	16
75 - 99	5	0
100 +	0	0
# of seminars	7	3
# of seminar positions available	252	
# of seminar positions filled	157	59
# of positions available in simulation courses	168	
# of simulation positions filled	111	47
# of positions available in faculty supervised clinical courses	20	
# of fac. sup. clin. positions filled	20	0
# involved in field placements	111	10
# involved in law journals	24	7
# in moot court or trial competitions	14	3
# of credit hrs required to graduate	88	

Faculty & Administrators

	Total		Men		Women		Minorities	
	Fall	Spr	Fall	Spr	Fall	Spr	Fall	Spr
Full-time	26	27	21	22	5	5	2	2
Other Full-Time	0	0	0	0	0	0	0	0
Deans, librarians, & others who teach > 1/2	1	1	1	1	0	0	0	0
Part-time	16	16	9	11	7	5	0	1
Total	43	44	31	34	12	10	2	3
Deans, librarians, & others who teach < 1/2	1	1	1	1	0	0	0	0

J.D. Enrollment & Ethnicity

	Men		Women		Fl-Time		Pt-Time		1st Yr		2nd Yr		3rd Yr		4th Yr		Total		JD Degrees Awarded
	#	%	#	%	#	%	#	%	#	%	#	%	#	%	#	%	#	%	
African-American	11	3.4	13	4.2	13	3.4	11	4.4	11	5.4	4	2.3	6	3.2	3	4.5	24	3.8	8
American Indian	0	0.0	0	0.0	0	0.0	0	0.0	0	0.0	0	0.0	0	0.0	0	0.0	0	0.0	0
Asian American	8	2.5	3	1.0	9	2.4	2	0.8	2	1.0	5	2.9	4	2.2	0	0.0	11	1.7	6
Mexican American	0	0.0	0	0.0	0	0.0	0	0.0	0	0.0	0	0.0	0	0.0	0	0.0	0	0.0	0
Puerto Rican	0	0.0	1	0.3	1	0.3	0	0.0	1	0.5	0	0.0	0	0.0	0	0.0	1	0.2	0
Hispanic American	12	3.7	6	2.0	13	3.4	5	2.0	5	2.4	4	2.3	9	4.8	0	0.0	18	2.8	10
Total Minorities	31	9.5	23	7.5	36	9.4	18	7.2	19	9.3	13	7.5	19	10.2	3	4.5	54	8.5	24
Foreign Nationals	2	0.6	1	0.3	2	0.5	1	0.4	0	0.0	1	0.6	2	1.1	0	0.0	3	0.5	0
Caucasian	293	89.9	282	92.2	343	90.0	232	92.4	186	90.7	160	92.0	165	88.7	64	95.5	575	91.0	194
Total	326	51.6	306	48.4	381	60.3	251	39.7	205	32.4	174	27.5	186	29.4	67	10.6	632		218

WESTERN NEW ENGLAND COLLEGE

GPA & LSAT Scores

	Full Time	Part Time	Total
# of apps	1,101	208	1,309
# admits	780	145	925
# of matrics	131	74	205
75% GPA	3.27	3.29	
25% GPA	2.79	2.63	
75% LSAT	151	151	
25% LSAT	144	144	

Tuition & Fees

	Resident	Non-resident
Full-Time	$17,366	$17,366
Part-Time	$12,820	$12,820

Living Expenses

Estimated living expenses for Singles

Living on campus	Living off campus	Living at home
N/A	$8,750	$4,680

Financial Aid

	Full-time		Part-time		Total	
	#	%	#	%	#	%
Total # of Students	381		251		632	
Total # receiving grants	71	18.6	32	12.7	103	16.3
Less than 1/2 tuition	67	17.6	31	12.4	98	15.5
Half to full tuition	1	0.3	1	0.4	2	0.3
Full tuition	3	0.8	0	0.0	3	0.5
More than full tuition	0	0.0	0	0.0	0	0.0
Median Grant Amount	$2,291		$1,803			

Informational & Library Resources

# of volumes & volume equivalents	338,029	# of professional staff	5
# of titles	40,877	Hours per week with professional staff	69
# of active serial subscriptions	4,513	Hours per week without professional staff	34
Study seating capacity inside the library	397	# of student computer work stations for entire law school	48
Square feet of law library	30,151	# of additional networked connections	0
Square feet of law school (excl. Library)	54,627	Require Laptop Computer?	N

Employment

	Total	%
Employment status known	200	92.6
Employment status unknown	16	7.4
Employed	175	87.5
Pursuing graduate degrees	0	0.0
Unemployed seeking employment	19	9.5
Unemployed not seeking employment	6	3.0
Type of Employment		
# employed in law firms	68	38.9
# employed in business & industry	54	30.9
# employed in government	37	21.1
# employed in public interest	5	2.9
# employed as judicial clerks	9	5.1
# employed in academia	2	1.1
Geographic Location		
# employed in state	61	34.9
# employed in foreign countries	0	0.0
# of states where employed	18	

J.D. Attrition (Prior Year)

	Academic	Other	TOTALS	
	#	#	#	%
1st Year	3	32	35	17%
2nd Year	0	5	5	2.6%
3rd Year	0	0	0	0.0%
4th Year	0	0	0	0.0%
TOTALS	3	37	40	5.8%

Bar Passage Rates

Jurisdiction	Massachusetts			Connecticut		
Exam	Sum 96	Win 97	Total	Sum 96	Win 97	Total
# from school taking bar for the first time	92	24	116	66	32	98
School's pass rate for all first-time takers	80%	58%	76%	85%	84%	85%
State's pass rate for all first-time takers	83%	76%	81%	84%	84%	84%

WHITTIER COLLEGE

3333 Harbor Boulevard
Costa Mesa, CA 92626
(714)444-4141
http://www.whittier.edu

ABA Approved Since 1978

The Basics

Type of School: Private
Term: Semester
Application deadline: 03/15
Application fee: $50
Financial Aid deadline: 06/01
Can first year start other than Fall? Yes
Student faculty ratio: 21.6 to 1
Does the University offer:
- housing restricted to law students? No
- graduate student housing for which law students are eligible? No

Faculty & Administrators

	Total		Men		Women		Minorities	
	Fall	Spr	Fall	Spr	Fall	Spr	Fall	Spr
Full-time	21	23	13	15	8	8	3	3
Other Full-Time	3	3	0	0	3	3	0	0
Deans, librarians, & others who teach > 1/2	0	0	0	0	0	0	0	0
Part-time	23	13	16	9	7	4	0	0
Total	47	39	29	24	18	15	3	3
Deans, librarians, & others who teach < 1/2	5	5	4	4	1	1	0	0

Curriculum

	Full time	Part time
Typical first-year section size	80	80
Is there typically a "small section" of the first year class, other than Legal Writing, taught by full-time faculty?	Yes	Yes
If yes, typical size offered last year	40	40
# of classroom course titles beyond 1st year curriculum	41	35
# of upper division courses, excluding seminars, with an enrollment:		
Under 25	28	24
25 - 49	9	5
50 - 74	13	4
75 - 99	3	2
100 +	0	0
# of seminars	8	3
# of seminar positions available	220	
# of seminar positions filled	95	44
# of positions available in simulation courses	660	
# of simulation positions filled	415	204
# of positions available in faculty supervised clinical courses	0	
# of fac. sup. clin. positions filled	0	0
# involved in field placements	96	40
# involved in law journals	55	15
# in moot court or trial competitions	56	22
# of credit hrs required to graduate	87	

J.D. Enrollment & Ethnicity

	Men		Women		Fl-Time		Pt-Time		1st Yr		2nd Yr		3rd Yr		4th Yr		Total		JD Degrees Awarded
	#	%	#	%	#	%	#	%	#	%	#	%	#	%	#	%	#	%	
African-American	15	4.7	25	7.9	18	4.9	22	8.3	17	6.7	12	6.7	10	6.7	1	1.9	40	6.3	10
American Indian	4	1.3	0	0.0	3	0.8	1	0.4	1	0.4	2	1.1	1	0.7	0	0.0	4	0.6	1
Asian American	44	13.8	49	15.6	60	16.3	33	12.4	49	19.4	16	8.9	22	14.8	6	11.1	93	14.6	29
Mexican American	31	9.7	24	7.6	36	9.8	19	7.1	18	7.1	23	12.8	11	7.4	3	5.6	55	8.7	14
Puerto Rican	0	0.0	1	0.3	0	0.0	1	0.4	0	0.0	1	0.6	0	0.0	0	0.0	1	0.2	0
Hispanic American	21	6.6	23	7.3	29	7.9	15	5.6	22	8.7	10	5.6	8	5.4	4	7.4	44	6.9	10
Total Minorities	115	35.9	122	38.7	146	39.6	91	34.2	107	42.5	64	35.6	52	34.9	14	25.9	237	37.3	64
Foreign Nationals	0	0.0	0	0.0	0	0.0	0	0.0	0	0.0	0	0.0	0	0.0	0	0.0	0	0.0	0
Caucasian	205	64.1	193	61.3	223	60.4	175	65.8	145	57.5	116	64.4	97	65.1	40	74.1	398	62.7	124
Total	320	50.4	315	49.6	369	58.1	266	41.9	252	39.7	180	28.3	149	23.5	54	8.5	635		188

GPA & LSAT Scores

	Full Time	Part Time	Total
# of apps	1,597	277	1,874
# admits	939	164	1,103
# of matrics	158	117	275
75% GPA	3.19	3.21	
25% GPA	2.55	2.59	
75% LSAT	154	153	
25% LSAT	148	145	

Tuition & Fees

	Resident	Non-resident
Full-Time	$20,014	$20,014
Part-Time	$12,022	$12,022

Living Expenses

Estimated living expenses for Singles		
Living on campus	Living off campus	Living at home
N/A	$14,958	N/A

Employment

	Total	%
Employment status known	150	89.8
Employment status unknown	17	10.2
Employed	115	76.7
Pursuing graduate degrees	3	2.0
Unemployed seeking employment	15	10.0
Unemployed not seeking employment	17	11.3
Type of Employment		
# employed in law firms	67	58.3
# employed in business & industry	30	26.1
# employed in government	8	7.0
# employed in public interest	2	1.7
# employed as judicial clerks	3	2.6
# employed in academia	4	3.5
Geographic Location		
# employed in state	91	79.1
# employed in foreign countries	1	0.9
# of states where employed	13	

Financial Aid

	Full-time		Part-time		Total	
	#	%	#	%	#	%
Total # of Students	369		266		635	
Total # receiving grants	147	39.8	88	33.1	235	37.0
Less than 1/2 tuition	134	36.3	82	30.8	216	34.0
Half to full tuition	9	2.4	3	1.1	12	1.9
Full tuition	4	1.1	3	1.1	7	1.1
More than full tuition	0	0.0	0	0.0	0	0.0
Median Grant Amount	$5,000		$3,000			

Informational & Library Resources

# of volumes & volume equivalents	297,614	# of professional staff	6
# of titles	108,520	Hours per week with professional staff	81
# of active serial subscriptions	4,952	Hours per week without professional staff	21
Study seating capacity inside the library	315	# of student computer work stations for entire law school	68
Square feet of law library	45,000	# of additional networked connections	225
Square feet of law school (excl. Library)	80,474	Require Laptop Computer?	N

J.D. Attrition (Prior Year)

	Academic	Other	TOTALS	
	#	#	#	%
1st Year	27	25	52	24%
2nd Year	7	9	16	9.5%
3rd Year	2	1	3	1.5%
4th Year	0	0	0	0.0%
TOTALS	36	35	71	11%

Bar Passage Rates

Jurisdiction	California		
Exam	Sum 96	Win 97	Total
# from school taking bar for the first time	113	23	136
School's pass rate for all first-time takers	63%	61%	63%
State's pass rate for all first-time takers	69%	62%	67%

WIDENER UNIVERSITY

4601 Concord Pike
P.O. Box 7474
Wilmington, DE 19803-0474
(302)477-2100
http://www.widener.edu/law/law.html

ABA Approved Since 1975

The Basics

Type of School: Private Term: Semester

Application deadline: 05/15

Application fee: $60

Financial Aid deadline: 04/15

Can first year start other than Fall? No

Student faculty ratio: 24.8 to 1

Does the University offer:
- housing restricted to law students? Yes
- graduate student housing for which law students are eligible? Yes

Faculty & Administrators

	Total		Men		Women		Minorities	
	Fall	Spr	Fall	Spr	Fall	Spr	Fall	Spr
Full-time	35	36	23	24	12	12	0	0
Other Full-Time	7	7	0	0	7	7	1	1
Deans, librarians, & others who teach > 1/2	5	5	3	3	2	2	0	0
Part-time	36	39	26	29	10	10	2	1
Total	83	87	52	56	31	31	3	2
Deans, librarians, & others who teach < 1/2	2	2	2	2	0	0	1	1

Curriculum

	Full time	Part time
Typical first-year section size	90	65
Is there typically a "small section" of the first year class, other than Legal Writing, taught by full-time faculty?	Yes	Yes
If yes, typical size offered last year	50	45
# of classroom course titles beyond 1st year curriculum	85	69
# of upper division courses, excluding seminars, with an enrollment:		
Under 25	19	54
25 - 49	31	34
50 - 74	13	9
75 - 99	8	4
100 +	2	2
# of seminars	20	21
# of seminar positions available	820	
# of seminar positions filled	327	312
# of positions available in simulation courses	761	
# of simulation positions filled	379	382
# of positions available in faculty supervised clinical courses	80	
# of fac. sup. clin. positions filled	61	19
# involved in field placements	134	49
# involved in law journals	245	51
# in moot court or trial competitions	110	32
# of credit hrs required to graduate	87	

J.D. Enrollment & Ethnicity

	Men		Women		Fl-Time		Pt-Time		1st Yr		2nd Yr		3rd Yr		4th Yr		Total		JD Degrees Awarded
	#	%	#	%	#	%	#	%	#	%	#	%	#	%	#	%	#	%	
African-American	17	2.6	28	5.1	23	3.1	22	4.9	21	5.5	8	2.1	8	2.4	8	8.2	45	3.8	16
American Indian	2	0.3	2	0.4	4	0.5	0	0.0	1	0.3	2	0.5	1	0.3	0	0.0	4	0.3	0
Asian American	7	1.1	13	2.4	13	1.7	7	1.6	7	1.8	6	1.6	6	1.8	1	1.0	20	1.7	4
Mexican American	0	0.0	1	0.2	1	0.1	0	0.0	1	0.3	0	0.0	0	0.0	0	0.0	1	0.1	0
Puerto Rican	2	0.3	3	0.5	3	0.4	2	0.4	2	0.5	0	0.0	3	0.9	0	0.0	5	0.4	2
Hispanic American	3	0.5	2	0.4	2	0.3	3	0.7	2	0.5	3	0.8	0	0.0	0	0.0	5	0.4	1
Total Minorities	31	4.8	49	9.0	46	6.1	34	7.6	34	9.0	19	4.9	18	5.4	9	9.2	80	6.7	23
Foreign Nationals	0	0.0	0	0.0	0	0.0	0	0.0	0	0.0	0	0.0	0	0.0	0	0.0	0	0.0	0
Caucasian	617	95.2	497	91.0	703	93.9	411	92.4	345	91.0	366	95.1	314	94.6	89	90.8	1114	93.3	350
Total	648	54.3	546	45.7	749	62.7	445	37.3	379	31.7	385	32.2	332	27.8	98	8.2	1194		373

GPA & LSAT Scores

	Full Time	Part Time	Total
# of apps	1,092	293	1,385
# admits	814	200	1,014
# of matrics	259	127	386
75% GPA	3.22	3.25	
25% GPA	2.72	2.66	
75% LSAT	151	152	
25% LSAT	145	145	

Tuition & Fees

	Resident	Non-resident
Full-Time	$17,820	$17,820
Part-Time	$13,380	$13,380

Living Expenses

Estimated living expenses for Singles		
Living on campus	Living off campus	Living at home
$11,620	$11,620	$8,020

Employment

	Total	%
Employment status known	350	92.1
Employment status unknown	30	7.9
Employed	279	79.7
Pursuing graduate degrees	5	1.4
Unemployed seeking employment	62	17.7
Unemployed not seeking employment	4	1.1
Type of Employment		
# employed in law firms	110	39.4
# employed in business & industry	64	22.9
# employed in government	36	12.9
# employed in public interest	1	0.4
# employed as judicial clerks	50	17.9
# employed in academia	3	1.1
Geographic Location		
# employed in state	51	18.3
# employed in foreign countries	0	0.0
# of states where employed	16	

Financial Aid

	Full-time		Part-time		Total	
	#	%	#	%	#	%
Total # of Students	749		445		1194	
Total # receiving grants	70	9.3	50	11.2	120	10.1
Less than 1/2 tuition	40	5.3	19	4.3	59	4.9
Half to full tuition	17	2.3	23	5.2	40	3.4
Full tuition	13	1.7	8	1.8	21	1.8
More than full tuition	0	0.0	0	0.0	0	0.0
Median Grant Amount	$8,577		$6,207			

Informational & Library Resources

# of volumes & volume equivalents	395,595	# of professional staff	10
# of titles	82,188	Hours per week with professional staff	77
# of active serial subscriptions	5,430	Hours per week without professional staff	30
Study seating capacity inside the library	461	# of student computer work stations for entire law school	162
Square feet of law library	41,590	# of additional networked connections	0
Square feet of law school (excl. Library)	164,127	Require Laptop Computer?	N

J.D. Attrition (Prior Year)

	Academic	Other	TOTALS	
	#	#	#	%
1st Year	25	47	72	16%
2nd Year	6	12	18	4.9%
3rd Year	0	6	6	1.6%
4th Year	0	0	0	0.0%
TOTALS	31	65	96	7.5%

Bar Passage Rates

Jurisdiction	Pennsylvania			New Jersey		
Exam	Sum 96	Win 97	Total	Sum 96	Win 97	Total
# from school taking bar for the first time	194	46	240	201	38	239
School's pass rate for all first-time takers	68%	65%	68%	80%	61%	77%
State's pass rate for all first-time takers	75%	76%	75%	78%	68%	77%

WIDENER UNIVERSITY-HARRISBURG

3800 Vartan Way
PO Box 69382
Harrisburg, PA 17106-9382
717-541-3900
http://www.widener.edu/law/law.html

ABA Approved Since 1989

The Basics

Type of School: Private   Term: Semester
Application deadline: 05/15
Application fee: $60
Financial Aid deadline: 04/15
Can first year start other than Fall? No
Student faculty ratio: 22.3 to 1
Does the University offer:
- housing restricted to law students? No
- graduate student housing for which law students are eligible? No

Faculty & Administrators

	Total		Men		Women		Minorities	
	Fall	Spr	Fall	Spr	Fall	Spr	Fall	Spr
Full-time	15	16	7	9	8	7	2	2
Other Full-Time	1	1	1	1	0	0	0	0
Deans, librarians, & others who teach > 1/2	2	2	2	2	0	0	0	0
Part-time	11	10	9	6	2	4	0	0
Total	29	29	19	18	10	11	2	2
Deans, librarians, & others who teach < 1/2	1	1	1	1	0	0	0	0

Curriculum

	Full time	Part time
Typical first-year section size	88	44
Is there typically a "small section" of the first year class, other than Legal Writing, taught by full-time faculty?	No	No
If yes, typical size offered last year	N/A	N/A
# of classroom course titles beyond 1st year curriculum	41	43
# of upper division courses, excluding seminars, with an enrollment:		
Under 25	42	24
25 - 49	17	9
50 - 74	7	3
75 - 99	7	1
100 +	1	0
# of seminars	9	9
# of seminar positions available	360	
# of seminar positions filled	140	147
# of positions available in simulation courses	416	
# of simulation positions filled	271	85
# of positions available in faculty supervised clinical courses	60	
# of fac. sup. clin. positions filled	32	8
# involved in field placements	93	52
# involved in law journals	95	16
# in moot court or trial competitions	66	9
# of credit hrs required to graduate	87	

J.D. Enrollment & Ethnicity

	Men		Women		Fl-Time		Pt-Time		1st Yr		2nd Yr		3rd Yr		4th Yr		Total		JD Degrees Awarded
	#	%	#	%	#	%	#	%	#	%	#	%	#	%	#	%	#	%	
African-American	1	0.4	7	4.0	2	0.7	6	4.1	3	2.4	2	1.5	1	0.6	2	6.3	8	1.8	3
American Indian	1	0.4	1	0.6	1	0.3	1	0.7	1	0.8	1	0.8	0	0.0	0	0.0	2	0.4	0
Asian American	4	1.4	1	0.6	4	1.3	1	0.7	1	0.8	3	2.3	1	0.6	0	0.0	5	1.1	2
Mexican American	1	0.4	0	0.0	0	0.0	1	0.7	0	0.0	0	0.0	0	0.0	1	3.1	1	0.2	0
Puerto Rican	1	0.4	0	0.0	1	0.3	0	0.0	1	0.8	0	0.0	0	0.0	0	0.0	1	0.2	1
Hispanic American	2	0.7	0	0.0	2	0.7	0	0.0	1	0.8	0	0.0	1	0.6	0	0.0	2	0.4	1
Total Minorities	10	3.6	9	5.1	10	3.3	9	6.1	7	5.6	6	4.5	3	1.9	3	9.4	19	4.2	7
Foreign Nationals	0	0.0	0	0.0	0	0.0	0	0.0	0	0.0	0	0.0	0	0.0	0	0.0	0	0.0	0
Caucasian	266	96.4	167	94.9	295	96.7	138	93.9	119	94.4	127	95.5	158	98.1	29	90.6	433	95.8	168
Total	276	61.1	176	38.9	305	67.5	147	32.5	126	27.9	133	29.4	161	35.6	32	7.1	452		175

WIDENER UNIVERSITY-HARRISBURG

GPA & LSAT Scores

	Full Time	Part Time	Total
# of apps	398	86	484
# admits	314	65	379
# of matrics	88	40	128
75% GPA	3.31	3.45	
25% GPA	2.57	2.65	
75% LSAT	151	156	
25% LSAT	144	147	

Tuition & Fees

	Resident	Non-resident
Full-Time	$17,820	$17,820
Part-Time	$13,380	$13,380

Living Expenses

Estimated living expenses for Singles		
Living on campus	Living off campus	Living at home
N/A	$11,620	$8,020

Financial Aid

	Full-time		Part-time		Total	
	#	%	#	%	#	%
Total # of Students	305		147		452	
Total # receiving grants	32	10.5	20	13.6	52	11.5
Less than 1/2 tuition	17	5.6	2	1.4	19	4.2
Half to full tuition	9	3.0	16	10.9	25	5.5
Full tuition	6	2.0	2	1.4	8	1.8
More than full tuition	0	0.0	0	0.0	0	0.0
Median Grant Amount	$7,980		$7,120			

Informational & Library Resources

# of volumes & volume equivalents	172,940	# of professional staff	5
# of titles	21,349	Hours per week with professional staff	77
# of active serial subscriptions	3,421	Hours per week without professional staff	27
Study seating capacity inside the library	358	# of student computer work stations for entire law school	48
Square feet of law library	20,587	# of additional networked connections	0
Square feet of law school (excl. Library)	69,292	Require Laptop Computer?	N

Employment

	Total	%
Employment status known	249	96.1
Employment status unknown	10	3.9
Employed	188	75.5
Pursuing graduate degrees	5	2.0
Unemployed seeking employment	51	20.5
Unemployed not seeking employment	5	2.0
Type of Employment		
# employed in law firms	72	38.3
# employed in business & industry	33	17.6
# employed in government	33	17.6
# employed in public interest	3	1.6
# employed as judicial clerks	34	18.1
# employed in academia	4	2.1
Geographic Location		
# employed in state	110	58.5
# employed in foreign countries	0	0.0
# of states where employed	12	

J.D. Attrition (Prior Year)

	Academic	Other	TOTALS	
	#	#	#	%
1st Year	6	17	23	15%
2nd Year	1	4	5	2.9%
3rd Year	1	3	4	2.2%
4th Year	0	0	0	0.0%
TOTALS	8	24	32	5.9%

Bar Passage Rates

Jurisdiction	Pennsylvania			New Jersey		
Exam	Sum 96	Win 97	Total	Sum 96	Win 97	Total
# from school taking bar for the first time	180	18	198	65	2	67
School's pass rate for all first-time takers	67%	44%	65%	74%	50%	73%
State's pass rate for all first-time takers	75%	76%	75%	78%	68%	77%

WILLAMETTE UNIVERSITY

245 Winter St. SE
Salem, OR 97301-3922
(503)370-6282
http://www.willamette.edu

ABA Approved Since 1938

The Basics

Type of School: Private Term: Semester
Application deadline: 03/15
Application fee: $50
Financial Aid deadline: Rolling
Can first year start other than Fall? No
Student faculty ratio: 18.6 to 1
Does the University offer:
- housing restricted to law students? No
- graduate student housing for which law students are eligible? Yes

Faculty & Administrators

	Total		Men		Women		Minorities	
	Fall	Spr	Fall	Spr	Fall	Spr	Fall	Spr
Full-time	18	18	14	14	4	4	0	1
Other Full-Time	3	3	0	0	3	3	0	0
Deans, librarians, & others who teach > 1/2	5	6	4	4	1	2	0	0
Part-time	5	15	4	7	1	8	0	2
Total	31	42	22	25	9	17	0	3
Deans, librarians, & others who teach < 1/2	1	1	1	1	0	0	0	0

Curriculum

	Full time	Part time
Typical first-year section size	90	0
Is there typically a "small section" of the first year class, other than Legal Writing, taught by full-time faculty?	Yes	No
If yes, typical size offered last year	22	N/A
# of classroom course titles beyond 1st year curriculum	77	0
# of upper division courses, excluding seminars, with an enrollment:		
Under 25	24	0
25 - 49	26	0
50 - 74	8	0
75 - 99	2	0
100 +	4	0
# of seminars	11	0
# of seminar positions available	265	
# of seminar positions filled	205	0
# of positions available in simulation courses	341	
# of simulation positions filled	334	0
# of positions available in faculty supervised clinical courses	32	
# of fac. sup. clin. positions filled	32	0
# involved in field placements	30	0
# involved in law journals	56	0
# in moot court or trial competitions	133	0
# of credit hrs required to graduate	88	

J.D. Enrollment & Ethnicity

	Men		Women		Fl-Time		Pt-Time		1st Yr		2nd Yr		3rd Yr		4th Yr		Total		JD Degrees Awarded
	#	%	#	%	#	%	#	%	#	%	#	%	#	%	#	%	#	%	
African-American	2	0.9	6	3.1	8	2.0	0	0.0	2	1.3	3	2.5	3	2.4	0	0.0	8	2.0	3
American Indian	1	0.5	2	1.0	3	0.8	0	0.0	2	1.3	0	0.0	1	0.8	0	0.0	3	0.7	3
Asian American	12	5.7	9	4.7	21	5.3	0	0.0	7	4.4	7	5.7	7	5.7	0	0.0	21	5.2	10
Mexican American	2	0.9	3	1.6	5	1.3	0	0.0	1	0.6	1	0.8	3	2.4	0	0.0	5	1.2	1
Puerto Rican	0	0.0	0	0.0	0	0.0	0	0.0	0	0.0	0	0.0	0	0.0	0	0.0	0	0.0	0
Hispanic American	2	0.9	2	1.0	4	1.0	0	0.0	1	0.6	2	1.6	1	0.8	0	0.0	4	1.0	1
Total Minorities	19	9.0	22	11.5	41	10.3	0	0.0	13	8.2	13	10.7	15	12.2	0	0.0	41	10.2	18
Foreign Nationals	5	2.4	2	1.0	7	1.8	0	0.0	2	1.3	3	2.5	2	1.6	0	0.0	7	1.7	1
Caucasian	187	88.6	168	87.5	350	87.9	5	100.0	143	90.5	106	86.9	106	86.2	0	0.0	355	88.1	155
Total	211	52.4	192	47.6	398	98.8	5	1.2	158	39.2	122	30.3	123	30.5	0	0.0	403		174

GPA & LSAT Scores

	Full Time	Part Time	Total
# of apps	776	2	778
# admits	572	2	574
# of matrics	158	2	160
75% GPA	3.50	0.00	
25% GPA	3.00	0.00	
75% LSAT	158	0	
25% LSAT	150	0	

Tuition & Fees

	Resident	Non-resident
Full-Time	$17,100	$17,100
Part-Time	$0	$0

Living Expenses

Estimated living expenses for Singles		
Living on campus	Living off campus	Living at home
$10,820	$10,820	$3,640

Employment

	Total	%
Employment status known	133	95.0
Employment status unknown	7	5.0
Employed	114	85.7
Pursuing graduate degrees	4	3.0
Unemployed seeking employment	14	10.5
Unemployed not seeking employment	1	0.8
Type of Employment		
# employed in law firms	71	62.3
# employed in business & industry	20	17.5
# employed in government	9	7.9
# employed in public interest	4	3.5
# employed as judicial clerks	8	7.0
# employed in academia	2	1.8
Geographic Location		
# employed in state	64	56.1
# employed in foreign countries	1	0.9
# of states where employed	18	

Financial Aid

	Full-time		Part-time		Total	
	#	%	#	%	#	%
Total # of Students	398		5		403	
Total # receiving grants	149	37.4	0	0.0	149	37.0
Less than 1/2 tuition	111	27.9	0	0.0	111	27.5
Half to full tuition	35	8.8	0	0.0	35	8.7
Full tuition	3	0.8	0	0.0	3	0.7
More than full tuition	0	0.0	0	0.0	0	0.0
Median Grant Amount	$7,000		$0			

Informational & Library Resources

# of volumes & volume equivalents	274,718	# of professional staff	6
# of titles	39,480	Hours per week with professional staff	68
# of active serial subscriptions	4,368	Hours per week without professional staff	45
Study seating capacity inside the library	398	# of student computer work stations for entire law school	44
Square feet of law library	38,552	# of additional networked connections	16
Square feet of law school (excl. Library)	64,171	Require Laptop Computer?	N

J.D. Attrition (Prior Year)

	Academic	Other	TOTALS	
	#	#	#	%
1st Year	5	13	18	13%
2nd Year	0	3	3	2.3%
3rd Year	0	0	0	0.0%
4th Year	0	0	0	0.0%
TOTALS	5	16	21	4.8%

Bar Passage Rates

Jurisdiction	Oregon			Washington		
Exam	Sum 96	Win 97	Total	Sum 96	Win 97	Total
# from school taking bar for the first time	88	7	95	31	13	44
School's pass rate for all first-time takers	75%	57%	74%	90%	85%	89%
State's pass rate for all first-time takers	77%	74%	77%	73%	82%	76%

WILLIAM AND MARY SCHOOL OF LAW

P.O. Box 8795
Williamsburg, VA 23187-8795
(757)221-3800
http://www.wm.edu/law

ABA Approved Since 1932

The Basics

Type of School: Public Term: Semester
Application deadline: 03/01
Application fee: $40
Financial Aid deadline: 02/15
Can first year start other than Fall? No
Student faculty ratio: 21.7 to 1
Does the University offer:
- housing restricted to law students? No
- graduate student housing for which law students are eligible? Yes

Faculty & Administrators

	Total		Men		Women		Minorities	
	Fall	Spr	Fall	Spr	Fall	Spr	Fall	Spr
Full-time	20	20	12	14	8	6	3	3
Other Full-Time	0	0	0	0	0	0	0	0
Deans, librarians, & others who teach > 1/2	4	4	4	4	0	0	1	1
Part-time	21	31	13	19	8	12	2	2
Total	45	55	29	37	16	18	6	6
Deans, librarians, & others who teach < 1/2	3	5	3	4	0	1	0	0

Curriculum

	Full time	Part time
Typical first-year section size	100	0
Is there typically a "small section" of the first year class, other than Legal Writing, taught by full-time faculty?	Yes	No
If yes, typical size offered last year	45	N/A
# of classroom course titles beyond 1st year curriculum	92	0
# of upper division courses, excluding seminars, with an enrollment:		
Under 25	38	0
25 - 49	19	0
50 - 74	6	0
75 - 99	7	0
100 +	1	0
# of seminars	24	0
# of seminar positions available	360	
# of seminar positions filled	246	0
# of positions available in simulation courses	496	
# of simulation positions filled	392	0
# of positions available in faculty supervised clinical courses	21	
# of fac. sup. clin. positions filled	17	0
# involved in field placements	30	0
# involved in law journals	123	0
# in moot court or trial competitions	32	0
# of credit hrs required to graduate	90	

J.D. Enrollment & Ethnicity

	Men		Women		Fl-Time		Pt-Time		1st Yr		2nd Yr		3rd Yr		4th Yr		Total		JD Degrees Awarded
	#	%	#	%	#	%	#	%	#	%	#	%	#	%	#	%	#	%	
African-American	31	11.0	45	18.8	76	14.6	0	0.0	21	12.4	33	18.0	22	13.2	0	0.0	76	14.6	17
American Indian	1	0.4	2	0.8	3	0.6	0	0.0	0	0.0	1	0.5	2	1.2	0	0.0	3	0.6	0
Asian American	6	2.1	11	4.6	17	3.3	0	0.0	3	1.8	8	4.4	6	3.6	0	0.0	17	3.3	7
Mexican American	0	0.0	0	0.0	0	0.0	0	0.0	0	0.0	0	0.0	0	0.0	0	0.0	0	0.0	0
Puerto Rican	0	0.0	0	0.0	0	0.0	0	0.0	0	0.0	0	0.0	0	0.0	0	0.0	0	0.0	0
Hispanic American	5	1.8	2	0.8	7	1.3	0	0.0	1	0.6	3	1.6	3	1.8	0	0.0	7	1.3	5
Total Minorities	43	15.3	60	25.1	103	19.8	0	0.0	25	14.7	45	24.6	33	19.8	0	0.0	103	19.8	29
Foreign Nationals	9	3.2	2	0.8	11	2.1	0	0.0	7	4.1	2	1.1	2	1.2	0	0.0	11	2.1	2
Caucasian	229	81.5	177	74.1	406	78.1	0	0.0	138	81.2	136	74.3	132	79.0	0	0.0	406	78.1	136
Total	281	54.0	239	46.0	520	100.0	0	0.0	170	32.7	183	35.2	167	32.1	0	0.0	520		167

WILLIAM AND MARY SCHOOL OF LAW

GPA & LSAT Scores

	Full Time	Part Time	Total
# of apps	2,330	0	2,330
# admits	688	0	688
# of matrics	171	0	171
75% GPA	3.53	0.00	
25% GPA	3.00	0.00	
75% LSAT	165	0	
25% LSAT	159	0	

Tuition & Fees

	Resident	Non-resident
Full-Time	$7,758	$17,574
Part-Time	$0	$0

Living Expenses

Estimated living expenses for Singles		
Living on campus	Living off campus	Living at home
$12,830	$12,830	$12,830

Employment

	Total	%
Employment status known	170	98.8
Employment status unknown	2	1.2
Employed	158	92.9
Pursuing graduate degrees	5	2.9
Unemployed seeking employment	3	1.8
Unemployed not seeking employment	4	2.4
Type of Employment		
# employed in law firms	96	60.8
# employed in business & industry	13	8.2
# employed in government	13	8.2
# employed in public interest	5	3.2
# employed as judicial clerks	29	18.4
# employed in academia	2	1.3
Geographic Location		
# employed in state	62	39.2
# employed in foreign countries	0	0.0
# of states where employed	27	

Financial Aid

	Full-time		Part-time		Total	
	#	%	#	%	#	%
Total # of Students	520		0		520	
Total # receiving grants	203	39.0	0	0.0	203	39.0
Less than 1/2 tuition	158	30.4	0	0.0	158	30.4
Half to full tuition	45	8.7	0	0.0	45	8.7
Full tuition	0	0.0	0	0.0	0	0.0
More than full tuition	0	0.0	0	0.0	0	0.0
Median Grant Amount	$2,000		$0			

Informational & Library Resources

# of volumes & volume equivalents	334,102	# of professional staff	7
# of titles	58,789	Hours per week with professional staff	64
# of active serial subscriptions	5,180	Hours per week without professional staff	73
Study seating capacity inside the library	428	# of student computer work stations for entire law school	76
Square feet of law library	36,522	# of additional networked connections	26
Square feet of law school (excl. Library)	31,738	Require Laptop Computer?	N

J.D. Attrition (Prior Year)

	Academic	Other	TOTALS	
	#	#	#	%
1st Year	0	8	8	4.0%
2nd Year	0	8	8	4.7%
3rd Year	0	1	1	0.6%
4th Year	0	0	0	0.0%
TOTALS	0	17	17	3.2%

Bar Passage Rates

Jurisdiction	Virginia		
Exam	Sum 96	Win 97	Total
# from school taking bar for the first time	87	6	93
School's pass rate for all first-time takers	93%	83%	92%
State's pass rate for all first-time takers	80%	66%	77%

WILLIAM MITCHELL COLLEGE OF LAW

875 Summit Avenue
St. Paul, MN 55105-3076
(612)227-9171
http://www.wmitchell.edu

ABA Approved Since 1938

The Basics

Type of School: Private   Term: Semester
Application deadline: 07/01
Application fee: $45
Financial Aid deadline: 03/15
Can first year start other than Fall? No
Student faculty ratio: 23.1 to 1
Does the University offer:
- housing restricted to law students? No
- graduate student housing for which law students are eligible? No

Curriculum

	Full time	Part time
Typical first-year section size	82	61
Is there typically a "small section" of the first year class, other than Legal Writing, taught by full-time faculty?	No	No
If yes, typical size offered last year	N/A	N/A
# of classroom course titles beyond 1st year curriculum	43	76
# of upper division courses, excluding seminars, with an enrollment:		
Under 25	37	40
25 - 49	31	29
50 - 74	12	8
75 - 99	8	13
100 +	0	1
# of seminars	4	15
# of seminar positions available	391	
# of seminar positions filled	77	281
# of positions available in simulation courses	766	
# of simulation positions filled	419	329
# of positions available in faculty supervised clinical courses	26	
# of fac. sup. clin. positions filled	26	0
# involved in field placements	175	72
# involved in law journals	53	21
# in moot court or trial competitions	84	19
# of credit hrs required to graduate	86	

Faculty & Administrators

	Total		Men		Women		Minorities	
	Fall	Spr	Fall	Spr	Fall	Spr	Fall	Spr
Full-time	31	30	23	22	8	8	3	3
Other Full-Time	0	0	0	0	0	0	0	0
Deans, librarians, & others who teach > 1/2	1	1	1	1	0	0	0	0
Part-time	76	78	44	51	32	27	6	2
Total	108	109	68	74	40	35	9	5
Deans, librarians, & others who teach < 1/2	2	2	1	1	1	1	0	0

J.D. Enrollment & Ethnicity

	Men		Women		Fl-Time		Pt-Time		1st Yr		2nd Yr		3rd Yr		4th Yr		Total		JD Degrees Awarded
	#	%	#	%	#	%	#	%	#	%	#	%	#	%	#	%	#	%	
African-American	23	4.2	17	3.5	12	2.4	28	5.3	18	5.5	6	2.2	8	2.6	8	6.3	40	3.8	9
American Indian	5	0.9	7	1.4	6	1.2	6	1.1	3	0.9	5	1.8	3	1.0	1	0.8	12	1.2	1
Asian American	20	3.6	21	4.3	18	3.5	23	4.3	13	4.0	9	3.3	14	4.5	5	3.9	41	3.9	19
Mexican American	5	0.9	4	0.8	5	1.0	4	0.8	4	1.2	2	0.7	2	0.6	1	0.8	9	0.9	2
Puerto Rican	2	0.4	0	0.0	1	0.2	1	0.2	1	0.3	0	0.0	0	0.0	1	0.8	2	0.2	0
Hispanic American	9	1.6	4	0.8	7	1.4	6	1.1	4	1.2	2	0.7	7	2.3	0	0.0	13	1.3	3
Total Minorities	64	11.6	53	10.9	49	9.6	68	12.8	43	13.1	24	8.8	34	10.9	16	12.6	117	11.3	34
Foreign Nationals	3	0.5	3	0.6	4	0.8	2	0.4	2	0.6	1	0.4	3	1.0	0	0.0	6	0.6	1
Caucasian	486	87.9	430	88.5	455	89.6	461	86.8	283	86.3	248	90.8	274	88.1	111	87.4	916	88.2	270
Total	553	53.2	486	46.8	508	48.9	531	51.1	328	31.6	273	26.3	311	29.9	127	12.2	1039		305

WILLIAM MITCHELL COLLEGE OF LAW

GPA & LSAT Scores

	Full Time	Part Time	Total
# of apps	937	0	937
# admits	694	0	694
# of matrics	200	135	335
75% GPA	3.49	3.31	
25% GPA	2.90	2.74	
75% LSAT	156	157	
25% LSAT	147	148	

Tuition & Fees

	Resident	Non-resident
Full-Time	$16,280	$16,280
Part-Time	$11,830	$11,830

Living Expenses

Estimated living expenses for Singles		
Living on campus	Living off campus	Living at home
N/A	$10,508	$4,678

Financial Aid

	Full-time		Part-time		Total	
	#	%	#	%	#	%
Total # of Students	508		531		1039	
Total # receiving grants	213	41.9	137	25.8	350	33.7
Less than 1/2 tuition	154	30.3	94	17.7	248	23.9
Half to full tuition	25	4.9	26	4.9	51	4.9
Full tuition	31	6.1	17	3.2	48	4.6
More than full tuition	3	0.6	0	0.0	3	0.3
Median Grant Amount	$5,340		$4,170			

Informational & Library Resources

# of volumes & volume equivalents	277,036	# of professional staff	7
# of titles	94,661	Hours per week with professional staff	85
# of active serial subscriptions	4,425	Hours per week without professional staff	21
Study seating capacity inside the library	672	# of student computer work stations for entire law school	73
Square feet of law library	58,000	# of additional networked connections	0
Square feet of law school (excl. Library)	142,000	Require Laptop Computer?	N

Employment

	Total	%
Employment status known	257	89.5
Employment status unknown	30	10.5
Employed	239	93.0
Pursuing graduate degrees	3	1.2
Unemployed seeking employment	15	5.8
Unemployed not seeking employment	0	0.0
Type of Employment		
# employed in law firms	112	46.9
# employed in business & industry	65	27.2
# employed in government	33	13.8
# employed in public interest	1	0.4
# employed as judicial clerks	24	10.0
# employed in academia	0	0.0
Geographic Location		
# employed in state	207	86.6
# employed in foreign countries	3	1.3
# of states where employed	14	

J.D. Attrition (Prior Year)

	Academic	Other	TOTALS	
	#	#	#	%
1st Year	0	19	19	6.6%
2nd Year	5	15	20	6.3%
3rd Year	3	2	5	1.5%
4th Year	0	0	0	0.0%
TOTALS	8	36	44	4.2%

Bar Passage Rates

Jurisdiction	Minnesota		
Exam	Sum 96	Win 97	Total
# from school taking bar for the first time	176	71	247
School's pass rate for all first-time takers	86%	80%	85%
State's pass rate for all first-time takers	92%	84%	91%

WISCONSIN, UNIVERSITY OF

975 Bascom Mall
Madison, WI 53706-1399
(608)262-2240
http://www.wisc.edu

ABA Approved Since 1923

The Basics

Type of School: Public   Term: Semester
Application deadline: 02/01
Application fee: $38
Financial Aid deadline: 03/01
Can first year start other than Fall? No
Student faculty ratio: 16.3 to 1
Does the University offer:
- housing restricted to law students? No
- graduate student housing for which law students are eligible? Yes

Faculty & Administrators

	Total		Men		Women		Minorities	
	Fall	Spr	Fall	Spr	Fall	Spr	Fall	Spr
Full-time	40	40	26	27	14	13	4	4
Other Full-Time	7	7	6	6	1	1	1	1
Deans, librarians, & others who teach > 1/2	4	4	4	4	0	0	0	0
Part-time	42	14	26	5	16	9	1	0
Total	93	65	62	42	31	23	6	5
Deans, librarians, & others who teach < 1/2	0	0	0	0	0	0	0	0

Curriculum

	Full time	Part time
Typical first-year section size	75	0
Is there typically a "small section" of the first year class, other than Legal Writing, taught by full-time faculty?	Yes	No
If yes, typical size offered last year	22	N/A
# of classroom course titles beyond 1st year curriculum	205	0
# of upper division courses, excluding seminars, with an enrollment:		
Under 25	92	0
25 - 49	43	0
50 - 74	15	0
75 - 99	3	0
100 +	3	0
# of seminars	63	0
# of seminar positions available	1,008	
# of seminar positions filled	972	0
# of positions available in simulation courses	246	
# of simulation positions filled	246	0
# of positions available in faculty supervised clinical courses	276	
# of fac. sup. clin. positions filled	276	0
# involved in field placements	203	0
# involved in law journals	334	0
# in moot court or trial competitions	121	0
# of credit hrs required to graduate	90	

J.D. Enrollment & Ethnicity

	Men		Women		Fl-Time		Pt-Time		1st Yr		2nd Yr		3rd Yr		4th Yr		Total		JD Degrees Awarded
	#	%	#	%	#	%	#	%	#	%	#	%	#	%	#	%	#	%	
African-American	36	8.3	43	11.3	76	10.2	3	4.7	17	6.9	36	12.0	26	9.8	0	0.0	79	9.7	25
American Indian	9	2.1	13	3.4	22	2.9	0	0.0	6	2.4	11	3.7	5	1.9	0	0.0	22	2.7	3
Asian American	17	3.9	12	3.2	27	3.6	2	3.1	9	3.6	10	3.3	10	3.8	0	0.0	29	3.6	7
Mexican American	0	0.0	0	0.0	0	0.0	0	0.0	0	0.0	0	0.0	0	0.0	0	0.0	0	0.0	0
Puerto Rican	0	0.0	0	0.0	0	0.0	0	0.0	0	0.0	0	0.0	0	0.0	0	0.0	0	0.0	0
Hispanic American	29	6.7	29	7.6	52	7.0	6	9.4	13	5.3	27	9.0	18	6.8	0	0.0	58	7.1	15
Total Minorities	91	21.1	97	25.5	177	23.7	11	17.2	45	18.2	84	28.1	59	22.2	0	0.0	188	23.2	50
Foreign Nationals	5	1.2	2	0.5	7	0.9	0	0.0	2	0.8	2	0.7	3	1.1	0	0.0	7	0.9	0
Caucasian	336	77.8	281	73.9	564	75.4	53	82.8	200	81.0	213	71.2	204	76.7	0	0.0	617	76.0	217
Total	432	53.2	380	46.8	748	92.1	64	7.9	247	30.4	299	36.8	266	32.8	0	0.0	812		267

GPA & LSAT Scores

	Full Time	Part Time	Total
# of apps	1,550	0	1,550
# admits	590	0	590
# of matrics	216	9	225
75% GPA	3.68	3.76	
25% GPA	3.27	2.89	
75% LSAT	163	161	
25% LSAT	154	154	

Tuition & Fees

	Resident	Non-resident
Full-Time	$5,910	$15,442
Part-Time	$4,924	$12,869

Living Expenses

Estimated living expenses for Singles		
Living on campus	Living off campus	Living at home
$9,725	$9,725	$5,545

Employment

	Total	%
Employment status known	247	91.5
Employment status unknown	23	8.5
Employed	227	91.9
Pursuing graduate degrees	5	2.0
Unemployed seeking employment	13	5.3
Unemployed not seeking employment	2	0.8
Type of Employment		
# employed in law firms	131	57.7
# employed in business & industry	26	11.5
# employed in government	35	15.4
# employed in public interest	10	4.4
# employed as judicial clerks	20	8.8
# employed in academia	3	1.3
Geographic Location		
# employed in state	148	65.2
# employed in foreign countries	2	0.9
# of states where employed	21	

Financial Aid

	Full-time		Part-time		Total	
	#	%	#	%	#	%
Total # of Students	748		64		812	
Total # receiving grants	104	13.9	0	0.0	104	12.8
Less than 1/2 tuition	4	0.5	0	0.0	4	0.5
Half to full tuition	42	5.6	0	0.0	42	5.2
Full tuition	0	0.0	0	0.0	0	0.0
More than full tuition	58	7.8	0	0.0	58	7.1
Median Grant Amount	$10,008		$0			

Informational & Library Resources

# of volumes & volume equivalents	470,162	# of professional staff	13
# of titles	230,434	Hours per week with professional staff	73
# of active serial subscriptions	4,937	Hours per week without professional staff	34
Study seating capacity inside the library	589	# of student computer work stations for entire law school	50
Square feet of law library	54,773	# of additional networked connections	0
Square feet of law school (excl. Library)	62,385	Require Laptop Computer?	N

J.D. Attrition (Prior Year)

	Academic	Other	TOTALS	
	#	#	#	%
1st Year	0	3	3	1.0%
2nd Year	4	6	10	3.5%
3rd Year	0	2	2	0.7%
4th Year	0	0	0	0.0%
TOTALS	4	11	15	1.7%

Bar Passage Rates

Jurisdiction	Wisconsin			Illinois		
Exam	Sum 96	Win 97	Total	Sum 96	Win 97	Total
# from school taking bar for the first time	All graduates were admitted to the Wisconsin bar via the diploma privilege.			23	5	28
School's pass rate for all first-time takers				96%	100%	96%
State's pass rate for all first-time takers				86%	84%	86%

WYOMING, UNIVERSITY OF

P.O. Box 3035
Laramie, WY 82071
(307)766-6416
http://www.uwyo.edu/law/law.htm

ABA Approved Since 1923

The Basics

Type of School: Public   Term: Semester

Application deadline: 04/01

Application fee: $35

Financial Aid deadline: 02/15

Can first year start other than Fall? No

Student faculty ratio: 15.3 to 1

Does the University offer:
- housing restricted to law students? Yes
- graduate student housing for which law students are eligible? Yes

Faculty & Administrators

	Total		Men		Women		Minorities	
	Fall	Spr	Fall	Spr	Fall	Spr	Fall	Spr
Full-time	12	12	8	8	4	4	0	0
Other Full-Time	0	0	0	0	0	0	0	0
Deans, librarians, & others who teach > 1/2	2	2	1	1	1	1	0	0
Part-time	5	9	3	4	2	5	0	0
Total	19	23	12	13	7	10	0	0
Deans, librarians, & others who teach < 1/2	1	1	0	0	1	1	0	0

Curriculum

	Full time	Part time
Typical first-year section size	80	0
Is there typically a "small section" of the first year class, other than Legal Writing, taught by full-time faculty?	No	No
If yes, typical size offered last year	N/A	N/A
# of classroom course titles beyond 1st year curriculum	52	0
# of upper division courses, excluding seminars, with an enrollment:		
Under 25	26	0
25 - 49	12	0
50 - 74	2	0
75 - 99	0	0
100 +	0	0
# of seminars	5	0
# of seminar positions available	50	
# of seminar positions filled	37	0
# of positions available in simulation courses	100	
# of simulation positions filled	93	0
# of positions available in faculty supervised clinical courses	64	
# of fac. sup. clin. positions filled	64	0
# involved in field placements	38	0
# involved in law journals	32	0
# in moot court or trial competitions	12	0
# of credit hrs required to graduate	88	

J.D. Enrollment & Ethnicity

	Men		Women		Fl-Time		Pt-Time		1st Yr		2nd Yr		3rd Yr		4th Yr		Total		JD Degrees Awarded
	#	%	#	%	#	%	#	%	#	%	#	%	#	%	#	%	#	%	
African-American	1	0.8	0	0.0	1	0.5	0	0.0	0	0.0	1	1.4	0	0.0	0	0.0	1	0.5	0
American Indian	0	0.0	1	1.1	1	0.5	0	0.0	1	1.2	0	0.0	0	0.0	0	0.0	1	0.5	2
Asian American	0	0.0	0	0.0	0	0.0	0	0.0	0	0.0	0	0.0	0	0.0	0	0.0	0	0.0	1
Mexican American	1	0.8	3	3.2	4	1.9	0	0.0	1	1.2	2	2.8	1	1.7	0	0.0	4	1.9	5
Puerto Rican	0	0.0	0	0.0	0	0.0	0	0.0	0	0.0	0	0.0	0	0.0	0	0.0	0	0.0	0
Hispanic American	0	0.0	0	0.0	0	0.0	0	0.0	0	0.0	0	0.0	0	0.0	0	0.0	0	0.0	0
Total Minorities	2	1.7	4	4.3	6	2.8	0	0.0	2	2.4	3	4.2	1	1.7	0	0.0	6	2.8	8
Foreign Nationals	1	0.8	0	0.0	1	0.5	0	0.0	0	0.0	1	1.4	0	0.0	0	0.0	1	0.5	1
Caucasian	116	97.5	90	95.7	206	96.7	0	0.0	80	97.6	67	94.4	59	98.3	0	0.0	206	96.7	59
Total	119	55.9	94	44.1	213	100.0	0	0.0	82	38.5	71	33.3	60	28.2	0	0.0	213		68

GPA & LSAT Scores

	Full Time	Part Time	Total
# of apps	441	0	441
# admits	267	0	267
# of matrics	82	0	82
75% GPA	3.41	0.00	
25% GPA	2.75	0.00	
75% LSAT	158	0	
25% LSAT	149	0	

Tuition & Fees

	Resident	Non-resident
Full-Time	$4,234	$9,322
Part-Time	$0	$0

Living Expenses

Estimated living expenses for Singles		
Living on campus	Living off campus	Living at home
$7,076	$7,076	$3,716

Financial Aid

	Full-time		Part-time		Total	
	#	%	#	%	#	%
Total # of Students	213		0		213	
Total # receiving grants	60	28.2	0	0.0	60	28.2
Less than 1/2 tuition	52	24.4	0	0.0	52	24.4
Half to full tuition	2	0.9	0	0.0	2	0.9
Full tuition	1	0.5	0	0.0	1	0.5
More than full tuition	5	2.3	0	0.0	5	2.3
Median Grant Amount	$1,668		$0			

Informational & Library Resources

# of volumes & volume equivalents	201,814	# of professional staff	3
# of titles	20,374	Hours per week with professional staff	62
# of active serial subscriptions	2,481	Hours per week without professional staff	45
Study seating capacity inside the library	248	# of student computer work stations for entire law school	31
Square feet of law library	30,000	# of additional networked connections	4
Square feet of law school (excl. Library)	30,060	Require Laptop Computer?	N

Employment

	Total	%
Employment status known	66	89.2
Employment status unknown	8	10.8
Employed	54	81.8
Pursuing graduate degrees	1	1.5
Unemployed seeking employment	11	16.7
Unemployed not seeking employment	0	0.0
Type of Employment		
# employed in law firms	24	44.4
# employed in business & industry	6	11.1
# employed in government	11	20.4
# employed in public interest	3	5.6
# employed as judicial clerks	10	18.5
# employed in academia	0	0.0
Geographic Location		
# employed in state	35	64.8
# employed in foreign countries	0	0.0
# of states where employed	0	

J.D. Attrition (Prior Year)

	Academic	Other	TOTALS	
	#	#	#	%
1st Year	3	7	10	13%
2nd Year	2	0	2	3.2%
3rd Year	0	0	0	0.0%
4th Year	0	0	0	0.0%
TOTALS	5	7	12	5.7%

Bar Passage Rates

Jurisdiction	Wyoming		
Exam	Sum 96	Win 97	Total
# from school taking bar for the first time	40	2	42
School's pass rate for all first-time takers	80%	100%	81%
State's pass rate for all first-time takers	76%	0%	76%

YALE UNIVERSITY

P.O. Box 208215
New Haven, CT 06520-8215
(203)432-1660
http://www.yale.edu/lawweb/lawschool

ABA Approved Since 1923

The Basics

Type of School: Private Term: Semester
Application deadline: 02/15
Application fee: $65
Financial Aid deadline: 03/15
Can first year start other than Fall? No
Student faculty ratio: 11.1 to 1
Does the University offer:
- housing restricted to law students? Yes
- graduate student housing for which law students are eligible? Yes

Faculty & Administrators

	Total		Men		Women		Minorities	
	Fall	Spr	Fall	Spr	Fall	Spr	Fall	Spr
Full-time	43	38	34	28	9	10	5	4
Other Full-Time	1	1	1	1	0	0	0	0
Deans, librarians, & others who teach > 1/2	2	2	2	2	0	0	0	0
Part-time	28	18	16	14	11	4	4	0
Total	74	59	53	45	20	14	9	4
Deans, librarians, & others who teach < 1/2	0	0	0	0	0	0	0	0

Curriculum

	Full time	Part time
Typical first-year section size	85	0
Is there typically a "small section" of the first year class, other than Legal Writing, taught by full-time faculty?	Yes	No
If yes, typical size offered last year	17	N/A
# of classroom course titles beyond 1st year curriculum	112	0
# of upper division courses, excluding seminars, with an enrollment:		
Under 25	32	0
25 - 49	22	0
50 - 74	12	0
75 - 99	2	0
100 +	9	0
# of seminars	35	0
# of seminar positions available	700	
# of seminar positions filled	343	0
# of positions available in simulation courses	175	
# of simulation positions filled	98	0
# of positions available in faculty supervised clinical courses	180	
# of fac. sup. clin. positions filled	146	0
# involved in field placements	27	0
# involved in law journals	400	0
# in moot court or trial competitions	107	0
# of credit hrs required to graduate	82	

J.D. Enrollment & Ethnicity

	Men		Women		Fl-Time		Pt-Time		1st Yr		2nd Yr		3rd Yr		4th Yr		Total		JD Degrees Awarded
	#	%	#	%	#	%	#	%	#	%	#	%	#	%	#	%	#	%	
African-American	23	7.0	30	12.3	53	9.2	0	0.0	18	9.6	16	7.6	19	10.9	0	0.0	53	9.2	17
American Indian	0	0.0	1	0.4	1	0.2	0	0.0	0	0.0	1	0.5	0	0.0	0	0.0	1	0.2	1
Asian American	46	14.0	34	13.9	80	14.0	0	0.0	23	12.2	31	14.8	26	14.9	0	0.0	80	14.0	24
Mexican American	5	1.5	3	1.2	8	1.4	0	0.0	4	2.1	3	1.4	1	0.6	0	0.0	8	1.4	0
Puerto Rican	2	0.6	5	2.0	7	1.2	0	0.0	4	2.1	2	1.0	1	0.6	0	0.0	7	1.2	1
Hispanic American	10	3.0	10	4.1	20	3.5	0	0.0	7	3.7	11	5.2	2	1.1	0	0.0	20	3.5	13
Total Minorities	86	26.1	83	34.0	169	29.5	0	0.0	56	29.8	64	30.5	49	28.0	0	0.0	169	29.5	56
Foreign Nationals	11	3.3	4	1.6	15	2.6	0	0.0	6	3.2	8	3.8	1	0.6	0	0.0	15	2.6	3
Caucasian	232	70.5	157	64.3	389	67.9	0	0.0	126	67.0	138	65.7	125	71.4	0	0.0	389	67.9	156
Total	329	57.4	244	42.6	573	100.0	0	0.0	188	32.8	210	36.6	175	30.5	0	0.0	573		215

GPA & LSAT Scores

	Full Time	Part Time	Total
# of apps	3,546	0	3,546
# admits	250	0	250
# of matrics	188	0	188
75% GPA	3.96	0.00	
25% GPA	3.78	0.00	
75% LSAT	175	0	
25% LSAT	168	0	

Tuition & Fees

	Resident	Non-resident
Full-Time	$23,940	$23,940
Part-Time	$0	$0

Living Expenses

Estimated living expenses for Singles		
Living on campus	Living off campus	Living at home
$11,090	$11,090	N/A

Employment

	Total	%
Employment status known	182	99.5
Employment status unknown	1	0.5
Employed	179	98.4
Pursuing graduate degrees	1	0.5
Unemployed seeking employment	2	1.1
Unemployed not seeking employment	0	0.0
Type of Employment		
# employed in law firms	66	36.9
# employed in business & industry	10	5.6
# employed in government	6	3.4
# employed in public interest	10	5.6
# employed as judicial clerks	85	47.5
# employed in academia	1	0.6
Geographic Location		
# employed in state	20	11.2
# employed in foreign countries	0	0.0
# of states where employed	31	

Financial Aid

	Full-time		Part-time		Total	
	#	%	#	%	#	%
Total # of Students	573		0		573	
Total # receiving grants	215	37.5	0	0.0	215	37.5
Less than 1/2 tuition	147	25.7	0	0.0	147	25.7
Half to full tuition	66	11.5	0	0.0	66	11.5
Full tuition	2	0.3	0	0.0	2	0.3
More than full tuition	0	0.0	0	0.0	0	0.0
Median Grant Amount	$9,300		$0			

Informational & Library Resources

# of volumes & volume equivalents	978,538	# of professional staff	18
# of titles	248,358	Hours per week with professional staff	87
# of active serial subscriptions	9,358	Hours per week without professional staff	81
Study seating capacity inside the library	250	# of student computer work stations for entire law school	73
Square feet of law library	60,401	# of additional networked connections	0
Square feet of law school (excl. Library)	52,291	Require Laptop Computer?	N

J.D. Attrition (Prior Year)

	Academic	Other	TOTALS	
	#	#	#	%
1st Year	0	0	0	0.0%
2nd Year	0	0	0	0.0%
3rd Year	0	0	0	0.0%
4th Year	0	0	0	0.0%
TOTALS	0	0	0	0.0%

Bar Passage Rates

Jurisdiction	New York		
Exam	Sum 96	Win 97	Total
# from school taking bar for the first time	67	15	82
School's pass rate for all first-time takers	97%	87%	95%
State's pass rate for all first-time takers	78%	67%	77%

YESHIVA UNIVERSITY

Benjamin N. Cardozo School of Law
55 Fifth Avenue
New York, NY 10003
(212)790-0200
http://www.yu.edu/csl/law

ABA Approved Since 1978

The Basics

Type of School: Private Term: Semester
Application deadline: 04/01
Application fee: $60
Financial Aid deadline: 04/15
Can first year start other than Fall? Yes
Student faculty ratio: 17.7 to 1
Does the University offer:
- housing restricted to law students? Yes
- graduate student housing for which law students are eligible? No

Faculty & Administrators

	Total		Men		Women		Minorities	
	Fall	Spr	Fall	Spr	Fall	Spr	Fall	Spr
Full-time	43	43	30	30	13	13	3	2
Other Full-Time	0	0	0	0	0	0	0	0
Deans, librarians, & others who teach > 1/2	2	2	1	1	1	1	0	0
Part-time	48	57	29	44	19	13	1	1
Total	93	102	60	75	33	27	4	3
Deans, librarians, & others who teach < 1/2	1	1	1	1	0	0	0	0

Curriculum

	Full time	Part time
Typical first-year section size	50	0
Is there typically a "small section" of the first year class, other than Legal Writing, taught by full-time faculty?	No	No
If yes, typical size offered last year	N/A	N/A
# of classroom course titles beyond 1st year curriculum	139	0
# of upper division courses, excluding seminars, with an enrollment:		
Under 25	57	0
25 - 49	31	0
50 - 74	19	0
75 - 99	8	0
100 +	17	0
# of seminars	44	0
# of seminar positions available	801	
# of seminar positions filled	630	0
# of positions available in simulation courses	494	
# of simulation positions filled	473	0
# of positions available in faculty supervised clinical courses	112	
# of fac. sup. clin. positions filled	104	0
# involved in field placements	273	0
# involved in law journals	245	0
# in moot court or trial competitions	60	0
# of credit hrs required to graduate	84	

J.D. Enrollment & Ethnicity

	Men		Women		Fl-Time		Pt-Time		1st Yr		2nd Yr		3rd Yr		4th Yr		Total		JD Degrees Awarded
	#	%	#	%	#	%	#	%	#	%	#	%	#	%	#	%	#	%	
African-American	25	5.2	27	6.3	52	5.7	0	0.0	15	5.6	22	7.7	15	4.1	0	0.0	52	5.7	8
American Indian	1	0.2	2	0.5	3	0.3	0	0.0	1	0.4	1	0.4	1	0.3	0	0.0	3	0.3	0
Asian American	39	8.0	36	8.4	75	8.2	0	0.0	33	12.3	22	7.7	20	5.5	0	0.0	75	8.2	19
Mexican American	0	0.0	0	0.0	0	0.0	0	0.0	0	0.0	0	0.0	0	0.0	0	0.0	0	0.0	0
Puerto Rican	10	2.1	8	1.9	18	2.0	0	0.0	5	1.9	6	2.1	7	1.9	0	0.0	18	2.0	0
Hispanic American	16	3.3	16	3.7	32	3.5	0	0.0	13	4.9	10	3.5	9	2.5	0	0.0	32	3.5	8
Total Minorities	91	18.8	89	20.7	180	19.7	0	0.0	67	25.0	61	21.5	52	14.4	0	0.0	180	19.7	35
Foreign Nationals	13	2.7	16	3.7	29	3.2	0	0.0	16	6.0	5	1.8	8	2.2	0	0.0	29	3.2	0
Caucasian	381	78.6	324	75.5	705	77.1	0	0.0	185	69.0	218	76.8	302	83.4	0	0.0	705	77.1	305
Total	485	53.1	429	46.9	914	100.0	0	0.0	268	29.3	284	31.1	362	39.6	0	0.0	914		340

GPA & LSAT Scores

	Full Time	Part Time	Total
# of apps	2,330	0	2,330
# admits	1,074	0	1,074
# of matrics	329	0	329
75% GPA	3.55	0.00	
25% GPA	2.99	0.00	
75% LSAT	159	0	
25% LSAT	151	0	

Tuition & Fees

	Resident	Non-resident
Full-Time	$20,000	$20,000
Part-Time	$0	$0

Living Expenses

Estimated living expenses for Singles		
Living on campus	Living off campus	Living at home
N/A	$18,038	$8,170

Financial Aid

	Full-time		Part-time		Total	
	#	%	#	%	#	%
Total # of Students	914		0		914	
Total # receiving grants	544	59.5	0	0.0	544	59.5
Less than 1/2 tuition	477	52.2	0	0.0	477	52.2
Half to full tuition	64	7.0	0	0.0	64	7.0
Full tuition	3	0.3	0	0.0	3	0.3
More than full tuition	0	0.0	0	0.0	0	0.0
Median Grant Amount	$4,000		$0			

Informational & Library Resources

# of volumes & volume equivalents	414,973	# of professional staff	6
# of titles	63,044	Hours per week with professional staff	62
# of active serial subscriptions	5,883	Hours per week without professional staff	26
Study seating capacity inside the library	513	# of student computer work stations for entire law school	106
Square feet of law library	37,012	# of additional networked connections	0
Square feet of law school (excl. Library)	84,988	Require Laptop Computer?	N

Employment

	Total	%
Employment status known	246	80.7
Employment status unknown	59	19.3
Employed	224	91.1
Pursuing graduate degrees	4	1.6
Unemployed seeking employment	12	4.9
Unemployed not seeking employment	6	2.4
Type of Employment		
# employed in law firms	131	58.5
# employed in business & industry	43	19.2
# employed in government	24	10.7
# employed in public interest	10	4.5
# employed as judicial clerks	14	6.2
# employed in academia	2	0.9
Geographic Location		
# employed in state	202	90.2
# employed in foreign countries	2	0.9
# of states where employed	8	

J.D. Attrition (Prior Year)

	Academic	Other	TOTALS	
	#	#	#	%
1st Year	2	15	17	5.9%
2nd Year	0	0	0	0.0%
3rd Year	0	0	0	0.0%
4th Year	0	0	0	0.0%
TOTALS	2	15	17	1.7%

Bar Passage Rates

Jurisdiction	New York		
Exam	Sum 96	Win 97	Total
# from school taking bar for the first time	260	32	292
School's pass rate for all first-time takers	77%	72%	77%
State's pass rate for all first-time takers	78%	67%	77%

Chapter Thirteen

Unapproved Law Schools

Below is a list of non ABA approved law schools as of October 1, 1997. A law school in the United States that is not approved by the ABA has either not applied for approval or does not satisfy the requirements of the ABA Standards for Approval of Law Schools. The list below is not comprehensive; but it is the most current data on record at the Office of the Consultant on Legal Education. You may wish to contact the bar admission authorities in the state(s) in which you intend to practice for more information on whether graduation from a law school that is not approved will qualify you to take the bar examination in that state. For your convenience, chapter six contains contact information for state bar examiners.

ALABAMA

Birmingham School of Law
923 Frank Nelson Building
Birmingham, AL

Miles Law School
P.O. Box 3800
Birmingham, AL 35208

Jones School of Law
Faulkner University
5345 Atlanta Highway
Montgomery, AL 36193-4601

CALIFORNIA

American College of Law
1717 S. State College Blvd.
Suite 100
Anaheim, CA 92806

Cal Northern
School of Law
2525 Dominic Drive, Suite F
Chico, CA 95928

California Pacific
School of Law
1600 Truxtun Avenue,
Suite 100
Bakersfield, CA 93301

* Chapman University
School of Law
1240 South State College Road
Anaheim, CA 92806

Empire College School of Law
3033 Cleveland Avenue
Suite 102
Santa Rosa, CA 95403

Glendale College of Law
220 North Glendale Avenue
Glendale, CA 91206

John F. Kennedy University
School of Law
547 Ygnacio Valley Road
Walnut Creek, CA 94596

Lincoln University
3000 S. Robertson Blvd.
Los Angelas, California 90034

New College of California
School of Law
50 Fell Street
San Francisco, CA 94102

Pacific Coast University
College of Law
440 Redondo Avenue #203
Long Beach, CA 90814

San Francisco Law School
20 Haight Street
San Francisco, CA 94102

Santa Barbara College of Law
911 Tremonto Road
Santa Barbara, CA 93101

Simon Greenleaf School of Law
3855 E. La Palma Avenue
Anaheim, CA 92801

Southern California
Institute of Law
Santa Barbara Campus:
1525 State Street, #202
Santa Barbara, CA 93101

University of La Verne
College of Law
21300 Oxnard Street
Woodland Hills, CA 91367

University of La Verne
College of Law
1950 Third Street
La Verne, CA 91750

University of West
Los Angeles
School of Law
1155 West Arbor Vitae Street
Inglewood, CA 90301-2902

Ventura College of Law
4475 Market Street
Ventura, CA 93001

Western State University
College of Law
P.O. Box 4310
1111 N. State CollegeBoulevard
Fullerton, CA 92631

DISTRICT OF COLUMBIA

* University of the District
of Columbia
4250 Connecticut Ave., N.W.
Building 48
Washington, D.C. 22008

FLORIDA

Florida Coastal School of Law
7555 Beach Blvd.
Jacksonville, FL 32216

University of Orlando
School of Law
6441 East Colonial Drive
Orlando, FL 32807

GEORGIA

John Marshall Law School
805 Peachtree Street, N.E.
Atlanta, GA 30308

KANSAS

President's College Law School
123 South Market Street
Wichita, KS 67202

MASSACHUSETTS

Massachusetts School of Law
Woodland Park
500 Federal Street
Andover, MA 01810

Southern New England
School of Law
874 Purchase Street
New Bedford, MA 02740-6232

PUERTO RICO

Eugenio Maria De Hostos
School of Law
GPO Box 1900
Mayaguez, Puerto Rico 00681

TENNESSEE

Nashville School of Law
2934 Sidco Drive
Nashville, TN 37204

VIRGINIA

Appalachian Regional
Law School
702 Park Avenue
Norton, VA 24273

** On February 3, 1998, just prior to the publication of this book, the ABA House of Delegates granted provisional approval to Chapman University School of Law and the University of the District of Columbia School of Law. For updates or corrections to this book, please visit the Section's website: http://www.abanet.org/legaled.*

Chapter Fourteen

Legal Education Statistics

Law School Attendance Figures, Fall 1997

		Full Time	Part Time	Total
First Year	Total	35,745	6,441	**42,186**
	Women	16,527	2,882	**19,409**
Second Year	Total	34,583	5,182	**39,765**
	Women	15,593	2,354	**17,947**
Third Year	Total	34,882	4,883	**39,765**
	Women	15,769	2,029	**17,798**
Fourth Year	Total	0	4,170	**4,170**
	Women	0	1,761	**1,761**
J.D. Total	Total	105,210	20,676	**125,886**
	Women	47,889	9,026	**56,915**
Post J.D.	Total	2,826	2,001	**4,827**
	Women	960	802	**1,762**
Other	Total	599	489	**1,088**
	Women	291	263	**554**
Grand Total	Total	**108,635**	**22,677**	**131,801**
	Women	**49,140**	**10,091**	**59,231**

Professional Degrees Conferred, 1997

		Full Time	Part Time	Total
J.D. / LL.B.	Total	35,432	4,682	**40,114**
	Women	15,580	1,972	**17,552**
LL.M.	Total	2,105	659	**2,764**
	Women	739	226	**965**
M.C.L. / M.C.J.	Total	148	1	**149**
	Women	52	0	**52**
S.J.D. / J.S.D.	Total	38	1	**39**
	Women	7	1	**8**
Other	Total	296	150	**446**
	Women	118	70	**188**
Total	Total	**38,019**	**5,493**	**43,512**
	Women	**16,496**	**2,269**	**18,765**

Teachers in Law Schools, Fall 1997

	Women	Minorities	Total
Full-Time	1,540	719	**5,395**
Part-Time	1,453	449	**5,166**
Deans & Administrators	2,004	540	**3,089**
Librarians	955	213	**1,443**

Legal Education and Bar Admission Statistics, 1963 - 1998

Academic Year	Number of Schools	First Year Enrollment	First Year Women Enrollment	Total J.D. Enrollment	Total J.D. Women Enrollment	Total [1] Overall Enrollment	Total LSAT Administrations	J.D. or LL.B. Awarded	Admissions to the Bar
1997 - 98	178[2]	42,186	19,409	125,886	56,915	131,801	NA	40,114	NA
1996 - 97	179	43,245	19,402	128,623	57,123	134,949	105,313	39,920	56,629
1995 - 96	178	43,676	19,462	129,397	56,961	135,595	114,756	39,271	56,613
1994 - 95	177[3]	44,298	19,312	128,989	55,808	134,784	128,553	39,710	57,875
1993 - 94	176	43,644	19,059	127,802	55,134	133,339	132,028	40,213	51,152
1992 - 93	176	42,793	18,325	128,212	54,644	133,783	140,054	39,425	57,117
!991 - 92	176	44,050	18,773	129,580	55,110	135,157	145,567	38,800	54,577
1990 - 91	175	44,104	18,592	127,261	54,097	132,433	152,685	36,385	43,286[5]
1989 - 90	75	43,826	18,722	124,471	53,113	129,698	138,865	35,520	47,174
1988 - 89	174	42,860	18,395	120,694	50,932	125,870	137,088	35,701	46,528
1987 - 88	175	41,055	17,506	117,997	48,920	123,198	115,988	35,478	39,918
1986 - 87	175[4]	40,195	14,491	117,813	47,920	123,277	101,235	36,121	40,247[5]
1985 - 86	175[4]	40,796	16,510	118,700	47,486	124,092	91,848	36,829	42,450[5]
1984 - 85	174	40,747	16,236	119,847	46,897	125,698	95,563	36,687	42,630
1983 - 84	173	41,159	16,049	121,201	46,361	127,195	105,076	36,389	41,684
1982 - 83	172	42,034	16,136	121,791	45,539	127,828	112,125	34,846	42,905
1981 - 82	172	42,521	15,811	120,879	43,245	127,312	119,291	35,598	42,382
1980 - 81	171	42,296	15,272	119,501	40,834	125,397	108,022	35,059	41,997
1979 - 80	169	40,717	13,490	117,297	37,534	122,860	113,145	34,590	42,756
1978 - 79	167	40,479	13,324	116,150	35,775	121,606	115,284	33,317	39,068
1977 - 78	163	39,676	11,928	113,080	31,650	118,557	127,760	33,640	37,302
1976 - 77	163	39,996	11,354	112,401	29,343	117,451	128,135	32,597	35,741
1975 - 76	163	39,038	10,472	111,047	26,020	116,991	133,316	29,961	34,930
1974 - 75	157	38,074	9,006	105,708	21,283	110,713	133,546	28,729	30,707
1973 - 74	151	37,018	7,464	101,675	16,303	106,102	135,397	27,756	30,879
1972 - 73	149	35,131	5,508	98,042	11,878	101,707	121,262	22,342	25,086
1971 - 72	147	36,171	4,326	91,225	8,567	94,468	119,694	17,006	20,485
1970 - 71	146	34,289	3,542	78,018	6,682	82,041	107,479	17,183	17,922
1969 - 70	144	29,128	2,103	64,416	4,485	68,386	74,092	16,733	19,123
1968 - 69	138	23,652	1,742	59,498	3,554	62,779	59,050	16,077	17,764
1967 - 68	136	24,267	1,179	61,084	2,769	64,406	49,756	14,738	16,007
1966 - 67	135	24,077	1,059	59,236	2,520	62,556	47,110	13,115	14,644
1965 - 66	136	24,167	1,064	56,510	2,374	59,744	44,905	11,507	13,109
1964 - 65	135[6]	22,753	986	51,079	2,056	54,265	39,406	10,491	12,023
1963 - 64	135	20,776	877	46,666	1,739	49,552	37,598	9,638	10,788

NOTES: Enrollment is in American Bar Association-approved schools as of October 1. The LSAT test year begins in June and ends in February of the following year. J.D. or LL.B. degrees are those awarded by approved schools for the academic year ending in the first year stated. Total new admissions to the bar include those admitted by office study, diploma privilege, and examination and study at an unapproved law school. The great bulk of those admitted were graduated from approved schools.

[1] Total overall enrollment includes post-J.D. and other.

[2] The District of Columbia School of Law is not included in this figure.

[3] Roger Williams not included.

[4] This number includes Oral Roberts University, Coburn School of Law, which terminated its program effective June 1, 1986. However, the Council advised it to retain degree-ranting authority for those former students who completed satisfactorily 30 additional hours in ABA-approved law schools by Sept, 1, 1988.

[5] Data was not complete for these years, thus figure is lower than prior years.

[6] Stanford enrollment not included.

30 Year JD Enrollment Trend

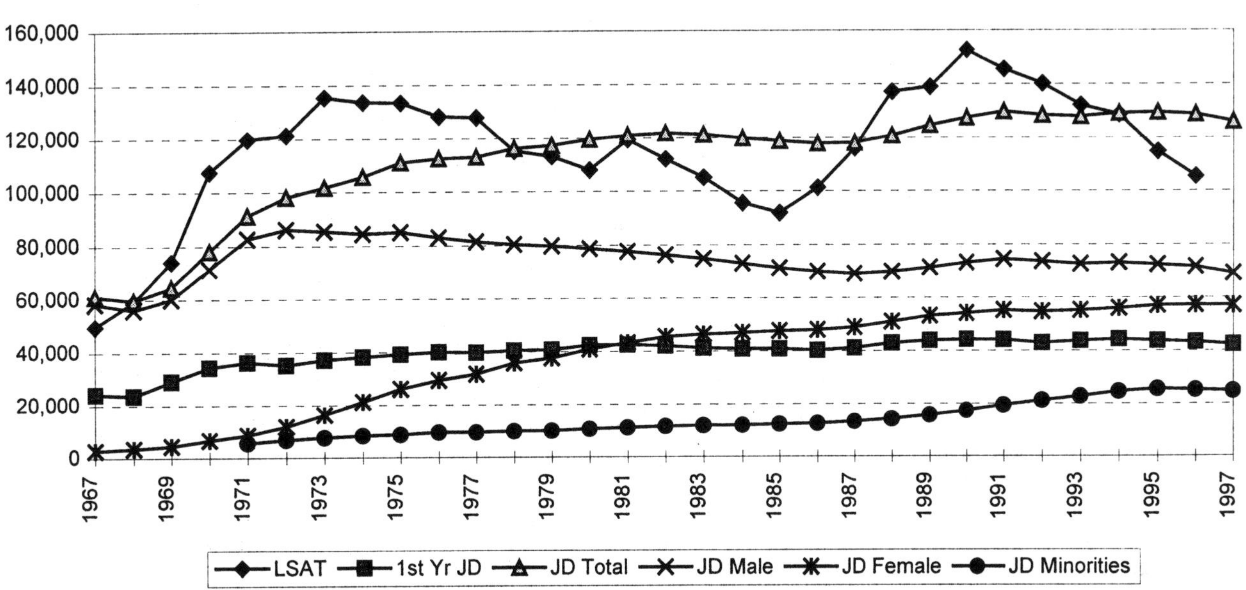

Law School Average Tuition
1987-1997

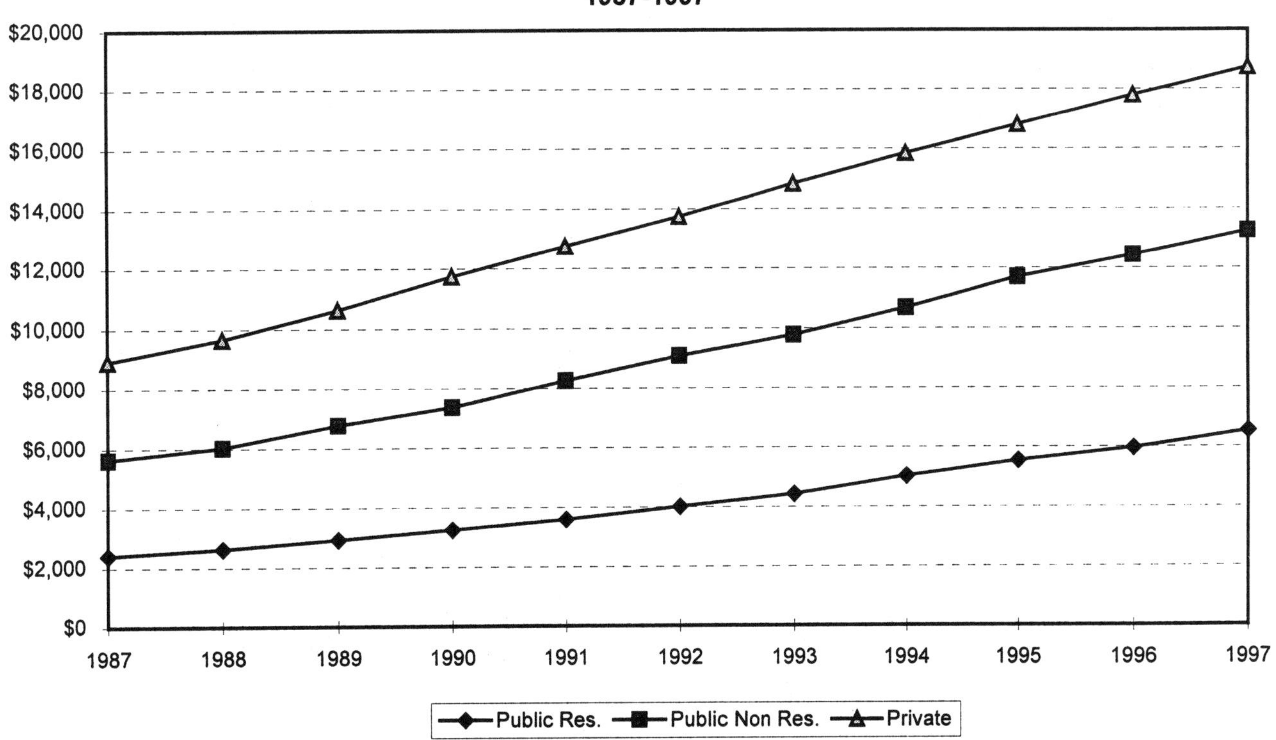

Survey of Minority Group Students Enrolled in J.D. Programs in Approved Law Schools, 1971 to Present

Enrollment Comparison: Fall 1997 vs. Fall 1996
By Rick L. Morgan, Data Specialist, ABA

The following observations resulted from a comparison of Fall 1997 enrollment and Fall 1996 enrollment. First, it should be noted that we effectively had one less school reporting data in 1997 than in 1996, because the District of Columbia School of Law is no longer in existence.

Total J.D. enrollment in the Fall 1997 was 125,886. This represents a decrease of 2,737 (2.1%) students from Fall 1996 when J.D. enrollment was 128,623. Total law school enrollment for Fall 1997 was 131,801, (2.3%) below total law school enrollment for 1996 (134,949). The entering class for the Fall 1997 semester (42,186) decreased 1,059 students (2.4%) from Fall 1996 (43,245).

Even though the entering class decreased by 1,059, the number of women entering law school actually increased this year to 19,409 which represented 46% of total first year students. Last year the entering class was made up of 44.9% women (19,402). First year male enrollment decreased 1,066 (4.5%) from a year ago. Total J.D. enrollment of women (56,915) decreased 208 from last year (57,123). The percentage of total J.D. enrollment which was female (45.2%) increased from last year's 44.4%.

1997 minority J.D. enrollment (24,685) decreased 594 (2.3%) over minority J.D. enrollment from 1996 (25,279). This year, first year minority students (8,493) decreased 229 (2.6%) from last year, 8,722.

Minorities constituted 19.6% of total J.D. students this year. For 1996 and 1995, minority enrollment represented 19.7%. Minority students accounted for 20.1% of the total entering class in 1997. In 1996, minorities represented 20.2% of the entering class.

Please note that the minority enrollment charts on pages 458 through 461 do not include students from the three Puerto Rican schools. J.D. Enrollment for the law schools in Puerto Rico was 1,710 for Fall 1997.

Total Minority Enrollment

Academic Year	No. of Schools Reporting	1st Year	2nd Year	3rd Year	4th Year	Total
1997-98	175/178	8,493	7,740	7,705	747	**24,685**
1996-97	176/179	8,722	8,009	7,869	679	**25,279**
1995-96	175/178	9,119	8,402	7,411	622	**25,554**
1994-95	174/177	9,249	7,633	7,124	605	**24,611**
1993-94	173/176	8,595	7,244	6,409	551	**22,799**
1992-93	173/176	8,070	6,682	6,032	482	**21,266**
1991-92	173/176	7,575	6,155	5,255	425	**19,410**
1990-91	172/175	6,933	5,325	4,676	396	**17,330**
1989-90	172/175	6,172	4,890	4,264	394	**15,720**
1988-89	171/174	5,565	4,408	3,911	411	**14,295**
1987-88	171/175	5,130	3,994	3,717	409	**13,250**
1986-87	171/175	4,738	3,839	3,648	325	**12,550**
1985-86	172/175	4,534	3,810	3,625	388	**12,357**
1984-85	171/174	4,429	3,725	3,432	331	**11,917**
1983-84	170/173	4,393	3,691	3,424	358	**11,866**
1982-83	169/172	4,421	3,624	3,217	349	**11,611**
1981-82	169/172	4,314	3,401	3,118	301	**11,134**
1980-81	168/171	4,124	3,215	2,976	260	**10,575**
1979-80	166/169	3,825	3,150	2,755	283	**10,013**
1978-79	164/167	3,801	2,925	2,902	324	**9,952**
1977-78	160/163	3,574	2,991	2,690	325	**9,580**
1976-77	160/163	3,698	2,892	2,641	358	**9,589**
1975-76	160/163	3,417	2,689	2,407	190	**8,712**
1974-75	154/157	3,373	2,630	2,173	196	**8,372**
1973-74	147/151	3,277	2,313	1,816	195	**7,601**
1972-73	144/149	2,947	2,041	1,619	123	**6,730**
1971-72	142/147	2,682	1,707	1,099	80	**5,568**

American Indian or Alaska Native Enrollment

Academic Year	No. of Schools Reporting	1st Year	2nd Year	3rd Year	4th Year	Total
1997-98	175/178	355	348	355	27	**1,085**
1996-97	176/179	391	397	310	18	**1,116**
1995-96	175/178	436	338	294	17	**1,085**
1994-95	174/177	377	283	290	12	**962**
1993-94	173/176	336	280	243	14	**873**
1992-93	173/176	313	243	206	14	**776**
1991-92	173/176	286	219	176	11	**692**
1990-91	172/175	224	185	129	16	**554**
1989-90	172/175	220	147	143	17	**527**
1988-89	171/174	177	165	149	8	**499**
1987-88	171/175	189	144	148	11	**492**
1986-87	171/175	176	155	148	9	**488**
1985-86	172/174	183	146	124	10	**463**
1984-85	171/174	173	135	111	10	**429**
1983-84	170/173	169	126	134	12	**441**
1982-83	169/172	154	134	110	8	**406**
1981-82	169/172	160	112	125	5	**402**
1980-81	168/171	163	138	107	7	**415**
1979-80	166/169	171	110	100	11	**392**
1978-79	164/167	145	110	124	11	**390**
1977-78	160/163	137	130	90	6	**363**
1976-77	160/163	133	87	75	6	**301**
1975-76	160/163	118	88	84	5	**295**
1974-75	154/157	110	90	65	0	**265**
1973-74	147/151	110	65	44	3	**222**
1972-73	144/149	79	48	4	42	**173**
1971-72	142/147	74	46	18	2	**140**

Asian or Pacific Islander Enrollment

Academic Year	No. of Schools Reporting	1st Year	2nd Year	3rd Year	4th Year	Total
1997-98	175/178	2,562	2,463	2,394	180	**7,599**
1996-97	176/179	2,695	2,451	2,380	180	**7,706**
1995-96	175/178	2,773	2,572	2,225	149	**7,719**
1994-95	174/177	2,740	2,247	2,087	122	**7,196**
1993-94	173/176	2,432	2,101	1,789	136	**6,458**
1992-93	173/176	2,235	1,873	1,618	97	**5,823**
1991-92	173/176	2,019	1,621	1,306	82	**5,028**
1990-91	172/175	1,753	1,343	1,134	76	**4,306**
1989-90	172/175	1,501	1,151	946	78	**3,676**
1988-89	171/174	1,282	954	825	72	**3,133**
1987-88	171/175	1,064	804	724	64	**2,656**
1986-87	171/175	929	685	650	39	**2,303**
1985-86	172/175	799	678	622	54	**2,153**
1984-85	171/174	766	610	600	50	**2,026**
1983-84	170/173	711	610	578	63	**1,962**
1982-83	169/172	731	593	562	61	**1,947**
1981-82	169/172	650	579	486	40	**1,755**
1980-81	168/171	641	485	473	42	**1,641**
1979-80	166/169	577	487	452	31	**1,547**
1978-79	164/167	557	435	398	34	**1,424**
1977-78	160/163	509	409	423	41	**1,382**
1976-77	160/163	484	439	378	23	**1,324**
1975-76	160/163	436	343	287	33	**1,099**
1974-75	154/157	432	322	288	21	**1,063**
1973-74	147/151	332	297	202	19	**850**
1972-73	144/149	299	218	144	20	**681**
1971-72	142/147	259	142	72	7	**480**

Black American Enrollment

Academic Year	No. of Schools Reporting	1st Year	2nd Year	3rd Year	4th Year	Total
1997-98	175/178	3,126	2,752	2,887	367	**9,132**
1996-97	176/179	3,223	3,013	2,991	315	**9,542**
1995-96	175/178	3,474	3,161	2,855	289	**9,542**
1994-95	174/177	3,600	3,000	2,771	310	**9,681**
1993-94	173/176	3,455	2,846	2,573	282	**9,156**
1992-93	173/176	3,303	2,603	2,465	267	**8,638**
1991-92	173/176	3,169	2,556	2,196	228	**8,149**
1990-91	172/175	2,982	2,222	2,023	205	**7,432**
1989-90	172/175	2,628	2,128	1,816	219	**6,791**
1988-89	171/174	2,463	1,913	1,728	217	**6,321**
1987-88	171/175	2,339	1,761	1,690	238	**6,028**
1986-87	171/175	2,159	1,800	1,735	200	**5,894**
1985-86	172/175	1,800	1,838	1,791	240	**6,052**
1984-85	171/174	1,735	1,878	1,686	177	**5,955**
1983-84	170/173	1,735	1,813	1,711	196	**5,967**
1982-83	169/172	2,217	1,827	1,623	185	**5,852**
1981-82	169/172	2,238	1,793	1,596	162	**5,789**
1980-81	168/171	2,144	1,684	1,531	146	**5,506**
1979-80	166/169	2,002	1,647	1,438	170	**5,257**
1978-79	164/167	2,021	1,565	1,572	192	**5,350**
1977-78	160/163	1,945	1,648	1,508	203	**5,304**
1976-77	160/163	2,128	1,654	1,488	233	**5,303**
1975-76	160/163	2,045	1,511	1,452	119	**5,127**
1974-75	154/157	1,934	1,587	1,329	145	**4,995**
1973-74	147/151	2,066	1,443	1,207	101	**4,817**
1972-73	144/149	1,919	1,324	1,106	74	**4,423**
1971-72	142/147	1,781	1,147	761	55	**3,744**

Mexican American Enrollment

Academic Year	No. of Schools Reporting	1st Year	2nd Year	3rd Year	4th Year	Total
1997-98	175/178	859	766	777	50	**2,452**
1996-97	176/179	861	768	751	49	**2,429**
1995-96	175/178	896	820	743	36	**2,495**
1994-95	174/177	902	739	719	42	**2,402**
1993-94	173/176	838	698	639	28	**2,203**
1992-93	173/176	807	744	683	24	**2,258**
1991-92	173/176	770	644	584	29	**2,027**
1990-91	172/175	768	624	527	31	**1,950**
1989-90	172/175	640	531	469	23	**1,663**
1988-89	171/174	656	510	458	33	**1,657**
1987-88	171/175	610	528	472	34	**1,644**
1986-87	171/176	564	486	431	31	**1,512**
1985-86	172/175	609	503	500	23	**1,635**
1984-85	171/174	607	538	486	30	**1,661**
1983-84	170/173	642	558	511	33	**1,744**
1982-83	169/172	628	573	491	47	**1,739**
1981-82	169/172	665	490	542	59	**1,756**
1980-81	168/171	659	501	498	32	**1,690**
1979-80	166/169	642	517	471	40	**1,670**
1978-79	164/167	606	471	510	62	**1,649**
1977-78	160/163	588	519	421	36	**1,564**
1976-77	160/163	591	465	463	69	**1,588**
1975-76	160/163	535	480	407	21	**1,443**
1974-75	154/157	568	439	338	17	**1,362**
1973-74	147/151	539	386	271	63	**1,259**
1972-73	144/149	480	337	238	17	**1,072**
1972-72	142/147	440	262	170	11	**883**

Puerto Rican Enrollment

Academic Year	No. of Schools Reporting	1st Year	2nd Year	3rd Year	4th Year	Total
1997-98	175/178	224	198	188	26	**636**
1996-97	176/179	206	213	238	29	**686**
1995-96	175/178	236	238	214	17	**705**
1994-95	174/177	263	244	186	25	**718**
1993-94	173/176	275	195	177	17	**664**
1992-93	173/176	202	193	177	15	**587**
1991-92	173/176	208	177	140	14	**539**
1990-91	172/175	183	153	158	12	**506**
1989-90	172/175	171	150	156	6	**483**
1988-89	171/174	168	156	141	13	**478**
1987-88	171/175	178	134	140	7	**459**
1986-87	171/175	183	152	130	6	**471**
1985-86	172/175	171	126	108	7	**412**
1984-85	171/174	132	137	123	15	**407**
1983-84	170/173	166	152	120	12	**450**
1982-83	169/172	171	130	105	12	**418**
1981-82	169/172	149	120	116	11	**396**
1980-81	168-171	158	135	141	8	**442**
1979-80	166/169	172	153	107	9	**441**
1978-79	164/167	184	126	104	9	**423**
1977-78	160/163	138	92	106	14	**350**
1976-77	160/163	118	95	105	17	**335**
1975-76	160/163	113	121	96	3	**333**
1974-75	154/157	119	91	59	3	**272**
1973-74	147/151	96	47	32	5	**180**
1972-73	144/149	73	40	25	5	**143**
1971-72	142/147	49	25	18	2	**94**

Other Hispanic American Enrollment

Academic Year	No. of Schools Reporting	1st Year	2nd Year	3rd Year	4th Year	Total
1997-98	175/178	1,367	1,213	1,104	97	**3,781**
1996-97	176/179	1,346	1,167	1,199	88	**3,880**
1995-96	175/178	1,304	1,273	1,079	114	**3,770**
1994-95	174/177	1,367	1,120	1,071	94	**3,652**
1993-94	173/176	1,259	1,124	988	74	**3,445**
1992-93	173/176	1,210	966	883	65	**3,124**
1991-92	173/176	1,123	938	853	61	**2.975**
1990-91	172/175	1,023	798	705	56	**2,582**
1989-90	172/175	1,019	783	734	51	**2,587**
1988-89	171/174	819	710	610	68	**2,207**
1987-88	171/175	750	623	543	55	**1,971**
1986-87	171/175	727	561	554	40	**1,882**
1985-86	172/175	589	516	477	50	**1,632**
1984-85	171/174	537	427	426	49	**1,439**
1983-84	170/173	458	432	370	42	**1,302**
1982-83	169/172	520	367	326	36	**1,249**
1981-82	169/172	452	307	254	24	**1,037**
1980-81	168/171	359	272	226	25	**882**
1979-80	166/169	261	236	187	22	**706**
1978-79	164/167	288	218	194	16	**716**
1977-78	160/163	257	193	142	25	**617**
1976-77	160/163	244	152	132	10	**538**
1975-76	160/163	170	146	81	9	**406**
1974-75	154/157	187	101	94	10	**392**
1973-74	147/151	128	70	59	4	**261**
1972-73	144/149	96	72	60	3	**231**
1971-72	142/147	79	62	35	3	**179**

Chapter Fifteen

Post J.D. Programs

Standard 307 of the ABA Standards for Approval of Law Schools states that a law school may not establish a degree in addition to its J.D. degree program without obtaining the Council's acquiescence. A law school may not establish a degree program in addition to its J.D. degree program unless it is fully approved, and the quality of its J.D. degree program exceeds the requirements of the Standards. The additional degree program may not detract from a law school's ability to maintain a sound J.D. degree program.

This book contains information concerning law schools that were operating as of October 1, 1997 and were approved by the ABA to confer the first degree in law. The approval status of an individual law school can change. Therefore, if you would like to confirm whether an individual law school is approved by the ABA at a specific time after October 1, you should contact the ABA directly. You can also access this information on the Section of Legal Education and Admissions to the Bar's website: http://www.abanet.org/legaled. For example, on February 3, 1998, just prior to the publication of this book, the ABA House of Delegates granted provisional approval to Chapman University School of Law and the University of the District of Columbia School of Law. In addition the Council of the Section acquiesced in advance degree programs from the following schools after October 1, 1997: American University School of Law, California Western School of Law, Golden Gate University School of Law, John Marshall Law School, University of Missouri-Columbia School of Law, University of Chicago School of Law, and Yeshiva University School of Law. For updates or corrections to this book, please visit the Section's website: http://www.abanet.org/legaled.

Alabama, University of
Taxation, LL.M.
Comparative Law, M.C.L.
General, LL.M

American University
International legal Studies, LL.M.

Arizona, University of
International Trade Law, LL.M.

Arkansas, Fayetteville
Agriculture Law, LL.M.

Baltimore, University of
Taxation, LL.M.

Boston University
Taxation, LL.M.
Banking, LL.M.
American Law, LL.M.

Brigham Young University
Comparative Law For Foreign Lawyers, LL.M.

California-Berkeley, Univ. of
General, LL.M.
General, J.S.D.

California-Davis, University of
United States Law (For Foreign Lawyers), LL.M.

California-Los Angeles, Univ. of
As Approved, LL.M. (For Non-US Students)

Capital University
Taxation, LL.M.
Business and Taxation, LL.M.

Case Western Reserve University
Taxation, LL.M.
U.S. Legal Studies, LL.M.

Chicago, University of
General, LL.M.
General, M.COMP
General, D.COMP
General, J.S.D.

Cleveland State University
General, LL.M.

Columbia University
General, LL.M.
General, J.S.D.

Connecticut, University of
U.S. Legal Studies, LL.M.

Cornell University
General, LL.M.
General, J.S.D.

Denver, University of
Taxation, LL.M.
Natural Resources, LL.M.
Amer. and Comp. Law, LL.M.

DePaul University
Taxation, LL.M.
Health Law, LL.M.

Duke University
Research, S.J.D.
U.S. Law For Int. Students, LL.M.

Emory University
General, LL.M.
Taxation, LL.M.
Litigation, LL.M.

Florida, University of
Taxation, LL.M.
Comparative Law, LL.M.

Fordham University
Banking Corp. and Finance Law, LL.M.
Int. Bus. and Trade Law, LL.M.

Franklin Pierce Law Center
Intellectual Property, LL.M.

George Washington University
General, LL.M.
Environmental Law, LL.M.
Govt. Procurement Law, LL.M.
Int. and Comparative law, LL.M.
Intellectual Property, LL.M.
Various, S.J.D.
Litigation & Dispute Resolution, LL.M.

Georgetown University
As Approved, S.J.D.
General, LL.M.
Advocacy, LL.M.
Int. and Comparative Law, LL.M.
Labor & Employment, LL.M.
Securities and Fin. Reg., LL.M.
Taxation, LL.M.
Common Law Studies, LL.M.

Georgia, University of
General, LL.M.

Golden Gate University
Taxation, LL.M.
International Legal Studies, LL.M.
International Legal Studies, S.J.D.

Hamline University
Foreign Lawyers, LL.M.

Harvard University
General, LL.M.
General, S.J.D.

Houston, University of
Int. Economic Law, LL.M.
Energy Environment and Natural Resources, LL.M.
Tax Law, LL.M.
Foreign Lawyer Program, LL.M.

Howard University
American Jurisprudence, LL.M.

Illinois Institute of Technology
Taxation, LL.M.
Int. and Comparative Law, LL.M.
Financial Services Law, LL.M.

Illinois, University of
General, J.S.D.
General, LL.M.

Indiana University - Bloomington
As Approved, LL.M.
Comparative Law, M.C.L.
Research, S.J.D.

Iowa, University of
Int. and Comparative Law, LL.M.

John Marshall Law School
Taxation, LL.M.
Intellectual Property, LL.M.
Comparative Legal Studies, LL.M.
Real Estate, LL.M.

Judge Advocate General's
Military Law, LL.M.

Lewis And Clark College
Environmental/ Natural Resources, LL.M.

Louisiana State University
As Approved, LL.M.
As Approved, M.C.L.

Loyola University-Chicago
Health Law, LL.M.
Child Law, LL.M.
Health Law, S.J.D.
Health Law, M.J.
Child Law, M.J.

McGeorge School of Law
Taxation, LL.M.
Business and Taxation, LL.M.
Transnational Bus. Practice, LL.M.

Miami, University of
Taxation, LL.M.
Estate Planning, LL.M.
Ocean and Coastal Law, LL.M.
International Law, LL.M.
Inter-American Law, LL.M.
Real Property & Land Dev., LL.M.
Comparative Law, LL.M.
General (For Foreign Law Graduates), LL.M.

Michigan, University of
As Approved, M.C.L.
As Approved, LL.M.
As Approved, S.J.D.

Minnesota, University of
American Law (For Foreign Lawyers), LL.M.

Missouri-Kansas City, Univ. of
General, LL.M.
Taxation, LL.M.
Urban Affairs, LL.M.

New York University
As Approved, J.S.D.
Corporate Law, LL.M.
International Legal Studies, LL.M.
Taxation, LL.M.
Trade Regulation, LL.M.
General Studies, LL.M.
International Taxation, LL.M.
Comp. Jurisprudence, M.C.J.
Labor Law, LL.M.

Northwestern University
Research, S.J.D.
Research, LL.M.

Notre Dame, University of
Int. and Comparative Law, LL.M.
Int. Human Rights, LL.M.
International Human Rights, J.S.D.

Pace University
Environmental Law, LL.M.
Environmental Law, S.J.D.

Pennsylvania, University of
As Approved, LL.CM.
As Approved, LL.M.
As Approved, S.J.D.

Pennsylvania State University
Comparative Law, LL.M.

Pepperdine University
Dispute Resolution-ADR, M.D.R.

Pittsburgh, University of
Int. and Comparative Law, LL.M.

Samford University
Comparative Law, M.C.L.

San Diego, University of
Taxation, LL.M.
General, LL.M.
Comparative Law, LL.M.

San Francisco, University of
International Transactions and Comparative Law, LL.M.

Seton Hall University
Health Law, LL.M.

Southern Methodist University
General, LL.M.
Comparative and Int. Law, LL.M.
Doctor of Science of Law, S.J.D.
Taxation, LL.M.

St. Louis University
Health law, LL.M.
American Law For Foreign Lawyers, LL.M.

St. Mary's University
Int. and Comparative Law, LL.M.
American Legal Studies, LL.M.

Stanford University
As Approved, J.S.D.
As Approved, J.S.M.

Temple University
General, LL.M.
Taxation, LL.M.
American Common Law Legal System & Comp. Law, LL.M.
Law & Humanities, Clinical Legal, LL.M.

Texas, University Of
General, LL.M.

Touro College
American Legal Studies, LL.M.

Tulane University
General, LL.M.
Admiralty, LL.M.
Energy & Environment, LL.M.
Comparative Law, M.C.L.
Comparative Law & Latin American Studies, M.C.L.
General, S.J.D.

Utah, University of
Environmental and Natural Resources, LL.M.

Vermont Law School
Environmental Law and Policy, M.S.E.L.

Villanova University
Taxation, LL.M.

Virginia, University of
General, LL.M.
General, S.J.D.
Judicial Process, LL.M.

Wake Forest University
American Law, LL.M.

Washington University
Taxation, LL.M.
Research, J.S.D.
Urban Studies, LL.M.
Master of Laws For Int., LL.M.

Washington, University of
Asian & Comparative Law, LL.M.
Law & Marine Affairs, LL.M.
Int. Environmental Law, LL.M.
Sustainable Int. Dev., LL.M.
Taxation, LL.M.
Asian & Comparative Law, Ph.D.

Wayne State University
General, LL.M.
Corporate and Finance, LL.M.
Labor Law, LL.M.
Taxation, LL.M.

Widener University
Corporate Law & Finance, LL.M.
Health Law, LL.M.

William and Mary, College of
American Legal System, LL.M.

William Mitchell
Taxation, LL.M.

Wisconsin, University of
As Approved, LL.M.
As Approved, S.J.D.
As Approved, M.L.I.

Yale University
General, LL.M.
General, J.S.D.

Admiralty
Tulane University, LL.M.

Agriculture Law
University of Arkansas - Fayetteville, LL.M

American Jurisprudence
Howard University, M.C.J.

American Legal System/ American Legal Studies
Touro College, LL.M
St. Mary's University, LL.M
William and Mary, College of, LL.M

American Law/ American & Comparative Law
Boston University, LL.M
Denver, University of, LL.M
Minnesota, University of, LL.M
Temple University (Common), LL.M

As Approved
Georgetown University, S.J.D.
Indiana University - Bloomington, LL.M.
Louisiana State University, LL.M
Louisiana State University, M.C.L.
Michigan, University of, LL.M
Michigan, University of, M.C.L.
Michigan, University of, S.J.D.
New York University, J.S.D.
Pennsylvania, University of, LL.M
Pennsylvania, University of, M.C.L.
Pennsylvania, University of, S.J.D.
Southern Methodist University, S.J.D.
Stanford University, J.S.D.
Stanford University, J.S.M.
Wisconsin, University of, LL.M
Wisconsin, University of, S.J.D.
Wisconsin, University of, M.L.I.

Asian and Comparative Law
Washington, University of, LL.M
Washington, University of, Ph.D.

Banking, Corporate, and Finance Law/ Financial Services
Fordham University, LL.M
IIT- Chicago Kent, LL.M

Banking Law Studies
Boston University, LL.M

Business and Taxation
McGeorge - University of the Pacific, LL.M
Capital University, LL.M

Child Law
Loyola - Chicago, LL.M
Loyola - Chicago, M.J.

Clinical Legal Education
Temple University, LL.M

Comparative Law/ Comparative Legal Studies/ Comparative Jurisprudence
Alabama, University of, M.C.L.
Florida, University of, LL.M
Indiana University - Bloomington, M.C.L.
John Marshall, LL.M
Miami, University of, LL.M
New York University, M.C.J.
Pennsylvania State University, LL.M.
Samford, M.C.L.
San Diego, University of, M.C.L.
Tulane University, M.C.L.

Corporate Law and Finance/ Corporate & Finance Law
New York University, LL.M
Wayne State University, LL.M
Widener University, LL.M

Energy, Environment/ Natural Resources
Denver, University of, LL.M
George Washington University, LL.M
Houston, University of, LL.M
Lewis and Clark, LL.M
Pace University, LL.M
Pace University, S.J.D.
Tulane University, LL.M
Utah, University of, LL.M
Vermont, MSEL

Estate Planning
Miami, University of, LL.M

General
Alabama, University of, LL.M
California - Berkeley, University of , LL.M
California - Berkeley, University of , J.S.D.
Chicago, University of, D.C.L.
Chicago,University of, LL.M
Chicago,University of, M.C.L.
Chicago,University of, S.J.D.
Cleveland State University, LL.M
Columbia University, LL.M
Columbia University, J.S.D.
Cornell University, LL.M.
Cornell University, S.J.D.
Emory University, LL.M
Georgetown University, LL.M
George Washington University, LL.M
Georgia, University of, LL.M
Illinois, University of, LL.M
Illinois, University of, J.S.D.
Missouri - Kansas City, University of, LL.M
New York University, LL.M
San Diego, University of, LL.M
Southern Methodist, LL.M
Temple University, LL.M.
Texas, University of, LL.M.
Tulane University, LL.M.
Tulane University, S.J.D.
Virginia, University of, LL.M.
Virginia, University of, S.J.D.
Wayne State University, LL.M.
Yale University, LL.M.
Yale University, J.S.D.

Health Law
DePaul University, LL.M
Houston, University of, LL.M.
Loyola - Chicago, M.J.
Loyola - Chicago, LL.M.
Loyola - Chicago S.J.D.
Saint Louis University, LL.M.
Seton Hall, LL.M.
Widener University, LL.M.

Intellectual Property
Franklin Pierce, LL.M.
George Washington University, LL.M.
Houston, University of, LL.M.
John Marshall, LL.M.

International/International and Comparative Law/Comparative and International Law/ International Legal Studies
American University, LL.M.
Georgetown University, LL.M.
George Washington University, LL.M.
Golden Gate, LL.M.
Golden Gate, S.J.D.
IIT - Chicago Kent, LL.M.
Iowa, University of, LL.M.
Miami, University of, LL.M.

New York University, LL.M.
Notre Dame, University of, LL.M.
Pittsburgh, University of, LL.M.
San Diego, University of, LL.M.
Southern Methodist University, LL.M.
St. Mary's, LL.M.

International Business and Trade Law/ Transnational Business Practice
Arizona, University of, LL.M.
Fordham University, LL.M.
McGeorge - University of the Pacific, LL.M.
San Francisco, University of, LL.M.

International Economic Law
Houston, University of, LL.M.

International Environmental Law
Washington, University of, LL.M.

International Human Rights
Notre Dame, University of, LL.M.
Notre Dame, University of, J.S.D.

Inter-American
Miami, University of, LL.M.

Judicial Process
Virginia, University of, LL.M.

Labor Law/Employment Law
Georgetown University, LL.M.
New York University, LL.M.
Wayne State University, LL.M.

Law and Marine Affairs
Washington, University of, LL.M.

Legal Studies
Connecticut, University of , LL.M.

Litigation/Trial Advocacy/Advocacy
Emory University, LL.M.
Georgetown University, LL.M. (clinical Fellows)
George Washington University, LL.M..

Military Law
Judge Advocate General's, LL.M..

Ocean and Coastal Law
Miami, University of, LL.M.

Real Estate
John Marshall, LL.M.

Real Property Land Development & Finance Law
Miami, University of, LL.M.

Research
Duke University, S.J.D.
Indiana University-Bloomington, S.J.D.
Northwestern University, LL.M.
Northwestern University, S.J.D.
Washington University, J.S.D.

Securities Regulation
Georgetown University, LL.M.

Sustainable International Development
Washington, University of, LL.M.

Taxation
Alabama, University of, LL.M.
Baltimore, University of, LL.M
Boston University, LL.M.
Case Western Reserve, LL.M.
Capital University, LL.M.
Denver, University of, LL.M.
DePaul University, LL.M.
Emory University, LL.M.
Florida, University of, LL.M.
Georgetown University, LL.M.
Golden Gate University, LL.M.
Houston, University of, LL.M.
IIT - Chicago Kent, LL.M.
John Marshall, LL.M.
McGeorge - University of the Pacific, LL.M.
Miami, University of, LL.M.
Missouri - Kansas City, University of, LL.M.
New York University, LL.M.
San Diego, University of, LL.M.
Southern Methodist University, LL.M.
Temple University, LL.M.
Villanova University, LL.M.
Washington University, LL.M.
Washington, University of, LL.M.
Wayne State University, LL.M.
William Mitchell, LL.M.

Trade Regulation
New York University, LL.M.

Urban Affairs
Missouri - Kansas City, University of, LL.M.

Urban Studies
Washington University, LL.M.

Programs for Foreign lawyers or international students, include. "U.S. Comparative Law"; "U.S. Legal Studies"
Brigham Young University, LL.M.
California - Davis, University of, LL.M.
California - Los Angeles, University of, LL.M.
Case Western Reserve, LL.M.
Duke University, LL.M.
Georgetown University, LL.M.
Hamline, LL.M.
Houston, University of, LL.M..
Miami, University of, LL.M.
Saint Louis University, LL.M.

GRADUATE DEGREES DEFINED

SECTION OF LEGAL EDUCATION AND ADMISSIONS TO THE BAR • ESTABLISHED 1893 • ABA

DEGREE	DEFINITION
LL.M.	Master of Laws
S.J.D.	Doctor of Juridical Science
J.S.D.	Doctor of the Science of Law
J.S.D.	Doctor of Jurisprudence
J.S.D.	Doctor of Juridical Science
J.S.M.	Master of the Science of Law
D.C.L.	Doctor of Comparative Law
M.C.L.	Master of Comparative Law
LL.C.M.	Master of Comparative Law
M.C.J.	Master of Comparative Jurisprudence
M.L.S.	Master of Library Science
M.A.L.S.	Master of American Legal Studies
M.L.I.	Master of Arts or of Science in Legal Institutions

Chapter Sixteen

Selected Statements

(What follows are several statements as adopted by the Council of the Section of Legal Education and Admissions to the Bar of the American Bar Association. To order a copy of the ABA Standards for Approval of Law Schools call (800) 285-2221. The cost is $12.00 plus shipping and handling. The information is also available on the Section's website at http://www.abanet.org/legaled)

Standard 101. BASIC REQUIREMENTS FOR APPROVAL.
A law school approved by the Association or seeking approval by the Association shall demonstrate that its program is consistent with sound legal education principles. It does so by establishing that it is being operated in compliance with the Standards.

Standard 211. EQUAL OPPORTUNITY EFFORT.
Consistent with sound legal education policy and the Standards, a law school shall demonstrate, or have carried out and maintained, by concrete action, a commitment to providing full opportunities for the study of law and entry into the profession by qualified members of groups, notably racial and ethnic minorities, which have been victims of discrimination in various forms. This commitment typically includes a special concern for determining the potential of these applicants through the admission process, special recruitment efforts, and a program that assists in meeting the unusual financial needs of many of these students, but a law school is not obligated to apply standards for the award of financial assistance different from those applied to other students.

Standard 212. INDIVIDUALS WITH DISABILITIES.
A law school may not discriminate against individuals with disabilities in its program of legal education. A law school shall provide full opportunities for the study of law and entry into the profession by qualified disabled individuals. A law school may not discriminate on the basis of disability in the hiring, promotion, and retention of otherwise qualified faculty and staff.

Standard 213. CAREER SERVICES.
A law school should provide adequate staff, space, and resources, in view of the size and program of the school, to maintain an active career counseling service to assist its students and graduates to make sound career choices and obtain employment.

Standard 301. OBJECTIVES.
(a) A law school shall maintain an educational program that is designed to qualify its graduates for admission to the bar and to prepare them to participate effectively in the legal profession.

(b) The educational program of a law school shall be designed to prepare the students to deal with both current and anticipated legal problems.

(c) A law school may offer an educational program designed to emphasize certain aspects of the law or the legal profession.

Standard 302. CURRICULUM.
(a) A law school shall offer to all students:

(1) instruction in those subjects generally regarded as the core of the law school curriculum;

(2) an educational program designed to provide its graduates with basic competence in legal analysis and reasoning, legal research, problem solving, and oral and written communication;

(3) at least one rigorous writing experience; and

(4) adequate opportunities for instruction in professional skills.

(b) A law school shall require of all students in the J.D. degree program instruction in the history, goals, structure, duties, values, and responsibilities of the legal profession and its members, including instruction in the Model Rules of Professional Conduct of the American Bar Association. A law school should involve members of the bench and bar in this instruction.

(c) The educational program of a law school shall provide students with adequate opportunities for study in seminars or by directed research and in small classes.
(d) A law school shall offer live-client or other real-life practice experiences. This might be accomplished through clinics or externships. A law school need not offer this experience to all students.

(e) A law school should encourage its students to participate in pro bono activities and provide opportunities for them to do so.

(f) A law school may offer a bar examination preparation course, but may not grant credit for the course or require it as a condition for graduation.

Standard 303. SCHOLASTIC ACHIEVEMENT; EVALUATION.
(a) A law school shall have and adhere to sound standards of scholastic achievement, including clearly defined standards for good standing, advancement, and graduation.

(b) The scholastic achievements of students shall be evaluated from the beginning of the students' studies.

(c) A law school shall not continue the enrollment of a student whose inability to do satisfactory work is sufficiently manifest so that the student's continuation in school would inculcate false hopes, constitute economic exploitation, or detrimentally affect the education of other students.

Standard 306. PARTICIPATION IN STUDIES OR ACTIVITIES IN A FOREIGN COUNTRY.
A law school may grant credit for student participation in studies or activities in a foreign country only if the studies or activities are approved in accordance with the Rules, Criteria, and Procedures as adopted by the Council.

Standard 401. QUALIFICATIONS.
(a) A law school shall have a faculty that possesses a high degree of competence, as demonstrated by its education, classroom teaching ability, experience in teaching or practice, and scholarly research and writing.

(b) A law school shall take reasonable steps to ensure the teaching effectiveness of its faculty.

Standard 501. ADMISSIONS.
(a) A law school's admission policies shall be consistent with the objectives of its educational program and the resources available for implementing those objectives.

(b) A law school shall not admit applicants who do not appear capable of satisfactorily completing its educational program and being admitted to the bar.

Interpretation 501-1:
A law school may not permit financial considerations detrimentally to affect its admission and retention policies and their administration. A law school may face a conflict of interest whenever the exercise of sound judgment in the application of admission policies or academic standards and retention policies might reduce enrollment below the level necessary to support the program.

Standard 502. EDUCATIONAL REQUIREMENTS.
(a) A law school shall require for admission to its J.D. degree program a bachelor's degree, or successful completion of three-fourths of the work acceptable for a bachelor's degree, from an institution that is accredited by a regional accrediting agency recognized by the Department of Education.

(b) In an extraordinary case, a law school may admit to its J.D. degree program an applicant who does not possess the educational requirements of subsection (a) if the applicant's experience, ability, and other characteristics clearly show an aptitude for the study of law. The admitting officer shall sign and place in the admittee's file a statement of the considerations that led to the decision to admit the applicant.

Interpretation 502-1:
Before an admitted student registers, or within a reasonable time thereafter, a law school shall have on file the student's official transcript showing receipt of a bachelors degree, if any, and all academic work undertaken. "Official transcript" means a transcript certified by the issuing school to the admitting school or delivered to the admitting school in a sealed envelope with seal intact. A copy supplied by the Law School Data Assembly Service is not an official transcript, even though it is adequate for preliminary determination of admission.

Standard 503. ADMISSION TEST.
A law school shall require all applicants to take an acceptable test for the purpose of assessing the applicants' capability of satisfactorily completing its education program. A law school that is not using the Law School Admission Test sponsored by the Law School Admission Council shall establish that it is using an acceptable test.

Standard 504. CHARACTER AND FITNESS.
A law school shall advise each applicant to secure information regarding the character and other qualifications for admission to the bar in the state in which the applicant intends to practice. The law school may, to the extent it deems appropriate, adopt such tests, questionnaires, or required references as the proper admission authorities may find useful and relevant, in determining the character and fitness of the applicants to the law school. If a law school considers an applicant's character qualifications, it shall exercise care that the consideration is not used as a reason to deny admission to a qualified applicant because of political, social, or economic views which might be considered unorthodox.

Standard 505. PREVIOUSLY DISQUALIFIED APPLICANT.
A law school may admit or readmit a student who has been previously disqualified for academic reasons upon an affirmative showing that the student possesses the requisite ability and that the prior disqualification does not indicate a lack of capacity to complete the course of study at the admitting school. In the case of admission to a law school other than the disqualifying school, this showing shall be made either by a letter from the disqualifying school, or if two or more years have elapsed since that disqualification, by the nature of interim work, activity, or studies indicating a stronger potential for law study. In each case, the admitting officer shall sign and place in the admittee's file a statement of the considerations that led to the decision to admit or readmit the applicant.

Interpretation 505-1:
The two year period begins on the date of the decision to disqualify the student for academic reasons. A review, appeal, or request for reconsideration of that decision is in the nature of post-decision remedies.

Interpretation 505-2:
A student who enrolled in a pre-admission program but was not granted admission is not a student who was disqualified for academic reasons under this Standard.

Standard 506. APPLICANTS FROM STATE-ACCREDITED LAW SCHOOLS.
(a) A law school may admit a student with advanced standing and allow credit for studies at a state-accredited law school if:

(1) the studies were "in residence" as provided in Standard 304, or qualify for credit under Standard 305; and

(2) the content of the studies was such that credit therefor would have been granted towards satisfaction of degree requirements at the admitting school.

(b) Advanced standing and credit hours granted for study at a state-accredited law school may not exceed one-third of the total required by an admitting school for its J.D. degree.

Standard 507. APPLICANTS FROM FOREIGN LAW SCHOOLS.
(a) A law school may admit a student with advanced standing and allow credit for studies at a law school outside the United States if:

(1) the studies were "in residence" as provided in Standard 304, or qualify for credit under Standard 305;

(2) the content of the studies was such that credit therefor would have been granted towards satisfaction of degree requirements at the admitting school; and

(3) the admitting school is satisfied that the quality of the educational program at the foreign law school was at least equal to that required by an approved school.

(b) Advanced standing and credit hours granted for foreign study may not exceed one-third of the total required by an admitting school for its J.D. degree.

Interpretation 507-1:
This Standard applies only to graduates of foreign law schools or students enrolled in a first degree granting law program in a foreign educational institution.

Standard 508. ENROLLMENT OF NON-DEGREE CANDIDATES.
Without requiring compliance with its admission standards and procedures, a law school may enroll individuals in a particular course or limited number of courses, as auditors, non-degree candidates, or candidates for a degree other than a law degree, provided that such enrollment does not adversely affect the quality of the course or the law school program.

Standard 509. BASIC CONSUMER INFORMATION.
A law school shall publish basic consumer information. The information shall be published in a fair and accurate manner reflective of actual practice.

Interpretation 509-1:
The following categories of consumer information are considered basic:

(1) admission data;

(2) tuition, fees, living costs, financial aid, and refunds;

(3) enrollment data and graduation rates;

(4) composition and number of faculty and administrators;

(5) curricular offerings;

(6) library resources;

(7) physical facilities; and

(8) placement rates and bar passage data.

Interpretation 509-2:
To comply with its obligation to publish basic consumer information under the first sentence of this Standard, a law school may either provide the information to a publication designated by the Council or publish the information in its own publication. If the school chooses to meet this obligation through its own publication, the basic consumer information shall be published in a manner comparable to that used in the Council-designated publication, and the school shall provide the publication to all of its applicants.

Interpretation 509-3:
All law schools shall have and make publicly available a student tuition and fee refund policy. This policy shall contain a complete statement of all student tuition and fees and a schedule for the refund of student tuition and fees.

Standard 510. STUDENT LOAN PROGRAMS.
A law school shall take reasonable steps to minimize student loan defaults, including provision of debt counseling at both the inception of a student's loan obligations and prior to graduation.

Interpretation 510-1:
The student loan default rates of a law school's graduates, including any results of financial or compliance audits and reviews, shall be considered in assessing the extent to which a law school complies with this Standard.

Interpretation 510-2:
The law school's obligation shall be satisfied if the university, of which the law school is a part, provides to law students the reasonable steps described in this Standard.

Standard 601. GENERAL PROVISIONS.
(a) A law school shall maintain a law library that is an active and responsive force in the educational life of the law school. A law library's effective support of the school's teaching, research and service programs requires a direct, continuing, and informed relationship with the faculty, students, and administration of the law school.

(b) A law library shall have sufficient financial resources to support the law school's teaching, research, and service programs. These resources shall be supplied on a consistent basis.

Standard 701. GENERAL REQUIREMENTS.
A law school shall have physical facilities and technological capacities that are adequate both for its current program of legal education and for growth anticipated in the immediate future.

Standard 703. RESEARCH AND STUDY SPACE.
A law school shall provide, on site, sufficient quiet study and research seating for its students and faculty. A law school should provide suitable group study rooms.

Rule 26. Release of Information Concerning Applications for Provisional or Full Approval of Law Schools.
In the case of schools seeking provisional or full approval, the staff persons of the American Bar Association may state:

(a) Whether or not a specific school has submitted an application to the American Bar Association for provisional approval.

(b) The procedural steps for consideration of an application, including:

(i) consideration of an application by the Accreditation Committee;

(ii) action by the Council upon the Accreditation Committee's recommendation and an explanation that action of the Council may not follow that of the recommendation made by the Accreditation Committee; and

(iii) action by the House of Delegates.

(c) After notification of the Accreditation Committee's action or the Council action, as the case may be, to the school, the staff may release the status of the school to the public, with the explanation of the procedural steps for consideration of an application as outlined in subparagraph (b) of this Rule.

Rule 28. Publication of List of Approved and Unapproved Schools.
The Council shall annually publish a complete list of all approved law schools and as many unapproved law schools as are known to the Consultant. The list shall be published annually in *ABA Approved Law Schools: Statistical Information on American Bar Association Approved Law Schools.* (This book.)

Statement of Good Practice on Impartiality and Propriety in the Process of Law School Accreditation
(A) Those who have significant responsibility in the process leading to accreditation of law schools serve a vital and quasi-judicial function in the legal system of the United States. It is important to the fair and effective functioning of the system of law school accreditation and to the maintenance of public and professional respect for that system that those who act in it act impartially and avoid even the appearance of impropriety.

(B) One who has significant responsibility in this system or who has had significant responsibility in this system within a period of two years past, as enumerated in paragraph "D" below should not serve as a consultant to a law school in any matter relating to:

(1) accreditation by the American Bar Association;

(2) membership in the Association of American Law Schools; or

(3) re-evaluation and continuation of American Bar Association accreditation or membership in the Association of American Law Schools.

(C) This restriction applies to service as consultant whether or not that service is for compensation. It does not apply to informal advice which an advisor renders (1) without fee; (2) informally and (3) which he or she discloses fully to the other members of the accreditation or membership body on which he or she serves or has served; nor does it apply to the routine or official advice and assistance which is rendered by members of a site evaluation team or hearing commission, by the Consultant on Legal Education to the American Bar Association, by the Executive Director of the Association of American Law Schools, or by persons acting on behalf of the Consultant or Executive Director, (4) or by a person acting in the normal course of his or her employment.

(D) This restriction applies to:

(1) members of the Accreditation Committee of the Council on Legal Education and Admissions to the Bar of the American Bar Association;

(2) the President, other Officers, members of the Board of Governors, and members of the Council of the Section of Legal Education and Admissions to the Bar of the American Bar Association;

(3) members of the Accreditation and Academic Freedom Committees of the Association of American Law Schools;

(4) the President and members of the Executive Committee of the Association of American Law Schools;

(5) members of the professional staff of the American Bar Association or the Association of American Law Schools, except as provided in paragraph "C" above;

(6) a member of a site evaluation team or hearing commission for either Association accepting appointment as a consultant to a law school that he or she has evaluated or conducted hearings on, in behalf of either Association within two years after the site evaluation or while either Association still has under consideration matters developed by the site evaluation, whichever is longer;

(7) the Executive Director of the Association of American Law Schools or other person acting on behalf of the Association of American Law Schools may not acquiesce in the appointment as consultant on readiness of any person who by this Statement should not accept appointment as a school's consultant.

(E) Service as a consultant for a law school does not disqualify a person from any of the offices or committees in paragraph "D." However, the officer or committee member should excuse himself or herself from participation in discussion, formal or informal, of the affairs of a school which he or she has served as consultant or employee and from taking part in any vote with respect to its status.

(F) A person who has served as a consultant or employee of a law school within two years prior to assuming a significant responsibility in the accreditation process should decline to participate in the determination of the accreditation status of the school with which he or she previously served.

(G) The Consultant on Legal Education to the American Bar Association, Executive Director of the Association of American Law Schools or either of them if they are acting cooperatively shall bring this regulation to the attention of persons who are nominated for or appointed to any of the positions enumerated in paragraph "D" above and to all persons who are holding these positions or who have held them within two years past, at the time the regulation becomes effective.

Adopted by the Council of the Section of Legal Education and Admissions to the Bar—December 10, 1977.

Adopted by the AALS Executive Committee—December 27, 1977.

Pass/Fail Grading

At its August, 1970 meeting the Council of the Section of Legal Education and Admissions to the Bar decided to endorse the following statement issued earlier by the Law School Admission Council on the impact of pass/fail grading by undergraduate colleges upon the law school admission process. This statement has also been endorsed by the Executive Committee of the Association of American Law Schools.

The adoption by an increasing number of colleges and universities of pass/fail or similar grading systems for some or all of their students' work has implications for the law school admissions process. When a student with a transcript bearing such grades seeks to enter law school, law school admissions committees will be deprived of data that have served them well in the past in making the admissions decision. In the belief that college and university faculties and administrations who are considering conversion of a conventional grading system to a pass/fail or some variant system may be interested in the possible effect of such grading systems upon their graduates who seek admission to law school, the Law School Admission Council issues this statement.

The Law School Admission Test (LSAT) was developed more than twenty years ago in response to an expressed need of law schools for additional data upon which to base their admissions decisions. Validity studies conducted over the years demonstrate that the LSAT score contributes significantly to the prediction of an applicant's grades in law school and thus aids in the making of the admissions decision. These studies show that the LSAT score and the undergraduate grade-point average are the two best quantitative predictors, and that when they are used together they are better than either used separately. College grades represent both academic competence and achievement; the LSAT score largely indicates academic competence—the kind relevant to the study of law. The academic achievement of an applicant to law school indicates the extent of his preparation and motivation for the study of law. It is apparent, then, that college grades make a significant contribution to prediction of law school grades that is not supplied by the LSAT score.

Where an applicant for admission to law school submits a transcript in which all or virtually all of his grades are on pass/fail basis, and submits no other indication of his level of achievement in college, the admissions committee can make little specific use of his college work in predicting his law school grades. This means that this prediction must be based on the LSAT score, even though the committee would much prefer not to place sole reliance on the test scores in making this prediction. Even when such a transcript is supplemented by a narrative evaluation of the applicant by several of his teachers and deans, the committee can make only limited use of the college work in predicting performance in law school. Like interviews, these evaluations give the committee some help in making the admissions judgment, but they are largely helpful in deciding which risks to take and which to reject.

Where the applicant for admission to law school submits a transcript containing some conventional grades and some pass/fail grades, the admissions committee can develop a grade-point average for that portion of the student's college work bearing the conventional grades. However, many admissions officers will not feel justified in assigning to that average the conventional weight. They may well assume that the student chose to receive a conventional grade in those courses in which he gauged his probabilities for a premium grade to be good. This indicates that his grade-point average so developed will overstate his academic competence and achievement as compared with the average of a student whose grades are all conventional. Furthermore, the committee may reasonably assume that the applicant did not make the same effort in the courses graded on a pass/fail basis as he did in those graded on the conventional basis. In short, a grade-point average based only upon the limited part of a student's work in which conventional grades were assigned seems to overstate in a compound way the student's general academic ability and achievement. Therefore, it is understandable that many admissions officers are already discounting such a grade-point average, and discounting it more if there is a large proportion of pass/fail grades.

The Council recognizes that the increased use of the pass/fail grading system—or some variant thereof—will mean that law school admissions committees and officers will place an increased reliance upon the LSAT score, a greater reliance than either the Council or law school admissions committee would like. The Council recognizes that there are many educational considerations to be taken into account by the faculty and administration in determining the appropriate grading system for that college or university. The Council, of course, respects the authority and judgment of the college and university faculty and administration in making that decision. The Law School Admission Council offers this statement concerning the effect of pass/fail grades upon the proper evaluation of a college graduate's application for admission to law school only in the hope that it may be useful to college faculties and administrations in determining what grading system to use.

Correspondence Study

The American Bar Association expressly disapproves of correspondence law courses as a means of preparation for bar examination and for practice. Before one pursues a correspondence law course, it is suggested that he first familiarize himself with the rules and regulations of the state in which he intends to practice and inquire whether correspondence law courses are acceptable under the applicable rules and regulations of the state and any governmental agency with which one expects to secure employment. Correspondence law school graduates may take the bar examinations only in California and even there only under special conditions.

Postponement of Graduation

WHEREAS, most state supreme courts require graduation from an ABA approved law school as a requisite for bar admissions in order to assure the public that persons representing them in legal matters have received a quality legal education, and

WHEREAS, some individuals begin and complete substantially all of their legal education at unapproved law schools, which law schools have been inspected for possible ABA provisional approval but are found not to meet the ABA Standards during the time of such attendance; and these individuals may then delay their formal graduation until after the law school received ABA provisional approval, and

WHEREAS, some law schools receiving ABA provisional approval have permitted students to delay their graduation until such approval was received by the school and have then awarded degrees dated subsequent to receipt of ABA provisional approval to such students,

THEREFORE, the Council of the Section of Legal Education and Admissions to the Bar hereby adopts a policy disapproving this practice, and requests that all provisionally approved law schools, all other schools seeking provisional approval, all law school site team members and all state bar admitting authorities be notified of this policy.

Law School Admission Fees

The American Bar Association Section of Legal Education and Admissions to the Bar condemns the practice of requiring persons seeking admission to a law school to pay a fee, in addition to the regular application fee, to be placed on a list of persons who will be admitted if additional places become available, commonly known as a "waiting list."

Rating of Law Schools

No rating of law schools beyond the simple statement of their accreditation status is attempted or advocated by the official organizations in legal education. Qualities that make one kind of school good for one student may not be as important to another. The American Bar Association and its Section of Legal Education and Admissions to the Bar have issued disclaimers of any law school rating system. Prospective law students should consider a variety of factors in making their choice among schools.

Propriety of Examination by Public Authority before Admission to Practice

A half century ago the American Bar Association adopted standards for legal education, the second of which is as follows:

> "The American Bar Association is of the opinion that graduation from a law school should not confer the right of admission to the bar, and that every candidate should be subject to an examination by public authority to determine his fitness."

The criticism of bar examinations, which is daily becoming more prevalent, makes it most appropriate for the Council of the Section of Legal Education and Admissions to the Bar and the Board of Managers of the National Conference of Bar Examiners to state their opinion on the matter of the so-called Diploma Privilege.

It is the position of the Council and Board that the above-quoted standard, adopted in 1921, is as valid today—perhaps more so with the mobility of law graduates—as it was at the time and that every applicant for admission to the bar should be subject to examination by public authority.

Very great progress has taken place in the caliber of legal education in the fifty years intervening since 1921. In part the improvement in legal education has been the result of experimentation in teaching techniques. Not all such experiments have proved successful. Public authority should not dictate teaching techniques but it should make sure that all applicants have the training necessary to adequately serve the public upon their admission.

Not only are law schools quite properly experimenting in teaching techniques but they are experimenting in curriculum content. Again, public authority should not dictate curriculum content but by examination should determine that the content of the applicant's education is such that upon admission he will be able to adequately serve the public. In one of the jurisdictions where graduates of certain law schools are admitted without examination, the Court found it necessary to a certain extent to dictate the curriculum content of those schools—an unfortunate limitation on the educational freedom of these schools.

Bar examinations themselves serve additional functions. They encourage law graduates to study subjects not taken in law school. They require the applicant to review all he has learned in law school with a result that he is made to realize the interrelation of the various divisions of the law—to view the separate subject courses which he took in law school as a related whole. This the curriculum of most law schools does not achieve. Also, it is the first time many of the applicants will have been examined by persons other than those who taught them, a valuable experience in preparation for appearing before a completely strange judge.

To reiterate, it is the position of the Council and the Board of Managers that there must be examination by public authority. This is not to say that public authority must not be very careful in its examination procedure to make sure that it is fulfilling its responsibilities. It should continually strive to make its methods of examination more effective so that the results will be the nondiscriminatory admission of none not qualified and the exclusion of none qualified, even though this requires the use of innovative examining techniques and constant consideration of the ever changing needs of our society. The necessity to train lawyers to represent all members of society is a continual challenge to teachers of law and legal education. To test this properly the examining authority can perform effectively and satisfactorily only if it makes responsive changes in its techniques.

Period of Time for Completion of Requirements to Obtain J. D. Degree

The normal maximum period for a full-time law student to complete requirements for a J.D. degree is five years. The normal maximum completion time for a part-time law student to complete requirements for a J.D. degree is six years.

Encouragement of Increased Emphasis on Pro-Bono Activities

Law Schools should make law students aware of the special needs of those persons often under-represented in legal matters, including minorities, the poor, elderly and handicapped members of society, facilitate student services to these groups and should instill a sense in their students of the profession's obligation to provide legal services to those who are unable to afford them.

Student Tuition and Fee Refund Policy

It is the policy of the Council that all law schools approved by the American Bar Association have and make publicly available an equitable student tuition and fee refund policy. This policy shall contain a complete statement of all student tuition and fees and a schedule for the equitable refund of student tuition and fees.

Policy on Timely Grading of Law School Examinations

The Council of the Section of Legal Education and Admissions to the Bar reports that as a result of the expressed concern of the Law Student Division concerning timely grading of examinations, the Consultant on Legal Education to the American Bar Association has conducted a survey of grading practices at all law schools approved by the American Bar Association. The Law Student Division proposal and resultant survey has promoted thoughtful discussion among the deans and faculties of ABA approved law schools. The Council urges that all law schools continue adoption and maintenance of timely grading practices of law school examinations. The Council is aware that on occasion, a faculty member may not honor their professional obligation in this regard. The Council urges enforcement by each school of its own adopted policies, and urges completion of the grading and notice provision to the students not later than 30 days following the last examination of the term.

Law School Policy Encouraging Faculty to Engage in Reasonable Post-Examination Review With Students

It is recommended that a law school have a policy encouraging faculty members to engage in reasonable post examination review with students, preferably individual review upon request. Absent good cause, students should also have a right to reasonably review their examination papers. This does not mean that faculty members are obligated to review examinations individually with all students in every course. A reasonable policy may take into account the workload of individual teachers, the number of examinations in the course, the academic needs of the particular students requesting review, and the availability of review in courses throughout the school. Faculty members may choose to carry out such a policy using alternative means, including engaging in individual review of examinations upon student's request, by holding a general review concerning the examination open to all students, or by providing an outline or exemplar of good examination answers. (June, 1990)

Student Complaints

It is the policy of the Council that each law school approved by the American Bar Association should communicate in written form to its students the manner in which it receives and responds to student complaints.

Chapter Seventeen

School Directory

Below is list of all the ABA approved law schools as of October 1, 1997. At that point there was 76 public ABA approved law schools and 102 private ABA approved law schools. For updates visit the ABA website at http://www.abanet.org/legaled.

AKRON, UNIVERSITY OF
C. Blake McDowell Law Center
Akron, OH 44325-2901
800-4akron-u
http://www.uakron.edu/law/index.html
Public

ALABAMA, UNIVERSITY OF
P.O. Box 870382
Tuscaloosa, AL 35487
(205)348-5117
http://www.law.ua.edu
Public

ALBANY LAW SCHOOL
80 New Scotland Avenue
Albany, NY 12208
(518)445-2311
http://www.als.edu
Private

AMERICAN UNIVERSITY
4801 Massachusetts Ave, NW
Washington, DC 20016
(202)274-4004
http://www.wcl.american.edu
Private

ARIZONA STATE UNIVERSITY
P.O. Box 877906
Tempe, AZ 85287-7906
(602)965-6181
http://www.asu.edu/law
Public

ARIZONA, UNIVERSITY OF
James E. Rogers Law Center
Tucson, AZ 85721-0176
(520)621-1373
http://www.law.arizona.edu
Public

ARKANSAS, FAYETTEVILLE, UNIVERSITY OF
Waterman Hall
Fayetteville, AR 72701-1201
(501)575-5601
http://law-gopher.uark.edu/arklaw
Public

ARKANSAS, LITTLE ROCK, UNIVERSITY OF
1201 McAlmont Street
Little Rock, AR 72202-5142
(501)324-9434
http://www.ualr.edu/~lawsch/index.htm
Public

BALTIMORE, UNIVERSITY OF
1420 North Charles Street
Baltimore, MD 21201
(410)837-4459
http://www.ubalt.edu/www/law
Public

BAYLOR UNIVERSITY
P.O. Box 97288
Waco, TX 76798-7288
(254)710-1911
http://www.baylor.edu/~Law
Private

BOSTON COLLEGE
885 Centre Street
Newton Centre, MA 02159
(617)552-8550
http://www.bc.edu/lawschool
Private

BOSTON UNIVERSITY
765 Commonwealth Ave
Boston, MA 02215
(617)353-3112
http://www.bu.edu/LAW
Private

BRIGHAM YOUNG UNIVERSITY
Provo, UT 84602
(801)378-4274
http://www.law.byu.edu
Private

BROOKLYN LAW SCHOOL
250 Joralemon Street
Brooklyn, NY 11201
(718)625-2200
http://www.brooklaw.edu
Private

CALIFORNIA WESTERN
225 Cedar Street
San Diego, CA 92101-3046
(619)239-0391
http://www.cwsl.edu
Private

CALIFORNIA-BERKELEY, UNIVERSITY OF
221 Boalt Hall
Berkeley, CA 94720
(510)642-1741
http://www.law.berkeley.edu
Public

CALIFORNIA-DAVIS, UNIVERSITY OF
School of Law
Davis, CA 95616-5201
(530)752-0243
http://www.kinghall.ucdavis.edu
Public

CALIFORNIA-HASTINGS, UNIVERSITY OF
200 McAllister Street
San Francisco, CA 94102
(415)565-4600
http://www.uchastings.edu
Public

CALIFORNIA-LOS ANGELES, UNIVERSITY OF
405 Hilgard Avenue
Los Angeles, CA 90095
(310)825-4841
http://www.law.ucla.edu
Public

CAMPBELL UNIVERSITY
P.O. Box 158
Buies Creek, NC 27506
(910)893-1750
http://webster.campbell.edu/culawsch
Private

CAPITAL UNIVERSITY
303 East Broad Street
Columbus, OH 43215
(614)236-6500
http://www.law.capital.edu
Private

CASE WESTERN RESERVE UNIVERSITY
Gund Hall
Cleveland, OH 44106-7148
(216)368-6350
http://lawwww.cwru.edu
Private

CATHOLIC UNIVERSITY OF AMERICA
Washington, DC 20064
(319)319-5140
http://www.law.cua.edu
Private

CHICAGO, UNIVERSITY OF
1111 East 60th Street
Chicago, IL 60637
(773)702-9494
http://www.law.uchicago.edu
Private

CINCINNATI, UNIVERSITY OF
P.O. Box 210040
Cincinnati, OH 45221-0040
(513)556-6805
http://www.law.uc.edu
Public

CITY UNIVERSITY OF NEW YORK
65-21 Main Street
Flushing, NY 11367
(718)340-4200
http://web.law.cuny.edu
Public

CLEVELAND STATE UNIVERSITY
Cleveland-Marshall College of Law
Cleveland, OH 44115-2223
(216)687-2344
http://www.law.csuohio.edu
Public

COLORADO, UNIVERSITY OF
Campus Box 401
Boulder, CO 80309-0401
(303)492-7203
http://www.colorado.edu/law
Public

COLUMBIA UNIVERSITY
435 West 116th Street
New York, NY 10027
(212)854-2640
http://www.columbia.edu/cu/law
Private

CONNECTICUT, UNIVERSITY OF
55 Elizabeth Street
Hartford, CT 06105
(860)570-5127
http://www.law.uconn.edu
Public

CORNELL UNIVERSITY
Myron Taylor Hall
Ithaca, NY 14853-4901
(607)255-3527
www.law.cornell.edu/admit/admit.htm
Private

CREIGHTON UNIVERSITY
2500 California Plaza
Omaha, NE 68178
(402)280-2872
http://www.creighton.edu/culaw
Private

DAYTON, UNIVERSITY OF
300 College Park Ave.
Dayton, OH 45469-2772
(937)229-3211
http://www.udayton.edu/~law
Private

DENVER, UNIVERSITY OF
7039 East 18th Street
Denver, CO 80220
(303)871-6000
gopher://gopher.cair.du.edu/1
Private

DEPAUL UNIVERSITY
25 East Jackson Boulevard
Chicago, IL 60604-2287
(312)362-8701
http://www.law.depaul.edu
Private

DETROIT COLLEGE AT MICHIGAN STATE UNIV.
368 Law College Bldg.
East Lansing, MI 48824-1300
(517)432-6819
http://www.dcl.edu
Private

DETROIT MERCY, UNIVERSITY OF
651 E. Jefferson
Detroit, MI 48226
(313)596-0200
website is under construction
Private

DRAKE UNIVERSITY
2507 University Avenue
Des Moines, IA 50311
(515)271-2824
http://www.drake.edu
Private

DUKE UNIVERSITY
P.O. Box 90362
Durham, NC 27708-0362
(919)613-7000
http://www.law.duke.edu
Private

DUQUESNE UNIVERSITY
900 Locust Street
Pittsburgh, PA 15282
(412)396-6280
http://www.duq.edu/law
Private

EMORY UNIVERSITY
Gambrell Hall
Atlanta, GA 30322-2770
(404)727-6816
http://www.law.emory.edu
Private

FLORIDA STATE UNIVERSITY
425 W. Jefferson Street
Tallahassee, FL 32306-1601
(850)644-3400
http://www.law.fsu.edu
Public

FLORIDA, UNIVERSITY OF
P.O. Box 117620
Gainesville, FL 32611
(352)392-9238
http://www.law.ufl.edu
Public

FORDHAM UNIVERSITY
140 West 62nd Street
New York, NY 10023-7485
(212)636-6875
http://www.fordham.edu/law/cle/law_main
Private

FRANKLIN PIERCE LAW CENTER
2 White Street
Concord, NH 03301
(603)228-1541
http://www.fplc.edu
Private

GEORGE MASON UNIVERSITY
3401 North Fairfax Drive
Arlington, VA 22201-4498
(703)993-8000
http://www.gmu.edu/departments/law
Public

GEORGE WASHINGTON UNIVERSITY
2000 H Street, N.W.
Washington, DC 20052
(202)994-7230
http://www.law.gwu.edu
Private

GEORGETOWN UNIVERSITY
600 New Jersey Avenue N.W.
Washington, DC 20001
(202)662-9000
http://www.law.georgetown.edu/lc
Private

GEORGIA STATE UNIVERSITY
P.O. Box 4037
Atlanta, GA 30302-4037
(404)651-2096
http://gsulaw.gsu.edu
Public

GEORGIA, UNIVERSITY OF
Herty Drive
Athens, GA 30602
(706)542-7140
http://www.lawsch.uga.edu
Public

GOLDEN GATE UNIVERSITY
536 Mission Street
San Francisco, CA 94105-2968
(415)442-6600
http://www.ggu.edu/law/
Private

GONZAGA UNIVERSITY
P.O. Box 3528
Spokane, WA 99220-3528
(509)328-4220
http://www.law.gonzaga.edu
Private

HAMLINE UNIVERSITY
1536 Hewitt Avenue
St. Paul, MN 55104
(612)523-2941
http://www.hamline.edu
Private

HARVARD UNIVERSITY
Cambridge, MA 02138
(617)495-1000
http://www.law.harvard.edu
Private

HAWAII, UNIVERSITY OF
2515 Dole Street
Honolulu, HI 96822
(808)956-8636
gopher://gopher.hawaii.edu/11/student/ca
Public

HOFSTRA UNIVERSITY
121 Hofstra University
Hempstead, NY 11549-1210
(516)463-5858
http://www.hofstra.edu
Private

HOUSTON, UNIVERSITY OF
4800 Calhoun
Houston, TX 77004-6371
(713)743-2100
http://www.law.uh.edu
Public

HOWARD UNIVERSITY
2900 Van Ness Street
Washington, DC 20008
(202)806-8000
http://www.law.howard.edu
Private

IDAHO, UNIVERSITY OF
6th & Rayburn
Moscow, ID 83844-2321
(208)885-6422
http://www.uidaho.edu/law
Public

ILLINOIS INSTITUTE OF TECHNOLOGY
Chicago-Kent College of Law
Chicago, IL 60661
(312)906-5000
http://www.kentlaw.edu
Private

ILLINOIS, UNIVERSITY OF
504 East Pennsylvania Avenue
Champaign, IL 61820
(217)333-0931
http://www.law.uiuc.edu
Public

INDIANA UNIVERSITY - BLOOMINGTON
211 S. Indiana Avenue
Bloomington, IN 47405
(812)855-7995
http://www.law.indiana.edu
Public

INDIANA UNIVERSITY - INDIANAPOLIS
735 West New York Street
Indianapolis, IN 46202-5194
(317)274-8523
http://www.iulaw.indy.indiana.edu
Public

INTER AMERICAN UNIVERSITY OF PUERTO RICO
P.O. Box 70351
San Juan, PR 00936-8351
(787)751-1912
http://www.derecho.inter.edu
Private

IOWA, UNIVERSITY OF
Melrose and Byington
Iowa City, IA 52242
(319)335-9034
http://www.uiowa.edu/~lawcoll
Public

JOHN MARSHALL LAW SCHOOL
315 S. Plymouth Ct.
Chicago, IL 60604
(312)427-2737
http://www.jmls.edu
Private

JUDGE ADVOCATE GENERAL'S SCHOOL
600 Massie Road
Charlottesville, VA 22903
(804)972-6300
http://www.jagc.army.mil
Public

KANSAS, UNIVERSITY OF
Green Hall
Lawrence, KS 66045
(785)864-4550
http://www.law.ukans.edu
Public

KENTUCKY, UNIVERSITY OF
209 Law Building
Lexington, KY 40506-0048
(606)257-1678
http://www.uky.edu/law
Public

LEWIS AND CLARK COLLEGE
10015 S.W. Terwilliger Blvd.
Portland, OR 97219-7799
(503)768-6600
http://lclark.edu/law/index.htm
Private

LOUISIANA STATE UNIVERSITY
210 Law Center
Baton Rouge, LA 70803
(504)388-8491
http://www.lsu.edu/guests/lsulaw/index.html
Public

LOUISVILLE, UNIVERSITY OF
Louis D. Brandeis School of Law
Louisville, KY 40292
(502)852-6879
http://www.louisville.edu/law/
Public

LOYOLA MARYMOUNT UNIVERSITY-LOS ANGELES
919 South Albany Street
Los Angeles, CA 90015
(213)736-1000
http://www.law.lmu.edu
Private

LOYOLA UNIVERSITY-CHICAGO
One East Pearson Street
Chicago, IL 60611
(312)915-7120
gopher://gopher.luc.edu/11/loyola/colleg
Private

LOYOLA UNIVERSITY-NEW ORLEANS
7214 St. Charles Avenue
New Orleans, LA 70118
(504)861-5550
www.loyno.edu/SchoolofLaw
Private

MAINE, UNIVERSITY OF
246 Deering Avenue
Portland, ME 04102
(207)780-4355
http://www.law.usm.maine.edu
Public

MARQUETTE UNIVERSITY
Sensenbrenner Hall
Milwaukee, WI 53201-1881
(414)288-7090
http://www.mu.edu/dept/law
Private

MARYLAND, UNIVERSITY OF
500 West Baltimore Street
Baltimore, MD 21201-1786
(410)706-3492
http://www.law.umaryland.edu
Public

MCGEORGE SCHOOL OF LAW
University of the Pacific
Sacramento, CA 95817
(916)739-7169
http://www.mcgeorge.edu
Private

MEMPHIS, UNIVERSITY OF
The University of Memphis
Memphis, TN 39152-6513
(901)678-2421
http://www.people.memphis.edu/~law
Public

MERCER UNIVERSITY
1021 Georgia Avenue
Macon, GA 31207
(912)752-2601
http://www.mercer.edu/~law
Private

MIAMI, UNIVERSITY OF
P.O. Box 248087
Coral Gables, FL 33124
(305)284-2394
http://www.law.miami.edu
Private

MICHIGAN, UNIVERSITY OF
Hutchins Hall
Ann Arbor, MI 48109-1215
(313)764-1358
http://www.law.umich.edu
Public

MINNESOTA, UNIVERSITY OF
229 19 Ave S.
Minneapolis, MN 55455
(612)625-1000
http://www.umn.edu/law/
Public

MISSISSIPPI COLLEGE
151 East Griffith Street
Jackson, MS 39201
(601)925-7100
http://www.mc.edu
Private

MISSISSIPPI, UNIVERSITY OF
Office of the Dean
University, MS 38677
(601)232-6900
http://www.olemiss.edu/depts/law_school
Public

MISSOURI-COLUMBIA, UNIVERSITY OF
203 Hulston Hall
Columbia, MO 65211
(573)882-6487
http://www.law.missouri.edu
Public

MISSOURI-KANSAS CITY, UNIVERSITY OF
5100 Rockhill Road
Kansas City, MO 64110
(816)235-1644
http://www.law.umkc.edu
Public

MONTANA, UNIVERSITY OF
Missoula, MT 59812
(406)243-4311
http://www.umt.edu/law
Public

NEBRASKA, UNIVERSITY OF
P.O. Box 830902
Lincoln, NE 68583-0902
(402)472-2161
http://www.unl.edu/lawcoll
Public

NEW ENGLAND SCHOOL OF LAW
154 Stuart Street
Boston, MA 02116
(617)451-0010
http://www.nesl.edu
Private

NEW MEXICO, UNIVERSITY OF
1117 Stanford, N.E.
Albuquerque, NM 87131-1431
(505)277-2146
http://www.unm.edu/~unmlaw
Public

NEW YORK LAW SCHOOL
57 Worth Street
New York, NY 10013-2960
(212)431-2100
http://www.nyls.edu
Private

NEW YORK UNIVERSITY
40 Washington Square South
New York, NY 10012
(212)998-6000
http://www.nyu.edu/law
Private

NORTH CAROLINA CENTRAL UNIVERSITY
1512 South Alston Avenue
Durham, NC 27707
(919)560-6333
http://www.nccu.edu/law
Public

NORTH CAROLINA, UNIVERSITY OF
Campus Box 3380
Chapel Hill, NC 27599-3380
(919)962-5106
http://www.law.unc.edu
Public

NORTH DAKOTA, UNIVERSITY OF
Centennial Drive
Grand Forks, ND 58202
(701)777-2104
http://www.law.und.nodak.edu
Public

NORTHEASTERN UNIVERSITY
400 Huntington Avenue
Boston, MA 02115
(617)373-5149
http://www.slaw.neu.edu
Private

NORTHERN ILLINOIS UNIVERSITY
DeKalb, IL 60115
(815)753-1420
http://www.niu.edu/claw
Public

NORTHERN KENTUCKY UNIVERSITY
Nunn Drive
Highland Heights, KY 41099
(606)572-5340
http://www.eku.edu/~chase
Public

NORTHWESTERN UNIVERSITY
357 East Chicago Avenue
Chicago, IL 60611
(312)503-8462
http://www.law1.nwu.edu/
Private

NOTRE DAME, UNIVERSITY OF
103 Law Building
Notre Dame, IN 46556
(219)631-6627
http://www.nd.edu/~ndlaw
Private

NOVA SOUTHEASTERN UNIVERSITY
3305 College Avenue
Fort Lauderdale, FL 33314-7721
(954)262-6100
http://www.nsulaw.nova.edu
Private

OHIO NORTHERN UNIVERSITY
525 S. Main Street
Ada, OH 45810-1599
(419)772-2205
http://www.law.onu.edu
Private

OHIO STATE UNIVERSITY
55 W. 12th Avenue
Columbus, OH 43210
(614)292-2631
http://www.acs.ohio-state.edu/units/law
Public

OKLAHOMA CITY UNIVERSITY
2501 North Blackwelder
Oklahoma City, OK 73106
(405)521-5354
http://www.okcu.edu/~law/home.htm
Private

OKLAHOMA, UNIVERSITY OF
300 Timberdell Road
Norman, OK 73019-5081
(405)325-4699
http://www.law.ou.edu
Public

OREGON, UNIVERSITY OF
1221 University of Oregon
Eugene, OR 97403-1221
(541)346-3852
http://www.law.uoregon.edu
Public

PACE UNIVERSITY
78 North Broadway
White Plains, NY 10603
(914)422-4210
http://www.law.pace.edu
Private

PENNSYLVANIA, UNIVERSITY OF
3400 Chestnut Street
Philadelphia, PA 19104-6204
(215)898-7483
http://www.law.upenn.edu
Private

PENNSYLVANIA STATE UNIVERSITY
Dickinson School of Law
Carlisle, PA 17013-2899
(717)240-5000
http://www.dsl.edu
Public

PEPPERDINE UNIVERSITY
24255 Pacific Coast Highway
Malibu, CA 90263
(310)456-4611
http://law.pepperdine.edu
Private

PITTSBURGH, UNIVERSITY OF
3900 Forbes Avenue
Pittsburgh, PA 15260
(412)648-1400
http://www.law.pitt.edu
Public

PONTIFICAL CATHOLIC UNIVERSITY OF PUERTO RICO
2250 Las Americas Avenue Suite 543
Ponce, PR 00731-6382
(787)841-2000
Private

PUERTO RICO, UNIVERSITY OF
P.O. Box 23349
San Juan, PR 00931-3349
(787)764-2680
Public

QUINNIPIAC COLLEGE
275 Mount Carmel Avenue
Hamden, CT 06518-1950
(203)287-3200
http://www.quinnipiac.edu/law
Private

REGENT UNIVERSITY
1000 Regent University Drive
Virginia Beach, VA 23464
(757)579-4040
http://www.regent.edu/acad/schlaw
Private

RICHMOND, UNIVERSITY OF
Law School
Richmond, VA 23173
(804)289-8189
http://law.richmond.edu
Private

ROGER WILLIAMS UNIVERSITY
Ten Metacom Avenue
Bristol, RI 02809
(401)254-4500
www.rwu.edu/law
Private

RUTGERS UNIVERSITY-CAMDEN
217 North Fifth Street
Camden, NJ 08102-1203
(609)225-6102
http://www-camlaw.rutgers.edu
Public

RUTGERS UNIVERSITY-NEWARK
15 Washington Street
Newark, NJ 07102-3192
(973)353-5561
http://www.rutgers.edu/rusln
Public

SAMFORD UNIVERSITY
800 Lakeshore Drive
Birmingham, AL 35229
(205)870-2701
http://www.samford.edu/schools/law
Private

SAN DIEGO, UNIVERSITY OF
5998 Alcala Park
San Diego, CA 92110-2492
(619)260-4527
http://www.acusd.edu/~usdlaw
Private

SAN FRANCISCO, UNIVERSITY OF
2130 Fulton Street
San Francisco, CA 94117-1080
(415)422-6586
http://www.usfca.edu
Private

SANTA CLARA UNIVERSITY
500 El Camino Real
Santa Clara, CA 95053
(408)554-4767
http://www.scu.edu/law
Private

SEATTLE UNIVERSITY
950 Broadway Plaza
Tacoma, WA 98402
(206)591-2275
http://www.law.seattleu.edu
Private

SETON HALL UNIVERSITY
One Newark Center
Newark, NJ 07102
(973)642-8500
http://www.shu.edu/law
Private

SOUTH CAROLINA, UNIVERSITY OF
Main and Greene Streets
Columbia, SC 29208
(803)777-6857
http://www.law.sc.edu
Public

SOUTH DAKOTA, UNIVERSITY OF
414 E. Clark Street
Vermillion, SD 57069-2390
(605)677-5443
http://www.usd.edu/law
Public

SOUTH TEXAS COLLEGE OF LAW
1303 San Jacinto
Houston, TX 77002-7000
(713)659-8040
http://www.stcl.edu
Private

SOUTHERN CALIFORNIA, UNIVERSITY OF
University Park
Los Angeles, CA 90089-0071
(213)740-7331
http://www.usc.edu/dept/law
Private

SOUTHERN ILLINOIS UNIVERSITY
Lesar Law Building
Carbondale, IL 62901-6804
(618)536-7711
http://www.siu.edu/~lawsch
Public

SOUTHERN METHODIST UNIVERSITY
P.O. Box 750116
Dallas, TX 75275-0116
(214)768-2618
http://www.smu.edu/~law
Private

SOUTHERN UNIVERSITY
P. O. Box 9294
Baton Rouge, LA 70813
(504)771-2552
website is under construction
Public

SOUTHWESTERN UNIVERSITY
675 South Westmoreland Avenue
Los Angeles, CA 90005-3992
(213)738-6710
http://www.swlaw.edu
Private

ST. JOHN'S UNIVERSITY
8000 Utopia Parkway
Jamaica, NY 11439
(718)990-6600
http://www.stjohns.edu/law
Private

ST. LOUIS UNIVERSITY
3700 Lindell Blvd.
St. Louis, MO 63108
(314)977-2766
http://lawlib.slu.edu
Private

ST. MARY'S UNIVERSITY
One Camino Santa Maria
San Antonio, TX 78228-8602
(210)436-3424
http://www.stmarylaw.edu
Private

ST. THOMAS UNIVERSITY
16400 N.W. 32 Avenue
Miami, FL 33054
(305)623-2320
http://www.stu.edu/law/lawmain.htm
Private

STANFORD UNIVERSITY
Crown Quadrangle
Stanford, CA 94305-8610
(650)723-2465
http://www-leland.stanford.edu/group/law
Private

STATE UNIVERSITY OF NEW YORK AT BUFFALO
John Lord'Brian Hall
North Campus
Buffalo, NY 14260
(716) 645-2053
http://www.buffalo.edu/law/js.html
Public

STETSON UNIVERSITY
1401 61st Street South
St. Petersburg, FL 33707
(813)562-7800
http://www.law.stetson.edu
Private

SUFFOLK UNIVERSITY
41 Temple Street
Boston, MA 02114-4280
(617)573-8155
http://www.suffolk.edu/law
Private

SYRACUSE UNIVERSITY
Syracuse, NY 13244-1030
(315)443-1962
http://www.law.syr.edu
Private

TEMPLE UNIVERSITY
1719 North Broad Street
Philadelphia, PA 19122
(215)204-7861
http://www.temple.edu/lawschool
Public

TENNESSEE, UNIVERSITY OF
1505 W. Cumberland Ave.
Knoxville, TN 37996-1810
(423)974-4241
http://www.law.utk.edu
Public

TEXAS, UNIVERSITY OF
727 E. Dean Keeton Street
Austin, TX 78705
(512)232-1200
http://www.utexas.edu/law
Public

TEXAS SOUTHERN UNIVERSITY
3100 Cleburne
Houston, TX 77004-3216
(713)313-1075
http://www.tsulaw.edu
Public

TEXAS TECH UNIVERSITY
1802 Hartford
Lubbock, TX 79409-0004
(806)742-3791
http://www.law.ttu.edu
Public

TEXAS WESLEYAN UNIVERSITY
1515 Commerce Street
Fort Worth, TX 76102
(817)212-4100
http://www.txwesleyan.edu
Private

THOMAS JEFFERSON
2121 San Diego Avenue
San Diego, CA 92110
(619)297-9700
http://www.jeffersonlaw.edu
Private

THOMAS M. COOLEY
217 South Capitol Avenue
Lansing, MI 48901
(517)371-5140
http://www.cooley.edu
Private

TOLEDO, UNIVERSITY OF
2801 West Bancroft
Toledo, OH 43606
(419)530-2882
http://www.utoledo.edu/law
Public

TOURO COLLEGE
300 Nassau Road
Huntington, NY 11743
(516)421-2244
http://www.tourolaw.edu
Private

TULANE UNIVERSITY
6329 Freret Street
New Orleans, LA 70118-
(504)865-5939
http://www.law.tulane.edu/
Private

TULSA, UNIVERSITY OF
3120 East Fourth Place
Tulsa, OK 74104
(918)631-2401
http://www.utulsa.edu/law
Private

UTAH, UNIVERSITY OF
332 South 1400 East Front
Salt Lake City, UT 84112-0730
(801)581-6833
http://info.law.utah.edu
Public

VALPARAISO UNIVERSITY
Valparaiso, IN 46383
(219)465-7829
http://www.valpo.edu/law/
Private

VANDERBILT UNIVERSITY
21st Avenue South
Nashville, TN 37240
(615)322-2615
http://www.vanderbilt.edu/law
Private

VERMONT LAW SCHOOL
Chelsea Street
South Royalton, VT 05068-0096
(802)763-8303
http://www.vermontlaw.edu
Private

VILLANOVA UNIVERSITY
299 North Spring Mill Road
Villanova, PA 19085-1682
(610)519-7000
http://www.law.vill.edu/vls
Private

VIRGINIA, UNIVERSITY OF
580 Massie Road
Charlottesville, VA 22903-1789
(804)924-7354
http://www.law.virginia.edu/index.htm
Public

WAKE FOREST UNIVERSITY
P.O. Box 7206
Winston-Salem, NC 27109-7206
(910)758-5435
http://www.wfu.edu
Private

WASHBURN UNIVERSITY
1700 College Avenue
Topeka, KS 66621
(785)231-1010
http://www.washburnlaw.wuacc.edu/school
Public

WASHINGTON AND LEE UNIVERSITY
Sydney Lewis Hall
Lexington, VA 24450-0303
(540)463-8400
http://www.wlu.edu
Private

WASHINGTON UNIVERSITY
1 Brookings Drive
St. Louis, MO 63130-4899
(314)935-6400
http://ls.wustl.edu
Private

WASHINGTON, UNIVERSITY OF
1100 NE Campus Parkway
Seattle, WA 98105-6617
(206)543-4551
http:/www2.law.washington.edu
Public

WAYNE STATE UNIVERSITY
468 Ferry Mall
Detroit, MI 48202
(313)577-3933
http://www.science.wayne.edu/~law
Public

WEST VIRGINIA UNIVERSITY
P.O. Box 6130
Morgantown, WV 26506-6130
(304)293-3199
gopher://wvnvm.wvnet.edu/11/wc/wvu
Public

WESTERN NEW ENGLAND COLLEGE
1215 Wilbraham Road
Springfield, MA 01119
(413)782-1412
http://www.law.wnec.edu
Private

WHITTIER COLLEGE
3333 Harbor Boulevard
Costa Mesa, CA 92626
(714)444-4141
http://www.whittier.edu
Private

WIDENER UNIVERSITY
4601 Concord Pike
Wilmington, DE 19803-0474
(302)477-2100
http://www.widener.edu/law/law.html
Private

WIDENER UNIVERSITY-HARRISBURG
3800 Vartan Way
Harrisburg, PA 17106-9382
717-541-3900
http://www.widener.edu/law/law.html
Private

WILLAMETTE UNIVERSITY
245 Winter St. SE
Salem, OR 97301-3922
(503)370-6282
http://www.willamette.edu
Private

WILLIAM AND MARY SCHOOL OF LAW
P.O. Box 8795
Williamsburg, VA 23187-8795
(757)221-3800
http://www.wm.edu/law
Public

WILLIAM MITCHELL
875 Summit Avenue
St. Paul, MN 55105-3076
(612)227-9171
http://www.wmitchell.edu
Private

WISCONSIN, UNIVERSITY OF
975 Bascom Mall
Madison, WI 53706-1399
(608)262-2240
http://www.wisc.edu
Public

WYOMING, UNIVERSITY OF
P.O. Box 3035
Laramie, WY 82071
(307)766-6416
http://www.uwyo.edu/law/law.htm
Public

YALE UNIVERSITY
P.O. Box 208215
New Haven, CT 06520-8215
(203)432-1660
http://www.yale.edu/lawweb/lawschool
Private

YESHIVA UNIVERSITY
55 Fifth Avenue
New York, NY 10003
(212)790-0200
http://www.yu.edu/csl/law
Private

Chapter Eighteen

Websites

Association of American Law Schools

AMERICAN BAR ASSOCIATION

American Association of Law Libraries

Access Group

National Conference of Bar Examiners

THE SECTION OF LEGAL EDUCATION AND ADMISSIONS TO THE BAR
http://www.abanet.org/legaled

Law School Admission Council

NALP

National Association for Law Placement

ABA Approved Law Schools
http://www.abanet.org/legaled/approved.html

1999 Edition

Give Us Your Thoughts

In an effort to improve future editions of this book, the ABA is actively seeking constructive criticism. Please take the time to complete this questionnaire, and return to Kurt Snyder, Office of the Consultant on Legal Education, 550 West North Street, Suite 349, Indianapolis, IN 46202. Thank You!

Name:____

Phone:____________________________, E-mail:______________________________

Gender:________, Race:________, Age:________

Where did you earn your undergraduate degree?________________________________

What law school will you attend?____

Please rate the following. One is the lowest and five is the highest.

For example,

NOT Very Helpful	Slightly Helpful	Helpful	More Than Helpful	Very Helpful
1	2	3	4	5

Chapter One, Introduction:

1 2 3 4 5

Chapter Two, ABA's Role in the Accreditation Process:

1 2 3 4 5

Chapter Three, Prelaw Preparation:

1 2 3 4 5

Chapter Four, Admissions Process:

1 2 3 4 5

Chapter Five, Finance & Debt Management:

1 2 3 4 5

Chapter Six, Bar Admissions:

1 2 3 4 5

Cut on Dotted Line

Continued on Next Page

Chapter Seven, Career Outlook:

1 2 3 4 5

Chapter Eight, Values of the Profession:

1 2 3 4 5

Chapter Ten, About the Data:

1 2 3 4 5

Chapter Eleven, Comparison Charts:

1 2 3 4 5

Chapter Twelve, School Profile, two page spread:

1 2 3 4 5

Chapter Fourteen, Legal Education Statistics:

1 2 3 4 5

Chapter Sixteen, Selected Statements:

1 2 3 4 5

How would you rate the value of this book?

1 2 3 4 5

How did you hear about this book?

____

How can we make the book better, especially on the schools' two page spread?

____

____

____

____

____

General Comments:

____

____

____

____

____

Cut on Dotted Line